IFIP Advances in Information and Communication Technology

536

Editor-in-Chief

Kai Rannenberg, Goethe University Frankfurt, Germany

IFIP – The International Federation for Information Processing

IFIP was founded in 1960 under the auspices of UNESCO, following the first World Computer Congress held in Paris the previous year. A federation for societies working in information processing, IFIP's aim is two-fold: to support information processing in the countries of its members and to encourage technology transfer to developing nations. As its mission statement clearly states:

> IFIP is the global non-profit federation of societies of ICT professionals that aims at achieving a worldwide professional and socially responsible development and application of information and communication technologies.

IFIP is a non-profit-making organization, run almost solely by 2500 volunteers. It operates through a number of technical committees and working groups, which organize events and publications. IFIP's events range from large international open conferences to working conferences and local seminars.

The flagship event is the IFIP World Computer Congress, at which both invited and contributed papers are presented. Contributed papers are rigorously refereed and the rejection rate is high.

As with the Congress, participation in the open conferences is open to all and papers may be invited or submitted. Again, submitted papers are stringently refereed.

The working conferences are structured differently. They are usually run by a working group and attendance is generally smaller and occasionally by invitation only. Their purpose is to create an atmosphere conducive to innovation and development. Refereeing is also rigorous and papers are subjected to extensive group discussion.

Publications arising from IFIP events vary. The papers presented at the IFIP World Computer Congress and at open conferences are published as conference proceedings, while the results of the working conferences are often published as collections of selected and edited papers.

IFIP distinguishes three types of institutional membership: Country Representative Members, Members at Large, and Associate Members. The type of organization that can apply for membership is a wide variety and includes national or international societies of individual computer scientists/ICT professionals, associations or federations of such societies, government institutions/government related organizations, national or international research institutes or consortia, universities, academies of sciences, companies, national or international associations or federations of companies.

More information about this series at http://www.springer.com/series/6102

Ilkyeong Moon · Gyu M. Lee
Jinwoo Park · Dimitris Kiritsis
Gregor von Cieminski (Eds.)

Advances in Production Management Systems

Smart Manufacturing for Industry 4.0

IFIP WG 5.7 International Conference, APMS 2018
Seoul, Korea, August 26–30, 2018
Proceedings, Part II

 Springer

Editors
Ilkyeong Moon ⓘD
Seoul National University
Seoul
Korea

Gyu M. Lee ⓘD
Pusan National University
Busan
Korea

Jinwoo Park
Seoul National University
Seoul
Korea

Dimitris Kiritsis ⓘD
EPFL
Lausanne
Switzerland

Gregor von Cieminski ⓘD
ZF Hungária Kft
Eger
Hungary

ISSN 1868-4238   ISSN 1868-422X   (electronic)
IFIP Advances in Information and Communication Technology
ISBN 978-3-030-07624-5   ISBN 978-3-319-99707-0   (eBook)
https://doi.org/10.1007/978-3-319-99707-0

This Springer imprint is published by the registered company Springer Nature Switzerland AG
The registered company address is: Gewerbestrasse 11, 6330 Cham, Switzerland

Preface

We have already experienced three major industrial revolutions since the 18th century. These revolutions brought innovation in productivity for industry, the public, and individuals. Surprisingly, another new industrial revolution, the fourth one, has been rapidly approaching us in every sector of industry. Key components of the fourth industrial revolution include big data analysis, artificial intelligence, and virtual and augmented reality. These components also had a huge impact on the manufacturing sector and research on production management. Therefore, the 2018 Advances in Production Management Systems Conference played a leading role in the academic field. The core of our contributions strive to realize smart production management for data-driven, intelligent, collaborative, and sustainable manufacturing. Our topics of interest include Global Supply Chain, Knowledge-Based Production Management, Collaborative Networks, Sustainability and Production Management, Industry 4.0, and Smart City.

We welcomed leading experts from academia, industry, and research institutes from all over the world to the 2018 Advances in Production Management Systems Conference in Seoul, Korea, to exchange ideas, concepts, theories, and experiences. A large international panel of experts reviewed all the papers and selected the best ones to be included in these conference proceedings. In this collection of papers, the authors provide their perspectives along with their concepts and solutions for the challenges that industrial companies are confronted with, to offer great opportunities, new technologies, collaboration, and developments.

The proceedings are organized in two parts:

- Production Management for Data-Driven, Intelligent, Collaborative, and Sustainable Manufacturing (Volume 1)
- Smart Manufacturing for Industry 4.0 (Volume 2)

We hope that our readers will discover valuable new ideas and insights in these proceedings. The conference was supported by the International Federation of Information Processing (IFIP) and was organized by the IFIP Working Group 5.7 on Advances in Production Management Systems, the Korean Institute of Industrial Engineers (KIIE), and the Institute for Industrial Systems Innovation at Seoul National University. We would like to thank all contributors for their research and for their willingness to share ideas and results. We are also indebted to the members of the IFIP Working Group 5.7, the Program Committee members, and Organizing Committee members for their support in the review of the papers. Finally, we appreciate the generous support from both the Korean Federation of Science and Technology

Societies (KOFST) grant funded by the Korean government and Korea Land and Housing Corporation.

August 2018

Ilkyeong Moon
Gyu M. Lee
Jinwoo Park
Dimitris Kiritsis
Gregor von Cieminski

Organization

Honorary Co-chairs

Dimtris Kiritsis	EPFL, Switzerland
Jinwoo Park	Seoul National University, Korea

Conference Chair

Ilkyeong Moon	Seoul National University, Korea

Advisory Committee

Byung Kyu Choi	KAIST, Korea
Chi Hyuck Jun	POSTEC, Korea
Kap Hwan Kim	Pusan National University, Korea
Tae Eog Lee	KAIST, Korea
Young Hoon Lee	Yonsei University, Korea

Program Co-chairs

Gregor von Cieminski	ZF Hungária Kft, Hungary
Gyu M. Lee	Pusan National University, Korea

Program Committee

Bhaskar Bhandarkar	Indian Institution of Industrial Engineering, India
Chen-Fu Chien	National Tsing Hua University, Taiwan
Shuo-Yan Chou	National Taiwan University of Science and Technology, Taiwan
Xuehao Feng	Zhejiang University, China
Chin-Yin Huang	Tunghai University, Taiwan
Szu-Hao Huang	National Chiao Tung University, Taiwan
Takashi Irohara	Sophia University, Japan
Yasutaka Kainuma	Tokyo Metropolitan University, Japan
Harish Kutemate	Indian Institution of Industrial Engineering, India
Bo Lu	Dalian University, China
Hiroaki Matsukawa	Keio University, Japan
Koichi Nakade	Nagoya Institute of Technology, Japan
Izabela Ewa Nielsen	Aalborg University, Denmark
Taeho Park	San Jose State University, USA
Subrata Saha	Institute of Engineering and Management, India
Biswajit Sarkar	Hanyang University, Korea

| Hongfeng Wang | Northeastern University, China |
| Ruiyou Zhang | Northeastern University, China |

Organizing Committee

Jung Woo Baek	Chosun University, Korea
Tai-Woo Chang	Kyonggi University, Korea
Yoon Seok Chang	Korea Aerospace University, Korea
Taesu Cheong	Korea University, Korea
Hyunbo Cho	POSTECH, Korea
Yong–Chan Choi	KAIST, Korea
Byung Do Chung	Yonsei University, Korea
Kwanghun Chung	Hongik University, Korea
Byung–Hyun Ha	Pusan National University, Korea
Kyu Hwan Han	Seoul National University, Korea
Yoo Suk Hong	Seoul National University, Korea
Young Jae Jang	KAIST, Korea
Bong Ju Jeong	Yonsei University, Korea
Hong-Bae Jun	Hongik University, Korea
Changmuk Kang	Soongsil University, Korea
Yuncheol Kang	Hongik University, Korea
Jun-Gyu Kang	Sungkyul University, Korea
Byung-In Kim	POSTECH, Korea
Byung Soo Kim	Incheon National University, Korea
Dongsoo Kim	Soongsil University, Korea
Duck Young Kim	UNIST, Korea
Hwa–Joong Kim	Inha University, Korea
Chang Seong Ko	Kyungsung University, Korea
Chulung Lee	Korea University, Korea
Dong Ho Lee	Hanyang University, Korea
Kangbok Lee	POSTECH, Korea
Kyungsik Lee	Seoul National University, Korea
Taesik Lee	KAIST, Korea
Dug Hee Moon	Changwon National University, Korea
Sang Do Noh	Sungkyunkwan University, Korea
Kun Soo Park	KAIST, Korea
Kwangyeol Ryu	Pusan National University, Korea
Jong–Ho Shin	Chosun University, Korea
Eun Suk Suh	Seoul National University, Korea

International Advisory Committee

Erry Yulian Triblas Adesta	International Islamic University Malaysia, Malaysia
Erlend Alfnes	Norwegian University of Science and Technology, Norway
Thecle Alix	IUT Bordeaux Montesquieu, France

Susanne Altendorfer-Kaiser	Montanuniversität Leoben, Austria
Farhad Ameri	Texas State University, USA
Bjørn Andersen	Norwegian University of Science and Technology, Norway
Eiji Arai	Osaka University, Japan
Frédérique Biennier	INSA Lyon, France
Umit S. Bititci	Heriot Watt University, UK
Magali Bosch-Mauchand	Université de Technologie de Compiègne, France
Abdelaziz Bouras	Qatar University, Qatar
Jim Browne	University College Dublin, Ireland
Luis Camarinha-Matos	Universidade Nova de Lisboa, Portugal
Sergio Cavalieri	University of Bergamo, Italy
Stephen Childe	Plymouth University, UK
Hyunbo Cho	Pohang University of Science and Technology, Korea
Gregor von Cieminski	ZF Hungária Kft, Hungary
Catherine Da Cunha	Ecole Centrale de Nantes, France
Frédéric Demoly	Université de Technologie de Belfort-Montbéliard, France
Shengchun Deng	Harbin Institute of Technology, China
Melanie Despeisse	Chalmers University of Technology, Sweden
Alexandre Dolgui	IMT Atlantique Nantes, France
Slavko Dolinšek	University of Ljubljana, Slovenia
Heidi Carin Dreyer	Norwegian University of Science and Technology, Norway
Eero Eloranta	Helsinki University of Technology, Finland
Soumaya El Kadiri	Texelia AG, Switzerland
Christos Emmanouilidis	Cranfield University, UK
Åsa Fasth-Berglund	Chalmers University, Sweden
Jan Frick	University of Stavanger, Norway
Paolo Gaiardelli	University of Bergamo, Italy
Adriana Giret	Universidad Politécnica de Valencia, Spain
Bernard Grabot	INP-ENIT (National Engineering School of Tarbes), France
Samuel Gomes	Belfort-Montbéliard University of Technology, France
Gerhard Gudergan	FIR Research Institute for Operations Management, Germany
Thomas R. Gulledge Jr.	George Mason University, USA
Hironori Hibino	Tokyo University of Science, Japan
Hans-Henrik Hvolby	Aalborg University, Denmark
Dmitry Ivanov	Berlin School of Economics and Law, Germany
Harinder Jagdev	National University of Ireland at Galway, Ireland
John Johansen	Aalborg University, Denmark
Toshiya Kaihara	Kobe University, Japan
Dimitris Kiritsis	Ecole Polytechnique Fédérale de Lausanne, Switzerland

Tomasz Koch	Wroclaw University of Science and Technology, Poland
Pisut Koomsap	Asian Institute of Technology, Thailand
Gül Kremer	Iowa State University, USA
Boonserm Kulvatunyou	National Institute of Standards and Technology, USA
Thomas R. Kurfess	Georgia Institute of Technology, USA
Andrew Kusiak	University of Iowa, USA
Lenka Landryova	Technical University of Ostrava, Czech Republic
Jan-Peter Lechner	First Global Liaison, Germany
Ming K. Lim	Chongqing University, China
Hermann Lödding	Hamburg University of Technology, Germany
Marco Macchi	Politecnico di Milano, Italy
Vidosav D. Majstorovich	University of Belgrade, Serbia
Adolfo Crespo Marquez	University of Seville, Spain
Gökan May	Ecole Polytechnique Fédérale de Lausanne, Switzerland
Jörn Mehnen	Strathclyde University Glasgow, UK
Hajime Mizuyama	Aoyama Gakuin University, Japan
Ilkyeong Moon	Seoul National University, Korea
Dimitris Mourtzis	University of Patras, Greece
Irenilza de Alencar Naas	UNIP Paulista University, Brazil
Masaru Nakano	Keio University, Japan
Torbjörn Netland	ETH Zürich, Switzerland
Gilles Neubert	EMLYON Business School Saint-Etienne, France
Sang Do Noh	Sungkyunkwan University, Korea
Manuel Fradinho Duarte de Oliveira	SINTEF, Norway
Jinwoo Park	Seoul National University, Korea
François Pérès	Université de Toulouse, France
Fredrik Persson	Linköping Institute of Technology, Sweden
Selwyn Piramuthu	University of Florida, USA
Alberto Portioli-Staudacher	Politecnico di Milano, Italy
Vittaldas V. Prabhu	Pennsylvania State University, USA
Ricardo José Rabelo	Federal University of Santa Catarina, Brazil
Mario Rapaccini	Florence University, Italy
Joao Gilberto Mendes dos Reis	UNIP Paulista University, Brazil
Ralph Riedel	TU Chemnitz, Germany
Asbjörn Rolstadås	Norwegian University of Science and Technology, Norway
David Romero	Tecnologico de Monterrey University, Mexico
Christoph Roser	Karlsruhe University of Applied Sciences, Germany
Martin Rudberg	Linköping University, Sweden
Thomas E. Ruppli	University of Basel, Switzerland
Krzysztof Santarek	Warsaw University of Technology, Poland

John P. Shewchuk	Virginia Polytechnic Institute and State University, USA
Dan L. Shunk	Arizona State University, USA
Riitta Smeds	Aalto University, Finland
Vijay Srinivasan	National Institute of Standards and Technology, USA
Johan Stahre	Chalmers University, Sweden
Kathryn E. Stecke	University of Texas at Dallas, USA
Kenn Steger-Jensen	Aalborg University, Denmark
Volker Stich	FIR Research Institute for Operations Management, Germany
Richard Lee Storch	University of Washington, USA
Jan Ola Strandhagen	Norwegian University of Science and Technology, Norway
Stanislaw Strzelczak	Warsaw University of Technology, Poland
Shigeki Umeda	Musashi University, Japan
Marco Taisch	Politecnico di Milano, Italy
Kari Tanskanen	Aalto University School of Science, Finland
Ilias Tatsiopoulos	National Technical University of Athens, Greece
Sergio Terzi	Politecnico di Milano, Italy
Klaus-Dieter Thoben	Universität Bremen, Germany
Jacques H. Trienekens	Wageningen University, The Netherlands
Mario Tucci	Universitá degli Studi di Firenze, Italy
Gündüz Ulusoy	Sabancı University, Turkey
Bruno Vallespir	University of Bordeaux, France
Agostino Villa	Politecnico di Torino, Italy
Hans-Hermann Wiendahl	University of Stuttgart, Germany
Joakim Wikner	Jönköping University, Sweden
Hans Wortmann	Groningen University, The Netherlands
Thorsten Wuest	West Virginia University, USA
Iveta Zolotová	Technical University of Košice, Slovakia

Marco Garetti Doctoral Workshop

Co-chairs

| Gyu M. Lee | Pusan National University, Korea |
| Ralph Riedel | TU Chemnitz, Germany |

Academic Reviewers and Participants

Gregor von Cieminski	ZF Hungária Kft, Hungary
Paolo Gaiardelli	University of Bergamo, Italy
Adriana Giret	Universidad Politécnica de Valencia, Spain
Gyu M. Lee	Pusan National University, Korea
Ming K. Lim	Chongqing University, China
Gökan May	Ecole Polytechnique Fédérale de Lausanne, Switzerland

Ralph Riedel   TU Chemnitz, Germany
David Romero   Tecnologico de Monterrey University, Mexico
Stanislaw Strzelczak   Warsaw University of Technology, Poland

Sponsors for APMS 2018

College of Engineering, Seoul National University
IFIP WG 5.7 Advances in Production Management Systems
Institute for Industrial Systems Innovation, Seoul National University
Korea Land & Housing Corporation
Korean Federation of Science and Technology Societies
Korean Institute of Industrial Engineers

Contents – Part II

Smart City Interoperability and Cross-Platform Implementation

Manufacturing Performance Management in Smart Factories

Industry 4.0 - Digital Twin

Industry 4.0 - Smart Factory

**Industry 4.0 – Collaborative Cyber-physical Production
and Human Systems**

Contents – Part I

Collaborative Networks

Smart Production for Mass Customization

Global Supply Chain - Supply Chain Management

Knowledge Based Production Planning and Control

Knowledge Based Engineering

Intelligent Diagnostics and Maintenance Solutions for Smart Manufacturing

Upgrading Legacy Equipment to Industry 4.0 Through a Cyber-Physical Interface

Hanna Jónasdóttir, Karishma Dhanani, Kenneth McRae,
and Jörn Mehnen$^{(\boxtimes)}$

University of Strathclyde, Glasgow G1 1XQ, UK
{hanna.jonasdottir,karishma.dhanani,k.mcrae,
jorn.mehnen}@strath.ac.uk

Abstract. With the recent developments of Industry 4.0 technologies, main-tenance can be improved significantly by making it "smart", proactive and even self-aware. This paper introduces a new cutting-edge interfacing technology that enables smart active remote maintenance right on the machine in real-time while allowing integration of smart automated decision making and Industrial Internet of Things to upgrade existing legacy equipment through latest Industry 4.0 technology. This interfacing technology enables remote sensing and actuation access to legacy equipment for smart maintenance by entirely non-intrusive means, i.e. the original equipment does not have to be modified. The design was implemented in a real-world manufacturing environment.

Keywords: Industry 4.0 · Legacy machine upgrade · Cyber-physical interface

1 Introduction

Ever since the first industrial revolution in the 18th century, industry has been con-stantly evolving and looking for solutions to increase efficiency and reduce cost. With emerging technologies, such as Big Data, Industrial Internet of Things (IIoT) and Augmented Reality (AR), industry can gain more insight into its processes than it has ever done before. One of the areas that are benefitting from this development is maintenance.

Historically, maintenance can be divided into three categories, i.e. unplanned maintenance, planned maintenance and condition-based maintenance (CBM), where CBM is the most recent development [1]. With the aforementioned technologies, pre-dictive and remote maintenance has been made easier, taking CBM one step further by using data analytics to predict failures. As smart technologies are getting more advanced, self-aware and self-maintained machine systems will be the logical next step [2].

Even though Industry 4.0 (I4) technologies have shown to be beneficial to industry [3], implementing I4 is still a challenge. One major challenge is related to data and data analytics [4, 5]. Security and model integration is also a major issue that needs to be considered when designing and implementing I4 technology in a life industrial envi-ronment [4–6].

The practical implementation of embedded devices in existing machine environ-ments often implies the need for manipulation of the target machine. This is often not

I. Moon et al. (Eds.): APMS 2018, IFIP AICT 536, pp. 3–10, 2018.
https://doi.org/10.1007/978-3-319-99707-0_1

desirable or possible for e.g. warranty reasons or simply because the process is too difficult, expensive or considered not safe. This need has also been highlighted in industry as companies have started implementing remote control programs in their equipment. By having remote access to machinery, machine downtime has been reduced as well as service cost [7].

This paper introduces a new, non-intrusive technology that leverages the availability of I4 technology for machine tools such as smart sensing and actuation while considering safety and security. The target area for demonstrating this new and in principle generically applicable interfacing technology is smart remote maintenance of CNC machine tools as it enables remote access to the machine from anywhere in the world.

2   Literature Review

Even though some companies have already started implementing Industry 4.0, there is still a long way to go [8]. Several approaches have been proposed to implement I4 technologies in industry. The 5C architecture as introduced by Lee et al. [9] is a step-by-step guideline divided into five layers for the implementation of Cyber-Physical Systems (CPS) in a manufacturing environment. Chien et al. [10] suggested a conceptual framework of Industry 3.5 to bridge the gap between Industry 3.0 and Industry 4.0. RAMI 4.0 [11] was developed to aid the integration of I4. The model is a map based on the Life Cycle Value Stream standard IEC 62890 and Hierarchy Levels standard IEC 62264 and IEC 61512 to address the actors needed for the implementation of I4.

As the definition of I4 varies between countries and research groups, different technologies have been suggested to upgrade factories to I4 level. Kang et al. [12] suggested that the key enabling technologies for I4 are: CPS, Internet of Things (IoT), 3D printing, Big Data, Cloud Computing, sensor, smart energy and holograms. Wang et al. [5] stated that IoT, Big Data, Cloud Computing and Artificial Intelligence (AI) are the main enablers of digitalization of industry. Zhou et al. [4] proposed that I4 could be realized through CPS, IoT technologies, Cloud Computing, Big Data and advanced analytics.

Radziwon et al. [13] define a Smart Factory as a manufacturing solution in a dynamic environment that can resolve production problems with flexible and adaptive processes. As maintenance is one of the factors of a factory life cycle [14], it is one of the key areas that need to be addressed when implementing I4. The emerging technologies allow for a shift towards remote maintenance of legacy equipment. Remote maintenance can be acquired in a few ways, i.e. remote maintenance system which accesses the health parameters of the machine and with remotely controlled robotics [15]. As Kang et al. [12] noted, many companies are still using legacy equipment, so the application guidelines and reference models need to take that into consideration. In this paper the term "legacy" is used in the sense of machine equipment that is not yet I4 ready and typically requires upgrading through Internet connectivity to allow access to advanced I4 technology. Typically, machine tools that are older than about 10 years will fall into that category, but even more modern machine tools do not utilize Industry 4.0 interconnectivity to its full extent.

Traditional human-machine interfaces (HMI) typically have only one feature, that is to visually display the system's outputs to a mechanical input. As industry moves towards CPS, the most important tools for HMI are mobile devices such as tablets [16]. By implementing tablets, the interaction with the machine moves from being performed on a keyboard or a mouse, to touch-screen interactions. Furthermore, mobile devices allow the user to access multiple machinery using only one device. Pacaux-Lemoine et al. [17] proposed a human-centered approach for the design and evaluation of manufacturing systems such as smart manufacturing systems. Harrison et al. [18] developed an engineering toolset for CPS. As a part of that toolset, CPS environment interfaces were developed, enabling remote access to machinery.

There has been significant research into using individual IoT devices, however, to gain the benefits of IoT, it is vital to incorporate the devices within bigger systems. With the Web of Things (WoT) [19], a device can be given a uniquely identifiable "existence" in the World Wide Web of physical things. WoT devices can be addressed through the web to receive or send data but also to sense and actuate other devices or components.

3   BAUTA

Remote maintenance is a key area benefitting from the changes of I4 [20]. With the I4 revolution, there have been many advances in creating devices which enable the integration of computing capabilities with physical objects [21]. This paper introduces BAUTA ("Bauta" is the Italian word for a classic Venetian mask) – an IIoT interface and technology which creates a smart platform to upgrade machines that have not been connected to the Internet yet using a minimal-invasive approach, i.e. the target machine does not need to be opened or manipulated in any ways. Although there are interface technologies such as RS232 [22] or advanced software tools such as MTConnect® [23], these interfaces are either slow or require in-depth technical knowledge or physical manipulation of the target machine.

Brecher et al. [24] suggested that in order for legacy machines to become part of the IIoT, they need to communicate with other systems within the factory as well as worldwide. The BAUTA physical interface (Fig. 1) mimics the interaction of a worker with the target machine preserving all existing safety features and standards around an existing machine. The BAUTA physical interface is also able to monitor specific parameters during any operation as well as interact physically with the target machine.

A systematic design process was used for the design of the device. The device has gone through several design consideration and the version presented in this paper is the second version of the device. The main challenges which had to be overcome in the design of the interface were to ensure a secure connection and selecting the appropriate mechanical actuators for the device. To avoid any exposure to physical attacks with the wireless connections within the system, passwords have been implemented at every interface. For this paper a legacy HAAS CNC machine with a standard CNC controller was used as generic representative for similar machine tools.

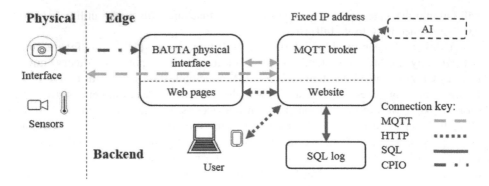

Fig. 1. The BAUTA cyber-physical system implementation

3.1 Design

Hardware

To remotely access legacy machinery, a physical interface is needed to allow the operator to interact with the equipment. To be a practical solution, it needs to be easy to install whilst not compromising the design of the machine or require electrical expertise to fit. To achieve this, the only physical connection used, were bolted mounting points on the controller.

The BAUTA interface mirrors the interaction of a worker with the controller by enabling external actuation of the keys on a CNC control panel. The design incorporates electro-mechanical actuators which match the key layout of the machine. Arbitrary virtual custom layouts of the keyboard can quickly be created from a template and mapped to the target machine keyboard. The physical BAUTA interface can be designed in parametric solid modelling and printed or machined through additive or subtractive manufacture, respectively. The front of the physical interface features an optional touch screen that allows the operator at the machine to still input commands directly if desired (Fig. 3), which are now mapped through the access software. However, the main task of the physical interface is to map remote commands or command sequences to the physical keyboard while collecting and sending any sensor data back to the remote operator for visual feedback or cloud-based maintenance analytics.

Edge Connection

For the physical interface to communicate with a web-based interface, the proposed architecture uses an IoT Edge processor to run a middleware software to transfer data. Through WoT technology modular sensors such as vibration, temperature and visual interface can become accessible through the web. The devices are connected through Wi-Fi, as no physical connections are required. For this implementation, an open source Edge processor (Raspberry Pi 3B+) was connected through eduroam® allowing remote operation through the academic web.

By following the WoT architecture, the sensors and actuators communicate within the system through MQTT [19], as it allows for a central broker which has a fixed IP address ensuring secure data transfer. The backend uses an HTTP application protocol with WebSockets [19] to transfer the data to and from a website which communicates immediately once the user interacts with the system.

User Interface

For the HMI, a web interface was chosen to allow easy access to any web browsing device as it can be used via any network connection to operate the system with the correct login details. This means that no specialist equipment or software is required. HTML webpages with WebSockets display the information and trends collected from the target machine for the operators to analyze (Fig. 2).

Use of prerecorded macro can be set up for maintenance tasks such as axis datuming and the set-up of feed rates. Setup functions like the loading of G-code from a file can also be processed.

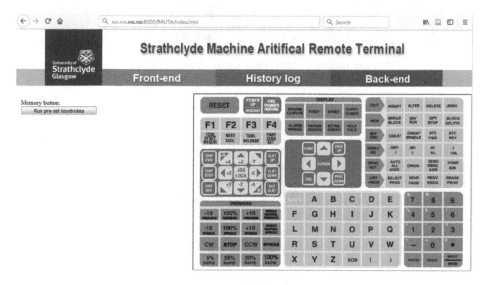

Fig. 2. View of the software displayed on a computer web browser.

3.2   Implementation

The physical interface and software was implemented at the Advanced Forming Research Center (AFRC) and University of Strathclyde on a HAAS control panel (Fig. 3). BAUTA successfully connected through eduroam® to the Cloud server and established its connection on the MQTT network automatically. This showed that the device can configure itself over a foreign network, given that it has Internet access. An Android® tablet was used to control the CNC machine over the Internet using the Web Interface shown in Fig. 2. Proximity to the machine is not required and that the machine could, in principle, be operated from anywhere in the world. To test the physical device, inputs were actuated from the front panel as shown in Fig. 3. All the trial commands were recorded on the log page along with user comments.

Fig. 3. Remote maintenance interface mounted on a HAAS control panel.

4   Conclusions

This paper presents a cutting-edge non-invasive cyber-physical interfacing technology which opens the world of Industry 4.0 through a new cyber-physical overlaying and augmenting approach, which to the authors' best of knowledge is a novel technology. The proposed cyber-physical prototype uses activation keys which can be controlled via the web to allow remote access to the target machine for maintenance activities. The device was successfully implemented on a control panel of a CNC machine, but detailed validation will be carried out in the future.

Future work will include integrating the system with Strathclyde University's new AI enabled smart modular sensors which will also unlock AR/VR capabilities for legacy machine tools. IEC 61499 [25] function blocks could be uploaded to interconnected BAUTA devices to create agile I4-process plans and create G-code in real-time. Furthermore, the design of the BAUTA device can be optimized by following a human-centered design process.

Acknowledgements. This work was supported by the Engineering and Physical Science Research Council (EPSRC) as part of an EPSRC HVMC Fellowship "BAUTA – A Non-invasive remote maintenance tool for legacy CNC machine tools". The authors would like to acknowledge the kind support by the Advanced Forming Research Centre (AFRC) at University of Strathclyde.

References

1. Martin, K.F.: A review by discussion of condition monitoring and fault diagnosis in machine tools. Int. J. Mach. Tools Manuf. **34**, 527–551 (1994). https://doi.org/10.1016/08906955(94)90083-3
2. Lee, J., Kao, H.-A., Yang, S.: Service innovation and smart analytics for Industry 4.0 and Big Data environment. Proc. CIRP **16**, 3–8 (2014). https://doi.org/10.1016/j.procir.2014.02.001

3. Choi, S., Kim, B.H., Noh, S.D.: A diagnosis and evaluation method for strategic planning and systematic design of a virtual factory in smart manufacturing systems. Int. J. Precis. Eng. Manuf. **16**, 1107–1115 (2015). https://doi.org/10.1007/s12541-015-0143-9
4. Zhou, K., Liu, T., Zhou, L.: Industry 4.0: towards future industrial opportunities and challenges. In: 2015 12th International Conference on Fuzzy Systems and Knowledge Discovery (FSKD), pp. 2147–2152. IEEE, Piscataway (2015). https://doi.org/10.1109/fskd.2015.7382284
5. Wang, S., Wan, J., Li, D., Zhang, C.: Implementing smart factory of Industrie 4.0: an outlook. Int. J. Distrib. Sens. Netw. **12** (2016). https://doi.org/10.1155/2016/3159805
6. Khan, M., Wu, X., Xu, X., Dou, W.: Big data challenges and opportunities in the hype of Industry 4.0. In: 2017 IEEE International Conference on Communications (ICC), pp. 1–6. IEEE, Piscataway (2017). https://doi.org/10.1109/icc.2017.7996801
7. PTC. Reducing Unscheduled Downtime and Customer Efficiency. https://www.ptc.com/-/media/Files/PDFs/IoT/Axeda-CS-Leica.ashx?la=en&hash=F070D368C6ABAC9E40D29-3FB7C698F196D04D295
8. Qin, J., Liu, Y., Grosvenor, R.: A categorical framework of manufacturing for Industry 4.0 and beyond. Proc. CIRP **52**, 173–178 (2016). https://doi.org/10.1016/j.procir.2016.08.005
9. Lee, J., Bagheri, B., Kao, H.-A.: A cyber-physical systems architecture for Industry 4.0-based manufacturing systems. Manuf. Lett. **3**, 18–23 (2015). https://doi.org/10.1016/j.mfglet.2014.12.001
10. Chien, C.-F., Hong, T., Guo, H.-Z.: A conceptual framework for "Industry 3.5" to empower intelligent manufacturing and case studies. Proc. Manuf. **11**, 2009–2017 (2017). https://doi.org/10.1016/j.promfg.2017.07.352
11. Hankel, M., Rexroth B.: The reference architectural model Industrie 4.0 (RAMI 4.0). ZVEI (2015)
12. Kang, H.S., et al.: Smart manufacturing: past research, present findings, and future directions. Int. J. Precis. Eng. Manuf. Green Technol. **3**, 111–128 (2016). https://doi.org/10.1007/s40684-016-0015-5
13. Radziwon, A., Bilberg, A., Bogers, M., Madsen, E.S.: The smart factory: exploring adaptive and flexible manufacturing solutions. Proc. Eng. **69**, 1184–1190 (2014). https://doi.org/10.1016/j.proeng.2014.03.108
14. Azevedo, A., Almeida, A.: Factory templates for digital factories framework. Robot. Comput.-Integr. Manuf. **27**, 755–771 (2011). https://doi.org/10.1016/j.rcim.2011.02.004
15. Roy, R., Stark, R., Tracht, K., Takata, S., Mori, M.: Continuous maintenance and the future – foundations and technological challenges. CIRP Ann. **65**, 667–688 (2016). https://doi.org/10.1016/j.cirp.2016.06.006
16. Gorecky, D., Schmitt, M., Loskyll, M., Zühlke, D.: Human-machine-interaction in the Industry 4.0 era. In: 2014 12th IEEE International Conference on Industrial Informatics (INDIN), pp. 289–294. IEEE, Piscataway (2014). https://doi.org/10.1109/indin.2014.6945523
17. Pacaux-Lemoine, M.-P., Trentesaux, D., Zambrano Rey, G., Millot, P.: Designing intelligent manufacturing systems through human-machine cooperation principles: a human-centered approach. Comput. Ind. Eng. **111**, 581–595 (2017). https://doi.org/10.1016/j.cie.2017.05.014
18. Harrison, R., Vera, D., Ahmad, B.: Engineering methods and tools for cyber-physical automation systems. Proc. IEEE **104**, 973–985 (2016). https://doi.org/10.1109/JPROC.2015.2510665
19. Guinard, D.D., Trifa, V.M.: Building the Web of Things: With Examples in Node.js and Raspberry Pi. Manning Publications Co, Greenwich (2016)

20. Masoni, R., et al.: Supporting remote maintenance in Industry 4.0 through augmented reality. Proc. Manuf. **11**, 1296–1302 (2017). https://doi.org/10.1016/j.promfg.2017.07.257
21. Shariatzadeh, N., Lundholm, T., Lindberg, L., Sivard, G.: Integration of digital factory with smart factory based on internet of things. Proc. CIRP **50**, 512–517 (2016). https://doi.org/10.1016/j.procir.2016.05.050
22. Electronic Industries Association, Engineering Department: Interface between data terminal equipment and data communication equipment employing serial binary data interchange. Electronic Industries Association, Engineering Department, Washington (1969)
23. MTConnect® Standard. Part 3.1 – Interfaces. http://www.mtconnect.org/standard-documents-2017/
24. Jeschke, S., Brecher, C., Meisen, T., Özdemir, D., Eschert, T.: Industrial internet of things and cyber manufacturing systems. In: Jeschke, S., Brecher, C., Song, H., Rawat, D. (eds.) Industrial internet of things, pp. 3–19. Springer, Cham (2017). https://doi.org/10.1007/978-3-319-42559-7_1
25. Function Blocks for Industrial-Process Measurement and Control Systems - Part 1: Architecture. IEC 61499 (2005)

Development of Maturity Levels for Agile Industrial Service Companies

Achim Kampker, Jana Frank$^{(\boxtimes)}$, Roman Emonts-Holley,
and Philipp Jussen

Research Institute for Industrial Management (FIR), RWTH Aachen University,
Campus-Boulevard 55, 52074 Aachen, Germany
Jana.Frank@fir.rwth-aachen.de

Abstract. Industrial service is currently undergoing tremendous changes, largely driven by the development of new technologies, in particular the advancing digitalization. Never before have organizations had more comprehensive and insightful data assets - and never before have the opportunities to fully exploit this potential been better. However, most companies are unaware of how they can make use of this potential and which development steps are necessary to react to the current situation. To change this, a maturity-based approach was developed which describes four development stages of an industrial service company from a technological, organizational and cultural point of view. The maturity model makes it possible to develop a digital roadmap that is tailor-made to each company, which helps to introduce Industrie 4.0 and transform industrial service companies into learning, agile organizations.

Keywords: Industrie 4.0 · Maturity model · Technical service
Service management · Culture · Organizational structure

1 Introduction

Recent developments in ICT (information and communication technologies) cause highly impactful changes in the industrial services sector. The digitization of service systems makes it possible to integrate ICT in different areas of a company, from sales and service provision to the development of entirely new services [1]. New technologies play a key role as tools for exploiting the changes brought about by digitization and Industrie 4.0 as an opportunity for industrial service. Networked, intelligent machines and plants cannot only control the production process automatically, but also schedule maintenance services and repairs by monitoring their own condition. With the help of remote technologies, it is also possible to undertake maintenance measures from a distance anytime. These and many other practical applications of ICT are just the beginning of an extensive revolution in the service sector [2]. The use of new technologies and the acquisition of knowledge from a target-oriented information processing change the distribution of responsibilities and working methods of companies significantly. New technologies are being introduced, but very few organizations did further changes, such as a fundamental structural and process reform to integrate new technologies to raise the full potential [3]. In the course of digitalization, organizational

I. Moon et al. (Eds.): APMS 2018, IFIP AICT 536, pp. 11–19, 2018.
https://doi.org/10.1007/978-3-319-99707-0_2

and cultural areas of a company must also be transformed. Although modern technologies make it possible to build an ever-growing database, harnessing the underlying potential depends just as much as on the organizational structure and culture in the company. For a service company, the overall objective should be to build a learning, agile service organization that can continuously adapt to a dynamic environment. For this purpose, traditional, hierarchical company structures and values need to be loosened. Nearly 60 percent of large companies are still traditionally managed – more than twice as many as medium-sized companies [4]. A simple reorganization is unlikely to suffice in most cases. Contemporary corporate identity precepts such as feedback orientation trust or fault tolerance can hardly be found among service companies [5].

New technologies in the industrial service sector also change the demands made on the company organization and corporate culture. The transfer of decision-making power to digital systems, the trust in data provided by these systems as well as the sharing of knowledge become crucial factors of success. The introduction of new technologies makes it possible to realize potentials in service, but only if employees accept these technologies, incorporate knowledge into systems and trust decision templates from systems. These technologies must be integrated efficiently into the existing organizational structure. On these grounds, a maturity model for industrial service was developed, which describes the development stages of a company from a technological, organizational and cultural point of view. It is constructed as a four-stage maturity model, whereby benefits for the company increase with each stage. The maturity model makes it possible to develop a digital roadmap, tailor-made to each company, which helps to introduce Industrie 4.0 and transform industrial service companies into a agile organization capable and willing to learn.

2   Fundamental Definitions and State of Research

The degree of maturity describes the maturity of a field of observation with regard to a specific method or a management model. Changing degrees of consistency between defined criteria and degrees of fulfillment of these criteria result in different levels of maturity. [6] So far, there are a variety of maturity models that assess the current state of digitalization and Industrie 4.0 in companies, such as the so-called acatech Industrie 4.0 Maturity Index. It is a standardized and well-established approach for the assessment of a company's status during its transformation towards becoming an agile company. The company is evaluated from technological, resource-related, organizational and cultural perspectives [7]. The maturity model is divided into six levels: computerization, connectivity, visibility, transparency, predictability and adaptability [7]. The acatech model refers primarily to manufacturing companies and not to service providers, which is why it does not give any indication of how industrial service is changing.

In the field of industrial service, there are primarily maturity models which describe the development stages of a company with regard to the service and spare parts portfolio, the professionalism and effectiveness of the organizational structure and the prevailing service processes [8, 9]. A source that considers all fields does not exist yet. Thus, this work contributes to close the research gab between Industrie 4.0 in the service sector and technological change and its impact on the structure and culture of a service company.

3 Methodology

The close cooperation with the project partners and the chosen practical method-ological approach is carried out as a combination of a workshop and in-depth literature review. The described acatech maturity index was used as a framework for the design of the maturity degrees. As mentioned before, it refers primarily to manufacturing companies and therefore does not give any indication of how industrial service is changing.

20 representatives of the German maintenance industry took part in the work-shop. In a first step, they were asked to describe their current technologies. Second, they were asked to discuss relevant future technologies, some of which are already being planned. Based on these results, it is possible to estimate which maintenance technologies are relevant in the near future. In a third step, the participants discussed about organizational changes through the introduction of new technologies by first agreeing on a short definition and delimitation of the two terms company culture and organizational structure. The result was a description of the organizational and cultural framework conditions under which technological developments in service can take place successfully. As a follow-up task to the workshop, the respective technologies as well as the framework conditions were assigned to the different levels of maturity, resulting in a maturity model for the industrial service, which describes four devel-opment steps towards an agile, learning service organization. The development stages are visibility, transparency, predictability and adaptability. They have been described in a holistic approach with regard to technology, organization and culture.

4 Industrial Service Maturity Model

The maturity level description is based on the different levels of technology devel-opment. Figure 1 provides an overview of the above-mentioned target variables.

As shown in Fig. 1, the use of preventive maintenance measures increased the availability of plants significantly as less reactive and more preventive maintenance is used. This causes a reduction in unplanned downtime, which cannot be avoided entirely though, as stage four shows - despite full automation. Based on available data, the maintenance plans may be subject to permanent change. The complexity of the interaction between production orders and maintenance requirements results in a sys-tem that enables constant recalculation of scenarios and simulations starting at level three. At the same time, decisions about the levels are increasingly taken over by systems, which in turn means that fewer and fewer employees are needed for admin-istrative activities.

In the following, the four maturity levels are described in detail. All descriptions follow the same scheme by first giving a brief overview of the technology of the stage and in the second step describing the maturity of the organization and culture based on the technological implications. For the organization, only the dimension *decision management* is considered. For company culture, the aspect of *decision processes* is described in an analogue way.

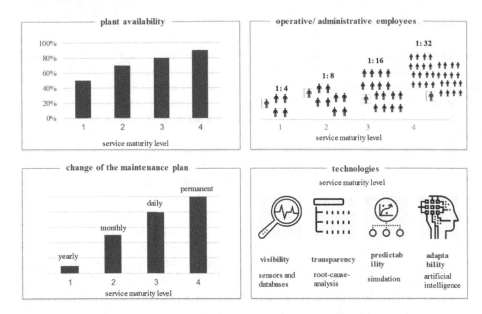

Fig. 1. Parameters of the maturity levels in industrial service

4.1   Visibility

Regarding the level of visibility, a condition monitoring system is the predominant technology. Data provides a complete picture of what is currently happening. Sensor, process and order data is read and manually evaluated in order to create a so-called digital twin of the machine, its mapping order status and the resources used. At this stage, only reactive or preventive maintenance measures are possible. They are based on wear and tear details or runtime-dependent intervals.

Technology

Machine Data

Vibration analysis, temperature data, performance data (voltage etc.), indirect performance data (lubricant, residual stress of the material). This data can be viewed in real-time via a dashboard and is also available historically via drill-down. Error messages are displayed in plain text to the machine operator and service provider. Based on an error message, the service provider can be commissioned. Depending on the contract, the service provider reports an error message directly to the machine operator.

Order Data

Orders are generated and scheduled as a preventive measure on the basis of machine data and manufacturer specifications. The planner of the service agent must schedule the orders manually. Each order contains all relevant order details: contact data, object data and object list, usage history, documents, material reservations and notifications. The customer can check the order status (in progress, planned, executed, etc.) in real time. The technician enters the following information in the system: time confirmation (directions, working time), material confirmation and service report.

Organization
Decisions can be made quickly and easily thanks to a sufficient data transparency. For the organization, this means that decisions must be based on data and hierarchies and release procedures become superfluous. This is problematic for companies with contractual liability. Managers must be responsible for decisions in order to ensure liability. At this point, contractual framework conditions must be created to secure decisions made by employees.

Culture
The employees base decisions and discussions on data. In doing so, Data-based decisions can be considered as having a higher value than personal opinions. Employees have to come to terms with the fact that everything is recorded in form of data. They also have to learn to trust this data and, at the same time, to question it critically.

4.2 Transparency

This level is characterized by root-cause-analysis, decision trees, data- and advanced analytics. In the case of the latter, the stored and aggregated data for the analysis of error causes is interlinked. Big Data is refined to so-called Smart Data. Technologically, the method of Edge Computing is used for this. Edge computing enables an acceleration of data streams, e.g. real-time data processing without latency times. This enables intelligent applications and devices to react to data almost immediately when it is created. This avoids delays. The systems are self-learning and present the user with a simple and intuitive way to combine different data sets. Data scientists and machine learning algorithms are indispensable for this task. The difference of this method to heuristic ones is the run-up time. Training a neural network requires great effort in the beginning. Once in operation, the system can deliver results in real-time. Heuristic methods require very little effort in the run-up phase, but can only achieve a result by running many calculations. This means that a long runtime can be expected for each request.

Technology
Machine Data
    The machine data described for the visibility level is automatically analyzed in the transparency level. Historical data of the machine is used for this purpose in order to automatically uncover correlations between the causes of faults. The failure of the bearing of an electric motor, for example, is a result of a combination of oil pressure, residual stress and torque. This conclusion was derived from historical data and checked by employees for meaningfulness.

Order Data
    Orders can be evaluated historically by the system, i.e. the necessity and time of the order can be automatically classified on a scale covering the options "optimal, too early, and too late". For this purpose, the performance data of the machine is compared before and after a maintenance service has been performed.

Organization
At this maturity level, human-machine interaction is of importance. The existing expert knowledge of the maintenance technician must be transferred to the system. The team structure of the operative unit changes due to the increase of the number of employees who may not have manual skills but possess mathematical-analytical skills. Teams must be able to get together quickly and work together locally in consideration of their competencies and the task to be solved. Decisions must be implemented extremely quickly, which affects hierarchical structures and release processes.

Culture
Employee knowledge influences the design of analysis models. This requires a willingness to share knowledge with the system and the understanding of the analysis models. The analysis models allow the detection of contexts, so that employees can draw conclusions. Information as the basis for decisions are available in a simpler form. Decisions can be made faster. Employees need to learn how to handle these faster available data-driven decisions.

4.3   Predictability

The forecasting ability level is characterized by the forecasting of events and predictive maintenance. Systems can predict scenarios with probabilities and provide them to the user. The user needs to evaluate them and then react accordingly. Historical data can be combined and evaluated and used for future predictions. For this purpose, forecasting methods are used that can analyze dynamic non-linear relationships between numerous parameters and, based on these, make forecasts for the future within a suitable period of time. The machines and systems are maintained proactively to minimize downtimes. Ideally, faults can be predicted before defects or failures occur. The actual occurrence of the fault can be prevented by the maintenance measures that are proactively initiated at an early stage. For reliable predictions regarding the condition of machines, systems and faults, it is necessary to collect large amounts of data. In addition to data from the machines, data from peripheral and environmental characteristics such as temperature or humidity levels is also collected. The actual result of the scenario must be closely observed and feed back into the system. This guarantees better forecasts. There is great potential for this maturity level: profitability increases through predictive maintenance because fewer reactive and preventive orders need to be carried out. As a result, machine downtime is reduced dramatically.

Technology
Machine Data
    The system records the status of the machine and can simulate various scenarios based on the planned orders. Thus, the system knows different future states of the machine. Recommendations for the optimal handling of the machine (on the part of production and service) can be issued by the system. Based on the objectives of the company, the service provider and the machine operator can select the right configuration. The current status of the machines or system components is displayed on a dashboard. Forecasting technology, in turn, creates risk profiles as to when and what disruption is to be expected. The forecast reports show in detail when which phases

begin and end, i.e. when the condition of the machine becomes critical. In this way, it is possible to determine when the time window during which maintenance should be carried out opens and closes in order to prevent unplanned breakdowns as far as possible and at the same time make optimum use of remaining service lives.

Order Data

Based on the created risk profiles and the forecast of when a plant condition will become critical, orders can be planned much better. This means that maintenance orders are planned based on the selected periods or scenarios. Periods refer to the lead time, which is determined according to the criticality of the investment. For a bottle-neck machine, for example, the calculated worst-case scenario is used, while the best-case scenario is selected for non-critical facilities. It is the responsibility of the customer and the scheduler to make these decisions. To this end, rules and frameworks should be defined in which the procedure and the systemic limits are shown and defined.

Organization

In this stage, the worker uses the expert systems that were filled based on the employee's knowledge. Decisions are thus prepared based on data and made available to the employee. Extreme flexibility of maintenance staff is required, as orders can change daily. Significantly greater competence and understanding of the planning content is required when setting up the system. Continuous testing of the scenarios at the beginning is necessary to determine the system limits.

Culture

The selection of a course of action and therefore the preparation of decisions is transferred to the machine. The work is no longer based on the knowledge and experience of the workers, but on the information and learning ability of the machine. However, willingness to cooperate requires trust in data and technology.

4.4   Adaptability

At this stage, decisions are made by the system. For this purpose, the data of the digital shadow is used in such a way that decisions with the greatest positive effects are made autonomously and without human intervention in the shortest time and the resulting measures are implemented. The service provider and the customer must set up a structured and clear set of rules. The system then takes over all of the planning as well as the settlement of the orders. Maintenance personnel can concentrate on the operational process. The planners can deal with strategic issues and develop better consulting services.

Technology

Machine and Order Data

All available data is processed and analyzed at all times.

Organization

Decisions are made by the system and they are available to the employee. All action is based on the planning of the system. Depending on the customer, the model and the contract design must be adapted. For safety reasons it is necessary that the dispatcher makes the decision and systemic liability issues are recorded in the contract.

Culture

Transferring decision-making powers to digital software systems creates certain restrictions regarding the employee's field of responsibility. Although the employee is the system designer as well as the inspector and exporter, he decides less autonomously than before because his decisions are system-oriented. Employees must therefore completely trust the systems, which guide and influence the decisions significantly.

5 Critical Reflection and Outlook

The described service maturity model is based on expert workshops as well as an in-depth literature review. In a first step, the maturity model describes the development stages of an industrial service provider on the way to becoming an agile, learning company. On this basis, one must define concrete recommendations for company measures, so that service enterprises can follow the path of maturity levels. For this purpose, it is necessary to disassemble the fields of action organization and culture in their dimensions and to assign the specific characteristics of the dimensions to the maturity levels. This is the only way to submit targeted recommendations for companies afterwards.

References

1. Herterich, M., Uebernickel, F., Brenner, W.: Industrielle Dienstleistungen 4.0. Springer, Wiesbaden (2016). https://doi.org/10.1007/978-3-658-13911-7
2. Martinsuo, M., Perminova-Harikoski, O., Turunen, T.: Strategic Change towards Future Industrial Service Business. https://tutcris.tut.fi/portal/files/4274023/strategic_change_towards_future_industrial_service_business.pdf. Accessed 01 Apr 2018
3. Petry, T.: Digital Leadership: Erfolgreiches Führen in Zeiten der Digital Economy. Haufe, Freiburg (2016)
4. Hermann, A., Löwer, P., Bohnenkamp, J., Stein, F.: Organigramm deutscher Unternehmen. http://assets.kienbaum.com/downloads/Organigramm-deutscher-Unternehmen_Kienbaum-Stepstone-Studie_2017.pdf?mtime=20170427131752. Accessed 01 Apr 2018
5. Baker, D., Kerry, D.: The two faces of uncertainty avoidance: attachment and adaptation. J. Behav. Appl. Manag. **12**(2), 128–142 (2011)
6. Ahlemann, F., Schroeder, C., Teuteberg, F.: Kompetenz-und Reifegradmodelle für das Projektmanagement. Grundlagen, Vergleich und Einsatz. https://www.researchgate.net/profile/Frank_Teuteberg2/publication/277323730_Kompetenz-_und_Reifegradmodelle_fur_das_Projektmanagement_Grundlagen_Vergleich_und_Einsatz/links/55678de308aeccd777378b12.pdf. Accessed 01 Apr 2018
7. Schuh, G., Anderl, R., Gausemeier, J., Ten Hompel, M., Wahlster, W.: Industrie 4.0 Maturity Index: Die digitale Transformation von Unternehmen gestalten. Herbert Utz Verlag, München (2016)

8. Geissbauer, R., Griesmeier, A., Feldmann, S., Toepert, M.: Serviceinnovation: Potenziale industrieller Dienstleistungen erkennen und erfolgreich implementieren. Springer, Wiesbaden (2016). https://doi.org/10.1007/978-3-642-21239-0
9. Burger, T., Ganz, W., Pezzotta, G., Rapaccini, M.: Service development for product services: a maturity model and a field research. In: 2011 RESER Conference, Productivity of Services Next Gen-Beyond Output/Input. Hamburg, Germany, 7–10 September 2011. Fraunhofer Verlag, Stuttgart (2011)

The Role of Internet of Services (IoS) on Industry 4.0 Through the Service Oriented Architecture (SOA)

Jacqueline Zonichenn Reis$^{(\boxtimes)}$ and Rodrigo Franco Gonçalves

Paulista University, São Paulo, Brazil
zonichenn@hotmail.com, rofranco212@gmail.com

Abstract. Many different concepts and approaches have been seen for an Industry 4.0 achievement. In the attempt of merging the theory to the practice, there are gaps to determine which concept or technology suits best the productive chain and what is really a pre-requisite to classify it as Industry 4.0. On scientific and empirical literature about this subject, the Internet of Services, IoS, has been mentioned as an important pillar for Industry 4.0, coupled with Internet of Things (IoT) and Cyber-physical systems (CPS). While IoT and CPS as well as their link with Industry 4.0 are detailed in many researches, a deeper understanding on the Internet of Services and its contribution for this scenario is still missing. This paper aims to fill this gap gathering concepts about the Internet of Services, how it is composed and what would be its role on the manufacturing environment. Through a deeper understanding about the origin of the term Internet of Services, there is an important concept that may explain how the Industry 4.0 operates in a business and technological perspective: the concept of SOA - Service Oriented Architecture.

Keywords: Internet of Services · Industry 4.0 · Service-Oriented Architecture

1 Introduction

After some years that Industry 4.0 was first coined, companies are still looking for the best approach and trying to understand this new paradigm. The manufacturers' dilemma is whether they should commit into Industry 4.0 and which technology would be the most suitable to adopt, considering the investment required and the benefits on productivity [1].

Historically, the first three industrial revolutions came as a result of mechanization, electricity and Information Technology respectively. Now, the introduction of the Internet of Things and the Internet of Services into the manufacturing environment leads to a fourth industrial revolution [2].

Although the Internet of Services is considered by many authors as one of the main pillars of Industry 4.0 [2–5], there is still a gap on the literature in addressing the full meaning of Internet of Services and its contribution on this new environment.

Comparing Internet of Services against the Internet of Things on literature about Industry 4.0, the number of papers reflect a more expressive focus on IoT while IoS is still not so explored.

I. Moon et al. (Eds.): APMS 2018, IFIP AICT 536, pp. 20–26, 2018.
https://doi.org/10.1007/978-3-319-99707-0_3

Moreover, Internet of Services brings itself a more intangible perspective which is natural from services [6]. While IoT deals with tangible objects, sensors and machines, the Internet of Services will cover a more abstract set of functionalities, bringing the concept of SOA, Service-Oriented Architecture.

Service-Oriented Architecture SOA is a logical model that reorganize software applications and infrastructure into a set of interacting services [7]. By exploring the concept of SOA, it is expected that the meaning of Internet of Services and Industry 4.0 becomes more clear, reinforcing the relevance of this study.

The aim of this research is characterize the Internet of Services explaining its composition and its role on Industry 4.0.

This paper is organized as follows: After this introduction, the second section brings the research method. The third section gives a contextualization on Industry 4.0. The forth section covers the foundation of Internet of Services and reveals the concept of Service Oriented Architecture. The fifth section links such concepts to the manufacturing environment, followed by a conclusion.

2   Research Method

This paper is a theoretical development based in bibliographic, but not systematic, review about Industry 4.0 and Internet of Services concepts, looking for the role of IoS in this new manufacturing environment.

An initial search was conducted using two comparative strings in the bases Google Scholar, Science Direct and Web of Science, looking for the relevance and originality of the subject.

Table 1. Boolean Strings used for the research

String	Finds		
	Google scholar	Science direct	Web of science
"Internet of Things" AND "Industry 4.0"	7660	492	252
"Internet of Services" AND "Industry 4.0"	579	61	9

As shown in Table 1, there are much less results when placing Internet of Services on the string.

Given the small number of resulting papers, the study becomes exploratory, without a specific inclusion or exclusion criteria for papers selection.

After gathering concepts that link the subjects Internet of Services and Industry 4.0, the study was refined into such correlations and a new model approach has been proposed for a smart manufacturing environment.

3   Industry 4.0

The term Industry 4.0, was rooted in the German federal government´s strategy in 2011 [2]. This German Government's initiative had the aim of gaining stronghold in global manufacturing by advanced application of information and communication systems. Through the application of new technologies in manufacturing, the entire factory environment becomes smart and enables mass customization [3].

Industry 4.0 is defined as a collective term for technologies and concepts of value chain organization [4]. Among this set of technologies, the protagonist ones would be Cyber Physical Systems, Internet of Things and Internet of Services [2–5]. Cyber Physical Systems (CPS) are sensors and actuators that monitor physical processes and create a virtual copy of the physical world. Over the Internet of Things, CPS communicate and co-operate with each other and humans in real time. Then through the Internet of Services (IoS), both internal and cross organizational services are offered and utilized by participants of the value chain [4].

The own promoters of the German program explain that Industry 4.0 involves the technical integration of IoT and IoS as enablers to create networks, incorporating the entire manufacturing process that convert factories into a smart environment [2].

As seen on Research Method section, while most papers in scientific literature cover Internet of Things, this paper focus on Internet of Services or IoS, addressing the service context and going beyond the infrastructure and connectivity domains.

4   Internet of Services

The term Internet of Services raised from the convergence of other two concepts: Web 2.0 and SOA - Service-oriented architecture [8]. The intersection of these two fields is the notion of reusing and composing existing resources and services.

The first concept, Web 2.0 is characterized by four aspects: interactivity, social networks, tagging and web services [9].

- Interactivity: this gain comes from two technologies: AJAX (Asynchronous Java-Script and XML) that allows the communication and the dynamic manipulation of data between a server and the Web browser;
- Social networks: the social networks up come based on common interests and make the information from each network available through different ways;
- Tagging: users can add a key-word as a tag to a certain Web content, making this tag easily reachable when searched by other users;
- Web Services: allow that other software make use of the features offered by a Web application, being available not only to people but also to machines.

The second concept that forms the Internet of Services is the Service Oriented Architecture – SOA [8]. SOA is a way of designing and building a set of Information Technology applications where application components and Web Services make their functions available on the same access channel for mutual use. In order to satisfy these requirements services should be [7]:

- Technology neutral: they must be invoked through standardized lowest common denominator technologies that are available to almost all IT environments. This implies that the invocation mechanisms (protocols, descriptions and discovery mechanisms) should comply with widely accepted standards.
- Loosely coupled: they must not require knowledge or any internal structures or conventions (context) at the client or service side.
- Support location transparency: services should have their definitions and location information stored in a repository such as UDDI and be accessible by a variety of clients that can invoke the services irrespective of their location.

4.1 Service Oriented Architecture - SOA

The Service Oriented Architecture – SOA - can be explained through two different angles. From a business perspective, it represents a set of services that improve the capability of the company to conduct business with customers and suppliers. From a technology perspective, it is a project philosophy characterized by modularity, separation of concerns, service re-uses, and composition, as well as a new programming method based [10].

Web Services technology constitutes the main vehicle for service-oriented architectures. Web Service is defined as "a software system designed to support interoperable machine-to-machine interaction over a network". It has an interface described in a machine-process format that informs what the service does and how to call its functions. Basically, Web Services on-line delivery functionalities (called *services*) offer simple input and output interfaces – hiding its internal structure and programming language – that can be used by other Web Service, software application or machine, as well as humans [11].

Through the concept of Service-Oriented Architecture, new applications can be assembled from the available components and services, like a LEGO®. In SOA, all applications in an organization can offer and consume services in a unique and integrated communication channel, called Enterprise Service Bus, as a simple way to facilitate integration [12].

5 Application of Service-Oriented Architecture on Industry 4.0

In the computer science domain, the service-oriented paradigm defines the principles for conceiving decentralized control architectures that decompose computational processes into sub-processes, called services. The focus of SOA is to leverage the creation of reusable and interoperable function blocks in order to reduce the amount of reprogramming efforts [13].

As a metaphor, it is like a shopping mall underground floor in which various services such as barber shop, cell phones repair, tailor's shop are offered in a same physical location, facilitating customer access.

In a cloud manufacturing system, various manufacturing resources and abilities can be intelligently sensed and connected into the wider Internet by means of SOA principles. As a result, the Service Oriented Manufacturing Systems (SOMS) emerges.

A promising approach to develop SOMS is the integration of multi-agent system (MAS) with Service Oriented Architectures (SOA) [14].

Within the Industry 4.0 it works as a service bus, as placed in Fig. 1, where different robots, machines and applications are available for the manufacturing process. The different services can be accessed, matched and integrated by discovery and composition applications creating a Service-Oriented Manufacturing Architecture (SOMA) which is an approach we developed for an Industry 4.0 smart manufacturing environment.

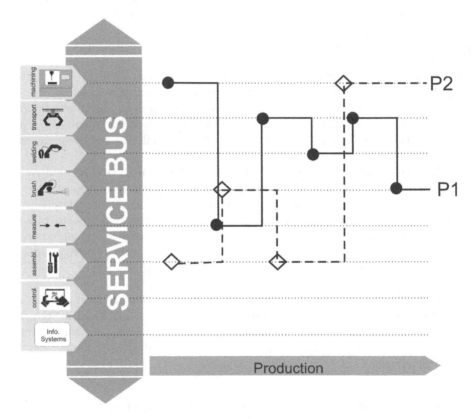

Fig. 1. Service-Oriented Manufacturing Architecture (SOMA). Source: the authors

On Fig. 1, instead of a traditional product-oriented environment, there is a service-oriented manufacturing. Both Process and Products (P1, P2) invoke the necessary services, which are shared through the Service Bus following a flexible and modular smart productive chain.

While making decisions by using its own sensors and actuators, the product itself can trace the better configurable line along the factory.

Also, by using this architecture, enterprises can generate their own manufacturing services for the participation on an external supply chain, in addition to the management of the internal supply chain. This generates the Internet of Services [15].

A similar approach called Intelligent Enterprise Service-based Bus (iESB) [16] have been proposed to interconnect several factories systems to each other. The architecture is based on Intelligent Services defined as independent pieces of software that are expected to provide a particular result, either produced by the Intelligent Service itself or by requesting support from other Intelligent Services. Our approach instead is exploring the interaction from the product or process within the factory, making use of the Industry 4.0 components that would be the Cyber Physical Systems or smart products.

Another similar SOA product-based models have been proposed [17], but not using the Service Bus. Moreover, they are prior to the Industry 4.0 model conception.

Our framework is based on the pillars of the Industry 4.0 such as Cyber Physical Systems, Internet of Things and Internet of Services. Moreover, we confirm from the study, that the Internet of Services is one of the main enablers to create networks and convert factories into a smart environment, what is achieved through the Service-Oriented Architecture.

6 Conclusion

This paper links the concepts of Industry 4.0, Internet of Services and Service-Oriented Architecture giving more emphasis to the service domain of manufacturing environment.

A service bus is illustrated to explain the idea of a Service-Oriented Manufacturing Architecture (SOMA), based on SOA, which is explained to better characterize the Internet of Services as one of the pillars of the Industry 4.0.

All manufacturing elements, like automated machine-tools, robots, human workers and information systems, have their functions available in the abstract form of services, exchanging data and instructions through the Service Bus.

References

1. Sanders, A., Elangeswaran, C., Wulfsberg, J.: Industry 4.0 implies lean manufacturing: research activities in industry 4.0 function as enablers for lean manufacturing. J. Ind. Eng. Manag. 9(3), 811 (2016)
2. Kagermann, H., Wahlster, H., Helbig, J.: Securing the future of German manufacturing industry: recommendations for implementing the strategic initiative INDUSTRIE 4.0 – Final Report of the Industrie 4.0 working group. Acatech – National Academy of Science and Engineering, pp. 1–82 (2013)
3. Satyro, W.C., Sacomano, J.B., da Silva, M.T., Gonçalves, R.F., Contador, J.C., von Cieminski, G.: Industry 4.0: evolution of the research at the APMS conference. In: Lödding, H., Riedel, R., Thoben, K.-D., von Cieminski, G., Kiritsis, D. (eds.) APMS 2017. IAICT, vol. 513, pp. 39–47. Springer, Cham (2017). https://doi.org/10.1007/978-3-319-66923-6_5
4. Hermann, M., Pentek, T., Otto, B.: Design principles for industrie 4.0 scenarios: a literature review. In: Working Paper No. 01/2015, Technische Universität Dortmund, Fakultät Maschinenbau and Audi Stiftungslehrstuhl - Supply Net, Order Management (2015)

5. Hofmann, E., Rusch, M.: Industry 4.0 and the current status as well as future prospects on logistics. Comput. Ind. **89**, 23–34 (2017)
6. Cardoso, J., Voigt, K., Winkler, M.: Service engineering for the internet of services. In: Filipe, J., Cordeiro, J. (eds.) ICEIS 2008. LNBIP, vol. 19, pp. 15–27. Springer, Heidelberg (2009). https://doi.org/10.1007/978-3-642-00670-8_2
7. Papazoglou, M.P.: Service-Oriented computing: concepts, characteristics and directions. In: International Conference on Web Information Systems Engineering et al (Orgs.), Proceedings/Fourth International Conference on Web Information Systems Engineering, WISE 2003. IEEE Computer Society (2003)
8. Schroth, C., Janner, T.: Web 2.0 and SOA: converging concepts enabling the internet of services. IT Prof. **9**(3), 36–41 (2007)
9. Treese, W.: Web 2.0: is it really different? NetWorker **10**(2), 15–17 (2006)
10. Ordanini, A., Pasini, P.: Service co-production and value co-creation: the case for a service-oriented architecture. Eur. Manag. J. **26**(5), 289–297 (2008)
11. W3C – World Wide Web Consortium. Web Services Architecture. https://www.w3.org/TR/ws-arch/
12. Bhadoria, R.S., Chaudhari, N.S., Tharinda Nishantha Vidanagama, V.G.: Analyzing the role of interfaces in enterprise service bus: a middleware epitome for service-oriented systems. Comput. Stand. Interfaces **55**, 146–155 (2018)
13. Gamboa, F.Q., Cardin, O., L'Anton, A., Castagna, P.: A modeling framework for manufacturing services in Service-oriented Holonic manufacturing systems. Eng. Appl. Artif. Intell. **55**, 26–36 (2016)
14. Giret, A., Garcia, E., Botti, V.: An engineering framework for service-oriented intelligent manufacturing systems. Comput. Ind. **81**, 116–127 (2016)
15. Tao, F., Cheng, Y., Xu, L., Zhang, L., Li, B.: CCIoT-CMfg: cloud computing and internet of things-based cloud manufacturing service system. IEEE Trans. Ind. Inf. **10**(2), 1435–1442 (2014)
16. Marin, C.A., et al.: A Conceptual Architecture Based on Intelligent Services for Manufacturing Support Systems, pp. 4749–4754. IEEE (2013)
17. Nagorny, K., Colombo, A., Schmidtmann, U.: A service- and multi-agent-oriented manufacturing automation architecture. Comput. Ind. **63**, 813–823 (2012)

Evaluating Impact of AI on Cognitive Load of Technicians During Diagnosis Tasks in Maintenance

Hyunjong Shin[✉] and Vittaldas V. Prabhu

Pennsylvania State University, University Park, State College, PA 16802, USA
hvs5026@psu.edu

Abstract. Even today, many maintenance activities are still done manually because maintenance is one of the most difficult areas to be automated in manufacturing. Many technicians spend their time on non-technical activities such as retrieving instructions from manuals. If AI (Artificial Intelligence) can alleviate some of these tasks, the time to diagnosis and repair can be shortened. However there are limited works about the effects of using AI during maintenance activities on a technician's cognitive load. Therefore, as an initiative, we conducted a pilot experiment with 10 participants to analyze the effects of the AI-based support system on diagnosis tasks in the manufacturing. In the experiment, participants were divided into two groups: the group used an AI-based support system and the other group used a Fault Tree (FT) based support system; two groups' mean task completion time and task load of participants using NASA Task Load were measured. According to the experiment results, the group which used the AI-based support system to diagnose the model completed task 53% lesser time than the group which used the FT-based support system. In addition, participants who used the AI-based support system reported relatively lower task loads compared to participants who used the FT-based support system. This experiment results imply that maintenance time and a variability can be reduced if an AI-based support system supports maintenance technicians.

Keywords: Smart maintenance · Artificial intelligence · Machine learning Naïve Bayesian · Diagnosis · Task load · Cognitive load · HAII

1 Introduction

Although maintenance activities are very critical in the manufacturing industry, only few maintenance activities are fully automated yet because it is one of the last areas to be automated in the manufacturing [1, 2]. Recent study also reports that over 30% of total workforce contributes to maintenance activities [3]. Maintenance activities are often composed of technical activities and non-technical activities. Retrieving instructions or information from manuals, for instance, take up about 45% of maintenance technicians' time [4]. Therefore, if a technology such as an AI can alleviate

I. Moon et al. (Eds.): APMS 2018, IFIP AICT 536, pp. 27–34, 2018.
https://doi.org/10.1007/978-3-319-99707-0_4

some of technicians' task by supporting their activities, the diagnosis and repair time will be shortened. However, AI must be cautiously implemented to the maintenance process because there was a case that an AI was meant to improve operators' performance but it, instead, acted as a barrier and created even more challenges [5, 6].

Since 1996, as AI has become more popular, the number of annually published AI papers has soared in the field of computer science; the annual investment in AI startups by venture capitals has increased six fold since 2000 [7]; more and more people are paying attention to the potential benefits of AI.

In the field of the manufacturing numerous AI related papers can be found. In the manufacturing, AI is often used to detect product quality problems [8]. For example, Nguyen et al. and Yang et al. used an AI to detect defective wafers in the semiconductor industry [9, 10]. Similarly, Liu and Jin used an AI to detect defective tail lights in the automobile industry [11]. Outside of detecting product quality problems, research has also investigated different applications of AI. Huang et al. used AI to diagnose vehicle fault. Hong et al. used AI to detect faults in the semiconductor manufacturing equipment [12]. Similarly Zhang et al. used AI to identify degradation machines and tools [13].

The usage of an AI is also studied in the field of the human factors. For example, Overmeyer et al., studied the cognitive load of the operator who commands autonomous vehicles through an AI agent [14]. Similarly Strayer et al. studied the cognitive load of drivers who used an intelligent personal assistant [5].

Therefore, to explore this issue, we conducted a controlled pilot experiment to investigate the effect of AI-based support system on diagnosis task in the maintenance process.

The rest of this paper is structured as follows. In Sect. 2, we explain the experiment that we conducted to evaluate the effect of the AI on the diagnosis task. Next, in Sect. 3, we present the results of the experiment. Lastly, in Sect. 4, we state discussion and conclusions of this experiment.

2 Experimental Design and Setup

A proximity sensor is widely used to detect the presence of an object in many automated machines. However, proximity sensors frequently fail in CNC (Computer Numerical Control) machines. In addition, even though a technician identifies that the cause of a machine failure is related to the proximity sensor, the maintenance activity is not as simple as replacing a proximity sensor. The technician must check conditions of all components such as cable, power, I/O board, and sensor itself in order to repair the machine. Therefore, in this experiment, the model operated by a proximity sensor is chosen to evaluate the effect of AI on diagnosis tasks in maintenance.

2.1 Experimental Task

Proximity Sensor Model. Every component in the proximity sensor model represents some component in a real industry machine as shown Table 1. The sensor in the experiment model detects whether the door in front of the sensor is closed or not. When the sensor detects the door, it shuts down the power to turn off the light. On the other hand, when there is no object, and every component is in working order, the light bulb is illuminated (See Fig. 1).

In the experiment, 4 components of the proximity sensor model were purposely in bad condition: battery, switch, light bulb and signal cable to light bulb. Then the participants were divided into two groups. The first group, also known as the FT group, were asked to diagnose problems and fix the model according to a fault tree-based support system. The participants in the second group, also known as the AI group, were asked to diagnose problems and fix the model according to an AI-based support system.

(a) When the Door is Closed – Light Off

(b) When the Door is Opened – Light ON

Fig. 1. Proximity sensor model

Table 1. Proximity sensor model setting

Real machine setting	Model setting	Malfunction
Sensor	Sensor	No
Power	Battery	Yes
Power switch	Switch	Yes
Sensor connection	Signal cable to light bulb	Yes
Cables	Cables	No
I/O board	Light bulb	Yes

Support Systems. Two support systems were provided to support participants' diagnosis tasks. The FT, which is a common practice to repair the machines in many small and medium enterprises, based support system helped participants diagnose the locations of problems by deductive failure analysis method. On the other hand, the AI-based support system helped participants diagnose the locations of problems based on the pre calculated probability using the Naïve Bayesians classifier method. The Naïve Bayesians classifier method is used in this experiment because the method is known to require less input, work great in practice even if NB assumptions doesn't hold, and good for showing casual relationship [1] (See Fig. 2).

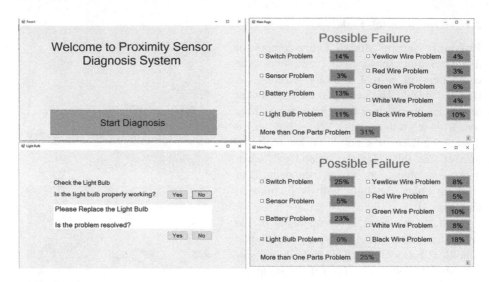

Fig. 2. AI-based support system interface

2.2 Participants

Five subjects were participated in each group. The total participants for this experiment were 10. The average age of participants in the FT and the AI group was 29.2 and 29.6 respectively. The youngest participant was 25 years old and the oldest was 32 years old. Of 10 participants, 80% of them were male. In each group, equal number of female participants was assigned to minimize gender effects. Twenty percent of the participants did not major in either engineering or science. All other participants' majors were either engineering or science.

2.3 Hypotheses

The following hypotheses were tested by using above experimental design and setup

- H1: The task completion time of the group which uses the AI-based support system will be shorter
- H2: The cognitive load of the group which uses the AI-based support system will be lower.

2.4 Experiment Procedures

Experiment participants are going to be divided into two groups depending on their assigned group and participated in the experiment as stated in Table 2.

Table 2. Experiment procedures

Step	Procedure	Description
1	Subject arrival	The subject will be introduced to the testing facility, locations of exits and restrooms will be provided
2	Eligibility verification	Subject eligibility will be checked prior to continuation. The requirements include: 18 years of age minimum and English speaking
3	Consent	A summary of the study will be given to participants. Participants will be allowed to ask questions about the study. Verbal consent will be obtained prior to continuation to the following steps
4	Demographic questionnaire	The subject will be asked to complete a short demographic questionnaire. Data collected with include: age, gender and major
5	Training session	The subject will attend a training session. Methods of using a multimeter and support system will be introduced using PowerPoint slides. The subject can ask any question during the training session
6	Break	The participant will take a break. The participant may go to the restroom and drink water during this time
7	Experiment	The subject will diagnose the problem of a simple circuit and correct the circuit accordingly with A.I. support or without A.I. support depending on the group that the participant is assigned
8	Work load questionnaire	A subjective workload questionnaire (NASA TLX) will be administered after the task, which includes six rating scales in total to measure workload along six different dimensions (mental demand, physical demand, temporal demand, effort, frustration, and performance)
9	Debrief	To conclude, subjects will be thanked and provided with monetary compensation. Any concerns or questions will be addressed

3   Experiment Results

Task Completion Time. Task completion time is the time that a participant takes to diagnose components and fix them accordingly. It is comprised of diagnosis time, such as using a diagnosis support system and a multimeter, and time to replace or fix components. By measuring the task completion time, the effect of the AI-based support system on diagnosis time can be identified.

The mean task completion time for the FT group was 372.4 s. The standard deviation of this group was 72.2. The mean task completion time of the AI group, on the other hand, was 176.4 s and its standard deviation was 21.1. The coefficient of variation for FT and AI group was 22% and 12% respectively. Based on the level of the coefficient of variation, the AI group had less variation in the task completion time. The

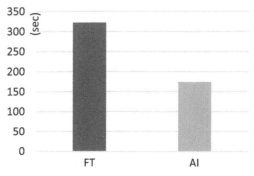

Fig. 3. Mean task completion time difference

mean task completion time difference between the two groups was 196 s (see Fig. 3). A two-sample t-test was used to test the difference between two groups. The calculated t-value was 5.83 and p-value was 0.004. Therefore at α equals to 0.05, we conclude that there was a mean task completion time difference between two groups.

NASA Task Load. The NASA Task Load index (TLX) is a subjective assessment tool that rates perceived workload of participants in order to assess a system. The TLX is divided into six subscales or categories: mental demand, physical demand, temporal demand, performance, effort and frustration. By measuring TLX, the effect of AI-based support system on operators' cognitive load and workload can be identified.

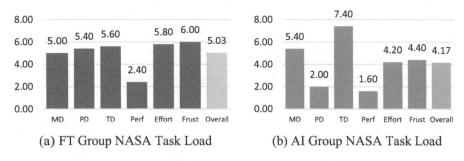

(a) FT Group NASA Task Load   (b) AI Group NASA Task Load

Fig. 4. The NASA TASK load of two groups: FT group and AI group

The average overall task load of the FT group was 5.03. For the FT group, the frustration load turned out to be the highest load among six sub-scales. The other loads were around 5.00 or above except the performance load. The average performance load for this group was 2.40. Furthermore, in average, the mental load was less than the physical load as shown in Fig. 4. On the other hand, the average overall task load for AI group was about 4.2. Most of the loads' levels were similar to the overall task load level. However, the temporal demand load was 1.5 times more than the overall task load. The second highest load was the mental load which was 5.40. Among six task loads, the performance load was the lowest (Fig. 5).

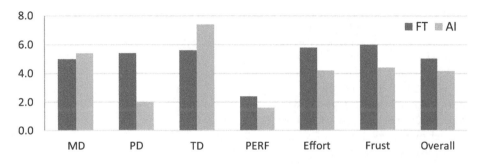

Fig. 5. NASA task load differences

A two-sample t-test was used to identify the significance of task load differences between the two groups. The two sample t-test revealed that none of task loads' differences were statistically significant at alpha 0.05. Although visually there were some differences between the two groups, the differences were not large enough to have statistical meaning.

Performance Accuracy. The performance accuracy (PA) was defined as the number of parts replaced divided by the number of malfunctioning parts. If PA is greater than one, it implies that the participant replaced unnecessary parts while they were diagnosing the model. Of 10 participants, none of them replaced unnecessary parts.

4 Discussion and Conclusions

The experiment that we conducted to investigate effects of the AI-based support system on maintenance reveals several interesting points.

First of all, the experiment result shows that the AI-based support system not only can reduce the diagnosis time but also can reduce the variation of the diagnosis time compared to the FT-based support system. This is possible that the AI-based support system allows participants to diagnose less numbers of parts compared to the FT-based support system if and only if the reliability of AI-based support system is high.

Secondly, AI-based support system must be carefully implemented to the maintenance process because the experiment result shows that the mean mental load of the AI group is higher than the mean mental of the FT group although the difference was not verified by the two-sample t-test.

In sum, the experiment showed that the AI-based support system can reduce the diagnosis time and increase the mental load of technicians. However, the above points must be carefully interpreted since these results are based on our preliminary experiment in which only 10 subjects participated. Since a prerequisite of a two-sample t-test is a normality and the normality could not be assumed with 10 participants, the result of the two-sample t-test has to be interpreted cautiously. In addition, the power test requires at least 8 participants for each group. Therefore, there is a possibility that participants in this experiment do not truly represent the population. This pilot experiment was conducted as part of an exploratory study. In the future study, several additional factors that might influence the cognitive load of a technician during the maintenance task will be included and investigated.

References

1. Langer, R., Li, J., Biller, S., Chang, Q., Huang, N., Xiao, G.: Simulation study of a bottleneck-based dispatching policy for a maintenance workforce. Int. J. Prod. Res. **48**, 1745–1763 (2010)
2. Sheikhalishahi, M., Pintelon, L., Azadeh, A.: Human factors in maintenance: a review. J. Qual. Maint. Eng. **22**, 218–237 (2016)

3. Kothamasu, R., Huang, S.H., Verduin, W.H.: System health monitoring and prognostics - a review of current paradigms and practices. In: Ben-Daya, M., Duffuaa, S., Raouf, A., Knezevic, J., Ait-Kadi, D. (eds.) Handbook of Maintenance Management and Engineering, pp. 337–362. Springer, London (2009)
4. Neumann, U., Majoros, A.: Cognitive, performance, and systems issues for augmented reality applications in manufacturing and maintenance. In: IEEE Virtual Real (VR 1998), pp. 4–11 (1998)
5. Wiener, E.L.: Human factors of advanced technology (glass cockpit) transport aircraft. (Nasa-Cr-177528), 222 (1989)
6. Wiener, E.L., Curry, R.E.: Flight-deck automation: promises and problems. Ergonomics 23, 995–1011 (1980)
7. Shoham, Y., Perrault, R., Brynjolfsson, E., Clark, J., LeGassick, C.: Artificial intelligence index, November 2017, p. 101 (2017)
8. Ademujimi, T.T., Brundage, M.P., Prabhu, V.V.: A review of current machine learning techniques used in manufacturing diagnosis. IFIP Adv. Inf. Commun. Technol. 513, 407–415 (2017)
9. Nguyen, D.T., Duong, Q.B., Zamai, E., Shahzad, M.K.: Fault diagnosis for the complex manufacturing system. Proc. Inst. Mech. Eng. Part O J. Risk Reliab. 230, 178–194 (2015)
10. Yang, L., Lee, J.: Bayesian belief network-based approach for diagnostics and prognostics of semiconductor manufacturing systems. Robot. Comput. Integr. Manuf. 28, 66–74 (2012)
11. Liu, Y., Jin, S.: Application of Bayesian networks for diagnostics in the assembly process by considering small measurement data sets. Int. J. Adv. Manuf. Technol. 65, 1229–1237 (2013)
12. Hong, S.J., Lim, W.Y., Cheong, T., May, G.S.: Fault detection and classification in plasma etch equipment for semiconductor manufacturing e-diagnostics. IEEE Trans. Semicond. Manuf. 25, 83–93 (2012)
13. Zhang, Z., Wang, Y., Wang, K.: Fault diagnosis and prognosis using wavelet packet decomposition, fourier transform and artificial neural network. J. Intell. Manuf. 24, 1213–1227 (2013)
14. Overmeyer, L., Podszus, F., Dohrmann, L.: Multimodal speech and gesture control of AGVs, including EEG-based measurements of cognitive workload. CIRP Ann. - Manuf. Technol. 65, 425–428 (2016)

An In-Process BSR-Noise Detection System for Car Door Trims

Woonsang Baek[iD] and Duck Young Kim[(✉)][iD]

Ulsan National Institute of Science and Technology, Ulsan, South Korea
dykim@unist.ac.kr

Abstract. The Buzz, Squeak, and Rattle (BSR) noises coming from car body parts are often caused by defective assembly. This paper presents an in-process BSR noise detection system for car door trims. A car door trim is slowly pressed down by a pneumatic pusher, and then the acoustic signals measured right above the door trim and on the four corners of the noise detection workstation are monitored for noise source localization by the time difference of arrival method and the relative signal strengths. Finally, the energy of BSR noise is examined by the discretized frequency information of the localized signals.

Keywords: In-process measurement · Inspection · Car door trim

1 Introduction

It has been reported that weak but still irritating noises coming from car body parts could disturb driver's attention, thereby incurring potential warranty claims. These noises are usually caused by the friction and irregular contact of mating surfaces between car parts due to defective parts, miss alignment, and incomplete assembly and called as BSR (Buzz, Squeak, Rattle) noises [1]. Many automakers thus have conducted sampling inspections by using an artificial vibration generator in an anechoic chamber.

This paper presents an in-process BSR noise detection system for car door trims. We estimate the BSR noise source by the time difference of arrival method and the relative signal strengths. The energy of BSR noise is examined by the discretized frequency information of the localized signals. The practical test results with real car door trims provide empirical support for the detection performance of the developed system.

2 System Configuration

The in-process BSR noise detection system was developed by consisting of (i) a sensor array of nine microphones, (ii) four parabolic microphones, (iii) a pneumatic pusher controlled by a gantry robot, (iv) a data acquisition system (NI cDAQ-9178™), and (v) a noise detection software.

A car door trim is slowly pressed down by a pneumatic pusher, and we collected the acoustic signals measured right above the door trim by a microphone array (called

I. Moon et al. (Eds.): APMS 2018, IFIP AICT 536, pp. 35–38, 2018.
https://doi.org/10.1007/978-3-319-99707-0_5

internal signals). Also the ambient sounds are collected with parabolic microphones on the four corners of the noise detection workstation.

2.1 Data Acquisition

The proposed in-process BSR detection procedure consists of the three main phases: (i) noise reduction, (ii) noise source localization, and (iii) abnormal noise detection. First, internal signals and external signals are collected from the sensor array and the parabolic microphones respectively. The inspection process noise, for example, movement noises of the pneumatic cylinder and actuators, was collected during the real inspection processes with a healthy car door trim for each 2 s recording time (Fig. 1).

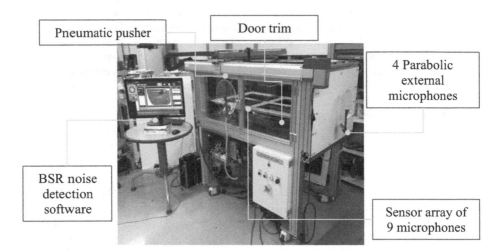

Fig. 1. The in-process BSR noise detection system.

2.2 Noise Reduction

The objective of this step is to reduce the external noises from the collected internal signal. In order to subtract the spectrum of the external noises, we apply a spectral subtraction method with the predefined attenuation factors. The spectrum of the denoised signal is then given by the multiplying the spectrum of internal signals and the attenuation factors. The attenuation factors here can be obtained by using the average of the time-frequency coefficients of the internal signal. However, in order to minimize musical noise after spectral subtraction, we used the empirical Weiner attenuation rule and can get the **S**, the spectrum of denoised signal as follows [2]:

$$\mathbf{S} = \left(1 - \lambda \left[\frac{1}{\xi + 1} \right]^{\beta_1} \right)^{\beta_2} \tag{1}$$

where the over-subtraction factors are $\beta_1, \beta_2 \geq 0$, $\lambda \geq 1$ $\lambda \geq 1$, and ξ is signal-to-noise ratio of the power spectrum. Note that we used the soft-thresholding method for determining the over-subtraction factors, and hence the following values are specified: $\beta_1 = 0.5, \beta_2 = 1$, and $\lambda = 5$.

2.3 Noise Source Localization

To examine the existence of unknown external noise, we localize noise sources by applying a hyperbolic function with the Time Difference Of Arrivals (TDOA) method, which is widely used for estimation of noise source location [3, 4]. We obtain a hyperbola by using the position information of a pair of microphones in the array and the arrival delay time. Generalized Cross-Correlation with Phase Transform method (GCC-PHAT) [5] is employed for efficient computation of delay time of arrival for noisy data.

Note that a hyperbola here implies the loci of possible locations of a noise source from the perspective of the total nine pairs of microphones. Then, we finally identify the location of a noise source by computing the average of intersection coordinates between all hyperbolas.

We consider that powerful source exists inside of the station. If the estimated location is outside of the array, we consider the powerful source exists outside of the station.

2.4 Abnormal Noise Detection

We investigate the existence of unknown internal noise in the denoised signal. To do this, the average energy of the signals captured during the 150 times inspection processes with a healthy car door trim is used as a reference.

The reference energy information for all microphones are compared with the energy information of the current localized internal signal. Any significant difference between the two energy information will lead us to conclude that an unknown internal noise, i.e. BSR noise, is detected.

3 Experimental Results

We conducted the inspection experiments with two types of car door trim: a faulty door trim known to emit a BSR noise and a healthy door trim. The inspection was done 96 times for each type of door trim. The result summarized in Table 1 shows that the correct decision rates for the faulty and the healthy door trims are 96.8% and 90.6% respectively. Nonetheless, the number of incorrect decisions cannot be negligible. As mentioned earlier, the spectral subtraction still left musical noises that often result in arbitrary energy value of a signal. Therefore, for the future study, we need to enhance the spectral subtraction method and develop a more detailed energy representation method for a signal.

Table 1. The experimental results of the total 192 inspections.

	Faulty door trim	Healthy door trim
Hit	93	0
Miss	3	0
False alarm	0	9
Correct rejection	0	87
Total	96	96
Correct decision (%)	96.8%	90.6%

4   Conclusion

This study presented the in-process BSR noise detection system for car door trims, which analyses acoustic signals acquired by a microphone array and parabolic microphones. The signal analysis was carried out by noise reduction and localization using a spectral subtraction method and a hyperbolic TDOA approach, followed by abnormal internal noise detection by the energy comparison of signals. The total 192 inspection results with real car door trims demonstrated the detection performance of the developed system.

For the future study, we will enhance the noise reduction method and develop a more detailed energy representation method for a signal. The localization method was applied only to check for the presence of external noise sources in this study. We will develop the method that can precisely estimate the defect location of the product in the process. We will also validate the system configuration by rearrangement of microphones and redesign of the pneumatic pusher.

References

1. Trapp, M., Chen, F.: Automotive Buzz, Squeak and Rattle: Mechanisms, Analysis, Evaluation and Prevention. Butterworth-Heinemann, Boston (2011)
2. McAulay, R., Malpass, M.: Speech enhancement using a soft-decision noise suppression filter. IEEE Trans. Acoust. Speech Signal Process. **28**, 137–145 (1980)
3. Gustafsson, F., Gunnarsson, F.: Positioning using time-difference of arrival measurements. In: Proceedings of 2003 IEEE International Conference on Acoustics, Speech, and Signal Processing, Hong Kong, vol. 6, pp. 553–556 (2003)
4. Mensing, C., Plass, S.: Positioning algorithms for cellular networks using TDOA. In: Proceedings of 2006 IEEE International Conference on Acoustics, Speech and Signal Processing, Toulouse, France, vol. 4, pp. 513–516 (2006)
5. Knapp, C., Carter, G.: The generalized correlation method for estimation of time delay. IEEE Trans. Acoust. Speech Signal Process. **24**, 320–327 (1976)

The Future of Maintenance Within Industry 4.0: An Empirical Research in Manufacturing

Irene Roda[(✉)], Marco Macchi, and Luca Fumagalli

Department of Management, Economics and Industrial Engineering,
Politecnico di Milano, Milan, Italy
irene.roda@polimi.it

Abstract. The recent advances in digital technologies are revolutionizing the industrial landscape. Maintenance is one of the functions that may benefit from the opportunities that emerge with the digital transformation of industrial processes. Nevertheless, until now very few research papers investigated on what digitalized manufacturing entails for maintenance organizations along both technical and social dimensions. The aim of this paper is to investigate the vision of the future of Maintenance within the industry 4.0 and to show empirical evidence on how manufacturing companies are approaching the digital transformation process of maintenance. An empirical investigation was developed through multiple case-study involving nine manufacturing companies in Italy. Findings emerge about the main perceived challenges by companies for the success of digital transformation of maintenance as well as the technological and organizational mechanisms that are used in ongoing innovative Maintenance projects.

Keywords: Maintenance · Digital transformation · Manufacturing
Industry 4.0

1 Introduction

In the current time, looking at manufacturing, digital transformation is affecting firms' strategy, its offerings, the IT infrastructure, the way to collaborate with partners, its organizational structure, overall process organization, and core competences, as well as the overall company culture [1]. Maintenance is a relevant function for the implementation of Industry 4.0-like solutions [2, 3] and predictive maintenance and its application in machine health prognosis are popular topics in the Industry 4.0-based CPS literature [4, 5]. Nevertheless, on one hand, it is notable that in both scientific and business literature on digitalised manufacturing, maintenance is barely considered, or is perceived narrowly, with its scope confined mainly to predictive maintenance and maintenance services [3, 6]. On the other hand, maintenance research [7, 8] has primarily approached digitalised manufacturing focusing on technical advancements.

This paper is founded on the idea that digitization requires to master both technology and organization, in order to build a Smart Maintenance system. The main objective is to investigate how maintenance may benefit from the opportunities that emerge with the digital transformation of industrial processes in accordance with the vision of Industry 4.0. A multiple case study was carried on, involving twenty

I. Moon et al. (Eds.): APMS 2018, IFIP AICT 536, pp. 39–46, 2018.
https://doi.org/10.1007/978-3-319-99707-0_6

managers (both technical (production and maintenance) and ICT managers) from nine companies in Italy. The findings allow: (i) investigating the visions about the future maintenance of industrial plants, and ii) showing empirical evidences on how manufacturing companies are approaching the digital transformation process of maintenance from technological and organizational perspectives.

The paper is organized as follows. Section 2 describes the scientific background of the research. Section 3 discussed the methodology that has been used. Section 4 reports the cross case study findings that are then discussed in Sect. 5. Section 6 is dedicated to conclusions.

2   Scientific Background

Scientific literature about the evolution of maintenance alongside the development of the communication and information technologies has grown since early 2000. Past concepts such as e-maintenance and Intelligent Maintenance Systems [8], have recently been enhanced by Industry 4.0 and the related key enabling technologies (Internet of Things, Cyber Physical Systems, etc.). Topics such as Condition-Based Maintenance and PHM are now under the scientific literature attention [5, 9, 10]. Nevertheless, in the existing literature there is a lack of understanding of what the realisation of digitalised manufacturing entails for maintenance organisations along both hard (technical) and soft (social) dimensions [3, 11].

In their recent paper [3], the authors clearly discuss the existing research gap between the expectations on digitalised manufacturing and the future role of maintenance. By addressing this gap, the authors implemented an empirical Delphi-based scenario planning study, identifying projections about potential changes of the internal and external environment for maintenance organisations by 2030. They identified eight probable scenarios describing the most probable future for maintenance organisations in digitalised manufacturing, as well as three wildcard scenarios (i.e. future events that are less likely to occur but could potentially have substantial impact on maintenance organisations). In detail, according to the authors, eight dominant themes are highly likely to influence maintenance organisations, which are: (i) data analytics, (ii) interoperable information systems, (iii) big data management, (iv) emphasis on education and training, (v) fact-based maintenance planning, (vi) new smart work procedures, (vii) maintenance planning with a systems perspective, and (viii) stronger environmental legislation and standards. Regarding the wildcard scenarios, the relevant themes identified are: (i) maintenance department, (ii) digital networks, and (iii) maintenance in social debate. As stated by the authors, their study provides guidance for further research and leaves margin for extending the geographic scope.

Based on such considerations, this research aims at verifying the identified scenarios by collecting opinions from experts of manufacturing companies in Italy, studying both their vision on the future role of maintenance within Industry 4.0 and how their companies are actually implementing the digital transformation process of maintenance considering both the organizational and technological dimensions. With respect to [3], this study not only involves maintenance experts but also Information & Communication Technology (ICT) and digitalization responsible in the companies.

3   Methodology

In this research, a multiple case study was developed. It allowed showing empirical evidences on how companies are approaching the digital transformation process of maintenance. In particular, nine companies have been selected from multiple industrial sectors. Within the identified panel, interviews were conducted to gather the opinions of various experts in each company, belonging both to the ICT area, and to the Operations and Maintenance area. In all, twenty experts were interviewed. Table 1 shows the panel of companies that was selected for this study.

Table 1. Case study: panel of involved companies

Company	Sector	Interviewees
A	Steel	• Maintenance Manager • Maintenance Engineering Director • R&D Director
B	Turbines	• Technical service Director
C	Steel	• Production Director • ICT Director • Maintenance Director
D	Tyres	• Global Maintenance Manager
E	Oil&Gas	• IT Digital Innovation & IT Operation corporate Director • Offshore Drilling and Digitalization R&D Director • Maintenance Director Offshore
F	Industrial gases	• Production Plants Director • Plant Director
G	Oil&Gas	• Digital projects Coordinator • Maintenance Director • Inspections Director
H	Steel	• Technical Function and Maintenance Director • R&D and data science Director • Maintenance Engineering Director
I	Mechanical	• Technical Functions Director • ICT Director

4   Cross Case Study Findings Analysis

Based on the undertaken analysis and coding of the interviews with the experts, the findings are presented hereafter through a cross-cases synthesis. In particular, in the first sub-section, findings about the vision of the future of Maintenance in the Industry 4.0, including expected benefits and foreseen barriers are reported. The second sub-section shows evidences on how companies are approaching the ongoing transformation process looking at both technological and organizational issues.

4.1   Vision, Expected Benefits and Barriers

Based on the considerations gathered about the future of Maintenance from the experts involved in the case study, data analysis and the definition of the role of the human factor are considered two fundamental issues referring to the future of Maintenance.

The two predominant visions are a data-centered maintenance vision and a human-centered maintenance vision. Regarding the first one, the interviewees highlighted the possibility of increasing knowledge and opening new perspectives for the company thanks to the availability and analysis of (big) data, that is also recognized as a challenge for the IT facing the management of large amounts of data (in so-called Data lakes).

The main weaknesses with this regard are the costs, which still characterize some advanced technological solutions, as well as the cost and difficulty of finding resources on the market with the necessary analytics and IT skills. Main threats of a data-centered maintenance are those linked to the exposure to the risk of cyber attacks, as well as the risk of losing contact with the physical dimension of industrial processes and assets, which leads to the need to secure the necessary competence based on engineering skills and know-how. Regarding the human-centered maintenance vision, the interviewees foresee the strength of the centrality of man, and human experience, allowing intelligence in the monitoring of the health status of the assets, as well as guaranteeing the capacity to adapt to changes (resilience). The main identified threat is represented by the potential resistance to change of people. Overall, the expected benefits of digitization of maintenance have been clearly identified by the companies interviewed, and they are the following (brackets indicate the number of companies in the panel that indicated the reference benefit, being shared in the opinion of the experts interviewed in each company):

- the possibility of improving the ability to predict the dynamics of production processes and/or asset degradation processes (9 companies),
- (consequently) the possibility of improving the reliability of plants (7 companies),
- the possibility of improving knowledge of production processes and/or asset degradation processes (6 companies),
- the possibility of improving efficiency in the use of maintenance resources (6 companies);
- the possibility of improving the safety of people (6 companies).

In addition to the benefits of digitization of maintenance, the findings of the case study reveal interesting evidence regarding the elements identified as main barriers, or rather, factors that can slow down the process of digital transformation of maintenance.

The most commonly indicated barriers by the experts interviewed are the following:

- lack of corporate culture towards decisions based on data/evidence (7 companies),
- lack of a structured collaboration in the digital network for a sustainable long-term project of digital transformation of maintenance (6 companies).

Interestingly, the two main barriers identified by respondents are of organizational nature. The first barrier highlights elements of the organization that are strongly impacted by the digital transformation: the corporate culture, in the first place, and the decision-making process, in second place. The second barrier concerns the entire network of actors involved in the value chain for the design of future Maintenance solutions (end-users, OEMs, technology suppliers, service providers, …). The emerging of this barrier is symptomatic of the importance that the respondents give to a structured collaboration for the development of future Maintenance projects. Respondents with responsibility in Operations and Maintenance, in addition to the two barriers mentioned above, identify an additional important organizational barrier, which is:

• the lack of skills and abilities of operators on digital technologies (4 O&M responsibles and 2 ICT responsibles).

The same maintenance managers or plant engineering managers then identify a further critical aspect that can slow down the digital transformation process of maintenance that is an economic-financial barrier, i.e.:

• the intrinsic difficulty in establishing the payback of an investment for the digital transformation of maintenance (7 companies).

Beyond the payback, some respondents underline the uncertainty on the impacts in the Total Cost of Ownership (TCO) of new equipment/instruments purchased to upgrade the infrastructure according to the paradigm of Industry 4.0.

The only technological barriers perceived as critical among the companies interviewed are:

• the lack of widespread standard solutions for new technologies,
• the potential lack of guarantees from current Cyber Security technologies on the complete effectiveness in data protection (experts from 4 companies agree on these elements).

4.2   Implementation Mechanisms of the Digital Transformation of Maintenance

The companies involved in the case study are companies that have undertaken a process of digital transformation of industrial processes, including a development program that involves maintenance. This aspect allowed the investigation on how they are approaching the digital transformation process of maintenance considering on-going projects. In particular, in next sub-sections the main findings that have been collected looking at organizational and technological issues, are presented.

Organizational Issues

The case study allowed investigating on the organizational aspects in the development of a Maintenance project under the Industry 4.0 paradigm. It was interesting to discover that, to undertake and conduct the digital transformation process of maintenance, most of the companies in the panel introduced new organizational solutions.

In particular, the focus has been placed on team-working as a primary organizational lever. With different levels of formalization, depending on the case, the tendency is to promote inter-functional teams, with multiple skills, combining the know-how of different business functions, selected according to the project objectives. The most common solution (seven companies) among the companies in the panel was the creation of inter-functional teams that involve, first of all, operations, maintenance and ICT management, while other solutions, if when the technical complexity requires it, include integration with other functions, such as Human Resources management, process technologies and plant automation.

Another organizational solution implemented by some companies interviewed concerns the introduction into the organizational structure of new roles and professional figures that bring complementary skills to those inherent to industrial processes, such as data scientists or experts of Industry 4.0. In some cases, the organizational position of the Chief Digital (Transformation) Officer is explicitly defined or, more generally, the focus is on the involvement of an innovation manager.

Technological Issues

The case study implementation also allowed investigating the role of the enabling technologies of Industry 4.0 for the digitization of maintenance.

Interestingly, what clearly emerges is how modeling and simulation are recognized a fundamental role for the future of maintenance (7 companies have indicated these technologies as relevant). Due to their intrinsic characteristics, these technologies let presume, in the future, the importance of defining the so-called digital twin of asset systems to support the maintenance processes. Other technology to which value is recognized for supporting the decision-making processes are the tools for monitoring conditions (8 companies). Sensors are also recognized (by 7 companies) as important infrastructural technology, without which it is not possible to undertake a real process of digital transformation. Technological solutions such as smart devices (e.g. smart watches) and, more generally, portable devices (such as tablets) are also recognized (by 6 companies) as important tools with an informative function, in particular, as support for operator in the shop floor. Augmented reality, is seen as an evolved technology (from 5 companies) which, however, will not be adopted in the near future. The Cloud, has received rather mixed opinions, with reference to the related problems of Cyber Security. In some cases, the Virtual reality is also mentioned for predominantly formative purposes, i.e. for training of operational staff, especially for plants located in countries where technical maintenance culture is not advanced. Finally, Artificial Intelligence (AI) and Business Intelligence (BI) analytics are two other technologies recognized as important (respectively by 5 companies) to provide an infrastructure to create decision support tools. Alongside modeling and simulation technologies, they can contribute their data analytics functions to the digital twin of the asset system.

5   Discussion of Findings

Referring back to the eight dominant themes that [3] identified in their work as highly likely to influence maintenance organisations, all of them came forth from the cross-case study findings analysis. Some of them appear to be more relevant than others, two of the three wildcard scenarios have actually emerged as relevant. Summarising, the relevance and centrality of data for the future of Maintenance that is identified in the study by [3], clearly emerged from the case study findings analysis as well. The challenge given by the achievement of high quality maintenance data and developing maintenance management systems that automatically transform big data into decision support is identified both in [3] and in the case study. In this study, the challenge is identified not only for Maintenance but also for the ICT function, facing the need of managing large amounts of data (in so-called Data lakes). From the case study, the role of the human factor as a core issue together with data for the future of Maintenance is confirmed. Not only, the need to keep up with technological development emerges but also, the need to secure the necessary engineering competence not to lose contact with the physical assets and the required technical knowledge to support decision-making.

Regarding the wildcard scenarios identified by [3], two of the three relevant themes identified, strongly emerged from the case studies, and they are: (i) maintenance department and (ii) digital networks.

Finally, one challenge that emerged from the case study implementation and that is not underlined in the study by [3] is the intrinsic difficulty in establishing the payback of an investment for the digitization of maintenance. Beyond the payback, some respondents underline the uncertainty on the impacts in the Total Cost of Ownership of new equipment/instruments purchased to upgrade the infrastructure according to the paradigm of Industry 4.0. This gives an evidence on the need for methodologies to be able to evaluate the cost-effectiveness of the new solutions.

6   Conclusions

This paper provides insights about the future role of Maintenance in the manufacturing sector within Industry 4.0. In particular, the objective is the investigation of how Maintenance may benefit from the opportunities that emerge with the ongoing digital transformation of industrial processes. To this aim, a case study involving nine companies and twenty experts belonging to both technical functions (operations and maintenance) and to ICT/innovation functions were involved. First of all, the research allowed identifying the main issues that will characterize the Maintenance in the future under the Industry 4.0 paradigm. The two core elements for the success of the digitalization of maintenance processes emerged and they are data and the human factor. Secondly, the research aimed at detecting empirical evidences on how manufacturing companies are actually approaching the digital transformation process of maintenance. Even in this case, relevant issues emerge not only of technological type but also organizational ones.

The development of further research (e.g. more case studies, a Delphi analysis etc.) would help better capturing and studying the alignment of business and technology goals in the target domain. The work complements the study by [3] in different ways. It enlarges the analysis to the Italian industrial context, it collects opinions not only from maintenance experts but also from experts with responsibility roles for the digitalization process and finally, it studies ongoing innovative maintenance projects. The case study was also developed more recently, starting from the second half of 2017 until beginning of 2018.

Acknowledgments. The research work was performed within the scope of TeSeM Observatory (www.tesem.net).

References

1. Pflaum, A.A., Michahelles, F.: The IoT and digital transformation : toward the data-driven enterprise. IEEE Pervasive Comput. **17**(1), 87–91 (2018)
2. Macchi, M., Roda, I., Fumagalli, L.: On the advancement of maintenance management towards smart maintenance in manufacturing. IFIP Adv. Inf. Commun. Technol. **513**, 383–390 (2017)
3. Bokrantz, J., Skoogh, A., Berlin, C., Stahre, J.: Maintenance in digitalised manufacturing: delphi-based scenarios for 2030. Int. J. Prod. Econ. **191**, 154–169 (2017)
4. Zheng, P., Wang, H., Sang, Z., Zhong, R.Y., Liu, Y., Liu, C., Mubarok, K., Yu, S., Xu, X.: Smart manufacturing systems for Industry 4.0: conceptual framework, scenarios, and future perspectives. Front. Mech. Eng. **13**(2), 1–14 (2018)
5. Lee, J., Ghaffari, M., Elmeligy, S.: Self-maintenance and engineering immune systems: towards smarter machines and manufacturing systems. Ann. Rev. Control **35**(1), 11–122 (2011)
6. Liao, Y., Deschamps, F., de Freitas Rocha Loures, E., Ramos, L.F.P.: Past, present and future of Industry 4.0 - a systematic literature review and research agenda proposal. Int. J. Prod. Res. **55**(12), 3609–3629 (2017)
7. Alaswad, S., Xiang, Y.: A review on condition-based maintenance optimization models for stochastically deteriorating system. Reliab. Eng. Syst. Saf. **157**, 54–63 (2017)
8. Guillén, A.J., Crespo, A., Macchi, M., Gómez, J.: On the role of prognostics and health management in advanced maintenance systems. Prod. Plan. Control **27**(12), 991–1004 (2016)
9. Moore, W.J., Starr, A.G.: An intelligent maintenance system for continuous cost-based prioritisation of maintenance activities. Comput. Ind. **57**(6), 595–606 (2006)
10. Jardine, A.K.S., Lin, D., Banjevic, D.: A review on machinery diagnostics and prognostics implementing condition-based maintenance. Mech. Syst. Signal Process. **20**(7), 1483–1510 (2006)
11. Pellegrino, J., Justiniano, M., Raghunathan, A.: Measurement science roadmap for prognostics and health management for smart manufacturing systems. NIST Adv. Manuf. Ser. **100**(2) (2016). Report number: 100-2

Modeling the Influence of Technician Proficiency and Maintenance Strategies on Production System Performance

Kai-Wen Tien[✉] and Vittaldas Prabhu

Pennsylvania State University, University Park, PA 16802, USA
kut147@psu.edu

Abstract. Maintenance tasks will be the latest automated part of a manufacturing system. Thus, the technician proficiency impacts manufacturing performance. We studied the influence of maintenance proficiency on both machine availability and manufacturing cycle times under three different maintenance strategies: run-to-failure (RTF), preventive maintenance (PM), and condition-based maintenance (CBM). To discuss scenarios in the same framework, we modeled a health-index based phase-type model and a probability model for imperfect maintenance being subject to technician proficiency. Finally, we simulated a single machine queueing model with different technician proficiency and maintenance strategies. The simulation results revealed that CBM could resist lower proficiency and keep higher availability and low manufacturing cycle times than RTF and PM.

Keywords: Condition-based maintenance · Imperfect maintenance
Maintenance proficiency

1 Introduction

Maintenance tasks will be the lastest automated segment of a manufacturing system. The quality of maintenance now still highly depends on the proficiency of maintenance technicians. Moreover, assigning appropriate maintenance technicians is crucial for maintaining productivity and throughput levels. For this purpose, Cabahug et al. provided a tool to classify maintenance proficiency into three different classes by three factors: years of relevant working experience on the machine, personal disposition, and operator reliability [1]. This classification can help the manager to select the best maintenance operator instead of only resting on manager's intuition and judgment. In addition, Edward et al. used the artificial neural network (ANN) to classify maintenance proficiency [2]. They claimed that the tool can achieve 89% accuracy by using ten significant variables.

Condition-based maintenance (CBM) has been studied in many different perspectives. Thanks for the cutting edge technologies such as the Internet of Things (IoTs) and big data analytics, CBM is ready for many different industries. Macchi et al. came up with a reflection that there is a huge potential for maintenance in this revolution, but maintenance is not yet advanced as it would be expected [3]. To assist industries on the

I. Moon et al. (Eds.): APMS 2018, IFIP AICT 536, pp. 47–54, 2018.
https://doi.org/10.1007/978-3-319-99707-0_7

pathway of smart manufacturing, Carolis et al. provided a maturity model for manufacturing companies to assess their digital readiness [4].

In addition, to assess the benefits of CBM, researchers are evaluating the influence of CBM in comparison of preventive maintenance (PM). Yu et al. provide a maintenance orientated approach to complex system design [5]. They claimed that the approach can reveal many nonobvious interactions between subsystems and produce designs which have lower life-cycle costs compared to traditional approaches. Jonge et al. reviewed the literature on the relative benefits of CBM over PM on three practical factors of CBM: (1) the effect of required planning time, (2) imperfect condition information, and (3) uncertain failure level. The results showed that the three practical factors could meaningfully impact the relative benefits of CBM to PM [6].

The human element is an unseparated part of maintenance, but only a few studies have discussed the changing of workforce planning during the smart manufacturing era. Koochaki et al. compare the impact of two strategies – CBM and Preventive Maintenance on workforce planning and scheduling [7]. Their results show that CBM is less efficient than Age-Based Replacement (ABR) on maintenance grouping, but CBM performs better with respect to total maintenance costs.

This work is motivated by the need of capturing the effect of technician proficiency and maintenance strategies on production performance. We investigated the impacts of maintenance proficiency on machine availability and manufacturing cycle times (CT) under three different maintenance strategies: run-to-failure (RTF), preventive maintenance (PM), and condition-based maintenance (CBM). Section 2 provides a phase-type model which describe machine deterioration and failures with machine health index. Moreover, its maintenance cycle time under RTF, PM, and CBM is described. In Sect. 3, we modeled imperfect maintenance being subjected to technician proficiency. In Sect. 4, we studied maintenance proficiency on machine availability and CTs using a simulation study. The conclusion is made in Sect. 5.

2   System Description and Assumptions

2.1   Health-Index-Based Phase-Type Deterioration Model

When studying CBM, we should discuss machine deterioration process. Health index (HI) is a practical tool to represent machine deterioration. It combines the data of operating observations, field inspections, and site and laboratory testing into a quantitative and object index as Fig. 1(a). Based on observation or other monitored data, the machine states is determined by a range of states from 1 to N (usually 10). HI model is suitable for a complex machine because it merges the senor information into one-dimension values. When IoT is introduced, it is likely to make HI more widespread and systematic rather than ad hoc.

Suppose a machine's HI is continuously monitored, we modeled the HI deterioration process to a phase-type model such as Fig. 1(b). The machine will stay in each HI for a period $1/\lambda_i$ before deteriorating to the next HI. Since, practically, the built HI might not be able to capture all failure modes, we model a Poisson failure rate μ_i in each HI, which represent the uncaptured failure modes, to represent the uncertainty of failure level. For example, the second failure in Fig. 1(a) happens before HI achieves the failure state.

When the HI reaches the failure state, the machine will be stopped for maintenance. After maintenance is done, the machine will recover to one of the previous states with probability α. Then the time to failure T_f can be formulated as a phase-type distribution [8] which distribution function is

$$F_{T_f}(t) = \Pr(T_f \le t) = 1 - \alpha\exp(St)\mathbf{1}. \tag{1}$$

α is a $N \times 1$ probability array, which represented the probability of the starting state. S is a $N \times N$ sub-generator matrix of the rate matrix. $\mathbf{1}$ represents an $N \times 1$ vector with every element being 1.

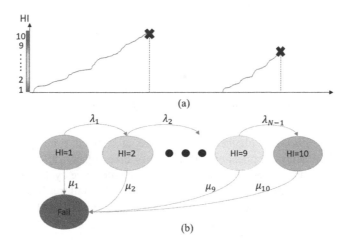

Fig. 1. The sample path of deterioration (a) process is modeled as a phase-type model (b).

2.2   Maintenance Cycle Under Different Strategies

Once the machine fails, the system will be stopped for "corrective maintenance". After the machine is repaired back to an acceptable condition, the machine will be restarted for production. The function of CBM and PM is to stop the machine in advance to prevent severe failure. However, some minor stoppages might be scheduled to avoid a severe one, which called "planned maintenance".

We define a maintenance cycle is a duration consisting of one time-to-stoppage and its corresponding maintenance time. When PM and CBM come in, the corresponding maintenance cycles are different. Define R_i is the time for i^{th} corrective maintenance; M_i is the time for i^{th} planned maintenance. We assume $\{R_i, i = 1, 2\ldots\}$ are i.i.d and $\{M_i, i = 1, 2\ldots\}$ are i.i.d. Usually, the mean and variance of R_i is much larger than M_i. Figure 1 illustrate a sample path of maintenance cycle. We assume that all sample paths of time-to-failure in the sub-plots are the same. The maintenance cycle is different under different maintenance strategies.

RTF strategy as Fig. 2(a) only allow maintenance to operate when the machine breakdown. The uptime in one maintenance cycle is as same as its lifetime distribution. Once the machine breaks down, corrective maintenance will be performed.

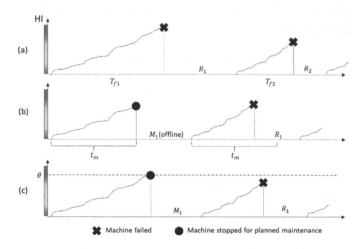

Fig. 2. A sample path of maintenance cycle under (a) RTF, (b) PM, and (c) CBM

PM strategy schedules planned maintenance at a fixed time t_m after the last maintenance. In practical applications, PM usually takes place offline (off production time), the planned maintenance time will not affect maintenance cycle times directly. In practice, PM cannot prevent the occurrence of all possible failures since the randomness behavior of failures. Therefore, the uptime in a maintenance cycle is $\min\{T_f, t_m\}$. In Fig. 2(b), the first time to failure was longer than t_m thus the machine is stopped for planned maintenance. But, the second time to failure was shorter than t_m therefore the machine was failed and corrective maintenance came in. In this paper, HI under PM was not used for maintenance decisions.

CBM strategy schedules planned maintenance when HI achieve threshold θ. Ideally, CBM can take place just before the failure. However, practically, CBM cannot prevent the occurrence of all possible failures because of the limitation of technologies or the high cost of monitoring all components. In Fig. 2(c), the first failure occurred at HI above threshold θ. Therefore, the machine stopped before the failure for planned maintenance. On the other hand, the second failure occurred when HI was lower than θ, so the corrective maintenance came to repair the machine.

3   Modeling Imperfect Maintenance Being Subject to Maintenance Proficiency

Maintenance performance, such as maintenance quality and maintenance time, highly depends on the skill of maintenance technicians. Maintenance proficiency does affect not only the length of maintenance but also maintenance quality. In this study, we assume that the distribution of maintenance time will not be affected by technician proficiency, but the maintenance is imperfect. Suppose maintenance can recover a machine from 'as new as good' and 'as bad as old'. It implies the HI of the recovered machine is between the old HI and HI = 1. Besides, perfect maintenance will bring a machine back to HI = 1.

Suppose the proficiency of maintenance technicians can be evaluated [1, 2, 9]. We defined a maintenance proficiency index p_{ipf}, which implies the probability of the machine can be successfully recovered by one HI from the previous HI during a maintenance. The probability of the recovered HI is defined as

$$P(HI_{new} = i) = \begin{cases} B(i - 1; HI_{old} - 1, 1 - p_{ipf}) & i \leq HI_{old} \\ 0 & i > HI_{old}. \end{cases} \quad (2)$$

$B(x; n, p)$ is the binomial probability mass function at x given n trials and the probability of success p. HI_{old} is the HI when maintenance took place; HI_{new} is the recovered HI after the machine got maintained. p_{ipf} is defined as probability that HI is the successfully recovered by one and it is a real value in (0, 1]. Instances of the distribution is illustrated in Fig. 3. If p_{ipf} is high, the machine is more likely to be repaired back to HI = 1. Otherwise, the machine tends to stay in HI_{old}.

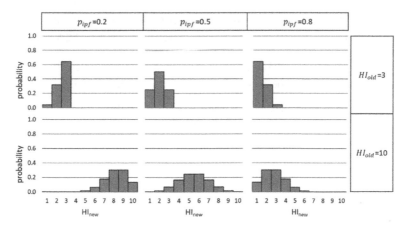

Fig. 3. Distribution of imperfect maintenance being subject to maintenance proficiency

4 A Simulation Study

In this section, we discuss the effect of maintenance proficiency on production performance under different maintenance strategies. CT is the time from a job arriving the machine to the job leaving the machine. It usually consists of two parts: queuing time and effective process time. CT is an indicator of production variation. If CT was large, the work-in-progress would be high under the same machine utilization.

4.1 Simulation Setting

We considered a machine which continuously monitored its healthiness. Its health states were scaled from 1 (perfect) to 10 (almost failed). The deterioration and failure rates are shown in Table 1. Practically, the information can be determined by expert experiences and/or machine history data. Figure 4 shows that the machine has a tube-shape hazard rate, which is typical for sophisticated machines.

The machine produced one type of product which process time is shown in Table 2. In the simulation, raw material arrival process time is a Poisson process. The machine utilization during available production time is set to be 0.8, which is common in most of the practical cases. R_i and M_i were set to be Gamma distributed given mean and variance in Table 2. The simulation had two phases. First, maintenance cycles were simulated by Monte Carlo method using MATLAB®. Then the simulated data were imported to the Machine Reliability Logic to a single machine queueing model in Simio®. The number of repetitions was set to be 50, the average of the 95% half widths over simulation means is less than 10%. Moreover, the simulation is run for 104 weeks (2 years) to generate enough samples since machine failures are rare events. For instance, the number of maintenance cycles under in RTF policy is around 70.

Table 1. Parameters of the phase-type model

HI	1	2	3	4	5	6	7	8	9	10
λ_i(1/hr)	0.100	0.050	0.030	0.010	0.010	0.010	0.040	0.100	0.500	0.000
μ_i(1/hr)	0.010	0.005	0.002	0.001	0.001	0.001	0.003	0.800	1.200	2.000

Table 2. Parameters of production & maintenance activities

	Process time (hours)	Corrective maintenance time (hours)	Planned maintenance time (hours)	Machine life time (hours)
Mean (hours)	1.00	16.00	2.00	258.00
Coef. of variation	0.00	1.00	0.50	0.75

4.2 Comparison of Maintenance Strategies

In this section, we compared the simulation results among different maintenance strategies and proficiency index. Here, t_m and θ were appropriately selected to minimize CT for different p_{ipf}. It should be noted that $p_{ipf} = 0$, which means the machine cannot recover from current HI with maintenance, is not realistic. Thus, we do not discuss the value in our simulation study. The results is shown in Fig. 5. RTF was most sensitive to proficiency index. Availability was around 94.10% and CT was around 6.60 h. When p_{ipf} was lower than 0.6, machine availability decreased and CT increased dramatically. On the other hand, the result of PM showed that it can resist imperfect maintenance more than RTF. Availability was around 96.20% and CT was around 5.5 h when $p_{ipf} \geq 0.5$. Its performance dropped once p_{ipf} was less than 0.5. The results of CBM told that CBM could keep high machine availability (96.91%–96.16%) and low CT (4.3–1.2 h) regardless of the proficiency index p_{ipf}. Because HI was continuous monitored, the machine stopped when HI excessed the threshold no matter how imperfect maintenance done previously.

It is unsuitable to conclude that CBM always works well in any possible situation because the performance of CBM is highly depended on its health index model. However, it is still worth to understand the effect of maintenance proficiency on production variation under different maintenance strategies with a simulation example. Moreover, we provided insight into modeling maintenance proficiency to compare different maintenance strategies.

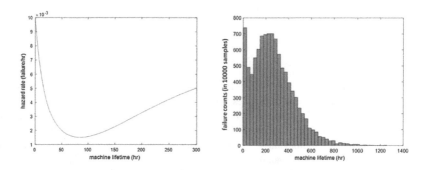

Fig. 4. Hazard function and distribution of time-to-failure

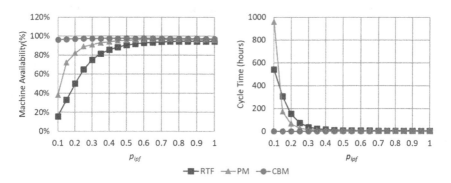

Fig. 5. Comparison of (a) machine availability and (b) manufacturing cycle times according to proficiency indices and maintenance strategies

5 Conclusion

This research investigated the impact of maintenance proficiency on production performance under three different maintenance strategies: RTF, PM, and CBM. To equivalently comparing the results, an HI-based phase-type model is proposed. Moreover, to discuss the impact of maintenance proficiency, we proposed a binomial probability model for imperfect maintenance being subject to maintenance proficiency index. Finally, we studied a simulation case. We compare CT and availability under the maintenance strategies with different proficiency index. The results show CBM was less sensitive than other two strategies. Even when maintenance proficiency is poor (p_{ipf} is close to zero), the performance of availability and CT were around 96.10% and 1.20 h. Since machine under CBM is continuous monitored, a poor maintenance can be detected.

In the future, we will first consider to model learning and forgetting curves into maintenance proficiency index since maintenance technicians will improve their maintenance proficiency when frequent for practicing increases. Secondly, we will study on how to assign maintenance technicians under different strategies or the mix to improve the overall system performance.

References

1. Cabahug, R.R., Edwards, D.J., Nicholas, J.: Classifying plant operator maintenance proficiency: examining personal variables (2004)
2. Edwards, D.J., Yang, J., Cabahug, R., Love, P.E.D.: Intelligence and maintenance proficiency: an examination of plant operators. Constr. Innov. **5**, 243–254 (2005)
3. Macchi, M., Roda, I., Fumagalli, L.: On the advancement of maintenance management towards smart maintenance in manufacturing. In: Lödding, H., Riedel, R., Thoben, K.-D., von Cieminski, G., Kiritsis, D. (eds.) APMS 2017. IAICT, vol. 513, pp. 383–390. Springer, Cham (2017). https://doi.org/10.1007/978-3-319-66923-6_45
4. De Carolis, A., Macchi, M., Negri, E., Terzi, S.: A maturity model for assessing the digital readiness of manufacturing companies. In: IFIP Advances in Information and Communication Technology. pp. 13–20 (2017)
5. Yu, B.Y., Honda, T., Zubair, S.M., Sharqawy, M.H., Yang, M.C.: A maintenance-focused approach to complex system design. Artif. Intell. Eng. Des. Anal. Manuf. AIEDAM **30**, 263–276 (2016)
6. de Jonge, B., Teunter, R., Tinga, T.: The influence of practical factors on the benefits of condition-based maintenance over time-based maintenance. Reliab. Eng. Syst. Saf. **158**, 21–30 (2017)
7. Koochaki, J., Bokhorst, J.A.C., Wortmann, H., Klingenberg, W.: The influence of condition-based maintenance on workforce planning and maintenance scheduling. Int. J. Prod. Res. **51**, 2339–2351 (2013)
8. Buchholz, P., Kriege, J., Felko, I.: Input Modeling with Phase-Type Distributions and Markov Models. Springer, Heidelberg (2014). https://doi.org/10.1007/978-3-319-06674-5
9. Edwards, D.J., Holt, G.D., Robinson, B.: An artificial intelligence approach for improving plant operator maintenance proficiency. J. Qual. Maint. Eng. **8**, 239–252 (2002)

Service Engineering Based on Smart Manufacturing Capabilities

How to Increase Share of Product-Related Services in Revenue? Strategy Towards Servitization

Ugljesa Marjanovic[1](✉)(iD), Bojan Lalic[1](iD), Vidosav Majstorovic[2](iD),
Nenad Medic[1](iD), Jasna Prester[3](iD), and Iztok Palcic[4](iD)

[1] Faculty of Technical Sciences, University of Novi Sad, Novi Sad, Serbia
{umarjano, blalic, nenad.medic}@uns.ac.rs
[2] Department for Production Engineering, University of Belgrade,
Belgrade, Serbia
vidosav.majstorovic@sbb.rs
[3] Faculty of Economics, University of Zagreb, Zagreb, Croatia
jprester@efzg.hr
[4] Faculty of Mechanical Engineering, University of Maribor, Maribor, Slovenia
iztok.palcic@um.si

Abstract. The process of creating value by adding services to product offerings, or servitization, has flourished in recent years. Manufacturing companies increasingly produce and provide services along with or instead of their traditional physical products. The provision of product-related services in emerging economies has been neglected and can tremendously improve understanding of service growth, especially in the field of billing. The aim of this study is to examine is it worthwhile for the manufacturing companies in transition countries to offer product-related services and what strategy should they pursue to build service business model. Our analysis used the Croatian, Serbian and Slovenian dataset from the European Manufacturing Survey conducted in 2015. Empirical results revealed that in manufacturing companies in transition countries product-related services can significantly increase share of revenue. Results indicate that management in manufacturing companies should directly invoice software development and revamping, and indirectly installation, and design, as product-related service to maximize firm's turnover and create a service business model.

Keywords: Product-related services · Turnover · EMS

1 Introduction

The process of creating value by adding services to product offerings [1], or servitization, has flourished in recent years [2]. Manufacturing companies increasingly produce and provide services along with or instead of their traditional physical products [3]. A notable reason for this movement is that the concept of servitization could enhance the competitiveness of a manufacturing company while simultaneously advancing economic conditions by higher share of turnover from selling services [1, 2]. Vast majority of manufacturers appear on the market as service providers [4]. Typical

I. Moon et al. (Eds.): APMS 2018, IFIP AICT 536, pp. 57–64, 2018.
https://doi.org/10.1007/978-3-319-99707-0_8

examples of the services provided include installation and training, after-sales services (i.e. product repair and maintenance, customer support and recycling), software development, remote support and modernization [5].

Services play a key role in developed economies [3], but in many transition countries the product related services are still in its infancy and present challenge for many manufacturing companies [6]. For a comprehensive analysis of servitization it seems therefore necessary to look at particular product-related service measuring the impact of services on performance of firms (i.e. turnover) [7]. Studies that deal with the assessment of whether adding additional services improves the financial performance of the firm, are scarce and more empirical research is needed in this area [8].

The aim of this study is to examine is it worthwhile for the manufacturing companies in three transition countries (i.e. Croatia, Serbia, Slovenia) to offer product related services and what billing strategy should they pursue: (i) service directly invoiced or (ii) indirectly (included in the product price).

2 Background and Related Work

2.1 Servitization

Servitization has become one of the most notable trend in recent years, and has been reflected in the changing structure of many advanced national economies, where services now account for the majority of national output [9]. Early studies reported that firms were adding service to their offering as a means of increasing competitiveness, turnover, and market power [1]. Servitization has evolved from 'goods or services' to 'goods and services'. Moreover, servitization involves more than just provision of more extensive services [10]. It involves firms' evolution in terms of specialization, vertical, horizontal and systematic integration [11]. This is seen as an enabler for value creation by blending services into overall strategies of the company [8]. Academics are almost unanimous in suggesting to product manufacturers to integrate services into their core product offerings since they can increase revenue, achieve higher margins, and accomplish stable source of income [12]. However, the provision of product-related services in emerging economies has been neglected and can tremendously improve our understanding of service growth [8, 13], especially in the field of billing [12].

In describing the service elements provided by manufacturing firms, several labels are used in the literature: industrial services, service strategy in manufacturing, product-related services, product-services, or after-sales services [12]. Focus of this paper is on product-related services, where business model is mainly oriented towards sales of products with additional service offerings [14]. Product-related services can serve as a differentiating characteristic which distinguishes firms within the same market. The distinctive strategy pattern is the ability of these firms to offer their customers unique problem solutions, integrating professional services and innovative products [7]. Most of the studies that deals with servitization are focusing on developed economies, while research in developing countries (e.g. Croatia, Serbia, Slovenia) are being neglected. Hence, focus on the specific situation of manufacturing companies in emerging economies is needed to compare to developed economies.

2.2 Research Questions

Based on literature review, the following research questions were proposed in attempt to identify the different effects of product-related services on manufacturing's firm performance:

- RQ1: Which product-related services increase share of revenue, when directly invoiced?
- RQ2: Which product-related services increase share of revenue, when indirectly invoiced (included in the product price)?

Figure 1 depicts the proposed model for our research questions. Product-related services presented in the model are identified based on exploratory interviews with practitioners and group discussions with experts in the field. All European Manufacturing Survey (EMS) consortium members were involved in this process, which resulted with a universal list of services which is transversal so that all manufacturing sectors can apply it indifferently of the product offered. Consequently, these product-related services were included in the EMS questionnaire. In the same manner, share of revenue was defined as the share of company revenue in the market [3, 7].

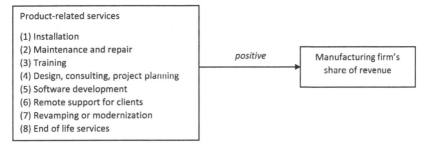

Fig. 1. Proposed model

3 Data and Methodology

Our analysis used Croatian, Serbian, and Slovenian dataset from the EMS conducted in 2015. Each survey has been carried out based on a proportionally size- and industry-based stratified random sample. Tables 1 and 2 depict the sample distribution across the participating European countries. EMS is a survey on the manufacturing strategies, the application of innovative organizational and technological concepts in production, and questions of servitization in European manufacturing industry [15–17]. The survey was conducted among manufacturing firms (NACE Rev 2 codes from 10 to 33) having at least 20 employees. The dataset includes 474 firms of all manufacturing industries. About 33.1% of the firms in the sample are small firms between 20 and 49 employees, another 50.6% of the firms have between 50 and 249 employees, and 16.3% of the firms have more than 250 employees. The largest industry in the sample is the manufacture of fabricated metal products (NACE 25; 19.2%), followed by manufacture of food products (NACE 10; 12.9%) and manufacture of machinery and equipment n.e. c. (NACE 28; 9.4%).

Tables 1 and 2 show that all constituting national samples of EMS have a reasonable representation for all firm sizes and a fair coverage of all manufacturing industries. The comparison between the firm size distribution of the subsamples of Croatian, Serbian, and Slovenian and the rest of EMS countries (e.g. Germany, Spain, Austria, the Netherlands) data shows no significant size bias. For all sub-samples, no significant differences compared to the rest of EMS countries data are revealed.

To analyze the relationships between product-related services and firm's revenue we employed a multivariate data analyzes.

Table 1. EMS database – distribution of firms by country and size

	Country sample		Firm size		
			20 to 49 employees	50 to 249 employees	250 and more employees
	%	n	n (%)	n (%)	n (%)
Croatia	21.9	104	31 (29.8)	47 (45.2)	26 (25.0)
Serbia	59.1	280	107 (38.2)	141 (50.4)	32 (11.4)
Slovenia	19.0	90	19 (21.1)	52 (57.8)	19 (21.1)
Total	100.0	474			

Table 2. Classification on manufacturing sectors according to share on total sample

NACE Rev. 2	Manufacturing industry	Share on total sample (%)
25	Manufacture of fabricated metal products, except machinery and equipment	19.2
10	Manufacture of food products	12.9
28	Manufacture of machinery and equipment n.e.c.	9.4
22	Manufacture of rubber and plastic products	8.4
27	Manufacture of electrical equipment	5.7
23	Manufacture of other non-metallic mineral products	5.3
13	Manufacture of textiles	4.3
29	Manufacture of motor vehicles, trailers and semi-trailers	4.3
14	Manufacture of wearing apparel	4.3
18	Printing and reproduction of recorded media	3.9
31	Manufacture of furniture	3.5
	Others	18.8

4   Results and Discussion

Table 3 presents two different regression models, for dependent variable (share of turnover), used to test research questions.

Table 3. Results of two different regression models

Product-related services	RQ1	RQ2
Installation	−.050	.923[***]
Maintenance and repair	.141	−.587[***]
Training	.228	−.973[***]
Design, consulting, project planning	.013	.199[***]
Software development	.299[**]	-.027
Remote support for clients	−.281	−.220
Revamping or modernization	.226[**]	.057
End of life services	.112[+]	.024
R	0.428	0.606
R^2	0.183	0.368
F	8.125	20.363
Sig.	0.000	0.000

Note: [***]$p < 0.001$; [**]$p < 0.01$; [*]$p < 0.05$; [+]$p < 0.1$

In regression model that tests first research question, the overall model was significant, adjusted R^2 = .183, F = 8.125, p < .001. Two predictors had a significant coefficient – Software development (B = .299, p < .01) and Revamping or modernization (B = .226, p < .01). Therefore, the results for our research question 1, "Which product-related services increase share of revenue, when directly invoiced?", indicate that manufacturing companies, in transition countries such as Croatian, Serbian, and Slovenian, can significantly increase share of revenue when directly invoicing product-related services (i.e. software development and revamping or modernization). Therefore, management in manufacturing companies should directly invoice *software development* and *revamping* as product-related service to maximize firm's turnover and create a service business model. While it is possible for a firm to provide product-related services within the context of a manufacturing operation, we found that firms that were directly billing services, such as maintenance and training, had not achieved higher share of turnover. This results are in line with previous studies [12]. It is not clear from our data, however, if the success of the two product-related services is due to the additional managerial focus these organizations received, or if, as we assume, cultural practices of customers in emerging markets are responsible for thwarting the other services investigated in this research (i.e. installation, maintenance, training, design and remote support).

Second regression model that tests research question 2, was also significant, with adjusted R^2 = .368, F = 20.363, and p < .001. Installation (B = .923, p < .001) and Design, consulting, project planning (B = .199, p < .001) had a coefficient that are positively and highly significant, thus supporting the idea to include them in the product price when billing to increase share of revenue. This result provides strong backing for managers in the manufacturing companies to indirectly include fees for services, such as *installation* and *design, consulting and project planning*, when provided invoices since they can significantly increase share of turnover. However, companies should not indirectly invoice services such as *maintenance and repair*, and *training* since they will significantly decrease firm's share of revenue. This does not mean that firms should not increase turnover when offering such services but will struggle to achieve service growth in overall revenue. Our results indicate that manufacturing firms offering *maintenance and repair*, and *training* are still more product rather than service-oriented companies.

Based on results, some of the product-related services did not have statistically significant coefficients (i.e. remote support for clients, end of life services). These results imply that personnel responsible for management of product-related services in the manufacturing firms should reconsider their strategy since current business model is not providing a valuable way for reaching higher success. As suggested by Gebauer et al. [18], utilization of services in manufacturing firms represents the challenge, since some manufacturers find it extremely difficult to successfully exploit the potential of an extended service business. Companies should redesign the current service business model or withdraw *remote support for clients*, and *end of life services* from its service portfolio.

5 Conclusion

This study examines servitization strategies of the manufacturing companies. Consequently, this paper provides theoretical and practical implications on how and in what way product-related services impact a manufacturing firm's revenue structure. Empirical results indicate that product-related service (i.e. Installation, Design, consulting, project planning, Software development, and Revamping) significantly influence firm's share of revenue when invoiced directly and indirectly (included in the product price). The contribution of this research is the ability to offer recent, international and relevant empirical figures about servitization from the three transition countries Croatia, Serbia and Slovenia.

Our sample was collected from all manufacturing industries, and, perhaps due to the industry specificity, results could differ. Also, there are various aspects that should be taken into consideration for assessment of service impact on company's turnover (e.g. type of costumer served, seasonality, and promotion). Further research is necessary to assess the experience and challenges of companies with focus on one industry (i.e. the manufacture of fabricated metal products) and to consider different challenges in measuring impact of services provided by manufacturing companies. Development of these ideas could prove, especially useful to firms facing the challenges of such industry, specific services to improve their financial performance [19]. It is foreseen to conduct this type of research again over a certain period, as EMS is a survey which is carried out on a triennial basis. In this way, we will be able to measure to what extent introduction of services affect turnover of manufacturing companies over time. In addition, next EMS survey should include "smart services" which are offered based on ICT functionalities of the product. In this manner, research results could reveal the possible strategy for emerging economies to take a lead and get closer to developed countries.

Acknowledgement. This work is supported by funding of Croatian Science Foundation O-1861-2014 – 3535 Building competitiveness of Croatian Manufacturing.

References

1. Vandermerwe, S., Rada, J.: Servitization of business: adding value by adding services. Eur. Manag. J. **6**(4), 314–324 (1988)
2. Shimomura, Y., Nemoto, Y., Ishii, T., Nakamura, T.: A method for identifying customer orientations and requirements for product–service systems design. Int. J. Prod. Res. **56**(7), 2585–2595 (2017)
3. Dachs, B., Biege, S., Borowiecki, M., Lay, G., Jäger, A., Schartinger, D.: Servitisation of European manufacturing: empirical evidence from a large-scale database. Serv. Ind. J. **34**(1), 5–23 (2014)
4. Lay, G., Copani, G., Jäger, A., Biege, S.: The relevance of service in European manufacturing industries. J. Serv. Manage. **21**(5), 715–726 (2010)
5. Santamaría, L., Nieto, M.J., Miles, I.: Service innovation in manufacturing firms: evidence from Spain. Technovation **32**(2), 144–155 (2012)
6. Crozet, M., Milet, E.: Should everybody be in services? The effect of servitization on manufacturing firm performance. J. Econ. Manage. Strategy **26**(4), 820–841 (2017)
7. Kinkel, S., Kirner, E., Armbruster, H., Jager, A.: Relevance and innovation of production-related services in manufacturing industry. Int. J. Technol. Manage. **55**(3–4), 263–273 (2011)
8. Kowalkowski, C., Gebauer, H., Oliva, R.: Service growth in product firms: past, present, and future. Ind. Mark. Manage. **60**, 82–88 (2017)
9. Johnstone, S., Wilkinson, A., Dainty, A.: Reconceptualizing the service paradox in engineering companies: is HR a missing link? IEEE Trans. Eng. Manage. **61**(2), 275–284 (2014)
10. Kowalkowski, C., Kindström, D., Alejandro, T.B., Brege, S., Biggemann, S.: Service infusion as agile incrementalism in action. J. Bus. Res. **65**(6), 765–772 (2012)
11. Gao, J., Yao, Y., Zhu, V.C.Y., Sun, L., Lin, L.: Service-oriented manufacturing: a new product pattern and manufacturing paradigm. J. Intell. Manuf. **22**(3), 435–446 (2011)
12. Oliva, R., Kallenberg, R.: Managing the transition from products to services. Int. J. Serv. Ind. Manag. **14**(2), 160–172 (2003)
13. Luoto, S., Brax, S.A., Kohtamäki, M.: Critical meta-analysis of servitization research: constructing a model-narrative to reveal paradigmatic assumptions. Ind. Mark. Manage. **60**, 89–100 (2017)
14. Tukker, A.: Eight types of product – service system: eight ways to sustainability? Bus. Strategy Environ. **260**, 246–260 (2004)
15. Lalic, B., Majstorovic, V., Marjanovic, U., Delić, M., Tasic, N.: The effect of industry 4.0 concepts and e-learning on manufacturing firm performance: evidence from transitional economy. In: Lödding, H., Riedel, R., Thoben, K.-D., von Cieminski, G., Kiritsis, D. (eds.) APMS 2017. IAICT, vol. 513, pp. 298–305. Springer, Cham (2017). https://doi.org/10.1007/978-3-319-66923-6_35

16. Lalic, B., Medic, N., Delic, M., Tasic, N., Marjanovic, U.: Open innovation in developing regions: an empirical analysis across manufacturing companies. Int. J. Ind. Eng. Manage. **8** (3), 111–120 (2017)

17. Lalic B., Anisic Z., Medic N., Tasic N., Marjanovic U.: The impact of organizational innovation concepts on new products and related services. In: Proceedings of 24th International Conference on Production Research - ICPR, pp. 110–115, DEStech Publications, Inc., Poznan (2017)

18. Gebauer, H., Fleisch, E., Friedli, T.: Overcoming the service paradox in manufacturing companies. Eur. Manag. J. **23**(1), 14–26 (2005)

19. Visnjic, K.I., Van Looy, B.: Servitization: Disentangling the impact of service business model innovation on manufacturing firm performance. J. Oper. Manage. **31**(4), 169–180 (2013)

A Hybrid Forecasting Framework with Neural Network and Time-Series Method for Intermittent Demand in Semiconductor Supply Chain

Wenhan Fu$^{(\boxtimes)}$ (iD), Chen-Fu Chien (iD), and Zih-Hao Lin

Department of Industrial Engineering and Engineering Management,
National Tsing Hua University, Hsinchu, Taiwan
s103034467@m103.nthu.edu.tw

Abstract. As the primary prerequisite of capacity planning, inventory control and order management, demand forecast is a critical issue in semiconductor supply chain. A great quantity of stock keeping units (SKUs) with intermittent demand patterns and distinctive lead-times need specific prediction respectively. It is difficult for companies in semiconductor supply chain to manage intricate inventory systems with the changeable nature of intermittent (lumpy) demand. This study aims to propose an integrated forecasting approach with recurrent neural network and parametric method for intermittent demand problems to support flexible decisions in inventory management, as a critical role in intelligent supply chain. An empirical study was conducted with product time series in a semiconductor company in Taiwan to validate the practicality of proposed model. The results suggest that the proposed hybrid model can improve forecast accuracy in demand management of semiconductor supply chain.

Keywords: Demand forecasting · Intermittent demand · Combining forecasts
Neural network · Semiconductor supply chain

1 Introduction

Semiconductor industry is a capital-intensive industry that demand fulfilment and capacity utilization significantly affect the revenue and profit of semiconductor companies [1, 2]. With the development of the technology, the semiconductor industry has become highly vertically integrated. The segments of "Vertical Disintegration" in semiconductor supply chain consist of IC design, wafer fabrication, and packaging and testing. In semiconductor supply chain management, one of the biggest challenges is to forecast the demand pattern of a great number of products. For various industries such as electronics, automotive and aircraft, stock keeping units with intermittent demand accounts about 60% of the total stock value [3]. There are several categories of semiconductor products based on physical design such as ICs, op-amp, capacitor, transistors, resistor, diodes etc. Numerous sub-categories exist in each specific category with great number of products per sub-category.

© IFIP International Federation for Information Processing 2018
Published by Springer Nature Switzerland AG 2018. All Rights Reserved
I. Moon et al. (Eds.): APMS 2018, IFIP AICT 536, pp. 65–72, 2018.
https://doi.org/10.1007/978-3-319-99707-0_9

Semiconductor companies need to make specific demand forecasting product by product as critical input of inventory control and ordering strategy. Each customer from downstream asks for types of component products at the same time. There are some gaps in semiconductor product demand forecasting: insufficient downstream information, low trade-off in market analysis and intermittent demand occurrence.

This research aims to propose a hybrid demand forecasting approach based on historical sales information to capture the intermittent pattern of semiconductor products demands as a part of to support flexible decisions in intelligent supply chain. In particular, an empirical case was employed to validate the model's effectiveness and compared with other classic methods. The proposed decision framework and process will assist decision makers in demand forecasting faced with historical data deficiency and demand uncertainty.

The remainder of this study is organized as follows. Section 1 introduces the background, significance and motivation of this research. Section 2 reviews demand categorization and intermittent demand forecasting. Section 3 proposes the research framework to make classification and forecasting of semiconductor products. Section 4 presents an empirical study in a leading semiconductor distributer in Taiwan to validate the proposed approach. Section 5 concludes with discussions and points out future research directions.

2 Literature Review

2.1 Demand Pattern Categorization

In semiconductor components management, thousands of different components have highly diverse usage individually [4]. Various demand patterns of the spare part causes a great segment in the inventory cost semiconductor components distributor [5]. Whereas, it's not practical to do a deep research to fit a demand pattern for each component, for there are too many components and that would cause a highly computational cost which is not efficiency. Thus, some categorization methods are built up to group the products, and they are invented to identify the appropriate forecasting method for the classification result.

Eaves and Kingsman [6] proposed a demand classification method, considering transaction variability, demand size variability and lead-time variability. However, there is not quantified method to classify the demand pattern. Syntetos et al. [7] used some mathematical proof to quantify the classification matrix. They proposed two cutoff value for calculate different demand pattern. One is the inter-demand interval (ADI = 1.32) It's used to identify the demand intervals. The other one is coefficient of demand variation (CV2 = 0.49). It can be used to identify whether the demand various is highly. The demand pattern can be classified into four types using this two-cut value. Lolli et al. [8] proposed a multi-criteria framework based on analytical hierarchy process (AHP) to classify and control inventory with intermittent demand.

2.2   Intermittent Demand Forecasting

Intermittent demand refers to demand pattern that appears randomly with high percentage of zero values between non-zero demand occurrences. The fluctuant nature of intermittent demand time-series render typical forecasting methods challenging to operate. Croston [9] presented an exponential smoothing based intermittent demand forecasting method by estimating separate extrapolation of non-zero demand size and demand interval between successive occurrences. Syntetos and Boylan [10] claimed that the original Croston's method was biased and made a modification with approximately unbiased demand/period estimates. Teunter et al. [11] developed a new decomposition method that updates the non-zero demand size and the demand incident probability separately.

Some artificial intelligence approaches were applied in intermittent forecasting problem. Gutierrez et al. [12] proposed a neural network modelling in lumpy demand forecasting and compares the performance of neural networks to traditional methods. Kourentzes [13] proposed dynamic demand rate forecasts with neural networks to capture potential interactions between the non-zero demand occurrences and zero demand intervals. Lolli et al. [14] applied single-hidden layer neural network trained back-propagation and extreme learning machines for forecasting intermittent demand and test it on industrial time series.

Though artificial intelligence method performs well in demand forecasting, neural network modelling and forecasting needs large amount of training data with high computing cost, which is rare for industrial company with off-line operation. Thus, how to balance the trade-off between traditional forecasting method with small sample data and neural network approaches worked with big data is a crucial issue. With effective evaluation and categorization of demand patterns, it will be supposed to improve forecasting accuracy with relatively low computing cost for real-time decision-making.

3   Methodology

To handle the deficient downstream information and intermittent demand occurrence for semiconductor products, we designed a hybrid demand forecasting framework for products/items in semiconductor supply chain which is shown in Fig. 1. First, we define the problem that semiconductor products with different demand patterns need to be forecasted in the mechanism. As two representatives of artificial intelligent and time series model for intermittent demand forecasting, recurrent neural network and SBA are applied in forecasting method construction stage. Then we use RFQV (Recency, Frequency, Quantity and Variance) analysis based on RFM (Recency, Frequency and Monetary Value) model [15] as the feature to classify products by demand feature. Each product is categorized into one subset and it is changeable with time moving. Finally, three accuracy matrices are performed for result evaluation and interpretation.

3.1 Problem Definition

Semiconductor companies usually maintain demand planning and inventory control weekly for thousands of products (with lead-time from 6–12 weeks) to keep customer service levels and combine predictions into orders for the component vendor.

The present problem is to establish an effective demand forecasting mechanism for all products in the light of their different characteristics since none of existing model can handle the diversity features of product demands.

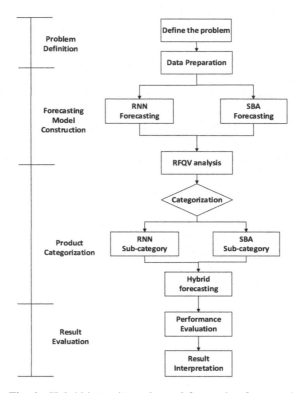

Fig. 1. Hybrid intermittent demand forecasting framework

3.2 Forecasting Model Construction

Two original forecasting models were occupied used at forecasting model construction stage in our framework. First is Recurrent Neural Network (RNN) for time series demand forecasting. The other is Syntetos-Boylan Approximation (SBA) [10], a typical representative of parametric time series method.

Suppose the demand series of product is $X = (x_1, x_2, \ldots\ldots, x_n)$, the intermittent demand series of product (X) is split into two variables: non-zero demand $C = (c_1, c_2, \ldots\ldots, c_n)$, and demand interval $I = (i_1, i_2, \ldots\ldots, i_n)$, where n means sales time points. The forecasting model construction process are illustrated as follows:

Step 1: select specific product number $C = (c_1, c_2, \ldots \ldots, c_n)$, $I = (i_1, i_2, \ldots \ldots, i_n)$.
Step 2: set sample length: number of times that sample point is taken, e.g. sample length = 4, training sample $z_1 = (z_1, z_2, z_3, z_4)$.
Step 3: set lead time for predicted time interval (e.g. lead = 3, $c_7 = (i_2, i_3, i_4, i_5)$ to forecast i_8).
Step 4: Move the interval length and demand before and after the moving average $(z_1 = \frac{c_1 + c_2 + c_3}{3})$.
Step 5: Divide the interval length and demand by the maximum period (scaled to 0–1)
Step 6: The pre-processed data is divided into C and I. Each model is trained for adaptive parameter settings constants.
Step 7: Combining predicted demand into single values based on prediction intervals.

In particular, for adaptive parameter settings constants of SBA and RNN model. For SBA model, the mathematical formulation to update prediction are:

$$
\begin{cases}
c_{t+1} = \alpha x_t + (1 - \alpha) + c_t \\
i_{t+1} = \alpha q + (1 - \alpha) + c_t \quad \text{if } x_t \neq 0 \\
y_t = \frac{c_{t+1}}{i_{t+1}} \left(1 - \frac{\alpha}{2}\right)
\end{cases}
\tag{1}
$$

$$
\begin{cases}
c_{t+1} = c_t \\
i_{t+1} = i_t \quad \text{if } x_t = 0 \\
y_{t+1} = y_t
\end{cases}
\tag{2}
$$

where q means the non-zero interval still time t, α is a smoothing parameter which can be adjusted between 0 and 1, y_t is the predicted demand in time t.

For RNN model, we added the structure of the neural network to three layers and used LSTM to replace the general recurrent neurons as shown in Fig. 2. The LSTM has a special structure in the recursive layer. The memory area consists of memory cells and gates. The purpose of the gate is to control the transmission of messages.

LSTM computes the input $X = x_1, x_2, \ldots \ldots, x_n$ according to the following formula to the output $Y = (y_1, y_2, \ldots \ldots, y_n)$ with $t = 1, 2, \ldots, n$:

$$
i_t = \sigma(W_{ix}x_t + W_{im}m_{t-1} + W_{ic}c_{t-1} + b_i)
\tag{3}
$$

$$
f_t = \sigma\left(W_{fx}x_t + W_{fm}m_{t-1} + W_{fc}c_{t-1} + b_f\right)
\tag{4}
$$

$$
c_t = f_t \odot c_{t-1} + i_t \odot g(W_{cx}x_t + W_{cm}m_{t-1} + b_c)
\tag{5}
$$

$$
o_t = \sigma(W_{ox}x_t + W_{om}m_{t-1} + W_{oc}c_t + b_o)
\tag{6}
$$

$$
m_t = o_t \odot h(c_t)
\tag{7}
$$

$$
y_t = \emptyset\left(W_{ym}m_t + b_y\right)
\tag{8}
$$

where W represents a weight matrix (e.g., W_{ix} is a matrix from the input gate to the input), b is a vector of errors (e.g. b_i is a vector of errors in input layers), σ is a logic and transfer function, *i, f, o, c, m* represent the input layer vector, the forgetting layer vector, the output layer vector, the cell activation vector, and the output activation vector respectively. The above vectors all have the same dimension, while $\odot$ denotes the element-to-element multiplication. *g* is a hyperbolic tangent function as the activation functions for cell input and cell output. Finally, $\emptyset$ is the network output activation function.

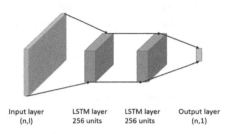

Input layer   LSTM layer   LSTM layer   Output layer
(n,l)   256 units   256 units   (n,1)

Fig. 2. Recurrent neural network structure

3.3 Product Categorization

It's crucial to select appropriate demand features for demand categorization of semiconductor products from historical sales recording dataset. Semiconductor products, especially component products like ICs, were made as part of electronic end-products like smart phone. The physical characters of such products have no influence in its demand sales.

For product value analysis, recency and frequency are favorable for inventory manager while quantity is more meaning than monetary for low unit price in semiconductor industry. Considering inter-demand interval and coefficient of demand variation are widely used in spare parts classification [7], we adjust RFM to RFQV (recency, frequency, quantity and coefficient of variation) for analyzing and evaluating product demand potentiality in the future. We separated the products by demand pattern through decision tree classification with the RFQV features. The response objective of demand pattern classification is the individual accuracy of SBA and RNN respectively. To customize the forecasting methods to fit the two categories, SBA and RNN with their rules in RFQV features. Thus, different kind products embedded with their corresponded forecasting method and combined as hybrid forecasting framework with two or more models.

3.4 Result Evaluation

For evaluation and interpretation of demand forecasting model, three different accuracy metrics: mean square Error, absolute error and mean absolute scaled error were used for validation. Root mean square error (RMSE), measures the average of the squares of the errors or deviations, is the common criterion for the demand forecast accuracy. Since RMSE enlarge extreme point's error in calculation, we use mean absolute error (MAE) that relatively robust to extreme value to balance the performance. In addition, mean absolute scaled error (MASE) [16] is a metric never undefined or infinite for non-trivial cases and is proper for evaluate intermittent demand series, which is common seen in semiconductor products.

4 Case Study

To demonstrate the effectiveness of the proposed model, an empirical study was conducted in a semiconductor company in Taiwan. The experiment data included weekly demand time series 78 products recording for 2 years. In data preparing stage, we separated dataset into three parts: training data for 1-year period, validation data for half-year and testing data for the last half-year.

Since the proposed model is a hybrid of RNN and SBA, we compared the forecasting results with these two approaches independently while the model used in empirical company- moving average and other two common-used methods (Croston and TSB) were added for performance evaluation. We devise data-driven adaptive parameter settings for constants in those models during the validation process to avoid overfitting.

The performance comparison includes three forecasting accuracy metrics on average for different methods on the testing period dataset are presented in Table 1. The results show that the proposed hybrid method performs better in all three accuracy criteria while the computing time cost is much less than RNN method. Thus, classification mechanism of product demand pattern can improve current prediction accuracy with limit computing cost.

Table 1. Performance comparison of different methods

Method	MASE	RMSE	MAE
Moving average	1.334	1374.7	814.6
Croston	1.114	1248.9	644.5
TSB	1.170	1241.0	648.7
SBA	1.077	1157.6	606.8
RNN	1.058	1161.9	600.6
Proposed	0.845	1035.8	588.1

5 Conclusions

In this study, a hybrid forecasting approach with recurrent neural network and time series method is proposed for irregular demand problems to support flexible decisions in inventory management, as a critical role in intelligent supply chain. The results in empirical study suggest that the proposed hybrid forecasting with product categorization can improve forecast accuracy in semiconductor product demand management. This study is also a typical case showing the combination decision solution embedded with both traditional model and artificial intelligence method, which can even better than AI only approach in some field. Future research can be done to enhance the forecasting approach in different scenarios (such as sufficient/deficient historical data) or import new ensemble operator instead of classification in combining forecast stage.

Acknowledgements. This research is supported by Ministry of Science and Technology, Taiwan (MOST106-2622-8-007-002-TM1; MOST 105-2218-E-007-027).

References

1. Chien, C.-F., Chen, C.-H.: A novel timetabling algorithm for a furnace process for semiconductor fabrication with constrained waiting and frequency-based setups. OR Spectr. **29**(3), 391–419 (2007)
2. Chien, C.-F., Dou, R., Fu, W.: Strategic capacity planning for smart production: decision modeling under demand uncertainty. Appl. Soft Comput. **68**, 900–909 (2018)
3. Bacchetti, A., Saccani, N.: Spare parts classification and demand forecasting for stock control: investigating the gap between research and practice. Omega **40**(6), 722–737 (2012)
4. Mönch, L., Uzsoy, R., Fowler, J.W.: A survey of semiconductor supply chain models part III: master planning, production planning, and demand fulfilment. Int. J. Prod. Res. (2017, in press). https://doi.org/10.1080/00207543.2017.1401234
5. Chuang, H.H.-C., Chang, H.L., Hsu, P.-C.: Improving the performance of inventory control–taking W company as an example. In: The 17th International Conference on Electronic Business, Dubai, UAE, pp. 289–292 (2017)
6. Eaves, A.H., Kingsman, B.G.: Forecasting for the ordering and stock-holding of spare parts. J. Oper. Res. Soc. **55**(4), 431–437 (2004)
7. Syntetos, A.A., Boylan, J.E., Croston, J.D.: On the categorization of demand patterns. J. Oper. Res. Soc. **56**(5), 495–503 (2004)
8. Lolli, F., Ishizaka, A., Gamberini, R., Rimini, B.: A multicriteria framework for inventory classification and control with application to intermittent demand. J. Multi-Criteria Decis. Anal. **24**(5–6), 275–285 (2017)
9. Croston, J.D.: Forecasting and stock control for intermittent demands. Oper. Res. Q. **23**(3), 289–303 (1972)
10. Syntetos, A.A., Boylan, J.E.: The accuracy of intermittent demand estimates. Int. J. Forecast. **21**(2), 303–314 (2005)
11. Teunter, R.H., Syntetos, A.A., Zied Babai, M.: Intermittent demand: linking forecasting to inventory obsolescence. Eur. J. Oper. Res. **214**(3), 606–615 (2011)
12. Gutierrez, R.S., Solis, A.O., Mukhopadhyay, S.: Lumpy demand forecasting using neural networks. Int. J. Prod. Econ. **111**(2), 409–420 (2008)
13. Kourentzes, N.: Intermittent demand forecasts with neural networks. Int. J. Prod. Econ. **143**(1), 198–206 (2013)
14. Lolli, F., Gamberini, R., Regattieri, A., Balugani, E., Gatos, T., Gucci, S.: Single-hidden layer neural networks for forecasting intermittent demand. Int. J. Prod. Econ. **183**, 116–128 (2017)
15. Fader, P.S., Hardie, B.G., Lee, K.L.: RFM and CLV: Using iso-value curves for customer base analysis. J. Market. Res. **42**(4), 415–430 (2005)
16. Hyndman, R.J.: Another look at forecast-accuracy metrics for intermittent demand. Foresight: Int. J. Appl. Forecast. **4**(4), 43–46 (2006)

Constructing a Metrology Sampling Framework for In-line Inspection in Semiconductor Fabrication

Chen-Fu Chien⬥, Yun-Siang Lin(✉)⬥, and Yu-Shin Tan

Department of Industrial Engineering and Engineering Management,
National Tsing Hua University, Hsinchu 30043, Taiwan, R.O.C.
yunsianglin@gmail.com

Abstract. Due to the shrinking IC device geometries and increasing inter-connect layers, process complexity has been rapidly increasing and leads to higher manufacturing costs and longer cycle time. Thus, in-line metrology is set at various steps to inspect the wafer in real time, which often causes lots of inspection costs and also increases cycle time. This study aims to develop a framework for in-line metrology sampling to determine the optimal sampling strategy in the light of different objectives to reduce extra cost and cycle time.

Keywords: Bayesian decision analysis · Sampling frequency · WIP metrology
Inspection · Quality control · Equipment efficiency

1 Introduction

In the wafer fabrication process, a number of inspection and measurement stations are set to monitor the process parameters and to find the problems in the early stage [1]. Due to limited capacities and costs for in-line wafer inspection, only certain wafers are inspected among a specific number of lots. Considering the high inspection cost [2], an effective sampling strategy for allocating the finite capacity has always played a huge role in yield management [3]. Meanwhile, given the characteristics of the semi-conductor industry, such as short product life cycles, changing demand of customers, keen competition in the market, and high manufacturing cost, a semiconductor com-pany should seek to cut back on unnecessary inspection cost and production time to increase the overall profit.

Although there are several existing studies for IC sampling strategy [4] in defect/particle inspection, little research has addressed with metrology sampling [1, 5] regarding the critical dimension or thin film. In-line metrology was to inspect the WIP in real time. Even though virtual metrology becomes popular recently [6], enterprises do not trust in this technology due to its uncertainty. Currently, the sampling metrology numbers and sampling frequency are still decided via the engineers' experience, and may vary from person to person.

The purpose of this study is to develop a full decision framework for statistically determining the optimal sampling strategy for in-line inspection in wafer fabrication. Moreover, we also explored how different sampling strategies could affect the cost of

© IFIP International Federation for Information Processing 2018
Published by Springer Nature Switzerland AG 2018. All Rights Reserved
I. Moon et al. (Eds.): APMS 2018, IFIP AICT 536, pp. 73–80, 2018.
https://doi.org/10.1007/978-3-319-99707-0_10

quality (COQ) and conducted an empirical analysis in a semiconductor factory. The constructed model and result may effectively help the engineers to decide the optimal sampling frequency in terms of product types and the cost of quality, which could enable full utilization of the machines and improve the product yield.

The remains of this paper are organized as follows: Sect. 2 reviews the studies related to the fundamentals of proposed framework. Section 3 shows the proposed method. Section 4 presents an empirical study. Section 5 concludes of the developed method and discussion on further studies to deal with the complex in-line metrology sampling process.

2 Fundamental

The notations used in this research are defined as follows.

θ_w: nature state of a wafer
θ_L: nature state of a lot
$\pi(\theta_{wi})$:   prior probability of a wafer in state i
$\pi(\theta_{Li})$:   prior probability of a lot in state i
A_w: set of actions in a wafer
A_L: set of actions in a lot
N_d: total number of dies in a wafer
N_w: total number of wafers in a lot
n_d: sample size for a wafer
n_w: sample size for a lot
k_d: number of out of spec dies in sampled dies
y: number of bad wafers in sampled wafers
z: number of rejection wafers in sampled wafers
$\delta_1(x)$:   decision rule for an inspected wafer
$\delta_2(z)$:   decision rule for an inspected lot
c_1:   acceptance number of a wafer
c_2:   acceptance number of a lot
v: sampling frequency
C_q: cost of per lot quality loss
C_s: sampling cost per lot

In practice, it costs tremendously to inspect every wafer in every lot. Without full-inspection, engineers only can infer the true quality of the product by prior probability, a subjective judgment of possibility, or by the latest evidence from sampled wafers and dies in a lot. According to the evidences, engineers may revise prior probability to posterior probability and determine proper actions: reject or accept a lot. Baye's theorem illustrate the revision of probability as

$$P(H|E) \propto P(H) \cdot P(E|H)$$

A decision to take appropriate actions based on sample data and the probability revision is call "Bayesian decision analysis".

2.1 Bayesian Decision Analysis

Bayesian decision discusses how to get extra information form appropriate sampling method, and update expected loss for feasible schemes from extra information to select a scheme with the minimum expected loss. According to Bayesian Theorem, decision makers can revise prior probability based on the sample information, and reappraise the expected value of each alternative. Chien, Hsu, Peng and Wu [4] applied Bayesian decision analysis and proposed a heuristic framework for sampling the particle or defect in wafer fabrication to provide the best sampling frequency and control limits. In addition, Chien, Wang and Wang [7] used Bayesian decision analysis to construct a IC final testing strategy for enhancing overall operational effectiveness. Figure 1 [8] shows a conceptual framework of Bayesian decision analysis.

There are three basic decision elements in Baye's decision analysis: parameter space, sample space and action space. Parameter space Ω is composed of possible states of nature θ_j, i.e., $\Omega = \{\theta_j\}$. We assume that there is a set of possible actions, a jointly constituting the action space A (i.e., $A = \{a_i\}$). Sample space is composed of sampled data.

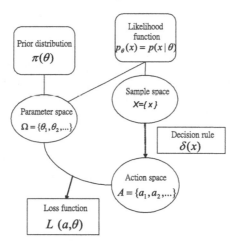

Fig. 1. Bayesian decision analysis [8]

When θ is not exactly know, we can get prior probability $\pi(\theta_j)$ of θ based on some mixture of subjective judgments and objective evidence. In many circumstances we may have some additional information provided from sample data x, with likelihood function $p_\theta(x)$ obtained from an experiment whose outcomes depend on the value θ. If we ignore prior information of θ, sample data alone can be used for choosing the action. Let the decision rule $\delta(x)$ specify the action in A corresponding to the evidence data x. That is, $\delta(x)$ is a decision rule that maps X to A. Furthermore, there is a function $L(a, \theta)$ defined on the $A \times \Omega$ space, where $L(a, \theta)$ measures the loss which arises if we take action a when the state of nature is θ.

Any decision rule $\delta(.)$ can be assessed in terms of long-term expected loss; that is, the average loss for different data might arise. For any decision rule $\delta(x)$, we consider the risk function as follows:

$$R(\delta(x), \theta) = \int_x L(\delta(x), \theta) \, p_\theta(x) \, dx \qquad (1)$$

If in addition to sample data, one may weigh the risk function by $\pi(\theta)$ and compute the summary measure (e.g. expected risk) as a basis for choosing between different decision rules. That is, Baye's risk is defined as follows:

$$r(\delta, \pi) = \int_\Omega \int_x L(\delta(X), \theta) \cdot p_\theta(x) \cdot \pi(\theta) \cdot dx \cdot d\theta \qquad (2)$$

The best decision rule is the one that has the minimum mean risk with respect to variations in θ; that is,

$$\min_\delta r(\delta, \theta) \qquad (3)$$

3   Approach

The proposed framework of sampling strategy is constructed based on Bayesian decision analysis as shown in Fig. 2. In particular, three Bayesian decision elements in the proposed sampling framework are defined as follows.

Parameter space is the true quality of population and comprises two states: θ_1 = good and θ_2 = bad since the true quality would either meet or fail quality requirement. Sample space X indicates the unqualified number in sample n drawn from population N. Action space contains two actions: a_1 = accept and a_2 = reject. Depend on decision rule (acceptance sampling plan) $\delta(x)$, if random variable x is lower than a criteria which is determined in advance we will accept this population. Otherwise, we will reject this population.

First, let us consider a sampling plan in a wafer. Suppose there are N_d dies in a wafer. The parameter space of a wafer θ_w consists of two states: θ_{w1} = good wafer and θ_{w2} = bad wafer since the true quality of a wafer would either meet or fail quality requirement. n_d dies are drawn from a wafer to inspect and x denotes the number of dies that do not meet quality requirement. According to the decision rule $\delta_1(x)$, $x \leq c_1$ means that we do not have sufficient evidence to reject this wafer conform to our requirement, we should not reject this wafer. Otherwise, $x > c_1$ means the wafer does not meet our requirement and thus should be rejected. A wafer state of nature includes good and bad state, $\Omega_w = \{\theta_{w1} = \text{good wafer}, \theta_{w2} = \text{bad wafer}\}$, and $\pi(\theta_{w1}) = p(good \, wafer)$, $\pi(\theta_{w2}) = p(bad \, wafer)$. Action space in a wafer is $A_w = \{a_1 = accept, a_2 = reject\}$ and sample space x is the possible unqualified number of dies in n_d dies.

Similar to a wafer, the state of nature of a lot consists of good lot and bad lot, i.e., $\Omega_L = \{\theta_{L1} = \text{good lot}, \theta_{L2} = \text{bad lot}\}$, and $\pi(\theta_{L1}) = p(good \, lot)$ $\pi(\theta_{L2}) = p(bad \, lot)$. Action space in a lot is $A_L = \{a_1 = accept, a_2 = reject\}$ and sample space y is the possible unqualified number of wafers in n_w wafers that are drown form a lot with N_w wafers.

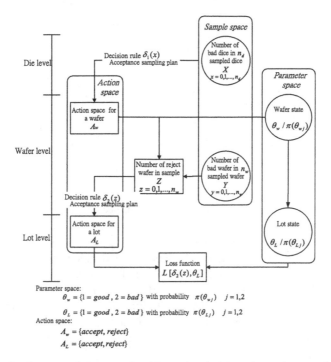

Fig. 2. Conceptual framework of Bayesian decisions for an inspected lot

However, in wafer fabrications, in-line metrology inspection is executed by sampling some wafers in an inspection lot and some dies in every sampled wafer, then integrate the decision result from individual sampled wafer to determine accept or reject this lot. Thus, in addition to basic Bayesian decision elements, there is an extra random variable z accounts the number of being rejected wafers in sample n_w wafers. Not only the decision making of a wafer, but number of bad wafers in our sampled n_w wafers also effect z. Combine random variable z and decision rule $\delta_2(z)$ in a lot, if the value z is less than acceptance quality level c_2 we think that every wafer in the lot is meet quality requirement and accept this lot. Otherwise, if the value z exceed c_2, we will reject this lot.

Because the nature state of a wafer uncertainly, and N_w wafers comprise a lot, it means that the state of a lot also uncertainly. Based on nature state of a wafer or a lot, a decision making is possible to make wrong and increase the producer risk or consumer risk simultaneously. The producer risk is meant that the wafer or lot was rejected under the wafer or lot was good. The consumer risk is meant that the wafer or lot was accepted under the wafer or lot was bad (Fig. 3).

$$\text{Producer risk} = p(\text{reject a product} \mid \text{product is good}) = \alpha$$
$$\text{Consumer risk} = p(\text{accept a product} \mid \text{product is bad}) = \beta$$

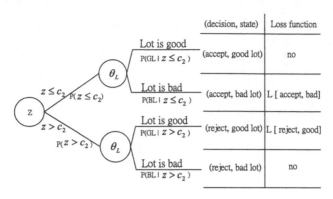

Fig. 3. Decision tree for a inspected lot

Under the combination (accept, bad) we will have a loss L [*accept*, *bad*] because we accept a bad lot. Since the action "accept" a lot decided based on decision rule $\delta_2(z)$, L [*accept*, *bad*] can be revised as a function of $\delta_2(z)$ as L [$\delta_2(z)$, *bad*]. Similarly, loss function of the combination (reject, good) L [*reject*, *good*] can be revised as a function of $\delta_2(z)$ as L [$\delta_2(z)$, *good*]. The remaining combinations of (accept, good) and (reject, bad) imply that decision maker takes right action and no loss will occur.

According to Eq. (1), we derive a pair of long-term expected loss $R(\delta_2(z)$, *good*) and $R(\delta_2(z)$, *bad*) for a inspected lot. Moreover, the Baye's risk $r(\delta_2(z), \pi_L)$ can be calculated by weighting the risk function $R(\delta_2(z)$, *good*) and $R(\delta_2(z)$, *bad*) with π_L(good lot) and π_L(bad lot) for a inspected lot. Finally, an optimal decision rule $\delta_2^*(z)$ with the minimum Baye's risk in all feasible decision rules under given conditions can be determined.

In addition, not all of products can be inspected. We assume the lot not inspected is good, but it may not always be true in really setting. There is a case that the lot is unqualified and we pass it because we do not inspect it. It brings a yield loss C_q from the gap between good and bad lot. For a long time, the expected yield loss of a non-inspected lot is π(bad lot) $\times C_q = r(B)$.

With sampling frequency v, we will inspect a lot again after $(v-1)$ lots. Between two sampling lots, the quality loss is $r(\delta_2^*(z), \pi_L) + (v-1)r(B)$. On the other hand, we need to consider sampling cost when sample a lot to inspect every time. Sampling cost consists of fixed sampling cost F and variant sampling cost S. If we sampled n_w wafers to inspect from a lot, then the sampling cost for a sample is

$$C_s = F + n_w \times S \tag{5}$$

In order to determine the best sampling frequency v, we tradeoff sampling costs and quality cost with a function $E(\text{cost}) = f(\delta_2, \pi_L, v)$.

The best sampling frequency is that with the minimum $E(\text{cost})$.

4 An Empirical Study

4.1 To Change the Sampling Inspection Plan and Frequency

From Fig. 4, we can find that given the same number of inspected wafers n_w, the greater the sampling frequency v is, the less influence inspected dies n_d have on the quality loss cost. On the other hand, with the same n_d, the greater v is, the less influence n_w have on the quality cost loss.

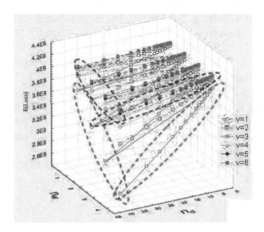

Fig. 4. The influence of the sampling strategy and frequency on E(Loss)

5 Conclusion and Further Study

This study proposed a general in-line metrology sampling framework for semiconductor manufacturing. The proposed framework can assist the decision maker in determining all parameters for in-line sampling strategy with different lot size and process capability. Moreover, the sampling acceptance level for a wafer and lot can also be decided.

However, not all in-line inspection station has the same process capability. Further study should be done to allocate the inspection resource to different inspection stations with different capability. Therefore, further studies need to decrease sampling rate at non-critical or with either stable or high process capability stations. On the other hand, increase sampling frequency at critical or low process capability stations. By the way, we can reduce cost of sampling and quality loss, decrease cycle time to increase throughputs.

References

1. Nduhura-Munga, J., Rodriguez-Verjan, G., Dauzere-Peres, S., Yugma, C., Vialletelle, P., Pinaton, J.: A literature review on sampling techniques in semiconductor manufacturing. IEEE Trans. Semicond. Manuf. **26**(2), 188–195 (2013)
2. Gudmundsson, D., Shanthikumar, J.G.: Improving the deployment of inspection tools; tutorial on inspection capacity and sample planning. In: IEEE International Symposium on Semiconductor Manufacturing, ISSM 2005, pp. 410–413. IEEE (2005)
3. Gudmundsson, D.: Inspection and metrology capacity allocation in the full production and ramp phases of semiconductor manufacturing (2005)
4. Chien, C.-F., Hsu, S.-C., Peng, S., Wu, C.-H.: A cost-based heuristic for statistically determining sampling frequency in a wafer fab. In: Semiconductor Manufacturing Technology Workshop, pp. 217–229. IEEE (2000)
5. Chien, C.-F., Hsu, C.-Y.: UNISON analysis to model and reduce step-and-scan overlay errors for semiconductor manufacturing. J. Intell. Manuf. **22**(3), 399–412 (2011)
6. Khan, A.A., Moyne, J.R., Tilbury, D.M.: An approach for factory-wide control utilizing virtual metrology. IEEE Trans. Semicond. Manuf. **20**(4), 364–375 (2007)
7. Chien, C.-F., Wang, H.-J., Wang, M.: A UNISON framework for analyzing alternative strategies of IC final testing for enhancing overall operational effectiveness. Int. J. Prod. Econ. **107**(1), 20–30 (2007)
8. Sainfort, F.: Eualuation of medical technologies: a generalized ROC analysis. Med. Decis. Making **11**(3), 208–220 (1991)

Maturity Models for Digitalization in Manufacturing - Applicability for SMEs

Stefan Wiesner[1]([✉]), Paolo Gaiardelli[2], Nicola Gritti[2], and Gianluca Oberti[2]

[1] BIBA - Bremer Institut für Produktion und Logistik GmbH at the University of Bremen, Hochschulring 20, 28359 Bremen, Germany
wie@biba.uni-bremen.de
[2] Università degli Studi di Bergamo, 24044 Dalmine, BG, Italy
https://www.unibg.it/

Abstract. Digitalization is a challenging topic for manufacturing SMEs. Besides improving their technological base, they have to keep the business offer attractive, e.g. by bundling their products with smart services. In addition to limited resources, often the necessary knowledge is missing to select the right technologies and develop attractive services based on their functionality. Due to the resulting high risks, SMEs neglect the chances of digitization and lose competitiveness. To start with, they need a maturity assessment model that can help them understand their level of readiness to implement aspects, such as Industry 4.0. In order to identify and fit such a model for SMEs, already existing assessment methods were analyzed according to a series of selected dimensions linked to SMEs features. The evaluation result illustrates requirements that have to be addressed by a new maturity model suitable for SMEs attempting digitalization.

Keywords: Industry 4.0 · Smart services · SMEs · Maturity model

1 Introduction

A firm's competitive position is determined by the ability to innovate its product portfolio and the time required to bring new products to the market. This increasing customer willingness to ask for new features and the rapid dynamization of the manufacturing environment are main drivers behind digitalization. As a consequence, Industry 4.0 has the aim to integrate sensors, machines, workpieces, and IT systems along the value chain beyond a single enterprise. These connected systems can interact with one another using standard Internet-based protocols and analyze data to predict failure, configure themselves, and adapt to changes [1].

Together with the technological advance, manufacturers are required to develop assets that can quickly adapt to new requirements from the customers through services. Unfortunately, there are many firms that consider themselves as a builder of things and that state their gross margin, revenues and other key performance indicators solely in term of "the product". When companies have begun to wrap value-adding services around their product, their competitive advantage is only temporary with regard to the

I. Moon et al. (Eds.): APMS 2018, IFIP AICT 536, pp. 81–88, 2018.
https://doi.org/10.1007/978-3-319-99707-0_11

technological development. The services have to be based on the new digital possibilities to become smart services [2]. They go beyond the kinds of upkeep and upgrades the firm may be bundling with the product, both in their value to customers and in their cost efficiency to the company.

In many European countries, small and medium-sized enterprises (SMEs) are the backbone of the manufacturing sector. For example, Italy has over four million enterprises in industry, services and construction with almost 11 million employees, and with an average size per firm of only 3.04 employees [3]. With more than 53% of value added and approximately 63% of employment, SMEs in Germany provide the majority of jobs and value added in the non-financial business economy, similar to the rest of the EU [3]. In order to remain competitive in this increasingly dynamic environment, SMEs have to provide adequate smart services, depending on the maturity of the company. This requires adopting the right technological options from the vast number of different alternatives summarized under digitalization. Although their dimensions foster creativity and the flexibility, problems in the development of smart services could arise because of the under-capitalization and the delay in identifying the best strategy for what concerns the technology choice [4]. Following the above challenges and issues, the aim of this paper is to analyze if existing maturity models are suitable for digitalizing SMEs and the possible drawbacks that have to be taken into account when developing a new improved maturity model for SMEs following Industry 4.0.

2 Methodology and Research Design

Although literature encourages companies to develop servitization strategies in a digitalization context, providing several methodologies and tools to assess the maturity level of smart services, it offers little guidance how SMEs have to cope with a smart servitization journey. In order to answer this question, a two stage research, aiming at the creation of a theoretical model that highlights the main characteristics of maturity models in Industry 4.0 for SMEs, was conducted. First of all, an extensive research on the most cited dimensions that characterise barriers and challenges in SMEs was carried out. At the same time a literature review using the search terms ("Industry 4.0" OR "Industrie 4.0") AND ("maturity model" OR "maturity assessment") in titles and abstracts was realised starting from interdisciplinary search engines as Scopus and Google Scholar. Matching the two analyses achieved the identification of the most appropriate maturity models for our research and the creation of an initial conceptual model able to explain the different attributes of maturity models supporting smart servitization of SMEs. Having created this initial model, we presented it to a panel of academic and industrial experts to validate its consistency with SMEs characteristics. The crosscheck was carried out separately and the obtained feedback compared and unitedly agreed among the experts and researchers, in order to construct the final version of the model which is presented later in this paper.

3 State of the Art Analysis

The use of new digital technologies and the acquisition of knowledge will inevitably lead to new types of work and ways of working. This will necessitate changes to the structures within companies and the relationships between companies and will revolve around networks of manufacturing resources that are autonomous, capable of controlling themselves in response to different situations, self-configuring, knowledge-based, sensor equipped and spatially dispersed [5]. As a key component of this vision, smart factories will be embedded into inter-company value networks and will be characterized by end-to-end engineering. The goal of this integration is to deliver an end-to-end solution [6]. Industry 4.0 capabilities help to incorporate individual customer and product specific features into the design, configuration, ordering, planning, production, operation and recycling phases, dramatically reducing the time between an event occurring and the implementation of an appropriate response [5].

3.1 Challenges for Manufacturing SMEs in Digitalization

While SMEs are often not led by a professional manager, they usually have a great capacity for improvisation [10]. Therefore, SMEs have a high potential for digitalization but they're also exposed to failure risk and greater financial constraints compared to the big companies [11]. The result is often a focus on sectors with medium (or medium-low) technology level, where the competitiveness is mainly based on price. While every fourth German manufacturing company already uses Industry 4.0 applications, from sensors to big-data to industrial 3D printing, the shift of business models from analogue to digital is an enormous challenge for SMEs. The companies must be open to new partnerships, as no vendor controls the whole process from sensor to invoice [7, 8]. Therefore, a fundamental criterion for a suitable maturity model is its general *adaptability to SMEs organizational structure*. It should support an agile company, enabling rapid decision-making and adaptation processes throughout every part of the business and across all business process areas [5].

According to a study among 420 German SMEs, the majority of the companies see a great potential in digitalization and invests between two and five percent of their sales. But there are still numerous challenges, which must be overcome. Many participants cite security, data protection, and loss of control over their own data, costs, time, or the high implementation effort as reasons for slowing things down. Examples of concrete implementations are still missing. Many digitization efforts would still fail because of the employees, who sometimes have little motivation or are not open to new ideas. Complex, incomprehensible technology and standstill after first developments are mentioned as well [9]. Thus, a suitable maturity model should not to be too complicated to be understood (*simplicity*), explaining the overall idea of digitalization and its related concepts, clarifying uncertainties instead of creating new ones. This includes *implementation easiness* as well.

The specific needs of SMEs, initially include information on the possibilities of digitalization, and subsequently providing guidance through the first steps of the transformation. They experience problems to identify concrete fields of action, programs and projects [12]. The benefits of Smart Manufacturing have to be shown by success stories how it can be applied in SMEs. Required resources include motivation, training, road mapping and support on the actual implementation. Rather than fascination for technology, it needs to be assured that solutions yield the profits they are supposed to [11]. Consequently, an important function of a maturity model is the *guidance provided* for SMEs on how to attain a higher level of maturity in their specific domain and to continue in the right direction with their business strategy. It should allow them to position their business against external trends and give a guideline to select suitable technological and smart service options.

Strongly linked to the uncertainty about digitalization concepts, the *knowledge requirements* to use a maturity model is crucial for its suitability for SMEs. A high initial knowledge constitutes a sort of entry barrier. This has been confirmed in semi-structured interviews with practitioners and researchers. Companies perceive the concepts of Industry 4.0 as highly complex with no strategic guidance offered and lack a clear idea of Industry 4.0 resulting in uncertainty regarding benefits and outcomes [12].

3.2   Model for Maturity Assessment and Technology Selection

One of the first obstacles encountered by companies approaching digitalization is to understand their level of maturity, generally defined as "state of being complete, perfect or ready" [13] for this transformation. The objective of maturity assessment models is to provide means for assessing a company's current maturity to implement aspects of Industry 4.0 and identifying concrete measures to help them achieve a higher maturity stage in order to maximize the benefits [5].

In the literature it is possible to find several models with this aim but, in order to streamline the process, it has been decided to focus the attention on four models that are currently adopted (according to a survey among manufacturing SMEs in the territory) in the countries where the researchers come from: Italy and Germany. The choice of these models simplifies, in addition, their analysis as, in the past, the authors of this paper were involved in the creation of one of them.

Furthermore, the Italian economy is based on SMEs, as the 99.9% of Italian firms belongs to this category [16], which means that this target is surely relevant. This fact will not exclude, with any doubt, a broader discussion in the future thanks to the inclusion of additional models.

1. Schumacher et al. (2016): *"Maturity model for assessing Industry 4.0 readiness and maturity of manufacturing enterprises"* [12]
   The model includes three distinct phases: an initial phase to create complete understanding of the domain of Industry 4.0, a core development phase to design and architect the model's structure as well as a practically applicable tool and an implementation phase to validate the resulting tool in real life application.
2. Jarrahi et al. (2017): *"Smart service strategies in industry 4.0: a proposal of a readiness assessment methodology"* [14]
   This model is based upon the main drivers that characterize business and operational transformation in Industry 4.0 and smart service-based strategies. The methodology aims to assist companies through smart servitization in the Industry 4.0 scenario by adapting the most appropriate smart service strategies.

3. Lichtblau (2015): *"IMPULS - Industrie 4.0-Readiness"* [15]

   The model provided by IMPULS involves an online self-check tool that lets one calculate an Industry 4.0 scorecard. Companies can find out where they are already well prepared for Industry 4.0 and where they still have room for improvement. This readiness model is based on key principles like smart products and services.

4. Schuh et al. (2017): *"Industrie 4.0 Maturity Index. Managing the Digital Transformation of Companies"* [5]

   The maturity assessment model by Acatech takes as an input the current situation and the corporate strategy of the firm in order to provide a digital guidance roadmap as output, with a step-by-step approach to achieving the benefits that reduces the investment and implementation risks for the company.

3.3 Applicability of Existing Industry 4.0 Maturity Models for SMEs

Table 1 below includes a brief evaluation of the four above-mentioned models according to the dimensions that we have identified as fundamental to perform an Industry 4.0 maturity assessment suitable for SMEs in Sect. 3.1.

Table 1. Applicability evaluation of I4.0 maturity models for SMEs

Method	Schumacher	Jarrahi	Lichtblau	Schuh
Simplicity & Implementation easiness	●	●	●	◑
Knowledge requirements	◔	◑	◐	◕
Importance of Organizational Issues	◕	◑	◑	●
Guidance provided	○	◑	○	●

The main advantage of *Schumacher*'s model [12] is its transparency, which makes it quite simple to understand, thanks to its maturity assessment questionnaire and formula. Some background knowledge is very important at the earliest stage, as it's the basis for the establishment of evaluation weights. Its basic technical and implementation requirements are quite suitable for SMEs. The main reason behind the simplicity of *Jarrahi*'s model [14] is the use of a questionnaire to classify the company in one of four levels. The model requires the user to have a medium knowledge level to better assess the maturity. A basic guidance is provided according to the level in which the company is classified. *Lichtblau's* model [15] requires very little time and resources involvement, being based on an online tool. It requires medium digitalization knowledge from the people that are going to fill the form to be consistent with the actual situation of the SME. Once again, there is a lack of guidance regarding the I4.0 framework. The completeness and broadness of *Schuh*'s model [5] require quite heavy time and resource involvement. It doesn't require a special kind of initial knowledge. The inclusion of strategic objectives in the analysis make this model suitable for every company dimension, thanks also to the very detailed and tailored guidance provided according to the company's objectives.

4   Requirements for a New SME Industry 4.0 Maturity Model

Following the evaluation that we have performed, it is possible to identify important similarities among the four models. These common dimensions are crucial and they provide the starting point for identifying requirements to develop a new Industry 4.0 maturity model useful for SMEs.

The company's *strategy and organizational structure* is present in each model, they all agree that one important point to understand the maturity level of a company is looking at its strategy. The new model should take into account the long term strategy of the company and build a step by step development process, which can help SMEs to identify their specific strategic goal within the constraints. The guidance provision should be aligned with the pre-established strategic objective of the SME and consider also the addition of some intermediate milestones.

The digital transformation into a learning, agile company in Industry 4.0 requires a change in *leadership and culture*. Companies will be unable to achieve the desired agility if they simply introduce digital technologies without also addressing their corporate culture. Instead, they must begin by deciding how they want their company to do things in the future and which skills their employees will require. The new model should find a simple and clear way to assess employees' willingness to change work behavior. It shouldn't require employees to change their work behavior too rapid.

For digitalization companies have to determine how they can contribute to satisfying the end *customer*'s needs. Even if the company doesn't itself deliver directly to the end customer, its product or service still forms part of the end customer's solution. The better the contributions made to this solution by the individual partners, the more successfully the companies in question will be able to differentiate themselves from the competition. The new model should find a clear and concise way to identify whether the company is focusing on the B2B or B2C customer needs. Therefore, the model should provide guidance for a periodical check of end user satisfaction.

In order to generate and analyze data and implement the corresponding decisions, the SMEs resources must acquire certain competencies or be upgraded with the relevant *technological* components. The new model should contain a straightforward method (weighted ranking) to assess the technological level of the company within the Industry 4.0 framework. Guidance should rationalize technology investments as the levels advance in order to avoid drastic expenses.

Last but not least, the model shouldn't require a high level of knowledge to identify the SME in one of the strategic levels. In addition it should provide information about the benefits of each level.

5 Summary and Outlook

This paper has presented an overview of the special challenges digitalization creates for SMEs. It has been illustrated that one of the major obstacles for these kind of companies is to assess their current situation regarding technology and smart service implementation, as well as to receive guidance on possible strategic development paths towards digitalization. Simplicity, the knowledge required, suitability for SME organization and the guidance provided have been identified as prerequisites for such methods. Four existing Industry 4.0 maturity models have been analyzed for their compliance towards these prerequisites. As no individual model could fully satisfy all prerequisites, requirements for a new SME maturity model have been derived.

After translating SMEs features into requirements and deciding which dimensions to include, in a next step the objective is to build a new SMEs-tailored maturity model. This model will specifically help SMEs to select the right technologies according to their maturity and provide guidance to develop value-adding smart services for their products. The first target of this model are Italian SMEs operating in the manufacturing sector, which often fail to grasp the overall concept of digitalization and all the opportunities coming with it, mainly because of the broadness of this topic. The model will be evaluated through application in several of these industrial cases.

References

1. Rüßmann, M., et al.: Industry 4.0: the future of productivity and growth in manufacturing (2015). Accessed 9 Apr 2018
2. Allmendinger, G., Lombreglia, R.: Four strategies for the age of smart services. Harv. Bus. Review **83**(10), 131–134, 136, 138 passim (2005)
3. European Commission: SBA Fact Sheet 2016 (2016). Accessed 31 May 2018
4. Bottoncini, A., Pasetto, A., Rotondi, Z.: Sviluppo e prospettive dell'industria 4.0 in italia e ruolo strategico del credito. 51-66 Paginazione/Argomenti, No 4 (2016): maggio - agosto (2016). https://doi.org/10.14276/1971-8357.516
5. Schuh, G., Anderl, R., Gausemeier, J., ten Hompel, M., Wahlster, W. (eds.): Industrie 4.0 maturity index. managing the digital transformation of companies. Acatech STUDIE. Utz, Herbert, München (2017)
6. Kagermann, H., Helbig, J., Hellinger, A., Wahlster, W.: Umsetzungsempfehlungen für das Zukunftsprojekt Industrie 4.0. Deutschlands Zukunft als Produktionsstandort sichern; Abschlussbericht des Arbeitskreises Industrie 4.0. Forschungsunion; Geschäftsstelle der Plattform Industrie 4.0, Berlin, Frankfurt/Main (2013)
7. Pütter, C.: Digitalisierung im Mittelstand: Probleme mit digitalen Geschäftsmodellen (2018)
8. Witsch, K., Kerkmann, C.: Industrie 4.0 light. Handelsblatt, 23–24 April 2018
9. Adelmann, S.: Transformation mit Hindernissen (2017)
10. Wiesner, S., Nilsson, S., Thoben, K.-D.: Integrating requirements engineering for different domains in system development – lessons learnt from industrial SME cases. Procedia CIRP **64**, 351–356 (2017). https://doi.org/10.1016/j.procir.2017.03.013
11. Thoben, K.-D., Wiesner, S., Wuest, T.: "Industrie 4.0" and smart manufacturing – a review of research issues and application examples. IJAT **11**(1), 4–16 (2017). https://doi.org/10.20965/ijat.2017.p0004

12. Schumacher, A., Erol, S., Sihn, W.: A maturity model for assessing Industry 4.0 Readiness and maturity of manufacturing enterprises. Procedia CIRP **52**, 161–166 (2016). https://doi.org/10.1016/j.procir.2016.07.040
13. Hanks, P., Pearsall, J., Stevenson, A.: Oxford Dictionary of English. Oxford University Press, Oxford (2010)
14. Jarrahi, F., Pezzotta, G., Cimini, C., Gaiardelli, P.: Smart service strategies in Industry 4.0. A proposal of a readiness assessment methodology. In: The Spring Servitization Conference 2017 "Internationalisation through Servitization", pp. 232–240. Aston University (2017)
15. Lichtblau, K.: Industrie 4.0 - Readiness. Impuls-Stiftung (2015)
16. Rapporto Cerved PMI (2017)

The Impacts of Quick Response in a Dual-Channel Supply Chain

Huihui Zhang and Danqin Yang[✉]

School of Economics and Management,
Nanjing University of Science and Technology, Nanjing 210094, China
yangdanqin@163.com

Abstract. We consider the quick response (QR) in a dual-channel supply chain in which a manufacturer sells products through both its own direct channel and a retailer. With QR, the retailer has an opportunity to reorder after the random demand is realized and the manufacturer is able to reproduce after that. We characterize the equilibrium decisions for each channel and investigate the impacts of QR on the decisions and profits. Through numerical analysis, we show that QR may be beneficial to the manufacturer whereas either increases or decreases the optimal expected profit of the retailer. In addition, the supply chain is able to achieve Pareto improvement with QR under certain conditions.

Keywords: Dual-channel supply chain · Quick response · Game theory

1 Introduction

With the development of e-commerce, it is a growing trend for manufacturers to open up direct channels. Many papers showed that operating direct channel may increase the profits of a firm and its downstream enterprise (Arya et al. 2007; Dumrongsiri et al. 2008). Plenty of companies have established dual-channel networks, such as Apple and Huawei. In last decades, products' life cycles are increasingly shortened and some categories are eliminated from the market so quickly that it's not sensible to keep too many stocks in both direct and retail channel. The quick response originated in the US apparel industry aims to respond to the demand changes better. Iyer and Bergen (1997) evaluated the effect of reducing delivery time through QR and found that QR can increase the retailer's profit while damage the manufacturer's profit. The fast fashion retailer, Zara's practice shows that QR is a critical factor for reducing the inventory risk. Although the QR systems may increase the cost of manufacturers and retailers, it mitigates the demand uncertainty and increases the sales profits.

Retailers can postpone product ordering until the time closer to the selling season making the demand forecasts and corresponding inventory decisions match better (Fisher et al. 2001). Caro and Martínez-de-Albéniz (2010) considered the retailer competition with demand spillover and found the QR is more profitable when the demand uncertainty is higher or the cross-temporal demand correlations are bigger. Li and Ha (2008) assumed the competitive manufacturers rely on initial inventory and QR ability to solve the problem of demand uncertainty. Lin and Parlaktürk (2012) analyzed the value of QR in supply chain with one manufacturer and two competing retailers.

I. Moon et al. (Eds.): APMS 2018, IFIP AICT 536, pp. 89–96, 2018.
https://doi.org/10.1007/978-3-319-99707-0_12

None of the above literature studied QR in dual-channel supply chain and our paper fills this gap. Our paper is the first to investigate QR in a dual-channel supply chain. Also, almost all literature only considers QR for sellers, whereas we study the pricing and inventory strategy assuming that QR is applied by the retailer and the manufacturer simultaneously. Furthermore, we show that the manufacturer's profit may be improved and the supply chain could achieve Pareto improvement under QR.

2   The Basic Model

We develop a two-stage dynamic programming model in dual-channel supply chain in which the second stage is a static game. The manufacturer sells products through its own direct channel at the direct price p_m and the retailer at the wholesale price w. The quantity reserved for the direct channel (i.e., direct inventory) is q_m. The retailer decides to order q_r units and sells to consumers at the retail price p_r. Due to demand uncertainty, both channels may be out of stock during the selling season. In that case, QR allows the manufacturer to start a possible QR production with a quantity of q'_m (i.e., QR inventory) and the retailer to place a possible QR order with a quantity of q'_r. The unit early and QR production cost of the manufacturer is c and c_{qr}, where $c_{qr} > c$. For a unit QR order, the retailer is charged by $w + e$, where e is the QR order fee, indicating that the retailer pays more for the QR order than the initial order. After the selling season, unsold products are disposed by a unit salvage value s. As is shown in Fig. 1, the sequence of the events is as follows:

(i)   In the first stage, the manufacturer decides the wholesale price w;
(ii) In the second stage, the manufacturer jointly decides the direct price p_m and the direct inventory q_m, and meanwhile the retailer jointly decides the retail price p_r and initial order quantity q_r.

All decisions above were decided before the selling season. We will use the notations listed in Table A 1 in the Appendix to define our problem.

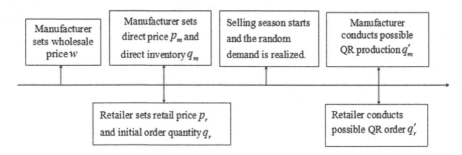

Fig. 1. The sequence of the events in the QR model.

Similar to Li et al. (2016), the demand function of the direct and retail channel is given by $d_m = (1 - \theta)(a + \varepsilon) - rp_m + tp_r$ and $d_r = \theta(a + \varepsilon) - rp_r + tp_m$. θ is the retailer's market share. The demand includes the certain part a and the random part ε which distributes on $U[-b,b]$ where $0 \leq b < a$. According to Li et al. (2012), the demand of many products, e.g., agricultural seeds and festival souvenirs, conforms to the uniform distribution if the life cycle is short and the demand intervals can be inferred from the past data. To provide an transformation of the inventory decisions, we define z_m, z_r and z_{mr} as inventory factors representing the product quantity ordered to satisfy the stochastic portion of the demand, where $q_m = (1 - \theta)(a + z_m) - rp_m + tp_r$, $q_r = \theta(a + z_r) - rp_r + tp_m$ and $q_m + q_r = a + z_{mr} - (r - t)(p_m + p_r)$.

We assume the scenario where the retailer is out of stock before the manufacturer as RO, whereas the scenario where the manufacturer is out of stock before the retailer as MO. Whether stock-out occurs in the retailer or the manufacturer, it will be meet completely in both direct and retail channels through QR. In RO, if $z_r < \varepsilon \leq z_{mr}$, the retailer places QR order with a quantity of q_r' where $q_r' = \theta(\varepsilon - z_r)$ and the manufacturer does not start QR production. For $\varepsilon > z_{mr}$, QR is conducted on both channels where $q_m' = \varepsilon - z_{mr}$, $q_r' = \theta(\varepsilon - z_r)$ and for $\varepsilon \leq z_r$, neither channel will conduct QR. In MO, if $z_m < \varepsilon \leq z_r$, the manufacturer conducts QR production with a quantity of q_m' where $q_m' = (1 - \theta)(\varepsilon - z_m)$ while the retailer does not place QR order. QR is conducted on both channels if $\varepsilon > z_r$, and is not conducted by either channel if $\varepsilon \leq z_m$.

According to the above, the manufacturer's expected profit in RO is:

$$
\begin{aligned}
\pi_m^{qr} =& p_m E(d_m) + wq_r + (w + e)q_r' - c(q_m + q_r) - c_{qr}q_m' + sE(q_m - d_m)^+ \\
&+ s \int_{z_r}^{\theta z_r + (1-\theta)z_m} (\theta z_r + (1 - \theta)z_m - \varepsilon)f(\varepsilon)d\varepsilon
\end{aligned}
\tag{1}
$$

where $E(\cdot)$ is the expectation operator and $x^+ = \max(x, 0)$. The manufacturer's expected profit in MO is:

$$
\pi_m^{qr} = p_m E(d_m) + wq_r + (w + e)q_r' - c(q_m + q_r) - c_{qr}q_m' + sE(q_m - d_m)^+ \tag{2}
$$

The retailer's expected profit is the same in both scenarios which is:

$$
\pi_r^{qr} = p_r E(d_r) - wq_r - (w + e)q_r' + sE(q_r - d_r)^+ \tag{3}
$$

Note that we use the superscript 'qr' to represent the scenario with QR throughout this paper. By using backward induction, we can obtain the global optimum solutions in Propositions 1–2. Proofs of all propositions are given in the Appendix.

Proposition 1 With QR, given a wholesale price w of the first stage, the optimal direct price $p_m^{qr*}(w)$, direct inventory $q_m^{qr*}(w)$, retail price $p_r^{qr*}(w)$ and initial order quantity $q_r^{qr*}(w)$ are given by:

(a) If $\quad w \geq w_E, \quad p_m^{qr*}(w) = \bar{p}_m^{qr*}(w), \quad q_m^{qr*}(w) = \bar{q}_m^{qr*}(w) = (1 - \theta)(a + \bar{z}_m^{qr*}(w))$
$\quad -r\bar{p}_m^{qr*}(w) + t\bar{p}_r^{qr*}(w), p_r^{qr*}(w) = \bar{p}_r^{qr*}(w), q_r^{qr*}(w) = \bar{q}_r^{qr*}(w)$;

(b) If $w < w_E, p_m^{qr*}(w) = \tilde{p}_m^{qr*}(w), q_m^{qr*}(w) = \tilde{q}_m^{qr*}(w) = (1 - \theta)(a + \tilde{z}_m^{qr*}) - r\tilde{p}_m^{qr*}(w)$
$\quad + t\tilde{p}_r^{qr*}(w), p_r^{qr*}(w) = \tilde{p}_r^{qr*}(w), q_r^{qr*}(w) = \tilde{q}_r^{qr*}(w)$;

where $w_E = \frac{c-s}{c_{qr}-c}e + s$, $\bar{p}_m^{qr*}(w) = \tilde{p}_m^{qr*}(w) = \frac{[2(1-\theta)r + \theta t]a + 3rtw + 2r(r-t)c}{4r^2 - t^2}$, $\bar{p}_r^{qr*}(w) =$
$\tilde{p}_r^{qr*}(w) = \frac{[2\theta r + (1-\theta)t]a + (2r^2 + t^2)w + t(r-t)c}{4r^2 - t^2}$, $\bar{q}_r^{qr*}(w) = \tilde{q}_r^{qr*}(w) = \theta(a + \bar{z}_r^{qr*}(w)) -$
$r\bar{p}_r^{qr*}(w) + t\bar{p}_m^{qr*}(w)$, $\bar{z}_m^{qr*}(w) = \frac{2b}{1-\theta}\left(\frac{c_{qr}-c}{c_{qr}-s} - \frac{\theta e}{w+e-s}\right) - b$, $\bar{z}_r^{qr*}(w) = \tilde{z}_r^{qr*}(w) =$
$\frac{2be}{w+e-s} - b$ and $\tilde{z}_m^{qr*} = 2b\frac{c_{qr}-c}{c_{qr}-s} - b$.

Considering the optimal responses to the wholesale price, we obtain the optimal wholesale price for the manufacturer in the following proposition.

Proposition 2. With QR, the optimal wholesale price w^{qr*} is given by:

(a) For $\bar{w}^{qr} \geq w_E$, the manufacturer sets $w^{qr*} = \bar{w}^{qr}$;
(b) For $\bar{w}^{qr} < w_E < \tilde{w}^{qr}$, the manufacturer sets $w^{qr*} = w_E$;
(c) For $\tilde{w}^{qr} \leq w_E$, the manufacturer sets $w^{qr*} = \tilde{w}^{qr}$, where

$\bar{w}^{qr}$ and $\tilde{w}^{qr}$ satisfy $\theta a - rp_r^{qr*} + tp_m^{qr*} + \frac{\theta(z_r^{qr*} + b)^2}{4b} + \frac{2r^2 + t^2}{4r^2 - t^2}\left[t(\bar{p}_m^{qr*} - c) - r(\bar{w}^{qr} - c)\right] = 0$ and $\theta a - rp_r^{qr*} + t\tilde{p}_m^{qr*} + \frac{\theta(z_r^{qr*} + b)^2}{4b} + \left[t(\tilde{p}_m^{qr*} - c) - r(\tilde{w}^{qr} - c)\right]\frac{2r^2 + t^2}{4r^2 - t^2}$
$- \frac{2b\theta e(c_{qr} - c - e\frac{c_{qr}-s}{\tilde{w}^{qr}+e-s})}{(\tilde{w}^{qr} + e - s)^2} = 0$.

The manufacturer and the retailer have the same relative shortage costs when the value of wholesale price is w_E. If $\bar{w}^{qr} > w_E$, the retailer's relative shortage cost is smaller than that of the manufacturer. Thus, the retailer will be easier to be out of stock than the manufacturer and the equilibrium occurs in RO. Similarly, if $\tilde{w}^{qr} < w_E$, the manufacturer's relative shortage cost is smaller than that of the retailer which results in a lower direct inventory so that the equilibrium occurs in MO.

Next, we consider the benchmark model with no QR. The sequence of events is the same as that in QR model except for not requiring the last stage. Similarly, we solve it by using backward induction. The manufacturer's expected profit is:

$$\pi_m = p_m E[\min(q_m, d_m)] + wq_r - c(q_m + q_r) + sE(q_m - d_m)^+ \tag{4}$$

The retailer's expected profit is:

$$\pi_r = p_r E[\min(q_r, d_r)] - wq_r + sE(q_r - d_r)^+ \tag{5}$$

Proposition 3. Assume $(1 - \theta)(a - b) - rc > 0$ and $\theta(a - b) - rw > 0$, we have

(a) For a given wholesale price w, the optimal direct price, retail price, direct inventory and initial order quantity are given below:

$$p_m^*(w) = \frac{[2(1 - \theta)r + \theta t]a + 3rtw + 2r(r - t)c}{4r^2 - t^2}$$
$$- \frac{2r(1 - \theta)(z_m^*(w) - b)^2 + \theta t(z_r^*(w) - b)^2}{4b(4r^2 - t^2)},$$

$$p_r^*(w) = \frac{[2\theta r + (1-\theta)t]a + (2r^2 + t^2)w + (r-t)tc}{4r^2 - t^2}$$
$$- \frac{(1-\theta)t(z_m^*(w) - b)^2 + 2\theta r(z_r^*(w) - b)^2}{4b(4r^2 - t^2)},$$

$$q_m^*(w) = (1-\theta)(a + z_m^*(w) - rp_m^*(w) + tp_r^*(w)),$$
$$q_r^*(w) = \theta(a + z_r^*(w)) - rp_r^*(w) + tp_m^*(w),$$

where $z_m^*(w) = 2b\frac{p_m^*(w) - c}{p_m^*(w) - s} - b$ and $z_r^*(w) = 2b\frac{p_r^*(w) - w}{p_r^*(w) - s} - b$;

(b) The optimal wholesale price satisfies the following first-order condition:

$$\theta(a + z_r^*) - rp_r^* + tp_m^* + [t(p_m^* - c) - r(w^* - c)]A(w^*)$$
$$+ \theta(w^* - c)\frac{2bA(w^*)(w^* - s) - b(p_r^* - s)}{(p_r^* - s)^2}$$
$$= 0,$$

$$A(w^*) = \frac{(2r^2 + t^2 - 2\theta r\frac{2b(w^* - s)}{(p_r^* - s)^2})(4r^2 - t^2 - 2(1-\theta)r\frac{2b(c-s)^2}{(p_m^* - s)^3}) + (1-\theta)t\frac{2b(c-s)^2}{(p_m^* - s)^3}(3rt - \theta t\frac{2b(w^* - s)}{(p_r^* - s)^2})}{(4r^2 - t^2 - 2\theta r\frac{2b(w^* - s)}{(p_r^* - s)^3})(4r^2 - t^2 - 2(1-\theta)r\frac{2b(c-s)^2}{(p_m^* - s)^3}) - (1-\theta)t\frac{2b(c-s)^2}{(p_m^* - s)^3}\theta t\frac{2b(w^* - s)}{(p_r^* - s)^2}}.$$

3   The Impacts of Quick Response

In this section, we study the impacts of QR in the dual-channel supply chain by numerical examples. The default values of all parameters are given by $a = 2000$, $b = 500$, $r = 50$, $t = 40$, $s = 0.2$, $c = 1$, $c_{qr} = 1.5$ and $e = 0.5$. Firstly, we explore the effects of QR on the optimal decisions and profits of the manufacturer and the retailer for different retailer's market share θ in Figs. 2–4.

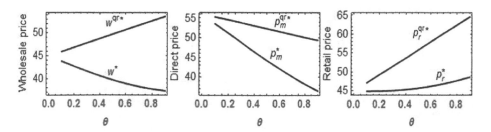

Fig. 2. The impact of QR on the optimal wholesale price, direct price and retail price.

We can obtain some interesting observations from Fig. 2. We find that the optimal wholesale price in QR model is substantially larger than that in no QR model. For the manufacturer, providing QR policy to the retailer brings higher production cost gives the reason to propose higher wholesale price. Naturally, the optimal selling prices of both channels are higher with QR. The optimal retail price increases in the retailer's market share because the optimal wholesale price increases in it. The optimal direct price decreases as the retailer's market share increases since the effect of its reduced market share outweighs that of the increased wholesale price.

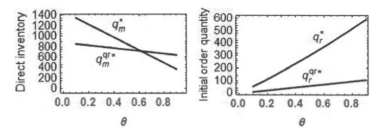

Fig. 3. The impact of QR on the optimal direct inventory and initial order quantity.

For the manufacturer, QR production allows him to decrease the direct inventory while the retailer's QR order prompts to increase it. From Fig. 3, we find that with QR, the manufacturer's optimal direct inventory is lower than that with no QR when the retailer's market share is low because the effect of QR production exceeds that of the QR order. However, if θ is sufficiently big, the effect of QR order exceeds that of QR production and the optimal direct inventory is higher than that with no QR. For the retailer, the higher optimal wholesale price and retail price results in lower initial order quantity. Therefore, the retailer's initial order quantity will be greatly reduced in contrast to that without QR.

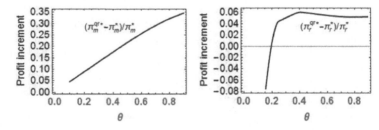

Fig. 4. The impact of QR on the increment of the optimal expected profit of the manufacturer and the retailer.

Form Fig. 4, we find that QR is beneficial to the manufacturer. This is because QR increases the expected sales revenue of both direct and retail channel. Although the manufacturer's production cost increases, it is less than the increase in sales revenue. Moreover, the manufacturer's expected profit increment increases in the retailer's market share. For the retailer, the expected profit might increase or decrease. When the retailer's market share is low, QR hurts the retailer, for the reason that the sales revenue increment is less than the procurement cost increment incurred by the QR. As the market share increases, the outcome is reversed and the retailer will benefit from QR. It's interesting to find that there exists Pareto improvement by QR when the market share of the retailer is sufficiently high. That is, QR is easier to implement in this case than other situations because both the manufacturer and the retailer will benefit from QR so that accept it.

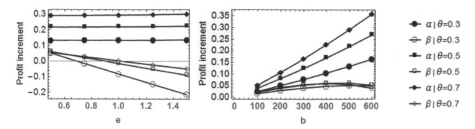

Fig. 5. The impacts of e and b on the increment of the optimal expected profits of the manufacturer and the retailer, where $\alpha = (\pi_m^{qr*} - \pi_m^*)/\pi_m^*$, $\beta = (\pi_r^{qr*} - \pi_r^*)/\pi_r^*$.

From Fig. 5, we show that the manufacturer's optimal expected profit increment with QR increases in the QR order fee, while that of the retailer decreases in it. When the value of e is small, the retailer benefits from QR. Once the QR order fee exceeds a threshold, the retailer's performance turns worse. We also show that the threshold will increase in the retailer's market share. This is because the retailer's expected sales revenue of QR order increases in its market share. Thus, QR achieves Pareto improvement with a sufficiently small QR order fee. This implies that QR may not be successful when it is hard to executive, e.g., the QR order fee is high. The manufacturer should reduce QR order fee as much as possible to prompt QR.

We find that the manufacturer's optimal expected profit increment increases in the random demand fluctuation range, while that of the retailer first increases in it and then decreases in it. We can explain it as follows: if the random demand is small, the impact from the retailer's increased sales income of QR order decreases; otherwise, the impact from the increased procurement cost increases. Therefore, if the market demand fluctuates too much, it is better for the retailer not to accept QR because the manufacturer may set a high wholesale price.

4 Conclusions

The literature on quick response has widely focused on tradition retail channel supply chain and firms' competition while we investigate the value of quick response in a dual-channel supply chain consisting of a manufacturer and a retailer. In this paper, we give the equilibrium decisions and profits of both channels. Our numerical results demonstrate that with QR strategy, the manufacturer could set a higher wholesale and direct price. The retailer reduces the initial order quantity significantly and set a higher retail price. For the manufacturer, direct inventory may not necessarily be reduced because of the retailer's QR order. We show that the manufacturer may be benefits from quick response because QR makes the manufacturer's sales revenue of direct and retail channel increase substantially. However, the retailer's expected profit will either be increased or decreased because the retailer has increased sales revenue and procurement cost as well. Finally, we find that QR could achieve Pareto improvement if the retailer's market share is high, the QR order fee is low, or the random demand fluctuation range is either not too big or too small. In the future, considering an endogenous QR wholesale price is a valuable research issue. It would also be interesting to study how strategic consumer behavior influences the value of quick response in a dual-channel supply chain.

Acknowledgement. This work is supported by (i) National Natural Science Foundation of China under grant 71771123; (ii) Social Science Foundation of Jiangsu Province under grant 15GLC006.

References

Arya, A., Mittendorf, B., Sappington, D.: The bright side of supplier encroachment. Mark. Sci. **26**(5), 651–659 (2007)

Dumrongsiri, A., Fan, M., Jain, A., et al.: A supply chain model with direct and retail channels. Eur. J. Oper. Res. **187**(3), 691–718 (2008)

Iyer, A.V., Bergen, M.E.: Quick response in manufacturer-retailer channels. Manage. Sci. **43**(4), 559–570 (1997)

Fisher, M., Rajaram, K., Raman, A.: Optimizing inventory replenishment of retail fashion products. Manufact. Serv. Oper. Manage. **3**(3), 230–241 (2001)

Caro, F., Martínez-de-Albéniz, V.: The impact of quick response in inventory-based competition. Manufact. Serv. Oper. Manage. **12**(3), 409–429 (2010)

Li, Q., Ha, A.Y.: Reactive capacity and inventory competition under demand substitution. IIE Trans. **40**(8), 707–717 (2008)

Lin, Y.-T., Parlaktürk, A.: Quick response under competition. Prod. Oper. Manage. **21**(3), 518–533 (2012)

Li, B., Hou, P.W., Chen, P., et al.: Pricing strategy and coordination in a dual channel supply chain with a risk-averse retailer. Int. J. Prod. Econ. **178**, 154–168 (2016)

Li, K., Zhang, Y.D., Yan, J.Y.: Supply chain coordination under uniformly distributed market demand—A double contract based on reward and punishment. Chin. J. Manage. Sci. **20**(3), 131–137 (2012)

Ryan, J.K., Sun, D., Zhao, X.: Coordinating a supply chain with a manufacturer-owned online channel: a dual channel model under price competition. IEEE Trans. Eng. Manage. **60**(2), 247–259 (2013)

Petruzzi, N.C., Dada, M.: Pricing and the news vendor problem: a review with extensions. Oper. Res. **47**(2), 183–194 (1999)

Smart Service Lifecycle Management:
A Framework and Use Case

Mike Freitag[1]([✉]) and Stefan Wiesner[2]

[1] Fraunhofer IAO, Nobelstraße 12, 70569 Stuttgart, Germany
mike.freitag@iao.fraunhofer.de
[2] BIBA – Bremer Institut für Produktion und Logistik GmbH at the University
of Bremen, Hochschulring 20, 28359 Bremen, Germany

Abstract. This paper focuses on the growing importance of offering Smart Services by manufacturing companies, which are enabled through the increasing amount of data available following Industry 4.0 implementation. Gradually, product-oriented industries are turning into service-oriented industries, where customers are much more involved in developing and delivering services than in developing and delivering products. The ability to offer Smart Services creates a competitive advantage for a company, as it can provide individually configured value-added services to the customer. However, expert interviews and work with industrial use cases show that the knowledge how to realize such Smart Services is still rudimental, in spite of high expectations. Therefore, a Smart Service Lifecycle Management is introduced, formalizing the support needs of the industry and the phases of the lifecycle in a framework, covering business, service and network elements. Parts of this framework has been successfully applied to develop a Monitoring Service for an industrial use case in video surveillance.

Keywords: Smart Service · Industry 4.0 · Service Lifecycle
Service Engineering · Product-Service System

1 Introduction

For manufacturing companies it is becoming increasingly important to offer services in addition to their products. Thereby, it is possible to focus on new target groups through innovative business models [1, 2]. Gradually product-oriented industries are turning into service-oriented industries where customers are much more involved in developing and delivering services than in developing and delivering products [3–5].

The implementation of Industry 4.0 is a catalyst and accelerator of change. For these reasons, integrated development of products and services is becoming increasingly important [6, 7]. On this way the dependencies and interactions between the product and the service along their lifecycles are getting relevant for companies when they want to servitize their business [6, 7]. An example of such an integrated approach are Smart Services. For example they can help gather and evaluate information and data, simplify machine maintenance processes or optimize industrial value chains. This causes profound changes for manufacturing companies in the medium and long term.

I. Moon et al. (Eds.): APMS 2018, IFIP AICT 536, pp. 97–104, 2018.
https://doi.org/10.1007/978-3-319-99707-0_13

By offering an attractive bundle of smart products and smart services the companies can creates a unique selling points in an addressed market niche [8, 9]. The customer receives a solution instead of products. It reduce complexity on the customer side and it guaranties a defined service level.

2 Product and Service Lifecycle Management

The main objective of a Product Lifecycle Management (PLM) and Service Lifecycle Management (SLM) is to provide a sound information basis to plan, control and coordinate processes and take decisions along the lifecycles of products and services. A holistic view of both PLM and SLM is necessary to involve all relevant aspects of the enterprise for an integrated development and management of PSS [3, 4].There are different concepts for Product Lifecycles and Product Lifecycle Management, for example concepts that are marketing driven and consider phases like development/ introduction, growth, maturity and decline [10, 11]. Many of those approaches structure the lifecycles in the following main phases:

- Beginning of Life: Product Ideation, Design/Engineering, Realization/Production/ Manufacturing and Logistics/Distribution.
- Middle of Life: Use and Maintenance/Service/Support.
- End of Life: Re-use, Recycling, Remanufacturing, and Disposal.

Most traditional approaches assume that phases and steps in the lifecycle are connected in a sequential mono-directional manner, a waterfall cascading model. However, in dynamic environments there could be loops, parallels and multi-directional processes, e.g. closed loop PLM [11]. On the one hand this provides flexibility for the interactions with SLM on the other hand it increases complexity.

Service Lifecycle Management is a part of Service Science, Management and Engineering (SSME), which address the challenges coming from the servitization process [1, 2]. A Service Lifecycle Management creates a connection between Management and Engineering and is an important discipline for providing and contributing specific knowledge about service. The three main phases are shown in the following [17–19]:

- Service creation: Service Ideation.
- Service Engineering: Service Requirement Analysis, Design, Implementation, and Testing.
- Service Operation: Service Delivery and Evolution.

For a PSS lifecycles of products and services are linked and, as a consequence, the lifecycle managements have to be aligned to those links or even integrated. Freitag et al. provide more detailed information [19].

3 Industry 4.0 and Smart Service

This section focuses on the relationship between Product Lifecycle Management, e.g. in a factory based on Industry 4.0, and the Service Lifecycle Management, e.g. based on a Smart Service. Here in this paper the Product-Service System (PSS) consists of a combination of Industry 4.0 and Smart Service. Figure 1 illustrates the relationship along a Smart Service Lifecycle.

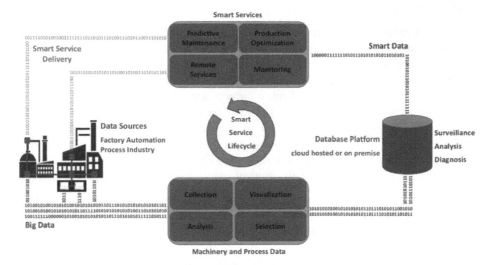

Fig. 1. Smart Service Lifecycle, adopted from [12]

In a networked factory, sensors from machines continuously send data to a database platform. Depending on the type of sensor, for example temperature, humidity or energy consumption can be measured. Depending on the configuration, the data transmission of the numerous measurement results (Big Data) can be done in real time or at fixed intervals, e.g. once a day. All transmitted data are stored on the selected platform. Not only the measured values are recorded, but also the associated metadata such as the date of the measured value and the serial number of the machine. This entire data pool is analyzed and structured at fixed intervals by using software. Only on the basis of this structured data (Smart Data) Smart Services – such as process optimizations or predictive maintenance plans – can be proposed [13]. This creates added value for the customer, even in monetary terms. The customer thus receives an individually configured service based on the collected and structured data of his machines. Based on acatech (2018) Smart Services can be defined as follows "Smart Services are connected physical or data-driven services that allow individual offerings to the customer" [14].

4 Empirical Evidence About Smart Service Expectations in Manufacturing Industries

In 16 expert interviews [15] conducted – mostly with representatives from small and medium-sized German enterprises – there were hardly any mentions of previously used Smart Services. However, the interviewed experts provided a first insight into the future expectations in the field of Smart Services in manufacturing industries. The following types of Smart Services have been mentioned several times:

- Remote Services,
- Production Optimization Services,
- Predictive Maintenance Services and
- Monitoring Services.

The vast majority of companies would like to offer Smart Services via service platforms in the future. On a European level, the PSYMBIOSYS research project has been working with four industrial use cases to support their transformation from product manufacturers to Product-Service System (PSS) providers [16]. An example of a Monitoring Service is given in Sect. 6, which aims at the development of video analysis and archiving Smart Services. Intended Smart Services for the other three use cases include: Production Optimization in the machine tool industry, Monitoring Services for office furniture to offer user-centric renovation projects and Production Optimization Services for the fashion industry. The support needs of the industrial partners have been analyzed to identify general requirements for the realization of these Smart Services [16], e.g.:

- Formalized PSS ideation platform
- Mechanisms to test and monitor tools and services
- Advanced PSS modelling
- New Business Models based on product servitization

A Smart Service Lifecycle Management framework, which structures the above elements among others from the idea to the replacement of a Smart Service is described in the next section.

5   Development and Management of Smart Service

One approach to develop and manage such a Smart Service Lifecycle as shown in Fig. 1 is the introduction of a Smart Service Lifecycle Management [17, 18]. This Lifecycle Management does not only depict the development perspective of a Smart Service, but also the Management of the Business Model and the Network. Figure 2 illustrates this.

There are three levels of Smart Service Lifecycle Management: Business Model Management, Smart Service Management and Network Management. These three levels contain a total of 28 development modules [18], which help to manage the Lifecycle of a Smart Service from Idea Creation to Delivery and Replacement.

The Smart Service lifecycle begins with an ideation stage. However, the process is not focused just on the service, but targets the Smart Service as a holistic solution. Therefore, also the Business Model and Network are considered. The same is true for the requirements stage. Starting from the market requirements, IT and partner needs for the solution will be defined. During conception, the Business Model, service and infrastructure, as well as the network are designed in parallel. Iterative feedback loops ensure design compatibility. The implementation comprises the realization of the tangible and intangible components of the Smart Service. Similar to conception, product and service realization is separated, but iterative testing of the results ensures that

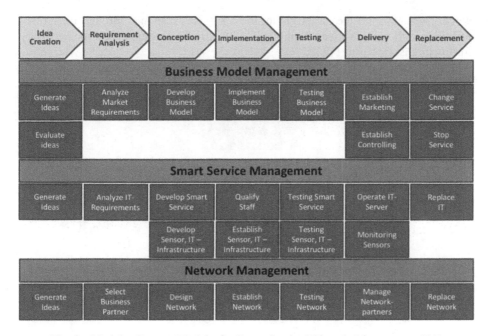

Idea Creation	Requirement Analysis	Conception	Implementation	Testing	Delivery	Replacement
Business Model Management						
Generate Ideas	Analyze Market Requirements	Develop Business Model	Implement Business Model	Testing Business Model	Establish Marketing	Change Service
Evaluate ideas					Establish Controlling	Stop Service
Smart Service Management						
Generate Ideas	Analyze IT-Requirements	Develop Smart Service	Qualify Staff	Testing Smart Service	Operate IT-Server	Replace IT
		Develop Sensor, IT – Infrastructure	Establish Sensor, IT – Infrastructure	Testing Sensor, IT – Infrastructure	Monitoring Sensors	
Network Management						
Generate Ideas	Select Business Partner	Design Network	Establish Network	Testing Network	Manage Network-partners	Replace Network

Fig. 2. Modular Process Model of a Smart Service Lifecycle Management [14]

they can be combined. As soon as this is verified, the Smart Service can be delivered to the user. Should the Smart Service not be able to fulfil its intended function anymore, it will be replaced. Here it will be decided, if the Smart Service can be changed by replacing IT or Network, or if it has to be stopped [19].

The above framework has been applied to configure a Smart Service Lifecycle Management by an aviation company, which is described in the following Sect. 6.

6 Use Case FTI

First, the company FTI will be briefly introduced, and then it will be described how the selected Smart Service has been developed step by step [19, 20].

The FTI Engineering Network GmbH specializes in the development of camera systems for aviation. The company thus supports the safe operation of aircraft and actively contributes to the development and improvement of security and entertainment subsystems. As a certified company, the portfolio ranges from individual components to customized complete systems.

The development activities in the area of Smart Services are driven in particular by the desired video-based surveillance solutions in aircraft. In terms of easy integration into the aircraft and maximum scalability, the monitoring system is based on a modular system architecture. It is also proving beneficial for the addition of smart services to the product portfolio due to possible separation between the flying device and the infrastructure on the ground. It is therefore possible to develop a customer-specific Smart

Service. Depending on the target group, these services convince through their functionalities and their innovative billing models [19, 20]. The basic idea for the necessary
infrastructure is shown in Fig. 3.

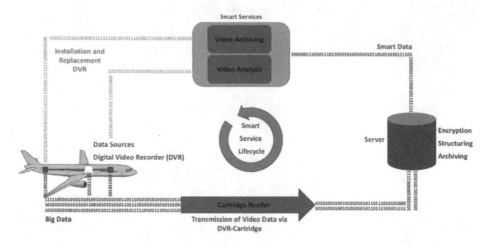

Fig. 3. Smart Service Lifecycle of FTI Engineering Network GmbH

After the aircraft landing, all data from the Digital Video Recorder (DVR) are
transferred to an archiving server. For this purpose, the memory module (Memory
Cartridge) must be removed from the DVR and inserted into a mobile reading device
(Cartridge Reader). The Cartridge Reader can be connected via standard interfaces to
standard computer platforms. A video analysis software allows access to the encrypted
video data. The software will also provide access to the services that will be unlocked
for each user and billed according to their usage. In this context, the server will provide
the database needed to run the services. Taking into account the use by different
customers, the server will ensure the strict separation of company data. The customer
does not have to provide any specific computer technology - only an internet connection is needed. Interesting price models will keep costs down for the customer while
generating new revenues for FTI [15].

To develop and manage this new Smart Service, the Smart Service Lifecycle
Management – described above – was used. So far 10 of the 28 modules have been
selected and adapted to FTI. First pilot customers in the aviation industry have already
used both video analysis and video archiving. At the end it was validated by FTI that
the Service Lifecycle Management can structure the developing process and integration
of the customer in the development process, e.g. to identify the right business model
and accepted Service Level Agreement.

7   Summary

This paper has depicted the growing importance of offering Smart Services by manufacturing companies, which are enabled through the increasing amount of data
available following Industry 4.0 implementation. The ability to offer Smart Services

creates a competitive advantage for a company, as it can provide individually configured value-added services to the customer. However, expert interviews and work with industrial use cases shows that the knowledge how to realize such Smart Services is still rudimental, in spite of high expectations. Therefore, a Smart Service Lifecycle Management is introduced, formalizing the support needs of the industry and the phases of the lifecycle in a framework, covering business, service and network elements. Parts of this framework have been successfully applied to develop a Monitoring Service for an industrial use case in video surveillance.

Although the Smart Service Lifecycle Management has also been tested with good results in other use cases, it is important to mention that it only provides a conceptual framework for Smart Service realization. In future research, methods and tools have to be further developed to support every element of the lifecycle for companies aiming to offer Smart Services. Standardized interfaces are needed to provide a seamless workflow along the lifecycle and between the different systems for the product, service, business and networking aspects.

Acknowledgements. This work has been partly funded by the European Commission through the FoF-Project "PSYMBIOSYS" (No. 636804) and by the German Federal Ministry of Education and Research (BMBF) through the Project "iSrv. Intelligente Servicesysteme" (No. 169110). The authors wish to acknowledge the Commission, the Ministry and all the project partners for their contribution.

References

1. Spohrer, J.C., Maglio, P.P.: Toward a science of service systems. In: Kieliszewski, C.A., et al. (eds.) Handbook of Service Science, pp. 157–194. Springer, New York (2010). https://doi.org/10.1007/978-1-4419-1628-0_9
2. Freitag, M., Ganz, W.: InnoScore® service. Evaluating innovation for product-related services. In: Service Research & Innovation Institute (eds.) Annual SRII Global Conference 2011, Proceedings IEEE, Piscataway, NJ, pp. 214–221 (2011)
3. Qu, M., Yu, S., Chen, D., Chu, J., Tian, B.: State-of-the-art of design, evaluation, and operation methodologies in product service systems. Comput. Ind. **77**, 1–14 (2016)
4. Pezzotta, G., Pirola, F., Pinto, R., Akasaka, F., Shimomura, Y.: A service engineering framework to design and assess an integrated product-service. Mechatronics **31**, 169–179 (2015)
5. Pezzotta, G., Pinto, R., Pirola, F., Ouertani, M.Z.: Balancing product-service provider's performance and customer's value: the service engineering methodology (SEEM). Proc. CIRP **16**, 50–55 (2014)
6. Wiesner, S., Freitag, M., Westphal, I., Thoben, K.-D.: Interactions between service and product lifecycle management. Proc. CIRP **30**, 36–41 (2015)
7. Westphal, I., Freitag, M., Thoben, K.-D.: Visualization of interactions between product and service lifecycle management. IFIP Adv. Inf. Commun. Technol. **2015**(460), 575–582 (2015)
8. Goedkoop, M.J., van Halen, C.J.G., te Riele, H.R.M., Rommens, P.J.M.: Product service systems, ecological and economic basics. Report for Dutch Ministries of Environment (VROM) and Economic Affairs (EZ) (1999)
9. Tukker, A.: Eight types of product–service system: eight ways to sustainability? Experiences from SusProNet. Bus. Strategy Environ. **13**(4), 246–260 (2004)

10. Stark, J.: Product Lifecycle Management: 21st Century Paradigm for Product Realisation. Springer, New York (2011). https://doi.org/10.1007/978-0-85729-546-0
11. Kiritsis, D.: Closed-loop PLM for intelligent products in the era of the internet of things. Comput. Aided Des. **43**(5), 479–501 (2011)
12. ZVEI (The German Electrical and Elektronic Industry Association). https://www.zvei.org/fileadmin/user_upload/Presse_und_Medien/Publikationen/2016/Dezember/Industrie_4.0__Smart_Services/Industrie-40-Smart-Services.pdf. Accessed 02 Apr 2018
13. Wiesner, S., Thoben, K.-D.: Cyber-physical product-service systems. In: Biffl, S., Lüder, A., Gerhard, D. (eds.) Multi-Disciplinary Engineering for Cyber-Physical Production Systems, pp. 63–88. Springer, Cham (2017). https://doi.org/10.1007/978-3-319-56345-9_3
14. acatech Homepage. http://www.acatech.de/fileadmin/user_upload/Baumstruktur_nach_Website/Acatech/root/de/Projekte/Laufende_Projekte/Smart_Service_Welt/BerichtSmartService_mitUmschlag_barrierefrei_HW76_DNK2.pdf. Accessed 09 Apr 2018
15. iSrv. Intelligente Servicesysteme. https://www.isrv.info/. Accessed 09 Apr 2018
16. Wiesner, S., Nilsson, S., Thoben, K.-D.: Integrating requirements engineering for different domains in system development – lessons learnt from industrial SME cases. Proc. CIRP **64**, 351–356 (2017)
17. Freitag, M., Kremer, D., Hirsch, M., Zelm, M.: An approach to standardise a service life cycle management. In: Zelm, M., van Sinderen, M., Pires, L.F., Doumeingts, G. (eds.) Enterprise Interoperability, pp. 115–126. Wiley, Chichester (2013)
18. Freitag, M., Hämmerle, O.: Smart service lifecycle management. Ein Vorgehensmodell für produzierende Unternehmen **106**(7/8), 477–482 (2016). wt Werkstattstechnik online
19. Freitag, M., Hämmerle, O., Hans, C.: Smart service lifecycle management in der Luftfahrtindustrie. In: Smart Services und Internet der Dinge: Geschäftsmodelle, Umsetzung und Best Practices, pp. 73–89. Carl Hanser Verlag, München (2017)
20. Hans, C., Kirste, S., Westphal, I., Wiesner, S.: Product-service systems – neue Marktpotenziale für den Mittelstand. In: Jahresbericht der Gemeinnützigen Gesellschaft zur Förderung des Forschungstransfers e.V., pp. 22–27. https://www.gfft-portal.de/wp-content/uploads/2017/11/2015_2016-Jahresbericht_0.pdf. Accessed 08 June 2018

acatech Industrie 4.0 Maturity Index – A Multidimensional Maturity Model

Violett Zeller[1], Christian Hocken[2], and Volker Stich[1(✉)]

[1] Institute for Industrial Management (FIR), RWTH Aachen University,
Campus-Boulevard 55, 52074 Aachen, Germany
{violett.zeller,volker.stich}@fir.rwth-aachen.de
[2] i4.0MC – Industrie 4.0 Maturity Center, Campus-Boulevard 55, 52074
Aachen, Germany

Abstract. Manufacturing companies worldwide recognized the high potential of Industrie 4.0 in order to increasing production efficiency. Key benefits include creation of integrated systems, networked products and improvement of service portfolios. However, for many companies deriving and evaluating necessary measures to use Industrie 4.0 potentials represents a major challenge. This paper introduces the "acatech Industrie 4.0 Maturity Index" as an approach to meet this challenge. The development of multidimensional maturity model intents to provide companies an assessment methodology. The aim is to capture the status quo in companies in order to be able to develop individual roadmaps for the successful introduction of Industrie 4.0 and manage the transformation progressively.

Keywords: Industrie 4.0 · Maturity model · Agile company
Manufacturing companies

1 Introduction

Production have been influenced crucially by digitalization in recent years that this progress is incomparable with any previous technical development. This process enables the initiation of the fourth industrial revolution – abbreviated by "Industrie 4.0" [1].

Concept and vision of Industrie 4.0 is often defined as "real-time, high data volume, multilateral communication and interconnectedness between cyber-physical systems and people", in order to realize self-optimizing business processes [3]. This depiction of Industrie 4.0 does not only seem to be very complex, but concentrates also primarily on a technological understanding with the objective that manufacturing companies achieve a competitive advantage. The fundamental economic lever of Industrie 4.0 lies in stimulating business processes through necessary decisions and real-time adaptations [2]. Short decision-making processes are determined fundamentally by the huge economic disposition of data and information.

Combined with adequate organizational conditions, companies are able to react faster to growing market dynamics, to develop new products more quickly and precisely in accordance with customer requirements and to launch them with a considerable lead on markets [4, 5, 9]. Therefore, an agile company is able to adapt constantly

I. Moon et al. (Eds.): APMS 2018, IFIP AICT 536, pp. 105–113, 2018.
https://doi.org/10.1007/978-3-319-99707-0_14

to changing conditions using suitable technologies and organizational learning as well as is capable of permanently occupying digital control points.

In cooperation with research institutes, industrial partners and the acatech – the national academy of science and engineering - the "acatech Industrie 4.0 Maturity Index" was designed to support manufacturing companies to identify individual, customized recommendations for action in order to realize the transformation [3].

2   Methodology of the acatech Industrie 4.0 Maturity Index

The main difference between the approach presented here and other maturity models or indexes is a holistic view and the direct correlation to the company goals. The model's approach is based on a succession of maturity levels, i.e. *value-based development stages* (see Sect. 2.1) that help companies navigate their way through every stage in the digital transformation, from the basic requirements for Industrie 4.0 to full implementation. Since a company desired target state will depend on its business strategy, it is up to each company to decide which maturity level represents the best balance between costs, capabilities and benefits for its own individual circumstances, taking account of how these requirements change over time in response to changes in the business environment and the company's strategy. To ensure that all aspects of manufacturing companies are taken into account, the model's structure is based on the "Production and Management Framework" by [6]. The framework's four *structural areas* enable a comprehensive analysis and set out a number of guiding principles.

In the following, the underlying model of the acatech Industrie 4.0 Maturity Index is illustrated. First, the stages of development, which describe capabilities of a company in order to achieve the full potential of Industrie 4.0, are explained. Then, Sect. 2.2 considers the four structural areas of resources, information systems, culture and organizational structure, which are vital to be considered for the transformation into a learning, agile company. Afterwards the model's application in a manufacturing company is exemplified in Sect. 3.

2.1   Value-Based Development Stages – Industrie 4.0 Maturity Levels

The basic structuring of Industrie 4.0 into successive stages presented below in Fig. 1 to provide manufacturing companies an overview of the required activities for digitalization. The subdivision and explanation of the individual stages as well as the necessary measures serve as support so that companies can better place the impending change in their own company context.

The development path is based on *computerization* (1), which is the starting point for digitization and refers to the targeted use of information technologies. In most companies, the computerization stage is largely in a highly advanced state and is particularly used for the efficient design of repetitive activities, as it enables cost-effective production with low error rates and generates the necessary precision, which is indispensable for the production of many modern products [3, 9]. Achieving the *connectivity* level (2), the targeted or isolated use of IT is replaced by networked components, whereby IT systems are interconnected and represent a projection of the corporate core business processes. A complete integration between IT (information technologies) and OT (operative technologies) levels has not yet taken place; however, interfaces to business IT are provided by parts of implemented OT [3, 11, 12].

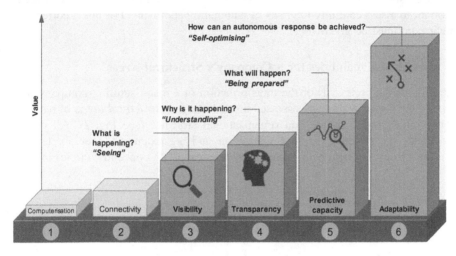

Fig. 1. Value-based development stages of Industrie 4.0 – Industrie 4.0 Maturity Levels [3]

Based on this, a digital *visibility* (3) is established with the help of sensors, which enable recording of processes from start to finish with a high amount of captured data. Processes states are no longer limited to individual areas, such as in a production cell, but can be extended to a production system or the entire company in real time in order to create a digital model, also known as the "digital shadow" [7]. This digital shadow, which is to be understood as a basic element for the subsequent maturity levels, helps to show what is happening in the company (real time) and enables data-based decision-making in management [3, 7, 9]. For a better causal understanding of processes, it is necessary to create further *transparency* (4) about the correlations in data stocks. The recognition and interpretation of interdependencies through the digital shadow requires the analysis of the collected data in the respective context using engineering knowledge. Process knowledge is more and more required to support more complex decisions, which are based on semantic connections and aggregation of data and its corresponding classification in a certain context. This process is supported fundamentally by new technologies for the analysis of mass data. Building up, the *predictive* capability level (5) enables simulation of different future scenarios and identification of those that are most likely. To this end, the digital shadow is projected into future-based scenarios and evaluated according to probability of occurrence. This enables companies to anticipate upcoming events, make decisions in time and take adequate reaction measures. Although measures usually still have to be initiated manually, the effects of a disruption can be limited in time due to the time gained through the prewarning. Reducing such disruptions or planning variance, which represent unexpected events in the business process, enables more robust operation. The ability to *adapt* (6) can enable an automatic reaction to expected machine failures or delays in delivery through a modified sequence in production planning. If a company manages to exploit data of the digital shadow in such a way that decisions are made autonomously, with the best positive results in the shortest possible time and the corresponding measures are taken, then stage six of the model has been successfully implemented [5]. It is, however, important to assess carefully the risks of automating approvals. For this a correct cost-benefit ratio must be given.

2.2 Required Capabilities for a Company's Structural Areas

The skills that are relevant for the transformation of a manufacturing company into a learning, agile organization are assessed through the *four structural areas* of resources, information systems, culture and organizational structure (see Fig. 2). All of them characterize the structure of an organization and are examined over six levels of Industrie 4.0 development path, which is represented by six concentric circles in Fig. 2.

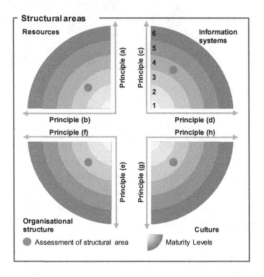

Fig. 2. Structure of the structural areas [3]

Each structural area is divided by two *principles*, each of which - depending on the benefit-oriented development levels - successively builds up skills. These skills guide the further development of the manufacturing company. The degree to which the abilities are implemented determines the maturity level of each principle. The maturity levels of the two principles are summarized and together they represent the evaluation of the structural area, which is oriented on the development levels.

The structural area *resources* includes all physical, tangible resources. This contains, for example, employees of a company, machinery and systems, the tools and materials used and the final product. The aim is to design resources that enable an interface between the physical and digital worlds in addition to pure functional fulfilment, thereby creating a digital shadow that forms the basis of the learning process for optimizing agility.

The two principles dividing this structural area are differentiated into *digital competence* and *structured communication*. "Digital competence" (a) characterizes the generation of data and its target-oriented independent processing into information by resources with corresponding technical components. This facilitates an information-driven way of working, based on feedback from the process environments and not on forecast-based planning specifications. The skills of digital competence also include the use of embedded systems and the retention of digital competence, which can only be successful, if attention is paid to promoting interdisciplinary thinking and action by employees - if they are increasingly integrated into the innovation process. Through "structured communication" (b) collected information is linked and creates an overall picture. An efficient communication can be defined and interface designed in order to support decision-makers. [3, 7, 8]

With the help of employees, information technologies and data information is available within *information systems* in accordance to economic criteria. Many manufacturing companies do not make sufficient use of data. The decisive factor is the insufficient processing of the collected data into information and its subsequent provision to the employees, which is why the first principle includes the *processing and preparation of data* (c) for decision support. This requires, among other things, context-based information provision, data storage and application-oriented interfaces in order to provide a technical infrastructure for real-time use of data and information ultimately [10]. In the context of the second principle, it is a question of *integration for optimized data (d)* use and increased agility under the primary aspect of data sharing within the value chain.

The transformation to a learning, agile company is achieved through the technologies explained above and the implementation of an appropriate *organizational structure*. In this model, the organizational structure refers on the one hand to the *internal corporate organization* (e) in the form of organizational structures and processes, and on the other hand describes the positioning in the *value network* (f). In contrast to the structural area *culture* described below, the organizational structure establishes mandatory rules that organize collaboration both within the company and externally. A high degree of individual responsibility on the part of employees is characteristic of the organic internal organization, which is why a highly skilled workforce is of fundamental importance for such an organizational form. Especially the so-called "flexible communities", i.e. the fast formation of organizational units to solve a specific task, represent an important capability of agile organizations. In addition, the bundling of the high degree of personal responsibility through motivating target systems and their orientation towards customer benefit is important, which is particularly feasible through agile management. Whether a company is in a position to cooperate within networks can be determined by, among other things, achieving shorter reaction times to changing market requirements by bundling competencies in line with demand [3].

A company's agility is highly dependent on the behaviour of its employees. Companies will be unable to achieve the desired agility if they simply introduce digital technologies without also addressing their corporate culture. In this context, two directions for changing corporate culture can be mentioned: *willingness to change (g)* and *social collaboration (h)*. The first term refers to the willingness of employees to continuously analyze and, if necessary, adapt their own behavior. This willingness to adapt within the framework of readiness for change goes along with the prerequisite of being able to recognize opportunities for change and then initiate appropriate measures. In addition, it is advantageous to see mistakes not as a problem, but as a treasure or as an opportunity for positive change and a certain openness for innovations as well as a willingness to undergo continuous further training. The term social collaboration refers to the consideration of knowledge as a decisive guideline for action, which implies that an ideal state is characterized by making decisions based on knowledge [8].

For each structural area, specific Industrie 4.0 skills must be achieved with regard to the development stages. In this regard, a holistic assessment for manufacturing companies is realized.

3   Application of the acatech Industrie 4.0 Maturity Index

The application of the acatech Industrie 4.0 Maturity Index consists of three successive phases (see Fig. 3) [3]. The first phase serves to determine the current maturity stage of the company, for which an examination of the existing Industrie 4.0 capabilities conducted according to the considered business process (e.g. production, logistics, service) and structural areas. The second phase aims - and based on the corporate strategy - to determine the target development stage with a view to the subsequent transformation process. A gap analysis helps to identify the missing required capabilities that still need to develop. These will depend on the current development stage ascertained in phase 1 and the target state that the company wishes to achieve by the end of the transformation.

Finally, the derivation of appropriate measures and incorporating them into a roadmap for the development of the identified capabilities in the third phase takes place.

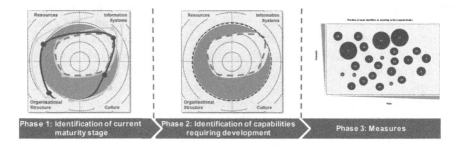

Fig. 3.   Application of the acatech Industrie 4.0 Maturity Index [3]

3.1   Phase 1: Identifying the Current Industrie 4.0 Development Stage

The company's location results from the six value-based development stages for Industrie 4.0 (see Sect. 2.1) and the skills dedicated to them. For an appropriate assessment, the consortium has developed a questionnaire, with approx. 600 questions for the business processes *engineering, production, logistics, service, sales* and *marketing.* An inspection of a production plant can give a first impression of the processes, followed by a detailed evaluation of the business processes. The as-is analysis and the questionnaire is conducted based on the order processing process, which forms the framework situation for the evaluation of existing skills. With the help of a questionnaire evaluation the Industrie 4.0 Maturity Index and Levels can be identified for each structural area.

3.2 Phase 2: Capabilities to Be Acquired

For the evaluation, the answers to the questionnaire shape the basis for the evaluation of the current situation of the company by the radar image (see Fig. 3). This display can be used to make quick statements about the average level of maturity and to clarify inconsistencies with regard to the characteristics of the four structural areas. The dependencies of the structural areas determine consistent development in all structural areas as an essential goal. This is the basis for the recommendation for companies to approach the resulting areas of action and to strive for a consistent maturity stage across all four structural areas and in this way to use the maturity stage (achieve maturity stage consistency). With regard to some areas, such as complex logistical processes, whose effectiveness is particularly determined by organizational performance. There may be some operating areas or functions where the majority of the available benefits are achieved without the requirement for balance and equal levels of maturity among the four structural areas [3].

3.3 Phase 3: Identifying Concrete Measures

The next step is to derive measures addressing areas identified as requiring action. Necessary measures can be deduced from the missing capabilities evaluating the four structural areas. By evaluating individual processes, many individual measures can be dedicated, which makes it easier for companies to create a digital roadmap.

In defining strategic objectives for a company, identified measures are worked out precisely. Achieving the targeted stages of development, in turn, aims to support the realization of the strategic objectives formulated at the outset. This enables decision-makers in manufacturing companies not only to identify at a glance the measures needed to achieve a higher maturity level, but also the interdependencies between identified measures. The purpose of this presentation is also to simplify the creation of a digitization roadmap by determining the order in which measures are implemented in terms of time and costs [3].

To date, the Maturity Index has been applied in 26 companies and their plants. The effort is essentially still very high (3-day workshop at the plant and 3–5 days evaluation). however, the organizations receive individual industry 4.0 roadmaps with many measures that help to reach the next level of maturity in all dimensions.

4 Conclusion and Outlook

In the context of Industrie 4.0, agile action and real-time changes become a company's strategic success factor. The acatech Industrie 4.0 Maturity Index provides companies a supporting tool for transformation into a learning, agile company. It describes six benefit-oriented development stages for four key areas of each company, each of which delivers additional benefits to the company. This approach can be used to develop a digital roadmap precisely tailored to the needs of each individual company in order to help them master the digital transformation across all involved relevant business units. In addition, the findings and the model can be used to developed tools and best practices that assist companies with the concrete shaping of the transformation. In this context, this specific procedure should be developed for different industrial sectors so that recommendations can be made as precisely as possible and to reflect the differences between individual industries.

The model developed is based on the principle of continuous learning and requires additional information resulting not only from validations but also from interaction and exchange with interested industrial and research partners [9].

References

1. Schuh, G., Jordan, F., Maasem, C., Zeller, V.: Industrie 4.0: Implikationen für produzierende Unternehmen. In: Gassmann, O., Sutter, P. (eds.) Digitale Transformation im Unternehmen gestalten. Geschäftsmodelle, Erfolgsfaktoren, Handlungsanweisungen, Fallstudien. Hrsg.: Hanser, München 2016, pp. 39–58
2. Schmitz, S., Wenger, L.: Acatech Industrie 4.0 Maturity Index: Welche Fähigkeiten sind im Wandel entscheidend? In: IT&Production, vol. 5, pp. 54–55 (2017)
3. Schuh, G., Anderl, R., Gausemeier, J., ten Hompel, M., Wahlster, W. (eds.): Industrie 4.0 Maturity Index. Managing the Digital Transformation of Companies (acatech STUDY), p. 21. Herbert Utz Verlag, Munich 2017
4. Infosys. Industry 4.0. The state of the nations. 1. Aufl. Hg. v. Infosys Ltd. Bangalore (2015)
5. Wee, D., Kelly, R., Cattel, J., Breunig, M.: Industry 4.0. How to navigate digitalization of the manufacturing sector. Hg. v. McKinsey (2015)
6. Boos, W., Völker, M., Schuh, G.: Grundlagen des Managements produzierender Unternehmen. In: Schuh, G., Kampker, A. (eds.) Strategie und Management produzierender Unternehmen. Handbuch Produktion und Management 1. VDI-Buch, pp. 1–62. Springer, Heidelberg (2011). https://doi.org/10.1007/978-3-642-14502-5_1
7. Bauernhansl, T., Krüger, J., Reinhart, G., Schuh, G.: WGP-Standpunkt Industrie 4.0. Hg. v. Wissenschaftliche Gesellschaft für Produktionstechnik Wgp e. V
8. Zühlke, D.: Die Cloud ist Voraussetzung für Industrie 4.0. Präsentation. VDI. VDI-Pressegespräch anlässlich des Kongresses "AUTOMATION 2013". Baden-Baden, 25 June 2013
9. Schuh, G., Potente, T., Thomas, C., Hauptvogel, A.: Steigerung der Kollaborationsproduktivität durch cyber-physische Systeme. In: Bauernhansl, T., ten Hompel, M., Vogel-Heuser, B. (eds.) Industrie 4.0 in Produktion, Automatisierung und Logistik, pp. 277–296. Springer, Wiesbaden (2014). https://doi.org/10.1007/978-3-658-04682-8_14
10. Hering, N., et al.: Smart Operations. Hg. v. FIR an der RWTH Aachen. Aachen (2015)

11. Vogel-Heuser, B.: Herausforderungen und Anforderungen aus Sicht der IT und der Automatisierungstechnik. In: Bauernhansl, T., ten Hompel, M., Vogel-Heuser, B. (eds.) Industrie 4.0 in Produktion, Automatisierung und Logistik, pp. 37–48. Springer, Wiesbaden (2014). https://doi.org/10.1007/978-3-658-04682-8_2

12. Kaufmann, T., Forstner, L.: Die horinzontale Integration der Wertschöpfungskette in der Halbleiterindustrie. Chancen und Herausforderungen. In: Bauernhansl, T., ten Hompel, M., Vogel-Heuser, B., Vogel-Heuser, B. (eds.) Industrie 4.0 in Produktion, Automatisierung und Logistik, pp. 359–367. Springer, Wiesbaden (2014). https://doi.org/10.1007/978-3-658-04682-8_18

An Analysis of the Impact of Industrie 4.0 on Production Planning and Control

Uwe Dombrowski and Yannick Dix[✉]

Institut for Advanced Industrial Management,
Technische Universität Braunschweig, 38106 Brunswick, Germany
{u.dombrowski,y.dix}@tu-bs.de

Abstract. The Production Planning and Control of industrial companies is often based on an inaccurate data basis. The increasing availability and quality of data through the technologies and elements of Industrie 4.0 open up promising potentials for increasing efficiency. This paper presents the impacts of Industrie 4.0 technologies and elements on Production Planning and Control that have been studied by a deductive research design. Through a quantitative analysis of these impacts, an orientation for the choice of Industrie 4.0 technologies and elements is provided in order to support the planning activities of the PPC in a targeted manner.

Keywords: Production Planning and Control · Logistics objectives
Industrie 4.0 · Digital Transformation

1 Introduction

With the aim of increasing competitiveness, manufacturing companies face the challenge to produce an increasing number of variants with a short delivery time and a high schedule reliability. These market challenges result in a significant increase in the complexity of planning and controlling the manufacturing process. Recent studies show that more than 2/3 of the companies are not up to the future challenges of their Production Planning and Control (PPC) [1].

The technologies and elements of the Industrie 4.0 open up promising potentials to address these challenges [2, 3]. Although the potentials of increasing data availability and data quality are obvious, the effects of Industrie 4.0 elements on the individual PPC modules and on the logistics objectives were not analyzed in detail. Based on a quantitative analysis, this article is intended to give an overview on this.

2 Production Planning and Control Within the AIM Reference Model

The reference model for the factory operation of the Institute for Advanced Industrial Management includes the *Product Development Process* and the *Order Management Process* [4]. The Production Planning and Control is assigned to the Order Management Process, which describes the planning, production, and sales of customer orders.

I. Moon et al. (Eds.): APMS 2018, IFIP AICT 536, pp. 114–121, 2018.
https://doi.org/10.1007/978-3-319-99707-0_15

The planning and controlling tasks of the PPC are group into several PPC modules. Figure 1 illustrates the classification of the PPC modules within the Order Management Process as well as the logical sequence of these modules to each other.

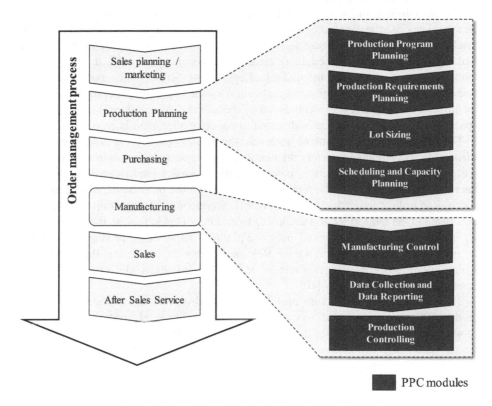

Fig. 1. Modules of Production Planning and Control

The **Production Program Planning** represents the starting point of the PPC. Based on past sales volumes and known customer orders, the production program is defined by quantity to be produced for every product and for every planning period [5]. The results of this task are documented in a sales plan, which contains the quantity of finished products (gross primary requirements). In the subsequent inventory planning, a stockholding strategy is developed. From the gross primary requirements of the product groups, the period-related net primary requirements (planned production quantity) are derived. For this purpose, the gross primary requirements are reduced by the not reserved inventories.

Based on the net primary requirements, the **Production Requirements Planning** is responsible for calculating the required materials (dependent requirements). In this context, a distinction can be made between deterministic, stochastic, and heuristic requirements planning [6, 7].

In the **Lot Sizing**, the calculated net primary requirements of an article are aggregate into manufacturing orders considering the holding costs and ordering costs. The lot sizing can be carried out by static (e.g. EOQ formula), dynamic (e.g. Wagner-Whitin-Algorithm) and stochastic (e.g. order point inventory) methods [8, 9].

The **Scheduling and Capacity Planning** is responsible for determining the planned start dates and the planned completion dates of the operations. In addition, the task of Scheduling and Capacity Planning is to determine the capacity requirements for each planning period. First, a schedule is created by assigning planned start dates and planned completions dates to the individual operations. Subsequent capacity planning reviews the medium- and short-term realization of the previous planning results. For this purpose, the capacity demand induced by the schedule is compared to the available capacity. If a capacity overload is detected, a capacity alignment is required [10].

The **Manufacturing Control** includes the *Order Generation* and the *Order Release* [5]. This module transfers the planning results to manufacturing orders. In the case of make-to-order production, customer orders usually lead directly to an order generation in the amount of the requested quantity. On the other hand, if the company produces an order anonymously (make-to-stock production), the generation of an order takes place in the defined lot size according to an Order Generation Method. The Order Generation determines the planned input and planned output of the production. Finally, the orders are released by an Order Release Method. Considering the short-term availability of resources, the order release defines the time from which processing of a manufacturing order can start [10].

Through the **Data Collection and Data Reporting**, relevant manufacturing data for the PPC is recorded and reported back to a higher-level control system. The reported data forms the basis for the **Production Controlling**. By comparing target and current values (e.g. completion date of an order), adjustment requirements to the PPC can be identified, considering the strategic company objectives. Based on the reported data, the target times (e.g. throughput time for selected operations) can also be adjusted so that an improved data basis can be used in subsequent planning processes.

3   Impact of Industrie 4.0 on Production Planning and Control

The vision of Industrie 4.0 describes the real time, intelligent and digital networking of people, equipment and objects for the management of business processes and value-creating networks [11]. The potential for PPC can generally be attributed to improved data availability and quality. Based on real-time data, for example, short-term interventions in the PPC can be made to counter events that are difficult to predict. In this context, it is already apparent that decision-making for short-term planning in particular can be supported by the use of Industrie 4.0 technologies. Furthermore, decisions that require a large number of input variables can be positively influenced by the improved data availability.

While the improved data availability and quality merely describe the potential for PPC in a general way, the influence of individual Industrie 4.0 technologies and elements on the PPC has not been comprehensively analyzed. So the question, which

Industrie 4.0 technologies should be implemented, in order to support individual PPC modules, remains unanswered. Current use cases give an idea of the potential, but without discussing the success of the technologies used for the PPC modules. Likewise, the influences of these technologies on the logistics objectives are only superficially analyzed. In this context, it becomes apparent that the improved data availability and quality basically offers advantages, but the resulting potential for the production planning and control has so far only been insufficiently specified. Thus, in practice, the question arises as to how the improved data availability and quality can be translated into economic success in the form of precise and reliable planning results.

Although digitization is currently widely discussed in both science and economy, there is no consistent definition of the structure of Industrie 4.0 [12]. Against this background, the Bundesverband Informationswirtschaft, Telekommunikation und neue Medien e. v. (Bitkom) defines five technology fields (TF). The technology fields *Cyber-Physical Systems* (1), *Cloud Computing* (2), *Smart Factory* (3), *Robust Networks* (4), and *IT Security* (5) are assigned individual Industrie 4.0 technologies [13]. Since this paper focuses on Production Planning and Control, it is expedient to limit the Industrie 4.0 model according to Bitkom. Because Robust Networks and IT Security do not reveal any direct potential for the PPC, this paper uses the technology fields of Cyber-Physical Systems, Cloud Computing and Smart Factory. The technologies fields of the Robust Networks (broadband internet, mobile communications, mobile devices) and IT Security (data privacy, information security) form the basis for ensuring a high degree of reliability, availability and security for communication and data exchange between different IT systems. Both technology fields thus are the basis for Cyber-Physical Systems, Cloud Computing, and Smart Factory [14, 15].

Table 1. Chosen elements of Industrie 4.0 according to [13]

Elements	TF	Explanation
Sensors & actuators	1	Controlling and moving an object or system
RFID	1	Wireless and sightless identification of objects
Networked objects	1	Objects with the ability to process and exchange data
M2M[1]-interaction	1	Exchange of information between machines with each other
Visualization	2	Visualization of key performance indicators
Virtualization	2	Integration of real objects in digital models
HMI[2]	2	User interface for interaction between human and machine/software program
ERP Enhancement	2	Application-specific enhancement of the ERP system with digital instruments
Real-time data	3	Collection and processing of data in real time
Big Data	3	Analysis of large and unstructured datasets
Apps	3	Applications on mobile devices to control the production

[1]Machine-to-maschine, [2]human machine interface

Consequently, this paper focuses on the Industrie 4.0 elements listed in Table 1. In addition to [13], the technology field Cyber-Physical Systems was assigned the technology *RFID* (radio frequency identification). In order to be able to consider company-specific enhancements of the ERP system, the technology field Smart Factory was supplemented by the element *ERP Enhancement*.

4   Potential for the Production Planning and Control

Based on current use cases, the potentials of Industrie 4.0 technologies and elements listed in Table 1 were analyzed for the separate PPC modules (Fig. 1). As this article focuses on the planning activities of the Production Planning and Control, the PPC modules *Data Collection and Data Reporting* and *Production Controlling* are not considered in detail below. While the Data Collection and Data Reporting includes all measures to collect production data and make it available at the place of processing [16], this paper is intended to answer the question as to which PPC module this data is beneficial for.

Thus, the focus is on the remaining PPC modules in order to show which Industrie 4.0 technologies and elements can be used to increase efficiency within the PPC. The database for this analysis is based on 38 application-related publications in prestigious journals from 2007 to 2017, whereby the focus was on publications in the field of Production Planning and Control. First, the required information for each PPC module was identified. Subsequently, the output variables of the listed Industrie 4.0 elements (Table 1) were collected and analysed through a literature search. Based on a matching of output variables (Industrie 4.0 element) and input variables (PPC module), the impact of an Industrie 4.0 element was derived for the corresponding PPC module. If a match between output variables and input variables could be determined, a positive impact was assumed. Otherwise, no effect was suspected between Industry 4.0 element and PPC module. Thus, real-time data (output: e.g. *work in progress* for each workstation) can help significantly increase order release efficiency, provided that it is aligned with bottleneck systems [5]. In this case, a positive impact on the module Manufacturing Control can be observed, since the order release is to be assigned to this module. Figure 2 summarizes the results of this analysis. Depending on the PPC modules, the number of sources (y-axis) was plotted for each Industrie 4.0 element (x-axis), which indicates an increase in efficiency of the PPC modules.

It has been shown that Scheduling and Capacity Planning as well as Manufacturing Control can benefit significantly from the elements of the Industrie 4.0, because the decision making process for these planning activities is largely based on current production information. This information can be collected in particular by the elements Sensors & Actuators, RFID and Networked objects. The relatively minor impact on the other modules is due to various characteristics. While Production Program Planning is strategic planning, Production Requirements Planning and Lot Sizing are based on simple mathematical operations, so that they have a low planning complexity. Therefore, no significant increases in efficiency can be achieved due to the improved data availability and quality of the Industrie 4.0 elements.

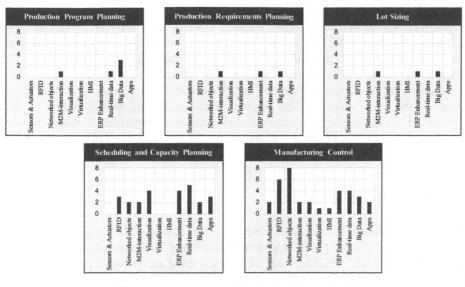

Fig. 2. Positive impact of Industrie 4.0 elements on PPC modules

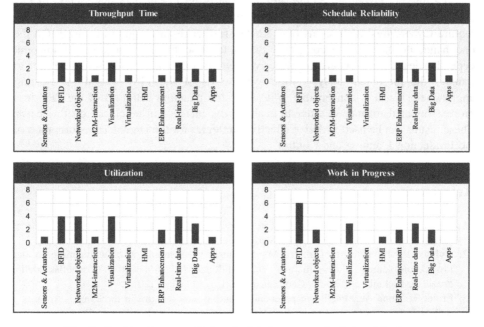

Fig. 3. Positive impact of Industrie 4.0 elements on logistics objectives

Based on this, the potential of an Industrie 4.0 element for improving logistics objectives was examined. An example in this context is an increase in schedule reliability by the use of networked objects. Considering their planned completion dates, subsequent operations and required resources, orders can dynamically prioritize themselves in front of a workstation. Because schedule reliability can be significantly influenced by the choice of a priority rule [5], networked objects can contribute to improving this logistics objective. A summary of the results is shown in Fig. 3, whereby the representation is to be interpreted in analogy to Fig. 2.

With regard to the improvement of logistics objectives by the use of Industrie 4.0 elements, there is consistently high potential. Because the logistics objectives can be significantly influenced by the operative control, this recognition can be traced back to the high potential of the Production Control (Fig. 2). Nevertheless, differences between the separate Industrie 4.0 elements can be identified.

5 Summary

Industrie 4.0 offers comprehensive potential for increasing efficiency in Production Planning and Control. So far, these potentials have only been reduced to the increasing availability and quality of data. Based on a quantitative analysis, this paper shows the potentials of Industrie 4.0 elements for the separate PPC modules as well as for the logistics objectives. With the aim of improving the planning quality of the PPC, this paper offers new perspectives.

The missing taxonomy of Industrie 4.0 has proved critical in the context of this article. If we consider that the elements of Cloud Computing (e.g. real-time data) require Cyber-Physical Systems (e.g. RFID), further research questions arise. On the one hand, the need for a consistent model to describe the structure and inherent dependencies of the elements can be derived. On the other hand, it seems appropriate to transfer the presented analysis to the processes of the PPC. Based on existing approaches [17], it is conceivable to describe the planning activities of the PPC in a process-oriented manner in order to evaluate the increase in efficiency on this basis. These results can be used to derive effective strategies for the Digital Transformation of the Production Planning and Control.

References

1. Nyhuis, P., et al.: Aktuellen Herausforderungen der Produktionsplanung und -steuerung mittels Industrie 4.0 begegnen. PZH-Verlag, Garbsen (2016)
2. Nyhuis, P., Hübner, M., Quirico, M., Schäfers, P., Schmidt, M.: Veränderung in der Produktionsplanung und -steuerung. In: Handbuch Industrie 4.0 – Geschäftsmodelle, Prozesse, Technik, pp. 31–50. Carl Hanser Verlag, München (2017)
3. Erola, S., Sihna, W.: Intelligent production planning and control in the cloud – towards a scalable software architecture. In: 10th Conference on Intelligent Computation in Manufacturing Engineering. Flexible Automation and Intelligent Manufacturing Conference 2016, pp. 571–576 (2016)
4. Dombrowski, U., Mielke, T. (eds.): Ganzheitliche Produktionssysteme – Aktueller Stand und zukünftige Entwicklung. Springer, Heidelberg (2015). https://doi.org/10.1007/978-3-662-46164-8

5. Lödding, H.: Handbook of Manufacturing Control – Fundamentals, Description, Configuration. Springer, Berlin (2013). https://doi.org/10.1007/978-3-642-24458-2
6. Wiendahl, H.-P.: Betriebsorganisation für Ingenieure. Carl Hanser, München (2008)
7. Magad, E.L., Amos, J.M.: Total Materials Management – Achieving Maximum Profits Through Materials/Logistics Operations. Springer, Boston (1995). https://doi.org/10.1007/978-1-4684-6450-4
8. Haase, K.: Lotsizing and Scheduling for Production Planning. Springer, Heidelberg (1994). https://doi.org/10.1007/978-3-642-45735-7
9. Schneider, H.: Operative Produktionsplanung und -steuerung. Oldenburg, München (2005)
10. Wiendahl, H.-P.: Load-Orientated Manufacturing Control. Springer, Berlin (1995). https://doi.org/10.1007/978-3-642-57743-7
11. Dombrowski, U., Richter, T.: Supplementing lean production systems with information and communication technologies. In: 26th International Conference on Flexible Automation and Intelligent Manufacturing Conference, pp. 654–661 (2016)
12. Dombrowski, U., Richter, T., Krenkel, P.: Wechselwirkungen von Ganzheitlichen Produktionssystemen und Industrie 4.0. Zeitschrift für wirtschaftlichen Fabrikbetrieb **112**(6), 430–433 (2017)
13. Bundesverband Informationswirtschaft, Telekommunikation und neue Medien e. V.: Industrie 4.0 – Volkswirtschaftliches Potenzial für Deutschland. Studie, Berlin (2014)
14. Kritenbrink, T.: Sicherheit in der Industrie 4.0 – Realitätscheck und Ausblick. Industrie 4.0 Management (4), 29–32 (2017)
15. Baumer, S.: Verlässliche eingebettete Systeme für Industrie 4.0. Zeitschrift für wirtschaftlichen Fabrikbetrieb **109**(4), 264 (2014)
16. Zäpfel, G.: Grundzüge des Produktions- und Logistikmanagements. Oldenburg Verlag, München (2001)
17. Schmidt, M., Schäfers, P.: The Hanoverian supply chain model: modelling the impact of production planning and control on a supply chain's logistic objectives. Prod. Eng. **11**(4–5), 487–493 (2017)

The Strategic Landscape of Industry 4.0

Børge Sjøbakk[(⊠)]

SINTEF Technology and Society, P.O. Box 4760 Torgarden,
7465 Trondheim, Norway
borge.sjobakk@sintef.no

Abstract. We are currently on the marks of Industry 4.0. Characterized by increased digitalization and automation, it is expected to overturn traditional business models and supply chains. Industry 4.0 initiatives have already made significant impact on industry, and will continue to do so in the years to come. While the concept of Industry 4.0 gains a foothold, there is no clear idea of how it should be addressed by companies. The transformation is without a doubt a strategic imperative that requires long-term commitment. Instead of investing in new technologies in an ad hoc manner, companies need to adopt a systematic approach to address technological opportunities throughout the supply chain. There exist many different and, in some cases, conflicting opinions about the scope of such an approach, what it should contain, its point of departure, etc. This paper synthesizes such views into a framework that depicts the strategic landscape manufacturing companies are facing at the outset of their digital journey. The framework can be used to position and discuss companies' digitalization and automation initiatives with respect to business-, manufacturing-, supply chain-, and digital strategy.

Keywords: Industry 4.0 · Factory of the future · Digital supply networks

1 Introduction

We are currently on the marks of Industry 4.0. Characterized by increased digitalization and automation, it is expected to overturn traditional business models and supply chains. Industry 4.0 initiatives have already made significant impact on industry, and will continue to do so in the years to come. The topic is virtually on every manufacturing company's agenda, as many (rightly) feel they are left with no choice but to go with the flow to remain competitive. History has shown that organizations that ignore the need for change are rapidly forced out of the market [1]. Currently, early adopters are implementing new technologies at a fast pace, and build capabilities that enable them to increase their lead [2]. Although the full shift toward Industry 4.0 may not be realized in decades, some argue that key advances will be established and winners and losers will emerge in the next five to ten years [3]. Therefore, to remain competitive, companies will need to accelerate their efforts towards Industry 4.0 [2].

While the concept of Industry 4.0 gains a foothold, there is no clear idea of how it should actually be addressed by companies [1]. In the past 10 to 15 years many companies have made large technology investments which have helped to standardize and improve the efficiency of fragmented processes [4]. Implementation of digital

I. Moon et al. (Eds.): APMS 2018, IFIP AICT 536, pp. 122–127, 2018.
https://doi.org/10.1007/978-3-319-99707-0_16

initiatives in silos or through a technology centric approach are persisting trends [5]. Even though these companies might realize short-term benefits from ad-hoc implementation of state-of-the-art digital technologies, they are likely to miss out on greater opportunities [1] – such as transparency and seamless planning and execution throughout the extended supply chain [4].

Although there is no common understanding of how organizations should adapt to Industry 4.0, such a transformation is without a doubt a strategic imperative that requires long-term commitment [1]. Instead of investing in new technologies in an ad hoc manner, companies need to adopt a systematic approach to address technological opportunities throughout the supply chain [6, 7]. There exist many different and, in some cases, conflicting opinions about the scope of such an approach, what it should contain, its point of departure, etc. The purpose of this paper is to synthesize such views into a framework that depicts the strategic landscape manufacturing companies are facing at the outset of their digital journey. Companies can use the framework to position and discuss their digitalization and automation initiatives with respect to business-, manufacturing-, supply chain-, and digital strategy.

The remainder of the paper is structured as follows. First, the research method is described. This is followed by a brief overview of Industry 4.0, including an understanding of the term and the technology trends constituting it, as well as two underlying transformations of Industry 4.0 – from traditional factories and supply chains to Factories of the Future and Digital Supply Networks, respectively. Thereafter, the multi-faceted strategic landscape is presented. Finally, the results are discussed and concluded.

2 Research Method

The strategic landscape of Industry 4.0 is proposed based on a study of publicly available reports from leading global management consulting companies. The reports were identified through Google searches for <company name> + <keywords> in the fall 2017. The keywords used were 'Industry 4.0', 'digital supply chain' and 'digital factory'. A total of 32 reports were studied for definitions and recommendations, especially emphasizing strategic issues related to the transformation towards Industry 4.0. Different views have been synthesized into the framework presented in this paper.

Business reports as a genre have a set of unique features, including funnel-shaped overall structure, topical organization, lack of emphasis on description of methods, and heavy stress on recommendations, which separate them from research articles [8]. As business reports typically lack method descriptions, their validity is lower than that of most research articles. Using such reports as a data source therefore limits the research quality. However, the sole purpose of this research was to study available advice to a practical situation; how to approach Industry 4.0 strategically. In this respect, business reports are especially relevant, as they typically provide the readers, who are usually members of the business community, with necessary information to advice action in practical situations [8]. Finally, it is worth noting that such reports often adopt a positive tone to inspire confidence and optimism in problem-solving [8]. They are persuasive, as their authors are eager to sell their services to the readers. For this reason, there may be more emphasis on pros rather than cons in the reports. This should not pose a problem for this paper, as pros and cons of Industry 4.0, digitalization and automation are not within the scope of the research.

3   Industry 4.0

Industry 4.0 is a vision of the industrial production of the future [3]. '4.0' refers to a fourth industrial revolution expected to be realized by cyber-physical production systems that merge real and virtual worlds. It is a further developmental stage in the organization and management of the manufacturing industry, succeeding mechanical production powered by water and steam in the end of the 18th century (first industrial revolution), mass production enabled by electrical energy in the start of the 20th century (second industrial revolution) and further automated production through application of electronics and IT since the 1970s (third industrial revolution) [9]. While the concept of Industry 4.0 is widely used across Europe, commentators in the US and other parts of the English-speaking world also use terms like 'internet of things', the 'internet of everything' or the 'industrial internet' to describe the digital transformation which traditional manufacturing and production methods are in the middle of [9].

Industry 4.0 is triggered by digital technologies that have a disruptive impact on manufacturing companies' business models, the way they operate and create customer value [1]. Different terms are used to describe the trending technologies driving Industry 4.0. Boston Consulting Group [3] defines nine technology trends constitute the building blocks of Industry 4.0: The Industrial Internet of Things; big data and analytics; the cloud; simulation; augmented reality; autonomous robots; additive manufacturing; cybersecurity, and; horizontal and vertical system integration.

Industry 4.0 arises simultaneously with the coalesce of technologies into a digital ecosystem [1], and the terms 'digitalization' and 'Industry 4.0' are often used concomitantly – even though digitalization, which has already impacted all parts of society for years, has a much larger range than industrial production. For Industry 4.0, digitalization is specially related to connectivity and interaction among parts, machines and humans, which is expected to transform the design, manufacturing, operation and service of products and production systems [3]. Examples of new or improved ways of operating include predictive decision making through big data; reduced complexity through increased coordination; new forms of collaboration and coordination (e.g. sharing economy); flexibility in when and where to manufacture (e.g. micro customization) and digitally enhanced contribution to human productivity, from human judgement to machine intelligence [1, 10].

The new digital ecosystem is changing the way products are designed, created and delivered to customers [11]. While smart products, services and innovation are expected to leverage company growth, supply chains and factories are the main efficiency drivers of the new industrial paradigm [1]. Arguably, the transformation towards Industry 4.0 is a transformation of both factories and supply chains – from traditional factories to 'smart' [1], 'digital factories' [7] or 'factories of the future' [12], and from traditional supply chains to 'digital supply networks' [11, 13]. These future-states are commonly characterized by a high degree of automation, integration and extensive information sharing. Efforts must be made both internally and externally to achieve this. For instance, products need to be developed in an integrated manner to ensure design for automated production, and core suppliers need to be involved when acquiring and developing tools for real-time information sharing and decision making throughout the supply chain.

4 Strategic Landscape

As noted in the Introduction, the transformation towards Industry 4.0 is a strategic imperative that requires a systematic approach. There exist different opinions of how the imminent technological opportunities should be addressed in a strategic manner.

Roughly speaking, two 'schools' have been identified when addressing strategies for digitalization and automation. The first advocates that the starting point for any digital journey is the definition of the company's digital vision and the resulting strategy [14]. This digital strategy sets the direction for a digital operating model, and in turn which digital technologies that should be used to digitalize core processes [5]. The second school argues that instead of developing digital strategies, companies should rethink their manufacturing and supply chain strategies in the light of digital technologies that enable e.g. increased flexibility and scalability [7, 15]. In addition, some narrow the scope even further. For instance, to drive value and avoid incorrect insights from all the data that is currently gathered, some argue that companies should develop an enterprise data management strategy driven by business goals [16]. It is possible to envision that other digital technologies could have similar technology strategies. Finally, business goals are above the constantly shifting technology landscape [16]. Therefore, regardless of school of thought, it is generally agreed that any adoption of technology should in some way be linked to desired business outcomes [5, 7, 10].

The Industry 4.0 strategy is located somewhere in between the two digitalization schools. Some simply state that companies need to define a tailored Industry 4.0 strategy to master the challenges of implementation [2]. Some go further in stating that the digital vision is the starting point to Industry 4.0 [1], which would imply that the digital vision sets the direction for the Industry 4.0 strategy. However, a clear relationship between the Industry 4.0 strategy and other strategies has not been identified. In the previous section it was argued that the transformation towards Industry 4.0 is a transformation of both factories and supply chains. With the same reasoning, it is proposed that an Industry 4.0 strategy is in fact the sum of a manufacturing and supply chain strategy enabled by digital technologies.

From this, a 'strategic landscape' of Industry 4.0 is proposed (Fig. 1). The dashed vertical line is used to separate the two schools of thought proposed above. The left-hand side of the line has a strong emphasis on digitalization (often, for the sake of digitalization), while the right-hand side sees digitalization as something that enables manufacturing and supply chain strategies to contribute more to business strategy, models and goals. The equal- and plus signs are used to show how the sum of the digitally enabled manufacturing and supply chain strategy amounts to an Industry 4.0 strategy. At the rightmost side of the landscape are specific technology strategies, which are driven by business strategy, and may instruct how to treat specific technologies. An example is the data management strategy mentioned above.

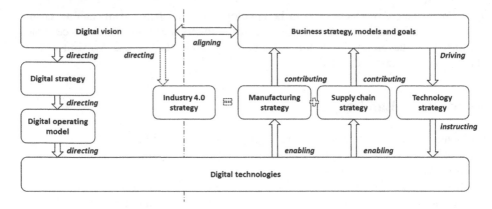

Fig. 1. The strategic landscape of industry 4.0

5   Discussion and Conclusion

The strategic landscape (Fig. 1) illustrates what many companies are facing at the outset of their digital journey; a myriad of partly conflicting opinions about how to approach Industry 4.0 and related topics. As such, it can be argued that its contribution lies in refining the problem, rather than bringing the answers to it. Still, there are some takeaways. First, a company should question whether it needs a dedicated Industry 4.0 strategy if it already has a manufacturing and/or supply chain strategy. The question of how digital technologies may serve as enablers is something that can be treated directly in these strategies, instead of in an additional Industry 4.0 strategy. On the other hand, if a company lacks a manufacturing and/or supply chain strategy, an Industry 4.0 strategy may serve this purpose. Further, a company could benefit from having a digital vision even if it does not develop a digital strategy, a digital operating model, and so on. For example, such a vision could dictate the company's policy about adopting new technology early versus only using mature technology. Alignment with business strategy, models and goals is always key. Finally, there is a question of what school is the best to follow. While the left-hand side of the strategic landscape may be more fit for the Netflixes and Spotifys of the world, some production companies may still find value in developing digital strategies and operating models. As seen in the framework, it is important to ensure that the technological directions that come out of these strategies and models are not in conflict with the technological trajectories best fit for manufacturing and supply chain management.

When companies have found their position in their strategic landscape, they must add content to their strategies. While this is largely company-specific, some topics are likely to be relevant for multiple companies. Further research includes identifying these topics and developing guidelines for strategy development within the strategic landscape. This could provide companies with a more systematic approach towards Industry 4.0. After all, "digital is too critical to a company's competitiveness to be left to chance" [7].

Acknowledgements. This work has been conducted within the project SmartChain funded by the Research Council of Norway. The author would like to thank the participants of the project for valuable discussions and feedback while developing the framework.

References

1. Bechtold, J., Kern, A., Lauenstein, C., Bernhofer, L.: Industry 4.0 - The Capgemini Consulting View. Sharpening the Picture beyond the Hype. Capgemini Consulting (2014)
2. Lorenz, M., Küpper, D., Rüßmann, M., Heidemann, A., Bause, A.: Time to Accelerate in the Race toward Industry 4.0. Boston Consulting Group (2016)
3. Rüßmann, M., et al.: Industry 4.0: The Future of Productivity and Growth in Manufacturing Industries. Boston Consulting Group (2015)
4. Hajibashi, M., Bhatti, A.: Supply Chain for a New Age. Accenture (2017)
5. Raab, M., Griffin-Cryan, B.: Digital Transformation of Supply Chains: Creating Value – When Digital Meets Physical. Capgemini Consulting (2011)
6. Ebner, G., Bechtold, J.: Are Manufacturing Companies Ready to Go Digital? Understanding the Impact of Digital. Capgemini Consulting (2012)
7. Rasmus, R., Nichols, J.: Digital Factory: Cracking the Code to Success. Accenture (2017)
8. Yeung, L.: In search of commonalities: some linguistic and rhetorical features of business reports as a genre. Engl. Specif. Purp. **26**, 156–179 (2007)
9. Schlaepfer, R.C., Koch, M.: Industry 4.0: Challenges and Solutions for the Digital Transformation and Use of Exponential Technologies. Deloitte (2015)
10. Schmidt, B., Rutkowsky, S., Petersen, I., Klötzke, F., Wallenburg, C.M., Einmahl, L.: Digital Supply Chains: Increasingly Critical for Competitive Edge. AT Kearney (2015)
11. Mussomeli, A., Gish, D., Laaper, S.: The Rise of the Digital Supply Network: Industry 4.0 Enables the Digital Transformation of Supply Chains. Deloitte (2016)
12. Küpper, D., Kuhlmann, K., Köcher, S., Dauner, T., Burggräf, P.: The Factory of the Future. Boston Consulting Group (2016)
13. Hanifan, G., Sharma, A., Newberry, C.: The Digital Supply Network: A New Paradigm for Supply Chain Management. Accenture (2014)
14. Hégelé, M., Tarnopolski, J., Aggarwal, P.: Digital Supply Chain Planning in Chemicals: Mastering Six Capabilities to Win. Accenture (2016)
15. Hanifan, G.L.: Is Your Supply Chain a Growth Engine? It Could Be If You Leverage Digital Technologies. Accenture (2015)
16. Alexander, M., Brody, P., Chadam, J., Cookson, C., Little, J., Meadows, B.: Digital Supply Chain: It's all about that Data. EY (2016)

Online Life Cycle Assessment for Fluid Power Manufacturing Systems – Challenges and Opportunities

Marcel Rückert[✉], Stephan Merkelbach, Raphael Alt,
and Katharina Schmitz

Institute for Fluid Power Drives and Systems, RWTH Aachen University,
Campus-Boulevard 30, 52074 Aachen, Germany
marcel.rueckert@ifas.rwth-aachen.de

Abstract. Increasing demands for highly flexible production, e.g. mass customization, as well as the production industries' search for new business models, enabled by big data, pose completely new requirements and challenges for modern components of manufacturing systems. Challenges range from plug and produce to digital twin as well as reconfiguration. To meet the requirements of customers and industry alike, components within a manufacturing line need to be smart to communicate with each other and support the operator during the whole life cycle. In order to optimize the value chain, transparent machine costs as well as the carbon footprint of a component and system are highly relevant. Because of their high power density and controllability, fluid power actuators are prime components in manufacturing systems. In this work, the product life cycle of a modern electro hydraulic actuator for state of the art manufacturing systems is defined. Based on this framework, an assessment is made on state of the art actuators with the focus on life cycle costing and the carbon footprint. Subsequently, requirements for future developments are derived for each part of the product life cycle.

Keywords: Life cycle assessment · Digital twin · Total cost of ownership
Carbon footprint · Fluid power · Compact hydraulic drives

1 Introduction

Mass customization caused by the costumers' demand for highly individualized products as well as a shortening of the product life cycle poses new challenges for the manufacturing industry. These challenges can be met with flexible production systems, transparent machine costs and smart components. In order to achieve smart production systems, the idea of "Industrial Internet of Things" (IIoT) or "Industrie 4.0" (I4.0) was introduced [1] with the goal to fuse computational power (embedded systems) and mechatronic systems to implement an internet based machinery network. One primary target is that information of all participating instances of a specific manufacturing process are available in real-time, so that an ideal value-added flow can be identified [2]. As an approach for the discription of IIoT, it can be categorized into four different aspects: Vertical integration, horizontal integration, integrated engineering and the

© IFIP International Federation for Information Processing 2018
Published by Springer Nature Switzerland AG 2018. All Rights Reserved
I. Moon et al. (Eds.): APMS 2018, IFIP AICT 536, pp. 128–135, 2018.
https://doi.org/10.1007/978-3-319-99707-0_17

human role [3, 4]. With a successful implementation of IIoT, the estimated reduction in part production costs are approximately 70%, see [2].

Fluid power components play an important role in manufacturing machines due to their compact size and high power density. Another advantage compared to electro-mechanical drives is the simple realizability of linear motions with cylinders. Most of the times, fluid power components act as actuators for presses, injection molding machines and other highly relevant manufacturing systems [5]. Figure 1 shows a commonly used electro hydraulic actuator (EHA) and the integration into a calibration press. The EHA itself consists of an electric motor, a pump, a switching valve, an accumulator and a cylinder, all located within close proximity to reduce installation space.

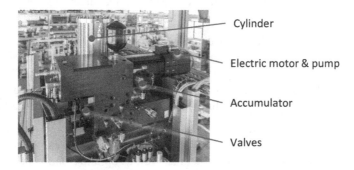

Fig. 1. Electro hydraulic actuator (EHA) integrated into a calibration press, after [6]

With increasing performance requirements, space optimization and increasing complexity of tasks, the correct planning of an EHA is highly relevant. Especially for the initial planning, information on life cycle costs of the product are important. Figure 2 shows the typical stages: Planning, development, production, commissioning, usage and reconfiguration.

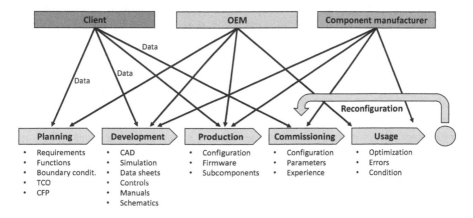

Fig. 2. Life cycle of an electro hydraulic actuator (EHA) for a smart manufacturing

Planning - During the planning phase, boundary conditions and functions are defined that need to be fulfilled by the component. Based on these requirements, a suitable component can be selected. In case of an EHA, electro mechanical drives are an option as well. For this selection, additional soft factors such as the total cost of ownership (TCO) and the carbon footprint (PCF) influence the result, see [7]. Based on the assigned operation, a choice is made.

Development - The development of a component such as an EHA is highly complex due to the interaction of different subparts as well as the installation space restrictions. In order to use an optimal design, CAD-Software as well as 1D and multidimensional simulation approaches are chosen. Another important part is the selection of suitable subcomponents for the task.

Production - Production refers to the assembly and manufacturing of all necessary parts into a working EHA.

Commissioning - With an increasing component complexity, the commissioning is still predominantly done manually. This requires a deep integration of the commissioning engineer (CE) into the production process. Assistant systems can help the CE to reduce the level of complexity and support the transition of a CE into a system engineer [1, 4]. After the commissioning, the EHA is fully operational and can be used for manufacturing purposes inside a machine.

Usage - During the usage, the condition in which the EHA is in can be monitored to ensure the functioning of the whole system as well as optimize and adjust production parameters. Highly flexible production requires low downtime. Therefore, predictive maintenance also plays an important role.

Reconfiguration - If the manufacturing process changes, or the EHA is supposed to be installed into another manufacturing machine, reconfiguration has to be done. Here, the disassembly and refitting takes place. Afterwards, the commissioning has to be performed again, ensuring the connectivity with other components of the new manufacturing system.

During the product life cycle, different entities access and provide data regarding the component, see Fig. 2. These entities can be OEMs, component manufacturers or clients. Today, data and information is primarily stored decentrally regarding location and time with the need of manual data transfers. To make information more accessible for relevant entities and therefore make the usability of an EHA more efficient and flexible, fluid power components need to get smart.

In this paper, current technological possibilities for fluid power components regarding the online accessibility of data and life cycle assessment are analyzed. Afterwards, potential for necessary developments is introduced in order to define the role of fluid power components within intelligent manufacturing systems and mass customization.

2   State of the Art

With the goal being an intelligent manufacturing system, every instance of the value chain needs to be able to communicate with each other as well as generate data for condition monitoring purposes. As of today, a lot of manufacturing systems do have incompatible communication between the participants resulting in unstructured and locally distributed data. Therefore, the relations between each component is only known to the respective worker. This prevents the planning of optimized production routes for manufactured parts, making the whole system unflexible and the components passive elements in the value chain. A path of a part is only dictated by the technical staff, because many systems do not have any intelligence or experience. The comparison of the above described state I3.0 with the goal of I4.0 is depicted in Fig. 3. Here, lack of knowledge due to unstructured and only locally available data creates unflexible systems. With the need of mass customization and smart and green manufacturing systems, a modern information and communication technology (ICT) needs to be applied to all subsystems for a standardized communication between random participants of the manufacturing system. This results in the possibility of machine learning and intelligent systems, which can optimize the path of a part through the value chain autonomically, creating cyber physical systems (CPS).

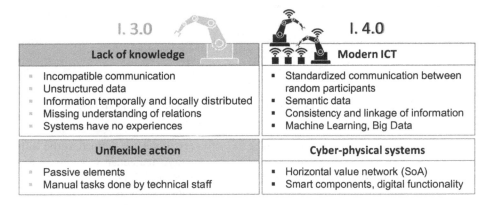

I. 3.0	I. 4.0
Lack of knowledge	**Modern ICT**
• Incompatible communication • Unstructured data • Information temporally and locally distributed • Missing understanding of relations • Systems have no experiences	• Standardized communication between random participants • Semantic data • Consistency and linkage of information • Machine Learning, Big Data
Unflexible action	**Cyber-physical systems**
• Passive elements • Manual tasks done by technical staff	• Horizontal value network (SoA) • Smart components, digital functionality

Fig. 3. Comparison of Industry 3.0 and 4.0 [8]

Data gathered in this process as well as during the whole product life-cycle is necessary to assess and calculate transparent machine costs. The knowledge enables system engineers to efficiently design smart and green manufacturing systems. For this, a life cycle analysis together with the total cost of ownership and the carbon footprint of the component needs to be done.

In the following, state of the art methodologies to analyze a product life cycle are reviewed with regards to the total cost of ownership as well as the carbon footprint.

2.1 Life Cycle Analysis in Fluid Power

In the past, different studies concerning the life cycles of fluid power equipment have been undertaken. These studies focus on two main impacts. The economic efficiency of different drives has to be evaluated and compared. Nowadays, the ecological impacts of the drives are added to the analysis as these factors become more and more important to manufacturers. In the future, the data necessary for the analysis of the economical as well as the ecological efficiency needs to be added to a digital twin of the EHA to ensure permanent monitoring. The unique characteristics of life cycle analysis regarding fluid power components are in the accounting of the driving fluids (oil and air). Here, manufacturing, maintenance, environmental effects and natural resources need to be accounted for. Getting the numbers right for these aspects is crucial for obtaining valid results.

Life Cycle Costing - The course of an analysis of the Life Cycle Costs (LCC) of different drives and some results will be discussed in the following. There are many different approaches for the analysis of LCC. In general, the steps followed during the analysis are comparable in every approach. An industrial standard is given in [9]. This approach is shown in Fig. 4.

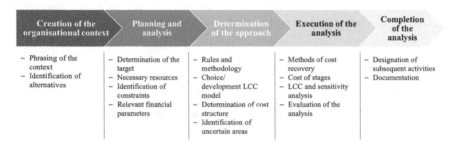

Fig. 4. Course of an LCC-analysis according to DIN EN 60300-3 [9]

No matter which approach is used, the LCC of every product is defined as the sum of five main cost blocks: Acquisition, installation, energy, maintenance & repair and recycling. The partitions of these main blocks vary between different drives as well as between different applications. An exemplary comparative study between electrome-chanical (EM) and pneumatic (PN) linear drives was performed at the Institute for Fluid Power Drives and Systems (IFAS) in [7]. Results for the normalized LCC of these drives are shown in Fig. 5.

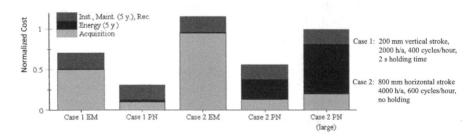

Fig. 5. Comparison of the normalized LCC for electromechanical and pneumatic linear drives as presented in [7]

It is obvious, that the choice of drives has a large influence on the acquisition as well as on the energy costs whereas installation and maintenance are not of great importance for the comparison between the drives. Information about the driving energy or the necessary maintenance cycles to ensure availability should be made accessible in the digital twin to optimize the usage and to reduce overall costs for the industrial user.

Carbon Footprint Analysis - Due to the increasing importance of environmental matters and climate change in particular, nowadays, many companies are interested in the Product Carbon Footprint (PCF) of the drives used in their applications. Analogue to the estimation of the LCC of products, there are many different approaches for the estimation of the PCF. One approach is given in the international guideline ISO T/S 14067. This guideline presents an approach which is similar to a complete Life Cycle Analysis (LCA) but limited to the effects on global climate. In this case, the LCA has to be executed in four main steps, shown in Fig. 6.

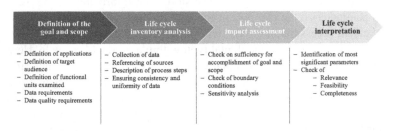

Fig. 6. Course of an LCA-analysis according to ISO 14044 and 14067 [10]

In order to realistically assess a components' total costs, access to data throughout the whole life-cycle needs to be available. Therefore, one of the most important steps towards intelligent manufacturing systems is the centralized storage of data. In the following chapter, required information for each step are analyzed and listed as well as the necessity of having a digital twin is discussed.

3 Digital Twin and Required Data for EHAs

In order to calculate the TCO and PCF in the planning phase, information regarding the product are required throughout its' life cycle. In each step, different information become relevant and it is of high importance that the access to information regarding future steps in the life cycle of a component are accessible for an optimal assessment of transparent costs.

Development and Production - The development and production of a component is an interaction of the OEM as well as the (sub-) component manufacturer. Therefore definitions on what materials are used need to be communicated and stored. Additionally, the processing, energy used, assembly, production time and cost are influencing factors for life cycle costing.

Commissioning - During the commissioning, parameters used to tune the component such as valve configurations have to be recorded. This way, a holistic commissioning data-base can be introduced accounting for the collected experience of every individual commissioning engineer, supporting the path towards a system engineer. If data is available, the concept of plug and produce can be realized, see [11].

Usage - Data collected from the actual load cycles is highly relevant but also highly sensible since it gives information about the manufacturing process itself. Especially for the calculation of the TCO, informations on the load cycles (stroke, load, time, acceleration, number of duty cycles per time unit and energy used per load cycle) need to be recorded. Additional working appliances (compressed air, oil) as well as maintenance cycles and effort are of interest as well. Fluid maintenance such as filtering, cooling and oil change influences both TCO and PCF. Necessary data in form of models needs to be captured and stored.

Reconfiguration - During reconfiguration, new boundary conditions and functions are defined. Therefore, no new data needs to be stored but information on usage data are required to parameterize the component towards its' new task.

To make data accessible, a digital twin of the real component is required.

Figure 7 depicts the role of the digital twin within a product life cycle. Here, information of every step are stored in a digitally and every entity has access and can provide additional data. The digital twin is an exact copy of the component storing purpose and all interactions in a way, that OEMs and component manufacturers can get required data without interfering with the know-how of the manufacturing company. In case of fluid power components such as an EHA, the model of the axis itself is not sufficient enough compared to electromechanical drives. Here, the working fluid has to be considered in production, commissioning and maintenance models. This poses a defining barrier since data regarding fluids is not easily available. One current focus of research is to provide an easy to use implementation of fluid data for TCO and PCF tools.

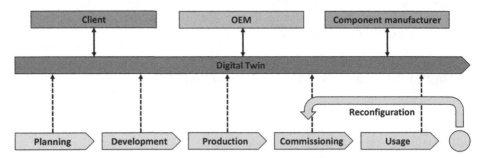

Fig. 7. A digital twin of an EHA helps to reduce complexity and provides structured information of the whole product life-cycle for future planning.

The digital twin poses the opportunity for all stakeholders to monitor and evaluate the TCO and PCF of an EHA during the whole life cycle including an estimation of the remaining life span of the component and the working fluid. By using a digital twin, this assessment can be made online.

4 Summary and Conclusion

With the need of mass customization and highly flexible manufacturing systems as well as green manufacturing, components have to adapt to new requirements. As a prime actor, EHAs are used in a wide range of manufacturing machines. Due to the complexity and variety of subcomponents, an assessment regarding the life cycle cost of an EHA is difficult to make.

In this paper, a look into the different sections of the life cycle of an EHA was performed with a state of the art analysis regarding the TCO and PCF. Based on this analysis, requirements are formulated in order to gather data during the whole product life cycle. With the help of a digital twin, future planning and design of new fluid power actuators can be significantly improved and machine costs can be optimized based on the duty cycle.

To achieve transparent costs, challenges like big data and the resulting security issues regarding cycle times in manufacturing as well as uniform communication standards for all machine components need to be tackled. Fluid power components in general can help realising intelligent and green manufacturing systems.

References

1. Kagermann, H., et al.: Industrie 4.0: Mit dem Internet der Dinge auf dem Weg zur 4. Industriellen Revolution. In: VDI Nachrichten, Nr. 13-2011. VDI Verlag GmbH (2011)
2. Wissenschaftliche Gesellschaft für Produktionstechnik (WGP), WGP-Standpunkt Industrie 4.0 (2016)
3. VDI/VDE: Statusreport - Referenzarchitekturmodell Industrie 4.0 (RAMI4.0) (2015)
4. BITKOM, VDMA, ZVEI, Umsetzungsstrategie Industrie 4.0 (2015)
5. Michel, S., Weber, J.: Energy-efficient electrohydraulic compact drives for low power applications, Proceedings of the Bath/ASME 2012 Symposium on Fluid Power and Motion Control FPMC2012, Bath, UK (2012)
6. https://www.boschrexroth.com/en/xc/industries/machinery-applications-and-engineering/machine-tools-forming-and-separating/references/frey/frey. Accessed 19 Apr 2018
7. Merkelbach, S., Murrenhoff, H., et al.: Pneumatische und elektromechanische Linearantriebe - Ein Vergleich der TCO, O + P Oelhydraulik und Pneumatik (in German Language) (2017)
8. Alt, R., et al.: A survey of industrial internet of things in the field of fluid power – basic concept and requirements for plug-and-produce. In: Bath/ASME 2018 Symposium on Fluid Power and Motion Control, FPMC 2018, Bath, UK (2018, unpublished)
9. DIN - Deutsches Institut für Normung e.V. DIN EN 60300-3-3 Dependability management - Part 3-3: Application guide - Life cycle costing, Beuth Verlag (in German Language), Berlin (2014)
10. DIN - Deutsches Institut für Normung e.V. DIN EN ISO 14044 Environmental management - Life cycle assessment - Requirements and guidelines, Beuth Verlag, Berlin (2006)
11. Profanter, S., et al.: OPC UA for Plug & Produce: Automatic Device Discovery Using LDS-ME (2017)

Summary and Conclusions

Smart City Interoperability and Cross-Platform Implementation

Study on the Utilization of Digital Manufacturing for Production Operations

Masahiro Shibuya[1]([⊠]), Kenichi Iida[2], and Koki Mikami[3]

[1] Tokyo Metropolitan University, 6-6 Asahigaoka, Hino, Tokyo, Japan
mshibuya@tmu.ac.jp
[2] Hokkaido Industrial Research Institute, Kita-19 Nishi-11,
Kita-ku, Sapporo, Japan
[3] Hokkaido University of Science,
4-1, Maeda 7-jo 15-chome, Teine-ku, Sapporo, Japan

Abstract. Digital manufacturing (DM), which has developed rapidly in recent years, is premised on use in planning operations, and it is not utilized in production operation. There are many challenges to the application of DM in production operations, such as the incapacity of a supervisor at a work site to effectively implement the manufacturing-line model developed using a DM, in a planning operation. Therefore, we propose a system that makes it possible to redesign work plans and support improvement activity by simply inputting values in accustomed standardized work tables, namely, process capacity tables, standardized work tables, and standardized work combination tables, of three types of workers, instead of inputting a large quantity of complicated parameters. Less examination time is desirable at production sites, and we added a tool that enabled the graphical display of execution processes and results. Moreover, we added a system that made it possible to alter Microsoft Excel database inputs, such as the number or arrangement of DM processing machines. This paper describes the proposed system and its method of implementation.

Keywords: Digital manufacturing · 3 kinds of standardized work tables
Improvement operation

1 Introduction

Technical developments for the realization of a "Smart Factory," which is an advanced factory substantiating the different manufacturing strategies (e.g., Industry 4.0, industrial Internet, cloud manufacturing) proposed by various countries, is flourishing. IEC 62832 (Digital Factory DF), which is aimed at the integrated management of physical and virtual spaces by digitizing the whole factory, is advocated. The method, called Digital Twin, was proposed by Grieves in 2003. Based on this idea, a concept is being developed to reproduce the physical manufacturing space in real time by digitization and to make the control and management of real factories easier. In German Industry 4.0, the optimization of all processes related to the manufacturing industry by CPS (Cypher Physical System) is underway. Some large enterprises (e.g., Siemens,

I. Moon et al. (Eds.): APMS 2018, IFIP AICT 536, pp. 139–145, 2018.
https://doi.org/10.1007/978-3-319-99707-0_18

Dassault, and PTC) use Digital Twin to support their customer services with state-of-the-art technology (e.g., aerospace technology for aircraft maintenance, etc.).

Tao classified the factory evolution process to achieve coalescence of physical and virtual spaces into four stages. Digital Twin is the fourth stage; the present is the third stage, in which physical and virtual spaces interact with each other. What is imperative in the third stage is production technique support using 3D CAD called Digital Manufacturing (DM). This method was developed to support the shortening of development periods by front-loading activities from product development by concurrent engineering to production preparation and process mounting.

Digital Manufacturing (DM), which has rapidly developed in recent years, is premised on its application in "planning operation," and will not be utilized in "production operation." To utilize DM in "production operation," the supervisor at a work site must be able to understand the manufacturing line model made by DM and possess the ability to modify it for factory improvement. Many experts say that manufacturing line simulators are difficult to master and are now experts' tools. In the Japanese manufacturing industry, the structure in which workers independently advance toward the achievement of their goals using various kinds of management tables of their own and repeating the PDCA cycle is widely used.

Therefore, we first examined how to utilize DM at a production site, rather than aiming for Digital Twin directly. For small and medium-sized enterprises unfamiliar with ICT, we thought it necessary to develop a mechanism that supports production re-design and improvement activities by inputting values into three kinds of workers' accustomed standardized work tables (process capacity tables, standardized work tables, and standardized combination tables) with click of a button, instead of inputting a large quantity of complex parameters. In this mechanism, based on the production plan made at an office, a virtual line is constructed for DM, and evaluation and improvement are conducted. Our aim is the development of a mechanism which makes it possible to seamlessly transfer the values in the process capacity table to the parameters of machines, such as the processing machines on the virtual line. The user can make the best standardized work combination table just by clicking a button. In the next step, we aim to utilize this system by feedbacking the actual operation and production information to the virtual production model, re-evaluating it, and connecting the results to factories in operation.

The purpose of this study is to create a mechanism which makes it possible to modify the original production plan (proposal) to obtain the best one suited for the manufacturing site using DM, and utilizing it effectively in the PDCA cycle.

2 Production Management Problems in Terms of Production Sites

2.1 How to Conduct Production Planning and Management

In some enterprises, the production management department of the corporate office makes the production plans, and the factory is forced to manage production according to these plans. Many of the plans made at the office side are medium schedule, and at the factory side small schedule such as when to start or finish must be made. Figure 1 shows a scene of production management. The center of the figure shows the PDCA cycle. Because the production management department makes long-term plans, it also examines process design, line design, etc. The outline is shown in the right and left of the Plan part (PLAN00).

Based on the production plan (PLAN00) made at the office side, the factory supervisor creates the process capacity table, determines the various production efficiencies of each process, modifies the plan into a practicable one by experience, decides the tackt time, and finally makes three kinds of standardized work tables. The factory is operated on the basis of the standardized work tables. The output is separately recorded, and utilized for evaluation and improvement.

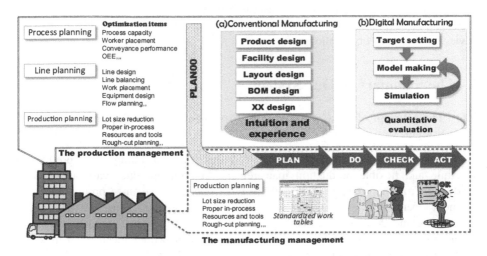

Fig. 1. Comparison between conventional and proposed production management operations.

2.2 New Production Management

Figure 1(a) shows the conventional method of starting the manufacturing of a new product. Figure 1(b) shows the method of using DM, which has become the focus of attention recently. As shown in the figure, in the stage PLAN00 of production plan management (office side), a practicable virtual line is constructed. Then, the parameters are modified to meet the target values; after repeated simulation, the new factory is quantitatively evaluated. This makes it possible to come up with an appropriate plan for the manufacturing site because the ordinary separated "process design" and "line design" are mutually connected, and to shorten the period of development and production preparation because the examination of items requiring intuition or experience, "visualization" and "optimization," can be realized in a shorter time.

Many enterprises utilize DM for the purpose of operating a highly efficient manufacturing line within a short time. DM has numerous functions, but the functions "process design," "line design," and "line operation design" are mainly utilized. The left of Fig. 1 PLAN00 shows optimization items which are important in production planning. Examining these items one by one takes a long time from model making to evaluation; thus, it is difficult to modify the model. The range of DM use is limited because of its high cost, but with its spread, attention is now being paid on how to create an autonomous control mechanism using the analysis results of worksite data.

Some shop-floor uses of DM include workability evaluation, layout re-examination, and line balance evaluation. The primary purpose of these evaluations is identify problems or bottlenecks in lines and processes before mass production, and verifying the measures in advance. Therefore, these must be finished before the start of manufacturing. What is necessary to effectively utilize DM on the shop floor is the development of a support system that makes it possible to easily conduct "minor adjustments in production preparation," "minor adjustment by improvement," etc., using the three kinds of standardized work tables as a user interface based on the worksite supervisor's experience and intuition, and, in the years ahead, information obtained from various devices and factory observations.

3   The Summary of Our System

3.1   The Concept of the Continuous Improvement Activity Support System

Small and medium-sized manufacturers requires quick planning of a production schedule and flexible production management for "multiproduct variable quantity production"; at the production sites, the way to effectively advance production management operations is a problem that needs to be solved. Thus, we have been researching and developing a "continuous improvement activity support system" in order to create a simple production management system whose mechanism makes it possible to collect production-site information using IoT, effectively utilize the PDCA cycle for production activities, conduct evaluation using DM, and utilize the results for re-designing production plans (Fig. 2). The design enables handling of the needs of each worksite by adding necessary functions, as shown by the wheel in Fig. 2.

Information inside the factory is gathered using IoT in the PDCA, as shown in the left of Fig. 2, and analyzed by DM, after which minor adjustments are made for production. When the production plan is very different from the present conditions, another one is made using O2O in the figure right.

3.2   Overview of the Proposed System

This system stores, in the simulation model, necessary information interpreted by DM based on the process order shown in the process capacity table. Therefore, the user can conduct evaluation and examination, modify the production plan for a practicable one, and reflect the results in the PDCA cycle (see Fig. 2). The factory simulation software DELMIA Quest was used in DM. Production planning was conducted with little input

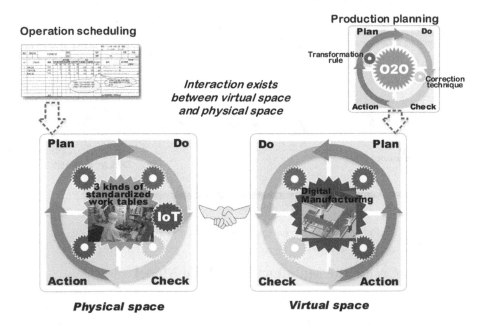

Fig. 2. Relationship between the continuous-improvement activity support system and three types of standardized work tables.

for given data (items, machines, work in progress, delivery requests, etc.) and adjustment parameters, by using the online to offline (O2O) technique. The right part of Fig. 2 shows a Microsoft Excel (hereby referred to as Excel) process capacity table made from the planning results.

Figure 3 shows the procedure to make a manufacturing line model using the data of standardized work tables on Excel; however, on Quest, this model can be concisely made. On Excel standardized work tables, the work order, work time, connecting order of machines, work contents, and other parameters are entered as the port. Because these contents are parameters imperceptible by Quest, by making a link between the conversion system and Excel, they are converted to BCL commands, which enables Quest to perceive the contents on Excel.

The conversion system analyzes the commands converted using the BCL program and redefines the execution order and other factors to develop a Quest model. Moreover, the system is given the role of controlling Quest. The system boots Quest and generates a manufacturing line model by transferring and executing the control command.

Quest has the function to back-end process the commands sent from the transmission system, and to front-end process the tool for both the visualization of execution results of the model and various predictions.

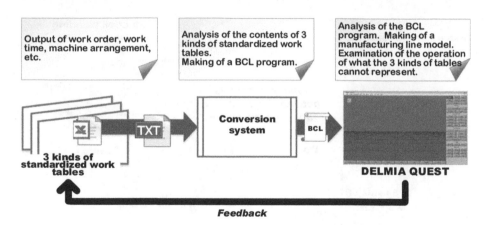

Fig. 3. Relationship between Excel, the conversion system, and Quest.

4 How to Create the Manufacturing Line Model

The user selects a standardized work combination table using the conversion system, and then, the system analyzes the read-in parameters for BCL command conversion. Quest analyzes and executes this control command, and a manufacturing-line model matched to the standardized work combination table is created (see Fig. 4). The conversion system judges the input contents and provides the production method logic, such as lot production, to the created model. Quest reads the particular execution time appointed by the user, and the created model automatically starts simulation.

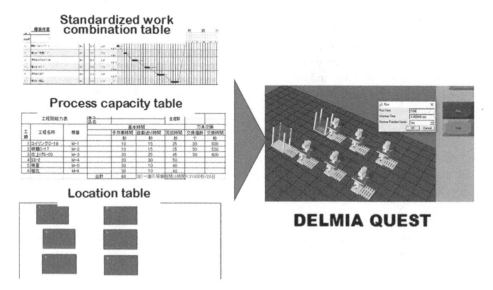

Fig. 4. Images of manufacturing-line model development using standardized work tables.

The trial system was examined at a labor-intensive factory. Our target was a part of the sheet metal processing line to manufacture parts for heating stoves. Figure 5(a) shows the layout of the target line. The rounded rectangles denote the processing machines, such as welders and press machines. The workers in this region moved and used a necessary processing machine to manufacture each part.

First, we made the three types of standardized work tables for the factory, and subsequently, we operated the system. On specifying a particular table, the model was displayed on Quest, as shown in Fig. 5(b). This factory used Lot Size 1 for production. We conducted evaluation considering Lot Size 10, because our investigation noted a large occurrence of waiting periods in this zone. The examination using the visualization tool showed that two more pieces could be manufactured in the case of Lot Size 10 (Fig. 5(c)).

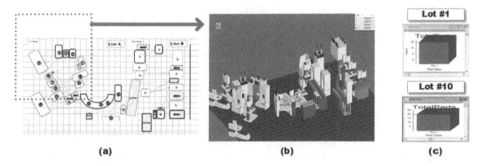

(a)   **(b)**   **(c)**

Fig. 5. Images of the examination of the steel metal processing using our trial system. (a) Layout of the target line, (b) automatic modelling of Worker A's work position, and (c) examination using the proposed visualization tool.

5 Conclusion

This paper proposes a system that makes it possible to automatically generate a DM model from three types of standardized work tables. The system realized the following:

- Generation of a DM model from three types of standardized work table
- Examination of the lot production system
- Determination of operation rates and load ratio on the line model
- Storage of the standardized work tables and the line model
- Storage of the history of operation and examination

These results proved that this system makes it possible to modify the production plan to attain optimization by using DM at a production site.

Semantic Interoperability and Open IoT APIs for Smart Cities Applications

Prodromos Kolyvakis[1(✉)], Christian Mader[2], and Dimitris Kiritsis[1]

[1] École Polytechnique Fédérale de Lausanne (EPFL), Lausanne, Switzerland
{prodromos.kolyvakis,dimitris.kiritsis}@epfl.ch
[2] Fraunhofer Institute for Intelligent Analysis and Information Systems (IAIS),
St. Augustin, Germany
christian.mader@iais.fraunhofer.de

Abstract. As the percentage of the total population living in urban regions is increasing, new challenges for the cities of the future arise. Smart Cities emerged as a solution to these challenges building on the strength of intelligent information, communication technologies and Internet of Things. In this work, we discuss the importance of semantic technologies as well as open IoT APIs for the future Smart Cities applications. Through an illustrative application, we demonstrate that both of the aforementioned technologies ease the computational burden of implementation, foster programming sustainability and create the necessary conditions so as to rapidly harness the available information and extract knowledge out of it. At the same time, the application's implementation lies in accordance with the latest IoT architectural recommendations such as Visual Programming interfaces for Service Composition, conformance with Big Data technologies and the latest IoT programming paradigms.

Keywords: Smart Cities applications · Semantic interoperability
Open APIs

1 Introduction

The percentage of the total population living in urban regions is increasing rapidly, and is estimated to reach 66% in 2050, according to a demographic estimate by the United Nations [19]. This growing mass movement of people to urban areas engenders various challenges for the cities of the future with regard to human health, air pollution, traffic congestion, waste management, etc. [2]. Intelligent information and communication technology (ICT) can tackle these challenges by making use of data from myriads of (end-user) devices connected to the Internet of Things (IoT), as well as existing data sources, with the goal to combine and analyze this data and use the results as a basis for future guidelines and decisions.

© IFIP International Federation for Information Processing 2018
Published by Springer Nature Switzerland AG 2018. All Rights Reserved
I. Moon et al. (Eds.): APMS 2018, IFIP AICT 536, pp. 146–154, 2018.
https://doi.org/10.1007/978-3-319-99707-0_19

By integrating all the aforementioned technologies, the notion of "Smart City" aims at optimizing "the efficiency of city operations and services and connect to citizens" [8]. Nonetheless, while the Smart City innovation brings value to the citizens by fostering sustainability and safeguarding environmental concerns, it creates various research challenges such as interoperability and cross-platform implementation. To enforce interoperability across heterogeneous systems and cross-platform implementations, IoT standards and semantic technologies have been proposed as a solution to simplify interoperability.

In this paper, a Smart City application is introduced, implemented in a way that conforms with the recent trends in IoT interoperability and Smart Cities applications. In parallel, through this application applications, an attempt is made to shed more light on the importance of semantic technologies as well as open IoT APIs for realizing a sustainable Systems-of-Systems ecosystem. The rest of this paper is structured as follows: Sect. 2 introduces the key enabling technologies for Smart Cities and discusses the role that semantic technologies and IoT standards will have to play in future IoT. Section 3 outlines a specific class of applications that we consider prototypical to illustrate the challenges. Section 4 presents the approach and Sect. 5 provides the implementation details. Finally, Sect. 6 closes the paper sketching future work.

2   Related Work

Santana et al. [18] have identified four main enabling technologies that are pervasive across all the state-of-the-art Smart Cities platforms. Specifically, they have identified: *(a)* Internet of Things [4,12], as a network of physical devices and smart objects that will serve as data sources for the various Smart Cities applications; *(b)* Big Data [10] to facilitate the storage and processing of the vast amount of data received by the cities; *(c)* Cloud Computing [3], offering elastic computing capabilities for the plethora of services and data; *(d)* Cyber-Physical Systems [13,21], that enable the interaction between the various systems and the city environment. Nonetheless, for sustaining an open innovation ecosystem for Smart Cities which would build upon the System-of-Systems paradigm, several authors [4,5,9,12] have argued that semantic technologies and open IoT standards constitute one of the catalytic factors that will permit the success and further development of Smart Cities' applications and services. Semantic technologies as well as open IoT communication protocols and data formats ensure an interoperable communication across heterogeneous systems of systems, and constitute a key facilitator for IoT [9,12].

3   Scenario Overview

The application under consideration is to provide a system that recommends citizens a number of places ("points of interest" (POI)) that have better environmental conditions compared to the places where they are currently located. Such a point of interest may, for instance, have higher temperature and lower humidity on a cold winter day and therefore constitutes a better environment for the citizen. The scenario's business value lies in its potential for generalization. Points of interest may also be inferred by taking traffic data into account to identify congested areas. Furthermore, the notion can be extended to areas of interest, warning citizens for instance, of particularly polluted regions or acute security threats. The approach and implementation method we present in this work can also be applied to support these applications.

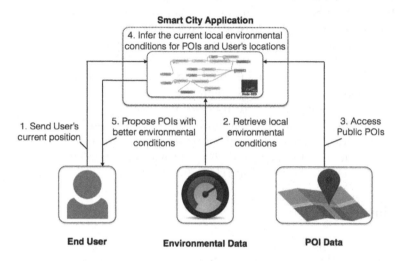

Fig. 1. Overview of the Smart City application.

From a technological perspective, this scenario illustrates how the different enabling technologies that were identified in Sect. 2 can be used to provide solutions to the various Smart Cities challenges. Figure 1 illustrates an overview of the proposed solution. We describe the processing steps by introducing the following scenario:

An end user is interested in finding POIs with better environmental conditions. For that reason, she/he subscribes to implemented Smart City application and accepts to send her/his geo-coordinates (step 1 on Fig. 1). In the next step, the application receives the user data, and in parallel requests for local environmental data (temperature and humidity) and POIs near the region where the user is currently on (steps 2 and 3 on Fig. 1). Based on the retrieved data, the application infers the local environmental conditions for the POIs and the user locations (step 4 on Fig. 1), and sends back the result to the user (step 5 on Fig. 1).

This simplistic scenario can be further be extended to include different kinds of data sources such as traffic data, pollution data, etc. Despite its simplicity, however, it can illustrate various key aspects that Smart Cities applications face. This application scenario includes a variety of different communication transactions across different and heterogeneous data provides (that may include cyber-physical systems) and data consumers. At the same time, the amount of data that the Smart City application receives can quite easily grow significantly enough so that the use of Big Data technologies will be a non-negotiable decision. Similarly, the end users, the environmental data as well as the POI data all provide geo-coordinates information. This raises the importance of sharing a common semantic description of this information so as to facilitate the information integration.

4 Approach

Visual programming languages and frameworks are increasingly used in the IoT era [6]. One typical example is Node-RED[1]; an open source visual programming tool, implemented by the IBM Emerging Technology organization. Node-RED, is based on Node.js and constitutes a mature visual programming framework that has gained large attention by the IoT community. It ships with a large set of nodes ("building blocks") and allows the programing to be performed in a "drag and drop" way. Deployment of programs implemented this way ("flows") in the runtime can be performed with just a single press of a button. In our prototype implementation, Node-RED constitutes a key component of our proposed solution, that allows a *browser-based visual programming* of the Smart Cities applications.

However, the fact that Node-RED is based on JavaScript, restricts the type of computations that can be performed. For instance, although there are programming libraries for performing numerical computations in JavaScript such as stdlib[2], programming languages such as R, Python, Julia [16] are more popular to perform various data-science related tasks. For that reason, the Node-RED environment was extended with a Python node that allows the execution of Python code inside the Node-RED environment. The node acts a proxy to well-known Python modules and libraries such as NumPy [20], SciPy [11], scikit-learn [15], PyTorch [14], as well as frameworks that provide a Python API such as TensorFlow [1].

To allow for the execution of SPARQL queries to be performed in a generic and graphically coherent way, inside the Node-RED environment, we created a Node-RED node and made it publicly available[3]. The implementation is based on the Python node and on the Python RDFlib[4] module. In addition, we use a MongoDB[5] database for storing the sensor data. Semantic technologies and open IoT communication and adherence to data format standards are key for

---

[1] https://nodered.org.
[2] https://stdlib.io.
[3] https://github.com/prokolyvakis/node-red-contrib-sparql.
[4] https://github.com/RDFLib/rdflib.
[5] https://www.mongodb.com.

an interoperable IoT. In particular, the standards O-MI (Open Messaging Interface)[6] and O-DF (Open Data Format)[7], provided by *the Open Group*, were used as they provide a means for standardized communication and data formatting and offer support for semantic annotations. A recent overview of these standards is provided by Robert et al. [17].

5   Implementation and Discussion

We implement the scenario described in Sect. 3 for a specific use case in Lyon, focusing on temperature and humidity as the main characteristics of an individual citizen's environmental situation. To acquire temperature and humidity data for the city of Lyon, the public API of Netatmo[8] is used. Figure 2 illustrates the workflow as implemented in Node-RED. The nodes "Get Netatmo Token" and "Lyon Netatmo" extract temperature and humidity sensor data. To retrieve various points of interest, we make use of the Sophox service[9], which allows the simultaneous execution of queries both to OpenStreetMap and Wikidata. The query is illustrated in Listing 1.

A description of the terms used in OpenStreetMap can be found in [7]. The process is illustrated in the node "OpenStreetMap Query". Finally, all these sensor data are stored in a MongoDB database. To get the citizen's position we use an O-MI call and parse the received response. The process is illustrated in the node "Read O-MI Node" and "Parse O-DF Message". In the next step, the geo-coordinates are extracted ("Extract Geo-coordinates" on Fig. 2) and the closest POIs that have better environmental position than the place that the user currently is are computed ("Find closest POIs"). The aforementioned action is achieved by running a geospatial query on the MongoDB database. Finally, the result is visualized on Node-RED and can be seen on Fig. 3. In Sect. 3, it was briefly discussed how this Smart City application shows the importance of the various Smart Cities enabling technologies that were introduced in Sect. 2. Since the focus of this paper is on the IoT interoperability, we will focus in the rest of this section on the importance of using standardized Open APIs and Semantic technologies for the Smart City Applications. Figure 2 already illustrated different communication transactions and data formats between the different information providers to the Smart City application. To access the temperature and humidity data, the Netatmo's RESTful API was used which provided the sensor data as JSON payloads. In the case that the coverage of these data were inadequate for the user's location under consideration, more sensor solution providers should be considered by the application. The communication layer as well as the data formats of these systems would be different from the ones used by the Netatmo company. What is more, the terms as well as the

---

[6] https://publications.opengroup.org/c14b.

[7] https://publications.opengroup.org/c14a.

[8] https://dev.netatmo.com; Netatmo is a French company specializing on smart product solutions, including smart weather stations, smart smoke detectors.

[9] https://sophox.org/bigdata/.

```
PREFIX osmt:  <https://wiki.openstreetmap.org/wiki/Key:>
PREFIX wd:    <http://www.wikidata.org/entity/>
PREFIX osmm:  <https://www.openstreetmap.org/meta/>

SELECT ?marketLoc ?marketName (?amenity as ?layer) ?osmid
WHERE {
# We are only interested in these types of amenities
        VALUES ?amenity { "kindergarten" "school"
                          "university" "college" }
# Find anything with tag "amenity",
# and that has a name and location
        ?osmid osmt:amenity ?amenity ;
               osmt:name ?marketName ;
               osmm:loc ?marketLoc .
# Get the center of Lyon City from Wikidata
        wd:Q456 wdt:P625 ?myLoc .
# Calculate the distance,
# and filter to just those within 5km
BIND(geof:distance(?myLoc, ?marketLoc) as ?dist)
FILTER(?dist < 5)
}
```

Listing 1. Example of a SPARQL query to extract POIs.

semantics of these different data formats may differ too. For that reason, we have chosen to use the Open Messaging Interface as well as the Open Data Format, provided by the Open Group. These allow the application to access the user's data in a common and standardized way. At the same time, it makes the visual programming easier as the communication across different systems can be achieved with only two nodes. On the contrary, each time a new sensor provider should be taken into account special consideration should be given so as to establish the communication.

Moreover, as it was already mentioned in Sect. 3, a common semantic layer between the different data payloads is extremely important so as to establish a common understanding. For instance, using different terminology and formatting while representing latitude, longitude and altitude information requires an additional programming effort so as to transform them in a common representation. In parallel, semantically annotated data allow for advanced inferencing and for complex queries across different data sources, as it was illustrated in Listing 1. It is important to also note that the key enabler that allowed the information fusion between the knowledge graphs of OpenStreetMap and Wikidata was the common way of representing the geo-coordinates information.

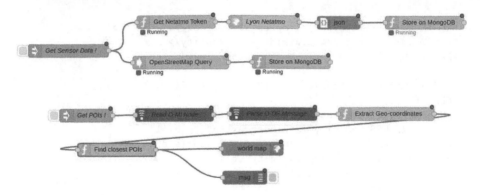

Fig. 2. Node-RED flow of the proposed solution.

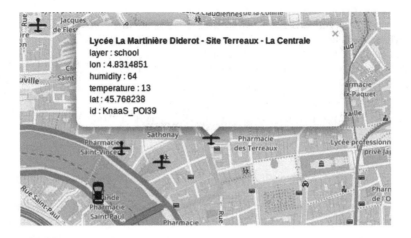

Fig. 3. Visualization of POIs with better environmental conditions.

6 Conclusion and Outlook

Semantic and IoT technologies are among the key enabling technologies to tackle the challenges of future citizens, caused by increasing population in urban areas. In this paper, we presented an approach and documented the implementation of a Smart City application, using a visual programming framework and leveraging heterogeneous data sources that conform to open IoT and semantic Web standards. The application allows evaluating the benefits of these technologies in an IoT context. In our future work we will further validate the approach by covering more advanced applications and data sources, including extensive experimentation and evaluation.

Acknowledgments. This project has received funding from the European Research Council (ERC) under the European Union's Horizon 2020 research and innovation programme (grant agreement No 688203; bIoTope). This paper reflects the authors' view only, and the EU is not responsible for any use that may be made of the information it contains.

References

1. Abadi, M., et al.: TensorFlow: a system for large-scale machine learning. In: Proceedings of the 12th USENIX Symposium on Operating Systems Design and Implementation (OSDI), Savannah, Georgia, USA (2016)
2. Ahvenniemi, H., Huovila, A., Pinto-Seppä, I., Airaksinen, M.: What are the differences between sustainable and smart cities? Cities **60**, 234–245 (2017)
3. Armbrust, M., et al.: A view of cloud computing. Commun. ACM **53**(4), 50–58 (2010)
4. Atzori, L., Iera, A., Morabito, G.: The internet of things: a survey. Comput. Netw. **54**(15), 2787–2805 (2010)
5. Barnaghi, P., Wang, W., Henson, C., Taylor, K.: Semantics for the internet of things: early progress and back to the future. Int. J. Semant. Web Inf. Syst. (IJSWIS) **8**(1), 1–21 (2012)
6. Blackstock, M., Lea, R.: IoT mashups with the WotKit. In: 2012 3rd International Conference on the Internet of Things (IoT), pp. 159–166. IEEE (2012)
7. Codescu, M., Horsinka, G., Kutz, O., Mossakowski, T., Rau, R.: OSMonto - an ontology of OpenStreetMap tags. State of the map Europe (SOTM-EU) (2011)
8. Contributors W: Smart City – Wikipedia, the Free Encyclopedia (2018). https://en.wikipedia.org/w/index.php?title=Smart_city&oldid=830028080. Accessed 12 Mar 2018
9. Främling, K., Kubler, S., Buda, A.: Universal messaging standards for the IoT from a lifecycle management perspective. IEEE Internet Things J. **1**(4), 319–327 (2014)
10. John Walker, S.: Big data: a revolution that will transform how we live, work, and think (2014)
11. Jones, E., Oliphant, T., Peterson, P.: {SciPy}: open source scientific tools for {Python} (2014)
12. Kiritsis, D.: Closed-loop plm for intelligent products in the era of the internet of things. Comput.-Aided Des. **43**(5), 479–501 (2011)
13. Kiritsis, D., Bufardi, A., Xirouchakis, P.: Research issues on product lifecycle management and information tracking using smart embedded systems. Adv. Eng. Inf. **17**(3–4), 189–202 (2003)
14. Paszke, A., et al.: Automatic differentiation in PyTorch (2017)
15. Pedregosa, F., et al.: Scikit-learn: machine learning in Python. J. Mach. Learn. Res. **12**, 2825–2830 (2011)
16. Piatetsky, G.: R, python duel as top analytics, data science software-KDnuggets 2016 software poll results (2016). http://www.kdnuggets.com/2016/06/r-python-topanalytics-data-mining-data-science-software.html
17. Robert, J., Kubler, S., Le Traon, Y., Främling, K.: O-MI/O-DF standards as interoperability enablers for industrial internet: a performance analysis. In: 42nd Annual Conference of the IEEE Industrial Electronics Society, IECON 2016, pp. 4908–4915. IEEE (2016)

18. Santana, E.F.Z., Chaves, A.P., Gerosa, M.A., Kon, F., Milojicic, D.S.: Software platforms for smart cities: concepts, requirements, challenges, and a unified reference architecture. ACM Comput. Surv. (CSUR) **50**(6), 78 (2017)
19. UNPD: World urbanization prospects: The 2014 revision. United Nations Department of Economics and Social Affairs, Population Division, New York (2015)
20. van der Walt, S., Colbert, S.C., Varoquaux, G.: The NumPy array: a structure for efficient numerical computation. Computi. Sci. Eng. **13**(2), 22–30 (2011)
21. White, J., Clarke, S., Groba, C., Dougherty, B., Thompson, C., Schmidt, D.C.: R&d challenges and solutions for mobile cyber-physical applications and supporting internet services. J. Internet Serv. Appl. **1**(1), 45–56 (2010)

Towards a Smart Manufacturing Maturity Model for SMEs (SM³E)

Sameer Mittal[1], David Romero[2], and Thorsten Wuest[1(✉)]

[1] Industrial and Management Systems Engineering,
Benjamin M. Statler College of Engineering and Mineral Resources,
West Virginia University, Morgantown, WV, USA
samittal@mix.wvu.edu, thwuest@mail.wvu.edu
[2] Tecnológico de Monterrey, Monterrey, Mexico
david.romero.diaz@gmail.com

Abstract. This paper proposes a new Smart Manufacturing Maturity Model for small and medium-sized Enterprises (SM³E). The SM³E maturity model supports SMEs during the challenging digital transformation journey and paradigm shift towards Smart Manufacturing and Industry 4.0 on three-axis: (i) organizational dimensions, (ii) toolboxes, and (iii) maturity levels. The SM³E maturity model development was based on a literature and critical review as well as interviews conducted during industrial visits. During these visits, SME specific requirements were collected, assessed and taken into account during the development of the SM³E maturity model. Overall, an analysis of maturity levels, based on the working methods and toolboxes of our SM³E maturity model will help SMEs to progress towards Smart Manufacturing and Industry 4.0.

Keywords: Digitalization · SMEs · Industry 4.0 · Smart manufacturing
Intelligent manufacturing · Maturity model · Working methods
Toolboxes · Toolkit

1 Introduction

Small and Medium-sized Enterprises (SMEs), especially those in the manufacturing sector, have always been considered as the backbone of the economy [1–4] for both developed and developing countries. However, their perspective has not always been taken into account when it comes to the framing of appropriate *Industry 4.0 policies.* Similarly is the case for the *guidelines of Smart Manufacturing Initiatives* in countries such as the U.S. (i.e., Smart Manufacturing), Germany (i.e., Industrie 4.0) and South Korea (i.e., Smart Factory) where specific directions for SMEs are missing [5, 6]. These *SM Initiatives* aim at accelerating the growth of the economy by capitalizing on the new *digital engines of growth* (e.g., connectivity, intelligence, and flexible automation) offered by the Fourth Industrial Revolution (I4). Nevertheless, by not considering the perspective of SMEs, their confined growth might have adverse effects on the overall growth of the economy and creation of true smart global value chains.

Maturity models are capable of identifying a set of "conditions when the examined objects reach the best (perfect) state for their intended purpose" [7]. Although literature

I. Moon et al. (Eds.): APMS 2018, IFIP AICT 536, pp. 155–163, 2018.
https://doi.org/10.1007/978-3-319-99707-0_20

shows several SM/Industry 4.0 maturity models for large enterprises [e.g., 8–16], it fails to present an SME perspective. The organizational dimensions and maturity levels for large enterprises need to be altered to reflect the different requirements of SMEs. Thus far, there are no "self-assessment methods" for SMEs, which support their digital transformation. Therefore, SMEs are often forced to either hire external experts (e.g., consultants or service providers), and thus straining their already limited resources, or slow down their activities to ramp-up their Smart Manufacturing (SM) journey.

This paper is divided into five sections. Section 1 presents the overall research problem. Section 2 identifies the research gap based on current literature and critical review augmented by interviews conducted during industrial visits to SMEs. Section 3 introduces our SM³E maturity model, a three-axis model composed by organizational dimensions, toolboxes and maturity levels. Section 4 presents an exemplary application of the SM³E maturity model's 'cloud/storage toolbox' towards the development of the SM capability 'data-driven decision making'. Section 5 concludes the paper with a summary of the results, limitations and an outlook on future work.

2 Literature Review

The most popular, based on citations, *maturity models* in the literature [8–16] do not sufficiently reflected an *SME specific perspective* and their unique requirements when it comes to adopting the SM/Industry 4.0 paradigm. Table 1 depicts nine current maturity models that mainly cater for large enterprises and do not represent SMEs' specific requirements. Only [10] has partially considered an SME perspective, but falls short in clearly defining 'organizational dimensions', thus making its utilization unrealistic for SMEs. Hence, *organizational dimensions* represent the organizational areas and/or enterprise functions of an organization, and the *maturity levels* provide a stepwise approach towards "maturity" in each of these organizational dimensions [17].

Table 1. Maturity models' dimensions and levels

Paper	Organizational dimensions	Maturity levels	SME persp.
[8]	*Nine* dimensions: strategy, leadership, customers, products, operations, culture, people, governance, and technology	Not defined	Not considered
[9]	*Four* dimensions: organizational maturity, information technology maturity, performance management maturity, and information connectivity maturity	Activity maturing scoring scale based on a task-score of 0 to 9: not performed (0), initial (1), managed (3), defined (5), qualitative (7), optimizing (9)	Not considered
[10]	Not defined	*Three* stage maturity model: initial, managed, and defined	Considered

(*continued*)

Table 1. (*continued*)

Paper	Organizational dimensions	Maturity levels	SME persp.
[11]	*Six* dimensions: strategy and organization, smart factory, smart operations, smart products, data-driven services, and employees	*Six* stage maturity model: outsider, beginner, intermediate, experienced, expert, top performer	Not considered
[12]	*Seven* dimensions: digital business models and customer access, digitization of product and service offerings, digitization and integration of vertical and horizontal value chains, data & analytics as core-capability, agile IT architecture, compliance security, legal and tax, and organization employees and digital culture	*Four* stage maturity model: digital novice, vertical integration, horizontal collaborator, and digital champion	Not considered
[13]	*Four* dimensions: resources, information systems, organization structure and organizational culture	*Six* stage maturity model: computerization, connectivity, visibility, transparency, predictability, and adaptability	Not considered
[14]	*Four* dimensions: information infrastructure, (incl. hard/software), controls & devices (e.g., sensors, actuators, motor controls, switches, and feed & receive data), networks (enabling information exchange), and security policies	*Five* stage maturity model: assessment, secure and upgraded network and controls, defined and organized working data capital, analytics, and collaboration	Not considered
[15]	*Five* dimensions: asset management, data governance, application management, process transformation, and organizational alignment	*Six* level (0–5) maturity model: incomplete, performed, managed, established, predictable, and optimizing	Not considered
[16]	*Three* dimensions: smart products and services, smart business processes, and strategy and organization	*Four* level (0–3) maturity model: absence, existence, survived, and maturity	Not considered

3 Towards a Smart Manufacturing Maturity Model for SMEs

Maturity models often define each of their levels in terms of components and sub-components, and the validity of these elements is mainly confirmed with the help of industrial surveys [18]. This makes *maturity models* a viable option to support manufacturing SMEs towards successfully realizing SM/Industry 4.0 capabilities.

Our proposed *SM³E maturity model* is a three-axis model (see Fig. 1), addresses five key organizational areas and/or enterprise functions of an SME, from now on referred to as *organizational dimensions* (X-axis), includes a modular toolkit composed of seven individual complementary *toolboxes* (Y-axis), which supports a stepwise approach through five *maturity levels* (Z-axis).

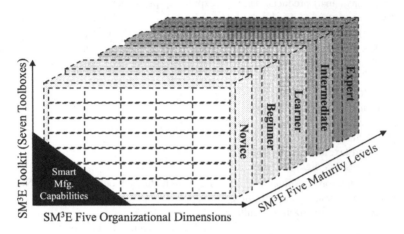

Fig. 1. The Smart Manufacturing Maturity Model for SMEs (SM³E)

By adopting our *SM³E maturity model,* an SME will be able to assess and place itself in one of five maturity levels for each of its five key organizational dimensions. Thus, the SME would be able to identify the input and/or support required to reach the next level of maturity in an organization dimension, which can be provided by dedicated toolboxes. A toolbox enables an SME to perform more sophisticated activities in the respective dimension(s). The next sub-sections detail each of the three-axes of the *SM³E maturity model: organizational dimensions, maturity levels and toolboxes.*

3.1   SM³E Organizational Dimensions

SM is about the connectivity, virtualization, and data utilization of manufacturing systems and beyond. The main focus is on manufacturing operations' performance. However, there are other organizational dimensions, beyond the purely technical ones, that have not yet been included in current maturity models. An example of such non-technical organizational dimensions is "finance". In order to truly support a holistic digital transformation of an enterprise those have to be reflected in the maturity model as well. Hence, in order to provide the best possible support to an SME that is willing to start its *SM journey,* the SME must be holistically informed about all the benefits of achieving the highest maturity level of the respective organizational dimensions. This information will build confidence and motivate the SME to move towards the development of SM/Industry 4.0 capabilities. SMEs have to balance different factors stemming from the evolution of manufacturing systems [19]. We took this into careful consideration when designing the organizational dimensions and sub-dimensions included in the SM³E maturity model (see Table 2). They all were selected based on the alignment with an SME perspective and their specific requirements and are aimed to "mimic" the typical organization structure and basic enterprise functions of a small business for easier adoption by SME managers during the SM journey.

Table 2. Organizational dimensions and sub-dimensions of SM³E maturity model

Dim.	Finance	People	Strategy	Process	Product
Sub-dim.	• Cost-benefit analysis • Budgeting and costs control • Investments risk and returns management	• Leadership • Customer feedback • Safety and ergonomics • Training and education	• Knowledge management • Decision Support/decision making • Standards • Legal/tax policies • Sustainability guidelines • Government regulations	• Quality control • Job scheduling • Repair and maintenance • Machines operation • Flexibility	• Logistics • New product development • Packaging • Modularity • Time to market

Dimension 1: Finance. This dimension is focussing on how the SME is managing its economics (i.e., financial accounting). Existing data is often managed in the form of balance sheets, income statements, cash flow statements, and investment portfolios. Cost-benefit analysis, budgeting, and costs control, as well as investments risk and return management, are the SME's primary concerns (sub-dimensions). In this sense, an *accounting computer-based information system* can provide a transparent and secure method *(data)* to help SMEs to manage their *SM project.*

Dimension 2: People. This dimension considers different organizational and cultural aspects such as an encouraging "leadership" and vision towards SM/Industry 4.0 [8, 20]. An organizational culture that is prepared to learn and evolve as well as to look ahead is positive for employee motivation [9, 11, 13, 15], and "customer feedback" in product development [8]. However, there may be some additional sub-dimensions that organizations need to consider, such as employees "safety and ergonomics" practices in order to have more productive employees and avoid medical expenditure due to occupational accidents. Here, *data* exists in the form of payroll-sheets (e.g., number of employees) and work schedules-sheets (e.g., workhours, shifts), which can help SMEs to better manage the personnel involved in their *SM project.* Moreover, allowing employees to attend workshops and seminars will help them to embrace new working methods and technologies, and up-skill/re-skill themselves (i.e., training and education) for the new Industry 4.0 workplace.

Dimension 3: Strategy. This dimension has been previously discussed in the literature [8, 16]. However, this dimension might overwhelm SMEs since they are more likely to focus on tactics and operations to run their daily business. When it comes to the *SM journey,* the most important 'strategy' for an SME, currently missing in literature, is how to utilize its data strategically (i.e., data/information/knowledge management).

Unlike many large enterprises, SMEs do not have an enormous amount of data readily available. However, SMEs have the versatile expertise of their employees, who often work in different domains and if their experience is augmented by supporting data (i.e., other computer-based enterprise information systems), the SME might be able to make better decisions. Similarly, "decision-making" should involve employees from different areas, rather than just relying on the instinct and limited market research of the SME managers. Moreover, SMEs are not always fully aware of the "industrial standards" they need to obey – e.g., new "legal & tax policies", "sustainability guidelines", and "government regulations" that might benefit their growth (i.e., incentives). Therefore, 'strategy' is another important dimension of our SM^3E model, where data occurs in the form of targets, performance metrics, ranks, etc.

Dimension 4: Process. The steps involved in the transformation of a product from raw material to final product fall under the 'process' organizational dimension. This dimension has been considered by [20] as a key element for measuring the potential of an SME for becoming a smart factory. The key aspects (or sub-dimensions) of this organizational dimension are: "quality control", "job scheduling", "repair and main-tenance", "machines operation", and "flexibility" [21]. Furthermore, *data* exists in the form of process parameters, machine downtimes, etc., documented in manuals and spreadsheets. Therefore, it is important to provide clear instructions to support employees in the execution of the key business processes of a manufacturing SME (i.e., sales, manufacturing, and delivery).

Dimension 5: Product. This organizational dimension includes the business activities (or sub-dimensions) of "logistics", "new product development", "packaging", "product modularity", and "time to market" [21]. In this case, *data* exists in the form of product specifications, the number of products, etc. The 'product' organizational dimension considers product logistics inside and outside the shopfloor environment, the development of new products, and making the product(s) available by reducing the time-to-market.

3.2   SM³E Maturity Levels

The SM^3E model acknowledges the common number of levels in maturity models (e.g., CMMI), and considers the following five levels: (i) *Novice* represents organizations, largely unaware of the SM/Industry 4.0 paradigm, (ii) *Beginner* signifies a recent awareness and basic notion of the SM/Industry 4.0 paradigm, (iii) *Learner* stands for an SME that has started to experiment with SM/Industry 4.0 technologies, (iv) *Intermediate* implies successful pilot projects with SM/Industry 4.0 technologies in different organizational domains, finally (v) *Expert* embodies an SME deploying SM/Industry 4.0 technologies in a strategic way, and therefore it might be referred to as an "SME 4.0".

3.3   SM³E Toolkit (Toolboxes)

A *toolkit* is a set of methods, tools, and practices that can lead towards a final goal [22]. The SM^3E *maturity model toolkit* is composed of *seven toolboxes:* (i) manufacturing/fabrication toolbox, (ii) design and simulation toolbox, (iii) robotics and automation toolbox, (iv) sensors and connectivity toolbox, (v) cloud/storage toolbox, (vi) data analytics toolbox, and (vii) business management toolbox (please read [22] for details on the *SM toolkit*). The rationale behind these seven toolboxes is to include various technologies, skills and business practices that can serve both the technical and managerial aspects required in an SME to adopt the SM/Industry 4.0 paradigm.

4 Exemplary Usage of the SM³E Cloud/Storage Toolbox

Due to pages length limitation, only the application/usage of the *SM³E maturity model's cloud/storage toolbox* will be detailed in this paper as an example. The *toolbox* focuses on "data/information storage support" as an enabler for "data-driven decision making", and it needs different "input requirements" depending on its maturity level like registers, logbooks and spreadsheets (novice), built-in hard drives (beginner), shared hard drives (HDs) (learners), cloud computing (intermediate), and fog computing (expert) in order to create a "data-rich environment" to successfully support decision- making in an *SM environment* (see Table 3).

Table 3. SM³E maturity model's cloud/storage toolbox

Dimension	Novice	Beginner	Learner	Intermediate	Expert
Finance	Store financial data using spreadsheets	Store financial data using hard drives	Store financial data using shared HDs	Store financial data using cloud	Store financial data using fog
People	Store people's data using spreadsheets	Store people's data using hard drives	Store people's data using shared HDs	Store people's data using cloud	Store people's data using fog
Strategy	-	-	-	-	-
Process	Store process data using spreadsheets	Store process data using hard drives	Store process data using shared HDs	Store process data using cloud	Store process data using fog
Product	Store product data using spreadsheets	Store product data using hard drives	Store product data using shared HDs	Store product data using cloud	Store product data using fog

Table 3 illustrates that not all organizational dimensions, in this case 'strategy', are affected by the cloud/storage toolbox. Additionally, some toolboxes may depend on other toolboxes/toolbox to perform their function. For example, the data stored in Table 3 have to be analyzed with the help of *data analytics toolbox* to truly create a "data-driven decision making" capability. The first level (novice) of *data analytics toolbox* is data collection, which is performed by the *cloud/storage toolbox*. The other maturity levels are data cleaning (beginner), data integration (learner), data reduction (intermediate) and data transformation (expert) respectively. These maturity levels are performed utilizing various statistical, optimization, machine learning, and artificial intelligence techniques. In case an SME uses only registers, logbooks and spreadsheets for their data collection, they can only support some short-term decision making processes, like planning for the number of products to be manufactured, the scheduling of workers shifts, etc. They will not be able to know the exact position of their product within the supply chain (i.e., traceability). On the other hand, if they can store data in the cloud (intermediate level), they might be able to get the shared and updated data from their customers, and therefore, they might be able to make better medium- and long-term decisions on the number of products to be produced and the scheduling of workers shifts. Similarly, they may now have the capability to know the location of their products across the supply chain. As an SME shifts towards the 'expert' maturity level, its overall awareness of its operational system increases. Thus, leading to a better, more mature, "data-driven decision making" capability.

5   Results, Limitations and Future Work

This paper introduced our *new SM^3E maturity model* composed of five organizational dimensions, seven toolboxes and five maturity levels aimed at support manufacturing SMEs in their digital transformation towards SM/Industry 4.0.

An exemplary case based on the *SM^3E maturity model's cloud/storage toolbox* was presented to showcase how data is stored and utilized based on the different organizational dimensions and maturity levels. This includes the use of different technologies from the *toolboxes* in order to create a "data-driven decision making" capability for the SME. Furthermore, it was illustrated how the different *SM^3E maturity model's toolboxes* work together, in this case, to enhance the "data-driven decision making" capability in the discussion, i.e., the *data analytics toolbox* with the *cloud/storage toolbox*.

The limitation of this paper is that it presents only one (digital) capability: "data-driven decision making", which can be performed by deploying in this case the cloud/storage toolbox in combination with the data analytical toolbox.

Future work will focus on the refinement and validation with SMEs of the proposed *SM^3E maturity model,* and the later development of the adoption guidelines.

References

1. Husin, M.A., Ibrahim, M.D.: The role of accounting services and impact on SMEs performance in manufacturing sector from east coast region of malaysia: a conceptual paper. Procedia-Soc. Behav. Sci. **115**, 54–67 (2014)
2. Tuyon, J., et al.: The role of microfinance in development of micro enterprises in Malaysia. Bus. Manag. Q. Rev. **2**(3), 47–57 (2011)
3. Jankowska, B., Götz, M., Główka, C.: Intra-cluster cooperation enhancing SMEs' competitiveness - the role of cluster organisations in Poland. Investiga. Reg. **39**, 195–214 (2017)
4. Schiersch, A.: Inefficiency in the German Mechanical Engineering Sector. DIW Berlin, Discussion Paper No. 1949 (2009)

5. Maier, A., Student, D.: Industrie 4.0 - Der Große Selbstbetrug (2015). (in German). http://www.manager-magazin.de/magazin/artikel/digitale-revolution-industrie-4-0-ueberfordert-deutschen-mittelstand-a-1015724.html
6. Balasingham, K.: Industry 4.0: securing the future for german manufacturing companies. Master's thesis, University of Twente (2016)
7. Wendler, R.: The maturity of maturity model research: a systematic mapping study. Inf. Softw. Technol. **54**(12), 1317–1339 (2012)
8. Schumacher, A., Erol, S., Sihn, W.: A maturity model for assessing industry 4.0 readiness and maturity of manufacturing enterprises. Procedia CIRP **52**, 161–166 (2016)
9. Jung, K., Kulvatunyou, B., Choi, S., Brundage, M.P.: An overview of a smart manufacturing system readiness assessment. In: Nääs, I., et al. (eds.) APMS 2016. IAICT, vol. 488, pp. 705–712. Springer, Cham (2016). https://doi.org/10.1007/978-3-319-51133-7_83
10. Ganzarain, J., Errasti, N.: Three stage maturity model in SME's toward Industry 40. J. Ind. Eng. Manag. **9**(5), 1119–1128 (2016)
11. Lichtblau, K., et al.: IMPULS-Industrie 4.0-Readiness. Impuls-Stiftung des VDMA, Aachen-Köln (2015). http://www.impuls-stiftung.de/documents/3581372/4875835/Industrie+4.0+Readniness+IMPULS+Studie+Oktober+2015.pdf/447a6187-9759-4f25-b186-b0f5eac69974
12. Geissbauer, R., Vedso, J., Schrauf, S.: Industry 4.0: Building the Digital Enterprise. Global Industry 4.0 Survey. PricewaterhouseCoopers (PwC), Munich (2016). https://www.pwc.com/gx/en/industries/industries-4.0/landing-page/industry-4.0-building-your-digital-enterprise-april-2016.pdf
13. Schuh, G., Anderl, R., Gausemeier, J., Hompel, M., Wahlster, W.: Industrie 4.0 Maturity Index (2017). http://www.acatech.de/fileadmin/user_upload/Baumstruktur_nach_Website/Acatech/root/de/Publikationen/Projektbeichte/acatech_STUDIE_Maturity_Index_eng_WEB.pdf
14. Rockwell Automation: The Connected Enterprise Maturity Model (2014). http://literature.rockwellautomation.com/idc/groups/literature/documents/wp/cie-wp002_-en-p.pdf
15. Gökalp, E., Şener, U., Eren, P.E.: Development of an assessment model for industry 4.0: industry 4.0-MM. In: Mas, A., Mesquida, A., O'Connor, R.V., Rout, T., Dorling, A. (eds.) SPICE 2017. CCIS, vol. 770, pp. 128–142. Springer, Cham (2017). https://doi.org/10.1007/978-3-319-67383-7_10
16. Akdil, K.Y., Ustundag, A., Cevikcan, E.: Maturity and readiness model for industry 4.0 strategy. In: Ustundag, A., Cevikcan, E. (eds.) Industry 4.0: Managing The Digital Transformation. SSAM, pp. 61–94. Springer, Cham (2018). https://doi.org/10.1007/978-3-319-57870-5_4
17. Pöppelbuß, J., Röglinger, M.: What makes a useful maturity model? A framework of general design principles for maturity models and its demonstration in business process management. In: 19th European Conference on Information Systems, Paper No. 28 (2011)
18. Lasrado, L.A., Vatrapu, R., Andersen, K.N.: Maturity models development in is research: a literature review. In: IRIS Selected Papers of the Information Systems Research Seminar in Scandinavia, vol. 6 (2015)
19. Tao, F., Cheng, Y., Zhang, L., Nee, A.Y.: Advanced manufacturing systems: socialization characteristics and trends. J. Intell. Manuf. **28**(5), 1079–1094 (2017)
20. Lee, J., Jun, S., Chang, T.W., Park, J.: A smartness assessment framework for smart factories using analytic network process. Sustainability **9**(5), 794–808 (2017)
21. Weyer, S., Schmitt, M., Ohmer, M., Gorecky, D.: Towards industry 4.0: standardization as the crucial challenge for highly modular, multi-vendor production systems. IFAC-PapersOnLine **48**(3), 579–584 (2015)
22. Mittal, S., Romero, D., Wuest, T.: Towards a smart manufacturing toolkit for SMEs. In: Proceedings of the 15th International Conference on Product Lifecycle Management (2018)

An Order Control Policy in Crowdsourced Parcel Pickup and Delivery Service

Yuncheol Kang$^{(\boxtimes)}$

Department of Industrial Engineering, Hongik University,
Wausan-ro 94, Mapo-gu, Seoul, South Korea
yckang@hongik.ac.kr

Abstract. Crowdsourced parcel delivery service has progressed dramatically by actively incorporating innovative technologies and ideas. Yet, maximizing profitability of this new type of delivery service becomes another challenge for service providers as market grows. In this paper we study a service order control policy to maximize profitability from a service provider perspective. Specifically, we suggest an order admission control approach that determines acceptance or rejection of an incoming order according to its profitability characteristics. For this, we model the problem as an average reward Semi-Markov Decision Process and utilize reinforcement learning to obtain an optimal order control policy that maximizes overall profitability of a service provider. Through numerical illustrations, we show that our suggested approach outperforms traditional methods, especially when the order arrival rate is high. Thus, smart order management is an important component of parcel pickup and delivery services.

Keywords: Reinforcement learning · Crowdsourced parcel delivery
Planning and decision-makings · Admission control · Smart logistics

1 Introduction

Since emergence of Industry 4.0, a crowdsourced parcel delivery service based on the idea of the sharing economy and just-in-time delivery, a multitude of scholars from different perspectives [1–3] have investigated the utility of this concept. First, crowdsourced parcel delivery is cost efficient in that it uses a shared resource. Second, it can provide more customized services, that is, pickup and delivery at the time a customer specifies. Lastly, it is eco-friendly since fewer vehicles are required to perform the given delivery service, thereby reducing the environmental pollution caused by high volume traffic and oversized delivery vehicles. There are three mainstream transport models that are classified by their type of vehicle: Taxi [4], multi-model, and private vehicle. Among these, the private vehicle is the most flexible and efficient, with the route and ability for pickup and delivery totally dependent on the driver's will. In addition, a private vehicle can support multiple pickup and delivery with less constraints, compared to other transport models. Lee et al. studied a private vehicle routing problem with an integrated decision-making framework that could handle both on-demand parcel delivery and green logistics, such as considering fuel consumption and

I. Moon et al. (Eds.): APMS 2018, IFIP AICT 536, pp. 164–171, 2018.
https://doi.org/10.1007/978-3-319-99707-0_21

gas emissions [5]. In particular, they argue that managing orders in a "smart" way is as important as optimizing operational aspects, such as maximizing profits and minimizing costs occurring in logistics systems. In their study, they assume that the incoming order can be effectively controlled to maximize profitability. Namely, an incoming order that enters a crowdsourced parcel delivery system can be either accepted or declined depending on the profitability associated with that parcel and its delivery. This order control problem maximizes benefits and minimizes costs and is defined and solved through a Markov Decision Process (MDP)-based admission control approach, which decides optimal sequence decisions and whether to include new incoming requests into the appointment schedule [6, 7].

In this paper we focus on optimizing operational costs occurring during conducting on-demand crowdsourced parcel delivery business. Specifically, we use a reinforcement learning approach to effectively manage delivery of orders, thereby maximizing profitability for the delivery business. In the next section, we define a problem that we consider in this paper. Then we suggest a reinforcement learning approach to efficiently solve the problem and illustrate the approach with some numerical examples to reveal the underlying characteristics of the suggested order control algorithm.

2   Problem Definition

To begin with, let us consider a single vehicle routing problem (VRP) with soft time windows and multiple on-demand pickup and delivery constraints. Unlike a traditional VRP problem, we assume that information about traveling locations and due-dates are not known to a service provider in advance. In other words, an order can arrive at any time without prior notice. An order contains information about when and where to travel to pickup and deliver a parcel. Once an order arrives, an order control system decides whether to accept the order with consideration for profitability in executing the order. If the order control system accepts the order request, it then schedules pickup and delivery of the parcel into the routing schedule. For the criteria for determining order acceptance, we consider both vehicle information and parcel information. For vehicle information, we consider the current available capacity and the "busyness" of the current schedule. For parcel information, we consider traveling distance and due-date for pickup and delivery as well as the parcel's load. An order could be rejected due to lack of profitability. If order control rejects the order, it may requote the parcel service. In the following section, we show how this type of problem can be modeled as a sequential decision-making problem, which is an MDP-based model.

3   Model Formulation

From an order control perspective, orders keep arriving at random with random quote conditions. With every order arrival, the order control system needs to decide whether to accept or reject the order. From a modeling perspective, this is a typical form of a sequential decision-making problem formulated as a MDP problem. The classical form of MDP, however, is often intractable. To avoid this difficulty, a reinforcement learning (RL) approach is used to solve the MDP problem, and it is often combined with the function approximation technique, which boosts computational efficiency. In this section we define an MDP model for the problem and RL approach to efficiently solve the model we formulate.

3.1   MDP Model for Order Management

As for the ingredients in the MDP problem, we need to define *state*, *action*, and *reward*. First, a vehicle's information and a parcel's information can be regarded as *state*, denoted as $s \in S := \vartheta \cup \zeta$ where ϑ and ζ represent a set of vehicle information and parcel information, respectively. A set of vehicle information, ϑ, consists of available capacity and "busyness" of the schedule at the current time. A set of parcel information, ζ, consists of due-date and traveling distance for pickup and delivery of the parcel and the load of the parcel. In particular, such parcel information is assumed to be unavailable until the corresponding order arrives, which can be regarded as an *event* in our system. Next, an *action*, denoted by $a \in A$, takes place in reference to an incoming order, that is, acceptance as is or rejection of the order. The best action is determined by comparing the benefits of acceptance with that of rejection. Such benefit is defined as a *reward* in the MDP setting and denoted by r, which is governed by S and A. With all these elements, we want to obtain an optimal policy that maximizes average reward in executing orders over the long run.

Theoretically, such an MDP model can be formulated as Bellman's equation and solved optimally by using several algorithms, such as value iteration, policy iteration, or linear programming in an infinite horizon of decision settings. Practically, however, the MDP model suffers from the curse of dimensionality, that is, solving the model becomes intractable as the size of problem increases. In our case, the combination of possible state ϑ and ζ exceeds 10 million, which is impossible to be solved by using a conventional algorithm. Besides, we assume that an order arrives randomly, and its acceptance will be determined at each arrival point in the system. Therefore, inter-decision time is not consistent; thus, the problem needs to be modeled as Semi-MDP (SMDP), which has more complex computational structures. In the following section, we suggest RL with the function approximation approach to solve this model.

3.2   Reinforcement Learning (RL) Approach

Q-learning, one of the RL approaches, is an iterative learning algorithm that learns from numerous trials by simulating actions, thus obtaining the best policy for a specific situation. Usually, Bellman's equation can be solved optimally using the Q-learning approach. In this paper the original version of the Q-learning approach is tailored for solving an average reward SMDP problem. Bertsekas proves that a regular Markov chain can be transformed into a Markov chain with an artificial terminate state, and the optimal policy of average reward SMDP for both cases is identical. Such a transformed model is called a stochastic shorted path (SSP) problem and is highly tractable, compared to the original problem [8]. This SSP problem can be solved in a Q-learning form as follows:

$$Q(i, a) = (1 - \alpha)Q(i, a) + \alpha \left[r(i, a, j) - \rho t(i, a, j) + \mathbb{I}_{j \neq i^*} \max_{v \in A(j)} Q(j, v) \right] \quad (1)$$

Here $i, j \in S$ and $i^* \in S$ is an artificial terminate state. α stands for a step size for an iterative algorithm. $t(i, a, j)$ stands for sojourn time from the state i to state j, and ρ is an estimated average reward, which is updated iteratively with accumulated reward and time [9]. $\mathbb{I}_{j \neq i^*}$ is 1 when $\neq i^*$, otherwise 0.

Once an order arrives, its acceptance is determined by comparing the Q value of acceptance with the Q value of rejection. If $Q(s, a_{accept})$ is greater than $Q(s, a_{reject})$ then the system accepts the order, otherwise the order is rejected. The difference between the two Q values is defined as the "additional-fee-for-acceptance." In the case of rejection, the "additional-fee-for-acceptance" becomes a positive value, which means the order would be accepted (i.e., the rejection decision overturned) if the customer were to pay an amount greater than or equal to the "additional-fee-for-acceptance" value. This value is denoted as $\delta(s)$ and defined as follows:

$$\delta(s) = \begin{cases} Q(s, a_{reject}) - Q(s, a_{accept}), & \text{if } Q(s, a_{reject}) > Q(s, a_{accept}) \\ 0, & \text{otherwise} \end{cases} \quad (2)$$

Namely, overturning the rejection decision requires $\delta(s)$ as an additional price. If the incoming order is rejected with higher $\delta(s)$, we can argue that the order is less attractive to the service provider. Meanwhile, if the order is rejected with lower $\delta(s)$, the rejected decision may be overturned and the order accepted by slightly changing the quote conditions, which makes the order more attractive.

RL can be more efficient in solving models when it incorporates a function approximation scheme. A popular approximation approach is to utilize an Artificial Neural Network (ANN) to efficiently retrieve and store enormous number pairs consisting of state and action. Although the detailed scheme is not included in this paper due to page limits, interest readers are referred to the relevant literature [8–11].

4 Numerical Illustration

This section describes the order control algorithm suggested in this paper and presents some numerical illustrations. For convenience, we consider a single vehicle routing problem with soft time windows. Since the order planning and route scheduling part is separated, choosing which route scheduling algorithm is trivial, i.e., no matter which route algorithm is used, the planning trend does not change. In this paper, we use the algorithm which was developed for deriving on-demand just-in-time delivery schedules based on the continuous variable feedback control approach [12].

4.1 Experimental Scenarios

In Table 1 we summarize the experimental conditions used for the illustration. All locations and due-date for pickup and delivery are randomly generated under the given condition in Table 1. For representing "busyness" of the schedule, we define the penalty parameter, ξ, as the summation of the deviation between scheduled time and appointment time of all current accepted orders (i.e., earliness or tardiness from the original schedule). Large ξ means the current delivery schedule is far from the original appointed due-date. In that case we impose a high penalty for the order, and this will increase the cost for executing the order, thereby lowering the chances of it being accepted. Here, a cost consists of delivery distance and parcel load, ξ penalty, and due-date. As (1) the vehicle travels longer, (2) due-date is tighter, (3) the current schedule becomes busier (i.e., high level of deviations between scheduled and appointed time) and (4) the parcel is heavier, we assume the cost for carrying the corresponding order increases. The lower and upper bounds related to cost were set at $4.99 and $10, respectively, by referring to the related literature [13].

Table 1. Experimental conditions

Parameter	Value
Arrival rate	Varies from 1 to 10 per minute
Vehicle capacity (lbs)	400
Delivery space	20 mile by 20 mile
Due-date	0.5, 1, 1.5, 2, 4, 6, 8, and 12 h after current time
ξ penalty	No penalty (<0.5 h difference), Light (0.5–1 h difference), Heavy (2> hour difference), Maximum (>3 h difference)
Load of a parcel (lbs)	10, 20, 30, 40

4.2 Experiment Results and Discussions

With RL and all of the conditions mentioned above, we calculated average reward and the ratio of admission when a new order arrives by varying the arrival rate of the order. The detailed results are shown in Table 2. From the results, we could see the average reward increases gradually as the arrival rate increases. Intuitively, this result is reasonable in that we expect more incoming orders as the arrival rate increases, thereby contributing to increased average reward.

Meanwhile, we could also see the ratio of admission tends to be lower as the arrival rate increases, even though average reward increases at that time. This result can be interpreted as our model tending to choose more profitable orders from among the many incoming orders.

For comparison purposes, we consider a simple heuristic algorithm. The rule of the algorithm is that we accept a parcel as long as vehicle capacity remains. Namely, the algorithm only rejects an order when the capacity becomes full. Intuitively, this type of heuristic makes sense in that the worker can easily apply the rule on site. From a simulation result of the algorithm, however, we saw that average reward decreases as the arrival rate increases. If the system follows this rule, the vehicle's capacity becomes full as the arrival rate increases. "Full" capacity means increasing fuel costs, thereby lowering profitability to carry the orders.

Table 2. Average reward and admitted ratio by arrival rate

Arrival rate	Average reward ($)	Admitted ratio
1	1.752317895	1
2	2.030466464	0.605830336
3	1.680257417	0.507339358
4	2.120772918	0.535525655
5	2.464457988	0.208630454
6	3.669486354	0.354101483
7	3.453952971	0.58208095
8	3.133908961	0.541404358
9	4.774441287	0.252209083
10	8.397353574	0.340053004

In terms of "additional-fee-for-acceptance", we plotted three cases that have different arrival rate values (λ = 2, 6, and 10) in Fig. 1. In the case of a low arrival rate (λ = 2), we observe δ does not significantly change across the range of capacity, meaning that the attractiveness of rejecting the order is trivial in most cases. Intuitively, this result makes sense since we may not need to be "choosy" when an order arrives intermittently. Also, we observe low level of δ for the case of low arrival rate, compared to higher arrival cases. Low δ means a minimal additional fee will lead to overturning the rejected decision. In other words, even if an order is rejected for some reason(s), it can be relatively easy to have the order accepted by paying a little more.

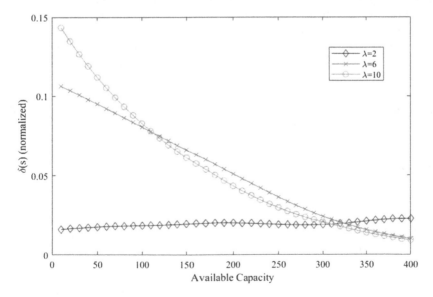

Fig. 1. "Additional-fee-for-acceptance" given available capacity

However, this trend changes when the arrival rate is high ($\lambda = 6$ and 10). In this case a high level of δ is observed at a lower level of remaining capacity, meaning that a rejected order carries a higher fee for the rejection to be overturned and the order to be accepted. Our algorithm becomes "choosy" in accepting an order when available capacity decreases. This can be interpreted as follows: given the case of highly frequent arrival events, if we have little available capacity, the system does not accept any orders since it expects greater profitability will result from order rejection and requoting at a higher price for order acceptance. Meanwhile, if there is enough room to load additional parcels, overturning rejected orders is possible by paying a little more.

5   Conclusion and Future Research

In this paper we study order control for maximizing profitability for a crowdsourced parcel pickup and delivery service. We show how the MDP-based control approach can be applied to this type of problem. We use a tailored RL approach with an adaptation of function approximation to efficiently solve the SMDP problem, which is often intractable in determining optimal policy. From the numerical results we gained some insights on how order control policy behaves as a variety of parameters such as arrival rate or available capacity changes.

Although we consider only two actions for this problem, that is, *accept* or *reject* the parcel, we can further add other types of actions. In particular, in the case of rejecting an order, we regard this as the starting point for negotiating with a customer. In other words, the order control system may suggest that the customer resubmit the order with at least one of the following conditions: (1) select different time slot with greater availability or (2) pay higher price for order. Thus, we may need to guide the customer by presenting different quote conditions until the request can finally be accepted. In addition, this paper only deals with a single vehicle routing problem but can be extended to a multiple vehicle routing problem [14], which represents the future direction of this research.

Acknowledgements. This work was supported by the National Research Foundation of Korea (NRF) grant funded by the Korea government (MSIP) (No. 2017R1C1B1005354).

References

1. Wang, G., Gunasekaran, A., Ngai, E.W., Papadopoulos, T.: Big data analytics in logistics and supply chain management: certain investigations for research and applications. Int. J. Prod. Econ. **176**, 98–110 (2016)
2. Davenport, T.H., Glaser, J.: Just-in-time delivery comes to knowledge management. Harv. Bus. Rev. **80**, 107–111 (2002)
3. Lai, K., Cheng, T.E.: Just-In-Time Logistics. Routledge, Abingdon (2016)
4. Li, B., Krushinsky, D., Reijers, H.A., Van Woensel, T.: The share-a-ride problem: People and parcels sharing taxis. Eur. J. Oper. Res. **238**, 31–40 (2014)
5. Lee, S., Kang, Y., Prabhu, V.V.: Smart logistics: distributed control of green crowdsourced parcel services. Int. J. Prod. Res. **54**, 6956–6968 (2016)

6. Wu, C.-H., Chien, W.-C., Chuang, Y.-T., Cheng, Y.-C.: Multiple product admission control in semiconductor manufacturing systems with process queue time (PQT) constraints. Comput. Ind. Eng. **99**, 347–363 (2016)
7. Kim, C., Dudin, S.: Priority tandem queueing model with admission control. Comput. Ind. Eng. **61**, 131–140 (2011)
8. Bertsekas, D.P., Tsitsiklis, J.N.: Neuro-dynamic programming: an overview. In: Proceedings of the 34th IEEE Conference on Decision and Control, pp. 560–564. IEEE (1995)
9. Gosavi, A.: Simulation-based optimization: an overview. In: Gosavi, A. (ed.) Simulation-Based Optimization. ORSIS, vol. 55, pp. 29–35. Springer, Boston, MA (2015). https://doi.org/10.1007/978-1-4899-7491-4_3
10. Sutton, R.S., Barto, A.G.: Reinforcement Learning: An Introduction, 2nd edn. MIT Press, Cambridge (2017)
11. Bertsekas, D.P.: Dynamic Programming and Optimal Control. Athena Scientific, Belmont (1995)
12. Lee, S., Prabhu, V.V.: Just-in-time delivery for green fleets: a feedback control approach. Transp. Res. Part Transp. Environ. **46**, 229–245 (2016)
13. Rougès, J.-F., Montreuil, B.: Crowdsourcing delivery: new interconnected business models to reinvent delivery. In: 1st International Physical Internet Conference, pp. 1–19 (2014)
14. Kafle, N., Zou, B., Lin, J.: Design and modeling of a crowdsource-enabled system for urban parcel relay and delivery. Transp. Res. Part B Methodol. **99**, 62–82 (2017)

Node and Edge Surveillance Using Drones Considering Required Camera Altitude and Battery Charging

Ivan Kristianto Singgih[1,2], Jonghwa Lee[1], and Byung-In Kim[1(✉)]

[1] Department of Industrial and Management Engineering,
Pohang University of Science and Technology (POSTECH),
Pohang, Republic of Korea
{ivanksinggih, jet226, bkim}@postech.ac.kr
[2] Department of Industrial Engineering,
Sepuluh Nopember Institute of Technology, Surabaya, Indonesia

Abstract. In this study, a drone routing problem is studied, in which several drones are used to perform an initial surveillance on an area after a disaster. During the surveillance, observations are performed by taking photos of nodes representing populated areas and road segments in the network using cameras installed on the drones from two different altitudes. More target nodes and edges can be observed by the drones from the higher altitude, but with low photo quality, while high photo quality can be obtained from the lower altitude, but within a smaller observation range. Each drone has a limited battery capacity and may need to return to the base for charging. Developed methods for the well-known arc-routing and vehicle routing problems cannot be directly used to solve the considered problem. This study aims to route the drones efficiently to perform the observation and satisfy the required photo quality for all target nodes and edges, while minimizing the total time required to perform the surveillance. This paper is the first study which considers the multiple-drone routing problem with different flying altitudes and battery charging process. The problem is formulated as a mixed integer programming model and numerical experiments are provided. Various important future research topics in this drone surveillance routing problem are also identified, which are necessary for providing basics for the development of algorithms to deploy the drones efficiently.

Keywords: Drone routing · Battery charging · Altitude · Photo quality Surveillance

1 Introduction

In this study, a multiple drone node-and-arc-routing problem is investigated. In the problem, each of the target nodes and edges must be observed by taking photos with low or high quality photo using drones. The target nodes and edges can be observed by drones at two altitudes [1]. Flying at the lower altitude allows the drones to obtain photos with high quality, but within a smaller observation range. Meanwhile, flying at the higher altitude restrict the drones to only produce observation photos with low

I. Moon et al. (Eds.): APMS 2018, IFIP AICT 536, pp. 172–180, 2018.
https://doi.org/10.1007/978-3-319-99707-0_22

quality, but allows the drones to capture more target nodes and edges. Performing observations of target nodes and edges at appropriate altitudes can reduce the total surveillance times and this is important in this post-disaster surveillance.

The problem is related to the arc routing problems, which have been studied by many researches including [2–5]. However, only few papers including [1, 6, 7] have studied drone observation at multiple altitudes. Waharte and Trigoni [1] and Zorbas et al. [7], the most related researches, proposed heuristic algorithms to perform search and rescue operations using drones and studied an optimal drone placement to minimize the cost while assuring the complete surveillance of all targets.

Different with the previous researches, we explicitly consider the drone routing problem at two altitudes by modeling all drone movements throughout the network. This paper is the first study on the drone routing problem at two altitudes for observing nodes and edges, which considers required observation quality and battery recharging. This paper focuses on introducing this new routing problem, in which different altitudes of drone flying determine the captured photo quality. This problem is different from well-known arc routing problem and vehicle routing problem because in those previous problems, any target node or edge requires direct visit, whereas the considered problem of this paper assumes that target nodes and edges require indirect visit (camera watching) and multiple observations of nodes and edges are possible from a single point visit. In addition, changing the flying altitude allows to change the observed area, which allows faster surveillance process.

This paper is organized as follows: The problem is defined in Sect. 2. The mathematical model is presented in Sect. 3. Numerical experiments are presented in Sect. 4. Finally, conclusions are given in Sect. 5.

2 Problem Definition

In this study, a network (S, E) is considered, where $S = \{1, 2, \ldots, \psi\}$ and $E = \{1, 2, \ldots, e\}$ represent the sets of target nodes and edges on the ground that must be observed. In a disaster area, the nodes to be observed in S are distribution centers, residential area, and road intersections. The edges in E are roads connecting the nodes. After a disaster occurrence, it is necessary to deliver supplies from the distribution centers to the residential areas. It is necessary to perform the surveillance on the nodes in order to assess the availability of the supplies at the distribution centers, the magnitude of disaster at residential areas along with the number of people in those area, and the possibility to use the roads and intersections in the post-disaster period. The surveillance is performed by taking photos using several drones. Photos with high quality must be captured for important nodes and edges, while other nodes and edges with less importance can be observed using photos with low quality.

The drones travel on a network (N, A), where N is the set of the depot and points, and A is the set of arcs. Set N includes the depot indices (0 for start depot and $2s + 1$ for end depot), a set of drone observation points at the lower altitude ($S_{low} = \{1, 2, \ldots, s\}$), and another set of drone observation points at the higher altitude $\left(S_{high} = \{s+1, s+2, \ldots, 2s\}\right)$. Observation points in S_{low} and S_{high} have the same horizontal positions with the target nodes on the ground. The set of arcs, A, includes a set of arcs for observation at lower altitude (E_{low}), a set of arcs for observation at higher altitude (E_{high}), arcs connecting both depot indices, arcs connecting each depot index with each observation point, and arcs connecting observations points at different altitudes.

Observations using drones are performed at two altitudes with different sizes of covered areas, as shown in Fig. 1. Travelling at a lower altitude allows the drones to observe less number of target nodes and edges, and drone movements at a higher altitude enable the drones to observe more number of target nodes and edges. The observation of some target edges may not be possible from any point. In that case, drones are required to flight through arcs above them to perform the observation. The required photo quality for each target node and edge must be satisfied. The total observation time must be minimized while each drone's flight duration is limited by its battery level.

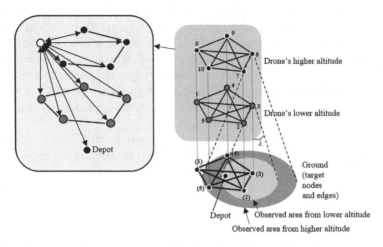

Fig. 1. Drone observation at two altitudes with different sizes of covered areas.

3 Mixed Integer Programming Model

The problem is formulated as a mixed integer programming (MIP) model as follows:

Sets:

K set of drone routes, $K = \{1, 2, \ldots, ld\}$

R set of individual drones, $R = \{1, 2, \ldots, l\}$

O_i set of target nodes covered when a drone performs the observation at point i, $i \in S_{low} \cup S_{high}, O_i \subset S$

P_i set of target edges covered when a drone performs the observation at point i, $i \in S_{low} \cup S_{high}, P_i \subset E$

π_{ij} set of target edges covered when a drone performs the observation at arc(i, j) at the higher altitude, $(i, j) \in E_{low}, \pi_{ij} \subset E$

μ_{ij} set of target edges covered when a drone performs the observation at arc(i, j) at the higher altitude, $(i, j) \in E_{high}, \mu_{ij} \subset E$

Parameters:
b battery charging time at the depot
d maximum possible number of routes per individual drone
$f_{0,k}$ initial battery level of a drone for route k at depot 0
g_{ij} reduced battery level during movement from depot or point i to depot or point j
q_h 1, if the required photo quality captured for node h is high; 0, otherwise, $h \in S$
r_{qy} 1, if the required photo quality captured for edge (q,y) is low; 0, otherwise, $(q,y) \in E$
t_{ij} required time for a drone to travel from depot or point i to depot or point j, $i \in N \backslash \{2s+1\}, j \in N \backslash \{0\}$

Decision variables:
a_{ik} the arrival time of a drone in route k at the depot or point i
c_{qy} 1, if edge (q,y) is covered by a drone observation at its higher altitude; 0, otherwise, $(q,y) \in E$
f_{ik} the battery level of a drone in route k at the depot or point i
m_{qy} 1, if edge (q,y) is covered by a drone observation at its lower altitude; 0, otherwise, $(q,y) \in E$
n_{qy} 1, if edge (q,y) is covered by a drone visit to any depot or point at the higher altitude; 0, otherwise, $(q,y) \in E$
u_h 1, if the photo quality captured for node h is high; 0, otherwise, $h \in S$
v_{qy} 1, if the photo quality captured for edge (q,y) is high; 0, otherwise, $(q,y) \in E$
w_{qy} 1, if edge (q,y) is covered by a drone visit to any depot or point at the lower altitude; 0, otherwise, $(q,y) \in E$
x_{ijk} 1, if a drone travels from stop i to stop j in route k; 0, otherwise, $i \in N \backslash \{2s+1\}, j \in N \backslash \{0\}, i \neq j$
z the latest arrival time of drones at depot $2s+1$
α_h 1, if node h is covered by any drone; 0, otherwise, $h \in S$
β_{qy} 1, if edge (q,y) is covered by any drone; 0, otherwise, $(q,y) \in E$
γ_{ih} 1, if node h is covered by a drone visit at point i at the lower altitude; 0, otherwise, $i \in S_{low}, h \in S$
δ_{ih} 1, if node h is covered by a drone visit at point i at the higher altitude; 0, otherwise, $i \in S_{high}, h \in S$
ε_{iqy} 1, if edge (q,y) is covered by a drone visit at point i at the lower altitude; 0, otherwise, $i \in S_{low}, (q,y) \in E$
θ_{iqy} 1, if edge (q,y) is covered by a drone visit at point i at the higher altitude; 0, otherwise, $i \in S_{high}, (q,y) \in E$

The formulated MIP is as follows:

$$\min \ z \tag{1}$$

$$\text{s.t. } \gamma_{ih} \geq x_{ijk}, \quad \forall i \in S_{low}, j \in N \backslash \{0\}, k \in K, h \in O_i \tag{2}$$

$$\gamma_{ih} \geq x_{jik}, \quad \forall i \in S_{low}, j \in N \backslash \{2s+1\}, k \in K, h \tag{3}$$

$$\sum_k \left(\sum_{j \in N \backslash \{0\}} x_{ijk} + \sum_{j \in N \backslash \{2s+1\}} x_{jik} \right) \geq \gamma_{ih}, \quad \forall i \in S_{low}, h \in O_i \tag{4}$$

$$\gamma_{ih} = 0, \quad \forall i \in S_{low}, h \in S - O_i \tag{5}$$

$$u_h \geq \gamma_{ih}, \quad \forall h \in S, i \in S_{low} \tag{6}$$

$$\sum_{i \in S_{low}} \gamma_{ih} \geq u_h, \quad \forall h \in S \tag{7}$$

$$\alpha_h \geq u_h, \quad \forall h \in S \tag{8}$$

$$u_h + \sum_{i \in S_{high}} \delta_{ih} \geq \alpha_h, \quad \forall h \in S \tag{9}$$

$$\varepsilon_{iqy} \geq x_{ijk}, \quad \forall i \in S_{low}, j \in N \backslash \{0\}, k \in K, (q,y) \in P_i \tag{10}$$

$$\varepsilon_{iqy} \geq x_{jik}, \quad \forall i \in S_{low}, j \in N \backslash \{2s+1\}, k \in K, (q,y) \in P_i \tag{11}$$

$$\sum_k \left(\sum_{j \in N \backslash \{0\}} x_{ijk} + \sum_{j \in N \backslash \{2s+1\}} x_{jik} \right) \geq \varepsilon_{iqy}, \quad \forall i \in S_{low}, (q,y) \in P_i \tag{12}$$

$$\varepsilon_{iqy} = 0, \quad \forall i \in S_{low}, (q,y) \in E - P_i \tag{13}$$

$$w_{qy} \geq \varepsilon_{iqy}, \quad \forall (q,y) \in E, i \in S_{low} \tag{14}$$

$$\sum_{i \in S_{low}} \varepsilon_{iqy} \geq w_{qy}, \quad \forall (q,y) \in E \tag{15}$$

$$m_{qy} \geq x_{ijk}, \quad \forall (i,j) \in E_{low}, (q,y) \in \pi_{ij}, k \in K \tag{16}$$

$$\sum_k \sum_{(i,j);(q,y) \in \pi_{ij}} x_{ijk} \geq m_{qy}, \quad \forall (i,j) \in E_{low} \tag{17}$$

$$v_{qy} \geq w_{qy}, \quad \forall (q,y) \in E \tag{18}$$

$$v_{qy} \geq m_{qy}, \quad \forall (q,y) \in E \tag{19}$$

$$w_{qy} + m_{qy} \geq v_{qy}, \quad \forall (q,y) \in E \tag{20}$$

$$\beta_{qy} \geq v_{qy}, \quad \forall (q,y) \in E \tag{21}$$

$$\beta_{qy} \geq w_{qy}, \quad \forall (q,y) \in E \tag{22}$$

$$\beta_{qy} \geq m_{qy}, \quad \forall (q,y) \in E \tag{23}$$

$$v_{qy} + n_{qy} + c_{qy} \geq \beta_{qy}, \quad \forall (q,y) \in E \tag{24}$$

$$\alpha_h \geq 1, \quad \forall h \in S \tag{25}$$

$$\beta_{qy} \geq 1, \quad \forall (q,y) \in E \tag{26}$$

$$u_h \geq q_h, \quad \forall h \in S \tag{27}$$

$$v_{qy} \geq r_{qy}, \quad \forall (q,y) \in E \tag{28}$$

$$\sum_{j \in N \setminus \{0\}} x_{0,j,k} = 1, \quad \forall k \in K \tag{29}$$

$$\sum_{i \in N \setminus \{2s+1\}} x_{i,2s+1,k} = 1, \quad \forall k \in K \tag{30}$$

$$\sum_{i \in N \setminus \{2s+1\}} x_{imk} - \sum_{j \in N \setminus \{0\}} x_{mjk} = 0, \quad \forall k \in K, m \in S_{low} \cup S_{high} \tag{31}$$

$$a_{ik} + t_{ij} \leq a_{jk} + M(1 - x_{ijk}), \quad \forall i \in N \setminus \{2s+1\}, j \in N \setminus \{0\}, k \in K \tag{32}$$

$$z \geq a_{2s+1,k}, \quad \forall k \in K \tag{33}$$

$$f_{ik} - g_{ij} \geq f_{jk} - M(1 - x_{ijk}), \quad \forall i \in N \setminus \{2s+1\}, j \in N \setminus \{0\}, k \in K \tag{34}$$

$$a_{2s+1,r+wl} + b \leq a_{0,r+(w+1)l}, \quad \forall r \in R, w \in \{0,1,\ldots,d-1\} \tag{35}$$

$$f_{ik}, a_{ik} = \text{positive integer} \tag{36}$$

$$c_{qy}, m_{qy}, n_{qy}, v_{qy}, w_{qy}, \beta_{qy}, u_h, \alpha_h, x_{ijk}, \gamma_{ih}, \delta_{ih}, \varepsilon_{iqy}, \theta_{iqy} = \text{binary} \tag{37}$$

The objective function (1) minimizes the total time required to perform observations of all nodes and edges. Constraints (2)–(7) assure photo quality captured at each node and constraints (15)–(25) ensure photo quality captured at each edge. In order to check whether target nodes are observed from points at the higher altitude, some constraints are written as same as Constraints (2)–(6), except that γ_{ih} is replaced with δ_{ih} and S_{low} with S_{high}. These constraints together with Constraints (2)–(9) and (25) ensure that each node is observed by at least one drone. In order to check whether target edges are observed from points at the higher altitude, some other constraints are written as same as Constraints (10)–(17) and Constraint (22)–(23), respectively, except that ε_{iqy} is replaced with θ_{iqy}, w_{qy} with n_{qy}, m_{qy} with c_{qy}, π_{ij} with μ_{ij}, S_{low} with S_{high}, and E_{low} with E_{high}. These constraints with Constraints (10)–(24) and (26) enforce that each edge is observed by at least one drone. Constraints (27) and (28) restrict that the requested photo quality at each target node and edge must be satisfied. Constraints (29) and (30) indicate that each drone should start and finish its travel at the depot.

Constraints (31) are the flow conservation constraints. Constraints (32) update the arrival time of drone k at depot or point j if the drone travels from depot or point i to depot or point j. Constraints (33) obtain the completion time of all drone operations. Constraints (34) measure the battery level of drone k after its travel from depot or point i to depot or point j. Constraints (35) ensure that the next departure time of drone k is larger than its previous arrival time at depot and its required battery charging time. Constraints (36)–(37) are the binary and integer constraints.

4   Numerical Experiments

In this study, advantages of considering two altitudes for drone movements (LH case) are shown by contrasting it with their movements in the lower altitude only (L case), in which observations with high quality are assured. Comparison with cases in which the drones only travel at the higher altitude is not considered because in this case, the drones can only obtain photos with low quality and more travel time is required to visit the points at the higher altitude. Moreover, this case is already considered as a part of the LH case.

Two data sets with different characteristics are considered. Each data set consists of five instances. In the first and second data sets, four and five target nodes are observed, as shown in Table 1. In both sets, two drones are considered and each drone can travel twice. Required photo qualities for nodes and edges are randomly generated. Target points and edges that can be observed from points are preset. It is assumed that a drone travels through an arc can observe the target edge below the travelled arc. Networks of target nodes and edges, and drones' travels for Instance 10 are presented in Fig. 1.

Parameters used in both experiments are listed as follows: λ in Fig. 1 is 60° [7] and $f_{0,k}$ is 360 min [8]. The drones are considered to fly at 44 m and 70 m altitudes in order to perform observations on target nodes within a spherical area with radius of 14 and 22 m from the observation point, as shown in Fig. 1. Values for q_h, r_{qy}, and t_{ij} are randomly generated between 0 and 1, 0 and 1, and [7, 27] minutes, meanwhile values for g_{ij} are assumed to be equivalent with t_{ij}. Value of b is set to 1 min. The MIP solutions are obtained using CPLEX 12.6.0. All experiments were performed on an Intel® Core™ i5-6400 CPU at 2.70 GHz with 8 GB RAM. Computational time for each instance is limited to 30 min. The experiment results are presented in Table 2. It is necessary to understand that optimal solutions in L cases are only optimal for the cases in which the lower altitude in the drone network is considered. In LH cases, drones visit more points at the higher altitude, which allows the drones to observe more target nodes and edges and reduces the total required travel times to observe all target nodes and edges, while satisfying the required photo qualities for target nodes and edges. The advantage of performing observation in lower and higher altitudes to reduce the total observation time is proven, with average gap equal to −4.6%, compared when the observations are performed only at lower altitude.

Table 1. Parameter settings for data sets

Data set	Set of target nodes	Set of depot indices	Set of observation points at lower altitude	Set of observation points at higher altitude
Data set 1 (Instances 1–5)	{1, 2, 3, 4}	{0, 9}	{1, 2, 3, 4}	{5, 6, 7, 8}
Data set 2 (Instances 6–10)	{1, 2, 3, 4, 5}	{0, 11}	{1, 2, 3, 4, 5}	{6, 7, 8, 9, 10}

Table 2. Experiment results

Instances	L	LH	Gap(%)
1	93(Optimal)	93(UB), 1(LB)	0
2	163(Optimal)	163(UB), 1(LB)	0
3	155(Optimal)	147(UB), 1(LB)	−5.2
4	95(Optimal)	95(UB), 1(LB)	0
5	112(Optimal)	112(UB), 1(LB)	0
6	165(Optimal)	165(UB), 1(LB)	0
7	285(UB), 175(LB)	185(UB), 1(LB)	−35.1
8	136(Optimal)	145(UB), 1(LB)	6.6
9	126(Optimal)	126(UB), 1(LB)	0
10	165(Optimal)	145(UB), 1(LB)	−12.1
Average			−4.6

5 Conclusions

In this study, a multiple drone routing problem at two different altitudes are discussed. The drones perform observations of target nodes and edges that require minimum or maximum photo qualities. In addition, the drones have limited battery level and need to return to depot for a battery charging process. The objective was to minimize the total observation times. An MIP model was developed. Experiment results show the advantages of performing observations at two altitudes instead of only at the lower altitude. Efficient heuristic algorithms will be developed in the near future.

For further researches related with drone routing, a drone network design problem is necessary to be studied. In this drone network design, various decision variables can be considered, such as observation altitudes and horizontal positions of the observation points at each altitude. Finding the best observation altitude is also necessary to determine the best observation range and the appropriate altitude that allow the drones to visit those points, while performing the observations in a short time. Possible collisions between the drones must be avoided, especially if the visited points are located close to each other.

References

1. Waharte, S., Trigoni, N.: Supporting search and rescue operations with UAVs. In: Proceedings of the International Conference on Emerging Security Technologies, pp. 142–147. IEEE Computer Society, Washington (2010). https://doi.org/10.1109/est.2010.31
2. Damodaran, P., Krishnamurthi, M., Srihari, K.: Lower bounds for hierarchical chinese postman problem. Int. J. Ind. Eng. 15(1), 36–44 (2008)
3. Prins, C., Labadi, N., Reghioui, M.: Tour splitting algorithms for vehicle routing problems. Int. J. Prod. Res. 47(2), 507–535 (2009). https://doi.org/10.1080/00207540802426599
4. Liu, T., Jiang, Z., Geng, N.: A memetic algorithm with iterated local search for the capacitated arc routing problem. Int. J. Prod. Res. 51(10), 3075–3084 (2013). https://doi.org/10.1080/00207543.2012.753165
5. Chen, L., Chen, B., Bui, Q.T., Hà, M.H.: Designing service sectors for daily maintenance operations in a road network. Int. J. Prod. Res. 55(8), 2251–2265 (2017). https://doi.org/10.1080/00207543.2016.1233363
6. Symington, A., Waharte, S., Julier, S., Trigoni, N.: Probabilistic target detection by camera-equipped UAVs. In: Proceedings of 2010 IEEE International Conference on Robotics and Automation, pp. 4076–4081. IEEE, Alaska (2010). https://doi.org/10.1109/robot.2010.5509355
7. Zorbas, D., Pugliese, L.D.P., Razafindralambo, T., Guerriero, F.: Optimal drone placement and cost-efficient target coverage. J. Netw. Comput. Appl. 75, 16–31 (2016). https://doi.org/10.1016/j.jnca.2016.08.009
8. Donateo, T., Ficarella, A., Spedicato, L., Arista, A., Ferraro, M.: A new approach to calculating endurance in electric flight and comparing fuel cells and batteries. Appl. Energy 187, 807–819 (2017). https://doi.org/10.1016/j.apenergy.2016.11.100

How to Choose the Greenest Delivery Plan: A Framework to Measure Key Performance Indicators for Sustainable Urban Logistics

Adriana Giret[1]([✉]), Vicente Julián[1], Juan Manuel Corchado[2],
Alberto Fernández[3], Miguel A. Salido[1], and Dunbing Tang[4]

[1] Universitat Politècnica de València, Valencia, Spain
agiret@dsic.upv.es
[2] Universidad de Salamanca, Salamanca, Spain
[3] Universidad Rey Juan Carlos, Madrid, Spain
[4] Nanjing University of Aeronautics and Astronautics, Nanjing, China

Abstract. The sustainability of urban logistics is an important issue for rapidly growing cities worldwide. Although many cities and research works have developed strategies to move people more efficiently and safely within the urban environment, much less attention has been paid to the importance of optimizing the delivery of goods to people at work and home taking into account sustainable goals. In this work we propose a framework that aids to register and measure a set of sustainable Key Performance Indicators (KPIs) for delivery routes and plans in urban zones. The approach is general and based on a set of well defined KPIs from the specialized research field.

Keywords: Urban logistics · Green supply chains · KPIs

1 Introduction

Urban logistics [1] is essential to the functioning of modern urban economies. Cities are places of consumption relying on frequent deliveries of groceries and retail goods, express deliveries to businesses, and a fast-growing home delivery market. European cities (as most of worldwide cities) are forced to tackle a wide range of urban traffic problems: first of all the big challenge of reducing traffic congestions, CO2, pollutant emissions, and energy consumption. According to the European Environment Agency, cities emit 69% of Europe's CO2 and urban transport accounts for 70% of the pollutants and 40% of the greenhouse gas emissions from European road transport (European Environment Agency). On the other hand, cities have to guarantee to citizens not only the overall accessibility to the different city and transport services, but also an efficient urban logistic with respect to the economic and environmental factors. According to

© IFIP International Federation for Information Processing 2018
Published by Springer Nature Switzerland AG 2018. All Rights Reserved
I. Moon et al. (Eds.): APMS 2018, IFIP AICT 536, pp. 181–189, 2018.
https://doi.org/10.1007/978-3-319-99707-0_23

this, the Transport Policy White Paper[1] set up the CO2 free urban logistics as one of the 10 objectives to reach by the 2030. The EU guidelines for "Developing and Implementing a Sustainable Urban Mobility Plan", aims to provide realistic and simple guidelines for city stakeholders and technicians, for developing a Sustainable Urban Logistics Plan focused on the optimization of urban logistics processes in order to reduce the related energy consumption and environmental impacts yielding its economic sustainability.

There is today a considerably growing consensus on the idea that more sustainable urban logistic operations and significant benefits in terms of energy efficiency can be achieved by an appropriate mix of different measures such as: urban consolidation centres, optimized urban logistic transport and delivery plans, use of clean vehicles and low emission technologies, focused regulation framework, public incentive/qualification policies, last mile and value added services, integration of city logistics processes within the overall urban mobility planning and management. To aid in these measures and focusing mainly on delivery plans in this paper a framework for scoring sustainable plans is proposed. Our work is motivated on the need to register and measure Key Performance Indicators (KPIs) that can help stakeholders and practitioners to mark and select those urban logistic delivery plans that optimizes sustainable goals.

2 Sustainable Urban Logistic and How to Measure Its Performance

Cities are places of consumption, production, and distribution of material goods. Urban logistics [1] includes all activities ensuring that the material demands of these activities are satisfied. It includes all goods movements generated by the economic needs of local businesses, that is, all deliveries and collection of supplies, materials, parts, consumables, mail and refuse that businesses require to operate [4]. As a city hosts a great number of different economic sectors, it is provisioned by hundreds of different supply chains, making urban logistics very complex and diverse. Over the past two decades delivering goods into cities has become a challenge with cities getting overly congested and traffic jams resulting in expensive logistics bottlenecks. Studies show that the cost of congestion now in terms of time wasted in traffic and fuel consumption is very high, almost 200% more than what it was in the 1980s. Pollution, lack of parking bays, and warehousing costs are all restraints that are contributing to the economic cost of urban logistics.

The concept of Sustainable Urban Logistic (or Sustainable Last Mile Logistic) is closely related with that of Sustainable Supply Chains. A Sustainable Supply Chain is one that performs well on both traditional measures of profit and loss as well as on an expanded conceptualization of performance that includes social and natural dimensions [8]. In the specialized literature a large number

---

[1] https://www.eesc.europa.eu/sites/default/files/resources/docs/pp-white-paper-transport-may16-en.pdf.

Table 1. Sustainable urban logistics' key performance indicators [6]

Urban logistics KPIs		
Economic dimension	Environmental dimension	Social/societal dimensions
Service rate	Greenhouse gas emission rate	Inhabitants satisfaction rates
Logistics costs	Energy consumption	Employment creation rates
Customers' satisfaction rate	Congestion	Reclamation rate
Number of vehicles	Noise level	
Delivery times		
Economic viability rates		
Number of deliveries		
Economic savings		
Number of delivery platforms		
Delay rates		
Vehicles' loading rates		
Maintenance rates		
Number of ruptures of charge		
Time delay due to congestion		

of works related with measuring the economic performance of logistics solutions can be found. Nevertheless, less works that mix all the aspects of sustainable logistics were reported. Among the few, but interesting, works found in the literature we base our study on the list of 21 indicators proposed by Morana in [6]. The list is in turn built from two other works [2,3]. The concrete details on why are these concrete KPIs included in the list can be found in [6], nevertheless it is important to point out that the proposed list was built based on an in-depth study on urban logistics experts, practitioners and stakeholders. The Morana list, see Table 1 includes three types of measurement that reflect the three dimensions of sustainable development, that is economic, environment and social/societal. Despite the usefulness of these KPIs there is a lack of a conceptual model (ontology) that can aid the stakeholders to register all the information relevant to measure these KPIs in order to facilitate working with them and better integrate into transportation models.

In this work we propose a framework that allows to capture these KPIs into an ontology for Intelligent Transportation Systems providing in this way an easy to use approach to measure them and using these KPIs in applications that want to find optimized sustainable urban delivery plans.

3   An Ontology to Capture Sustainable KPIs in Urban Logistics

The Intelligent Transportation System Ontology (ITSO) we propose is based on the work of [7]. Nevertheless, other works such as [10] that proposes two ontologies for way-finding with multiple transportation modes, and [5] in which a system is proposed based on public transportation ontology, were also taken into account for the ontology definition. The ITSO is complete in terms of the six dimensions defined in [7] and extended with the sustainable specific attributes and/or relationships that are key in order to register the sustainable KPIs of Table 1 and to realize the optimized movement of materials in the city. Moreover, it is ready to use and provided as an XML description file easy to read and process by any type of software application. Following the ontology is described with special focus on its original elements.

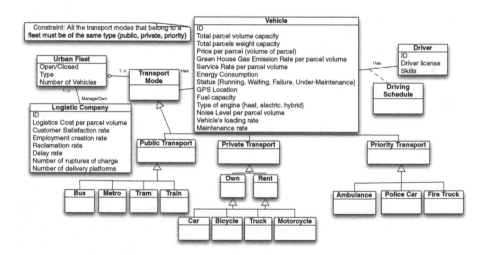

Fig. 1. Main ontology concepts of the Intelligent Transportation System Ontology

Figure 1 shows the different ontology concepts that built up the model and deal specifically with the transportation multi-modality or transportation mode and the sustainable KPIs related with the Vehicles definition and the Logistic Company characterization. The three dimension KPIs of Table 1 are included for vehicles and logistic company. In the proposed ontology there are three modes. (i) Public to which pertain the modes that are provided by transportation operators, with transportation lines running in a transportation network following a schedule (see Fig. 2 for a detailed view). This mode is included in order to allow logistic deliveries using the public transportation system in urban areas. (ii) Private to which pertain Cars, Bicycles, Trucks (the particular features of the trucks are registered in the class Truck, in this way different type of trucks

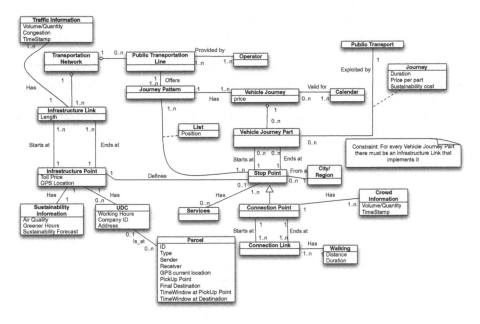

Fig. 2. Ontology definition of the Transportation Network

are allowed depending on the fleet requirements for LMD), and Motorcycle that can again be Owned or Rented by citizens/users. (iii) Priority to which pertain special type of transports such as: Ambulance, Police Car and Fire Truck. This last transportation mode is included in order to provide a complete transportation model, but this mode cannot be used by Logistic Companies for delivery purposes.

An Urban Fleet (see Fig. 1) is defined as a group of transports in which all the transports belong to the same Transportation Mode. It can be Open or Close. An Open Urban Fleet is one that can change dynamically, i.e. a transport owner can decide to enter or exit the fleet at any time. A Close Urban Fleet is one in which no new transport owners can decide to enter the fleet in a dynamic fashion. A Logistic Company manages or owns one or many Urban Fleets. Its associated features for the KPIs registry are Logistics Cost per parcel volume, Customer Satisfaction rate, Employment creation rate, Reclamation rate, Delay rate and Number of ruptures of charge. The values for these features can be calculated and/or measured using different mechanism depending on the concrete application that uses the ITSO. For example the Customer Satisfaction rate can be measured by means of customer polls.

Figure 2 presents the Transportation Network ontology. It is defined by the set of Infrastructure Links that defines the transportation infrastructure itself and the set of Public Transportation Lines that runs in the network. An Infrastructure Links connects Infrastructure Points. Every Infrastructure Link has a Traffic Information associated that is used in order to infer recommendations to the users about timing issues when intending to move trough the given Infrastructure Link, the Congestion KPI is registered using this concept. Moreover, every Infrastructure Point is associated with Sustainability Information about Air Quality, "Greener" Hours to navigate the point, and Sustainability Forecast (mainly about CO2 data). The Sustainability Information is intended to be taken into account by for example a recommender model when analyzing the sustainability cost for the overall system for the given itinerary (a route made up of connected Infrastructure Links).

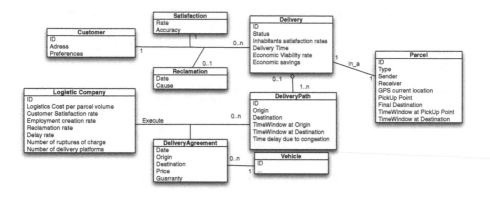

Fig. 3. Users, deliveries and parcels

Finally Fig. 3 shows the specification for the Deliveries. The rest of the KPIs associated with the concrete material/parcel that is being delivered are included as attributes of the Delivery and DeliveryPath concepts.

4   Measuring KPIs

In this section we describe the measurement module of the framework in order to complete the ITSO with a complete definition of its measuring methods. The methods we describe in this section are those for measuring the KPIs from the delivery plans (a set of DeliveryPaths, see Fig. 3) provided by Logistic Companies. These methods are appropriate for applications seeking to optimize delivery plans (in Sect. 5 a case study is presented).

From Fig. 3 a Delivery Plan $Plan(P)$ for a Parcel P is an ordered non-empty set of DeliveryPaths $DPath$.

$$Plan(P) = \{DPath_1, \ldots, DPath_n\}, \text{ where } n \geq 1$$

Each $DPath$ has an associated DeliveryAgreement that links the Logistic Company and the Vehicle that transport the Parcel in the given DeliveryPath. This connection of concepts must be navigated in order to measure, for example, the Green Gas Emission rate KPI (GGER-KPI) for a given Delivery Plan and, in this way, compare different plans in order to choose the greenest one.

$GGER - KPI(Plan(P)) =$
$\sum_{i=1}^{n} DPath_i.DeliveryAgreement.Vehicle.GreenHouseGasEmissionRate$

On the other hand, if the goal is to measure the Customers' Satisfaction rate KPI (CSR-KPI) for a given Logistic Company, the following formula must be calculated.

$CSR - KPI(LogisticCompany) =$
$\sum_{i=1}^{m}((LogisticCompany.Plan_i.Satisfaction.Rate)*$
$(LogisticCompany.Plan_i.Satisfaction.Accuracy))$, where $m \geq 1$

and represents all the deliveries executed by the given Logistic Company.

The Energy consumption KPI (EC-KPI) is calculated as follows

$EC - KPI(Plan(P)) =$
$\sum_{i=1}^{n} DPath_i.DeliveryAgreement.Vehicle.EnergyConsumption$

The Congestion KPI (C-KPI) is measured with the following formula

$C - KPI(Plan(P)) =$
$\sum_{i=1}^{n} <DPath_i.Origin, DPath_i.Destination>.TrafficInform.Congestion$

The tuple $<DPath_i.Origin, DPath_i.Destination>$ defines an Infrastruc-tureLink, see Fig. 2, and helps to retrieve the Traffic Information.

Due to space limitation in this paper not all the formulas for all the KPIs are described, but the process to build them is easy and similar to those described in this section.

5   A Case Study: Last Mile Delivery a Crowd Logistic Approach

In this section we shortly describe an application that uses the ITSO presented in this paper in order to implement a crowdsourcing approach for Last Mile Delivery. Crowd Shipping, these two words together form an increasingly familiar and emerging concept among those interested in transportation, logistics and urban mobility. In the spirit of collaborative economics, the idea behind crowdshipping is using ordinary citizens - on foot, by bicycle or by any means of transportation available to them - to make deliveries. Entrepreneurs, couriers, and consumers simply need to sign up in an application to connect. Crowdshipping can com-plement truck deliveries with lighter, easier-to-maneuver vehicles, as more and more cities impose restrictions on truck traffic. Crowdshipping can save compa-nies money - as they no longer need to set up a carrier structure - and can be a new source of income for many people. Our approach is named *CALMeD SURF* [9] and is based on crowdsourcing, taking advantage of the movements of the citizens in the urban area, that move for their own needs. This application is addressed as a mobile phone app for: customers that want to deliver a parcel, and users that want to serve as occasional deliverers in an urban area. The main idea is that the users register in the application (as customer or deliverer), and *CALMeD SURF* will locate them in the city on real-time. In this way, when there is a parcel delivery request, the system uses a graph, that is dynamically generated from the active users and the instantiated ITSO, where each node is either a user (a potential deliverer, and/or customer) or a delivery center/office. The system proposes optimized parcels delivery paths (measuring the associated KPIs of previous sections) to the crowd of potential deliverers (those who are closest to the calculated delivery path) to participate. If some of the potential deliverers rejects the proposal, it calculates an alternative path (i.e. a new path and a new set of potential deliverers) in order to achieve the parcel delivery goal. The calculated path may include several deliverers that may pass the parcel from one to another (connecting sub-paths). One of the optimization criteria used by the system, closely related with the goal of minimizing the harm to the environment, is to minimize the deviation of the deliverers from the path to their own destinations and to maximize the use of sustainable transportation modes (mainly bicycles). Trying in this way to minimize new emissions originated by movements that are solely used for parcel deliveries. This case study is a successful example of the usefulness of ITSO in optimized delivery plans for sustainability goals, achieving an optimization of 30% in the Green House Gas Emission rate KPI and reducing by 35% the Service rate KPI.

6   Conclusion and Future Works

In this paper a framework that aids to register and measure a set of sustainable Key Performance Indicators (KPIs) for delivery routes and plans in urban zones was proposed. The approach is general and based on a set of 21 well defined KPIs from the specialized research field. Moreover a case study was also presented illustrating the usefulness of the proposed approach when building optimized delivery plan solutions for sustainable goals. As ongoing work we are tuning the measuring mechanism for the proposed KPIs (mainly in terms of fast search algorithms) and implementing a library of optimized SW approaches that can take into account multiple KPIs into different domains. A complete validation phase is also devised as future work.

Acknowledgement. This research is supported by research projects TIN2015-65515-C4-1-R and TIN2016-80856-R from the Spanish government.

References

1. Gonzalez-Feliu, J., Semet, F., Routhier, J.L.: Sustainable Urban Logistics: Concepts, Methods and Information Systems. Springer, Heidelberg (2014). https://doi.org/10.1007/978-3-642-31788-0
2. Griffis, S., Goldsby, T., Cooper, M., Closs, D.: Aligning logistics performance measures to the information needs of the firm. J. Bus. Logist. **48**, 35–56 (2007)

3. Gunasekaran, A., Kobu, B.: Performance measures and metrics in logistics and supply chain management: a review of recent literature (1995–2004) for research and applications. Int. J. Prod. Res. **45**, 2819–2840 (2007)
4. Macharis, C., Melo, S.: City distribution and Urban freight transport: Multiple perspectives. Edward Elgar Publishing, Cheltenham (2011)
5. Mnasser, H., Oliveira, K., Khemaja, M., Abed, M.: Towards an ontology-based transportation system for user travel planning. 12th IFAC Proc. Vol. **43**(8), 604–611 (2010)
6. Morana, J., Gonzalez-Feliu, J.: A sustainable urban logistics dashboard from the perspective of a group of operational managers. Manag. Res. Rev. **38**(10), 1068–1085 (2015)
7. de Oliveira, K.M., Bacha, F., Mnasser, H., Abed, M.: Transportation ontology definition and application for the content personalization of user interfaces. Expert Syst. Appl. **40**(8), 3145–3159 (2013)
8. Pagell, M., Wu, Z.: Building a more complete theory of sustainable supply chain management using case studies of 10 exemplars. J. Suppl. Chain Manag. **45**, 37–56 (2009)
9. Rebollo, M., Giret, A., Carrascosa, C., Julian, V.: The multi-agent layer of calmed surf. In: Proceedings of the 5th International Conference on Agreement Technologies (2017)
10. Timpf, S.: Ontologies of wayfinding: a traveler's perspective. Netw. Spat. Econ. **2**(1), 9–33 (2002)

Developing an Advanced Cloud-Based Vehicle Routing and Scheduling System for Urban Freight Transportation

Sotiris P. Gayialis[✉], Grigorios D. Konstantakopoulos,
Georgios A. Papadopoulos, Evripidis Kechagias, and Stavros T. Ponis

National Technical University of Athens,
Iroon Polytechniou 9, 157 80 Athens, Greece
{sotga, staponis}@central.ntua.gr,
{gkonpoulos, gpapado, eurikechagias}@mail.ntua.gr

Abstract. In today's challenging sector of logistics and transportation, companies, seek to adapt software which leads to efficient solutions at an acceptable cost. Conventional routing software is developed to solve vehicle routing problem and help managers and planners in decision making. Simultaneously, specific constraints and different VRP (Vehicle Routing Problem) variants are considered each time, such as the Capacitated, the Multi Depot and the Pickup and Delivery VRP. However, the last few years the need for more reliable deliveries and better customer services arose. In addition, reducing travel distance, travel cost and environmental impact are important factors encountered in urban freight transportation. Therefore, routing software needs to take into account multiple constraints. Such constraints are traffic congestion, speed limits, transportation regulations and restricted zones. These constraints affect mainly Time dependent VRP, VRP with Time Windows, Dynamic VRP and Green VRP. Data collection and processing are essential in routing software for solving these variants and offering the best solution. The methods for solving these problems, along with technological achievements, including cloud computing, can lead to efficient, easily adaptable routing software. Such software solutions can eventually render companies with complex transportation and logistics problems, competitive. The scope of this paper is to describe the concept and methodological approach for the development of such a routing and scheduling system, operating in a cloud environment. The definition of its requirements and the development of the system is the main purpose of an ongoing research project, being in its first stages of system's analysis and design.

Keywords: Vehicle routing problem · Scheduling
Urban freight transportation · City logistics · Routing software
Software as a service (SaaS) · Cloud software

1 Introduction

Logistic professionals have faced the Vehicle Routing Problem (VRP) in practice, ever since multi-drop freight carrying vehicles were introduced. VRP is still encountered in our days, mainly in the domain of transportation and logistics and it is one of the most

I. Moon et al. (Eds.): APMS 2018, IFIP AICT 536, pp. 190–197, 2018.
https://doi.org/10.1007/978-3-319-99707-0_24

widely studied topics in the field of Operational Research [1]. Still, theoretical research in the field of vehicle routing started in 1959, when Dantzig and Ramser [2] posed the "truck dispatching problem", utilizing hand calculations and a linear programming formulation in order to find a near optimal solution with four routes to a problem of twelve drop points. Extended research has been achieved in the field of VRP and plethora of articles have been published, as described by Braekers et al. [1]. In spite of all this research into vehicle routing, there is no single algorithm that optimally solves every problem. Algorithms and methods have been developed for optimally solving certain classes of vehicle routing and scheduling problems, tackling only a single issue in order to minimize the number of variables under consideration, in order to simplify real-life business cases.

Routing of vehicles and scheduling of deliveries from distribution centers to several drop points, is affected from multiple variables and constraints such as vehicle capacity, number of depots, traffic conditions, regulations and other restrictions. Traffic congestion in urban areas along with various time restrictions make the optimization of routing and scheduling operation particularly difficult. Furthermore, restrictions for minimizing CO_2 emissions, which depend on truck speed, have been recently taken into consideration [3]. All these variables and constraints are identified and connected with multiple VRP variants such as the Capacitated VRP, the Multi Depot VRP and the Dynamic VRP. These variants, along with the VRP with Time Windows, the Time Dependent VRP and the Green VRP, are some of the most studied topics from researchers [4, 5], concerning logistics companies as well.

The need for software which can combine all the above VRP variants and attribute an optimal solution, giving priority to specific variants has appeared. Conventional information systems are usually designed case by case, having many issues in fields of system elasticity, while the purchase of hardware and software is of outmost need [6]. However, the main disadvantage these systems present is in the absence of real time data and big data analytics, which can contribute in solving specific time dependent VRP variants and offering more reliable solutions.

On the other side, routing Software as a Service (SaaS), which is a software distribution model in which a third-party provider hosts applications and makes them available to customers over the Internet, have become very popular nowadays as they provide (i) Big Data Analytics [7], (ii) Flexible Payments, (iii) Scalable Usage, (iv) Automatic Updates and (v) Accessibility and Persistence [8]. Such software can offer both reliable deliveries and minimization of costs, mainly, due to the usage of advanced algorithms in powerful servers and due to the advantages of big data analytics.

The aim of the described ongoing research is the development of a routing and scheduling SaaS, covering the contemporary requirements of logistics companies, offering simultaneously a holistic approach in the cases of static and dynamic vehicle routing and scheduling. This holistic approach makes the system innovative, as there is no such a system described in the literature.

In the remainder of this paper, the contribution of big data and internet of things (IoT) in VRP is presented in Sect. 2. Section 3, introduces the system development approach and the conceptual model of the routing and scheduling SaaS as part of the ongoing research project. In Sect. 4 conclusions and further research are discussed, featuring the next steps of the research in order to develop an advanced cloud-based vehicle routing and scheduling system for urban freight transportation.

2 Big Data and Internet of Things in VRP Software

The concepts of Big Data and Internet of Things (IoT) are not just buzzwords. They are new approaches to unify everything in our world and analyze various data under a common infrastructure [9]. Massive quantities of data, relevant to businesses and to services, both in private and public sector can easily be collected, due to technological advances which are simultaneously the reason of the explosion big data appear [10]. Objects such as electronics, sensors, software and network connectivity are related to IoT and to the big data phenomenon as too.

The main differences big data present compared with traditional data are in (i) volume (ii) velocity and (iii) variety [11]. In cases, such as the vehicle routing and scheduling of deliveries, in which, traffic conditions change dynamically, and the re-routing of vehicles sometimes seem necessary to avoid delays and improve deliveries, the speed of data creation is significant, for decision makers. Furthermore, big amount of data can lead to better statistical analysis and better forecast and prediction models of traffic, calculating travel time between delivery points. Travel time is essential for static vehicle routing as well as for the dynamic routing, when exceptional cases appear. In the case of static routing, historical data are used for defining the initial routes of vehicles, using forecasting methods. Furthermore, real-time data are used when the distribution of products has started, in order to avoid traffic congestion and simultaneously, delays of deliveries.

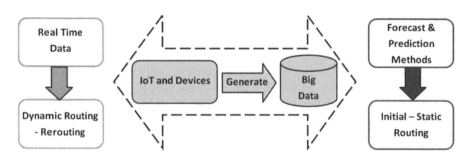

Fig. 1. Data, methods and decision making for vehicle routing and scheduling

In order to receive the desired outcome and be able to develop a vehicle routing SaaS system, solving specific variants of the VRP and leading to reliable deliveries without despising constraints, big amount of data is required. Simultaneously, data analysis, which refers to the techniques used to analyze and acquire intelligence from big data [12], is crucial, as without it, data cannot be reclaimed to the maximum extent. Global Positioning System (GPS) signal and sensors can provide enormous amount of data, related to the location, the speed of vehicles and their direction as well [10]. Real-time data of vehicles locations in addition with real-time traffic data can adjust delivery estimates in order to detect inconsistencies of schedules and required modifications. Figure 1 describes the way through which traffic data are collected using various data inputs like public or private traffic management services, or even existing equipment in vehicles for route tracking. Forecasting and prediction methods are used for the static routing of vehicles in order to offer data for expected traffic and delivery. Finally, Fig. 1 encompasses the important role that real time data play in the rerouting of vehicles. Through this procedure better decision making for vehicle routing and scheduling is accomplished and efficient deliveries are succeeded. The significance of using big data in the described routing and scheduling software is presented in the next section.

3 Developing a Routing and Scheduling System

3.1 System Development Approach

This paper reports ongoing work and initial results from a project in Greece which aims to enhance the capabilities of routing and scheduling operations of Transportation and Logistics companies. The system presented in this paper is intended to support the decisions of the static routing and scheduling problem, as well as the dynamic aspects of the problem and is being developed in the context of the research project "SMARTRANS". The project participants include (i) a major technological University responsible for the theoretically informed analysis and design of the new system, the development of the algorithms for the static and dynamic routing problem, and the creation of methods for traffic data collection and analysis, (ii) an IT company implementing the system and applying technological solutions of the theoretical design, and (iii) a Greek logistics company as an industrial partner for testing and validating the system.

The research project's phases are presented in Fig. 2, including four main phases. The first phase is the preparation phase of a comprehensive literature review concluding to the "state of the art" of three main research areas: VRP variants for the static and dynamic problem, the algorithms for solving them, forecasting methods for travel time estimation in order to schedule the deliveries and innovative big data techniques for traffic data collection in a dynamic way (see also the "Research" perspective in Fig. 3). The forecasting and prediction methods which are developed use historical traffic and delivery data, making assumptions about the future. However, through computer simulation the performance of these methods can be studied while the set of initial parameters change, leading to significant and more accurate results. Information technologies for routing software and cloud-based application are analyzed as well.

The design and analysis of Business Process Models of logistics companies are also included in preparation phase, leading to requirements analysis, which are the system's services, constraints, and goals that are established through consultation with the system users. Often, one requirement generates or constrains other requirements. In order to ensure that services/features are delivered properly, system requirements need to specify both services and features of the system and the necessary functionality [13]. Use case scenarios are also developed based on business processes, in order to test and validate the implementation in later phases, leading to the identification of functionality with potentially improvement.

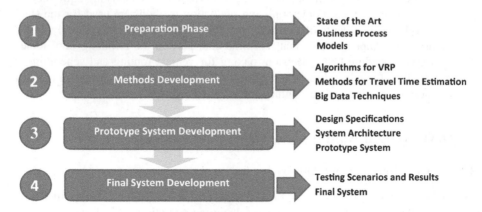

Fig. 2. Research project's phases and outcomes

Preparation phase has been completed and algorithms for the static and dynamic VRP are being developed in order to support the decisions for the scheduling of deliveries in real-life companies. Forecasting methods for travel time estimation in urban environment, as well as big data techniques for real-time traffic data collection and processing will be devolved in the second phase (methods development). The third and fourth phases will be carried out after the first year of the project and will finally conclude to the advanced and innovative system, described in the next section and in Fig. 3.

3.2   System Design Concept

The designed system for vehicle routing and scheduling of the deliveries integrates both static and dynamic version of the VRP, as depicted in Fig. 3 in the "Outputs" perspective of the conceptual model. The software, using the outcome of the VRP algorithms, is able to solve static VRP, in which, information does not change during deliveries, choosing the best scenario among all the alternative ones. The static routing provides alternative scenarios of deliveries based on different objectives of the VRP. System user can decide for the most preferable scenario or let the system choose the optimum, based on a combination of constraints and parameters for the variants of the VRP. These parameters and constraints are related to capacity (weight, volume and height), time windows, driving hours and road regulations and restrictions. The objective function is complex, as the optimization is not related only to the mini-mization of travel distance and the number of vehicles. It is also vital to minimize travel costs and carbon dioxide emissions, while maximizing customer service and accuracy of deliveries.

All these parameters are inputs ("Inputs" perspective) in solving the problem. In addition, inputs also include the customer orders, the available vehicles (which in turn have specific weight and volume capacities) and the depots. Real time traffic data are gathered from various applications such as Google Maps, HERE WeGo Maps and from traffic police reports. These data are stored to the system, processed, and finally contribute in the development of a forecasting and prediction model of travel times. This functionality can assist the calculation of travelling time of each route in a more accurate way, leading to feasible routes and deliveries, especially in traffic congestion cases.

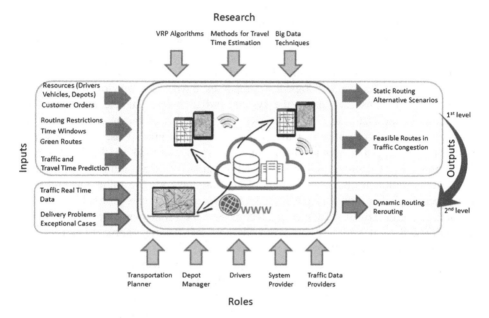

Fig. 3. Overview of the vehicle routing and scheduling system design concept

Real time data of traffic and exceptional cases can be collected using big data techniques in order to re-route the vehicles during deliveries, as accidents and delays can cause delivery problems which eventually lead to penalties. This functionality refers to the Dynamic VRP (DVRP) and is distinguished as a second level routing in Fig. 3.

The main roles involved, contributing and using directly the software are: (i) transportation planners and depot managers, who receive the outcome of the software, edit the created solution, and finally provide the initial routing of vehicles and scheduling of deliveries, (ii) drivers, who receive the routing and scheduling in a front-end device, such as tablets and mobile devices, (iii) system providers, which is the IT company, providing all the above functions and applications, as well as, maintaining and supporting the software, and finally (iv) traffic data providers, who support the whole procedure, by providing the appropriate data for travel time prediction and dynamic routing.

The technical solution of the system is based on the cloud computing concept, as the system runs on the cloud under the responsibility of the system provider. Every user of the routing and scheduling system can access its functionality as a software service (SaaS).

4   Conclusions and Further Research

This paper presents the development phases and the conceptual design of an integrated web-based software solution to support transportation operations of contemporary logistics companies in order to effectively schedule their deliveries under various parameters and time dependent constraints.

The methodological approach for system implementation is presented in Fig. 2. According to the first phase (preparation phase), the "state of the art" has concluded to the conceptual design of the system, presented in Fig. 3. In addition, business process models of transportation and logistics companies have been developed in order to conduct requirements analysis of the system and to investigate the parameters and constraints of the static and dynamic VRP. The analysis of business processes will drive the design specifications of the new system in the third phase of the research. State of the art results, along with requirements analysis will be the input for the development of algorithms for the static and dynamic vehicle routing and scheduling problem, as well as for the development of big data methods for traffic data collection and processing. The first and the most important note that can be made for further research is the design of system's architecture and the implementation of a prototype for testing and validation purposes (third phase of the research approach) and later the implementation of the final system (fourth phase).

The final outcome of the presented approach and conceptual design will be an innovative system for vehicle routing and scheduling in urban environment, which is characterized by heavily and often unpredictable traffic congestion. The system's innovative characteristics include the formation of the time dependent vehicle routing and scheduling problem, taking into consideration various parameters and restrictions like traffic congestion, working hours and state regulations in a holistic way, the algorithms for solving this problem and the forecasting methods for the calculation of travel times. Finally, the service provision through a web-based interface will make the system globally accessible, user friendly and relatively easy to implement even in smaller scale logistics companies.

Acknowledgments. This research has been co-financed by the European Union and Greek national funds through the Operational Program Competitiveness, Entrepreneurship and Innovation, under the call RESEARCH – CREATE – INNOVATE (project code: T1EDK-00527 and Acronym: SMARTRANS)

References

1. Braekers, K., Ramaekers, K., Van Nieuwenhuyse, I.: The vehicle routing problem: state of the art classification and review. Comput. Ind. Eng. **99**, 300–313 (2016)
2. Dantzig, G.B., Ramser, J.H.: The truck dispatching problem. Manag. Sci. **6**(1), 80–91 (1959)
3. Salimifard, K., Raeesi, R.: A green routing problem: optimising CO_2 emissions and costs from a bi-fuel vehicle fleet. Int. J. Adv. Oper. Manag. **6**(1), 27–57 (2014)
4. Eksioglu, B., Vural, A.V., Reisman, A.: The vehicle routing problem: a taxonomic review. Comput. Ind. Eng. **57**(4), 1472–1483 (2009)
5. Konstantakopoulos, G.D., Gayialis, S.P.: Vehicle routing problem for urban freight transportation: a review. In: Vlachopoulou, M., Kitsios, F., Kamariotou, M. (eds.) 6th International Symposium and 28th National Conference on Operational Research, pp. 14–20 (2017)
6. Chen, L., Zheng, X., Chen, G.: A system architecture for intelligent logistics system. In: 2013 International Conference on Cloud Computing and Big Data (2013)
7. Yu, W.D., Gottumukkala, A., Senthailselvi, D.A.: Distributed big data analytics in service computing. In: 2017 IEEE 13th International Symposium on Autonomous Decentralized Systems (ISADS 2017), pp. 55–60 (2017)
8. Vidhyalakshmi, R., Kumar, V.: CORE framework for evaluating the reliability of SaaS products. Future Gener. Comput. Syst. **72**, 23–36 (2017)
9. Madakam, S., Ramaswamy, R., Tripathi, S.: Internet of things (IoT): a literature review. J. Comput. Commun. **3**, 164–173 (2015)
10. Speranza, M.G.: Trends in transportation and logistics. Eur. J. Oper. Res. **264**(3), 830–836 (2018)
11. Gandomi, A., Haider, M.: Beyond the hype: big data concepts, methods, and analytics. Int. J. Inf. Manag. **35**(2), 137–144 (2015)
12. Sang, G.M., Xu, L., de Vrieze, P.: Simplifying big data analytics systems with a reference architecture. In: Camarinha-Matos, Luis M., Afsarmanesh, H., Fornasiero, R. (eds.) PRO-VE 2017. IAICT, vol. 506, pp. 242–249. Springer, Cham (2017). https://doi.org/10.1007/978-3-319-65151-4_23
13. Sommerville, I.: Software Engineering, 9th edn. Pearson Education, London (2007)

Lease Contract in Usage Based Remanufactured Equipment Service System

H. Husniah[1], U. S. Pasaribu[2], and B. P. Iskandar[2(✉)]

[1] Langlangbuana University, Bandung, Indonesia
hennie.husniah@gmail.com
[2] Bandung Institute of Technology, Bandung, Indonesia
bermawi@mail.ti.itb.ac.id

Abstract. In this paper we study a usage based lease contract for remanufactured equipment as an implementation of product service system. Under this lease contract, the equipment is leased for a period of Γ with a maximum usage, U. If the usage of the equipment exceeds U at time Γ, then lessee will be charged some additional cost. Otherwise there will be no additional cost. The price of the lease contract for the remanufactured equipment is much cheaper than that of a new one. As a result, the lease contract for the remanufactured equipment would be a more attractive option to the lessee. The decision problem for the lessee is to select the best option suitable to its requirement, and the decision problem for the lessor is find the optimal maintenance policy and the price for each length of periods offered. We provide numerical examples for illustrating the optimal decisions for the lessee, and the lessor, which maximizes the expected profit for each party.

Keywords: Remanufactured · Lease · Usage based service system
Preventive maintenance · Game theory

1 Introduction

In recent global economy, a manufacturing company cannot just provide products alone to the customers, in order to remain competitive, but it needs to offer solutions for their businesses. An innovative way to achieve this is to offer a package of product and services called as a product-service system (PSS). [1] defines PSS as "an integrated product and service offering that delivers value in use". As a result, under PSS, there is a significant shift from a "traditional" product oriented model which provides products alone (or selling products) to a "service oriented" model (e.g. selling either product usage or performance) that will give the opportunity for the manufacturing company to gain competitive advantage [2]. This shift also contributes to reducing associated environmental impacts (i.e. refurbishment, remanufacturing and recycling of durable products, which save more energy and reduce waste through the product's life) and the volume of goods in the economy to the sufficiency strategies and establish long-term relations with customers. The others effect of the PSS are reducing lifecycle impacts of products and services through product servicing, remanufacturing and recycling [3]. Research of lease contracts in PSS have been studied by many researchers (See [4–7]).

I. Moon et al. (Eds.): APMS 2018, IFIP AICT 536, pp. 198–205, 2018.
https://doi.org/10.1007/978-3-319-99707-0_25

Since leasing equipment (rather than purchase it) becomes a common practice in company that functioning equipment as generating revenue. It also has many positive points i.e. saving on initial investment, flexibility on equipment upgrading, and cost reduction in maintenance and inventory [8]. Moreover study lease contract (LC) that involves both lessee and lessor has been attracted by many researchers. A comprehensive review of LC from the lessor's or lessee's perspective can be found in [9]. For the case where the study is done from the lessor and lessee point of views then a game theory formulation is needed to modelling the decision problems (See [10]).

The LC for the new lease item, can be found in [8, 11] to name a few, whilst [12, 13] examined the lease contract for used items. Finally, [14] considered lease options which include a remanufactured equipment. When the equipment is used intensively (or with high usage) per unit of time, the usage experienced affects significantly the deterioration of the equipment. This indicates the need to consider age and usage in modelling the failure and also defining the lease contract which involves two parameters –i.e. age and usage limits (called a two dimensional lease contract). We are aware only the works by [15, 16] belong to this group. In [15] the period of the contract is always the same with a maximum usage rate whilst [16] consider a two dimensional lease contract for maximum age or usage.

In this paper, we study a usage based lease contract for remanufactured equipment as an implementation of product service system. We consider a multi-period LC in which each period has a time limit but no usage limit. However, if the usage exceeds the maximum usage allowed in the contract, then the lessee has to pay some additional cost. In general, Original Equipment Manufacturer or OEM (as a lessor) offers not only a LC for a brand new equipment but also a LC for a remanufactured one. As the price of the LC for the remanufactured equipment is much lower than the price of a new one, and hence it would be a more attractive option to the companies. This paper deals with a multi period lease contract for a remanufactured equipment (such as dump trucks) in which the price scheme of LC gives some incentive for the lessee when the equipment is leased for more than one periods.

The paper is organised as follows. In Sect. 2 we give model formulation for the two dimensional lease contract studied. Sections 3 and 4 deal with model analysis and the optimal decisions for the lessor and the lessee. In Sect. 5, we provide with a numerical example. Finally, we conclude with topics for further research in Sect. 6.

2 Model Formulation

In this section, we first define a new LC, describe failure model, formulate a preventive maintenance policy and its effect on reliability, and then obtain the expected profit for a lessor and a lessee.

Notations:

$\Omega = [0, \Gamma) \times [0, \infty)$	Lease coverage region	P	Lease contract price
N	Number of PM during lease contract	C_b	Annual cost
T_r	The time to the first failure of the remanufactured equipment	C_p	Preventive maintenance cost
y	Usage rate	C_r	Average repair cost
$F(t, \alpha_r); f(t, \alpha_r)$	Distribution function and density function for T_r	δ_y	Preventive maintenance level
$\lambda(t, \alpha_r), \Lambda(t, \alpha_r)$	Hazard function and cumulative hazard function	U_y	Total usage in $[0, m\Gamma)$
$E[\pi_y]; E[\phi_y]$	Expected profit for a lessor, and for a lessee	$m\Gamma$	Lease contract periods, $\Gamma > 0$ and $m = 1, 2, \ldots$
$J^1(K, \delta_y), J^2(K, \delta_y)$	Expected preventive maintenance and minimal repair cost		

2.1   Multi-period Lease Contract

A lessee will lease the equipment for one or more periods, and use with a constant usage rate over the LC periods. A different lessee may have a different usage rate. A LC studied for a remanufactured equipment for period of $m\Gamma(\Gamma > 0$ and $m = 1, 2, \ldots)$ with a maximum usage ($U_{\max}$) (e.g. km travelled/time period or machine-hours/time period). For a given lessee (or usage rate y), if the total usage at the end of a lease period, U_y exceeds $U_{\max}$ (See Fig. 1), then the lessee (or customer) will be charged an additional cost which is proportional to $\varphi = Max\{0, U_y - U_{\max}\} = Max\{0, y\Gamma - U_{\max}\}$ for one period. This additional cost is viewed as a compensation to the lessor as larger usage rate ($U_y > U_{\max}$) results in more failures under LC and hence higher maintenance cost.

2.2   Modelling Failure

In general, most products at the end of the first life or end-of-use have a low reliability (or their reliability is below the threshold value of reliability R^*). Remanufacturing involves disassembly, cleaning, and refurbishment or replacement of parts to improve the reliability of the equipment to a like-new one or it improve the reliability of the product to at least the same level of the threshold reliability. Let T_r be the time of the first failure the remanufactured product. $F(t)$ is the distribution function for T_r. If $F(t)$ is given by Weibull distribution function with $F(t, \alpha_r) = 1 - e^{-(t/\alpha_r)^\beta}$, then the reliability of the remanufactured product is $R(t, \alpha_r) = 1 - F(t, \alpha_r) = e^{-(t/\alpha_r)^\beta}$. As $R(t, \alpha_r) \geq R^*$, then we have $\alpha_r \geq t/\{(\sqrt[\beta]{-\ln R^*}\}$.

We model failure of the remanufactured product as follows. It is considered that failure is not only influenced by age but also usage. Let Y be the constant usage rate for a given customer (e.g. $y = 120$ km/day for a dump truck). For a given customer (or usage rate, y), let $r_y(t)$ be the conditional hazard function which is a non-decreasing function of t (the age of the truck) and y. An accelerated failure time (AFT) model is proposed to model the effect of age and usage rate on degradation of the truck. In AFT model the distribution function for T_y is given by $F(t, \alpha_y)$, with a scale parameter given by $\alpha_y = (y_0/y)^\rho \alpha_r$ where y_0 is a nominal usage rate, α_r is the scale parameter when the truck is used in a normal mode. If the lessee uses the equipment with the usage rate exceeding the normal value, $y > y_0$, then $\alpha_y > \alpha_r$ or the equipment will deteriorate faster, otherwise when $y < y_0$ then it goes slower. Let T_y be the time to first failure of the remanufactured product for a given lessee. The distribution function for T_y is given by $F_y(t)$. Let $N_y(t)$ be the number of failures in $(0, t]$ for a given y. If all failures under the LC are minimally repaired and repair times are very small relative to the mean time between failures, then $N_y(t)$ is a non-homogeneous Poisson process with intensity function $r_y(t)$. The cumulative hazard functions associated with $r_y(t)$ is given by $R_y(t) = \int_0^t r_y(x)dx$.

2.3 Modelling the Preventive Maintenance Effect

For a given customer with $Y = y$, PM is done periodically at $k\tau_y$, $k = 1, 2, \ldots$ where k is an integer value, and hence we have k disjoint intervals $-[0, \tau_y)$, $\ldots$, $[k\tau_y, (k+1)\tau_y = \Gamma)$. As in [16, 17], we model the impact of PM through the reduction in the intensity function –i.e. the reduction is δ_{yj} after PM at $t_j, j \geq 1$, and $\delta_{yj} = \delta_y$. As any failure occurring between PM is minimally repaired, then the expected total number of minimal repairs over $[0, \Gamma_0)$ or $([t_{j-1}, t_j), 1 \leq j \leq k)$ is given by

$$N = \sum_{j=1}^{k} \int_{t_{j-1}}^{t_j} r_{j-1}(t')dt'.$$

3 Analysis

We carry out the analysis to obtain the expected profit for the lessor, and the lessee.

3.1 Lessor's Expected Profit

The lessor's expected total cost consists of preventive maintenance cost and corrective maintenance cost. If $J^1(k_y, \delta_y)$ and $J^2(k_y, \delta_y)$ are the expected preventive maintenance cost and the expected total repair cost over the LC period $(0, m\Gamma], m = 1, 2, \ldots$ for a given usage rate y, respectively, then the expected total cost the lessor for m period LC, $\Psi[k_y, \delta_y]$ is given by

$$\Psi[k, \delta_y] = \sum_{i=1}^{m} \Pi_i[k, \delta_y]; \Pi_i[k, \delta_y] = J^1(k, \delta_y) + J^2(k, \delta_y) \tag{1}$$

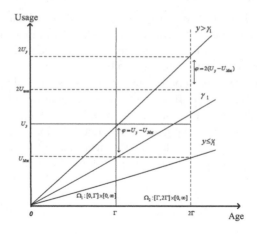

Fig. 1. A lease contract with m periods ($m\Gamma$, $m = 2$) and the maximum usage (U_{max})

Preventive Maintenance Cost

Let $C_{pm}(\delta_y)$ and C_r be the cost of the j-th PM and the cost of each minimal repair. If $C_{pm}(\delta_y) = C_0 + C_v\delta_y$ then the expected total PM cost over the LC period $(0, m\Gamma]$, $m = 1, 2, \ldots$ is given by

$$J^1(k_y, \delta_y) = \sum_{j=1}^{k} C_{pm}(\delta_y) = kC_0 + C_v \sum_{j=1}^{k} \delta_y \qquad (2)$$

Corrective Maintenance Cost

If C_r is the cost of each minimal repair, then

$$J^2(k, \tau_y, \delta_y) = C_r\left(R_y(\Gamma) - \sum_{j=1}^{k} (\Gamma - j\tau_y)\delta_y\right) \qquad (3)$$

After simplification for m = 1, we have the expected total cost of the lessor given by

$$\Psi[k, \delta_y] = C_r R_y(\Gamma) - \left\{ C_r \sum_{j=1}^{k} \left[(\Gamma - C_v/C_r) - j\tau_y\right]\delta_y - kC_0 \right\} \qquad (4)$$

Expected Total Revenue

The expected total revenue is the sum of the price of LC and some additional revenues due to the total usage of the equipment is greater than U_{max} (the maximum usage). The price of LC is dependent on the usage rate and the number of LC periods (m) given by

$$P(m) = P\{e^{-\varphi m}/e^{-\varphi}\} = P\left\{e^{-\varphi(m-1)}\right\} \qquad (5)$$

where $0 \leq \varphi < 1$ represents a discount parameter. This price function gives a discount price when $m \geq 2$. The additional revenues earned by the lessor is given by

$$\Phi(m, y) = C_d \sum_{j=1}^{m} Max\{0, (y \times j\Gamma - jU_{\max})\} \tag{6}$$

where C_d is the additional cost charged (e.g. $/km or $/page copied). $\Phi(m, y)$ is viewed as some additional revenues for the lessor. As a result, the expected profit is given by

$$E[\pi_y] = P(m) + \Phi(m, y) - \Psi[k_y, \delta_y] - mC_b^r \tag{7}$$

where C_b^r is the annual cost of the remanufactured equipment.

3.2 Lessee's Expected Profit

The lessee's expected profit is equal to the expected total revenue minus the total expected cost, that will be given as follows.

$$E[\phi_y] = K(m\Gamma) - P(m) - \Phi(m, y) \tag{8}$$

4 Optimization

Case 1: [Joint Optimization]

We consider that the lessee and lessor would like to work jointly to obtain a joint optimal profit. Then, the strategy set of the lessor and the lessee is given by $Q_y = \{(\delta_y, \tau_y, k_y, P, m) | 0 \leq \delta_y \leq 1, \tau_y \geq 0, k_y \geq 0\}$. Here the decision variables for the lessor are δ_y, τ_y, k_y, P, and m is for the lessee. Both players choose the set of strategies $q_y^* \in Q_y$ that solves $\max_q E[\Pi_y] = \max\{E[\phi_y] + E[\pi_y]\}$ where $E[\phi_y]$ and $E[\pi_y]$ are the total expected profit for the lessee and lessor. The coordination solution is obtained by solving the following problem.

$$\max_{\delta_y, \tau_y, k_y} E[\Pi_y] = \max_q \{E[\phi_y] + E[\pi_y]\}, \quad \text{s.t. } \delta_y, \tau_y, P > 0, and \ k_y, m > 0 (integer) \tag{9}$$

Case 2: [Non Cooperative Nash Game Theory]

Next, we consider a win-win decision situation for the lessee and lessor, and model using a Nash game theory formulation. In this scheme, the strategy set of the lessee and lessor are $Q_y^{nash} = \{(\delta_y, \tau_y, k_y, P, m) | 0 \leq \delta_y \leq 1, \tau_y \geq 0, k_y \geq 0\}$. If $E[\phi_y]$ and $E[\pi_y]$ are the total expected profit for the lessee and lessor, both players choose the set of strategies $q_y^* \in Q_y^{nash}$ that solves $\max_q E[\phi_y] = \max_q E[\pi_y]$ with the optimal values of the set of strategies $q_y^* \in Q_y^{nash}$ for the lessee and lessor by solving the following problem.

$$\max_{\delta_y,\tau_y,k_y} E[\phi_y] = \max_{\delta_y,\tau_y,k_y} E[\pi_y], \text{s.t.} \delta_y > 0, \tau_y > 0, k_y > 0 \, and \, integer \qquad (10)$$

5 Numerical Example

The parameter values used are: $R = 0.4$, $\beta = 1.5$, $\Gamma = 12$ (months), $U = 24$ (1×10^4 Km), ($\gamma = U/\Gamma = 1$), $y_0 = 1$, $\rho = 2$ and $C_v = 0.5C_m$, $C_a = 0.75C_r$, $\zeta = 12$ (units).

Table 1 shows optimal solutions for cases 1 and 2. In Case 1, as the usage rate increases, the profit gained for the lessor [lessee] increases [decreases], and the profit for the lessee is less than that of lessor started at y = 3.0 (as the additional cost charged to the customer is much bigger as y is larger (y > 2.5)). In contrast, the profit resulting from the Nash bargaining solution (Case 2) is always the same for both the lessor and the lessee for each y, and it decreases as y increases. This is due to the total profit generated by both parties decreasing as y increases (or more failures occur and hence bigger downtimes as the usage is larger). The joint optimization is favor the lessor. This is expected as the bargaining strategy shares equally the total profit generated.

Managerial Implementation
The results shows that implementation of the leasing concept connected to a product remanufactured can undoubtedly deliver economic benefits to the lessor and lessee. As it is not a new product, and hence a thorough preparation of a special marketing strategy that results in a customer acceptance is required. This is agreed with [3].

Table 1. Results for case 1 and case 2 with LC region 12 months (m = 1)

	Case 1: Joint optimization					Case 2: Non- cooperative nash game theory		
$\bar{y}$	k_y^*; τ_y^*; δ_y^*	$E[\pi_y]$; $E[\phi_y] \times 10^5$ [Lessor]; (lessee)	$E[\Pi_y] \times 10^5$	$P \times 10^5$		k_y^*; τ_y^*; δ_y^*	$E[\pi_y] = E[\phi_y] \times 10^5$ [Lessor]; (lessee)	$P \times 10^5$
2.0	17; 0.95; 0.09	[3.0]; [9.2]	13.2	1.6		2; 3.09; 0.19	[5.36]; [5.36]	5.45
2.5	24; 0.47; 0.15	[5.9]; [6.6]	14.3	3.0		4; 2.08; 0.31	[4.72]; [4.72]	4.82
3.0	31; 0.37; 0.25	[10.0]; [2.46]	15.9	5.2		5; 1.78; 0.49	[3.77]; [3.77]	3.88
3.2	34; 0.33; 0.26	[12.4]; [0.406]	16.8	6.3		6; 1.55; 0.56	[3.29]; [3.29]	3.41

6 Conclusion

In this paper we have studied a usage based lease contract for remanufactured equipment such as dump trucks. Under this lease contract, the equipment is leased for a period of Γ and a maximum usage, U. We find the optimal solution jointly (joint optimization) for both parties, and then seek the optimal decisions using a Nash game theory formulation. One can model the decision problems for the lessor and the lessee using a Stackelberg game theory formulation, and consider a subsequent of LC periods in which the usage pattern may change significantly from period to period (this is due to a different lessee leases the equipment). These two topics are currently under investigation.

Acknowledgements. This work is funded by the Ministry of Research, Technology, and Higher Education of the Republic of Indonesia through the scheme of "PUPT 2018" with contract number SP DIPA-042.06.1.401516/2018.

References

1. Neely, A.: Exploring the financial consequences of the servitization of manufacturing. Oper. Manag. Res. **1**(2), 103–118 (2008)
2. Kindström, D., Kowalkowski, C.: Service innovation in product centric firms: a multidimensional business model perspective. J. Bus. Ind. Mark. **29**(2), 96–111 (2014)
3. Mont, O., Dalhammar, C., Jacobsson, N.: A new business model for baby prams based on leasing and product remanufacturing. J. Cleaner Prod. **14**(17), 1509–1518 (2006)
4. Besch, K.: Product-service systems for office furniture: barriers and opportunities on the European market. J. Cleaner Prod. **13**(10–11), 1083–1094 (2005)
5. Lindahl, M., Sundin, E., Sakao, T.: Environmental and economic benefits of integrated product service offerings quantified with real business cases. J. Cleaner Prod. **64**, 288–296 (2014)
6. Yalabik, B., Chhajed, D., Petruzzi, N.C.: Product and sales contract design in remanufacturing. Int. J. Prod. Econ. **154**, 299–312 (2014)
7. Lieckens, K.T., Colen, P.J., Lambrecht, M.R.: Network and contract optimization for maintenance services with remanufacturing. Comput. Oper. Res. **54**, 232–244 (2015)
8. Jaturonnatee, J., Murthy, D.N.P., Boondiskulchok, R.: Optimal preventive maintenance of leased equipment with corrective minimal repairs. Eur. J. Oper. Res. **174**, 201–215 (2006)
9. Murthy, D.N.P., Jack, N.: Extended Warranties, Maintenance Service and Lease Contracts. Series in Reliability Engineering. Springer, London (2014)
10. Bhaskaran, S.R., Gilbert, S.: Implications of channel structure for leasing or selling durable goods. McCombs Research Paper Series No. IROM-01-07 (2007)
11. Pongpech, J., Murthy, D.N.P.: Optimal periodic preventive maintenance policy for leased equipment. Reliab. Eng. Syst. Saf. **91**, 772–777 (2006)
12. Pongpech, J., Murthy, D.N.P., Boondiskulchok, R.: Maintenance strategies for used equipment under lease. J. Qual. Maintenance Eng. **12**, 52–67 (2006)
13. Yeh, R.H., Kao, K.C., Chang, W.I.: Preventive maintenance policy for leased products under various maintenance costs. Expert Syst. Appl. **38**(4), 3558–3562 (2011)
14. Aras, F., Gullu, R., Yurulmez, S.: Optimal inventory and pricing policies for remanufacturable leased products. Int. J. Prod. Econ. **133**, 262–271 (2011)
15. Hamidi, M., Liao, H., Szidarovszky, F.: Non-cooperative and cooperative game-theoretic models for usage-based lease contracts. Eur. J. Oper. Res. **255**, 163–174 (2016)
16. Iskandar, B.P., Husniah, H.: Optimal preventive maintenance for a two dimensional lease contract. Comput. Ind. Eng. **113**, 693–703 (2017)
17. Yeh, R.H., Kao, K.C., Chang, W.I.: Optimal maintenance policy for leased equipment using failure rate reduction. Comput. Ind. Eng. **57**(1), 304–309 (2009)

Manufacturing Performance Management in Smart Factories

Increasing Rate of Diffusion of Innovation in Supply Chain: Targeting the Early Adopters in UK Supply Chain

S. Y. Lee[1], M. K. Lim[2(✉)], D. Food[3], and J. Hu[1]

[1] Coventry University, Coventry CV1 5FB, UK
[2] Chongqing University, Chongqing 400044, China
Ming.lim@cqu.edu.cn
[3] University of Warwick, Coventry CV4 7AL, UK

Abstract. Innovations (technology and software) had revolutionized the modern supply chain and bring numerous benefits. Nevertheless, not all party in a supply chain is ready to embrace and adopt the innovations when they are first released due to the substantial risk and uncertainty. Early adopters however are bold enough to take the risk in trying an innovation and later lead the late adopters in using the said innovation, which also act as a motivator in helping to spread and diffuse that innovation. This research aimed to look for characteristics of early adopters in UK supply chain at the firm level, specifically within purchasing of software innovation. It is discovered that the early adopters in UK supply chain fit the description that was put forward by various researchers stating that early adopters are quick, bold and take the risk in purchasing a new software that is just released to the market even if they are expensive. They will advise other company to buy a good software. They however do not exhibit clear traits in their company profile, in terms of size, age and type of industry. The profile of the purchasing manager(s) in the firm also fail to exhibit distinct characteristics in term of gender and age. The media habit and software usage, as well as methods to gather information about new software, however reveal some positive results. They are willing to join any group in social media and they use most social media apart from LinkedIn.

Keywords: Early adopter · Supply chain · Diffusion of innovations

1 Introduction

1.1 Innovations and Supply Chain

As recently as 1990s, supply chain operations were highly disorganised and inefficient where average time for a company to process and deliver merchandise from warehouse inventory to a customer ranged from 15 to 30 days, due to inefficiencies in orders preparation, processing, picking and delivery. Thankfully, impregnations of innovations had successfully introduced massive changes to the incompetent operations, for example, commercialisation of technology such as computer, internet and information transmission system as well as development of Software such as Enterprise Resources

I. Moon et al. (Eds.): APMS 2018, IFIP AICT 536, pp. 209–214, 2018.
https://doi.org/10.1007/978-3-319-99707-0_26

Planning software (ERP) had effectively minimised the problems faced in supply chain. Apparently, innovations could revolutionise the supply chain and make supply chain to be more efficient [1].

1.2   Diffusion of Innovations and Role of Early Adopters

Despite of the numerous benefits innovations can offer, research shown that not all party in a supply chain is ready to embrace and adopt the innovations when they are first released due to the substantial risks and uncertainties [2]. Analysis of several hundred of major innovations over past two centuries shows that the time an innovation takes to be mature (also known as rate of diffusion) for different innovations are different, with a typical span between ten to fifty years between innovation and successful diffusion [3].

This delayed in diffusion rate is because as high as 84% of people in the population possess high degree of scepticism and a small risk appetite, causes them to not adopt an innovation when it is first introduced to them [2]. Rogers [2] in his model of Diffusion of Innovations (DOI), shows that innovation can only diffuse after a critical mass of adopters had existed, where the proportion of firms already using an innovation would increase the rate of diffusion by exerting competitive pressures among late adopters.

Drawing from the literature, it is hypothesised that identifying the early adopter helps in attaining critical mass quicker and catalyse diffusion of innovation. Nevertheless, there is a gap falling short in studying the characteristics of early adopters in supply chain to help in accretion of critical mass of adopters. Existing research mostly focus on general or macro-level characteristics of early adopters, where its application on micro-level supply chain company, especially focusing on purchasing of software innovation, is scarcely studied. This research thus aimed at closing the gap by looking for early adopters at the firm level, in SC specifically in the UK, within purchasing of software innovation. Subsequently extract their characteristics from various dimensions, such as company profile, profile of purchasing manager(s) in the company, company's media habit, and methods of gathering information about new software. This can contribute by ensuring fast diffusion of innovation in supply chain which ultimately benefit the entire supply chain in the UK.

1.3   Characteristics of Early Adopter at the Firm Level

Researchers that studied on characteristics of early adopters shows that they possess distinctive attitude towards innovations. At the firm level, early adopters are found to be higher in rate of purchasing an innovation compared to late adopters (i.e.: they adopt higher number of innovations from an available pool of innovations within a given period) [4]. They are bold and take the risk in purchasing a new software that is just released to the market (i.e. having larger risk appetite or risk tolerance) that allows them to adopt technologies that may ultimately fail. The financial resources are one of the factors that increase their risk tolerance by helping them to absorb the cost in case of failures. They are richer and insensitive to price of the innovations, which causes them to use the best quality innovations regardless of the price, as the cost of failures can be easily absorbed. They are also better educated, more literate, have higher social status and more upward social mobility, making them have tendency to advise others, as they enjoy being respected by his/her peers and enjoy having a reputation for successful and discrete use of innovative ideas [2].

In the context of organisational/company, size was found to be the common characteristics possessed by early adopters' company but empirical evidence regarding the impact of size shows mixed results. Also, due to imbalance in nature of income distribution, early adopter is richer and able to afford an innovation, where more consumers (late adopters) can only afford it when the price of an innovation falls. They are also generally found to have founded for a long time compared to the late adopters' firm (i.e.: more senior and consequently more experienced and possesses higher degree of opinion leadership, social status, financial liquidity and connection to knowledge and financial providers). Besides, different type industries (primary/secondary/tertiary/ quaternary) were found to positively correlate with level of innovations adoption [5].

Other than that, gender and age of a purchasing manager were also found to correlate with the innovations adoption and its diffusion, with gender being positively correlated with diffusion rate and vice versa for age. They also tend to have higher degree of centralisation (i.e.: decisive power concentrate on few individuals). Further, they are socially active and inclines towards creating reviews around product they like or dislike and tend to utilise technology to aid their daily operation more than a late adopter. Whether or not these observations can be observed in UK supply chain, especially within the purchasing of innovations, is the primary focus of this research [6].

2 Method

2.1 Sampling and Data Collection

Data for the study were obtained from online survey of 500 SC executives from micro companies and SMEs in the UK. The SC executives were invited to participate in this study using LinkedIn social media. A total of 60 valid responses were received (a 12% response rate). The low response rate might be attributed to the length of questionnaire and the fact that no follow up was used to improve the response rate.

2.2 Profile of Responding Companies

The responding firms present in all industry sectors [11.1% in Primary (raw material extraction), 46% in secondary (manufacturing), 28.6% in tertiary (service), and 9.5% in quaternary (high tech)]. The distribution of companies in terms of their age (or years of establishment) is almost equal (57.1% founded less than 50 years and 42.9% founded at least 50 years). The respondents' seniority ranged from lower management, manager and senior management (28%, 58%, and 14% respectively). As our study used a self-administered questionnaire, this mix is very important to provide responses that is free from cognitive biases, as the respondents from senior management position would be responding to survey that present themselves in a favourable manner.

2.3   Measurement of Early Adopters

The key sampling element in the study was the early adopter. This group of adopters was identified through one closed-question on the questionnaire, where respondents are asked to select their level of agreement using 5-point scale (1 = "strongly disagree" and 5 = "strongly agree") towards the statement: "my company consider itself as an Early Adopter". Of the 60 respondents, 3 respondents (5%) identified themselves as early adopters who "strongly agree" with the statement. It is these 3 respondents who were classified in this study as "Early adopters" and whose responses were contrasted with the other 57 respondents (95%) to examine possible differences in several dimensions. This 1:19 ratio of respondents of Early adopters compared to the late adopters differ from the general distribution proposed by Rogers [2] in model of DOI, which is 1:39. However, the distribution discovered from this study compared very favourably with recent findings reported by Cecere [7].

3   Results and Discussion

For each of the dimension, differences in responses between early adopters and late adopters (remainder of the samples) were investigated. Since both independent and dependent variables were treated as nominally scaled variables, bivariate chi-square analysis was used to investigate frequency differences in the responses. Specifically, comparisons were made of the number of early adopters and late adopters in various dimensions. The attitude towards innovation for both early adopters and late adopters were explored. Among five attitudes investigated, four exhibit significant chi-square scores ($p \leq 0.05$) which similar to the theory that was put forward by Rogers [2]. Early adopters in UK supply chain tend to advise other company to buy software ($X^2 = 38$), bold and take the risk in purchasing a new software that is just released ($X^2 = 24.4$), buy a new software more quickly than others when it is released ($X^2 = 5.12$), and using the best quality software even if it is expensive ($X^2 = 5.12$). However difference in price sensitivity between early adopters and late adopters could not be observed in adopters in the UK supply chain (Table 1).

The differences in company profile between early adopters and late adopters however cannot be statistically proven to be significant. A guideline to differentiate the early adopters and the late adopters in UK supply chain (result with $p > 0.05$) could not be established. From the result obtained, the theory that was put forward by researchers stating that larger organisation adopt technology faster could not be replicated in this study, signifying that business size was not a significant indicator in identifying early adopter in UK supply chain. Other than that, theory stating that early adopters at the firm level generally wealthier and had been founded for a long time cannot be observed in this research (more percentage of late adopters being founded longer than early adopter). Same goes to the relationship between innovations adoption level and the type of industries (primary/secondary/tertiary/quaternary), as well as the gender and age of purchasing manager(s) in the UK supply chain, could not be verified in this research. The findings of media habit and software used by early adopters in UK supply chain shows that they are willing to join any virtual group in social media ($X^2 = 5.15$),

Table 1. Characteristics of early adopters vs. late adopters.

Category	Early adopters (n = 3) (%)	Remainder of the sample (n = 57) (%)	X^2
More than 100 employees	100	85	0.56
Founded more than 50 years old	33	43	0.16
Generate more than £700 k turnover	100	85	0.523
Involved internationally	100	87	0.434
Listed in the list of fortune 500	67	33	1.45
Involved in primary industry	67	46	0.293
Involved in secondary industry	33	29	0.468
Involved in tertiary industry	0	9	0.967
Involved in quaternary industry	0	10	0.38
Male only manager, which is:	100	84	0.193
A male	100	46	1.14
A group dominated by male	0	38	1.02
Female only manager, which is:	0	16	0.193
A female	0	13	0.156
A group dominated by female	0	3	0.028
Manager age below 30 years old	0	2	0.047
Manager age between 30–35 years old	0	18	0.449
Manager age between 35–40 years old	50	23	0.782
Manager age between 40–45 years old	50	36	0.153
Manager age between 45–50 years old	0	16	0.375
Manager age above 50 years old	0	5	0.095
Social media active (create posts)	100	79	0.775
Express fondness of products	100	66	1.5
Beta tester	100	54	2.42
Willingness to join group	100	26	5.15[a]
Software utiliser, which is:	100	84	0.569
Inventory optimisation	100	72	1.12
Transportation and Logistics	67	57	0.098
Planning	67	77	0.152
Distribution Management	33	49	0.275
E-commerce	67	62	0.0295
Gather info via social media, which is:	100	42	3.81[a]
Facebook	67	57	0.095
Twitter	33	64	0.977
LinkedIn	67	100	4.96[b]
Gather info via word of mouth	67	35	1.26
Gather info via colleague	67	35	1.26
Gather info via summit/event	67	54	0.188
Gather info via magazine	33	23	0.165

[a] $P < 0.05$; [b] $P < 0.01$; [c] $P < 0.001$

but the traits such as social media active and express fondness of products in that platform is unable to be observed. The willingness to participate in software Beta and tendency to utilise software and the type of software utilised were unable to be confirmed. Lastly, social media was found to be the mostly used method for early adopters in UK supply chain to gather information about new software (apart of using word of mouth/colleague/summit or event/magazine). They however do not use LinkedIn as much as late adopter in gathering information about new software.

4 Conclusion

It is discovered that the early adopters in UK supply chain fit the description that was put forward by Rogers [2] and various researchers, stating that early adopters are quick, bold and take the risk in purchasing a new software that is just released to the market even if they are expensive. They will use the best quality software and will advise other company to buy a software. They however do not exhibit clear traits in their company profile. The profile of the purchasing manager(s) in the firm also fail to exhibit distinct characteristics in term of gender and age. The media habit and software usage, as well as methods to gather information about new software, however reveal some positive results. Early adopters in the UK supply chain are willing to join any group in social media. It is recommended to look for them using social media apart of LinkedIn. A practical implication drawn from this research is the ways to look for early adopters in the UK supply chain, based on dimensions investigated in the research. It should be noted that early adopters do not exhibit clear traits in their company profile, for example size, age and type of industry, gender and age of purchasing manager(s). Practitioner are advised to look for early adopters from dimensions other than the dimensions stated from above. Future research will look into building the profile of early adopters in UK supply chain from other dimensions, as well as exploring the factors that causes the early adopters do not exhibit certain characteristics as anticipated.

References

1. Bowersox, D.: Supply Chain Logistics Management, 4th edn. McGraw-Hill, New York (2013)
2. Rogers, E.M.: Diffusion of Innovations, 5th edn. Free Press, New York (2003)
3. Nakicenovic, N.: The automobile road to technological change: diffusion of the automobile as a process of technological substitution. Technol. Forecast. Soc. Change **29**(4), 309–340 (1986)
4. Subramanian, A., Nilakanta, S.: Organizational innovativeness: exploring the relationship between organizational determinants of innovation, types of innovations, and measures of organizational performance. Omega **24**(6), 631–647 (1996)
5. Tornatzky, L.G., Fleischer, M., Chakrabarti, A.K.: Processes of Technological Innovation. Lexington books, Lanham (1990)
6. Morris, M.G., Venkatesh, V.: Age differences in technology adoption decisions: implications for a changing work force. Pers. Psychol. **53**(2), 375–403 (2000)
7. Cecere, L.: https://www.linkedin.com/pulse/doug-oberhelman-learns-lesson-lora-cecere. Accessed 22 Feb 2018

The Interaction of Global Networks in Their Evolutions: A Longitudinal Case Study

Yang Cheng[1($\boxtimes$)] and Ruihong Gao[2]

[1] Department of Materials and Production,
Aalborg University, Aalborg, Denmark
cy@business.aau.dk
[2] Faculty of Business Administration,
Osaka University of Economics, Osaka, Japan

Abstract. Based on a longitudinal study of two companies, this paper investigates the evolution of manufacturing, supply, and strategic networks and suggests it can be viewed as a long-term, stepwise, expansive, iterative and interactive process and thereby, can be called "interactive evolution of constructs and networks". It is further found that the evolution of plants and manufacturing networks is more closely linked with the evolution of suppliers and supply networks, and vice versa; the evolution of JVs and strategic networks can be linked with the evolutions of plants/suppliers and manufacturing/supply networks, but depending on the purposes behind the establishment of JVs. Finally, this paper proposes short-term and long-term solutions to manage different networks holistically.

Keywords: Manufacturing network · Supply network · Strategic network

1 Introduction

Since the 1980s, it has been impossible for manufacturing companies to withstand the trend of globalisation. There are generally three modes for manufacturers to globalise their operations [1]. The first mode is the so-called **dominant equity mode**, which allows full ownership and control. The explosively increased FDI have further resulted in the widespread restructuring of manufacturing systems, moving from a focus on the plant to one on the manufacturing network. A manufacturing network, defined as a coordinated aggregation (network) of intra-firm plants/factories located in different places, is normally studied as a wholly owned and internal network in which all plants are under full financial control [1, 2].

Meanwhile, it has also become more accepted for manufacturing companies to globalise their operations by following the second mode, i.e. the **diffused governance mode**, which lacks ownership and has only limited possibilities for control. This development has further pushed companies into new relationships and made the subjects of supply chain/network become more relevant and required [3]. A supply network, defined as a network of connected and interdependent organisations mutually and cooperatively working together to manage the flow of goods and services from original supply sources to end users, is normally analysed as an external (inter-firm)

I. Moon et al. (Eds.): APMS 2018, IFIP AICT 536, pp. 215–222, 2018.
https://doi.org/10.1007/978-3-319-99707-0_27

network with facilities owned by different organisations and characterised by sets of purposeful and connected exchange relationships [1].

The last mode is the **balanced mode**, which emphasizes shared ownership, equal partnership and balanced contracts, and appears in the forms of strategic alliance (SA) and joint venture (JV). The prevalence of SA and JV further stimulates more considerations on strategic networks. A strategic network exists within and is an integral part of the overall inter-firm supply network. It goes beyond intra-firm manufacturing network and refers to inter-firm collaboration with external partners, but it mainly addresses long-lasting inter-organisational relationships [4].

The rationale for choosing specific modes is not necessarily guided by the same principles and the managements of manufacturing network, supply network, and strategic network are usually discussed independently [2, 3]. The existing studies generally do not adequately address in a systematic manner the complex interactions between the evolutions of different networks. Nevertheless, any company in the practice that intends to establish a global operations structure might adopt three modes simultaneously. Therefore, this paper aims to address such a cognitive gap and develop an in-depth understanding of the interactions between the evolutions of manufacturing network, supply network, and strategic network by exploring RQ1, i.e. *how the evolution of one type of network affects other networks*. This issue has become ever more urgent to manufacturing companies in the context of today's business environment. Companies could be out of business if they do not analyse and adjust the operations of their networks holistically and proactively. Thus, this paper also aims to explore RQ2, i.e. *how to manage different networks in a holistic way*.

2   Literature Review

2.1   Manufacturing, Supply, and Strategic Networks

Setting its root in the disciplines of operations management, the research on manufacturing network seeks to extend the boundaries of traditional manufacturing systems from a single plant towards a multi-plant system and further, to globally dispersed and coordinated plant networks [5]. Thus, manufacturing network can still be seen as a manufacturing system, but certainly with many different characteristics from the classic model. Two types of decisions can generally be distinguished related to manufacturing network: those concerning "configuration", which primarily addresses structural decisions to design a network, and those related to "coordination", which primarily addresses infrastructural links among plants [1].

Similar to manufacturing network, supply network also has its own missions, architectures, mechanisms, and strategy processes, but, differently, the research on supply network sets its roots in physical distribution and material management. It tends to analyse the network as external with facilities owned by different organisations [1, 3] and focuses on the links between the nodes (and specifically distribution nodes), whereas manufacturing network research tends to focus on the (manufacturing) nodes themselves [1]. Accordingly, compared to studies on manufacturing network, the research in the field of supply network has quite different focuses in addition to physical distribution and material management, such as customer relationship management, customer service management, demand management, procurement, and so on. Similar to other areas in management, these focuses appear to generally fall into two broad streams: the "hard" system-dominated focuses that deal with technological and infrastructural issues and the "soft" people-focused focuses that deal with social relationships [6].

SAs and JVs are integral part of the overall inter-firm supply network and as such, the management of them is directly related to the characteristics of these inter-firm supply networks and the embeddedness a firm exhibits in such networks. Accordingly, recent academic inquiry has directed attention to examining SA and JV from a network perspective [4]. The strategic network area is examined by different streams of research: (1) the emergence of strategic networks, answering why and how firms build strategic networks [7]; (2) the configuration of strategic networks; (3) the formation of strategic networks, exploring the formation of relationships and the formation processes [8]; and (4) the management of strategic networks with the emphases on the capability of strategic network, management approaches and tools, and the performance assessment of strategic networks [7, 8].

2.2 Literature Analysis, Theoretical Gaps, and Research Questions

According to the above review, it is obvious that the literature on manufacturing network, supply network, and strategic network is well established, but three research gaps can still be identified. First, according to the definitions of networks stated early in the introduction, intra-firm plant, inter-firm SA and JV, and other inter-firm organisations can be respectively viewed as the basic constructs of manufacturing network, strategic network, and supply network. However, the two levels of analysis, i.e. construct level and network level, are usually discussed independently to reduce the complexity of research on manufacturing, strategic, and supply networks. Some of more recent studies in the area of manufacturing network attempted to address this gap, but they are still limited in the domain of manufacturing network. To our knowledge, there is no research addressing how the development of SAs, JVs, and other inter-firm organisations affects the plants within a manufacturing network and leads to changes of that manufacturing networks, or vice versa. This actually implies the second research gap, i.e. the studies on manufacturing, strategic, and supply networks are limited within their own domains, and the interaction between different networks is not well addressed. However, there is abundant empirical evidence that the manufacturing industry is currently transforming from plant based manufacturing system centralised or dispersed within one country to plant networks with geographic dispersion and operational integration owned by a multinational corporation and from the traditional vertically-integrated value chain to collaboration between specialised independent companies [3]. Thus, it is important to discuss different networks in a holistic framework. Some studies have addressed this issue [5, 9], but they neglect the fact that individual subsidiaries and affiliates, joint ventures, strategic alliances, independent suppliers, and distribution channels have gradually developed to be manufacturing networks, strategic networks, and supply networks, which is the third gap. Addressing the above gaps, this paper aims to investigate the interaction between manufacturing, strategic, and supply networks in their evolution, specifically paying attention to both construct and network levels. Two research questions listed in the Introduction are expected to be answered.

3 Research Methodology

In order to answer the "how" questions formulated above, the case study was selected as the primary research method and mainly used for an explorative purpose [10]. To obtain the understandings on the interactions between different networks in their evolution in depth, this paper chose to specifically focus on a sample of two case companies from the same industry, i.e. machine tool industry, but with different size and from different countries. One of the case companies, i.e. FFG, is the third biggest manufacturer of machine tools in the world, in terms of more than 5000 employees, 50 production bases in 10 countries, and 37 machine tool brands. The other case company, i.e. TM, is relatively small with around 510 employees, but has been developing and producing machine tools since 1961. In fact, TM is one of the most important partners of FFG. They have established several JVs together, which brings the opportunity to investigate the development of a strategic network from both sides.

Empirical data was collected between 2010 and 2017 following a three-step approach. First, longitudinal secondary sources were analysed. Second, the researchers visited the headquarters and the facilities of two case companies in China, Taiwan, Japan, and Italy to conduct interviews. More than 20 interviews were conducted with group chairmen, presidents, general managers, production managers, and global sourcing managers, each of which typically spanned three to four hours. Finally, combing the data from different sources, case reports were written, returned to the interviewees for verification, and finalised after several rounds.

Data analysis was carried out simultaneously with data collection, creating an iterative process between the interviews, literature reviews and analysis. More specifically, it followed the framework analysis approach proposed by [10].

4 Case Analysis and Discussion

4.1 Interactive Evolution of Constructs and Networks

In FFG and TM, the evolution of their plants and manufacturing networks generally followed the approach described in [11]. In both companies, their overseas plants were mainly established for low-cost labour and market proximity, but they evolved gradually and simultaneously. From a plant perspective, these plant evolutions were often interdependent. As the portfolios of products and processes flowed among plants, strategic roles of related plants (i.e. transferors and receivers) were being changed simultaneously and gradually. From a manufacturing network perspective, inter-related evolutions of plants can also lead to the portfolio of plants being changed from time to time, which represented the transformation of the configurations of manufacturing networks and further triggered the redevelopment of coordination mechanism of manufacturing networks.

Meanwhile, the evolution of plants and manufacturing networks in two case companies further influenced, as well as being influenced by, the evolution of suppliers and supply networks. When FFG established its first plant in China, it initially imported components from Taiwan and Japan, but soon asked its Taiwanese and Japanese suppliers to relocate to China, in order to support its local production operations. Differently, TM chose to establish a JV with FFG and heavily rely on the suppliers developed by FFG when it entered the Chinese market. Otherwise, it might also have to import components from Japan. Nevertheless, TM treated the JV, i.e. FT-China, as its own plant. After accumulating proper capabilities, both FT-China and the Chinese plant of FFG were given more responsibilities to produce more products by using more complicated processes. Along with more products/processes being transferred to their Chinese facilities, it became natural for FFG and TM to have more local suppliers, since for FFG not all of its suppliers in Taiwan and Japan followed its footprint and started operating in China; and for TM more cost reduction might be achieved by engaging more local suppliers. Nevertheless, both companies had to help local suppliers to develop their capabilities, in order to supply their specific production. After accumulating their capabilities and proving their viability, the Chinese suppliers were given more production tasks and used to replace the suppliers from other places, which at the same time led to the changes in the supply network configuration. Meanwhile, the development of the Chinese suppliers in turn triggered more products/processes being transferred to the Chinese plants and FT-China, making them responsible for producing more kinds of and more complicated products. TM even outsourced more production activities to its suppliers. The manufacturing networks of both companies were accordingly, reconfigured.

Furthermore, the evolution of JVs and strategic networks in two case companies was also closely linked with the evolutions of plants/suppliers and manufacturing/supply networks, but in different manners depending on the purposes behind the establishment of JVs. First, FFG established FT-China with TM, as well as the other JV with TM and a Japanese supplier, for the purpose of learning. The development of these JVs gradually facilitated the other plants of FFG improving their capabilities by transferring technological and managerial knowledge to them. In this case, these JVs were more like centres of excellence to FFG and hereby contributed to the evolution of its plants and manufacturing network directly. Second, TM established JVs mainly for the purpose of initially penetrating into new markets and later expanding in those markets. It treated JVs as its own plants and as a part of its manufacturing network. Along with the development of these JVs, more products/processes were transferred from TM's plants to it, which accordingly led to the evolution of plants/suppliers and manufacturing/supply networks of TM as discussed above. Third, similarly, FFG established the other JV in Japan with TM (i.e. FT-Japan) for the purpose of penetrating into new market. Nevertheless, the development of this JV did not have much influence on the evolution of plants/suppliers and manufacturing/supply networks of both companies, since this JV was established mainly for selling FFG's products in Japan and ensuring TM could provide necessary after-sales services and maintenance. Finally, FFG also established JVs with some of its Chinese suppliers for the purpose of helping them improving their capabilities, which accordingly contributed to the evolution of these suppliers and further led to the reconfigurations of supply network, as well as the evolution of plants and manufacturing network, as discussed above. Nevertheless, no matter which purposes JVs were established for, their development and success generally triggered both companies to establish more JVs and extend their strategic networks.

4.2 How to Manage Different Networks in a Holistic Way?

It is indeed difficult to manage different networks in a holistic way, as there are too many elements that need to be considered. Alternatively, we can attempt to address what are the unique benefits that might not be obtained without running different networks holistically. Then, the question becomes identifying the unique benefits and ensuring companies can obtain them from operating different networks holistically.

In the near-term, companies can benefit from operating different networks holistically in terms of three aspects, as demonstrated in the empirical cases. First, operating different networks holistically allows plants, suppliers, and JVs learn more from each other, and thereby accelerates learning and moves down the learning curve quickly. Sharing knowledge among different constructs and networks is essential for obtaining this benefit. Second, operating different networks holistically enhances the ability of a company to pool resources, capacities, and capabilities in multiple network constructs, and hence copes with variability of demand and production processes. Sharing resources, capacities, and capabilities is the key for enjoying this benefit. Third, operating different networks holistically facilitates more coordinated planning and responsiveness among different network constructs, and thereby reduces potential mistakes and creates better alignments between manufacturing, supply, and strategic networks. In this case, information sharing among different constructs and networks is necessary. Comparatively speaking, it is obvious that the key to obtain these benefits is *Sharing*. Then, exploring how to stimulate sharing among different networks is pivotal for answering how to manage different networks in a holistic way in near-term. The empirical case study of FFG provides some good demonstrations, showing the sharing among different networks can be stimulated from both configuration and coordination perspectives. From the configuration perspective, FFG established three manufacturing bases in Hangzhou, China. It not only placed all its Chinese plants in these manufacturing bases, but also invited its suppliers and partners to place their plants there. In doing so, FFG would benefit from cluster effect, facilitate sharing among different networks, and ensure that every entity in the networks can work together in a mutually complementary multifaceted manner. From the coordination perspective, FFG appointed regional managers, whose responsibilities included visiting plants, suppliers, and JVs in the regions in a regular basis, tracking their development, acting as a broker to coordinate them and as a bridge to link them with other regions and headquarters.

In the long-term, companies can benefit from managing different networks in a holistic way, only when they continuously optimise the allocation of production and procurement among their plants, suppliers, and JVs. In order to continuously optimise the allocation of production and procurement among their plants, suppliers, and JVs, companies have to monitor various factors frequently, integrate them as a whole, distinguish or predict their every (possible) change, address the implications of their evolution and interaction. The factors that can influence the allocation of production and procurement among plants, suppliers, and JVs are as follows: (1) *The development of product and process.* In FFG and TM, new products and processes are normally developed, improved, and manufactured in their lead-plants or JVs initially. During the course of their life cycles, their production gradually becomes mature and standard, which further enable transferring them to other plants, JVs, and even suppliers; (2) *Capability development of plant, supplier, and JV.* As demonstrated in FFG and MT, plants, suppliers, and JVs normally start their operations from simple products and basic processes due to the fact that they do not have the capabilities to handle complicated production tasks. However, they are able to develop their own competencies based on the accumulation of their experiences with simple operations and the supports from headquarters and partners. Once they are capable and qualified, more (complicated) production activities can be allocated to them, both intra-firm and inter-firm; (3) *Change of external environment of construct location.* Location conditions of plants, suppliers, and JVs change dynamically, which might have positive and negative impacts on the allocation of production and procurement. For example, TM established and moved some of its production to FT-China, because on the one hand the Japanese domestic market has become mature and entered into a decreasing phase; on the other hand the Chinese market has grown rapidly. Similarly, FFG established its first plant in China due to the advantage of low cost labour and the potential of Chinese markets. Afterwards, it continuously upgraded its Chinese plants because China developed at a faster pace in the last decades. This also explained why TM set up International Purchasing Office in China, purchased more from Chinese and Taiwanese suppliers, and extended its supply networks in China and Taiwan rather than in Thailand, even though it also produced there. Nevertheless, the above three factors enable the re-allocation of production and procurement activities, but real changes have to be eventually driven by top management when they recognise opportunities and attempt to make relevant; (4) *high-level strategic decisions*, including relocating production activities among existing plants, suppliers, and JVs; relocating procurement activities among existing suppliers; establishing new plants and JVs to accommodate relocated production; acquiring/merging plants and JVs to accommodate relocated production; closing plants and JVs; supporting the development of plants, suppliers, and JVs.

5   Conclusion

Based on a longitudinal study of two companies, this paper bridges the gaps identified in the existing literature about the evolution of manufacturing, supply, and strategic networks by exploring how the evolution of one type of network affects other networks and how to manage different networks in a holistic way. It is suggested that the evolution can be viewed as a long-term, stepwise, expansive, iterative and interactive process and, thereby, can be called "interactive evolution of constructs and networks". It is further found that the evolution of plants and manufacturing networks is more closely linked with the evolution of suppliers and supply networks, and vice versa; the evolution of JVs and strategic networks can be linked with the evolutions of plants/suppliers and manufacturing/supply networks, but depending on the purposes behind the establishment of JVs. Finally, this paper proposes short-term and long-term solutions to manage different networks holistically.

This paper's findings and discussions were based on case studies of one Taiwanese and one Japanese companies. The small sample size obviously limits generalisation of the presented conclusions. Besides, the evolution of global networks is closely related to the activities across international boundaries, it becomes imperative to have discussions on the variables such as international culture, administration, geographical challenges and economic situation.

References

1. Cheng, Y., Farooq, S., Johansen, J.: International manufacturing network: past, present, and future. Int. J. Oper. Prod. Manag. **35**(3), 392–429 (2015)
2. Cheng, Y., Chaudhuri, A., Farooq, S.: Interplant coordination, supply chain integration, and operational performance of a plant in a manufacturing network: a mediation analysis. Supply Chain Manag.: Int. J. **21**(5), 550–568 (2016)
3. Cheng, Y., Johansen, J.: Operations network development: internationalisation and externalisation of value chain activities. Prod. Plann. Control **25**(16), 1351–1369 (2014)
4. Carnovale, S., Rogers, D.S., Yeniyurt, S.: Bridging structural holes in global manufacturing equity based partnerships: a network analysis of domestic vs. international joint venture formations. J. Purchasing Supply Manag. **22**(1), 7–17 (2016)
5. Shi, Y., Gregory, M.: Emergence of global manufacturing virtual networks and establishment of new manufacturing infrastructure for faster innovation and firm growth. Prod. Plann. Control **16**(6), 621–631 (2005)
6. Burgess, K., Singh, P.J., Koroglu, R.: Supply chain management: a structured literature review and implications for future research. Int. J. Oper. Prod. Manag. **26**(7), 703–729 (2006)
7. Wassmer, U.: Alliance portfolios: a review and research agenda. J. Manag. **36**(1), 141–171 (2010)
8. Grimm, C., Knemeyer, M., Polyviou, M., Ren, X.: Supply chain management research in management journals: a review of recent literature (2004–2013). Int. J. Phys. Distrib. Logistics Manag. **45**(5), 404–458 (2015)
9. Ernst, D., Kim, L.: Global production networks, knowledge diffusion, and local capability formation. Res. Policy **31**(8–9), 1417–1429 (2002)
10. Yin, R.: Case Study Research: Design and Methods. Sage Publications, Inc., Thousand Oaks (2003)
11. Cheng, Y., Farooq, S., Johansen, J.: Manufacturing network evolution: a manufacturing plant perspective. Int. J. Oper. Prod. Manag. **31**(12), 1311–1331 (2011)

Measuring Similarity for Manufacturing Process Models

Hyun Ahn[1] and Tai-Woo Chang[2(✉)]

[1] Division of Computer Engineering, Kyonggi University,
Gyeonggi 16227, Republic of Korea
hahn@kgu.ac.kr
[2] Department of Industrial and Management Engineering/Intelligence
and Manufacturing Research Center, Kyonggi University,
Gyeonggi 16227, Republic of Korea
keenbee@kgu.ac.kr

Abstract. In manufacturing companies, it is vital to manage their manufacturing processes in order to ensure high quality of products and manufacturing consistency. Because so-called smart factories interconnect machines and acquire processing data, the business process management (BPM) approach can enrich the capability of manufacturing operation management. In this paper, we propose BPM-based similarity measures for manufacturing processes and apply them to the processes of a real factory. In addition to the structural similarity of the existing studies, we suggest a production-related operation similarity. Our contribution is considered on the assumption that a manufacturing company adopts the BPM approach and it operates a variety of manufacturing process models. The similarity measures enable the company to automatically search and reutilize models or parts of models within a repository of manufacturing process models.

Keywords: Manufacturing process · Business process management
Process similarity · BPMN

1 Introduction

As the evolution of manufacturing systems has been progressed rapidly, manufacturing companies are able to effectively perform the product lifecycle management (PLM) that includes planning, designing, and manufacturing for their products. Nevertheless, it is still challenging for large-scale manufacturing companies to manage a vast array of their manufacturing processes. Although ICT technologies (e.g., computer-aided manufacturing) have been introduced to promote technical support to the manufacturing operation management (MOM), more comprehensive methodology should be adopted to fully support manufacturing-process-centric management activities.

The business process management (BPM) approach can be one of the promising solutions to tackle this hurdle. BPM aims to continually improve processes through automation of the BPM lifecycle that consists of modeling, execution, monitoring, and redesign through optimization. By applying this approach, manufacturing companies

I. Moon et al. (Eds.): APMS 2018, IFIP AICT 536, pp. 223–231, 2018.
https://doi.org/10.1007/978-3-319-99707-0_28

will benefit from well-defined methodologies, standards, and process-centric engineering practices for optimizing their manufacturing processes.

In this paper, we propose process similarity measures for manufacturers that adopt the BPM approach. To this end, we first describe the transformation from document-based manufacturing process data into BPMN-compliant manufacturing process models. Then, we will describe the similarity measures with illustrative models designed with the basis of real manufacturing processes for thermocouple probe products.

2 BPMN-Based Manufacturing Process Modeling

The Business Process Model and Notation (BPMN) is one of the most outstanding standards for modeling business processes. It has a rich set of element types that can fully represent the context of a business process. Moreover, this standard can be easily extended, and it has been applied to modeling problems in various domains.

Manufacturing companies conventionally possess manufacturing process charts and bill-of-materials (BOM) specifications to define and manage their manufacturing processes. In case of the Republic of Korea, the KSA 3002 standard [1], which is for manufacturing process chart standard, has been used in manufacturing industries. However, it provides only a set of graphical symbols, and there is no technical support for the modeling and automatic executions of manufacturing processes.

A BOM specification contains detailed information about the components (e.g., materials, parts, subassemblies and end products) of each needed to manufacture a particular product. However, it is not sufficient to understand a production flow of a manufacturing process. A manufacturing process consists of a set of manufacturing operations, which have precedence relationships with other preceding and/or successive operations. In this regard, we additionally exploit BOMO (Bill of Material Operations [2]) concept to define production-flow-oriented information of manufacturing process examples.

As shown in Table 1, each operation (e.g., wire welding) consumes a set of components and produces an intermediate component or end product. The preceding operation information provides an execution ordering of the operations within a manufacturing process. Through these basic ingredients of manufacturing process data (process chart, BOM, and BOMO), we can organize structures for manufacturing processes.

To create process models for manufacturing processes, we apply the BPMN standard and extend its notations. The BPMN standard has a variety of its extensions, but there is a lack of modeling notations for the manufacturing domain. In spite of a few studies presented BPMN extensions for manufacturing processes [3], these extensions do not cover the whole context of the manufacturing domain due to the absence of uniformity. Accordingly, we define a minimal set of BPMN notations that suffices to model the examples we present in this paper (Table 2).

Regarding the control-flow aspect, we limit the notations to focus on the examples including only sequential and parallel control-flow patterns. However, we need to add

Table 1. BOMO data of the product examples

End product	Operation ID	name	Component	Intermediate component	Preceding operation
PROBE-01	OP6	Packaging	SUB-05, PACK-01, PACK-04, PACK-06, PACK-13, PACK-17	PROBE-01	OP5
	OP5	Insulation (cement)	SUB-04, MATL-11	SUB-05	OP4
	OP4	Housing	SUB-03, PART-08, PART-18, PART-19	SUB-04	OP3
	OP3	Wire injection	SUB-01, SUB-02	SUB-03	OP1, OP2
	OP2	Quartz tube winding	PART-15, MATL-02, MATL-04	SUB-02	–
	OP1	Wire welding	MATL-03, MATL-05, MATL-06	SUB-01	–
PROBE-02	OP6	Packaging	SUB-08, PACK-01, PACK-03, PACK-10, PACK-14, PACK-17	PROBE-02	OP5
	OP5	Insulation (cement)	SUB-07, MATL-09, MATL-10, MATL-13	SUB-08	OP4
	OP4	Housing	SUB-04, SUB-05, SUB-06, PART-02, PART-04, PART-18, PART-19	SUB-07	OP3, OP8, OP9
	OP3	Wire injection	SUB-01, SUB-02	SUB-04	OP1, OP2
	OP8	Bar welding	PART-09, PART-19	SUB-05	–
	OP9	Sealing	SUB-03, PACK-02, PACK-05	SUB-06	OP7
	OP7	Fastening	PART-10, MATL-01, MATL-07	SUB-03	–
	OP2	Quartz tube winding	PART-15, MATL-02, MATL-04	SUB-02	–
	OP1	Wire welding	MATL-05, MATL-06	SUB-01	–

extra notations for other patterns, such as selective and repetitive patterns to facilitate modeling of sophisticated types of manufacturing processes and systems. Figure 1 shows a modeling result of the examples. Both models represent the manufacturing processes for thermocouple products in the same category. In the next section, we will describe the overall procedure of measuring similarity by taking these models as an example.

Table 2. BPMN notations for manufacturing process models

Notation	Element type	Description
⭕	Start event	A *Start event* indicates where a particular manufacturing process will start.
⭕	End event	An *End event* indicates where a manufacturing process will terminate.
(op)	Operation	An *Operation* is a generic term for manufacturing tasks. Each *Operation* can be performed by machines and/or human workers.
(comp)	Component	A *Component* is a generic term for raw materials, assemblies, and parts needed to manufacture a product.
⬥	Parallel gateway	A *Parallel gateway* is used to create and synchronize disjunctive flows which proceed in parallel fashion.
→	Sequence flow	A *Sequence flow* is used to show the order that operations will be performed in a manufacturing process.
┄┄▶	Component association	A *Component association* is used to link components (e.g., material, part) and operations.

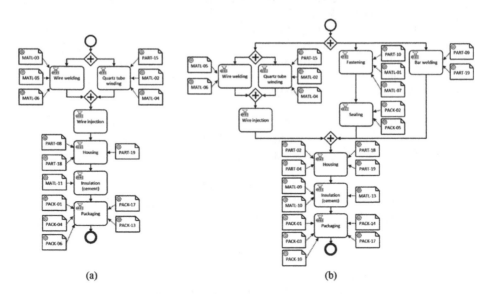

(a)   (b)

Fig. 1. Transformed BPMN manufacturing process models

3   Similarity Measure

Our measuring method of similarity encompasses two sub-concepts of similarity: operation similarity and structural similarity. In this section, we describe an operational procedure of the method with the example models of Fig. 1 to confirm the applicability of our method.

3.1 Preliminaries

We denote a set of manufacturing process models as $\mathbf{M} = M_1, \ldots, M_n$ with n indicating the number of manufacturing process models, a set of operations as $\mathbf{OP} = OP_1, \ldots, OP_m$ with m indicating the number of operations, and a set of components as $\mathbf{C} = C_1, \ldots, C_l$ with l indicating the number of components. We also introduce a mapping function $\delta(\mathbf{OP}) \rightarrow \wp(\mathbf{C})$ that maps from an operation OP_k^i to input components of OP_k^i which are a subset of total components, where $OP_k^i \in \mathbf{OP}$ is the operation OP_k in the process model M_i.

3.2 Operation Similarity

Although many similarity concepts have been proposed for business processes, the manufacturing process has many features that distinguish it from the business process. In particular, production-related factors, which determine the characteristics of a manufacturing process, must be addressed in measuring similarities.

The operation similarity we introduce in this paper is a similarity concept based on associations between operations and components that is one of these influential factors. Mostly, each operation requires a group of certain components to produce end products or intermediary components. Based on this feature, we can calculate a similarity between operations of the same type in different processes. If two operations are the same type of operations but have associations with different component types, we consider two operations to have different characteristics. Mathematically, this similarity is based on the Jaccard coefficient, which is calculated by the division of the number of elements in the intersection set by the number of elements in the union set. Accordingly, the operation similarity between each operation OP_k in the process models M_i and M_j is calculated by Eq. 1.

$$J\left(OP_k^i, OP_k^j\right) = \frac{\left|\delta\left(OP_k^i\right) \cap \delta\left(OP_k^j\right)\right|}{\left|\delta\left(OP_k^i\right) \cup \delta\left(OP_k^j\right)\right|} \tag{1}$$

For example, there are two *Housing* operations (in Fig. 2) of the same type that is included in two different process models M_1 and M_2. The *Housing* operation in M_1 (Fig. 2(a)) is associated with the set of input components $\delta\left(OP_4^1\right) = \{\text{PART} - 08,$ PART $- 18$, PART $- 19\}$, that is different from the set of input components of the *Housing* operation in M_2 (Fig. 2(b)), $\delta\left(OP_4^2\right) = \{\text{PART} - 02, \text{PART} - 04, \text{PART} - 18, \text{PART} - 19\}$. Accordingly, the operation similarity between these two operations is $2/5 = 0.4$.

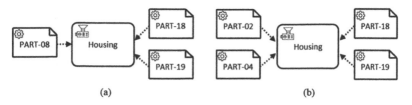

(a)   (b)

Fig. 2. Operation-component associations

In this regard, an operation similarity matrix including operation similarity mea-surements for all pairs of process models is defined as $X = (x_{rk}) \in \mathbb{R}^{\frac{n(n-1)}{2} \times m}$, where an element x_{rk} represents an operation similarity measure $J\left(OP_k^i, OP_k^j\right)$ between two operations of OP_k for the rth process model pair of the process models M_i and M_j.

Based on the above, the operation similarity matrix of the example equals to the row vector represented by $X = [0.67, 1, 0, 0.40, 0, 0.25, \ldots, 0]$ since the example con-tains only two process models. Operation similarity measurements affect the total similarity between two process models.

3.3   Structural Similarity

In this paper, we employ the similarity concepts of activity vector and transition vector similarities, both are presented in [5]. Accordingly, we redefine these similarity con-cepts to fit manufacturing process models and call them structural similarity.

The structural similarity has two parts: operation vector similarity and transition vector similarity, and these concepts are slightly different from the similarity concepts for business process models [5]. The total similarity is measured by putting these two similarities together.

Operation Vector Similarity. A manufacturing process comprises multiple operations that consume components and produce intermediate components or end products. Therefore, information indicating whether a specific operation is included in the pro-cess is the salient feature that characterizes manufacturing processes. An operation vector v_i^O is an m-dimensional vector, where each element $v_{k,i}^O$ is a binary value (0 or 1) representing whether the operation OP_k is included in the process model M_i.

$$v_i^O = \left[v_{1,i}^O, v_{2,i}^O, \ldots, v_{m,i}^O\right] \tag{2}$$

The operation vector similarity $sim_{ov}(M_i, M_j)$ is measured based on the Cosine coefficient. Given two operation vectors corresponding to two different manufacturing process models respectively (M_i and M_j), the Cosine coefficient quantifies the similarity between these two vectors.

$$sim_{ov}(M_i, M_j) = \frac{\sum_{k=1}^{m} v_{k,i}^O v_{k,j}^O x_{rk}}{\sqrt{\sum_{k=1}^{m} \left(v_{k,i}^O\right)^2 \sum_{k=1}^{m} \left(v_{k,j}^O\right)^2}} \tag{3}$$

x_{rk} is an operation similarity measurements of OP_k between M_i and M_j and it is a part of the numerator in the above equation. It implies that even if these vectors equal to each other, according to the operation similarities, the operation vector similarity varies from 1 to 0. For our example, the measured operation vector similarity is $sim_{ov}(M_1, M_2) = \frac{3.32}{\sqrt{54}} \approx 0.45$.

Transition Vector Similarity. The transition is the fundamental property of all kinds of process models which is formally represented as a directed acyclic graph (DAG). The causality of tasks (or operations) in a process model is established based on transitions between the tasks, and it is a main structural property of process models including manufacturing processes. For example, the first task in a process model precedes to all other tasks including a succeeding task directly following to the start task. Therefore, causal relationships between tasks are quantified and weighted through calculations of distance weights, and these are represented as a transition vector.

Let v_i^T, be a transition vector of process model M_i. v_i^T is a row vector containing $m \times m$ elements for all pairs of operations, where each element $v_{kl,i}^T$ represents a causal relationship between OP_k and OP_l, measured by the reverse of distance weight $d_{kl,i}^T$ between OP_k and OP_l.

$$v_i^T = \left[v_{11,i}^T, v_{12,i}^T, \ldots, v_{mm,i}^T \right] \tag{4}$$

$$v_{kl,i}^T = \frac{1}{d_{kl,i}^T} \tag{5}$$

The Cosine coefficient-based transition vector similarity $sim_{tv}(M_i, M_j)$ is measured by the following equation.

$$sim_{tv}(M_i, M_j) = \frac{\sum_{k=1}^{m} \sum_{l=1}^{m} v_{kl,i}^T \cdot v_{kl,j}^T}{\sqrt{\sum_{k=1}^{m} \sum_{l=1}^{m} \left(v_{kl,i}^T \right)^2 \sum_{k=1}^{m} \sum_{l=1}^{m} \left(v_{kl,j}^T \right)^2}} \tag{6}$$

Based on the above equation, the result of measuring transition vector similarity between M_1 and M_2 for our example is $sim_{tv}(M_1, M_2) = \frac{6.45}{8.32} \approx 0.78$.

The total similarity between process models M_i and M_j is measured by putting these two vector similarities $sim_{ov}(M_i, M_j)$ and $sim_{tv}(M_i, M_j)$ together and adding a balancing parameter $\alpha \in [0, 1]$ to blend them.

$$sim(M_i, M_j) = \alpha \cdot sim_{ov}(M_i, M_j) + (1 - \alpha) \cdot sim_{tv}(M_i, M_j) \tag{7}$$

For this example, the measured total similarity is $sim(M_1, M_2) \approx 0.62$ with the balancing parameter $\alpha = 0.5$.

4   Related Works

Many similarity measures have been suggested in the field of BPM to handle a large collection of process models. To support process design and modeling, different similarity measures have been proposed in order to find similar models and eventually to reuse and benchmark such models [4–6]. Searching process model [4, 7] that satisfies specific conditions is another application of process similarity.

Despite a rich set of previous studies contributed to the process similarity, there is still a lack of proper methods for manufacturing processes since BPM approach has not been actively discussed in the manufacturing industry. As slightly different applications, the similarity concept was applied to the problems of machine groupings [8] for the design of manufacturing systems. Compared to our similarity, these studies presented similarity measures that focus on relations between machines and components and therefore such measures are not process-centric. Therefore, to the best of our knowledge, our work is first attempt to measure similarities between manufacturing process models. Particularly, our similarity takes into account the relationships between operations and components for quantifying similarity among operations of the same type.

Overall, we believe that our similarity is distinguished from the existing similarity concepts in both fields of BPM and manufacturing. However, the proposed similarity should be more elaborate, possibly incorporating other factors that characterize manufacturing processes, such as production volume and operation time.

5   Conclusion

In this paper, we propose similarity measures for manufacturing processes, which are based on BPM approach. To facilitate the similarity measures, we presented the description of transformation from manufacturing data into BPMN process models. With the running example, we confirmed that our similarity measures are applicable to manufacturing process models. In conclusion, measuring similarities between manufacturing process models enables us to search and reuse models in the design of new manufacturing processes. We believe that our similarities provide an opportunity to aid various engineering issues such as clustering and re-engineering of manufacturing processes. As future works, we plan to conduct a case study that applied the BPM-based manufacturing process management and our approach to the manufacturing company.

Acknowledgement. This work was supported by the GRRC program of Gyeonggi province. (GRRCKGU2017-B01), Research on Industrial Big-Data Analytics for Intelligent Manufacturing.

References

1. KSA-3002 Standard. http://www.kssn.net. Accessed 04 Aug 2018
2. Jiao, J., et al.: Generic bill-of-materials-and-operations for high-variety production Management. Concurr. Eng. **8**(4), 297–321 (2000)
3. Zor, S., Leymann, F., Schumm., D.: A proposal of BPMN extensions for the manufacturing domain. In: Proceedings of 44th CIRP International Conference on Manufacturing Systems (2011)
4. Schoknecht, A., et al.: Similarity of business process models: a state-of-the-art analysis. ACM Comput. Surv. **50**(4), 52 (2017)
5. Jung, J.-Y., Bae, J., Liu, L.: Hierarchical clustering of business process models. Int. J. Innov. Comput. Inf. Control **5**(12), 1349–4198 (2009)

6. Akkiraju, R., Ivan, A.: Discovering business process similarities: an empirical study with SAP best practice business processes. In: Maglio, P.P., Weske, M., Yang, J., Fantinato, M. (eds.) ICSOC 2010. LNCS, vol. 6470, pp. 515–526. Springer, Heidelberg (2010). https://doi.org/10.1007/978-3-642-17358-5_35
7. Kunze, M., Weske, M.: Metric trees for efficient similarity search in large process model repositories. In: zur Muehlen, M., Su, J. (eds.) BPM 2010. LNBIP, vol. 66, pp. 535–546. Springer, Heidelberg (2011). https://doi.org/10.1007/978-3-642-20511-8_49
8. Gupta, T., Seifoddini, H.: Production data based similarity coefficient for machine-component grouping decisions in the design of a cellular manufacturing system. Int. J. Prod. Res. 28(7), 1247–1269 (1990)

Dynamic Rescheduling in Energy-Aware Unrelated Parallel Machine Problems

Sergio Ferrer[1], Giancarlo Nicolò[1], Miguel A. Salido[1(✉)], Adriana Giret[2], and Federico Barber[1]

[1] Instituto de Automática e Informática Industrial,
Universitat Politècnica de València, Valencia, Spain
{serfers,giani,msalido,fbarber}@dsic.upv.es
[2] Departamento de Sistemas Informáticos y Computación,
Universitat Politècnica de València, Valencia, Spain
agiret@dsic.upv.es

Abstract. Advance in applied scheduling is a source of innovation in the manufacturing field, where new results help industrial practitioners in production management. The literature of rescheduling problems for single-objective optimization is well study, while there is a lack of extensive studies for the case of rescheduling for multi-objective optimization, especially for energy aware scheduling. This paper extends a previous work over an energy aware scheduling problem, modelled from a real industrial case study, extending its manufacturing environment to a dynamic one. To this end, two rescheduling techniques are developed to tackle machines disruptions (greedy-heuristic and meta-heuristic). They are compared to existing approach thought manufacturing environment simulations. The results give insight to improve the production management in terms of rescheduling quality and computational time.

Keywords: Energy-aware rescheduling · Metaheuristics
Sustainable manufacturing

1 Introduction

Applied scheduling is the field of study that aims to fill in the gap between the scheduling theory and its application to real scenario, giving to production managers new and innovative solutions to face current trend in their domain of work. Of particular interest for the applied scheduling is the manufacturing domain, where one of the main application of the scheduling problems is in the context of optimizing the manufacturing line production. In this scheduling environment, the usual assumption is to analyse the problem as static, meaning that all the information of the scheduling problem does not change over time. While this assumption can be useful for theoretical results, when dealing with real scenario this assumption limits the possibility to concretely apply the developed static scheduling technique, because the only way to face environment disruption is to

© IFIP International Federation for Information Processing 2018
Published by Springer Nature Switzerland AG 2018. All Rights Reserved
I. Moon et al. (Eds.): APMS 2018, IFIP AICT 536, pp. 232–240, 2018.
https://doi.org/10.1007/978-3-319-99707-0_29

solve a new scheduling problem with substantial computational cost and lack of system responsiveness. To improve this situation the environment has to be considered as dynamic and faced with predictive-reactive scheduling strategies. In this way, a (predictive) scheduling solution is produced and when a disruption occurs a reactive strategy (rescheduling) is carried out to generate a new feasible solution.

Most of the literature works over rescheduling problems address scheduling environment in which the main objectives are related to production objectives (completion time, tardiness, lateness, etc.), while current trends in manufacturing are taking in to consideration more complex objectives, where environmental issues have to be addressed through the consideration of energy consumption in the optimization process (i.e. energy-aware scheduling problem) leading to the creation of the sustainable scheduling field of study. Even though the importance of sustainable scheduling is broadly affirmed through the scientific community [1,2,7], most of the current literature in this field is addressing static problems (predictive scheduling), while literature works related to dynamic environments are very few in comparison to the variety of possible dynamic rescheduling environments determined by the combinatorial combination between scheduling environments, optimization functions, constraints and analysed disruptions. [11] tackles a bi-objective single machine batch scheduling problem where the first objective is to minimize the makespan and the second is to minimize the total energy costs, by considering both the machine utilization and the economic cost. An integer programming model is proposed and then, an exact ϵ-constraint method is adapted to obtain the exact Pareto front. In [8], a simple multi-agent system model is proposed to decompose an energy-aware scheduling problem into smaller subproblems. In this approach, each agent solves a subproblem by using a Mixed Integer Linear Programming (MILP) model and the results are combined to obtain a global solution. A similar idea is proposed in [5] where a set of solving techniques are compared and job features are studied in order to tackle energy-aware scheduling problems.

The proposed work is an extension of a well-studied scheduling scenario derived from analysing a manufacturing real case of an injection moulding plastic industry [6]. This problem can be considered as an energy-aware unrelated parallel machine scheduling problem with machine-dependent energy consumption and sequence-dependent setup time. The current literature taking in consideration the problem under analysis, models it as a static environment (predictive scheduling), and no previous works have been developed to manage this problem as a dynamic one.

2   Description of the Scheduling Problem

The scheduling problem under analysis is the energy-aware unrelated parallel machine scheduling problems with machine-dependent energy consumption and sequence-dependent setup time. It was firstly introduced in [6] and better studied in [3–5,8]. In this problem, a set of orders, represented by jobs, has to be scheduled on a set of unrelated parallel machines. Each job has associated to its specific temporal and cost features: release date, due date and penalty cost. A job can be processed by one or more machines, where processing time and energy consumption of the job depends by the machine assigned to process it. Between the execution of two consecutive jobs over the same machine a setup time is needed, where its value depends on the jobs sequence and machine assigned to them. The problem is formally described as Mixed Integer Linear Programming model and the mathematical formulation is described in [6].

The problem is considered as multi-objective since there are three measures to be minimized, which are expressed as objective functions: the total weighted tardiness of the jobs $TT(s)$, the total energy consumption $EN(s)$, and the total setup time $ST(s)$. The solution s^* can be obtained by minimizing a 3-dimensional objective function:

$$s^* = \arg \min_{s \in S}[TT(s), EN(s), ST(s)] \tag{1}$$

where S denotes the feasibility space for the problem solution space.

3   Definition of Incidence

An "incidence" is an unpredictable event that transforms the original schedule into a non-executable plan, such as: breakdowns on machines, power cuts, work accidents, etc. The representation for an incidence is independent of its origin and nature. This means that the representation of an incidence only has information about its technical characteristics ignoring the reason for the incidence. An incidence i is represented by mean of 4 parameters: an identification number for the incidence, the point when the incidence occurs, the machine that is affected by this incidence and the time necessary to recover the affected machine. So, an incidence can be formally defined as:

$$i = [id_i, st_i, m_i, tts_i]$$

where

- id_i: an identification number for the incidence
- st_i (starting time): the time point when the incidence i starts
- m_i (machine): an integer representing the ID of the affected machine by i
- tts_i (time to solve): the necessary time to solve the incidence i. It has to be estimated by a human expert. From st_i to $st_i + tts_i$, the machine m will be inoperative.

3.1   A Greedy Rescheduling (GR) Algorithm

In contrast to a baseline technique, based on the propagation of the incidence along the schedule on the affected machine using a Right-Shift technique [10],

a new reallocation approach is proposed. It analyzes every affected job to determinate if it has to be moved to another machine and, if applicable, determine
what is the best machine and in which position to introduce this job. An "affected
job by an incidence" is defined as "Every job scheduled in the same machine in
which the incidence occurs and its execution time is scheduled after the incidence
starts". Formally, the set of affected jobs (AJ) by an incidence i is defined as:

$$AJ = \{j : y_{jm_i} = 1 \land st_j > st_i\} \tag{2}$$

For each affected job, it has to be analyzed if it is convenient to move it
to another machine or is more productive to wait until the machine is repaired.
Thus, the Best Available Machine (BAM) for each job is determined. If the BAM
of a job is the machine in which it is previously scheduled, the job will not be
moved, otherwise the job will be moved to its BAM.

Given a job j already scheduled in a machine k', we need to do the next
calculations to determinate its BAM. First, we need to study how the rest of
machines improve or worsen their performance when receiving job j, s.t. $\forall j \in AJ$:

$$\Delta_k = F(S_k + j) - F(S_k), \forall k \neq k' \in M_j \tag{3}$$

where:

- M_j: is the set of machines that can execute job j (see Sect. 2).
- S_k: is the schedule of machine k. S_k is a sorted list including all the jobs
  assigned to machine k. Formally:

$$S_k = \{j : y_{jk} = 1\} \tag{4}$$

- $F(S_k)$: is the multi-objective value resulting from the application of the evaluation function on the schedule S_k.
- $S_k + j$: is the resulting schedule from inserting the job j into schedule S_k in the
  best position inside S_k (determined by brute force). In this case, the symbol
  '+' represents the operator of adding a new job into an existing schedule into
  the best position inside it.
- Δ_k: represents how much the evaluation of the schedule S_k is worsened when
  job j is added into it.

Each Δ_k stores how much each machine k is deteriorated when receiving the job
j, so it can be selected the best machine k* with lower value:

$$k^* = argmin_{k \neq k'} \Delta_k \tag{5}$$

In this way, k* is selected as the best machine to receive job j, but j is already
in a machine k' that could event be better than k*. To evaluate how job j fits on
k', j is taken out from S'_k and an evaluation of how the machine k' performances
without j is carried out by:

$$\Delta_{k'} = F(S_{k'}) - F(S_{k'} - j) \tag{6}$$

where:

- $S_{k'} - j$: is the resulting schedule from extracting the job j from schedule S_k.

So, $\Delta_{k'}$ stores how much machine k' deteriorates its performance due to job j. So, finally, the BAM for a given job j can be defined as:

$$BAM = k \in \{k', k^*\} : k = argmin\Delta_k \tag{7}$$

If BAM is k' means that j is already in its best machine and it does not need to be reallocated in other machine to produce better results. By contrast, if BAM is k^* means that moving job j into k^* will produce a better performance $(\Delta_{k^*} < \Delta_{k'})$.

Given this BAM definition, Algorithm 1 presents the pseudo-code used to manage the incoming incidences into an existing schedule:

Algorithm 1. Rescheduling algorithm

INPUT: solution S and incidence I
OUTPUT: solution S with I inside and affected jobs by I reallocated
1: id ← I[0]; st ← I[1]; m ← I[2]; tts ← I[3]; # see section 3
2: affectedJobs ← $\{j : y_{jm} = 1 \wedge st_j > st_{id}\}$
3: Right-Shift(I,S) # Inserts incidence.
4: for job ∈ affectedJobs do {
5: $\Delta_k = F(S_k + j) - F(S_k), \forall k \neq m \in M_j$
6: $k^* = argmin_{k \neq m}\Delta_k$
7: $\Delta_m = F(S_m) - F(S_m - j)$
8: $BAM = k \in \{m, k^*\} : k = argmin\Delta_k$
9: if (BAM ≠ m) {moveJob(job, BAM) } }

Line 3 implements the Right-Shift repairing technique [10]. That means to apply the baseline before rescheduling starts in order to take into account the delay introduced by the incidence when evaluating the reallocation possibilities for each job. In line 9, the *moveJob* function moves the job to its BAM, both elements received as parameters. The position for the job inside its BAM is selected by brute-force: trying one by one all the possible places. Formally, the index i to introduce the job j into its BAM is selected as:

$$i = argmin_{0 \leq i < |S_{BAM}|}F(S_{BAM} + j, i) \tag{8}$$

where:

- S_{BAM} is the current schedule for machine BAM.
- $F(S_{BAM} + j, i)$ is the application of the evaluation function to the schedule S_{BAM} with the job j introduced in the position i by Right-Sift technique.

3.2   A Genetic Algorithm with GR Initialization (GA+GR)

In this section, a Genetic Algorithm (GA) for rescheduling a solution after an incidence is proposed. The main idea is to run a GA only with the affected jobs

(AJ) (Eq. 2) in order to preserve the solution before the incidence and trying to reschedule all the jobs after the incidence with the objective of minimizing the impact of the disruption. Notice that incidences are supposed to appear in the production environment while the scheduling is being already executed by the machines, therefore the decision to keep the previous jobs without rescheduling them is not really a decision but a constraint of the environment. A competitive GA to tackle this problem has been used in [5], where the GA is embedded in a multi-agent system. Taking this GA as a starting point and our definition of AJ, some modifications to them have been carried out:

- In order to reschedule the whole set of jobs that can be moved after the incidence, a new definition of AJ is presented: $AJ = \{j : st_j > st_i\}$ With this new definition, the whole set of jobs executed after the incidence is selected for the rescheduling, independently of the machine in which the job is scheduled, which allows the GA to explore a larger search space than the GR algorithm. The main idea behind this choice is to be able to compare two options of general rescheduling approaches: preserve as much as possible the previous solution (stability) by rescheduling only the jobs of the affected machine (done by GR) or to reschedule the whole solution after the incidence (done by this modification of GA).
- The *fitness* function of the GA is modified to contemplate the previous schedule to the solutions given by the GA in order to calculate the multi-objective function of the complete schedule. Notice that GA is executed only with the AJ as input, so the schedule given as solution only contains the AJ. Nevertheless, the evaluation of the solution needs the previous schedule (the one containing the *non affected jobs*) in order to decide the quality of a solution. In this way it is achieved that the GA solves a sub-problem of scheduling (only the problem containing the AJ) but it evaluates its solutions with respect the complete schedule
- The initialization of the GA is modified to create an initial population which includes the solution given by the GR algorithm. The incidences will be solved accumulatively (see Sect. 4), which implies that as incidences appear, the GR and the GA may have different solutions for each incidence. The GA executes the GR when initialized, which provides a greedy solution. This greedy solution is used as an individual of the initial population of the GA. This decision is given to guide the GA search with the previous solutions with allows to study if these solutions are replaced during the process by another better solutions or they are preserved during the whole process.

4   Evaluation

To evaluate the proposed system, a set of incidences was generated. The incidences were randomly generated over a machine and before the 75% of the total time in the schedule. This decision avoids the generation of incidences at the end of the schedule because when an incidence is introduced at the end of the schedule the set AJ may be empty or composed of few jobs. This situation does not show an objective comparison of the different techniques. Furthermore, the time needed to solve the incidence was randomly generated between 10% of the longest job assigned to the affected machine and its total processing time.

The incidences were solved accumulatively, which means that the solution of the incidence i was the schedule in which the incidence $i+1$ was introduced. By accumulating the incidences in the schedule, it can be compared how the different techniques absorb the incoming incidences as new disruptions arrive into the system.

The instances of the problem were taken from the benchmark proposed in [9] which presents 4 classes of instances depending on the number of jobs and machines per incidence: j30 with 4 machines and 30 jobs, j50 with 6 machines and 50 jobs, j100 with 10 machines and 100 jobs, and j250 with 20 machines and 250 jobs. The time needed to execute each technique is fixed to: baseline $= 0.2$ s, GR $= 2.3$ s, GA $= 30$ s and GA+GR $= 30$ s.

To test and compare the four techniques, a subset of the 10 largest instances per class were selected (40 instances). They were solved with the system proposed in [3] and the solutions given by this system were used as the input for our system.

Figures 1, 2, 3 and 4 show the results of applying the four techniques to each class of the problem. As shown on Fig. 1a, for small instances the GR algorithm obtained the best results, but as problem gets larger, the GA+GR algorithm got a better behavior than the rest of the techniques. It is also interesting to compare GA vs GA+GR since GA+GR maintained a better performance that GA in all cases, although both were very similar. This is due to the fact that the only difference between them is that GA+GR includes the greedy algorithm GR in each step. This difference could come from the fact that GA was designed in [5] to have a good performance in solving (not rescheduling) the instance and with a larger timeout (10 min) than the timeout fixed for the rescheduling tasks.

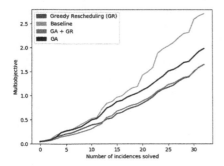

Fig. 1. Results on j30

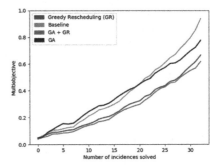

Fig. 2. Results on j50

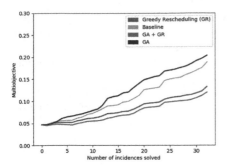 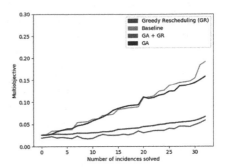

Fig. 3. Results on j100   **Fig. 4.** Results on j250

5   Conclusions and Future Works

In this paper, two different techniques for solving the rescheduling on the unrelated parallel machine problem have been proposed. The proposed GR algorithm obtained the best results for small instances of the problem, while the GA+GR algorithm obtained a better behavior when instances are larger leading to useful insight over which technique to use regarding the problem size. As future work, it is proposed to manage the incidences by a match-up technique to recover the original solution as soon as possible in order to improve stability of solutions.

Acknowledgements. The paper has been partially supported by the Spanish research project TIN2016-80856-R and TIN2015-65515-C4-1-R, and the ACIF/2017 Program of the Conselleria d'Educació (Generalitat Valenciana).

References

1. Bruzzone, A., Anghinolfi, D., Paolucci, M., Tonelli, F.: Energy-aware scheduling for improving manufacturing process sustainability: a mathematical model for flexible flow shops. CIRP Ann.-Manuf. Technol. **61**(1), 459–462 (2012)
2. Dai, M., Tang, D., Giret, A., Salido, M.A., Li, W.D.: Energy-efficient scheduling for a flexible flow shop using an improved genetic-simulated annealing algorithm. Robot. Comput.-Integr. Manuf. **29**(5), 418–429 (2013)
3. Nicolo, G., Ferrer, S., Salido, M.A., Giret, A., Barber, F.: A multi-agent framework to solve energy-aware unrelated parallel machine scheduling problems with machine-dependent energy consumption and sequence-dependent setup time. In: ICAPS 2018, Delft, The Netherlands (2018)
4. Nicolò, G., Salido, M., Giret, A., Barber, F.: Assessment of a multi agent system for energy aware off-line scheduling from a real case manufacturing data set. In: COPLAS 2016, p. 35 (2016)
5. Nicolo, G., Salido, M.A., Ferrer, S., Giret, A., Barber, F.: A multi-agent approach using dynamic constraints to solve energy-aware unrelated parallel machine scheduling problem with energy-dependent and sequence-dependent setup time. In: COPLAS 2017, pp. 31–37 (2017)

6. Paolucci, M., Anghinolfi, D., Tonelli, F.: Facing energy-aware scheduling: a multi-objective extension of a scheduling support system for improving energy efficiency in a moulding industry. Soft Comput. **21**, 1–12 (2015)
7. Plitsos, S., Repoussis, P.P., Mourtos, I., Tarantilis, C.D.: Energy-aware decision support for production scheduling. Decis. Support Syst. **93**(Suppl. C), 88–97 (2017). http://www.sciencedirect.com/science/article/pii/S016792361630166X
8. Tonelli, F., et al.: Assessment of mathematical programming and agent-based modelling for off-line scheduling: application to energy aware manufacturing. CIRP Ann. - Manuf. Technol. **65**, 405–408 (2016)
9. Tonelli, F., Evans, S., Taticchi, P.: Industrial sustainability: challenges, perspectives, actions. Int. J. Bus. Innov. Res. **7**(2), 143–163 (2013)
10. Vieira, G.E., Herrmann, J.W., Lin, E.: Rescheduling manufacturing systems: a framework of strategies, policies, and methods. J. Sched. **6**(1), 39–62 (2003)
11. Wang, S., Liu, M., Chu, F., Chu, C.: Bi-objective optimization of a single machine batch scheduling problem with energy cost consideration. J. Cleaner Prod. **137**, 1205–1215 (2016)

Information Support for Supplier Kit Preparation

Maria Kollberg Thomassen[1(✉)], Lars Skjelstad[1], and Erlend Gjønnes[2]

[1] SINTEF Technology and Society, S.P. Andersens veg 5,
7031 Trondheim, Norway
{maria.thomassen,lars.skjelstad}@sintef.no
[2] Orkel AS, Johan Gjønnes' veg 25, 7320 Fannrem, Norway
Erlend@orkel.no

Abstract. Information support in kit preparation is critical for the design of efficient kitting systems. Existing literature is dominated by studies that address in-house kitting and order picking support in warehouse settings and that are based upon laboratory experiments. This study explores critical aspects of information support for kit preparation outsourced to partners in the supply chain based upon empirical evidence of a web application for kitting adopted in a real-life case of a manufacturer and a supplier. Detailed insights to kitting efficiency, information sharing and user acceptance are presented. Critical aspects are identified primarily related to the relationship and interaction between companies, quality of information sharing, usefulness, parts identification efficiency, and joint improvement and development efforts. This work highlights the importance of considering supply chain information sharing in outsourced kitting.

Keywords: Parts logistics · Kitting · Supply chain collaboration

1 Introduction

Kitting is a materials handling policy, where components are delivered to the shop floor in pre-determined quantities that are placed together in dedicated containers, to avoid keeping components inventories at assembly stations [1]. The policy is especially suitable in mixed-model assembly situations, typically characterized by small batch sizes and large product variety, such as mass customization settings [2].

Efficient kit preparation is essential for high performance kitting systems. Information systems for picking support is recognized as a critical design factor [3, 4]. There is a large amount of research addressing order picking support in warehouse settings. Rapid developments of digitalization drives the adoption of smart digital tools, and several recent studies investigate the use of such tools in order picking [e.g. 5, 6]. However, printed picking lists are still common, and research dealing with information support in kit preparation situations is scarce (see for instance [7]).

Most empirical studies dealing with picking support are based upon laboratory experiments, and there is thus a need for more research on real-world adoption in industrial settings. Existing research is also mainly concentrated to in-house operations.

I. Moon et al. (Eds.): APMS 2018, IFIP AICT 536, pp. 241–248, 2018.
https://doi.org/10.1007/978-3-319-99707-0_30

Therefore, research on information support when kit preparation is outsourced to an external party, for instance when suppliers or third-party logistics providers are involved, is scarce.

The purpose of this research is to investigate key information support aspects for kit preparation in supply chain settings by exploring the adoption of such support in a real-life case. This work is expected to contribute to further development of information support when kitting operations are outsourced to a supplier or a third party.

Even though kitting may be related to logistics operations in business-to-consumer settings i.e. kit-to-customer, the scope of this study includes kit-to-manufacturing, that implies pulling parts together in kit containers which are delivered to the shop floor to support assembly operations [1].

2 Research Approach

A case study approach is applied including a literature review of key information support aspects for kit preparation and information sharing in supply chains. The empirical study focuses on the adoption of a support tool for kit preparation in a dyadic relationship with a manufacturing company and one of its key suppliers. The companies are selected due to their participation in a joint R&D project dealing with efficient logistics in the supply chain.

The companies have been involved in the research process; company representatives have served as main sources of data collection. Empirical findings have been documented and archived after discussions with the companies. Several sources of information have been combined; data is mainly collected by interviews, discussions and direct observations, in addition to data transcripts and e-mails. Key informants from the companies have confirmed the description of the case presented. Findings regarding relevant aspects in the case are also discussed in view of existing literature.

Empirical data was mainly collected from interviews, workshops and discussions with key informants, and factory visits in the companies between 2016 and 2018. About ten workshops of 2–4 h were held together with researchers and representatives of the two companies; the work group included the plant managers of both companies, the manufacturer's purchasing manager, the technical manager and the customer service representative of the supplier, and several employees in production, picking and goods reception. Most of the workshops were combined with factory visits.

Empirical information is also gathered from photos, documentation, presentations, data extracts from the manufacturer's ERP system and e-mails. Measurements data of kitting costs between September 2016 and December 2017 were gathered.

The manufacturing company, Orkel, assembles large machinery equipment and the supplier, Skala, delivers steel components to Orkel. Components, which are manufactured by laser cutting and bending of steel plates, are sorted into kits before delivered to Orkel. Complexity is high due to high variation in the number of parts per kit and sizes of parts and kits.

Orkel has developed a mobile web application, the Supplier Kitting Application (SKA), to support kitting at Skala. It is accessed via a tablet and shows order and kit information and drawings of components. A picker, who is responsible for kit preparation, mainly uses traditional printed paper lists to identify parts. Each part is also marked with a laser printed number to facilitate identification. The main purpose of the SKA is to give the picker easy access to drawings of parts in case of uncertainty or difficulties finding parts and serves as a complement to paper lists.

3 Literature Review

3.1 Information Support in Kit Preparation

Kitting means delivering components and subassemblies to the shop floor in predetermined quantities that are placed together in specific containers and a kit is a specific collection of components and/or subassemblies that together support one or more assembly operations for a given product or shop order [1]. In kitting, materials are centrally stored and kits are typically prepared in a stockroom based upon a pick list, and are delivered to the assembly line according to production schedule [2].

Efficient preparation of kits is essential due to increased costs related to extra parts handling, labor intensive and non-productive work [2, 8]. Kitting efficiency is influenced by several factors, for instance the amount of kits, kitting area, picking sequence, storage and racks, batch size, kit container and carrier [3, 4, 9]. Also, information support is often recognized as a critical factor [3, 4]. It involves how the picker receives and understands information of which parts to pick for each order [3]. Issues may be related to how information is communicated to the picker and that experienced pickers with comprehensive understanding of underlying product structures tend to neglect the picking information [3].

Efficient support for pickers is a major challenge in warehouse operations. Due to rapid developments in automated and advanced order picking support, many companies have adopted pick-by-light and pick-by-voice systems and there is also a growing interest for pick-by-vision or augmented reality systems [10]. However, manual picking and printed lists is still used. Common aspects related to information picking support include picking time, picking error rate or accuracy and cognitive load [5–7, 10, 11]. Considerations should also be taken to user acceptance and motivation, learning success, technology acceptance, usability and ergonomics [10].

3.2 Supply Chain Information Sharing

Since it is beneficial to locate kitting operations close to the assembly line, it is often carried out in-house by the manufacturer [2]. Kitting operations can also be outsourced to an external party, for example a supplier or a third-party logistics services provider [12]. It is assumed that outsourced kitting operations may imply challenges related to information support. For example, a picker at a supplier may have more limited understanding of the manufacturers products and product structures compared to an in-house picker. It may also be more difficult to solve issues that may occur during kitting or have access to additional information due to physical distances between two different organizations. A supplier is dependent upon that the manufacturer provides necessary information to the supplier to perform kitting in an efficient manner.

Information-sharing is recognized as a key driver of supply chain integration and collaboration [13]. Even though information-sharing often involves manufacturers sharing demand information, plans and forecasts with suppliers, suppliers may also share information such as status information or delivery plans with their customers.

To ensure high usage of shared information its quality is critical; information must be accurate, convenient to access, reliable and in time [14, 15]. Information technology may be used to enhance quality as well as information sharing, and relationship quality in terms of for example trust or length, is further critical for information sharing, information quality and information technology [14].

4 Case Findings

4.1 Picking Efficiency and Accuracy

The manufacturer's measurements of supplier kitting costs, and the time for adopting the web application (mid-December 2016), are shown in Fig. 1. Overall, by the end of the measurement period (August 2017), average costs had decreased by about 29% compared to the period before the tool was introduced (mid-September to mid-December 2016), and by about 46% compared to the peak of average costs (February 2017).

It is probably not the web application alone that has contributed to reduced kitting costs, but rather several improvements that have been implemented. For example, the number of order lines per order has increased during the same period. Also, in June 2017, the delivery frequency was changed based upon completed kits instead of deliveries of completed orders and a new kitting area at the supplier plant was established.

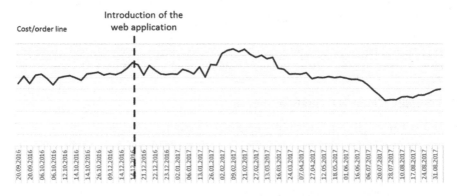

Fig. 1. Kitting cost per order line between September 2016 and August 2017

An explanation to increased costs is that the picker spent more time using the web application to identify parts in the beginning. The picker must use both hands to access the tablet, so it is not possible to pick at the same time. The application thus led to reduced efficiency on a short term. As the picker became more familiar with the tool and learned to identify parts without using the tool, he spent less time to use the tool.

In addition, even though the picker has no conception of product structure, he has trained his ability to visually recognize combinations of parts of the kits based upon the paper list only. Also, since the parts have printed identification number and are delivered directly to the kitting area for kitting the same or the following day as produced, the picker is exposed to a limited number of parts and numbers.

Efficiency is also affected by that the picker uses the tool to give feedback on kitting status to the manufacturer. It can be assumed that this has slowed down kitting as the picker stops picking to mark completed kits. However, this has led to that kits could be delivered more frequently, which in turn implied reduced work in progress.

Accuracy has not been measured since errors are generally rare. The web application may have contributed to higher accuracy, in combination with several other improvements in the kitting system including more frequent deliveries of kits, marking and organization of kits in pallets, and so on.

4.2   Information Sharing

The content of information provided by the manufacturer includes a list of orders with kit numbers and specification of parts of each kit, Fig. 2. The picker can choose to access drawings of each part to get a visual presentation of that part in case of uncertainty.

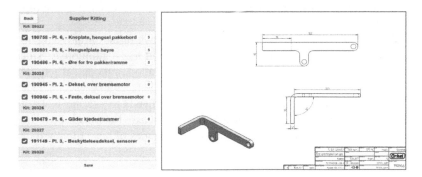

Fig. 2. Example screen shots from web application; list of kits and components and drawing of a component

Quality of information is ensured by that the manufacturer has developed the web application for the supplier and thus provides the necessary information via the application. It is integrated with the manufacturer's ERP system and updated files are continuously transferred to the database that is accessible via the web application. The manufacturer thus ensures that the picker always has online access to up-to-date information with the latest version of kit information and drawings.

The web application further provides additional value to the manufacturer; the manufacturer can easily get an overview of status of kit preparation at the supplier in real time. This requires that the picker checks out completed kits in the web application in a timely manner.

The web application has had a positive contribution to the collaborative relationship and communication between the companies; both companies experience positive value from the new kitting support and therefore they also invest in improving the web application.

The information content has not changed during the investigation. However, the companies have discussed how the web application can be further adjusted to substitute the use of the paper picking list at Skala and have started to test an updated version with more adjusted information, where specific materials and bended parts are specifically marked in the list.

The drawings have contributed to reducing the cognitive load of identifying parts. However, alternatives to detailed drawings have been discussed since the picker often only needs a basic visual conception of parts, related to size, form and geometry, rather than a full specification. Tests of using simple photos of parts in kits are planned and may substitute or serve as a simplified complement to detailed drawings. Photos may also give the picker an overview of the final kit, which is missing in the current version of the application.

4.3 User Acceptance

The picker has found the tool useful for kit preparation and has been motivated to use it. The tool is easy to use as the picker has not experienced any trouble to use it. The picker has gained more experience over time and has become less dependent of the web application, indicating positive learning effects.

The picker also gives feedback to the manufacturer of further improvements of the application. Moreover, the picker checks out completed kits continuously, since he is aware of that the manufacturer can access this information, although it requires extra time.

In view of ergonomics, the picker must use both hands to use the tablet and this interrupts the kitting activity. The companies have discussed alternatives to the tablet and plan to test the web application in various technologies of head mounted tablets to support kitting.

5   Discussion and Conclusion

The study shows how information support provided by a manufacturer can contribute to increase efficiency of supplier kitting operations. Key aspects identified include;

- the initiative is initiated by the manufacturer, with a good understanding of specific needs of the supplier for the development of the tool
- the supplier utilizes the information support as intended and finds it usable and useful
- the supplier uses the support as a learning tool, to improve the ability to recognize parts

- the supplier understands the information needs of the manufacturer and utilizes the tool to share information with the manufacturer
- the manufacturer ensures the quality of information sharing by ERP integration
- the companies prioritize and make joint efforts to improve kitting performance and parts supply efficiency
- the companies make joint efforts to utilize the tool to further develop information sharing practices

While existing research mainly deals with picking information support in in-house logistics and in laboratory settings, this study adds further insights to settings where kit preparation is outsourced based upon a real-life case of practical adoption. The identified aspects bring further details regarding supply chain considerations related to kit preparation. The study especially emphasizes the importance of information sharing and quality in supply chain integration and collaboration, which is also highlighted in existing supply chain research [14, 15]. The identified information sharing aspects provide additional understanding to kit preparation information support in outsourced situations.

Generally, findings are line with existing in-house logistics research highlighting efficiency gains from information support in kitting and picking situations [6, 7]. Findings also confirm that experienced pickers may have different picking support needs compared to the needs of less experienced pickers [3]. Findings further reveal how user acceptance seem to depend upon usability and usefulness of the support and reduced cognitive load. This is in line with research emphasizing the importance of human factors [10].

Aspects presented in this study may be used in further research on the development and implementation of information support for outsourced kitting situations. Managers may find the results useful for implementing kitting support in such settings.

Findings are based upon empirical data from one case. Further empirical research is suggested to develop more insight to how identified aspects vary in different outsourcing supply chain settings. Moreover, the aspect of changing picking efficiency and needs of information support over time was highlighted in this study. It is therefore suggested that further research should include longitudinal studies of information support adoption in practice. The study shows how an information support tool for kitting initiated by a manufacturer can contribute to improved material flows and enhanced collaboration with suppliers. Further research is planned to test several types of information support equipment, such as smart glasses and head-mounted tablets, for outsourced picking.

Acknowledgements. This work was supported by the User-driven Research based Innovation (BIA) program of the Research Council of Norway.

References

1. Bozer, Y.A., McGinnis, L.F.: Kitting versus line stocking: a conceptual framework and a descriptive model. Int. J. Prod. Econ. **28**(1), 1–19 (1992). https://doi.org/10.1016/0925-5273 (92)90109-K
2. Caputo, A.C., Pelagagge, P.M.: A methodology for selecting assembly systems feeding policy. Ind. Manag. Data Syst. **111**(1), 84–112 (2011). https://doi.org/10.1108/ 02635571111099749
3. Brynzér, H., Johansson, M.I.: Design and performance of kitting and order picking systems. Int. J. Prod. Econ. **41**(1), 115–125 (1995). https://doi.org/10.1016/0925-5273(95)00083-6
4. Hanson, R., Medbo, L.: Aspects influencing man-hour efficiency of kit preparation for mixed-model assembly. Proc. CIRP **44**, 353–358 (2016). https://doi.org/10.1016/j.procir. 2016.02.064
5. Funk, M., Mayer, S., Nistor, M, Schmidt, A.: Mobile in-situ pick-by-vision: order picking support using a projector helmet. In: Proceedings of the 9th ACM International Conference on PErvasive Technologies Related to Assistive Environments. ACM, New York (2016). https://doi.org/10.1145/2910674.2910730
6. Guo, A., et al.: A comparison of order picking assisted by head-up display (HUD), cart-mounted display (CMD), light, and paper pick list. In: Proceedings of the 2014 ACM International Symposium on Wearable Computers, pp. 71–78. ACM, New York (2014). https://doi.org/10.1145/2634317.2634321
7. Hanson, R., Falkenström, W., Miettinen, M.: Augmented reality as a means of conveying picking information in kit preparation for mixed-model assembly. Comput. Ind. Eng. **113**, 570–575 (2017). https://doi.org/10.1016/j.cie.2017.09.048
8. Kilic, H.S., Durmusoglu, M.B.: Advances in assembly line parts feeding policies: a literature review. Assem. Autom. **35**(1), 57–68 (2015). https://doi.org/10.1108/AA-05-2014-047
9. Kilic, H.S., Durmusoglu, M.B.: Design of kitting system in lean-based assembly lines. Assem. Autom. **32**(3), 226–234 (2012). https://doi.org/10.1108/01445151211244357
10. Reif, R., Walch, D.: Augmented & virtual reality applications in the field of logistics. Vis. Comput. **24**(11), 987–994 (2008). https://doi.org/10.1007/s00371-008-0271-7
11. Reif, R., Günthner, W.A., Schwerdtfeger, B., Klinker, G.: Evaluation of an augmented reality supported picking system under practical conditions. Comput. Graph. Forum **29**(1), 2–12 (2010). https://doi.org/10.1111/j.1467-8659.2009.01538.x
12. Klingenberg, W., Boksma, J.-D.: A conceptual framework for outsourcing of materials handling activities in automotive: differentiation and implementation. Int. J. Prod. Res. **48** (16), 4877–4899 (2010). https://doi.org/10.1080/00207540903067177
13. Cao, M., Zhang, Q.: Supply Chain Collaboration: Roles of Interorganizational Systems, Trust, and Collaborative Culture. Springer, London (2012). https://doi.org/10.1007/978-1-4471-4591-2
14. Li, S., Lin, B.: Accessing information sharing and information quality in supply chain management. Decis. Support Syst. **42**(3), 1641–1656 (2006). https://doi.org/10.1016/j.dss. 2006.02.011
15. Forslund, H., Jonsson, P.: The impact of forecast information quality on supply chain performance. Int. J. Oper. Prod. Manag. **27**(1), 90–107 (2007). https://doi.org/10.1108/ 01443570710714556

Real-Time Linked Open Data for Life Cycle Inventory

Jayakrishnan Jayapal(iD) and Senthilkumaran Kumaraguru$^{(\boxtimes)}$(iD)

Department of Mechanical Engineering, Indian Institute of Information
Technology, Design and Manufacturing, Kancheepuram, Chennai 600127, India
skumaran@iiitdm.ac.in

Abstract. The quality of data used for the Life Cycle Assessment (LCA) is of prime importance as they influence the outcomes of the impact assessments. Most of the LCI data has validity periods as the data gets outdated due to introduction of new technology and process. In order to replace outdated data with most recent value we have developed a device called EnBoX (Energy Baseline of X) for real-time power measurement and which would be used for generating Linked Open Data. In this paper a semantic web based Linked Open Data architecture is developed to update the sensed data into an LCI database. A case study is presented in this paper by updating an existing data base of injection moulding process with an Open LCI data base using the proposed method. The LCI data is open and could potentially eliminate the data validity issues arising out of conventional LCI data gathered over time. The work presented in this paper would be useful to manage sustainability performance of products/processes in an accurate manner.

Keywords: Life Cycle Assessment · Open data · Linked data
Life Cycle Inventory

1 Introduction

Life Cycle Assessment (LCA) is an approach to quantify the environmental impacts associated with all the stages of the product life. The LCA needs a long list of input and output impacts data at the unit process level and that is usually available in a database called Life Cycle Inventory (LCI) [1]. The existing LCI databases are developed by collecting the data manually at various stages by different people and consolidated by the LCI service providers. But the challenges of the existing data collection techniques are poor quality and accuracy of the data. To match with current data quality standards, specified in the ISO 14000 series standards, various service providers within the LCA community have developed different methodologies to improve the quality of Life Cycle Inventory (LCI) data and few researchers have used modern technologies like ICT (Information communication and Technologies) and IoT (Internet of Things) [7] as a tool for collection and assessment of data. So, in this paper we are proposing a real time open LCI data updated in the database using the concepts of linked data and semantic web [2]. More state of the art technologies related to the data collection in LCI is discussed in the following sections.

© IFIP International Federation for Information Processing 2018
Published by Springer Nature Switzerland AG 2018. All Rights Reserved
I. Moon et al. (Eds.): APMS 2018, IFIP AICT 536, pp. 249–254, 2018.
https://doi.org/10.1007/978-3-319-99707-0_31

2 Dynamic LCI and Semantic Based Life Cycle Impact Assessment

Usually LCA was done after collecting all related data. In contrast to the existing techniques, Remo et al. [3] presented a method to perform a web-based dynamic LCI and LCIA for manufacturing processes by implementing a system based on combining Labview and GaBi software, as well as MTConnect® standard for data collection. Similar to [3] Brandon et al. [4] have used a standardized LCA catalog that can express the semantic content of a data resource. By using this catalog, a user can generate LCI data by querying the requirement for the LCA. The query responses can be enriched through integration with linked data services that are in development or already exist.

Most of the existing LCI has three different flows material flow, water flow and energy flow. To implement sustainable manufacturing [5] in industries have to closely monitor the energy flow. So, we have limited our scope of our study to energy related flows in the LCI data.

2.1 IoT Based Device for Energy Monitoring

Few researchers [6–8] have developed the IoT based devices for monitoring the energy consumption and used the measured data for various downstream analysis. In home automation systems, Putta and Balamurugan [6] used IoT approach for continuous monitoring and control of the appliances far from their home using connected devices thus achieving Energy Efficiency (EE). Lidia et al. [7] presented an open IoT infrastructure that provides real-time monitoring in multiple school buildings. Shee et al. [8] introduced an IoT enabled software application for real-time monitoring of EE on manufacturing shop floors.

But all these data are static in nature and after over a period, the data may become outdated/invalid. So, we need a real-time open LCI data were the data values are updated in the database as the manufacturing facility in use. In order to solve the problem stated above we propose a systematic approach to develop a real-time open LCI in the following section.

3 Methodology

LCI development is creating an inventory of flows from and to the environment during product/process development, among all the flows our focus is on the energy flows. So here we present the development of an energy measurement device, its ability to push sensed data into the cloud and the overall architecture of the semantic annotation system that enriches the data from monitoring device for consumption by an LCA system. Figure 1 demonstrates the proposed framework for integrating the sensed data with the semantic Web to develop the open LCI database and detailed description of the architecture is given in the following sections.

3.1 Overall Architecture for Open LCI Data Preparation

In this frame work the primary stage is sensing the data from the device which we need to monitor for energy consumption. These connected devices can be any manufacturing facility that we use during the product development stage or in the product use stage. If we consider a bottle produced with polypropylene material by using the injection moulding process, the sensing device can be connected to the injection moulding machine to monitor the energy consumption during the production of the bottle in the shop floor.

Sensing Devices

During development of an LCI data sets we need to monitor different flows associated with the unit process like material input, energy consumption and emissions to the air, water and land. To monitor each flow we insist on different sensors, for example to measure the emission of particulate matter 2.5 to the environment we use light scattering sensors. But in this work, to monitor the energy consumption, we have used a non-invasive current sensor to calculate the total electric energy consumption by using a device known as EnBoX.

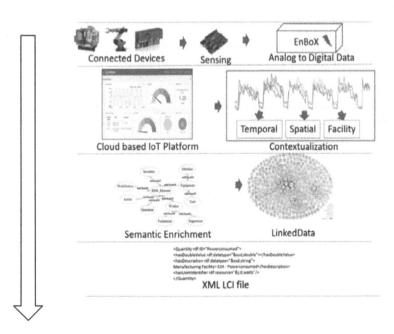

Fig. 1. Overall architecture of Open LCI data

Energy Measuring Device (EnBoX)

An IoT based device like [7] has been used to measure the energy consumption and we named it as EnBoX where X can be any equipment which can be used in manufacturing of the product. The Fig. 2 shows the overall system architecture.

EnBoX consist of an Arduino, a non-invasive current sensor, a rectifier circuit and a Wi-Fi module. Arduino is programed to calculate the power by multiplying the voltage

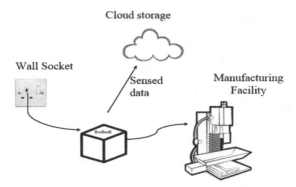

Fig. 2. Architecture of EnBoX

with the current sensor data. The Wi-Fi module will help us to push the derived sensor data in the IoT based cloud platform known as Ubidots.

Cloud Based IOT Platform
IOT based cloud platform is designed to store and analyze different data collected. In this work we used Ubidots as a cloud storage platform to store the real-time data that is sensed by the EnBoX.

Contextualization
The analog data generated from the EnBoX is semantically enriched in the cloud before it is published. Before content curation, the data are contextualized based on location, time and the manufacturing facility for which power is measured, so that anyone who queries data for a certain region/location or the manufacturing facility/equipment can get access to the data very easily.

Semantic Enrichment and Linked Data Preparation
The idea behind the Linked data is to increase the usefulness of data as it is interlinked with large amount of other data. On one hand, the connection enables qualitative annotations to promote interoperability, and thus avoid creating repetitive data with the help of the ontology prepared for an LCI input and output flows. The data already published on the semantic Web can be widely used by communities for the LCA. During the impact assessment using the open LCI data, the sensed data is updated based on the semantic web.

The enriched data can be probed using a RESTful server connection to the cloud and the data is presented to the user in an XML file unlike the SPINE and SPOLD formats used in conventional LCI data. One can perform LCIA with the data obtained from the Linked data.

3.2   Case Study

A representative LCI data from the NREL database is considered and its important flows, object and data properties (category, flow type, unit measured and amount) are used to prepare the case study ontology. The ontology created for both input and output flows are graphically represented in Fig. 3. Then the prepared ontology is presented as an XML LCI file. As and when the EnBoX is connected to equipment to monitor the energy consumption, the real-time values will be updated in the Open LCI database.

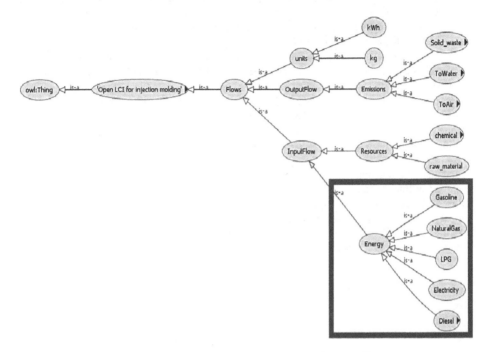

Fig. 3. Ontology for the LCI data (Color figure online)

As mentioned earlier, we are focusing only on the energy flows in the unit process, which is highlighted in the Fig. 3. Among the five-energy source EnBoX will measure the electricity consumption in real-time and represent the value in LCI database using an XML Schema for LCI data. Then the most recent value stored in the cloud platform can be updated to an LCI database periodically or when the user demands for the LCI data.

4   Conclusions

With the help of industry 4.0 tools and modern technologies like linked data and semantic web is used to develop a real-time open LCI data collection system, which helps to have pinpoint assessment of the product/process throughout its life cycle. The proposed system will reduce the cost incurred in the LCA process. However, this poses challenges in terms of sharing proprietary data over to large audience, cyber-security and repetitive sensed data for similar products and processes. Crowd sourcing also brings challenges in terms of peer-reviewing the LCI data which must be addressed. The future work is to develop connections to OpenLCA to perform impact assessment using the XML LCI Schema.

References

1. Finkbeiner, M., Inaba, A., Tan, R., Christiansen, K., Klüppel, H.-J.: The new international standards for life cycle assessment: ISO 14040 and ISO 14044. Int. J. Life Cycle Assess. **11** (2), 80–85 (2006)
2. Charalampidis, C.C., Keramopoulos, E.A.: Semantic web user interface - a model and a review. Data Knowl. Eng. **115**, 214–227 (2018)
3. Remo, A.P., Diogo, A.L., Eraldo, J., Ometto, A.R.: Dynamic system for life cycle inventory and impact assessment of manufacturing processes. CIRP Conf. Life Cycle Eng. **21**, 531–536 (2014)
4. Kuczenski, B., Davis, C.B., Rivela, B., Janowicz, K.: Semantic catalogs for life cycle assessment data. J. Clean. Prod. **137**, 1109–1117 (2016)
5. United States Environmental Protection Agency. Basic information on sustainable manufacturing (2009). https://www.epa.gov/sustainability/sustainable-manufacturing. Accessed 07 Apr 2018
6. Sindhuja, P., Balamurugan, M.S.: Smart power monitoring and control system through internet of things using cloud data storage. Indian J. Sci. Technol. **8**(19), 1–7 (2015)
7. Pocero, L., Amaxilatis, D., Mylonas, G., Chatzigiannakis, I.: Open source IoT meter devices for smart and energy-efficient school buildings. Hardware **1**, 54–67 (2017)
8. Tan, Y.S., Ng, Y.T., Low, J.S.C.: Internet-of-things enabled real-time monitoring of energy efficiency on manufacturing shop floors. Proc. CIRP **61**, 376–381 (2017)

The Construction Value Chain in a BIM Environment

Myrna Flores[1,3]($\boxtimes$), Ahmed Al-Ashaab[2], Oliver Mörth[2],
Pablo Cifre Usó[2], Harry Pinar[2], Fatimah Alfaraj[2], and Ming Yu[2]

[1] Lean Analytics Association (LAA), Carona, Switzerland
myrna.flores@epfl.ch
[2] Cranfield University, Cranfield, UK
[3] Ecole Polytechnique Fédérale de Lausanne (EPFL), Lausanne, Switzerland

Abstract. This paper provides the findings of a research project aiming to understand the current level of industrial awareness, challenges and lessons learned during the application of the BIM (Building Information Modelling) across the construction value chain. A literature review was conducted to gather the state of the art and latest trends about BIM fundamentals, different elements in a BIM application, BIM dimensions and BIM maturity levels, as well as the associated standards. Furthermore, the BIM environment was investigated and information related to the construction value chain was gathered as the foundation to carry out a field study in which 29 organizations located in six countries were interviewed through face to face sessions with different actors involved in variety of roles across the construction value chain to enable an interdisciplinary and global understanding.

Keywords: Construction value chain · BIM environment · Full collaboration

1 Introduction

Several actors are involved in construction projects, such as architecture designers, structure designers, system designers, material providers, contractors, end users and more. Typically, each project member has a different vision of the final asset, as the organization is involved in a different stage of the project and uses a different software, making it difficult to have a common understanding and an integrated and complete overview and data model. Different kinds of issues, such as isolated work, differences between reality and the client's vision, delay in delivery, additional costs and more, might occur at any phase of the project lifecycle (Design and Engineering, Construction, Operation, Maintenance and Demolition) due to the lack of communication and collaboration between all these actors. Therefore, there is a need to have a single representation of the asset to help create one common and shared vision. Hence, the construction community gave rise to the concept of building information modelling [1, 4, 5, 12].

Building Information Modeling (BIM) might be misunderstood, referring to it as the software with which companies design their individual components up to the fully integrated construction asset. Nevertheless, BIM goes beyond a technology, it requires

I. Moon et al. (Eds.): APMS 2018, IFIP AICT 536, pp. 255–262, 2018.
https://doi.org/10.1007/978-3-319-99707-0_32

a radical change in the mindset of how a construction project is carried out. One definition for BIM proposed by the World Economic Forum [17] is stated as follows: "BIM is a collaborative process in which all parties involved in a project use three-dimensional design applications, which can include additional information about assets' scheduling, cost, sustainability, operations and maintenance to ensure information is shared accurately and consistently, throughout total assets' lifecycles."

Adopting BIM requires an important change in the way the different actors involved in a construction project work together. Those actors represent the construction value chain. This paper presents a view of what the construction value chain could look like when collaborating in a BIM environment to help achieve benefits, such as cost and waste reduction impacting on faster projects delivery, risk reduction and more. The opportunity BIM is providing to the construction sector is the co-creation of one shared 3D-Model representing the physical and functional characteristics of an asset, including information that is frequently added, extracted, updated or modified, to provide a standardized information exchange. Therefore, BIM enables the integration of all the elements of the construction assets and therefore allows different actors to collaborate during the different stages of the construction project providing a way for an integrated team to make informed decisions. However, given that working approach is relatively new and has only recently become widely diffused, not all actors across the construction value chain have fully adopted BIM. Many clients still see BIM as merely a design tool and do not realize all its capabilities and advantages like, for example, in maintenance operations, where the data will be available and updated to schedule maintenance activities when required. BIM is one of the key drivers enabling the construction industry moving towards digitalization and the industry and government have started noticing its capabilities [1, 4, 5, 7, 8, 15].

This paper presents the summarized results of a BIM (Building Information Modelling) study that was conducted at Cranfield University, in collaboration with the Lean Analytics Association, and focuses on understanding the construction value chain within a BIM environment and on capturing the best practices in the industry as well as identifying the importance of its members.

Therefore, the research question to be answered by this study is as follows:

What is the current level of industrial awareness in the construction value chain about the application of BIM and which are the important enablers?

The research methodology is divided into the following four phases: Learn, Energize, Apply and Diffuse (LEAD). In the *Learn* phase, a literature review was conducted to obtain the state of the art of the current BIM fundamentals and BIM applications. In the *Energize* phase, a questionnaire was designed to help perform semi-structured interviews in a field study to capture current information from the industry. The data analysis of the field study in the *Apply* phase supported the understanding of the industrial perspective of BIM and its applications, and provided a general view of the construction value chain within a BIM environment. Finally, a final presentation, poster and this paper were developed as a part of the *Diffuse* phase.

2 BIM Fundamentals

A BIM model represents the physical and functional characteristics of an asset and consists of sub-models and BIM objects. Sub-models represent a model of one particular discipline, such as an architecture model, a structure model or a system model, and joining them together creates the actual BIM model. The National Building Specification points out that a BIM object represents the physical and functional characteristics of one component of the asset and contains geometric, technical, admin and functional information. Furthermore, a BIM application provides different elements, such as the modeling element, the technical element, the construction admin element, the simulation element and the business element. The modeling element includes the geometric modeling (2D and 3D) to visualize the shape of the buildings and their internal systems, such as the electrical system, the plumbing system etc., as well as the structure, system and clash analysis. Engineering data, such as material selection and specifications but also tolerances, are part of the technical element, whereas the construction admin element includes the bill of materials, the project plan, cost estimation, scheduling etc. The simulation of end-user operations, the management of the asset, environmental efficiency, sustainability, emergency and disaster events and the acoustic system are part of the simulation element, whereas the business element includes the feasibility study, contracts and legal management, return on investment, risk assessment etc. Different companies have managed to achieve different levels of implementation and integration of these elements, as well as different levels of collaboration. In a BIM environment, these are referred to as BIM maturity levels and dimensions [1, 5, 11].

As shown in Fig. 1, four maturity levels from 0 to 3 exist, where level 0 represents the lowest level of collaboration and is based on 2D and paper. It is very much a representation of the traditional manner in the construction sector and its disadvantages. Level 1 is an enhanced maturity level, where a 3D CAD model is developed and used to share the asset data but important technical and admin data is still missing. Level 2 is the start of real effective collaboration, where the BIM models consist of geometric, technical and admin data. Even though all actors use their own 3D CAD models, collaboration is achieved through sharing design information using a common file format. Typical dimensions for this level are 4D (time-related information and construction sequencing) and 5D (added cost aspect such as the purchasing, running and replacement cost). Level 2 has become compulsory as part of the government strategy in many countries such as the UK, the US, Singapore, etc. and several national and international standards have been developed. As visualized in Fig. 1, the UK has established four standards (BS1192, BS 7000, BS8541, PAS1192), required to complete work at level 2. However, the standards for level 0 and level 1 must also be met as fundamentals of level 2. In order to prove that companies work at level 2 and to obtain the trust of their clients and other actors of the value chain, certifications from formal standard bodies, such as BSI, are needed. However, at the moment, a BSI certification is not necessarily accepted by other countries, which puts the pressure on construction companies to have more certifications from different national standard bodies within the different countries they operate in. Therefore, creating international standards accepted by all actors in the construction value chain all over the world is the next necessary step. Level 3 is the top level and means full collaboration and full integration. There is only one shared model all parties across the construction value chain have access to in order to enable modification and improvement in real time. As visualized in Fig. 1, three new dimensions are associated with this top level. 6D is focused on the lifecycle management of the building and 7D is focused on sustainability. Finally, 8D represents accident preventions in which the UK government is very interested at the moment. Even though the UK government plans to reach level 3 by 2025, this is very optimistic from an industrial perspective [2, 3, 7–11, 14].

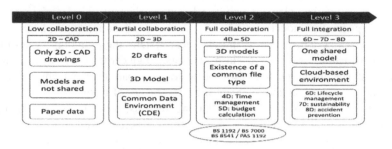

Fig. 1. BIM levels, dimension and required standards

Furthermore, in order to work properly in a BIM environment, every actor is required to use the same software to integrate the specific BIM elements for the work performed enabling the interoperability of data across the construction value chain. Currently, companies use more than one software to perform different types of work, such as concept design, architecture design, structure design and system design. This happens because designers are trained and have a lot of experience in a specific traditional software (non-BIM software) and feel uncomfortable working with any other kind of software even though its technical capability is higher than the traditional one's. This results in designers who do the same work twice, because the first design of the asset is done using traditional software and, subsequently, the whole asset is created a second time with a BIM software to add the technical and construction admin data and enable the actual collaboration. This results in additional time and increased cost which works against the expected benefits of using BIM. As of now, there is no single software available in the market capable of sufficiently covering every part of a project. This emphasizes the importance of efficient data exchange between the different BIM software applications. One of the findings was that the commercial software Revit, from Autodesk, is mainly used in the six countries within the scope of our research project: United Kingdom, Spain, Ireland, France, Saudi Arabia and Singapore and provides advantages in the structure and system design since it was developed by engineers. The second most used software is Archicad from Graphisoft which is preferred in architecture design since it was developed by architects and provides similar tools to traditional software. Another very important criterion for selecting a BIM software is its technical capability and the fact that this is the software used by the client. Using the same software across the construction value chain provides a lot of advantages as far as data compatibility is concerned, since open file formats such as IFC still cause a loss of data and, consequently, additional time and cost [1, 6, 15]. Figure 2 shows that from the sample of construction actors interviewed, 71.4% of the interviewees are using Revit and Fig. 3 the key challenges to implement.

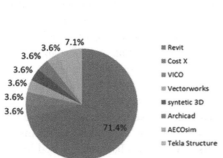

Fig. 2. BIM softwares used

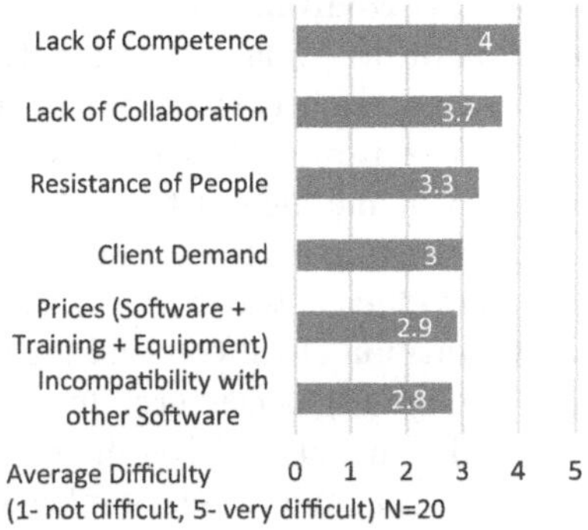

Fig. 3. Main BIM implementation challenges

3   The Construction Value Chain in a BIM Environment

Having understood the BIM environment, it appears that the focus lies on the end-to-end construction value chain, which integrates many different actors, each one providing value to the overall construction project. While the ideal construction value chain is perceived as linear with little complexity, the real construction value chain is a web of relationships and is, thus, complex and not linear. However, this work assumes a linear value chain including only the main phases: Design & Engineering, Construction, Operation, Maintenance & Renovation, and Demolition. These main phases have been identified through the literature review. A field study was conducted to understand the current industrial perspective of the construction value chain and to capture the current best practices and challenges in the industry.

A questionnaire was designed to help perform semi-structured interviews. In order to obtain sufficient amount of quantitative and qualitative information, interviews with diverse companies took place across six different countries around the world, including the United Kingdom, Ireland, France, Spain, Saudi Arabia and Singapore. These interviews involved actors from all disciplines across the construction value chain as well as directly related organizations, reaching the number of 29 companies: Architecture & Engineering (5), Construction (8), Consultancy (5), Materials & Elements Suppliers (4), Software, Standard and BIM Object providers (3) and Universities (4). Interviews were supported by a BIM expert from each organization. The respondents were BIM managers or designers in the case of architecture & engineering or construction companies, the person in charge of BIM applications when referring to materials & elements suppliers or software, standard and BIM object providers as well as professors and research fellows from architecture and engineering schools in the case of universities. This enabled the development of an interdisciplinary and global understanding of the construction value chain [13, 15, 16]. To gather quantitative information, the following question was asked:

Which of the following represents an important actor of the construction value chain in a BIM environment?

The result of the evaluation of the data collected for this question is visualized in Fig. 4, where the numbers represent the importance of ten given options corresponding to actors of the construction value chain in a BIM environment. The lowest relevance is represented by 1, the highest by 5. The graph demonstrates that the most important actor is the owner or investor, who is essential for the project to be launched. BIM enables a more efficient way to convince investors to start a project by providing more accurate information about cost and time at an early stage, as well as visualizing the final asset through augmented or virtual reality. Designers take the second place. At the moment, BIM is mainly used in the design phase as its true capabilities in terms of enabling full collaboration and the related benefits have not yet been recognized by all actors across the construction value chain. Even though BIM entails many benefits to improve maintenance, many owners still think BIM is merely a design tool. Maintenance might become more popular in the future when full collaboration and integration has been achieved and the mindset of each actor across the construction value chain has changed to see BIM not as a mere design tool but as an enabler of collaboration and integration. Suppliers are important for the construction value chain, but less important in a BIM environment. The reason for this is that the contractor determines the needed amount of goods and materials and sets the actual order. In terms of supplier selection, the contractor also has the final say and designers can only express their preferences. Finally, the demolition contractor has the lowest importance as an actor in the construction value chain in a BIM environment. That can be explained by the currently low number of companies in this field that are using BIM. However, this might also change in the future when BIM has reached its full maturity across the construction value chain. Figure 4 provides the findings showing which actors have a major role fostering a BIM collaborative environment.

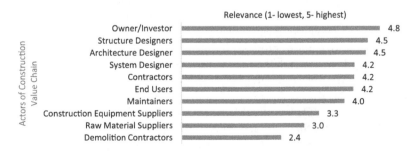

Fig. 4. Relevance of construction value chain actors fostering the BIM environment

The final construction value chain is visualized in Fig. 5. All actors have access to the BIM model as a single source of information, and each actor uses the model to finish their own work in the most efficient way. BIM can be used to design and analyze the asset, the structure (Finite Element Analysis) and the systems, such as the electrical system, the plumbing system, the climatic system, the acoustic system and the IT system (Mechanical and Electrical Analysis). Furthermore, the user experience should also be part of the design phase to provide an optimal solution. The main contractor but also subcontractors should use the same BIM model which provides everyone with the same information and enables off-site manufacturing, which also results in benefits such as time, cost, and risk reduction. The owner, operator and user of the building are provided with all asset information needed to use and manage it in the most efficient way.

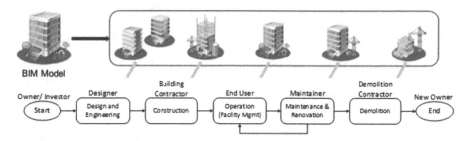

Fig. 5. Construction value chain in a BIM environment

Furthermore, BIM enables the creation of an accurate maintenance plan to prevent failures more efficiently and to eliminate them as fast as possible in case of any occurrence. However, as mentioned earlier, the different actors across the construction value chain have still not fully understood how to realize all benefits of BIM in terms of maintenance. Furthermore, even though BIM has not been fully implemented in the demolition industry yet, demolition contractors can use BIM to easily identify the best way an asset could be demolished. All these benefits are for the long term and are only achievable if BIM is fully adopted across the construction value chain and if the BIM applications are used properly to enable collaboration. Current challenges are the resistance to change, a lack of competence and expertise, incompatibility with other software and missing IT infrastructure [13, 15, 16].

4 Conclusion

The understanding of the reviewed literature related to the construction value chain and the captured industrial perspectives shown in Fig. 4 have led to the definition of the value chain in the BIM environment illustrated in Fig. 5. Therefore, gaining the real benefits of BIM by achieving full collaborations among the different construction actors is possible by understanding the construction value chain. This understanding should include the individual role and responsibilities as well as the value adding activities to the final definition and construction of the asset. Furthermore, this level of full collab-oration has not yet been achieved, since not all actors in the value chain have successfully adopted BIM or realized and understood its capabilities. As many governments are pushing the industry towards full collaboration and integration, all actors across the construction value chain will have to improve their BIM adoption and consistently implement it at each project to achieve this level within the expected time frame.

References

1. Bryde, D., Broquetas, M., Volm, J.: The project benefits of Building Information Modelling (BIM). Int. J. Project Manag. **31**, 971–980 (2012)
2. BS 1192: 2007+A2:2016 - Collaborative production of architectural, engineering and construction information – Code of practice. London: BSI Standards Limited (2016)
3. BS 8536-2:2016 - Briefing for design and construction – Part 2: Code of practice for asset management (Linear and geographical infrastructure). BSI Standards Limited, London (2016)
4. Design Buildings Wiki: Building information modelling BIM (2018)
5. Design Buildings Wiki: Collaborative practices for building design and construction (2018). https://www.designingbuildings.co.uk/wiki/Collaborative_practices_for_building_design_and_construction. Accessed 22 Apr 2018
6. GOV.UK: Creating a Digital Built Britain: what you need to know (2017). https://www.gov.uk/guidance/creating-a-digital-built-britain-what-you-need-to-know. Accessed 22 Apr 2018
7. Government of the United Kingdom: Industrial Strategy: government and industry in partnership - Construction 2025, London (2013). https://www.designingbuildings.co.uk/wiki/Building_information_modelling_BIM
8. Issa, R.R.A., Olbina, S.: Building information modeling: applications and practices. Rinker School of Construction Management, Florida (2015)
9. McPartland, R.: National Building Specification: BIM Levels Explained (2014). https://www.thenbs.com/knowledge/bim-levels-explained. Accessed 22 Apr 2018
10. McPartland, R.: National Building Specification: What are BIM Dimensions (2017). https://www.thenbs.com/knowledge/bim-dimensions-3d-4d-5d-6d-bim-explained. Accessed 22 Apr 2018
11. McPartland, R.: National Building Specification: What are BIM Objects (2017). https://www.thenbs.com/knowledge/what-are-bim-objects. Accessed 22 Apr 2018
12. NBS: National Building Specification: What is Building Information Modelling (BIM) (2016). https://www.thenbs.com/knowledge/what-is-building-information-modelling-bim. Accessed 22 Apr 2018
13. PAS 1192-2:2013: Specification for information management for the capital/delivery phase of construction projects using building information modelling. BSI Standards Ltd., London (2013)
14. PAS 1192-5:2015: Specification for security-minded building information modelling, digital built environments and smart asset management. BSI Standards Limited, London (2015)
15. Renz, A., et al.: Shaping the Future of Construction: A Breakthrough in Mindset and Technology. World Economic Forum, Cologny (2016)
16. Salman, A., Masce, A.: Building Information Modeling (BIM): Trends, Benefits, Risks, and Challenges for the AEC Industry. American Society of Civil Engineers (2011)
17. WEF. An Action Plan to Accelerate Building Information Modeling (BIM) Adoption, The World Economic Forum, February 2018

Performance Measurement in Sensorized Sociotechnical Manufacturing Environments

Emrah Arica[1(✉)], Manuel Oliveira[1], and Christos Emmanouilidis[2]

[1] Department of Economics and Technology Management,
SINTEF Technology and Society, Trondheim, Norway
{emrah.arica,manuel.oliveira}@sintef.no
[2] School of Aerospace, Transport and Manufacturing,
Cranfield University, Cranfield, UK
christosem@cranfield.ac.uk

Abstract. Industry 4.0 entails the digitization of the shopfloor operations combining technologies such as internet of things-enabled sensing, cyber-physical systems, data analytics, augmented reality, and wearable devices and robots that transform the manufacturing environment into a workplace of human-machine interactive symbiosis. With the digitization of the manufacturing environment, new opportunities emerge concerning performance measurement as new sources of real-time data become available, including data collated from the operator on the shopfloor. Traditionally, the human dimension had been disjoint from the situation analysis of shopfloor performance that drives evidence based decision making. This paper presents the features and advantages of performance measurement in human-workplace interactive manufacturing where detailed data on human performance is provided by sensors and utilized to improve the performance goals. The paper is concluded with a discussion on the impact of context information management for interactive manufacturing workplaces, as a means of delivering more informed situational awareness, a critical enabler for human-machine interaction, as well as for handling complexity in disparate data sources.

Keywords: Performance measurement · Manufacturing
Human-machine interaction

1 Introduction

Performance measurement contributes to identify the deviation from the targets, provide mechanisms for both top-down and bottom-up communication, and assess the competitive priorities and operational capacity of the firm [1]. Achieving these functions largely rely on capturing timely and accurate status information from the manufacturing environment composed of a complex ecosystem of processes, workers, machines, tools, robots, information systems and technologies. Such complexity also involves uncertainty and flexibility in the manufacturing processes, as well as a degree of decision-making autonomy on the shop floor, typified as sociotechnical manufacturing environments [2, 3]. In today's industry 4.0 sociotechnical manufacturing environments, a great deal of real time data can now be captured from machines and

I. Moon et al. (Eds.): APMS 2018, IFIP AICT 536, pp. 263–268, 2018.
https://doi.org/10.1007/978-3-319-99707-0_33

processes by information systems and technologies such as sensors. Sensorizing the workers is far behind this digitalization pace due to various reasons, such as lack of focus on human factor in performance measurement systems and privacy concerns. However, research indicates that human factor is an important mediator to achieve good performance results [4, 5]. As such, the correlation between the human performance and other performance dimensions should be better understood. Further research is therefore needed to study how workplaces with sensorized workers capturing detailed real time human data can be incorporated into performance measurement systems.

This paper proposes a conceptual framework for sensorized manufacturing environment and discusses its impact on performance measurement. A literature review is conducted, highlighting the scarcity of resources on the influence of industry 4.0 technologies on performance measurement. To the best of our knowledge, the potential performance impact of sensorizing humans has not been sufficiently discussed previously. Furthermore, the paper proposes a framework that can be utilized to develop adaptable and interactive workplaces with enhanced efficiency and worker well-being.

2 Manufacturing Performance Measurement

A manufacturing performance measurement system traditionally focuses on flow orientation with short throughput times and maximizing the internal efficiency in terms of both financial (e.g. cost) and non-financial measures (e.g. labor productivity) [6]. Alignment of financial and non-financial measures has gained importance with the introduction of balanced scorecard [7] and its derivations [8]. Many authors argue that non-financial performance measures have indirect but important impact on financial performance. One way of realizing the positive influence of non-financial measures on financial performance is through lean manufacturing practices [4]. This necessitates the incorporation of human factor into performance measurement frameworks and consideration of human resource-oriented metrics. However, traditional manufacturing performance measurement systems are criticized as they largely focus on technical measures and the human factor is largely ignored [9]. The pioneering empirical study of [5] on 163 plants indicates the necessity of joint optimization of both socially- and technically-oriented practices for achieving good performance results. Tracking, measuring, and improving human-oriented performance dimensions such as employee involvement, training, and information and feedback are closely linked with success in overall efficiency measures (e.g. productivity) and financial performance [5, 10]. Eliminating production wastes alone does not improve productivity, quality, or delivery performance, but reveals them [4]. There is need for involving shop-floor employees through information and actionable feedback to address the root causes of problems. As such, sociotechnical manufacturing environments require the convergence of social (e.g. reduced worker accidents, increased skills) and technical (e.g. increased productivity and quality) performance dimensions and objectives for optimized and improved company performance.

Research shows the positive correlation of employing enterprise information systems in manufacturing with shop floor performance dimensions [11]. Although manufacturing technologies and information systems have been utilized to manage and improve performance, there are still challenges in timely information acquisition and timely feedback [11]. The recent applications of Internet of Things (IoT) technologies (e.g. radio frequency Identification tags, embedded computing devices and sensors, actuators and mobile devices), along with IoT-oriented computing architectures are providing enablers for addressing such challenges. They are not only enabling more adaptive and reactive performance measurement systems, but also lead to the evolution of performance measurement systems by enabling timely information availability and accessibility. Relatively few recent studies focus on the latter aspect to develop smart performance measurement systems. Kumaraguru et al. [12] proposes a continuous performance measurement system integrated with real-time analytics. Hwang et al. [13] suggested an IoT-based performance management model that define the performance indicators consistent with the ISA95 automation standard, using manufacturing information systems such as MES. However, these studies are at the very early stages and consider the use of IoT technologies merely on objects and locations such as machines, production lines, and inventory areas. The focus is mainly on machine-oriented overall efficiency measures such as OEE, and on minimizing the deviation between targeted and actual performance. The impact of human performance and the interaction between different measures is not considered. The next section presents a performance measurement framework for sensorized manufacturing environment, where real time data can be captured both from humans and machines, enabling involvement of human factor in performance management frameworks.

3 Performance Measurement in Manufacturing Environments with Sensorized Workers

In Industry 4.0 manufacturing environments, the human worker can be directly sensorized by wearable devices, yielding more data in addition to what is accessible by means of information systems that support processes, machines, and robots. This will permit to assess the worker's state across multiple dimensions, including satisfaction, engagement, stress level, capabilities, skill, performance and experience. Motion sensors can detect movement and gestures that contribute to the definition of the psycho-physiological status. Through wearable devices, workers receive the support to bridge cognitive gaps they are experiencing. Examples of captured parameters are: breath/heart rate, skin conductance and movement of relevant body segments. From the analysis of the signals representing the multiple dimensions, it can be decided if an immediate action should be taken or if the detected conditions are not so serious as to require a long-term re-design of the workplace to improve the interaction between workers and the production system. This can help detecting when deviations occur that require interventions for physical and cognitive enhancements, making sense regarding the context if the underlying circumstances and can lead to improving operator performance and wellbeing. Furthermore, the symbiosis between workers and workplaces will be facilitated, making the interaction between the two comfortable and efficient. A conceptual framework for such manufacturing environment is depicted in Fig. 1 and described below.

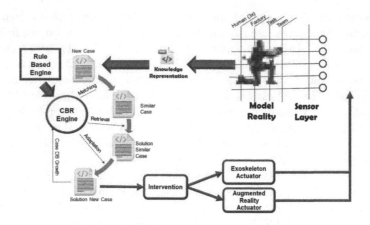

Fig. 1. A conceptual framework for sensorized manufacturing environment

The process starts with the capture of signals from different sources, including the operator on the shopfloor. The collated signals are used to create in the system a situation awareness of the work being carried out by the worker by means of digital representation of reality. The system then uses machine learning (e.g.: case based reasoning or similar approaches) to detect when deviations from the norm, including potential safety and ergonomics problems or cognitive deficits (e.g. lack of attention, tiredness, reduction of productivity) of workers are detected. The system triggers potential short-term interventions that address the nature of a deviation. Two examples are shown:

- An exoskeleton actuator is used to alleviate the physical stress and thereby mitigate the tiredness of the worker of handling heavy equipment or/and parts;
- An augmented reality actuator is triggered when signals indicate a decline in their attention, thus the system will reinforce with visual cues their focus of attention.

The interventions triggered are very context dependent, thus when the system is unable to find a resolution to an identified deviation with an existing intervention (e.g.: exoskeleton or augmented reality), the system registers the failure and triggers a long term intervention where a human stakeholder (e.g.: engineer) is required to use a set of tools for mining the data collated to determine the root cause of the deviation and devise a new short-term intervention, alternatively they may redesign the product, process or workplace. Such human-workplace interactive sensorized manufacturing environment are suggested to bring the following performance measurement system improvements:

Successful utilization of proactive leading performance indicators: The quality of commonly-used indicators (e.g. number of accidents) is questioned since they are historical in nature, reporting on activities that occurred in the past [9]. Such indicators are classified as lagging indicators in literature [14]. Lagging indicators are output oriented and aim to provide a snapshot of analysis of the historical data. Leading indicators aim to monitor if the tasks are being performed on track and to provide early warning signs for taking a proactive action to avoid unwanted events from occurring. An example of a leading indicator is the frequency of stress peaks of the workers, which provides a warning for a future work accident. A proactive action in this case could be taking a break. While leading indicators enable taking corrective actions towards performance objectives, lagging indicators primarily reveals the performance results.

Better understanding of causal relationships between measures: There is highly limited possibility to understand the cause-effect relationships of measures in today's performance measurement systems. This is usually done with trial and error approach, with lack of evidences. Capturing detailed real-time performance information from workers can also provide evidence-based links between various performance dimensions such as health, productivity, and quality. For example, it can now be better understood how the stress and fatigue levels of the workers correlates with sickness and absenteeism. How does the stress level influence the productivity? Is the worker achieving the daily quote at the cost of his/her health? How is the level of stress the person is feeling when getting the daily productivity quote? How is the quality influenced by the stress levels? Better understanding of such causal relationships also enables better alignment of different performance dimensions and better decisions. For example, reducing the daily productivity quote to reduce the absenteeism can on the long run increase productivity.

4 Discussion and Conclusion

This paper focused on the potential impact of employing industry 4.0 technologies, with emphasis on sensors and wearables, on performance measurement. Considerable challenges need to be addressed when introducing sensorized solutions for human performance measurement. First, situational awareness needs to be established, so that measurements are analysed, and recommendations or action triggers are initiated on the basis of the right context. Secondly, the complexity and disparity of data sources need to be managed, filtering out irrelevant data, while reinforcing attention via cues which are contextually relevant. Finally, concerns regarding the privacy and security of data related to human activity must be addressed. The latter should be considered at the design stage and relevant guidelines need to be followed to address privacy issues of human-centered manufacturing environments for all phases of data lifecycle management (Mannhardt et al. [15]). The first two challenges require further research on context information management, which is now recognized as of high importance in modern enterprise information systems and as such it is also relevant to the assessment of human performance in workplaces [16]. The typology of high level context identified in such information systems, namely user, environment, system, social, and business/service context is also relevant for human performance measurement. Further work is nonetheless needed to model this type of application-specific context with a particular emphasis on 'User Context' to capture key elements of human physical and sentiment situational awareness. For example, detecting worker stress during work activities has different contextual interpretation depending on the circumstances under which the worker operates. The context of operating under heavier than usual workload and tight constraints is quite different from that of a worker operating under low work load conditions and therefore any stress detection should be interpreted differently. Such analysis should then provide further guidance not also regarding the sensorization choices but also the sensor and context fusion approaches which would be applicable to performance measurement in sensorized sociotechnical manufacturing environments.

References

1. Nuthall, L.: Supply chain performance measures and systems. In: Gower Handbook of Supply Chain Management, pp. 248–266. Gower Publishing, Burlington (2003)
2. Wiers, V.C.S.: The relationship between shop floor autonomy and APS implementation success: evidence from two cases. Prod. Plann. Control 20(7), 576–585 (2009)
3. Arica, E., Haskins, C., Strandhagen, J.O.: A framework for production rescheduling in sociotechnical manufacturing environments. Prod. Plann. Control 27(14), 1191–1205 (2016)
4. Fullerton, R.R., Wempe, W.F.: Lean manufacturing, non-financial performance measures, and financial performance. Int. J. Oper. Prod. Manag. 29(3), 214–240 (2009)
5. Cua, K.O., McKone, K.E., Schroeder, R.G.: Relationships between implementation of TQM, JIT, and TPM and manufacturing performance. J. Oper. Manag. 19(6), 675–694 (2001)
6. Jonsson, P., Lesshammar, M.: Evaluation and improvement of manufacturing performance measurement systems-the role of OEE. Int. J. Oper. Prod. Manag. 19(1), 55–78 (1999)
7. Kaplan, R.S., Norton, D.P.: Using the balanced scorecard as a strategic management system. In: Harvard Business Review, Boston (1996)
8. Hoque, Z.: 20 years of studies on the balanced scorecard: trends, accomplishments, gaps and opportunities for future research. Br. Account. Rev. 46(1), 33–59 (2014)
9. Gomes, C.F., Yasin, M.M., Lisboa, J.V.: A literature review of manufacturing performance measures and measurement in an organizational context: a framework and direction for future research. J. Manuf. Technol. Manag. 15(6), 511–530 (2004)
10. Birdi, K., et al.: The impact of human resource and operational management practices on company productivity: a longitudinal study. Pers. Psychol. 61(3), 467–501 (2008)
11. Abdel-Maksoud, A., Dugdale, D., Luther, R.: Non-financial performance measurement in manufacturing companies. Br. Account. Rev. 37(3), 261–297 (2005)
12. Kumaraguru, S., Kulvatunyou, B., Morris, K.C.: Integrating real-time analytics and continuous performance management in smart manufacturing systems. In: Grabot, B., Vallespir, B., Gomes, S., Bouras, A., Kiritsis, D. (eds.) APMS 2014. IAICT, vol. 440, pp. 175–182. Springer, Heidelberg (2014). https://doi.org/10.1007/978-3-662-44733-8_22
13. Hwang, G., et al.: Developing performance measurement system for internet of things and smart factory environment. Int. J. Prod. Res. 55(9), 2590–2602 (2017)
14. Muchiri, P., et al.: Development of maintenance function performance measurement framework and indicators. Int. J. Prod. Econ. 131(1), 295–302 (2011)
15. Mannhardt, F., Petersen, S.A., Duarte de Oliveira, M.F.: Privacy challenges for process mining in human-centered industrial environments. In: Intelligent Environments (IE) (2018)
16. El Kadiri, S., et al.: Current trends on ICT technologies for enterprise information systems. Comput. Ind. 79, 14–33 (2016)

Industry 4.0 - Digital Twin

A Scheduling Tool for Achieving Zero Defect Manufacturing (ZDM): A Conceptual Framework

Foivos Psarommatis(✉) and Dimitris Kiritsis

École Polytechnique Fédérale de Lausanne, ICT for Sustainable Manufacturing,
EPFL SCI-STI-DK, Lausanne, Switzerland
foivos.psarommatis@epfl.ch

Abstract. Contemporary manufacturing landscape has changed and has become highly volatile and demanding. Product Life Cycle has significantly decreased because of the consumers' need for personalized products in shorter period of time. This need forced the manufacturers to produce smaller batches of highly diversified products instead of producing huge batches of the same product. These newly imposed production requirements made the manufacturers struggle to optimize their productions in such short period of time and therefore, these production requirements created the need for more efficient, productive and eco-friendly planning and scheduling. The solution to this problem can be given partially by a concept named "Zero Defect Manufacturing" (ZDM). The goal of ZDM is to eliminate defected parts and therefore achieving higher efficiency, eco-friendliness and lower production costs. There are four ZDM strategies that are interconnected with each other: detection, repair, prediction and prevention. The current research work focuses on the Beginning of Life of the product and considers the development of a dynamic Scheduling tool combined with an intelligent Decision Support System (DSS) that takes into consideration the ZDM strategies for eliminating defected parts during production. The elimination of defected parts would be done mainly by creating specific algorithms for predicting when a defect may occur and for taking the right decisions in order to prevent the defect occurrence. Finally, an industrial example is presented in order to illustrate the potential benefits of such an approach.

Keywords: Zero Defect Manufacturing · Defect prediction · Scheduling

1 Introduction and State of the Art

Nowadays, manufacturing environment is highly volatile and rapidly changing. Also the need of products is increasing exponentially, and therefore Product Life Cycle is shortened [1]. As a result, more products are required to be manufactured or remanufactured [2]. So far, manufacturers used to produce large batches of the same product, but these new market requirements forced them to produce small batches of different products. This production strategy created a problem to the manufacturers that they have never faced in the past. Manufacturers are producing so many different products leaving no room for production optimization, as it was happening so far. The result of

© IFIP International Federation for Information Processing 2018
Published by Springer Nature Switzerland AG 2018. All Rights Reserved
I. Moon et al. (Eds.): APMS 2018, IFIP AICT 536, pp. 271–278, 2018.
https://doi.org/10.1007/978-3-319-99707-0_34

this situation is high number of defected parts which are discarded, recycled or they are repaired if it is possible [3]. This approach increases the cost of the final product and the energy consumption, which may turn the production process non-profitable.

Global competition is very tough, therefore manufacturers must be able to provide innovative and intricate products of high quality, with less process iterations, and more cost competitiveness, if they want to survive. The existing manufacturing systems cannot completely satisfy these requirements because of their deterministic approach to decision-making in an uncertain environment [4].

1.1 Zero Defect Manufacturing Concept

Zero Defect Manufacturing (ZDM) is a concept in quality management introduced in the 1960s by the US Army department. It has now become common practice which aims at reducing the number of errors and defects made during the manufacturing process of a product and therefore, make the production process more cost efficient, more eco-friendly and competitive. ZDM refers to a state where waste is completely eliminated from the manufacturing process and where defects are reduced to the minimum [5]. The concept of ZDM consists of four main elements: detecting, repairing, predicting, preventing, and their interconnections can be seen in Fig. 1. Even though zero defects are not possible to achieve in practice, the quest relies on perfection in order to improve general quality of products and processes. Waste, defined as all the tools and processes that are unproductive and that do not create value or add cost to the final product or service, is meant to disappear.

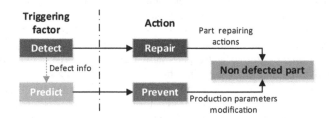

Fig. 1. Zero Defect Manufacturing elements

Many studies already worked on the way to achieve ZDM. In their study, Ferretti et al. [1] described a first classification of actions that can be implemented in all kind of manufacturing processes in order to reach the goal of a production with a low percentage of scrap pieces. They introduce two main categories of actions: (a) indirect actions, which are related to maintenance operations, training operators and raw material inspections, mainly and (b) the direct actions are directly performed on the manufacturing process itself, with two main possibilities, in-process or post-process actions.

ZDM is a very promising concept, but still there is no complete solution for the manufacturers. Most of the ZDM applications focus on optimizing processes on machine level and not to a higher level such us the scheduling level. Real-time events can disrupt the production, thus the scheduling tools are responsible for keeping production up to a certain level of efficiency.

1.2   Production Scheduling

Production scheduling is a very important and challenging problem in many manufacturing and process industries [6]. As information technology evolves, it allows to use real-time data in order to use them to solve dynamic, stochastic environment, complex manufacturing scheduling problems [7].

Dios and Framinan [8] investigated 99 computer based scheduling tools and their findings were very interesting, 41/99 tools were considering the objective of due dates fulfilment. Further to that other objectives commonly used are feasibility, resource usage, set up time reduction, make span and cycle time. On the other hand only 5/99 where considering the product quality [8], which is the primary case of ZDM. However, few papers take both manufacturing system scheduling and workforce scheduling into consideration [9].

Production systems operating in a highly dynamic environment where unpredictable events may occur and make the current schedule unfeasible [7]. Literature on dynamic scheduling has classified real-time events into two categories: (a) Resource – related and (b) Job – related [10]. This is mentioned because for applying ZDM a new category of real time events should be introduced and this is *"product related"* real time events.

2   Framework Architecture and Functionalities

Up to now, most of the approaches in management and maintenance of production systems were *"Machine oriented"*, but this has some limitations due to the fact that the outcome of a production system is a product. Therefore, in the context of the current work, a *"Product oriented"* approach is proposed and aligned with ZDM concept.

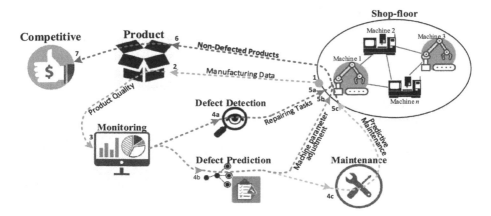

Fig. 2. Product oriented ZDM

Figure 2 illustrates the concept that it is proposed in order to address and reduce the product defects during production as it is imposed by ZDM.

The abovementioned concept can be implemented by integrating a DSS tool that complies with the ZDM objectives and mainly the "prediction" and "prevention" of a defect, into a dynamic scheduling tool.

The purpose is to provide a tool that will be capable to manage production with a more efficient way and able to cope with the contemporary production and market requirements. The difference with the current scheduling tools would be that instead for the scheduling tool to be "machine" oriented it would be "product" oriented and respond primarily to "product" related real time events, besides the other two categories.

Figure 3 illustrates the conceptual framework of the proposed tool with the informational flow among the scheduling tool, the DSS and the shop floor. The DSS will utilize real-time data from the shop floor in order to predict or detect a defect, then the outcome of the DSS is fed into the scheduling tool and the scheduling tool updates the schedule according to the suggestions that the DSS produced.

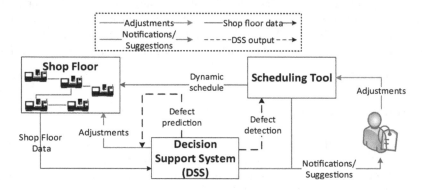

Fig. 3. Overall framework of the proposed tool

2.1 Decision Support System (DSS)

The DSS tool will consist of three individual components: (a) the defect detection module, (b) the defect prediction module and (c) decision making algorithms for suggesting a solution based on user-defined rules. Special attention needs to be given to both the defect prediction and the decision-making algorithms. The defect prediction module is a crucial part of the whole tool, because it is more efficient to prevent a defect before it happens. The figure below (Fig. 4) depicts the overall work flow of the defect prediction module.

This module will use real time data from the shop floor (product dimensional measurements, sensorial data, machine data etc.). Then based on specific "rule based" designed algorithms will analyze, identify and detect patterns, using user-adjusted parameters in order to fit to each individual use case. When a pattern is detected, up to a certain percentage (user defined), this percentage is fed on the decision-making

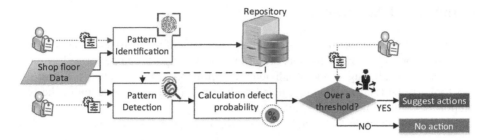

Fig. 4. Defect prediction overall work flow

algorithms in order to suggest solution for preventing the defect to occur. The final component is the defect detection, which by using the collected shop floor data will be able to detect defect and then the DSS will produce the required repairing tasks if it is repairable, and forward these tasks to the scheduling tool in order to re-schedule the production.

2.2   Scheduling Tool

When real time events, that disrupt the production, are happening the output of the DSS is fed into the dynamic scheduling tool along with the shop floor status and specification. The new schedule is produced according a specific set of user defined criteria. When the new schedule is produced, the Key Performance Indicators (KPIs) are calculated and if they are acceptable the updated schedule is released, otherwise the schedule is re-calculated with different criteria weights until KPIs are acceptable (Fig. 5).

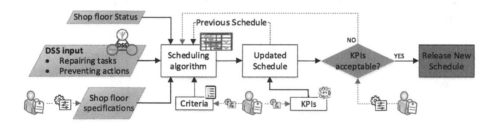

Fig. 5. Scheduling tool overall work flow

The primary criterion that the scheduling tool will consider for the production of the schedule is the product quality and afterwards all the other criteria and KPIs that each manufacturer has chosen. This is critical for the incorporation of ZDM concept to the scheduling tool. Also the novelty of the approach described above is the fact that the system will be tuned and operated based on "product" oriented events rather than "machine" oriented events which are dominantly used in such tools.

3   Industrial Application

The presented framework will be tested through two real life industrial use cases from a semiconductor and a hard metal manufacturer. The testing will be performed in three stages. At the beginning, the two individual components the Scheduling tool and the DSS tool will be tested and validated and at the final stage the integration of the two components will be tested and validated as well.

In order to illustrate the benefits of the proposed approach, a small example has been prepared in this scope utilizing data coming from the semiconductor manufacturer. The example considers three workstations (WS) for producing one type of product (P1). The WS1 and WS2 are manufacturing the two out of three components that P1 requires, component1 and component2 respectively (C1 and C2). P1 besides C1 and C2 requires also C3, which is an outsourced component. Afterwards, all the components going to the ws3 in order to be assembled. WS1 has defect ratio 2.3%, WS2 has 2.9% and WS3 has 4.1%. All the calculations will be done for an order of 100 parts, each's part materials cost 70 money units (MU) and requires 9.6 min to be produced. Further to that if, a defect occurs at ws1 or ws2 has 35% and 25% probability of being repaired whereas if a defect occurs in ws3 the assembled part cannot be repaired. The graph below (Fig. 6) illustrates the results from this example for four strategies production with repairing the defects (S1), without repairing the defects (S2), applying a defect prediction and repair the defected parts (S3) and finally applying defect prediction without repairing the defected parts (S4). All these strategies are compared with each other and with the normal production without defects. As it was expected the highest cost and latest order completion time is for S2. The S3 and S4 where considering a defect prediction probability of 60%. The outcome of this example in terms of cost is that S3 and S4 behave only 2.56% and 3.46%, respectively, worse than the ideal conditions whereas S1 and S2 have 6.16% and 8.21% respectively. The order completion time follows similar trend as the production cost. S3 and S4 are considering the proposed approach and shows better behavior than the S1and S2 with 3.69% and 4.93% respectively.

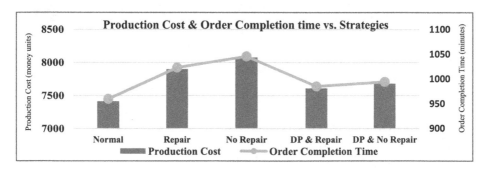

Fig. 6. Results from example case

4 Conclusions

The scheduling of a manufacturing system is a very important and critical problem and manufacturers face it every day. These days manufacturers are struggling to keep their productions up to a certain level of efficiency. This is because instead of producing large batches of the same product they produce smaller batches of multiple products. This situation leaves no time to manufacturers to optimize their production for a specific product. Driven by this need the current research work is proposed. There are numerous scheduling tools available in the literature but all of them are "machine" oriented, something that is not acceptable in the ZDM strategy. ZDM concept has as principle that everything are "product" oriented. Therefore, the proposed scheduling tool will be "product" oriented. Further to that, the integrated DSS besides the decision-making will have functionality to be able to predict when a defect will occur and therefore prevent it minimizing the production costs. The outcome of the current proposal would be to give to the manufactures a tool that will allow them to cope with the production of small batches of highly versatile products and at the same time keeping high quality standards. Furthermore, the results from the industrial example showed that there is a potential in such an approach especially in cases that the repair of a component is not feasible. Finally, this approach has some limitations in terms of the amount of data that are required in order to deliver the expected outcome.

Acknowledgments. The work presented in this paper is partially supported by the project Z-Factor which is funded by the European Union's Horizon 2020 program under grant agreement No 723906.

References

1. Ferretti, S., Caputo, D., Penza, M., D'Addona, D.M.: Monitoring systems for zero defect manufacturing. Proc. CIRP **12**, 258–263 (2013)
2. Zhou, L., Gupta, S.M., Kinoshita, Y., Yamada, T.: Pricing decision models for remanufactured short-life cycle technology products with generation consideration. Proc. CIRP **61**, 195–200 (2017)
3. Colledani, M., Coupek, D., Verl, A., Aichele, J., Yemane, A.: Design and evaluation of in-line product repair strategies for defect reduction in the production of electric drives. Proc. CIRP **21**, 159–164 (2014)
4. Manupati, V.K., Putnik, G.D., Tiwari, M.K., Ávila, P., Cruz-Cunha, M.M.: Integration of process planning and scheduling using mobile-agent based approach in a networked manufacturing environment. Comput. Ind. Eng. **94**, 63–73 (2016)
5. Myklebust, O.: Zero defect manufacturing: a product and plant oriented lifecycle approach. Proc. CIRP **12**, 246–251 (2013)
6. Ferris, M.C., Maravelias, C.T., Sundaramoorthy, A.: Simultaneous batching and scheduling using dynamic decomposition on a grid. INFORMS J. Comput. **21**, 398–410 (2009)
7. Ouelhadj, D., Petrovic, S.: A survey of dynamic scheduling in manufacturing systems. J. Sched. **12**, 417–431 (2009)
8. Dios, M., Framinan, J.M.: A review and classification of computer-based manufacturing scheduling tools. Comput. Ind. Eng. **99**, 229–249 (2016)

9. Qu, S., Wang, J., Govil, S., Leckie, J.O.: Optimized adaptive scheduling of a manufacturing process system with multi-skill workforce and multiple machine types: an ontology-based, multi-agent reinforcement learning approach. Proc. CIRP **57**, 55–60 (2016)

10. Vieira, G.E., Herrmann, J.W., Lin, E.: Analytical models to predict the performance of a single-machine system under periodic and event-driven rescheduling strategies. Int. J. Prod. Res. **38**, 1899–1915 (2000)

Predictive Maintenance Platform Based on Integrated Strategies for Increased Operating Life of Factories

Gökan May[1(✉)], Nikos Kyriakoulis[2], Konstantinos Apostolou[3], Sangje Cho[1], Konstantinos Grevenitis[3], Stefanos Kokkorikos[2], Jovana Milenkovic[3], and Dimitris Kiritsis[1]

[1] EPFL, ICT for Sustainable Manufacturing, EPFL SCI-STI-DK, Station 9, 1015 Lausanne, Switzerland
gokan.may@epfl.ch
[2] Core Innovation and Technology O.E, Athens, Greece
[3] ATLANTIS Engineering S.A., Thessaloniki, Greece

Abstract. Process output and profitability of the operations are mainly determined by how the equipment is being used. The production planning, operations and machine maintenance influence the overall equipment effectiveness (OEE) of the machinery, resulting in more 'good parts' at the end of the day. The target of the predictive maintenance approaches in this respect is to increase efficiency and effectiveness by optimizing the way machines are being used and to decrease the costs of unplanned interventions for the customer. To this end, development of ad-hoc strategies and their seamless integration into predictive maintenance systems is envisaged to bring substantial advantages in terms of productivity and competitiveness enhancement for manufacturing systems, representing a leap towards the real implementation of the Industry 4.0 vision. Inspired by this challenge, the study provides an approach to develop a novel predictive maintenance platform capable of preventing unexpected-breakdowns based on integrated strategies for extending the operating life span of production systems. The approach and result in this article are based on the development and implementation in a large collaborative EU-funded H2020 research project entitled Z-Bre4k, i.e. Strategies and predictive maintenance models wrapped around physical systems for zero-unexpected-breakdowns and increased operating life of factories.

Keywords: Industry 4.0 · Predictive maintenance · Big data
Asset management · Smart factories · Sustainable manufacturing
Industrial production

1 Introduction and State-of-the-Art

The requirement of competitiveness is a constant objective of manufacturers [1]. For a successful shift toward Industry 4.0, companies must constantly innovate and implement new methods and approaches enabling them to reduce operating costs and increase the availability and reliability of their production equipment [2]. For this

I. Moon et al. (Eds.): APMS 2018, IFIP AICT 536, pp. 279–287, 2018.
https://doi.org/10.1007/978-3-319-99707-0_35

reason, any downtime due to technical issues with the equipment needs to be avoided and, if occurring, decreased as much as possible [3]. On that vein, maintenance in general and predictive maintenance strategies in particular, are now facing significant challenges to deal with the evolution of the equipment, instrumentation and manufacturing processes they should support. Preventive maintenance strategies designed for traditional highly repetitive and stable mass production processes based on pre-defined components and machine behaviour models are no longer valid and more predictive-prescriptive maintenance strategies are needed. The success of those adaptive and responsive maintenance strategies highly depends on real-time and operation-synchronous information from the production system, the production process and the individual product, which should enrich and extend more traditional techniques and models.

To meet the requirements mentioned above and aligned with the Industry 4.0 key objectives toward eco-factories of the future [4, 5], this study provides a holistic framework and a comprehensive set of integrated strategies encompassing the whole manufacturing line for addressing the issue of asset management in smart factories of industry 4.0 in order to extend the life of production systems. Doing so, the research aims at providing an answer as to what could be the proper strategies and associated technologies to effectively minimize downtimes of manufacturing systems. A large collaborative EU-funded H2020 research project entitled Z-Bre4k [6] has been the main driver of the described approach and is designed for its validation. The project consortium is formed by 17 organisations across Europe including industrial pilot plants, academic institutions and technology providing companies.

To this end, novel strategies are designed in this research to be deployed at the field in order to prevent/predict/diagnose/remediate failures, estimate remaining useful life (RUL) of assets, manage alarms and mitigation actions, and synchronise with shop-floor operations and plant management systems while ensuring the safety of workers. The ultimate aim is to introduce and apply a holistic approach via integrated strategies to increase maintainability, accurately predict the condition and the RUL of networked machines, and adapt the performance to increase the operating life span of production systems.

2 Strategies for Increased Operating Life of Production Systems

The innovative synergies between online data gathering systems, real-time simulation models, data-based models and the knowledge management system form the main strategies which contribute to achieve zero breakdowns in manufacturing. In this context, the proposed solution comprises the introduction of eight (8) scalable strategies at component, machine and system level, all of which can be applied in the existing manufacturing plants with minimum interventions, targeting (1) the prediction occurrence of failure (Z-PREDICT), (2) the early detection of current or emerging failure (Z-DIAGNOSE), (3) the prevention of failure occurrence, building up, or even propagation in the production system (Z-PREVENT), (4) the estimation of the RUL of assets (Z-ESTIMATE), (5) the management of the aforementioned strategies through event modelling, KPI monitoring and real-time decision support (Z-MANAGE), (6) the replacement, reconfiguration, re-use, retirement, and recycling of components/assets (Z-REMEDIATE), (7) synchronizing remedy actions, production planning and logistics (Z-SYNCHRONISE), (8) preserving the safety, health, and comfort of the workers (Z-SAFETY). Each of the developed strategies are triggered based on predicting, detecting and assessing the impact of system level events that cause low performances, generate failures, and increase the costs. Figure 1 highlights the synergies and interactions between the eight Z-Strategies for building a novel predictive maintenance platform and the role of each strategy is further explained below.

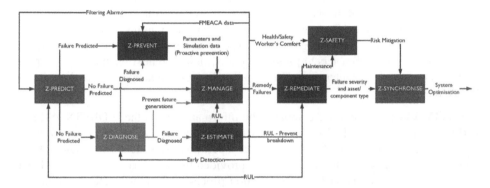

Fig. 1. Synergies and interactions between the eight Z-Strategies

Z-PREDICT: The events detected from the physical layer of the system are engineered into high value data that stipulates new and more accurate process models. Such an unbiased systems behaviour monitoring and analysis provides the basis for enriching the existing knowledge of the system (experience) learning new patterns, raising attention towards behaviour that cause operational and functional discrepancies (e.g. alarms for predicted failures) and the general trends in the shop-floor. The more the data pool is being increased the more precise (repeatability) and accurate the predictions will be. The estimations for the future states involve the whole production line – network of machines and components. The system can thus predict with high confidence the expected performance of components and their maintenance needs, predicting current or emerging failures, allowing better production planning and decision making on their RUL. Hence, the ability to optimise the manufacturing processes according to the RUL, production needs, and the maintenance operations is the key innovation to fulfil the industrial requirements.

Z-PREVENT: The prevention of failure occurrence strategy is based on the prediction strategy (i.e. degraded performance of assets or failure) realised across the shop-floor for condition monitoring of machinery and respective produced quality. The Z-PREDICT is predecessor of Z-PREVENT. The initial estimation of the future states is based on the simulation and modelling of the parameters. For each predicted failure or low performance (e.g. due to fatigue, wear), the responsible factors are identified and flagged through the FMEA system. The system analyses these factors based on an initial estimation, which after the simulation these are updated recursively. The result of this process is to avoid the building up or even propagation of a failure that leads to breakdown based on each recorded event both from previous and current states. The strategy thus prevents multiple alarm activations on similar failures.

Z-DIAGNOSE: This strategy is invoked when a current or an emerging failure is detected considering the condition at all three levels – machine, product, shop-floor. In such a scenario, an alarm is being triggered to flag the events that resulted in a failure or system performance degradation. By mapping the true reasons, the system is then able to avoid generating the failure or its emergence by weighting the system model. The strategy also involves more actions and processes to deal both with the generation of the diagnosed failure, and its severity increase to the next iterations as well as its impact to the production line. Depending on the criticality of the generated failure, the system can either adapt its parameters to prolong the RUL until the next maintenance, or plan to the production for maintenance. The final decision on the actions is based on the Z-MANAGE strategy.

Z-ESTIMATE: This strategy combines the information from the Z-DIAGNOSE and Z-PREDICT estimating the RUL of the assets. The estimated values are also combined with the information from the maintenance operations (physical examination from operators) as well as from the specifications provided from the manufacturer. The latter is used as the starting point for the estimation process, which after each iteration the deviation of the real-model from the physical model is reduced having an accurate virtual-model wrapped around the actual state of each machine and its components. The trends for the fatigue and wear rates provide a confident RUL estimation.

Z-MANAGE: This strategy is executing the overall supervision and optimisation of the system. The failures are processed with the Decision Support System (DSS) tools and are interfaced with Manufacturing Execution Systems (MES). False positives and false negatives are clustered within the Z-PREDICT and Z-PREVENT Strategies. To achieve so, the previous acquired knowledge and incidents are also processed to fine tune the system's performance. Additionally, the production is optimised by better scheduling (Z-SYNCHRONISE), taking into account the impact of each failure. The optimised scheduling and adaptability of the manufacturing improves the overall flexibility, placing a premium on the production systems, extending their operating life, while preserve increased machinery availability.

Z-REMEDIATE: This strategy involves the decision making in the event of a failure, which classifies and categorises the input in terms of criticality, type, etc. Based on the component/assets types (repairable-non repairable) and their RUL the strategy decides for the following: (1) replace, (2) reconfigure and/or re-use, (3) retire, and (4) recycle. This strategy triggers the Z-SYNCHRONISE and Z-SAFETY strategies from which the maintenance actions can be planned and organized.

Z-SYNCHRONISE: The predecessor Z-REMEDIATE strategy identifies the type of action required for diagnosed failures which are then fused with the Z-MANAGE output. This strategy synchronises all the remedy actions with internal and external supply-chain tiers, as well as with production planning and logistics. It is therefore responsible to shift the production from one machine to another due to failure or deteriorated condition/performance, acting as the "end-effector" thus leading to optimised scheduling and reduced costs by carrying out maintenance activities on time.

Z-SAFETY: This strategy is invoked to increased Health & Safety during Z-Bre4k shop-floor operations. Since most of the accidents occur during maintenance actions, the Z-SAFETY prevents any activation to the machine that is under investigation or repair. The "Safety-Mode" lifts any unauthorised control from the personnel for the whole duration of the maintenance. Apart from reducing the accidents Z-SAFETY also takes into account the comfort of the human personnel on the shop-floor, e.g. extreme heat or noise may be tolerable for the machines but not for humans. Therefore, the health & safety procedures are also taken into account towards the operation feedback of the whole production line.

3 Predictive Maintenance Platform Based on Z-Strategies

Manufacturing enterprises are pushed to take local actions: thinking globally however staying economically compatible within the local context. In order to achieve high precision manufacturing of complex products, there has to be a fundamental rethink on how to improve the operation of machines and improved controls. The improvement should not only concern the individual machines as isolated islands but encompass the totality of production process as a system of interrelated elements that seek to maximise efficiency,

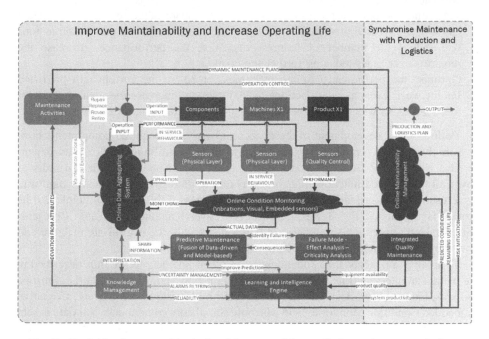

Fig. 2. Tools' landscape and logical architecture of the predictive maintenance platform

productivity, customer satisfaction; whilst at the same time eliminating waste and excess inventory. For that purpose, aligned with the Z-Strategies, a set of technologies and overall system architecture have been identified as a part of the proposed approach, following the method and procedures developed and proposed by May et al. [7].

The first high-level description to lead to the definition of the predictive maintenance platform consisted in identifying and classifying all components that can be called as the tools' landscape and logical architecture, i.e. conceptual view. Figure 2 presents this landscape by proposing a compact representation of the involved tools.

Based on the proposed approach and defined conceptual view of the system, in Z-Bre4k a novel predictive maintenance platform will be developed and demonstrated in three pilot plans proving its universal applicability for the achievement of zero breakdowns in manufacturing. Therefore, the predictive maintenance platform will:

- Introduce a novel design for predictive maintenance based on three levels: machine (network of components), product, and shop-floor (network of machines). It will reconfigure the system to increase its performance (shorter cycles), increase its quality, and its availability by the employment of eight strategies to maximise these factors.
- Make accurate predictions for the future states of the components/machines/systems by the employment of intelligent and adaptive simulators forecasting the generation of failures, the fatigue and wear levels, estimating the RUL triggering respective remedy actions. The condition monitoring will provide data about the actual status which will update the simulation results, increasing its accuracy. The DSS will synchronise the plans for maintenance, production and logistics.
- Estimate the RUL through its simulation capabilities, calling for maintenance and suggesting the optimal times to place orders for spare parts, reducing the related costs. The increased predictability of the system and the failure prevention actions will reduce the number of failures, maximise the performance, decrease the repair/recover times reducing further the costs.
- Optimise the performance of the machines, based on the current and predicted fatigue/wear levels allowing actions to maintain and increase the operating life of these assets, as well as to reduce the unexpected failures and breakdowns.

Following the development of the conceptual view, the required components have been highlighted in a preliminary architectural view, identifying services and dependencies within the Z-Bre4k platform. Later, new components were added in order to cover all the required functionalities of the resulting predictive maintenance platform. As a result, definitions, identifications and classification of the system principle and its process is presented in Fig. 3. Besides the defined overall architecture, Table 1 presents initial links on how these strategies are integrated within the overall architecture and how they are associated with each component of Z-Bre4k platform.

Z-Bre4k components, their functionality and their interactions are thus described in the overall architecture (Fig. 3). Initial data, generated by shop-floor assets (i.e. sensors, cameras, industrial/IoT devices, etc.) is collected by Condition Monitoring, Cognitive Embedded Condition Monitoring and Machine Simulators components. All data is sent to the Industrial Data Spaces (IDS) reaching the overall Z-Bre4k platform after which they are homogenized by the Semantic Framework and used by the components in a unified manner. Within the platform, users/employees are using HMI in order to add data and/or parameterize components. Specifically, FMECA (Failure mode, effects, and criticality analysis) component needs these inputs to calculate risks, Risk Priority Numbers (RPNs), criticality matrices and alerts in order to send data to DSS, that further generates and delivers strategies, recommendations, notifications, reports and updated schedules. Finally, M3 Gage, M3 Software and VRfx components are related to XYZ cloud points, 3D representations and visualization data of physical objects.

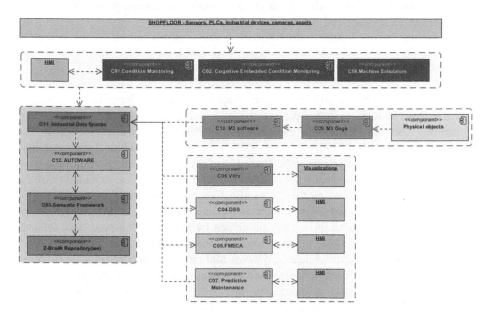

Fig. 3. Overall architecture of the predictive maintenance platform

Table 1. Z-Strategy and component association

No.	Z-Strategy	Components
1	Z-PREDICT	Condition monitoring, Machine simulators, VRfx, Predictive Maintenance
2	Z-PREVENT	Machine simulators, Predictive Maintenance, FMECA
3	Z-DIAGNOSE	Predictive Maintenance, FMECA
4	Z-ESTIMATE	Machine simulators, VRfx, Predictive Maintenance
5	Z-MANAGE	Predictive Maintenance, FMECA, DSS
6	Z-REMEDIATE	FMECA, DSS
7	Z-SYNCHRONIZE	AUTOWARE Communication Middleware
8	Z-SAFETY	DSS

The resulting Z-Bre4k system will be demonstrated in three key sectors with the strongest SME presence (i.e. automotive, food and beverage, consumer electronics) for a wide range of components and machines with different operational requirements and behaviours, illustrating the potential and full value of Z-Bre4k as a holistic framework to address predictive maintenance strategies for operation in high diversity of machinery (e.g. robotic systems, inline quality control equipment, injection moulding, stamping press, high performance smart tooling/dies and fixtures), including highly challenging and sometimes critical manufacturing processes (e.g. automated packaging industry, multi-stage zero-defect adaptive manufacturing of structural light-weight component for automotive industry, short-batch mass customised production process for consumer electronics and health sector).

4   Discussion and Concluding Remarks

The main goal of the predictive maintenance approach and implementation is to provide machine builders and designers (OEMs), industrial component suppliers and engineering software developers with novel solutions which will: (1) improve the performance of the manufacturing processes; (2) increase the machine maintainability; (3) provide predictions on damages/failures; (4) understand and interpret the source of the failures enhancing eventually the design process; (5) increase the availability of the machine builders while making them cost effective; and thus (6) increase OEE.

In this context, the study will: (a) act as a comprehensive and practical guide for optimizing production machineries and processes by implementing predictive maintenance principles; (b) transform machine tool and process related data into useful information that could support machinery prognosis and optimization strategies by enabling model-based control of machine tools based on actual machine life-cycle parameters.

Accordingly, the expected impacts are highlighted as follows: (1) improved predictive maintenance and system adaptability for manufacturing systems and processes; (2) new maintainability concepts based on predictive maintenance with improved machine reliability (MTBF) and reduced maintenance costs; and (3) incorporating intelligent systems and data analysis methods for achieving smart factories of Industry 4.0.

Future work will focus on implementing and validating the proposed approach on several use cases in different industries, demonstrating its ability to support major actors of the manufacturing sector to take advantage of the digital transformation.

Acknowledgements. This work has been carried out in the framework of Z-Bre4k Project, which has received funding from the European Union's Horizon 2020 research and innovation programme under grant agreement N° 768869.

References

1. Swanson, L.: Linking maintenance strategies to performance. Int. J. Prod. Econ. **70**(3), 237–244 (2001)
2. Wang, S., Wan, J., Li, D., Zhang, C.: Implementing smart factory of industrie 4.0: an outlook. Int. J. Distrib. Sens. Netw. **12**(1), 3159805 (2016)

3. Lee, J., Kao, H.-A., Yang, S.: Service innovation and smart analytics for industry 4.0 and big data environment. Procedia CIRP **16**, 3–8 (2014)
4. Lee, J., Bagheri, B., Kao, H.-A.: A cyber-physical systems architecture for Industry 4.0-based manufacturing systems. Manuf. Lett. **3**, 18–23 (2015)
5. May, G., Stahl, B., Taisch, M.: Energy management in manufacturing: toward eco-factories of the future – a focus group study. Appl. Energy **164**, 628–638 (2016)
6. Z-Bre4 k Project. https://www.z-bre4k.eu. Accessed 21 Mar 2018
7. May, G., Ioannidis, D., Metaxa, I.N., Tzovaras, D., Kiritsis, D.: An approach to development of system architecture in large collaborative projects. In: Lödding, H., Riedel, R., Thoben, K.-D., von Cieminski, G., Kiritsis, D. (eds.) APMS 2017. IAICT, vol. 513, pp. 67–75. Springer, Cham (2017). https://doi.org/10.1007/978-3-319-66923-6_8

Conceptual Design of a Digital Shadow for the Procurement of Stocked Products

Daniel Pause[✉] and Matthias Blum

Institute for Industrial Management (FIR), Aachen, Germany
daniel.pause@fir.rwth-aachen.de

Abstract. Industrie 4.0 and the consequent necessity of digitalization has also implications to the field of procurement, resulting in the so-called term of Procurement 4.0. Digitalization can be a valuable tool to increase the efficiency of the procurement organization and to exploit new opportunities of growth. A mandatory requirement to perform the digital transformation is an increased transparency along the procurement process chain. This paper aims to conceptualize a digital shadow for the procurement process in manufacturing industry as a basis for advanced data analytics procedures. The term digital shadow stands for a sufficiently accurate, digital image of a company's processes, information and data. This image is needed to create a real-time evaluable basis of all relevant data in order to finally derive recommendations for action. The formation of the Digital Shadow is thus a central field of action for Industrie 4.0 and forms the basis for all further activities.

Keywords: Procurement 4.0 · Digital shadow · Data analytics
Conceptual data model · Industrie 4.0 · Digital supply chain

1 Introduction

The rigid value chains are being transformed into highly flexible value networks. This lays out the platform for the end-to-end digitalization of the entire value chain [1]. Being a part of the value chain, procurement also has to adapt itself to the transformation of Industrie 4.0. As procurement acts as a direct interface between the company and suppliers, it holds the advantage of bringing the innovations into the company. This creates the opportunity for procurement to establish a better position within the entire network, both inside and outside of the company. This will result in the increase of the strategic importance of procurement. The digital transformation and the real-time availability will henceforth lead to the introduction of Procurement 4.0 [2].

"Procurement 4.0" or a "Supply Management 4.0" is a fundamental conceptual element of Industrie 4.0 as it connects the different supply chain partners and enables a dynamic and rapid cooperation and coordination beyond organizational boundaries [3]. To achieve this cooperation and coordination and to also improve the corporate processes, the company's data und their transparency is very essential. Therefore real-time as well as historical data must be evaluated. An exact digital mapping of all processes, information and data of a company is necessary. This digital mapping is called Digital

I. Moon et al. (Eds.): APMS 2018, IFIP AICT 536, pp. 288–295, 2018.
https://doi.org/10.1007/978-3-319-99707-0_36

Shadow [4]. In this paper we focus on the digital shadow for the procurement process in manufacturing industry.

The field of observation in this paper is the procurement of stocked products, for example C-parts. The ABC analysis is based on the finding that typically a relatively small percentage of goods in the warehouse make up a high proportion of the total inventory value. Typically, about 20% of the stock accounts for 70–80% of the total inventory value (A-parts). Another 10–15% of the stock value is tied by another 30% of the stock quantity (B-parts). The remaining 10–15% are represented by the C-parts, which usually account for about 50% of the amount [5]. The cost of procuring C-parts in comparison to the value of goods is usually disproportionately high. Ordering, warehousing, administration and internal goods movement often generate 80% of the costs, only 20% correspond to the material value [6]. Increased transparency in the procurement process by means of a digital shadow may be helpful to reduce procurement and storage costs of C-parts.

The remainder of this paper is organized as follows: First, a brief description about the impact of Industrie 4.0 on the procurement organization is given. The second chapter deals with the motivation for deriving a digital shadow for the Procurement of Stocked Products. In Sect. 3, the state of the art of a digital shadow as a basis for data analytics in the context of business intelligence is described and Sect. 4 derives a digital shadow based on corporate reference processes. Finally, we conclude in Sect. 5 and highlight future work.

2   Motivation

In this paper, the term analytics in association with business intelligence is defined as follows: It is understood as a scientific process of mathematical-logical transformation of data to improve decision making [7]. Depending on the maturity level of analytical skills, four stages of data analytics can be defined: descriptive, diagnostic, predictive and prescriptive analytics (see Fig. 1) [8, 9].

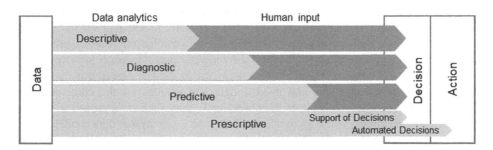

Fig. 1. Four stage model of the decision making assisted by data analytics [8]

The first stage, called descriptive analytics, answers the question "What happened?". Descriptive analytics aim at analyzing large amounts of data with the purpose of getting an insight and conclusion of what happened in the past. By analyzing interactions within the data diagnostic analytics pursue the question "Why did it happen?". Predictive and prescriptive analytics support proactive optimization. The question "What will happen?" is covered by predictive analytics. Future behavior is predicted by methods of pattern recognition and the use of statistics. Prescriptive analytics form the last stage and answer the question "What should be done?". Using optimization algorithms and simulation approaches concrete measures are suggested or even directly implemented without any human interaction [8].

In this paper the following research question will be answered: How can we increase transparency in cross-company procurement networks using the concept of the digital twin?

3   State of the Art

Although, several publications focus on approaches regarding data models which assist in planning and controlling the manufacturing process, a scientific investigation of a real-time representation of a product component in a procurement stage is only performed in very few research activities and not dealt with in detail. In the following section these approaches will be outlined.

The paper by the research corporation for production technology defines the Digital Shadow as a sufficiently exact mapping of processes in the production and development with the objective to create a basis that evaluates in real-time all relevant data. As a main challenge the paper points out the determination of the relevant data. It especially focusses on the state of technology and the corresponding challenges. In that sense the research corporation refers to multimodal data acquisition and data fusion as a means to achieve data faster and in a more reliable way. In contrast to our research, this research does no create a model to illustrate the minimum level of transparency which is required to put Procurement 4.0 into practice [10].

Schuh et al. emphasize in their paper the huge relevance that the Digital Shadow currently has in the production processes. Relating it to Industry 4.0 the paper points out that the Digital Shadow gained more importance following the development of Industry 4.0 as better possibilities to link and process data. Within the framework of digitalization not only the generation of data but especially its efficient use gains more importance. For the production process the relevant data can help to measure efficiency and progress and initiate changes. In the following the paper focusses on explaining how companies can create a Digital Shadow using the method of a migration path. This concept analyses the available and needed data and decides on the corresponding technology. In contrast to our paper, it consequently describes an approach to implement to corresponding technology while we focus on a conceptual data model [4].

Blum and Schuh define the Digital Shadow as a virtual representation of a product on the shop-floor that represents the relevant data in real-time. They focus on using real-time data as in other relevant papers concerning data models real-time data is neglected. As in our research, the paper also develops a data structure but they do not use the conceptual data model and they focus on order processing and do not consider procurement [11].

4 Deriving a Digital Shadow for Procurement Process

The methodology for deriving a digital shadow for the procurement of stocked products, as a first step, central business processes have to be defined. The SCOR model will be used as a regulation framework to derive basic business processes, related to stocked products. The second step comprises the derivation of a data structure as a basis for data analytics. To visualize the datastructure a conceptual data model will be used. This data model is a conceptual representation of data structures required to construct a database and a crucial tool to illustrate business requirements. However, hardware and software requirements are not considered.

4.1 Defining Processes in Procurement

As pointed out before, the first step before creating a data structure as a basis for data analytics procedures is defining the corporate processes in the field of procurement. The Supply Chain Operations Reference (SCOR) model by APICS SCC[1] is used as a reference model to define the basic procurement processes (see Fig. 2).

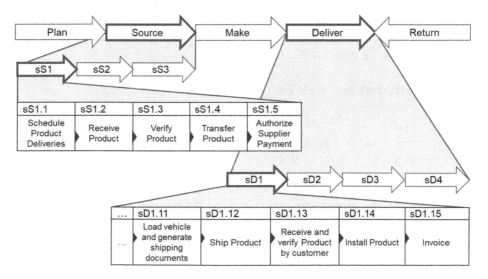

Fig. 2. "Source" and "Deliver" Processes of the Supply Chain Operations Reference (SCOR) model [12]

The SCOR model comprises different schematic process levels. The first level gives a definition of the scope and content of the SCOR model and the second level

---

[1] "APICS Supply Chain Council (APICS SCC) is a nonprofit organization [...] that maintains the Supply Chain Reference model (SCOR), the supply chain management community's most widely accepted framework for evaluating and comparing supply chain activities and performance" [12].

differentiates different configuration types. The third level finally describes operational processes. In Fig. 2, only the "source" and "deliver" processes relevant to the context of the work are presented in greater detail.

The field of "Source" is differentiated in different configuration types such as "Source Stocked Product" (sS1), "Source Make-to-Order Product" (sS2) and "Source Engineer-to-Order Product" (sS3). In the following, the configuration type of stocked products (sS1) will be considered. It is described as a "process of ordering, receiving and transferring raw material items, sub-assemblies, product and or services based on aggregated demand requirements. The intention of Source-to Stock is to maintain a pre-determined level of inventory for these materials, sub-assemblies or products. No customer reference or customer order detail is exchanged with the supplier, attached to or marked on the product, or recorded in the warehousing or ERP system for Source-to-Stock products" [12].

Since the procurement process represents the external boundary of the enterprise and communicates with external actors in the supply chain, the distribution process of the supplier or logistics service provider should also be considered. For this reason, the important processes regarding product shipping are listed. The configuration types within the field of "Deliver" are similar to "Source", however, there is an additional configuration type "Deliver Retail Product" (sD4). In the following, the configuration type of stocked products (sD1) will be considered. It is described as a "process of delivering a product that is sourced or made based on aggregated customer orders and inventory re-ordering parameters" [12].

4.2   Data Structure as a Basis for Data Analytics

Physical Level
According to the understanding of a production process, the process consists of different process steps which are needed to procure a product. Items are tracked in relation to the procurement plan, e.g., the transport vehicle. This enables the user to determine on which transport operations have been performed to complete the order. Based on the current operation the status of the order is logged. To calculate time related data (e.g. absolute procurement time, transition time) the status is needed. With this information conclusions about the current state of an order as well as ex post analysis are conducted. Based on the data record orders with the same production processes can be compared and reasons for deviations can be revealed.

Virtual Level
This section presents the derived data structure for the virtual representation of the transported goods during the procurement process as a basis for data analytics. For a comprehensive representation of an order in the purchasing department different aspects have to be considered. Besides tangible aspects (e.g. the good, transport vehicles, etc.) intangible aspects (e.g. purchasing plans, the geolocation, the status, etc.) are needed. The data structure is primarily developed for procuring stocked products. The derived data structure is presented in Fig. 3 and is described hereafter.

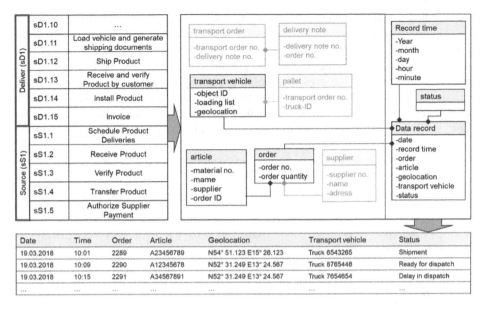

Fig. 3. Data structure for the purchasing of stocked products including example data sets

Time data specifies when the data was recorded and enables an entire data record from the start of monitoring until all processes are executed. Similar to an airplane's flight data recorder collected data is written inside a database in a specific time interval. As time data constitutes the leading characteristic among the collected data, corresponding data must refer to it. During the procurement process deviations from the schedule (e.g. geolocation and transport vehicle) may occur and can be detected in real-time. Order data includes the attributes order and product. The item order assigns a unique ID to each order and enables the traceability of an order during the procurement and delivery process. Furthermore, product ID is recorded to determine between different products of an order. Based on the integration of tracking technologies (e.g. GPS) a live tracking of an order is possible. Tracking the geolocation is necessary in order to ensure the routing of the order between two points. This enables to determine the current location of the order. Featured by the use of sensor technologies and a real-time routing, the status of an order between different steps in the procurement plan can be obtained.

5   Conclusion and Further Research

In this research paper a data structure for the procurement of stocked products is developed, which aims at providing a virtual representation of the transported goods during the procurement process. The digital shadow represents the relevant data (e.g., order, geolocation and status) in a time series format. After introducing the relevant processes for the procurement the structural framework of a data structure was derived.

For enabling the implementation of the model, practical implications have been carried out. This data structure is the foundation for the use of data analytics methods in the procurement environment. Therewith, conclusions about past incidents and a real-time status of an order contribute to improve procurement processes. Further research is needed to substantiate the presented solution principles. Directions of further work include the development of measures to improve the data quality (i.e., plausibility and consistency checks and the use of information provided by sensors), the handling of the geolocation and the development of a reference architecture.

Acknowledgements. The presented research is a result of the Cluster of Excellence (CoE) on "Integrative Production Technology for High-Wage Countries" funded by Deutsche Forschungsgemeinschaft (DFG). Within the CoE "Integrative Production Technology for High-Wage Countries" several institutes at RWTH Aachen University are conducting research on fundamentals of a sustainable production strategy. The authors would like to thank the German Research Foundation DFG for the kind support within the Cluster of Excellence „Integrative Production Technology for High-Wage Countries.

References

1. Kagermann, H., Anderl, R., Gausemeier, J., Schuh, G.: Industrie 4.0 im globalen Kontext. Strategien der Zusammenarbeit mit internationalen Partnern. acatech STUDIE (2016). http://www.acatech.de/fileadmin/user_upload/Baumstruktur_nach_Website/Acatech/root/de/Publikationen/Projektberichte/acatech_de_STUDIE_Industrie40_global_Web.pdf. Accessed 28 Feb 2018
2. Pellengahr, K., Schulte, A.T., Richard, J., Berg, M.: Pilot Study on Procurement 4.0. The Digitalisation of Procurement, Frankfurt (2016)
3. Glas, D.A., Kleemann, P.D.: The impact of industry 4.0 on procurement and supply chain management: a conceptual and qualitative analysis. Int. J. Bus. Manag. Invention 5(6), 55–66 (2016)
4. Schuh, G., Walendzik, P., Luckert, M., Birkmeier, M., Weber, A., Blum, M.: Keine Industrie 4.0 ohne den Digitalen Schatten. ZWF (2016). https://doi.org/10.3139/104.111613
5. Biedermann, H.: Ersatzteilmanagement. Effiziente ersatzteillogistik fur industrieunternehmen. Springer, Heidelberg (2008)
6. Engroff, B.: C-Teile-Management. AWF-Arbeitsgemeinschaft "Die Disposition - Strategien, Methoden und Organisation für eine effiziente und prozessorientierte Disposition" (2014). https://www.awf.de/wp-content/uploads/2014/12/C-Teilemanagement-awf.pdf
7. Knabke, T., Olbrich, S.: Towards agile BI: applying in-memory technology to data warehouse architectures. In: Innovative Unternehmensanwendungen mit In-Memory Data Management (2011)
8. FAIR ISAAC Coorporation: Business Intelligence and Big Data Analytics: Speeding the Cycle from Insights to Action Four Steps to More Profitable Customer Engagement. http://docplayer.net/3343658-Business-intelligence-and-big-data-analytics-speeding-the-cycle-from-insights-to-action-four-steps-to-more-profitable-customer-engagement.html. Accessed 15 Mar 2018
9. Sherman, R.: Business Intelligence Guidebook. From Data Integration to Analytics. Morgan Kaufmann, Waltham (2015)

10. Bauernhansl, T., Krüger, J., Reinhart, G., Schuh, G.: WGP-Standpunkt Industrie 4.0. https://www.ipa.fraunhofer.de/content/dam/ipa/de/documents/Presse/Presseinformationen/2016/Juni/WGP_Standpunkt_Industrie_40.pdf
11. Schuh, G., Blum, M.: Design of a data structure for the order processing as a basis for data analytics methods (2016). http://www.picmet.org/db/member/proceedings/2016/data/polopoly_fs/1.3251052.1472157052!/fileserver/file/680707/filename/16R0290.pdf. Accessed 7 Mar 2017
12. APICS SCC: Supply Chain Reference model (SCOR). https://www.apics.org/about/overview/about-apics-scc

A Framework Based on Predictive Maintenance, Zero-Defect Manufacturing and Scheduling Under Uncertainty Tools, to Optimize Production Capacities of High-End Quality Products

Paul-Arthur Dreyfus[1,2(✉)] and Dimitrios Kyritsis[1]

[1] ICT for Sustainable Manufacturing, EPFL,
EPFL SCI-STI-DK, Station 9, 1015 Lausanne, Switzerland
Paul.dreyfus@epfl.ch
[2] Artificial Intelligence Laboratory, EPFL,
EPFL IC IINFCOM LIA Station 14, 1015 Lausanne, Switzerland

Abstract. Nowadays exploiting the full potential of the humongous amount of data that manufactures can produce with their production means is a real challenge. Moreover, increasing production capabilities without large investments is a recurring objective for them. To reach this objective, many different strategies are in development i.e. zero-defect manufacturing, predictive maintenance and scheduling algorithms which deal with high uncertainty. In the end, they will all be implemented in industry. Their joined implementation in the industry is however missing a coherent framework that would allow to merge those different solutions. This paper proposes an approach that combines those three deeply interconnected technologies to bring a clean solution that significantly improves production capacity. This paper present the approach giving an idea of the possibilities and opportunities of the presented solution.

Keywords: Predictive maintenance · Tuning assistant
Zero-defect manufacturing · Automatic scheduling agent
Scheduling under uncertainty · Industry 4.0

1 Introduction and State of the Art

Like the three past major industrial changes, the worldwide industry is undergoing an in-depth mutation, leading to so called 4th industrial revolution or Industry 4.0. During the past few years, different countries around the world presented the development of smart factories as one of their long-term strategies such as the 'Industry 4.0' in Germany or the 'industrial Internet' in the United States.

Up to now, different solutions have been studied, and more or less successfully implemented, to augment production capabilities such as predictive maintenance

I. Moon et al. (Eds.): APMS 2018, IFIP AICT 536, pp. 296–303, 2018.
https://doi.org/10.1007/978-3-319-99707-0_37

or automatic scheduling agent. On that vein, predictive maintenance is one of the recent trends that implements machine learning techniques to tackle real industrial issues. This solution is very popular and even big services companies such as IBM provide predictive maintenance services. Our approach includes this solution, not as a whole, but as a component. Scheduling is the heart of a production floor and optimized scheduling is a major enabler for improvements in production capability. In this context, including automatic scheduling tool with predictive maintenance is a very interesting approach. As demonstrated by Liu et al. [10], those two components are tightly linked. Another approach known as zero defect manufacturing regroups different solutions which aim to reduce the number of rejected products as well as increasing the production capabilities. Raabe et al. [12] used one of those solution to show that it is possible and valuable to identify problems in the production line which lead to rejected products. The approach proposed in this study aims at creating one solution combining predictive maintenance, automatic scheduling and zero defect manufacturing.

2   Framework and Approach

Firstly, all three technologies which are tuning assistant, predictive maintenance and automatic scheduling are presented. Then the framework, which link them is explained.

2.1   Tuning Assistant for Zero Defect Manufacturing

Every machine needs to be tuned. The belief which describes machines that have to be tuned only one time to produce forever is far from reality. It is even more true for high-end industry with products aiming at tiny tolerances and with very accurate quality control, where small perturbations such as temperature change or small tools wearing can force to re-tune the machine. The keystone of a good production floor is, therefore, the group of machine operator and technician that control and tune machines. Actually, the tools that help them to tune machines are very basic. This is why product changeover can sometimes take weeks. A tuning assistant is a tool which is very effective to tune and help tuning the machine. It is a machine learning algorithm that will help technicians to produce conform pieces. First, it tunes automatically the machine when it is needed and second it gives critical information to technicians, helping them to tune the machine when it cannot be done automatically. This technology enter in one category of the zero defect manufacturing paradigm called: "Early Malfunction detection and analysis" [4]. Therefore, the machine is faster to tune during product changeover. It is more robust to well-known changes thanks to the algorithm that tunes the machine in real time. But also if there is a problem that cannot be automatically repaired by the tuning assistant, the production can quickly be stopped and the technician informed, so that the number of non-conform products is minimized and the machine re-launched in production as quickly as possible.

There is not a lot of documentation about this solution, Bufardi et al. [3] provides an example of real-time defect correction for non-conventional production machines, electrical discharge machining, using only two types of sensors. But it is to some extent hard to find publications on conventional production machines. However some publications propose interesting framework for tuning assistant [15]. A lot of Horizon 2020 project are actually working to find practical solutions to apply Zero defect manufacturing, like Z-fact0r or FOCUS.

In the approach presented, the tuning assistant is the first component. It is made of two independent blocks. The first one, i.e. "Estimation block" takes as input all the measurements from machine's sensors, the geometric tolerance measurement, the quality control feedback and possible alerts from technicians. It also receives conclusions of the tuning assistant working in the machine that did the previous operation, for instance, if the actual tuning assistant is working for the finishing stage, it will receive feedback from the tuning assistant working for the machining stage. This estimation block outputs first a vector of estimations describing the probability that the machine needs to be tuned, and second a vector of estimation of the time that those tuning are expected to take. Those outputs will go to the scheduling algorithm that will take the decision on either to tune or not the machine. The second block called "Tuning block" receives as input a tuning request explaining the type of tuning that need to be done. It will either do it automatically or help the technician to do it efficiently (Figs. 1 and 2).

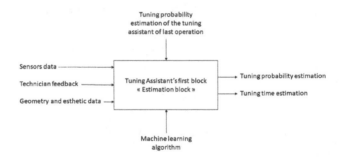

Fig. 1. IDEF0 of the first block of the tuning assistant component.

2.2 Predictive Maintenance with Machine Learning

All the production machines need to be repaired regularly, it is not rare to see highly stressed machines needing maintenance multiple times a month. Nowadays this reality is more obvious than ever with the increasing complexity of the equipment. Production time's losses added with maintenance cost can be very harmful to a company. Predictive maintenance is a strategy which, as illustrated in Fig. 3, aims to remove the time where the broken machine is waiting for reparation by predicting and preventing the failures before their occurrence.

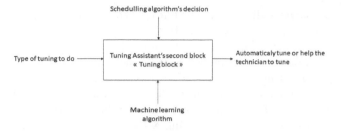

Fig. 2. IDEF0 of the second block of the tuning assistant component.

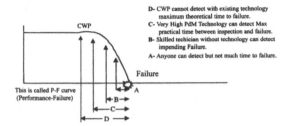

Fig. 3. The predictive maintenance strategy aim to detect early signals to predict failure and launch maintenance before the machine fail. CWP stand for critical wear point [9].

This strategy is quite old [11], it enters in the preventive maintenance strategy group, with for instance the planned maintenance strategy which plans the maintenance in function of suppliers' predictions. The particularity of Predictive maintenance is that machines' health is monitored in real time and future failures predicted, using multiple sensors and machine learning algorithms.

To implement it, relevant data have first to be identified. Usually, supervised algorithms are used for predictive maintenance, and so, labeled training data set have to be furnished which assume to clearly know which information to measure and when the production machine will fail. Several articles [1,2] describe the use of unsupervised machine learning algorithms permitting to detect the failure by measuring unusual behaviors, therefore compensating a possible lack of knowledge against a loss of accuracy. Actually, even if there are some articles looking at other types of data, such as acoustic signature [5], the most commonly studied feature is the vibration. Other information could be studied such as temperature measurement, flow measurements, electrical analysis, thickness measurement analysis, efficiency analysis, analysis of positions and alignments, etc. [8]. When the data is accessible, a machine learning algorithm has to search a possible relation between failures and measured information. Encountering the right algorithm is at the present time a hot topic, Pushe et al. [16] proposed a way to pre-process the data, enabling anomalies to be detected more easily. There are a lot of different algorithms [7,13] that are proposed by the literature, but there is no consensus on which one is the best in which case.

In this approach predictive maintenance is the Second fundamental component. In the classical approach it only takes data as input. In our approach, on top of data is added the estimated probability that tuning has to be done. This input is fed by tuning assistant block. As explained before, tuning assistant is not machine-centered but product centered, it detects from machine's data potential product nonconformities. Those nonconformities can sometime be an alert for some type of machine failure. Moreover, the Tuning assistant can also use, as input, the conclusions of previous tuning assistants, therefore it pre-process for the predictive maintenance algorithm a broader amount of data. The Predictive maintenance component outputs are firstly a vector of the estimation percentage of all the different failures, secondly a vector of estimation of the time that it will take to repair those failures (Fig. 4).

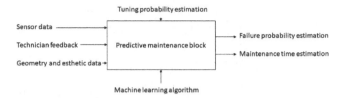

Fig. 4. IDEF0 of the predictive maintenance component.

2.3   Automatic Scheduling Under High Uncertainty

In this approach the last component is the automatic scheduling algorithm. It is the brain of the model, which takes into account uncertainty and decide to launch and schedule maintenance operation, authorizes machine tuning and plan changeover. Its Input are multiples, It takes all the outputs from the two others components that are predictive maintenance and tuning assistant's estimation block. Moreover, it takes all the classical information provided to scheduling algorithm such as production order, available resources, etc.

To decide to launch a maintenance, it computes the estimation of failures and the estimation of the time needed to correct those failures which also contain a lot of uncertainties. Taking into account potential tuning needs, the production pressure and more, the algorithm evaluates the risk and decide or not to plan maintenance. To decide if a machine need to be tuned, it uses the estimate of percentage of tuning and the estimation of the time it will take. Again taking into account other information such as production pressure or available resources, it decides or not to launch or to plan a tuning request. Doing so it sends the request to the second block of the tuning assistant.

Using all this information the automatic scheduling algorithm has to deal with a lot of uncertainty, thanks to existing algorithms which can optimize this kind of problems.

Automatic scheduling is a well known field, a lot of algorithm exist which model the problem, solve it and evaluate the solution to ensure its quality. A lot of those solutions are described by Manuel Dios in his review [6]. Even if we know how to include uncertainty into mathematical model such as two-stage stochastic programming, parametric programming, fuzzy programming, chance constraint programming, robust optimization techniques, conditional value-at-risk, and other forms of risk mitigation approaches [14], doing optimizing under high uncertainty is still challenging (Fig. 5).

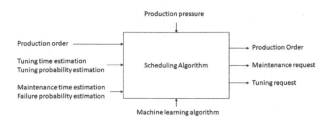

Fig. 5. IDEF0 of the automatic scheduling algorithm.

2.4   Framework

The approach proposed in this study, aims at integrating those three different technologies, i.e. product-centered tuning assistant, machine-centered predictive maintenance and finally production-centered automatic scheduling in a unique solution. As each one of them carries a lot of ambition, a huge effort is currently undertaken by the community in order to better understand them and so their implementation by the industry is only a few years away. However, no framework have been yet published to merge those technologies.

Going to the description of the framework, the first block is the tuning assistant which increases the productivity of the machine by detecting when to tune the machine and by tuning it automatically whenever is possible. It takes as

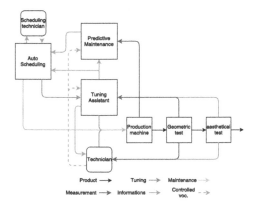

Fig. 6. Suggested approach to industry 4.0.

input all the output/conclusions of the previous tuning assistant, of the same production chain. The second one is the predictive maintenance block which increases the production capability by detecting when to do maintenance on the machine. It can use information from the tuning assistant to understand the link between product unconformity and predicted future failure. The robust automatic scheduling algorithm can use all this information to optimize, when to do maintenance, when to tune the machine and to schedule production orders. For each possible tuning or failure, the two first blocks will give a percentage of chance of happening, as well as a time estimation to repair/correct the problem. With all of this this last block will do the optimal choice in term of production optimization. The block diagram in Fig. 6 illustrates how these three technologies work together and communicate with their environment.

3   Discussion and Conclusion

The approach presented in this paper combine three ambitious technologies, i.e. tuning assistant, predictive maintenance and automatic scheduling algorithm, and it is now implemented in a case study of a high-end production company. Those technologies seem at first to be very different, but we theoretically found out that they can be very complementary. The first layer composed by tuning assistant and predictive maintenance is very challenging to implement in industrial study case. To be efficient machine learning technologies need a lot of labeled data. However, failure happen seldom and so gathering the theoretically good amount of data is not easily possible. Nowadays, this is one of the biggest limitation. Nonetheless, some solution are studied like on-line un-structured algorithm to tackle this challenge.

None of those are mastered, we still have a long journey to reach the final objective called the principle of digital twin. Due to the significant potential of the proposed approach significant, further research on the subject should be carried out to test, qualify and improve this solution.

Finally the macro solution merge three solutions that will reshape production floors such as machine oriented, product oriented and production oriented. An optimal production floor can be defined with those three ideas: Machine producing, Product conform and Production optimized.

References

1. Amruthnath, N., Gupta, T.: Fault class prediction in unsupervised learning using model-based clustering approach
2. Amruthnath, N., Gupta, T.: A research study on unsupervised machine learning algorithms for early fault detection in predictive maintenance. In: 5th International Conference on Industrial Engineering and Applications (2018)
3. Author, A.A., Author, B.B., Author, C.: Title of article. Title of Journal 10(2), 49–53 (2005)
4. Z-Fact0r Consortium: Zero defect manufacturing strategies toward on-line production management for European factories (2016)

5. Darius, Ş.M., Florin, B.C., Marius, B., Edit, T.K., Mihai, P.R.: Maintenance planning of the sewing needles of simple sewing machines
6. Dios, M., Framinan, J.M.: A review and classification of computer-based manufacturing scheduling tools. Comput. Ind. Eng. **99**(C), 229–249 (2016). https://doi.org/10.1016/j.cie.2016.07.020
7. Grall, A., Dieulle, L., Berenguer, C., Roussignol, M.: Continuous-time predictive-maintenance scheduling for a deteriorating system. IEEE Trans. Reliab. **51**(2), 141–150 (2002)
8. Keith Mobley, R.: An introduction to predictive maintenance / r. keith mobley (06 2018)
9. Levitt, J.: Complete Guide to Prevent and Predictive Maintenance. Industrial Press, New York (2003)
10. Liu, Q., Dong, M., Chen, F.: Single-machine-based joint optimization of predictive maintenance planning and production scheduling. Robot. Comput. Integr. Manuf. **51**, 238–247 (2018)
11. Mobley, R.K.: An Introduction to Predictive Maintenance. Butterworth-Heinemann, New York (2002)
12. Raabe, H., Myklebust, O., Eleftheriadis, R.: Vision based quality control and maintenance in high volume production by use of zero defect strategies. In: Wang, K., Wang, Y., Strandhagen, J.O., Yu, T. (eds.) IWAMA 2017. LNEE, vol. 451, pp. 405–412. Springer, Singapore (2018). https://doi.org/10.1007/978-981-10-5768-7_43
13. Sipos, R., Fradkin, D., Moerchen, F., Wang, Z.: Log-based predictive maintenance. In: Proceedings of the 20th ACM SIGKDD International Conference on Knowledge Discovery and Data Mining, KDD 2014, pp. 1867–1876. ACM, New York (2014). https://doi.org/10.1145/2623330.2623340
14. Verderame, P.M., Elia, J.A., Li, J., Floudas, C.A.: Planning and scheduling under uncertainty: a review across multiple sectors. Ind. Eng. Chem. Res. **49**(9), 3993–4017 (2010). https://doi.org/10.1021/ie902009k
15. Wang, K.S.: Towards zero-defect manufacturing (ZDM)-a data mining approach. Adv. Manuf. **1**(1), 62–74 (2013). https://doi.org/10.1007/s40436-013-0010-9
16. Zhao, P., Kurihara, M., Tanaka, J., Noda, T., Chikuma, S., Suzuki, T.: Advanced correlation-based anomaly detection method for predictive maintenance. In: 2017 IEEE International Conference on Prognostics and Health Management (ICPHM), pp. 78–83, June 2017

An Introduction to PHM and Prognostics Case Studies

Hong-Bae Jun$^{(\boxtimes)}$

Department of Industrial Engineering, Hongik University, Seoul 04066, South Korea
hongbae@gmail.com

Abstract. Large-scale systems such as plants should be operated with high reliability and availability because the downtime due to system failure has a significant influence on the manufacturing activity. Nowadays the emerging ICTs (Information Communication Technologies) and sensor technologies make it possible to monitor health status of important equipment of the plant and do diagnosis and prognosis for further suitable maintenance actions in real time, which leads to much concern on PHM (Prognostics and Health Management) or CBM (Condition-Based Maintenance). In this study, we briefly look through the concept of PHM and introduce prognostics case studies for plant equipment.

Keywords: Prognostics and Health Management
Condition-based maintenance · Plant equipment · Maintenance
Prognostics

1 Introduction

In general, maintenance is defined as all technical and managerial actions taken during usage period to maintain or restore the required functionality of a product or an asset. There have been various classifications of maintenance policies [1]. Simply, maintenance policies can be divided into breakdown maintenance and preventive maintenance. In the breakdown maintenance, the maintenance action is taken after some problems such as breakdowns in a product are found while the preventive maintenance periodically checks a product with a certain interval in order to prevent the abnormality of the product. The preventive maintenance is again classified into TBM (Time-based maintenance) and CBM (Condition-based maintenance) depending on the criteria for determining maintenance action; fixed time or mileage for TBM and product status for CBM. Recently, PHM (Prognostics and Health Management), the similar concept with CBM, has been highlighted with the concepts of Industry 4.0 and smart factory.

Large-scale systems such as plants should be operated with high reliability and availability because the downtime due to system failure has a significant influence on manufacturing activities. To meet such a demand, reliable and robust methods for monitoring, diagnosing, and predicting the abnormal

I. Moon et al. (Eds.): APMS 2018, IFIP AICT 536, pp. 304–310, 2018.
https://doi.org/10.1007/978-3-319-99707-0_38

status of important equipment, and making decision for appropriate maintenance actions are required. These are the core of PHM.

Recently, advanced IoT (Internet Of Things) technologies including internet-
aware smart sensors [2], embedded system [3], cloud-assisted IWN (Industrial
Wireless Network) [3], WSNs (Wireless Sensor Networks) [4], RFID (Radio Frequency Identification), and SCADA (Supervisory Control And Data Acquisition)
are expected to be rapidly used for gathering and monitoring the status data of
plant equipment during their usage period. In this environment, capturing the
status of plant equipment related to performance, operation and environmental
conditions, and detecting their anomalies in a real-time way become challenging
issues. The raw data from sensors need to be efficiently managed and transformed
to usable information through data fusion, which in turn must be converted to
predictive insights via knowledge discovery, ultimately facilitating automated or
human-induced tactical decisions or strategic maintenance policy.

Though the data gathering systems are becoming relatively mature, a lot of
innovative research need to be done on knowledge discovery from huge repositories of plant data. In this vein, recently the importance of PHM has been
highlighted and tried to be implemented in various domains. In order to apply
the concept of PHM into current maintenance policy and implement the PHM
system, first and foremost, it is prerequisite to understand what PHM is. In this
study, we briefly look through the concept of PHM and related previous works.
Then, we introduce prognostics case studies for three plant equipment.

2   PHM

In recent years, PHM has emerged as one of the key enablers for achieving efficient system-level maintenance and lowering life-cycle costs need [5,6]. It could
improve availability of critical engineering assets while reducing inopportune
spending and security risks [7]. The IEEE Reliability Society (www.phmconf.
org) defines PHM as "a system engineering discipline focusing on detection,
prediction, and management of the health and status of complex engineered systems". Furthermore, according to Sheppard et al. [8], PHM could be defined
as "a maintenance and asset management approach utilizing signals, measurements, models, and algorithms to detect, assess, and track degraded health, and
to predict failure progression". According to Chen et al. [9], PHM comes from the
U.S. DoE (Department of Energy) and the U.S. DoD (Department of Defense).
In the JSF (Joint Strike Fighter) program of U.S. DoD, the name PHM was
adopted.

Regarding PHM term, there are some similar terms used interchangeably:
e.g., predictive maintenance, prognostics, and CBM. Among them, the most
well-known terminology is CBM. Over the last decade, CBM has evolved into
the concept of PHM, due to its broader scope [7].

The purpose of PHM is to maximize the operational availability and safety
of the engineering asset that eventually improves security, reliability, availability
and mission success, and support a better ability to plan for maintenance events,

which leads to reduce the operation and maintenance cost [8,10,11]. The PHM can be done by (1) gathering product status data; (2) monitoring the product condition based on gathered data; (3) making a diagnosis of a product status; (4) predicting the remaining useful life of the product; and (5) executing appropriate actions such as repair, replace, and disposal based on reasonable decision making.

In general, the PHM system should have the capability of anomaly detection, fault diagnostics, fault prognostics, and health management. To get the capability, various methods have been considered, which could be mainly grouped into physics-based, data-driven, and hybrid approaches.

According to Vichare and Pecht [5], Luna [12], Zhang et al. [6], Sun et al. [13], and Javed [7], the following are the benefits of PHM (Table 1):

Table 1. Benefits of PHM

Domain	Benefits
Quality	- Maintain effectiveness through timely repair actions,
	- Improve system safety,
	- Increase system operations reliability and mission availability,
	- Increase availability,
	- Avoid consequences of failure by advance warning of failures,
	- Extend life/Reduce maintenance frequency,
	- Optimize resource use,
	- Decrease unnecessary maintenance actions,
	- Improve system safety (predict to prevent negative outcomes),
	- Improve qualification and assisting in the design and logistical support of fielded and future systems,
	- Improve decision making to prolong life time of a machinery
Cost	- Reduce system LCC (Life-Cycle Cost) by decreasing inspection costs, downtime, and inventory,
	- Reduce operational costs to optimized maintenance
Delivery	- Reduce lead time,
	- Minimize unscheduled maintenance,
	- Extend maintenance cycles

3   Previous Works

So far there have been several research works related to PHM or CBM or predictive maintenance. For example, Vichare and Pecht [5] presented the state-of-practice and the current state-of-research in the area of electronics PHM. In their work, examples for four approaches such as BIT (Built-In-Test), use of fuse and canary devices, monitoring and reasoning of failure precursors, and modeling accumulated damage based on measured life-cycle loads were provided.

Luna [12] provided a framework for organizing themes of PHM benefits by identifying overall categories for understanding the different types of impacts and benefits a PHM system can have from a logistics support perspective. They mentioned the benefits of PHM from the logistics support perspective: (1) Reduce lead time, (2) Avoid consequences of failure, (3) Extend Life/Reduce Maintenance Frequency, and (4) Optimize resource use. Cheng et al. [14] introduced the state-of-the-art sensor systems for PHM and the emerging trends in technologies of sensor systems for PHM. They discussed the considerations for sensor system selection for PHM applications, including the parameters to be measured, the performance needs, the electrical and physical attributes, reliability, and cost of the sensor system. Das et al. [10] discussed the essential steps for an effective PHM system. In their work, they described time and frequency domain features that can be extracted from raw sensor data. They also described a case study of implementing a PHM system for a high speed face milling CNC cutter. Pecht [15] presented an assessment of the state of practice in PHM of information and electronics rich systems. He presented a fusion prognostics approach, which combines or "fuses together" the model-based and data-driven approaches, to enable markedly better prognosis of remaining useful life. In order to illustrate the implementation of the fusion approach to prognostics, he carried out a case study of a printed circuit card assembly. Recently, Lee et al. [16] carried out a comprehensive review of the PHM field. They introduced a systematic PHM design methodology, 5S methodology, for converting data to prognostics information. They also presented a systematic methodology for conducting PHM as applied to machinery maintenance.

4   Prognostics Applications

This section introduces three case studies for prognostics that we have carried out until now. Table 2 shows the summary of case studies. In Cho et al. [17], we have introduced two approaches predicting the next failure time or identifying failure status of the gas compressor which is one of essential mechanical equipment in both onshore and offshore plants, based on gathered vibration data: Regression-based approach (Cho et al. [17]), and Bayesian network-based approach (Jun and Kim [18]). Furthermore, we have dealt with estimating the RUL (Remaining Useful Life) of the mooring line of an offshore plant based on

Table 2. Case studies of prognostics

Equipment	Sensor type	No. of sensors	Approach
- Compressor	- Vibration	- Single	- Regression-based [17]
		- Multiple	- Bayesian network-based [18]
- Mooring line	- Tension	- Single	- RUL estimation based on k-means, ARIMA, and Miner's rule [19]
- Electric generator	- Temperature	- Single	- DTW-based approach

gathered ocean environment data and mooring line tension data. For the mooring line case, we have developed a hybrid approach integrating data-driven and physics-based approaches. In the proposed approach, not only data analyzing methods such as k-means clustering method and ARIMA, but also tension damage calculation method by the Miner's rule has been applied to predict the RUL of the mooring line. For more details, please refer to Kim et al. [19]. In addition, we have developed an algorithm for estimating the RUL by analyzing the temperature sensor data of an electric generator using a DTW (Dynamic Time Warping) based approach.

Except the mooring line case, three cases are all data driven approaches. For the limited test data, the proposed approaches have been applied. As the result, we could see that the proposed approaches give some reliable results for prognosis. For example, in the case study of regression-based approach [17], we could see that the estimated next failure time is close to the real failure time. But, we could also find that the regression model based approach gave the poor performance when the remaining residual life time is relatively long [17]. In the Bayesian network based approach and DTW based approach, for the generated test examples, we could see that our methods give reasonable results. There must be some benefits in the plant industry from the plant operation and safety viewpoints since the suitable decision based on equipment prognosis result could be made, if this kind of PHM system is commercially applied in the real field. You may see the details of the test results in the relevant references [17–19].

5   Limitations and Discussion

This study introduced the case studies of prognostics algorithm for plant equipment with the PHM concept. Although we have looked the possibility of PHM approach with several case studies, there are still some limitations in applying its concept as follows.

First, the core algorithms of the PHM are to diagnose the current state of equipment based on the collected data and to predict RUL in the future. The accuracy of these algorithms is mostly affected by the amount and quality of the gathered data. When implementing PHM, if there are much amount of failure data available, data-driven algorithms could be applied. However, in reality, it was difficult to get the actual failure history. In our study, the proposed approaches have been tested based on limited real failure data or the generated data based on it. Thus, to prove the robustness of the approach, further exhaustive test should be done based on lots of real data.

Second, another limitation is that most algorithms mentioned in this study dealt with the single variable or single location problem. As the result, there is a limit to precisely predict the state of the equipment and the time of failure with only a single variable sensor data at one location of the equipment. To resolve this problem, the Bayesian network based approach could be applied to more high-level equipment based on the integrated failure propagation model of the target plant equipment to identify the multiple causes and failures in an integrated way.

With these limitations, the following point could be discussed: We could think of applying the PHM into not only maintenance but also other domains, e.g., product design improvement. For example, we can build a system to improve the design by reflecting the diagnostics and prognostics results of the PHM as well as the maintenance of the equipment by creating a closed link between design improvement and the PHM. The RUL value estimated at a certain time can be compared to the theoretical RUL of a product, calculated according to the difference between the designed lifetime and the equipment operating time. A comparison of these values tells us how adequately the equipment is being used. As a result, if the RUL is longer than the theoretical RUL, we can then let the equipment go without any maintenance actions or modify the severity of the mission profile for use with more intensive applications. Otherwise, PHM operations should be done. This kind of information could provide us with the feedback for product design improvement.

In order to develop a more accurate prognostics algorithm in the future, the following points should be considered. First of all, the cause-symptom-failure relations should be well defined for each equipment. To this end, the well-designed modeling method to represent this relations should be developed. Second, a clear definition of failure and a criterion for determining the failure of equipment, for example, thresholds, should be defined. Third, failure history data, sensor signal data at the time of failure, and operation related data should be integrated and continuously recorded and managed. Finally, when the equipment is operated at the beginning of its life, there will be only a few failure data, which leads to make estimating the RUL of the equipment impossible with considered prognostics algorithms. Therefore, it is needed to estimate the RUL in a different way. For example, in the early life stage of equipment, it is reasonable to estimate the RUL based on the reliability data provided by manufacturers. Then, if the failure history data is accumulated systematically, we need to apply a learning-based algorithm that improves the accuracy of the RUL prediction.

6 Conclusion

In this study, we have briefly looked into PHM concept and prognostics case studies. The purpose of PHM is to maximize the operational availability and reliability of the engineering system. Using PHM technologies, the companies could have the ability to prevent the unexpected abnormality of the engineering system during its usage lifetime. In the era of the fourth industrial revolution, the PHM is becoming an important component of system design and operation of complex systems. PHM is not a single technique and requires very complex and various interdisciplinary research techniques, which leads to take much time and efforts for PHM. Although this study did not introduce exhaustive and detailed PHM works, it could be a base for future PHM works.

Acknowledgments. This research was supported by Basic Science Research Program through the National Research Foundation of Korea (NRF) funded by the Ministry of Education (NRF-2017R1D1A1B03031633).

References

1. Shin, J.H., Jun, H.B.: On condition based maintenance policy. J. Comput. Des. Eng. **2**, 119–127 (2015)
2. O'Donovan, P., Leahy, K., Bruton, K., O'Sullivan, D.T.J.: An industrial big data pipeline for data-driven analytics maintenance applications in large-scale smart manufacturing facilities. J. Big Data **2**(25), 1–26 (2015)
3. Wang, S., Wan, J., Li, D., Zhang, C.: Implementing smart factory of Industrie 4.0: an outlook. Int. J. Distrib. Sens. Netw. **12**, 1–10 (2016)
4. Xu, L.D., He, W., Li, S.: Internet of things in industries: a survey. IEEE Trans. Ind. Inf. **10**(4), 2233–2243 (2014)
5. Vichare, N.M., Pecht, M.G.: Prognostics and health management of electronics. IEEE Trans. Compon. Packag. Technol. **29**(1), 222–229 (2006)
6. Zhang, H., Kang, R., Pecht, M.: A hybrid prognostics and health management approach for condition-based maintenance. In: The 2009 IEEE Conference Proceedings, pp. 1165–1169 (2009)
7. Javed, K.: A robust and reliable data-driven prognostics approach based on extreme learning machine and fuzzy clustering. Ph.D. thesis, Université de Franche-Comté (2014)
8. Sheppard, J.W., Kaufman, M.A., Wilmering, T.J.: IEEE standards for prognostics and health management. IEEE A&E Syst. Mag. **24**, 34–41 (2009)
9. Chen, Z.S., Yang, Y.M., Hu, Z.: A technical framework and roadmap of embedded diagnostics and prognostics for complex mechanical systems in prognostics and health management systems. IEEE Trans. Reliab. **61**(2), 314–322 (2012)
10. Das, S., Hall, R., Herzog, S., Harrison, G., Bodkin, M.: Essential steps in prognostic health management. In: IEEE Conference on Prognostics and Health Management Proceedings, pp. 1–9 (2011)
11. Jinyu, Z., Xianxiang, H., Wei, C.: Research on prognostic and health monitoring system for large complex equipment. In: IITA International Conference on Control, Automation and Systems Engineering Proceedings, pp. 1–6 (2009)
12. Luna, J.J.: Metrics, models, and scenarios for evaluating PHM effects on logistics support. In: Annual Conference of the Prognostics and Health Management Society Proceedings (2009)
13. Sun, B., Zeng, S., Kang, R., Pecht, M.G.: Benefits and challenges of system prognostics. IEEE Trans. Reliab. **61**(2), 323–335 (2012)
14. Cheng, S., Azarian, M.H., Pecht, M.G.: Sensor systems for prognostics and health management. Sensors **10**, 5774–5797 (2010)
15. Pecht, M.: A prognostics and health management for information and electronics-rich systems. In: Mathew, J., Ma, L., Tan, A., Weijnen, M., Lee, J. (eds.) Engineering Asset Management and Infrastructure Sustainability, pp. 19–30. Springer, London (2012). https://doi.org/10.1007/978-0-85729-493-7_2
16. Lee, J., Wu, F., Zhao, W., Ghaffari, M., Liao, L.: Prognostics and health management design for rotary machinery systems-reviews. Mech. Syst. Signal Process. **42**, 314–334 (2014)
17. Cho, S.J., Shin, J.H., Jun, H.B., Hwang, H.J., Ha, C.H., Hwang, J.S.: A study on estimating the next failure time of a compressor equipment in an offshore plant. Math. Probl. Eng. **2016**(8705796), 1–14 (2016)
18. Jun, H.B., Kim, D.: A Bayesian network-based approach for fault analysis. Expert Syst. Appl. **55**(5), 1350–1367 (2017)
19. Kim, Y.J., Seo, M., Jun, H.B., Ha, C.H., Shin, J.H.: A study on predictive algorithm for estimating the RUL of offshore plant equipment. In: TCIEAS Proceedings, pp. 1–10 (2016)

A Hybrid Machine Learning Approach for Predictive Maintenance in Smart Factories of the Future

Sangje Cho[1(✉)], Gökan May[1], Ioannis Tourkogiorgis[1],
Roberto Perez[2], Oscar Lazaro[3], Borja de la Maza[4],
and Dimitris Kiritsis[1]

[1] EPFL, ICT for Sustainable Manufacturing, EPFL SCI-STI-DK,
Station 9, 1015 Lausanne, Switzerland
Sangje.cho@epfl.ch
[2] GF Machining Solutions, Meyrin, Switzerland
[3] Innovalia, Bilbao, Spain
[4] TRIMEK, Zuia, Álava, Spain

Abstract. Advanced technologies based on Internet of Things (IOT) are blazing a trail to effective and efficient management of an overall plant. In this context, manufacturing companies require an innovative strategy to survive in a competitive business environment, utilizing those technologies. Guided by these requirements, the so-called predictive maintenance is of paramount importance and offers a significant potential for innovation to overcome the limitations of traditional maintenance policies. However, real shop-floors often have obstacles in providing insights to facilitate the effective management of assets in smart factories. Even if a significant amount of machine and process data is available, one of the common problems of these data is the lack of annotations describing the machine status or maintenance history. For this reason, companies have limited options to analyse manufacturing data, despite the capability of advanced machine learning techniques in supporting the identification of failure symptoms in order to optimize scheduling of maintenance operations. Moreover, each machine generates highly heterogeneous data, making it difficult to integrate all the information to provide data-driven decision support for predictive maintenance. Inspired by these challenges, this research provides a hybrid machine learning approach combining unsupervised learning and semi-supervised learning. The approach and result in this article are based on the development and implementation in a large collaborative EU-funded H2020 research project entitled BOOST 4.0 i.e. Big Data Value Spaces for COmpetitiveness of European COnnected Smart FacTories.

Keywords: Industry 4.0 · Predictive maintenance · Machine learning
Big data · Asset management · Smart factories · Sustainable manufacturing

I. Moon et al. (Eds.): APMS 2018, IFIP AICT 536, pp. 311–317, 2018.
https://doi.org/10.1007/978-3-319-99707-0_39

1 Introduction

As of today, modern industries require efficiency and convenience for management of the entire Product Life Cycle(PLC), in order to overcome intensely competitive business environment. Advances of IoT opens an efficient way to innovative predictive maintenance strategies in smart manufacturing environments, and these advanced technologies generate industrial big data. To exploit this big data, trend-oriented predictive maintenance tasks are carried out based on actual condition of machinery to avoid occurrence of failures, since advanced enabling technologies and wireless technologies open innovative capability to monitor very details of machines' status and behaviour. In that regard, even if predictive maintenance allows increasing business values and smart machining services, big data from various technologies should be effectively managed for interoperability via standards for merging and transformation of data. According to Lee, a successful shift toward more intelligent machines can be addressed considering five distinct issues as follows: Manager and Operator Interaction, Machine Feet, Product and Process Quality, Big Data and Cloud, and Sensor and Controller Network [1]. To address these issues, predictive maintenance pilots in the EU-funded H2020 research project entitled BOOST 4.0 [2] provides product innovation through a data-driven approach. These pilots are elaborated to integrate digital platforms and industrial things so as to foster collaboration considering the features of Industry 4.0 including (i) horizontal integration through value networks to facilitate inter-corporation collaboration, (ii) vertical integration of hierarchical subsystems inside a factory to create flexible and reconfigurable manufacturing system, and (iii) end-to-end engineering integration across the entire value chain to support product customization [3].

Meanwhile, data analytics through advanced machine learning techniques has been improved with the development of strong hardware and useful algorithms, supporting engineers to find trends and symptoms of failures in order to carry out maintenance tasks optimally. However, types and formats of data vary significantly depending on data sources. Most companies do not have the competence for management of such big data, and often record data without tags describing machine status and/or maintenance history. These constraints limit the application of machine learning algorithms and thus supervised learning and semi-supervised learning cannot be performed for data analytics. For this reason, this research provides a hybrid machine learning approach combining unsupervised learning and semi-supervised learning based on the development and implementation in the BOOST 4.0 project.

2 A Main Architecture for the Predictive Maintenance Pilot

Thanks to recent scientific and technological developments, most industrial practices try to employ a predictive maintenance policy instead of conventional Maintenance (i.e. corrective and/or preventive maintenance). According to Sullivan et al., independent surveys indicate that this predictive maintenance policy can lead to high return on investment, reduction in maintenance cost, elimination of breakdown, reduction in downtime and increase in production [4] since conventional maintenance policies incur low reliability of machines or needless maintenance tasks. However, the main constraints for application of predictive maintenance in BOOST 4.0 can be summarized as no maintenance history and heterogeneous data. Inspired by these constraints, the predictive maintenance pilot in BOOST 4.0 deals with a business case as follows:

- The target product is a milling machine in the shop floor
- Products produced by a milling machine can be measured by a Coordinate Measuring Machine (CMM) in the same shop floor
- Providers of milling machines and CMM machines are different, and machine data is collected by each machine provider
- The results of measurement are useful for the milling machine, but currently there is no intersection between two kinds of data
- The Data formats of the milling machine and the CMM machine are heterogeneous
- Milling machine data does not have maintenance indicator.

This pilot study consists of the following steps: (i) the acquisition and storage of data, (ii) data analytics on operating data and monitoring, (iii) continuous evaluation and prediction of the health status of the equipment as cyber-physical system (i.e. transform descriptors extracted previously in relevant behaviour models, allowing to represent the ways of functioning of the machine and the evolution of the equipment condition over time for detection and prognosis of failures), (iv) decision-making support by considering the context of use of the equipment.

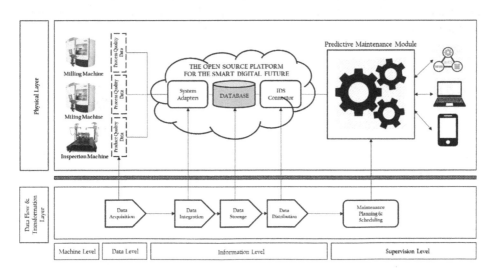

Fig. 1. An architecture for the predictive maintenance pilot

To address the concern of the acquisition and storage of data, application of the open source platform for the smart digital future considers data management (See Fig. 1). This open platform has the capacity of context management to merge heterogeneous data from milling machines and CMM machines. A system adapter in the open source platform will read all the data from milling and CMM machines.

Tracking ID of a product produced by milling machine, it will recognize relevant measurement data. Afterwards, it will update attribute values of defined entities which have the context of the shop floor. Context data will be managed by Context Blocker within IDS connectors. Context data from the shop floor will be accessible through IDS connect which is a back-end processor communicating with the milling machine predictive maintenance system. Depending on data security and requirements, IDS connector will send relevant data to the predictive maintenance system. The Predictive maintenance system will exploit distributed data for maintenance planning & scheduling. This system is in charge of data analytics on operating data and monitoring, evaluation and prediction of the health status, and decision-making support. On the other hand, the open source platform allows exploitation of a specific part of milling machine data for the CMM precision management system which is a part of an operation management pilot. In this context, this study focuses on the predictive maintenance application.

3 A Hybrid Approach of the Predictive Maintenance Pilot

This chapter describes the details of the predictive maintenance system for the pilot. As mentioned above, milling machine data have no maintenance indicator of any events. Therefore, available data limits application of machine learning algorithms and thus supervised learning and semi-supervised learning are not available for data analytics. For this reason, this research provides a hybrid machine learning approach combining unsupervised learning and semi-supervised learning (Fig. 2).

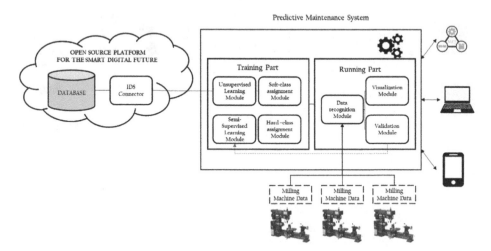

Fig. 2. A hybrid approach for the predictive maintenance pilot

The hybrid approach is comprised of two parts; a training part and a running part. The main role of the training part is to provide a probabilistic model to identify the status of machines. As a hybrid approach, this part has unsupervised learning module linked to soft-class assignment and semi-supervised learning module linked to hard-class assignment. Soft-class assignment initiates all the classes as inputs of an unsupervised learning module to overcome no maintenance indicator whereas hard-class assignment provides consistency of classes.

Based on the assignment modules, new data from milling machines could be used to identify if the machine status is normal or not. To provide a detailed explanation of procedures of data analytics, roles of each module are described below.

Receiving unlabelled training data sets (D_{1u}) which means they have no maintenance indicators from the open source platform, the training part will classify all the data set through an unsupervised learning module. Where the class indexes are k and $\pi_k = N_k/N$ (N_k: a number Dataset of class k, N is a total number of datasets), $\pi_k, \mu_k, \sum_k$ for each class k and $\mu_{D_{1u}}, \sum_{D_{1u}}$ are estimated. And then, where $x_n \in D_{1U}$, each of $\pi_k, \mu_k, \sum_k$ will be updated through the Expectation-Maximization (EM) [5] algorithm as follows:

$$\text{E step} : \gamma_{nk} = \frac{\pi_k N(x_n|\mu_k, \sum_k)}{\sum_{j=1}^{K} \pi_j N(x_n|\mu_j, \sum_j)} \tag{1}$$

$$\text{M step} : \mu_k^{new} = \frac{1}{N_k} \sum_{n=1}^{N} \gamma_{nk} x_n \tag{2}$$

$$\sum_k^{new} = \frac{1}{N_k} \sum_{n=1}^{N} \gamma_{nk}(x_n - \mu_k^{new})(x_n - \mu_k^{new})^T \tag{3}$$

$$\pi_k = \frac{N_k}{N} \tag{4}$$

The log likelihood can be estimated as follows:

$$\ln p(X|\mu, \sum, \pi) = \sum_{n=1}^{N} \ln\left\{ \sum_{k=1}^{K} \pi_k N(x_n|\mu_k, \sum_k) \right\} \tag{5}$$

In the case of $P[\mu_k \in D_{1u}] \geq w$ (where, w is a predefined acceptance parameter), the k class will be soft-assigned to a normal class because normal data set is overwhelming in all the data sets. Otherwise, it will be soft-assigned to an abnormal class. When new data sets (D_2) from active milling machines are delivered to the running part, the running part will estimate $\arg\max_k P[x_t \in C_k]$ $(x_t \in D_2)$. If $\max P[x_t \in C_k] \geq w$, d_2 will be assigned to Class k, and $\pi_k, \mu_k, \sum_k$ will be updated. Otherwise, d_2 will be reported as unidentified data set. The visualization module will display all the graphs with significant values to deliver results of analytics (See Fig. 3). Maintenance engineers will validate these results through dashboard and will give maintenance annotations

(D_{IL}) to abnormal/unidentified data sets. These maintenance annotations will go to the semi-supervised learning module this module will initiate classes based on D_{IL}. To update $\pi_k, \mu_k, \sum_k$ of each class k, where $x_n \in D_{1U}(D_1 = D_{1U} \cup D_{1L})$, E step of EM algorithm is as follows:

$$
\text{E step} : \gamma_{nk} =
\begin{cases}
\dfrac{\pi_k N(x_n|\mu_k, \sum_k)}{\sum\limits_{j=1}^{K} \pi_j N(x_n|\mu_j, \sum_j)} & \text{if } d_n \in D_{2U} \\[4ex]
1\,(k = y(n)) & \text{if } d_n \in D_{2L}
\end{cases}
\tag{6}
$$

M step and estimation of the log likelihood can be estimated following Eqs. (2), (3), (4) and (5).

Fig. 3. A dashboard of predictive maintenance system

Return values from the hybrid approach are presented in a dashboard (See Fig. 3). Considering how to show results of the proposed approach, the dashboard is comprised of three kinds of aspects, i.e. a summary of the machines, machines` KPI, and machine details. A summary of the machines shows a graph representing a rate of available machines, and abnormal machines with probability of failures. Moreover, machines` KPI indicates meaningful information such as failure probability, failure events, aging, warning events, and so on. Machine details display status of each machine. The hybrid approach allows extension of visualisation depending on validation process.

The resulting predictive maintenance system will be demonstrated in the milling machine scenario, and then, its scope will be extended with illustration of all the predictive maintenance pilots in BOOST 4.0 for a wide range of application.

4 Discussion and Concluding Remarks

The main purpose of this research was to provide a novel predictive maintenance approach for the predictive maintenance pilot of BOOST 4.0. This study addressed the problems caused by no maintenance annotations and heterogeneous data sources. To resolve the issue in an efficient way, this paper included an architecture exploiting the open source platform for the smart digital future for merging heterogeneous data from milling machines and CMM machines through context management. In addition, the hybrid predictive maintenance approach was proposed to overcome constraints of no maintenance annotations.

Accordingly, the implications for knowledge and practice could be summarized as follows: (i) the shop floor enables a high-value service for users of the equipment by avoiding downtimes through predictive knowledge. This service brings results of minimizing the total cost and offers optimization of material usage, and (ii) through increased equipment availability, as well as the manufacturing technology as a whole, will help customers to gain a competitive advantage where much unforeseen downtime reduces the profitable production time.

As for future work, the proposed approach will be implemented and validated on not only the milling machine case but also other predictive maintenance pilots within tasks of BOOST 4.0, demonstrating its capacity and potential to support maintenance engineers and machine operators.

Acknowledgements. This work has been carried out in the framework of BOOST 4.0 Project, which has received funding from the European Union's Horizon 2020 research and innovation programme under grant agreement N° 780732.

References

1. Lee, J., Kao, H.A., Yang, S.: Service innovation and smart analytics for industry 4.0 and big data environment. Procedia Cirp **16**, 3–8 (2014)
2. BOOST4.0 Project. http://boost40.eu/. Accessed 06 Apr 2018
3. Wang, S., Wan, J., Li, D., Zhang, C.: Implementing smart factory of industrie 4.0: an outlook. Int. J. Distrib. Sens. Netw. **12**(1), 3159805 (2016)
4. Sullivan, G., Pugh, R., Melendez, A.P., Hunt, W.D.: Operations & Maintenance Best Practices-A Guide to Achieving Operational Efficiency (Release 3) (No. PNNL-19634). Pacific Northwest National Laboratory (PNNL), Richland (2010)
5. Bishop, C.M.: Pattern Recognition and Machine Learning. Springer, New York (2006)

Skill Modelling for Digital Factories

D. Arena[1(✉)], F. Ameri[2], and D. Kiritsis[1]

[1] École Polytechnique Fédérale de Lausanne (EPFL),
SCI-STI-DK ME, Station 9, 1015 Lausanne, Switzerland
{damiano.arena,dimitris.kiritsis}@epfl.ch
[2] Department of Engineering Technology, Texas State University,
601 University Dr., San Marcos, TX 78666, USA
ameri@txstate.edu

Abstract. In the past two decades, the use of ontologies has been proven to be an effective tool for enriching existing information systems in the digital data modelling domain and exploiting those assets for semantic interoperability. Despite the presence of many databases for industrial skills and professions, a formal representation, namely, an ontology, which meets the requirements of an existing tool for skill and capability analysis called CaMDiF is missing. In this research, the MSDL ontology, used by the tool in its initial version, is extended by importing modules of upper level and mid level ontologies (BFO and Agent Ontology) and by developing a new ontology for industry skills and professions based on an existing non-ontological resource (O*NET). As a result, an overview of the enriched data structure is provided along with some discussions on a use case related to skill analysis enabled by the new CaMDiF's skill modelling features.

Keywords: Capability · Skill modelling · Ontology · Digital factory

1 Introduction

The increasing adoption of ontologies in industry is motivated by the need for enhancing the intelligence and interoperability of various business solutions in the context of Industry 4.0 paradigm. In particular, there is an emerging need for formal representation of industrial skills and professions in order to properly take into account the human resources while performing capability analysis for digital factories. In presence of formal and machine-interpretable models of human skills and profession, it is possible to conduct in-depth search and analysis on the available skills in a single factory or a group of factories and identify the areas of strength and weakness in terms of competencies.

Human skill is a complex, evolving, and multifaceted entity. To properly represent the semantics of human skills, a high level of expressivity and extensibility is called for. Ontologies, due to their logic-based underpinning, provide the required level of expressivity, formality, and flexibility for skill modelling.

Ontology Engineering refers to "The set of activities that concern the ontology development process and the ontology lifecycle, the methods and methodologies for ontology building, and the tool suites and languages that support them" [1].

© IFIP International Federation for Information Processing 2018
Published by Springer Nature Switzerland AG 2018. All Rights Reserved
I. Moon et al. (Eds.): APMS 2018, IFIP AICT 536, pp. 318–326, 2018.
https://doi.org/10.1007/978-3-319-99707-0_40

The employment of ontology engineering technologies in the area of industrial data and information modelling has opened the path for exploiting ontologies towards providing formal definitions of the elements and their types, properties and interrelationships that exist for the domain of discourse [2]. An extensible ontology dealing with worker competencies was proposed in [3]. In this work, the current state of the so-called General Competency Schema (GCS) is presented. This is an OWL ontology that aims to provide a representation for requirement relationships between competencies and their constituents that to enable inference of competencies. It also provides several metrics for competency measurement and for specifying levels of required competencies. A rather simple ontological model for representing, inferring, and validating competencies over time is presented in [4] as an extension of the Process Specification Language (PSL). The authors provide a detailed range of axioms and inference rules expressed in First Order Logic (FOL), moreover, addressing a non-trivial subject such as the reliability of the information sources for worker skills. In the first paper, authors state that the model is flexible and can be easily adapted to the organization need, however, the organization is not mentioned in the model, and thus, it is unclear what role it may play. Much the same applies to the second work where, again, the worker's context is not taken into account.

The current research aims to extend an existing tool for capability analysis of digital factories by introducing a worker-centred ontology-based module for skill and profession modelling. The document is structured as follows. Section 2 discusses the existing works and their relations with the current research. Section 3 introduces the proposed skill ontology and its modules. In Sect. 4, the extension of CaMDiF based on the skill ontology and two use cases are discussed briefly.

2 Relation to Current Research

2.1 CaMDiF

CaMDiF (Capability Modeling for Digital Factory) is a software framework that is used for ontological representation and analysis of capabilities of digital factories. The Digital Factory, as the digital twin of a physical factory, replicates the facility in terms of installed machinery, material handling equipment, human resources, and other production support systems, including both software and hardware.

The CaMDiF framework has a three-level architecture (Fig. 1). The main components of the data and knowledge layer are the capability ontology and the manufacturing capability thesaurus, external domain ontologies, and the libraries of manufacturing resources including CNC machine and 3D printer, factory, and supply chain libraries. The second layer is the semantic layer which is basically the Apache Jena semantic application suite which provides a set of Java libraries and Application Programming Interfaces (APIs). Jena allows programmers to create, edit, and manage semantic web ontologies using RDF graphs. Also, Jena provides the necessary interfaces for query and reasoning that are usually needed in semantic applications. The last layer is the application layer that has three main functions, namely, build, analyse, and match. The first implementation of CaMDiF does not address human skills as part of the company's capability model. This paper introduces an extension of CaMDiF in which enables manufacturing companies to add the capabilities offered by human resources to their company profiles.

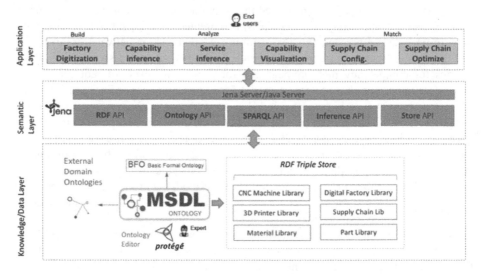

Fig. 1. The architecture of the CaMDiF framework

2.2 Profession and Skill Databases

A non-exhaustive list of the existing ontological and non-ontological resources (structured models, guidelines, etc.) is presented in Table **1** and described below.

ESCO is a wide classification by the *European Commission for Skills, Competencies, Qualifications and Occupations*. Available in TTL and XLS formats, it is of particular interest regarding transversal skills/competencies.

The *International Standard Classification of Occupations* is a universal mono-hierarchical classification scheme of occupation groups, compiled by the International Labour Organization (ILO). There have been published four versions of the classification since 1957, abbreviated to ISCO-58, ISCO-68, ISCO-88 and ISCO-08, respectively. Among others, the ISCO classification is used by the European Union and by its member nations as a basic scheme for the construction of national occupation classifications.

ASOC stands for the *Arab Standard Occupational Classification* and is known as Tasneef in Arabic. It is the occupational classification system that is being built in the Kingdom of Saudi Arabia in 2015. ASOC covers all occupations and jobs in the national economy, including occupations in the public and private sectors. The classification system is built based on ISCO-08 and is available in Arabic and English.

The Italian occupation classification *Classificazione delle Professioni* (CP) 2011 is based on ISCO-08 and available in two languages (IT, EN), latest version 2011.

The *Occupational Information Network* (O*NET) in the USA is supported by the US Department of Labor/Employment and Training Administration (USDOL/ETA). It is related to the UK occupation classification SOC. O*NET is a broad database of occupation descriptions and the respective skills, competencies, etc. needed for each of them. Each occupation is structured into Tasks, Tools used, Knowledge, Skills, Ability, Work Activities, Work Context, Job Zone.

The *European Dictionary of Skills and Competencies* (DISCO) II is an online thesaurus with currently more than 104,000 skill and competence terms and about 36,000 phrases in the fields of health, computing, social services, environmental protection and non-domain specific skills and competencies. Available in eleven European languages, DISCO is one of the largest collections of its kind in the education and labour market.

The *Répertoire Opérationnel des Métiers et des Emplois* (ROME), version 3, the French Occupation Classification has its own structure, thus it is not based on ISCO-08. The structure contains three levels: occupation categories, fields of work and the occupation term, to which all the occupations are assigned.

Table 1. Comparison of the existing skill databases

Resource	Format				Documented	Language(s)
	TTL	JSON	XLS	TXT		
ESCO	x		x		Yes	English
ISCO-08				x	Yes	English
ASOC			x		Yes	Arabic, English
CP 2011				x	Yes	Italian, English
O*NET			x	x	Yes	Multiple
DISCO II				x	Yes	English
ROMEV3		x	x		Yes	French

3 Ontology Modelling

The ontology used in this work has different modules, namely, BFO, Agent Ontology, MSDL, and ISPO, which are described in following sub-sections.

3.1 Description of BFO

Basic Formal Ontology (BFO) is used as the foundational, or upper, ontology in this work [5]. As a domain-neutral upper-level ontology, BFO adopts a view of reality and represents different types of entities that exist in the world and relations between them. BFO is deliberately designed to be very small and its most recent version, BFO 2.0, has 35 classes. There are two types of entities in BFO, namely, *Continuants* and *Occurrents*. *Continuants* are the entities that continue to persist through time while maintaining their identity whereas, *Occurrents* are the events or happenings in which *Continuants* participate. Apart from its realistic approach, BFO has multiple other unique features that make it an appropriate upper ontology for many domains. Firstly, BFO has a very large user base and it is widely used in a variety of ontologies. Secondly, BFO is very small and therefore, easy to use and easy to learn. Additionally, BFO is very well-documented and there are multiple tutorials, guidelines, and web forums for using BFO in ontological projects.

3.2   Description of MSDL

The capabilities of a Digital Factory are formally described using the MSDL ontology. Manufacturing Service Description Language (MSDL) is an ontology for representation of capabilities of manufacturing services. MSDL decomposes the manufacturing capability into four levels of abstraction, namely, company-level, shop-level, machine-level, and device-level [6]. MSDL was initially developed to enable automated supplier discovery in distributed environments with focus on mechanical machining services but the classes were intentionally designed to be generic enough to address a wide range of manufacturing processes and services.

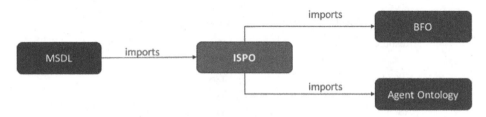

Fig. 2. Ontology network

3.3   Description of ISPO

Despite the existence of an ontological resource called ESCO, which provides a Turtle ontology-based classification for skills, distinguishing between skill/competence and knowledge elements by indicating the skill type, in this work, we present an ontological model generated from a non-ontological resource named O*NET, the structure of which better suits the needs of the new CaMDiF architecture presented in Sect. 3.1.

Starting from a list of unstructured information organized within an XSL document, an ad hoc MatLab© script has been designed and used to generate the class hierarchy based on O*NET's structure. Figure 3 shows the first two class levels of the Industry Skills and Professions Ontology (ISPO).

At its present state of development, the ISPO Ontology only contains *is a* relations and serves as a bridge between the MSDL and both BFO and Agent Ontologies Fig. 2. As a result, the ontology network (Fig. 4) exploits parts of MSDL, BFO, ISPO, and Agent Ontology for semantic data annotation, interpretation, and querying.

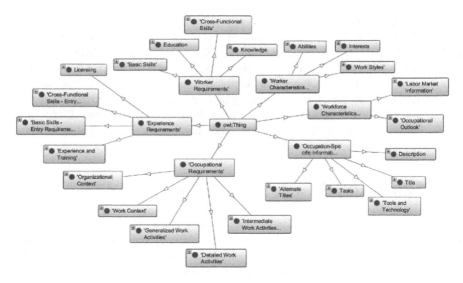

Fig. 3. First two class levels of ISPO

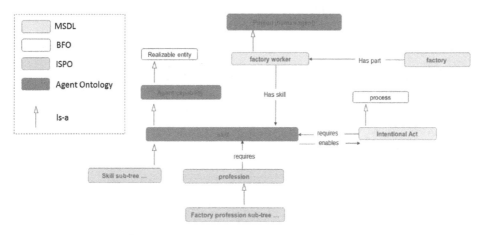

Fig. 4. Top-level class diagram of the ontology

3.4 Description of Agent Ontology

ISPO and MSDL both import the Agent Ontology in order to represent various agents and the roles they have in different contexts. The Agent Ontology is one of the eleven mid-level ontologies that together comprise the Common Core Ontologies (CCO). In the Agent Ontology, the class *Agent* is defined as "An Independent Continuant that is capable of performing Intentional Acts". The class *Agent* can represent both individual agents (Person) and coordinated groups of individuals (Organization). Another core class of the Agent Ontology that is reused in the present work is the *Occupation Role* class that is defined as "A Role that inheres in an Agent in virtue of the responsibilities that Agent is expected to fulfil within the context of some Act of Employment".

For example, a *Factory Operator*, as an individual agent, is a person that assumes the role of *Operator Role*, as a sub-class of *Occupation Role*. Agents can have both qualities and capabilities. The *Agent Capability* class is defined as a "Realizable Entity that inheres in an Agent to the extent of that Agent's capacity to realize it in Intentional Acts of a certain type". In the Agent Ontology, *Skill*, as a defined class in Agent Ontology, is an agent capability that inheres in a *Person*. The Agent Ontology does not provide any subclass of the *Skill* and *Occupation Role* classes. Therefore, ISPO extends the *Skill* and *Occupation Role* classes in order to cover a wide range of skills and professions in manufacturing organizations.

4   CaMDiF Extension with Skill Modelling Feature

The use of the abovementioned ontological models allows the extension of CaMDiF tool with skill modelling features. It enables semantics-driven capability and skill gap analysis for digital factories. Figure 5 shows the user interface implemented for addition of skills to the capability model of the digital factory in CaMDiF. Since *Skill* is a subclass of the *Disposition* class in BFO, its level should be measurable along some scale. In this work, an ordinal scale (low-medium-high) is chosen for specify the level of each available type of skill.

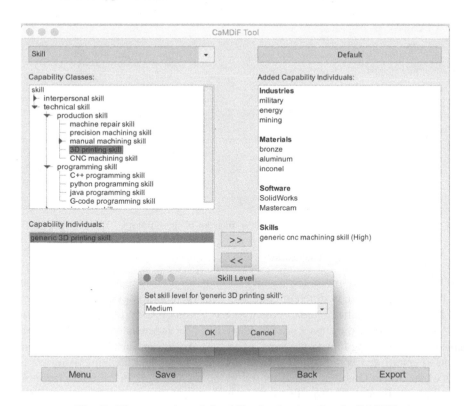

Fig. 5. The screenshot of the skill selection interface in CaMDiF

One utility of including skills ontology in CaMDiF is performing skill gap analysis. Skill gap analysis can be carried out through comparing the required skills for a particular manufacturing sector with the provided skills by the factories in CaMDiF's factory repository. The required skills can be obtained from the historical work orders available in the CaMDiF's work order repository. For example, CaMDiF's work orders can be queried to find the top ten skills required by all work orders in the aerospace sector. If the scope of the gap analysis is a single factory, then the gaps can be identified through subtracting the provided skills, by the factory, from the requested skills in the aerospace sector. The scope of gap analysis can be extended to cover all factories that provide precision machining services, for example. The identified skill gap informs the precision manufacturing sector about the new skills that need to be acquired in order to better serve the needs of customers from the aerospace industry.

In the current implementation of CaMDiF, the required skills for a given work order are asserted explicitly. However, in the future versions, it is possible to implement a mechanism for inferring the required skills for a given work order based on the part properties such as material, tolerances, and surface finishes as well as the required manufacturing processes for fulfilling the order.

5   Conclusions

In this paper, a new ontology for representation of manufacturing skills and professions was introduced and it was demonstrated how the ontology can be used for skill gap analysis in CaMDiF framework. The main contribution of this paper is to propose a modular, BFO conformant ontology for skill representation. The skill ontology can be used for formal description of the capabilities of digital factories. Formal skill representation is a major enabler for competency-based supply chain formation solution. The layered and modular structure of the ontology allows for seamless extension of the ontology in different sub-domains of manufacturing industry. One of the research issues that needs to be addressed in the future is automated extraction of required skills for manufacturing work orders.

Acknowledgement. This work was partially supported by the EU funded DILECO project (ID 785367).

References

1. Kiritsis, D.: Closed-loop PLM for intelligent products in the era of the Internet of Things. Comput.-Aided Des. **43**(5), 479–501 (2011)
2. Arena, D., et al.: Human resource optimisation through semantically enriched data. Int. J. Prod. Res. **56**(8), 1–23 (2018). https://doi.org/10.1080/00207543.2017.1415468
3. García-Barriocanal, E., Sicilia, M.-A., Sánchez-Alonso, S.: Computing with competencies: modelling organizational capacities. Expert Syst. Appl. **39**(16), 12310–12318 (2012)
4. Fazel-Zarandi, M., Fox, M.S.: An ontology for skill and competency management. In: FOIS (2012)

5. Arp, R., Smith, B., Spear, A.D.: Building Ontologies with Basic Formal Ontology. MIT Press, Cambridge (2015)
6. Ameri, F., Dutta, D.: An upper ontology for manufacturing service description. In: ASME 2006 International Design Engineering Technical Conferences and Computers and Information in Engineering Conference. American Society of Mechanical Engineers (2006)

Digital Twin Approach for Solving Reconfiguration Planning Problems in RMS

Kezia Amanda Kurniadi, Sangil Lee, and Kwangyeol Ryu[(✉)]

Pusan National University, Busan, South Korea
kyryu@pusan.ac.kr

Abstract. Reconfigurable Manufacturing System (RMS) appeared as a solution to high variation in customer demands allowing manufacturers to satisfy different amount of demands in different period. RMS satisfies demands by rapidly reconfiguring its hardware and software components, in order to quickly adjust its production capacity and functionality within a part family in response to sudden market changes or intrinsic system change depends on the demand of every single period. This reconfiguration process brings a critical issue within the RMS that is called as reconfiguration planning problems (RPP) introduced in this paper. With the rise of digital twin that has been a global issue, many companies or manufacturers are trying to integrate it into their production systems. There is a need of RMS to apply digital twin in order to hopefully improve the effectiveness and efficiency so that RPP can be automatically solved and controlled. The goal of this paper is to address the importance and requirement of the integration of digital twin simulation into RMS by providing comparison study between normal simulation program and digital twin simulation program. A case study is presented for comparison of two simulation models. Plant Simulation 11 is used for a normal simulation model, while Visual Components is used to build a digital twin simulation model.

Keywords: Reconfigurable manufacturing system · Digital twin
Simulation · Reconfigurable planning problem

1 Introduction

The process of RMS requires reconfiguring machines with exact number of its components to meet the demands. Demands that periodically change also cause the machines reconfigurations. The changes of machine reconfigurations in RMS are evoked by influencing factors, to new conditions by adapting the set of machines, as known as configurations in RMS. Hence, these reconfigurations are always connected to monetary and temporal expenses. Since reconfiguration process requires high expense, effort, and time. Reflecting at those conditions, the systematic and organized planning is very necessary in RMS, whether to minimize cost or/and save time and energy.

Therefore, the purpose of this research is firstly to introduce Reconfigurable Planning Problem (RPP) in RMS. The goal of this paper is to address the importance and requirement of the integration of digital twin simulation into RMS by providing

© IFIP International Federation for Information Processing 2018
Published by Springer Nature Switzerland AG 2018. All Rights Reserved
I. Moon et al. (Eds.): APMS 2018, IFIP AICT 536, pp. 327–334, 2018.
https://doi.org/10.1007/978-3-319-99707-0_41

comparison study between normal simulation program and digital twin simulation program. Since there said to be a need of simulation on digital twin to enable optimal decision-making in RMS [1]. Case study is presented for comparison study by using Plant Simulation 11 is used for normal simulation program, while Visual Components 2014 is used to build digital twin simulation program. The purpose is to find a conclusion whether digital twin is best to achieve more effective and efficient reconfigurable manufacturing system or not, as well as how to apply digital twin or other similar methodology in order to improve RMS. In this study, manufacturing process for making flip-flop is used as a case study. After experimentation of simulation model, the results will be analyzed to carry out the main objectives of the study.

2   Reconfigurable Manufacturing System

The reconfigurable manufacturing system (RMS) has emerged in the last few years in an attempt to achieve changeable functionality and scalable capacity [1]. Machine components, machines, cells, or material handling units can be activated, deactivated, modified, or interchanged as needed to respond quickly to changing requirements. In summary, an ideal RMS comprehends the advances of DMS and FMS [3]. RMS is marked by six core reconfigurable characteristics, as summarized below [4]:

- Customization (flexibility limited to part family)
- Convertibility (design for functionality changes)
- Scalability (design for capacity changes)
- Modularity (components are modular)
- Integrability (interfaces for rapid integration)
- Diagnosability (design for easy diagnostics)

Reconfigurable Machine Tools. Reconfigurable machine tools (RMTs) are designed for a specific range of operational requirements, and can be rapidly converted from one configuration to another. The world-first patent on RMT was issued in 1999 [2]. Figure 1 shows an arch-type RMT that was built by the ERC-RMS and exhibited in 2002 at the International Manufacturing Show in Chicago. It was designed to drill and mill on inclined surfaces in such a way that the tool is perpendicular to the surface.

Fig. 1. Reconfigurable machine tool (RMT) developed at the ERC-RMS [4]

3 Reconfigurable Planning Problem

In RMS, machine components, machines, cells can be added, removed, modified, or interchanged as needed to respond quickly to changing requirements. However the process of adding or removing machines is very impractical in real life. Therefore in this study, it is assumed that system reconfiguration involves the activation and deactivation of machines components among working stations between periods, in which the representing flowchart is shown in Fig. 2. As shown in Fig. 2, system throughput should be calculated first in order to determine whether it will satisfy the new demand or not. If the throughput cannot satisfy the demand, then the system requires activating additional machines. If the amount of next demand is less than the first demand, then machine/s may be deactivated since those machines will not be used to satisfy the new demand. To solve RP problems, the following notation and assumptions are used. Matlab 2013 is used to obtain the result of mathematical model.

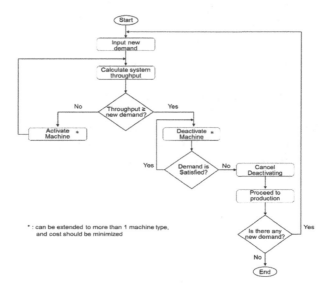

Fig. 2. Flowchart of machine reconfiguration in RMS

Notations:

I	Index of period ($i = 1, 2, ..., I$)
J	Index of working station ($j = 1, 2, ..., J$)
K	Index of machine type ($k = 1, 2, ..., K$)
N_i	Minimum number of total machines in period i
Q_i	Demands in period i
T_i	Working time in period i
TM_{ij}	Total number of machines in working station j in period i-1 (before activating/deactivating machines in period i)
α_k	Activation cost of machine type k ($\$$)

β_k Deactivation cost of machine type k (\$)
AD_{ijk} Number of machines type k activated in working station j in period i
RM_{ijk} Number of machines type k deactivated in working station j in period i
O_i System throughput in period i

Firstly, we have to calculate the N_i by dividing Q_i by T_i, as represented in Eq. 1.

$$N_i = \left\lceil \frac{Q_i}{T_i} \right\rceil \tag{1}$$

The objective function of reconfigurable planning is to minimize the Reconfiguration Planning cost (RP cost) which is the total summation cost of activating, deactivating, and purchasing newly bought machine, as expressed as in Eq. 2.

$$\text{Minimize} \sum_{i=1}^{I} \sum_{j=1}^{J} \sum_{k=1}^{K} \left[(AD_{ijk}\alpha_k) + (RM_{ijk}\beta_k) \right] \tag{2}$$

Assumptions:

- The processing time of each operation, capacity of machine, purchasing cost of machines, and demand are known.
- Conveyors are considered as a material handling system, and sensor is installed in each machine.
- All the machines within the same stage perform exactly the same sequence of tasks.
- There are reserved spaces for adding new machines in the stages and material handlers can be extended to deliver parts to the newly added machines.
- Company budget for buying new machines is enough for the reserved periods.

The objective function is subject to the following constraints.

- Total number of machines must be equal or larger than the minimum number of total machines in that period.

$$TM_{ij} \geq N_i \tag{3}$$

- Throughput constraints must be equal or larger than the demand.

$$O_i \geq \sum_{i=1}^{I} Q_i \tag{4}$$

4   Case Study

In this study, RMS logic will be applied into the manufacturing process of flip-flop. Sandal manufacturing is most likely labor intensive process and it cannot be fully automated. It requires craftsmanship in each phase of the production. The actual production plant assembles high quality unisex (for men and women) sandals. The size available varies from European size 36–40 (or: 235–255 mm) for women and

European size 40–44 (or: 255–275 mm) for men. Figure 3 shows the production sequence of two sandal products, Plain red flip-flop (R) and Couple flip-flop (C).

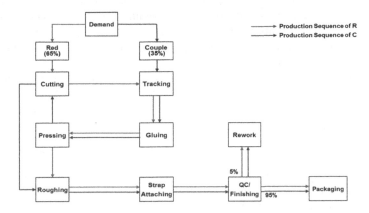

Fig. 3. Production sequence of two products (Color figure online)

The simulation model is driven by following assumptions:

- The demand/production mix is random with exponential distribution, in terms of sandal type, size, and quantity to be produced, as shown in Table 1. The total demand is separated into 65% R and 35% C.
- The input buffer policy in each station for stacking trolleys.
- Every station has an input buffer where trolleys are stacked up if they cannot be processed immediately. These buffers are simulated as queues. Each coming trolley is ranked based on its order number and, then, it is released following the FIFO rule (first in – first out) when the machine is free. In this way, each station will process all trolleys with the same order number.
- Working time is 10 h - a day.

Table 1. Demand list for 3 periods

Period	Demand (units)		
	Red (65%)	Couple (35%)	Total
1	293	158	451
2	59	33	92
3	132	72	204

The production strategy for the problem is make-to-order with the preorder duration of 1 day. Each day the company will receive new demand, and the company should satisfy the demand at the end of the day. The simulation is run for 1 working-month, and it is assumed that 1 month consists of 20-working days. At the end of QC work station, the result of defective and non-defective products are set to the ratio of 5:95, because the company wants to achieve 95% non-defective products. Before running the experiment, we should calculate the system throughput first, in order to set the range of demand. The value of demand should be smaller than system's maximum throughput. System throughput is the total amount of items produced by the system. By activating all machines and running the simulation, we can obtain the value of system's maximum throughput, which is 497 units per day. Based on the demand, we can calculate the total number of machines needed to satisfy the demand. For the comparison purpose, we only consider the first 3 periods only.

In Plant Simulation, every machine is built by using the provided machine/facility attributes that are already created inside the software. The machine capacity and operation time can be modified based on the requirements. Figure 4 shows the factory layout. The advantage of using Visual Component 2014 software is that there are several machine/facility that are very close with the real life attributes. Depending on what kind of company or factory that needs to be simulated, those provided features can be very helpful. However, in order to closely compare with real data used in Plant Simulation 11, machine cycle time was modified into as close as the Plant Simulation one. Figure 5 shows the factory layout.

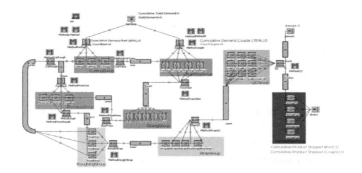

Fig. 4. Factory floor layout (Plant Simulation 11)

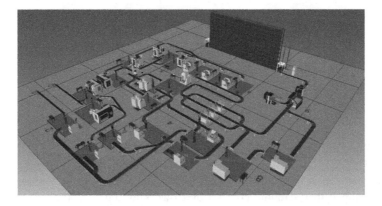

Fig. 5. Factory floor layout (Visual Components 2014)

Table 2 shows the processing time, and number of machines needed in Plant Simulation 11 based on the real data of company workers in Company X, while the processing time in Visual Components is already provided within the software. Assume that activation and deactivation cost for all machines are the same, activation cost is $10 and deactivation cost is $20. After doing the simulation on both programs for 20 days x 1-h, the result shows result summary of reconfiguration cost and number of working machine of each station is shown in Table 3. As shown in Table 3, total RP cost for Visual Components is lower than total RP cost for Plant Simulation 11.

Table 2. Processing time of work stations

Work station j	Processing time (minutes/pair)	Number of machines
1. Cutting	2	3
2. Pressing	2	3
3. Roughing	2	3
4. Strap attaching	3	4
5. Tracing	3	4
6. Gluing	4	5
7. QC/Finishing	7	9
8. Packaging	3	4
Total machines needed		35

Table 3. Comparison of simulation result and reconfiguration cost

Period	Working machine in station j								Number of active machine (AD)	Number of inactive machine (RM)	RP cost
	1	2	3	4	5	6	7	8			
Plant Simulation 11											
1	2	3	4	2	2	3	6	3	25	0	250
2	1	1	1	1	1	1	2	1	0	16	320
3	1	2	2	1	1	2	3	2	5	0	50
Total RP cost = 830											
Visual Components 2014											
1	2	3	4	2	2	3	6	3	25	0	250
2	1	1	1	1	1	1	2	1	0	16	320
3	1	1	1	1	1	2	2	2	2	0	20
Total RP Cost = 800											

5 Conclusion

This paper introduced a RP problem in order to anticipate any planning problem within RMS especially for the calculation of required machines to satisfy new demand, as well as presented the fact that digital twin can be and is being applied into RMS.

Configurations of machines are one of the most important issues needed for an efficient and effective RMS. Machine reconfigurations are very likely occur whenever the new demands inputted into the system. Reconfiguring machines which include activating/deactivating machines needs relatively high cost. Configurations of machines are the one of the most important key issue in order to achieve an efficient and effective RMS. By applying digital twin into the RMS, the real life application seems to be possible and the system will be able to be more organized and integrated through connecting all the physical devices, operators, and data.

However, in a real production facility, additional cost factors need to be taken into account as well, such as labor, tooling, utility, floor space, operating cost, and material handlers. Since a reconfiguration process usually requires shutting down of the production system, an extra cost will occur due to the production loss during the reconfiguration process. Other constraints should also be added, such as limited factory floor space, set-up cost, and others. The future result of this study can be complied not only in RMS but also in other manufacturing concept as well.

References

1. Koren, Y., Gu, X., Guo, W.: Reconfigurable manufacturing systems: principles, design, and future trends. Front Mech. Eng. **2**(5), 99–110 (2017)
2. Koren, Y.: General RMS charasteristics. Comparison with dedicated and flexible system. In: Dashchenko, A.I. (ed.) Reconfigurable Manufacturing Systems and Transformable Factories, pp. 27–46. Springer, Berlin (2006). https://doi.org/10.1007/3-540-29397-3_3
3. Koren, Y., Ulsoy, A.G.: Vision, principles and impact of reconfigurable manufacturing systems. Powertrain Int. **5**(3), 14–21 (2002)
4. Koren, Y.: Reconfigurable manufacturing system. CIRP Ann. Manuf. Tech. **48**, 527–540 (1999)
5. Wang, W., Koren, Y.: Scalability planning for reconfigurable manufacturing systems. J. Manuf. Syst. **31**(2), 83–91 (2012)
6. Deif, A.M., ElMaraghy, W.H.: A systematic design approach for reconfigurable manufacturing systems. In: ElMaraghy, H.A., ElMaraghy, W.H. (eds.) Advances in Design. Springer Series in Advanced Manufacturing, pp. 219–228. Springer, London (2006). https://doi.org/10.1007/1-84628-210-1_18
7. Aboufazeli, M.: Reconfigurable machine tools design methodologies and measuring reconfigurability for design evaluation. Master thesis, School of Industrial Engineering and Management, The Royal Institute of Technology, Sweden (2011)
8. Koren, Y., Shpitalni, M.: Design of reconfigurable manufacturing system. J. Manuf. Syst. **29**, 130–141 (2010)

Remaining Useful Life Estimation
for Informed End of Life Management
of Industrial Assets: A Conceptual Model

Marco Macchi, Irene Roda$^{(\boxtimes)}$, and Leonardo Toffoli

Department of Management, Economics and Industrial Engineering,
Politecnico di Milano, Milan, Italy
irene.roda@polimi.it

Abstract. The management of the End of Life phase of the lifecycle of industrial assets is more and more a relevant issue for companies dealing with aging assets. This paper provides a conceptual model that includes different aspects that should be considered by a comprehensive methodology to support an informed decision-making process in this regard. In particular, the work stems from the need of estimating the Remaining Useful Life (RUL) of an asset, for defining an Ageing Asset Strategy, through a multi-disciplinary approach instead of a purely technical one. To this end, the proposed model highlights the different End of Life types of an asset that should be considered for comprehensive RUL estimation methodology.

Keywords: Remaining useful life · Asset Management · Life extension
End of Life

1 Introduction

Nowadays, ageing assets represent a particular challenge for asset managers [1]. Society's inventory of capital goods is increasing as well as ageing in the western societies. This is very much the case for infrastructures like roads, railways, electric power generation, transport, and aircrafts [2] but also involves production facilities. Many manufacturing plants – at least in Europe – have been built in the years after the Second World War, and assets therein are currently approaching the end of their expected functional lives [3]. Ageing of asset systems is one of the reasons why physical Asset Management (AM) has become a more essential part of the organizations' activities during the last decades [4, 5]. Therefore, it is more and more important to define an effective Ageing Assets Strategy for companies managing capital assets. The implementation of such a strategy should provide asset managers with the tools they need to determine the most cost-effective strategy for the ageing assets under their stewardship [1].

As stated by [6], life extension is an alternative to conventional End of Life management strategies, such as decommissioning and replacement of capital equipment, and is gaining popularity in the last years. The decision of extending the life of an asset can potentially bring great economic advantages and value to asset owners,

I. Moon et al. (Eds.): APMS 2018, IFIP AICT 536, pp. 335–342, 2018.
https://doi.org/10.1007/978-3-319-99707-0_42

managers and stakeholders if all the necessary information is effectively collected to support it, and proper decision-making is applied. In fact, it is crucial for decision makers to have a holistic view on the current processes and issues involved in undertaking a life extension program.

Asset Life Extension processes generally include: definition of premises for the life extension program, assessment of asset condition, estimation of remaining useful life (RUL) and evaluation of different strategies for life extension [6–8].

The Asset Integrity Management (AIM) approach developed in the Oil&Gas industry, can be considered the predecessor of the ageing and life extension programs that are nowadays under discussion. According to [7], AIM and Asset Life Extension are overlapping facets of the same requirement to ensure offshore safety, with the former principally concerned with contemporaneous integrity management, and the latter requiring a forward-looking approach anticipating future changes, challenges and threats, and forecasting the consequences on an installation's risk profile. In the document by [7], a process to preserve asset integrity and extend its life is proposed and its main phases are: to understand the asset condition, to recognize ageing and obsolescence, to manage life extension. Even if the model does not analyze in depth how condition assessment and RUL estimation should be performed, it gives an important remark: there are not only forces related to physical degradation at work in an ageing of asset but obsolescence should be taken into account too in industrial installations.

Based on these premises, this research aims at proposing a conceptual model to estimate the Remaining Useful Life (RUL) for informed-decision making in End of Life Management (EOL) of industrial assets, identifying and considering different potential causes of ageing, relevant in order to define an Asset Strategy through a multi-disciplinary approach instead of a pure technical one. Section 2 shows findings from the literature analysis about EOL causes and RUL estimation approaches. Section 3 describes the proposed conceptual model. Section 4 is dedicated to the Conclusions.

2 Literature Analysis

Estimating the exact moment in which an asset would reach its EOL and therefore calculating its RUL is one essential step in the life extension process but it is not a trivial task [6–8]. RUL estimation is a key research topic of Condition Based Maintenance (CBM) and PHM ([9, 10]) but some gaps still exist, mainly related to the need of addressing the problem from a multi-disciplinary perspective and not only from a technical one [8]. In fact, one open issue in the literature is about ageing causes to be considered for RUL estimation in order to get to an indicator that can be used for informed AM decision-making, overcoming the pure physical ageing perspective of an asset.

For this reason, the first objective of this paper is to analyze and systematize the discussion about EOL causes. Secondly, the analysis of current approaches in literature for RUL estimation is presented.

2.1   End of Life Causes

In the studies on life extension of assets in the Oil&Gas industry [6, 7], the presence of two aspects when talking about ageing is hinted. Indeed, they suggest the separation between causes of ageing related to the physical condition of the asset and causes related to obsolescence, which can be linked to various factors other than physical degradation.

Other studies support this idea, by clearly stating the distinction of obsolescence from any type of physical degradation. For example, the work [11] demonstrated the presence of two forces of ageing with a case study distinguishing between what they call the traditional forces of mortality and the technology obsolescence. The work [12] recently confirmed this insight as they also asserted that the main reasons for the end of life of a system can be divided between physical ageing and wear, and obsolescence, that they define as the inability to satisfy increasing requirements of the users. Moreover, the authors identify three types of obsolescence, i.e., economic obsolescence, functional obsolescence and spare parts obsolescence, asserting that what other scholars have defined as technology obsolescence is one of the causes, possibly the most frequent, of the three obsolescence types.

Table 1 shows and classifies different types of EOL causes, adapting the work by [12] including other relevant literature.

Table 1. EOL causes classification

EOL causes	Type	Factors
Physical ageing	Physical degradation (the asset is unable to produce a predetermined quality or quantity of output)	Traditional ageing mechanisms as wear or corrosion
Obsolescence	Economic obsolescence (relative increase in the costs of operations)	Technology advance/other causes
	Functional obsolescence (the asset is unable to satisfy new requirements)	Changing needs of client/introduction of new regulations/other causes
	Diminishing manufacturing sources and material shortages (DMSMS) *(difficulty in repairing the asset)*	Spare parts unavailability/bankruptcy of suppliers/other causes

In detail, two main EOL causes can be defined: physical ageing and obsolescence. Physical ageing is considered as the main form of ageing by most of the literature, and its only cause is physical degradation increasing the failure risk. Most methodologies related to the RUL estimation are specifically dedicated to this type of EOL cause, as showed in the next section.

Obsolescence is the other EOL cause type and it can be classified into:

- Economic obsolescence, caused mainly by technology advance and emerging when the current asset is no more profitable if compared with a new equipment;

- Functional obsolescence, emerging when the asset is unable to satisfy the new requirements after the introduction of new regulations or a change in the market;
- Diminishing Manufacturing Sources and Material Shortage (DMSMS) obsolescence, mainly related to the obsolescence of the spare parts leading to difficulty in repairing the asset caused, mostly but not only, by technology advance.

2.2   Remaining Useful Life Estimation Approaches

Currently, the estimation of the RUL is a topic of extensive research efforts [13]. Assuming the RUL would be known exactly, an asset could be exploited generating optimal value for its owner, without any increased failures or costs. Furthermore, knowing the processes or incidents that cause the end of the assets useful life would allow the owner to take preventive measures to extend the asset's life [3, 13]. However, there are some weaknesses related to current approaches to estimate asset RUL. In particular, [3] highlighted two of those weaknesses.

- many approaches are limited to the technical aspects of the asset or to a mainly statistical approach to deterioration mechanisms;
- many quantitative attempts fail because of the quality and availability of data.

Hence, on one side there is the need for methods that adopt a multi-disciplinary approach, considering other ageing causes together with physical degradation, connected with obsolescence [8]. On the other side, there is need for methods suitable for situations in which limited or no quantitative data are available, for example methods based on the knowledge of experts [10].

Looking at the RUL estimation techniques in the literature, it is clear that most scholars focused their studies mainly on the development of quantitative methods to support condition-based maintenance programs [14–19]. These works have been grouped and defined generically as quantitative RUL estimation methods and techniques because their objective is to link one or more degradation mechanisms to the life of the asset element, mainly low levels of the asset decomposition (in a complex asset structure), to predict when it will fail. They are often complex methodologies and models concentrating on a specific part or assembly to develop a technique that works in certain conditions. Besides, they can be very precise when data are available but they are difficult to be applied when reliable data is scarce. Moreover, as already stated, they are mono-disciplinary since they are limited to the technical aspects of the asset. In [8], they recognized the importance for a multi-disciplinary approach for RUL prediction for Life Extension (LE) decision-making. Nevertheless, their model still focuses on the technical input to decision-making, by establishing a process for technical health assessment.

A group of scholars, starting from the difficulties that often emerge when using quantitative methodologies, tried to overcome them developing a model that considers also qualitative information along with quantitative data and that is multi-disciplinary [3]. In an attempt to make the RUL a multi-disciplinary practice, [3] propose a new methodology called Lifetime Impacts Identification Analysis that aims to identify the external impacts that could affect an asset's life in the future without trying to calculate the exact date of end of life. According to the authors it is important to consider four dimensions of ageing: (i) the technological perspective, which is related to the question for how long the asset (and/or its output) will comply with the existing technical specifications, (ii) the economic perspective, concerning the costs of operating and maintaining a piece of equipment, (iii) the compliancy perspective, that deals with the 'license to operate' of the company, and (iv) the commercial perspective, which considers whether the asset (and its production) are still able to fulfil the demands of the market. This methodology is an interesting starting point for research looking for comprehensive methodologies to support the EOL management of industrial assets.

3 Proposed Conceptual Model

Based on the analysis of the literature, the proposed conceptual model intends to provide the basis to develop a guide for asset managers to determine in a simple but systematic manner the RUL of an asset, enlarging the concept of RUL by considering different EOL causes together with the physical ageing. The proposed methodology is thought to facilitate a rigorous approach to address the problem, bearing in mind that each step of the process will require the application of systematic judgment and experience, to achieve informed decisions in the EOL phase and to eventually develop proper asset strategies.

The methodology is built on this simple postulate: while physical degradation is certainly causing the end of physical life, it is not the only way an asset can reach its EOL; starting from the definitions provided by the literature, different EOL types can be defined associated with different EOL causes. In particular, we define four types of EOL besides the end of physical life: (i) end of service level life, (ii) end of capacity life, (iii) end of financial life, (iv) end of maintainable life. In the reminder, each of it is described in detail and related to one type of EOL causes as defined in Table 1.

Regarding the physical ageing EOL cause, the EOL type can be identified as follows the EOL type can be identified as follows the EOL type can be identified as follows:

- End of physical life: it occurs when an asset is physically non-functioning (e.g., failed, collapsed, stopped working). Physical mortality failure occurs when the consumption of an asset caused by usage over time reduces performance to such an extent that the asset is unable to sustain performance at or above minimum requirements. A physical mortality failure could occur due to such things as age, wear and tear, environmental factors, accidental damage or operator error.

Regarding the *Functional Obsolescence* EOL cause, two types of EOL can be identified, related to external factors, and they are the following:

- End of service level life: it occurs when the expected levels of service have changed since the acquisition of the asset such that the performance requirements now imposed on the asset exceed the functional design capabilities of the asset. This could be due to changes in regulations (such as effluent, air, water quality or safety requirements) or due to changes in customer needs.

- End of capacity life: it occurs when the volume of demand placed on an asset exceeds its design capability.

Regarding the *Economic Obsolescence* EOL cause, one type of EOL can be identified, and it is:

- End of financial life: it occurs when an asset ceases to be the lowest cost alternative to satisfy a specified level of performance or service level, i.e. when the cost to sustain required performance from an asset under current O&M practices exceeds that of feasible alternatives (where the amortized cost to acquire plus the costs to operate and maintain a new or renewed asset is less than the operation and maintenance of the existing asset). This type of EOL is often driven by outdated technology or design.

Regarding the *DMSMS Obsolescence* EOL cause, one type of EOL can be identified, and it is:

- End of maintainable life: it occurs when it becomes inconvenient to maintain the asset either because the costs of spare parts are increasing or because spare parts are not available in the market. This type of EOL is strictly connected with the unavailability of spare parts which can be caused by the development of a new technology, by a supplier's bankruptcy or by the supplier's decision, e.g. not to produce anymore the parts. This type of EOL is also connected with the End of financial life since it can be related to an increase in the costs of operating the asset as a consequence.

The different EOL types have to be considered to estimate RUL through a complete evaluation, and it is needed that the asset managers identify which type of EOL will likely rise first. In fact, while all five causes are at work on an asset at all times, only one type of EOL is expected to be the most imminent in time. By this perspective, RUL is defined as the lowest expected life for a selected asset given its operating environment where that life is derived from a determination of the most imminent EOL type, i.e. minimum value among the different types of Time to EOL ($TT_{-x\ EOL}$):

$$RUL = Min\left(TT_{physical\ EOL},\ TT_{capacity\ EOL},\ TT_{service\ level\ EOL},\ TT_{financial\ EOL},\ TT_{maintainable\ EOL}\right)$$

$$(1)$$

Once the RUL is estimated, it enables to forecast the point in time at which the asset will likely end its life. This is relevant for asset strategy at its EOL: it can be used to evaluate the lead time to be considered as the horizon to define the EOL strategy to adopt (e.g. major repair, refurbishment or replacement).

Figure 1 summarizes the steps to estimate the RUL of an asset following the proposed model. The most challenging aspect is the way to estimate each $TT_{-x\ EOL}$ since, for each type of EOL, many factors may incur (see Table 1) and should be considered to estimate it in a quantitative way. Moreover, uncertainty must be managed. Therefore, adequate sources of information and knowledge should be available, to finally obtain the most likely EOL of the asset.

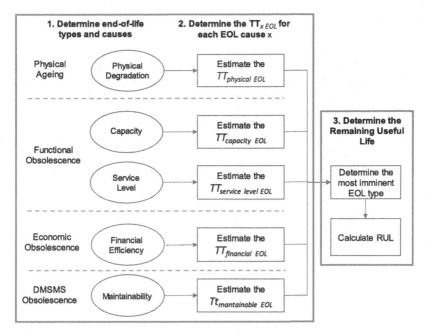

Fig. 1. Conceptual model for RUL estimation for informed decision-making

4 Conclusions

This paper discusses about the relevance of a comprehensive methodology to estimate the RUL of an industrial asset in order to support an informed decision-making process to manage its EOL phase. In fact, RUL estimation is a critical process for the definition of asset strategies at their EOL. Up to date, most RUL models that can be found in the literature focus on the physical ageing EOL cause. Very few attempts were made to estimate the impact of obsolescence on the assets EOL from a multi—disciplinary perspective. In this paper, different EOL causes are identified and classified and, based on that, a conceptual model is proposed including the EOL types that should be considered in a comprehensive methodology to be used for Asset Management decision making about the EOL of industrial assets. The proposed model can be used as a reference for future research on methods for decision and information support in EOL management of industrial assets. The model is intended to be conceptual and opens the path for future research on the methods that can be used for transferring the various aspects of End of life to Time to EOL and hence, to estimate the RUL through the proposed perspective. In fact, different methods can fit this model, either semi-quantitative like multi-criteria decision making supporting methods, either quantitative like the use of optimization based on consideration of optimal usage of the asset. The proposed model can be also useful in the context of Product-Service Systems both for the asset owner/operator and the OEMs [20] and future research on this aspect is envisioned by the authors.

References

1. IAM: Asset Management – an Anatomy (2012)
2. Budai, G., Dekker, R., Nicolai, R.P.: Maintenance and production: a review of planning models. In: Budai, G., Dekker, R., Nicolai, R.P. (eds.) Complex System Maintenance Handbook. Springer Series in Reliability Engineering, pp. 321–344. Springer, London (2008)
3. Ruitenburg, R.J., Braaksma, A.J.J., Van Dongen, L.A.M.: A multidisciplinary, expert-based approach for the identification of lifetime impacts in asset life cycle management. Procedia CIRP 22(1), 204–212 (2014)
4. CSN EN 16646: Maintenance within physical asset management. European Standard (2014)
5. Amadi-Echendu, J.E., Brown, K.: Definitions, Concepts and Scope of Engineering Asset Management (2010)
6. Shafiee, M., Animah, I.: Life extension decision making of safety critical systems: an overview. J. Loss Prev. Process Ind. 47, 174–188 (2017)
7. Oil&Gas-UK: Guidance on the Management of Ageing and Life Extension for UKCS Oil and Gas Installations, 1 (2012)
8. Vaidya, P., Rausand, M.: Remaining useful life, technical health, and life extension. Proc. Inst. Mech. Eng. Part O J. Risk Reliab. 225(2), 219–231 (2011)
9. Jardine A.K.S., Tsang, A.H.C.: Maintenance, replacement and reliability: theory and applications, Boca Raton (2006)
10. Si, X.-S., Wang, W., Hu, C.-H., Zhou, D.-H.: Remaining useful life estimation – a review on the statistical data driven approaches. Eur. J. Oper. Res. 213(1), 1–14 (2011)
11. Barreca, S.L., Kateregga, K.A.: Technology Life-Cycles and Technological Obsolescence. BCRI Inc., Birmingham (2000)
12. Lomakin, M.I., Murav'ev, A.V.: Managing the process of re-engineering of information systems based on integrated monitoring of obsolescence. Meas. Tech. 58(10), 1102–1106 (2016)
13. Guillén, A.J., Crespo, A., Macchi, M., Gómez, J.: on the role of prognostics and health management in advanced maintenance systems. Prod. Plan. Contr. 27(12), 991–1004 (2016)
14. Sobral, J., Guedes, S.C.: Preventive maintenance of critical assets based on degradation mechanisms and failure forecast. IFAC-PapersOnLine 49(28), 97–102 (2016)
15. Chen, X., Yu, J., Tang, D., Wang, Y.: Remaining useful life prognostic estimation for aircraft subsystems or components: a review. In: IEEE 2011 10th International Conference on Electronic Measurement and Instruments, pp. 94–98 (2011)
16. Okoh, C., Roy, R., Mehnen, J., Redding, L.: Overview of remaining useful life prediction techniques in through-life engineering services. Proc. CIRP 16, 158–163 (2014)
17. Animah, I., Shafiee, M.: Condition assessment, remaining useful life prediction and life extension decision making for offshore oil and gas assets. J. Loss Prev. Process Ind. 53, 1–12 (2016)
18. Wang, H.-K., Haynes, R., Huang, H.-Z., Dong, L., Atluri, S.N.: The use of high-performance fatigue mechanics and the extended Kalman/Particle Filters, for diagnostics and prognostics of aircraft structures. CMES: Comput. Model. Eng. Sci. 105(1), 1–24 (2015)
19. Wang, X., Rabiei, M., Hurtado, J., Modarres, M., Hoffman, P.: A probabilistic-based airframe integrity management model. Reliab. Eng. Syst. Saf. 94(5), 932–941 (2009)
20. West, S., Wuest, T.: A strategy for midlife upgrades to provide value for both the equipment operator and the supplier. In: Spring Servitization Conference (SSC 2017) (2017)

Heat Recovery Unit Failure Detection in Air Handling Unit

Manik Madhikermi[1(✉)], Narges Yousefnezhad[1], and Kary Främling[1,2]

[1] School of Science, Aalto University, P.O. Box 15400, 00076 Aalto, Espoo, Finland
{manik.madhikermi,narges.yousefnezhad}@aalto.fi
[2] Department of Computing Science, Umeå university, Umeå, Sweden
kary.framling@umu.se

Abstract. Maintenance is a complicated task that encompasses various activities including fault detection, fault diagnosis, and fault reparation. The advancement of Computer Aided Engineering (CAE) has increased challenges in maintenance as modern assets have became complex mixes of systems and sub systems with complex interaction. Among maintenance activities, fault diagnosis is particularly cumbersome as the reason of failures on the system is often neither obvious in terms of their source nor unique. Early detection and diagnosis of such faults is turning to one of the key requirements for economical and functional asset efficiency. Several methods have been investigated to detect machine faults for a number of years that are relevant for many application domains. In this paper, we present the process history-based method adopting nominal efficiency of Air Handling Unit (AHU) to detect heat recovery failure using Principle Component Analysis (PCA) in combination of the logistic regression method.

Keywords: Fault detection · Fault diagnosis · FDD
Logistic regression · PCA · Air handling unit · Heat recovery unit

1 Introduction

Air Handling Unit (AHU) is an integral functionality of any modern buildings that contributes to the well-being of its occupants. As energy prices sore up, operating these devices become costly. As a result of rising energy prices along with environmental concerns, building owners have become more and more interested in reducing the energy consumption of their buildings. In modern AHU, it is common to have Heat Recovery Units (HRU), especially in countries with cold climate like Finland. HRU helps to reduce energy consumption by extracting heat from waste air and employing it to heat the supply air.

Advancement in Computer Aided Engineering (CAE), manufacturing companies are producing complex AHUs with capabilities in computing, sensing, and actuating. Using these capabilities, maintenance of AHU is even more challenging as this equipment became a complex combination of systems and subsystems

© IFIP International Federation for Information Processing 2018
Published by Springer Nature Switzerland AG 2018. All Rights Reserved
I. Moon et al. (Eds.): APMS 2018, IFIP AICT 536, pp. 343–350, 2018.
https://doi.org/10.1007/978-3-319-99707-0_43

with complex interactions. Fault diagnosis is considered a complicated maintenance activity since there might be multiple reasons behind each failure and the
failure reasons are also often ambiguous in terms of their sources. By identifying
and diagnosing the faults to be repaired, building owners can benefit by reducing
energy consumption and improving operational performance. However, no matter how reliable the products (or equipment) are, they tend to deteriorate over
time and also occasionally fail due to real-world operating conditions under various degrees of stress. In order to make such assets economically and functionally
efficient, it is necessary to detect and diagnose such failures at early stages. Several failure detection techniques have been developed to detect different kinds
of failure such as cooling coil subsystem and sensor faults, as seen in literature
in Sect. 2. In this paper, we propose a process history-based method to detect
HRU failure following the generic principal of nominal efficiency. The novelty of
the proposed methodology is application of nominal efficiency to detect faulty
HRU hitherto unseen in the literature. The theoretical background and proposed
methodology are detailed in Sects. 3 and 4, respectively.

2 Fault Diagnosis in Air Handling Unit

Fault detection and diagnosis is a well-researched area. Several researchers have
examined and identified different techniques to detect and diagnose fault condition in AHU. Typically, these techniques have been broadly classified into
three categories [1]: quantitative model-based methods, qualitative model-based
methods, and process history-based methods. These methods belong to the same
generic class—data-driven methods. However, in general, extensive prior knowledge is required to apply quantitative and qualitative model-based methods.
They are also often device-specific and are difficult to be applied to other devices.
Therefore, process history-based methods are at the core of this study. Process
history-based methods are also known as black box models. Unlike model-based
methods that are based on physical principles, these methods are based on actual
data generated during usage. The relation between input and output are discovered during the learning phase of these methods. Several researchers have worked
on such methods for diagnosing failures on AHU.

Lee et al. [2] presented Artificial Neural Network (ANN) backward propagation method to detect the fault of cooling coil subsystem of AHU based on
dominant residual signature. Similarly, in 2012, Yonghua et al. [3] proposed a
method for diagnosing the sensor failure based on the regression neural network
with a combination of wavelet and fractal dimensions. In this method, three-
level wavelet analysis was applied to decompose the sensor measurement data,
and then each frequency band was extracted and used to depict the failure characteristics of the sensors which were then used to train the neural network to
diagnose sensor faults. Du et al. [4] introduced a detection method for drifting
sensor biases in an AHU using a combination of wavelet analysis along with the
neural network. PCA is another technique widely used to detect and diagnose
faults in AHU. For instance, Wang et al. [5] could present a PCA-based strategy to detect and diagnose sensor faults in the AHU. This strategy employed

squared prediction error as indices of fault detection and the Q-contribution plot to isolate faults in AHU. Similarly, Du et al. [6] employed PCA with Joint Angle Analysis (JAA) to detect and diagnose both fixed and drifting sensor biases in Variable Air Volume (VAV) systems. The Squared Prediction Error (SPE) plot based on PCA was used to detect the sensor fixed and drifting biases. Then, the JAA plot instead of conventional contribution plot was applied to diagnose the faults. Chen et al. [7] also proposed a method using PCA for detecting and identifying sensor bias, drifting, and failure in AHU. In his method, PCA is employed to identify correlation of measured variables in the heating/cooling billing system and reduce the dimension of measured data. SPE statistic was used to detect sensor faults in the system. Xiao et al. in [8] presented an expert-based multivariate coupling method by enhancing capabilities of PCA-based method in fault diagnosis by applying expert knowledge about the process concerned. This method develops unique patterns of typical sensor faults by analysing the physical cause-effect relations among variables, which are compared to fault symptoms reflected by the residual vectors of the PCA models with fault patterns to isolate sensor faults. Similarly, several other researchers such as Yan et al. [9] and Liang et al. [10] used model-based SVM to detect faulty condition in an AHU.

3   Theoretical Background

3.1   System Description

A typical AHU with a balanced air ventilation system, as shown in Fig. 1, includes the HRU, supply fan, extract fan, air filters, controllers, and sensors. The system circulates the fresh air from outside to the building by utilising two fans (supply side and extract side) and two ducts (fresh air supply and exhaust vents). Fresh air supply and exhaust vents can be installed in every room, but typically this system is designed to supply fresh air to bedrooms and living rooms, where occupants spend their most of time. A filter is employed to remove dust and pollen from outside air before pushing it into the house. The system also extracts air from rooms where moisture and pollutants are most often generated (e.g. kitchen and bathroom). One of the major components of the AHU is HRU, which is used to decrease energy consumption. The principle behind the HRU is to extract heat from extracted air (before it is removed as waste air) from the house and adopt it to heat the fresh air that is entering the house. HRU is a fundamental component of AHU which helps to recycle extracted heat. The main controllers in the system include the supply air temperature controller, which adjusts the temperature of the supply air entering house and Hru_output, which controls the heat recovery rate. In order to measure HRU efficiency, five temperature sensors are installed in AHU, which measure the temperature of circulating air at different parts of AHU (Table 1). In addition to sensor data, the HRU control state, supply fan speed, and extract fan speed can be collected from the system.

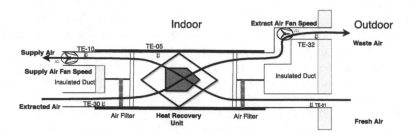

Fig. 1. Schematic diagram of air handling unit

Table 1. Air handling unit sensor details

Sensor name	Sensor description
T_{frs} (TE-01)	Temperature of fresh incoming air
T_{supH} (TE-05)	Temperature of supply air after HRU
T_{sup} (TE-10)	Temperature of supply air
T_{ext} (TE-30)	Temperature of extracted air
T_{wst} (TE-35)	Temperature of waste air
Hru_Output	State of HRU output controller
Sup_Fan_Speed	The current effective supply-side fan speed
Ext_Fan_Speed	The current effective extract-side fan speed

3.2   Principal Component Analysis (PCA)

Principal Component Analysis (PCA) is the statistical procedure mostly used for dimension reduction and orthogonal decomposition. A Principal Component (PC) is defined as a linear transformation of the original variables which are normally correlated, into a new set uncorrelated variables. If there are n observations with p variables, then the number of distinct PCs is $\min(n-1, p)$. This transformation is defined in such a way that the first PC has the largest possible variance, and each succeeding component in turn has the highest variance possible under the constraint that it is orthogonal to the preceding components. The first PC Y_1 is given by the linear combination of the variables $X_1, \ldots, X_p$ as seen in (1). Collectively, all of these transformations of the original variables to the PCs are given by (2). The rows of matrix A (loading matrix) are called the eigenvectors of matrix S_x derived from (3), the variance-covariance matrix of the original data. The elements of an eigenvector are the weights a_{ij}, known as loadings. The elements in the diagonal of matrix S_y (see (4)), the variance-covariance matrix of the PC, are known as the eigenvalues.

$$Y_1 = a_{11}X_1 + a_{12}X_2 + a_{13}X_3 + \ldots a_{1p}X_p = A_1 X_1 \tag{1}$$

$$Y = AX \tag{2}$$

$$S_x = \frac{X^T X}{(n-1)} \tag{3}$$

$$S_y = A S_x A^T \tag{4}$$

3.3   Logistic Regression (LR)

Logistic Regression (LR) was developed by David Cox in 1958 [11]. It is a statistical method to determine dependent dichotomous variables using one or more independent variables. It is a variation of ordinary regression method that is used when the dependent variable is dichotomous. The goal of LR is to find the best fitting model to describe the relationship between the dichotomous characteristic of the dependent variable and a set of independent variables [12]. LR generates the coefficients, standard errors, and significance levels of a formula to predict a logit transformation of the probability of presence of the characteristic of interest. The logit model of multiple LRs can be shown in (5) and the logit transformation is defined as the logged odds shown in (6).

$$logit(p) = b_o + b_1 X_1 + b_2 X_2 + b_3 X_4 + ... b_k X_k = ln(\frac{p}{1-p}) \tag{5}$$

$$odds = \frac{probability\,of\,presence\,of\,characteristic}{probability\,of\,absence\,of\,characteristic} = \frac{p}{1-p} \tag{6}$$

4   Methodology

The method of detection and diagnosis for HRU failure is shown in Fig. 2. This binary classification method is based on the nominal efficiency of AHU to detect failure of HRU using PCA and LR methods. The rationale behind such methodology is that there is a high number of dimensions and detecting faulty operation (HRU Failure) from normal operation is quite difficult. The nominal efficiency (μ_{nom}) of the HRU is a function of air temperatures in AHU, which is yielded by (7) [13]. To develop this model, the dataset contains 26700 instances of data with two types of information collected using architecture and interfaces described in [14] during "Normal" and "No Heat Recovery"states. One information regards the class label (i.e. "Normal": 18882 instances and "No Heat Recovery": 7818 instances) and the other contains different kinds of air temperature circulated by AHU (detailed in Table 1). Since Hru_output is set to "max" (i.e. it is a constant parameter) and HRU nominal efficiency is a function of air temperatures associated with AHU (see (7)), only temperature dimensions are considered in this analysis. In other words, these dimensions can be combined to measure the performance of HRU.

$$\mu_{nom} = \frac{T_{ext} - T_{wst}}{T_{ext} - T_{frs}} \tag{7}$$

As the first step, the collected dataset is split into "Train"and "Test" datasets. Second, the PCA model, based on nominal efficiency, is set up through the training dataset with five temperature dimensions. The corresponding matrix is denoted as:

$$X_{26700 \times 5} = \begin{pmatrix} T^1_{supH} & T^1_{frs} & T^1_{sup} & T^1_{ext} & T^1_{wst} \\ T^2_{supH} & T^2_{frs} & T^2_{sup} & T^2_{ext} & T^2_{wst} \\ \vdots & \vdots & \vdots & \vdots & \vdots \\ T^n_{supH} & T^n_{frs} & T^n_{sup} & T^n_{ext} & T^n_{wst} \end{pmatrix}$$

The primary PCs are identified based on eigenvalue which is calculated based on variance-covariance matrix of PCs (4). Eigenvector is applied to project "Train" and "Test" datasets into principle component subspace. The eigenvectors are computed based on the variance-covariance matrix of original data from (3). Since dependent variables (i.e. class) are dichotomous in nature, these data are adopted to train the LR model by merging the associated class with each instance of data. The LR model is trained with different cutoff values in order to improve its predictive performance. The cutoff value is defined as the threshold probability of whether a sample belongs to a particular class or not. Once the optimal cutoff value is selected, the "Test" datasets are used to evaluate the model performance. Different performance metrics and results are presented in the next chapter.

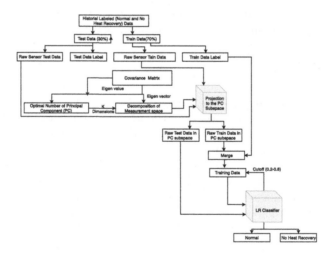

Fig. 2. Heat recovery failure detection methodology

5   Result and Conclusion

As stated, detection and diagnosis of HRU failure is performed by adopting the "Test" dataset. The accuracy of our proposed method for "Train" and "Test" at different cutoff values is shown in Fig. 3 (a). It is clearly seen that the model accuracy is increased from 95% to 97% when the cutoff is changed from 0.3 to 0.8. Detailed performance metrics such as methods Sensitivity and Specificity are presented in Table 2. It is worth noticing that the change in the cutoff value has effects on Sensitivity and Specificity.

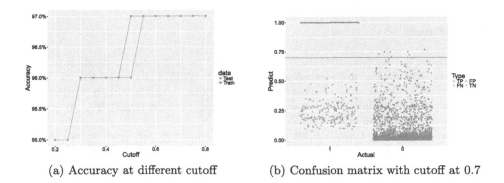

(a) Accuracy at different cutoff   (b) Confusion matrix with cutoff at 0.7

Fig. 3. Model results

Figure 3 (b) depicts the tradeoff between False Negative (FN) and False Positive (FP) for choosing a reasonable cutoff. If we increase the cutoff value, the number of True Negative (TN) increases and the number of True Positive (TP) decreases or in other words, if we increase the cutoff value, the number of FP is lowered, while the number of FN rises. Our main objective is to effectively detect HRU failure for immediate maintenance, thus we chose 0.7 as the final cutoff where the faulty HRU can be detected with 97% accuracy while maintaining perfect specificity of 100% along with 91% sensitivity.

Table 2. Performance metrics of proposed methodology to detect HRU failure

Cut-off value	Accuracy	Sensitivity	Specificity
0.2	0.95	0.95	0.95
0.4	0.96	0.91	0.98
0.6	0.97	0.91	0.99
0.8	0.97	0.91	1.00

In this paper, we presented the application of PCA in combination with LR to detect the HRU failure of the AHU based on nominal efficiency parameters. This method helps quick detection of faulty HRU, which aids to take quick action (such as maintenance of AHU) to avoid further damage. If such faults remain undetected, it may result in unwanted consequences such as wasting of energy and establishing an unhealthy living space. This study focuses on fault detection of a single component (i.e. HRU) of AHU using nominal efficiency. In future, we plan to extend this study to detect other types of fault that might occur in other components during the operation of AHU.

Acknowledgment. The research leading to this publication is supported by the European Union's Horizon 2020 research and innovation programme (grant 688203) and Academy of Finland (Open Messaging Interface; grant 296096).

References

1. Katipamula, S., Brambley, M.R.: Methods for fault detection, diagnostics, and prognostics for building systems-a review, part I. HVAC R Res. **11**(1), 3–25 (2005)
2. Lee, W.Y., House, J.M., Park, C., Kelly, G.E.: Fault diagnosis of an air-handling unit using artificial neural networks. Trans. Am. Soc. Heating Refrig. Air Cond. Eng. **102**, 540–549 (1996)
3. Zhu, Y., Jin, X., Du, Z.: Fault diagnosis for sensors in air handling unit based on neural network pre-processed by wavelet and fractal. Energy Build. **44**, 7–16 (2012)
4. Du, Z., Jin, X., Yang, Y.: Wavelet neural network-based fault diagnosis in air-handling units. HVAC R Research **14**(6), 959–973 (2008)
5. Wang, S., Xiao, F.: Detection and diagnosis of AHU sensor faults using principal component analysis method. Energy Convers. Manag. **45**(17), 2667–2686 (2004)
6. Du, Z., Jin, X., Wu, L.: Fault detection and diagnosis based on improved PCA with JAA method in VAV systems. Build. Environ. **42**(9), 3221–3232 (2007)
7. Chen, Y., Lan, L.: Fault detection, diagnosis and data recovery for a real building heating/cooling billing system. Energy Conver. Manag. **51**(5), 1015–1024 (2010)
8. Xiao, F., Wang, S., Xu, X., Ge, G.: An isolation enhanced pca method with expert-based multivariate decoupling for sensor FDD in air-conditioning systems. Appl. Therm. Eng. **29**(4), 712–722 (2009)
9. Yan, K., Shen, W., Mulumba, T., Afshari, A.: ARX model based fault detection and diagnosis for chillers using support vector machines. Energy Build. **81**, 287–295 (2014)
10. Liang, J., Du, R.: Model-based fault detection and diagnosis of HVAC systems using support vector machine method. Int. J. Refrig. **30**(6), 1104–1114 (2007)
11. Cox, D.R.: The regression analysis of binary sequences. J. Royal Stat. Soc. Ser. B (Methodol.) **20**(2), 215–242 (1958)
12. Yan, J., Lee, J.: Degradation assessment and fault modes classification using logistic regression. J. Manuf. Sci. Eng. **127**(4), 912–914 (2005)
13. Roulet, C.A., Heidt, F., Foradini, F., Pibiri, M.C.: Real heat recovery with air handling units. Energy Build. **33**(5), 495–502 (2001)
14. Främling, K., Holmström, J., Loukkola, J., Nyman, J., Kaustell, A.: Sustainable PLM through intelligent products. Eng. Appl. Artif. Intell. **26**(2), 789–799 (2013)

Industry 4.0 - Smart Factory

Towards Digital Lean Cyber-Physical Production Systems: Industry 4.0 Technologies as Enablers of Leaner Production

Daryl Powell[1]([✉]), David Romero[2], Paolo Gaiardelli[3], Chiara Cimini[3], and Sergio Cavalieri[3]

[1] Norwegian University of Science and Technology, Trondheim, Norway
daryl.j.powell@ntnu.no
[2] Tecnológico de Monterrey, Monterrey, Mexico
david.romero.diaz@gmail.com
[3] University of Bergamo, Bergamo, Italy
{paolo.gaiardelli,chiara.cimini,
sergio.cavalieri}@unibg.it

Abstract. Lean production emerged as an alternative way of organizing and managing manufacturing operations in the 1990s, following the close examination and promotion of the Toyota Production System as a better way of working. More recently, the advent of Industry 4.0 and its associated Cyber-Physical Production Systems has materialised novel ways of optimizing production operations. Though it is generally agreed that manufacturers should not neglect one of the aforementioned approaches in favour of the other, there remains uncertainty as to how Industry 4.0 technologies should be integrated with existing lean production programmes. This paper presents an overview of both approaches, and provides an exploratory study that examines the integration of Lean and Industry 4.0 in practice.

Keywords: Lean production · Digital lean manufacturing · Cyber-Physical Production Systems · Industry 4.0.

1 Introduction

With the purpose of increasing operational performance and competitive advantage, many manufacturing firms have developed and deployed *lean production programmes* with the ultimate goal of creating a culture of continuous improvement [1–3]. Recent developments towards the Fourth Industrial Revolution, or Industry 4.0 [4], now encourage manufacturers to look at/into advanced technologies, automation and digitalization as the next digital frontier for improving the *lean enterprise* and achieving operational excellence.

Toyota Motor Co. is recognized as the pioneer of what has become widely known as *lean production* – with the company's corporate philosophy: "The Toyota Way", firmly underpinning its operations model, "The Toyota Production System (TPS)". Sugimori et al. [5] was one of the first to describe the infamous TPS, describing it as two fundamental sub-systems: the Just-in-Time (JIT) system and Respect-for-Human

I. Moon et al. (Eds.): APMS 2018, IFIP AICT 536, pp. 353–362, 2018.
https://doi.org/10.1007/978-3-319-99707-0_44

(RFH) system. Furthermore, a description of the principles and behaviours underlying the "Toyota Way" philosophy can be found in Liker [6], who describes Toyota's managerial approach as a set of 14 core "lean" principles. Some examples of these are *"use only reliable, thoroughly tested technology that serves your people and processes"* and *"make decisions slowly by consensus, thoroughly considering all options"*. These specific examples support the notion that Toyota, as a company, is a slow adopter of new technology. However, one should by no means dismiss the new opportunities presented by emerging Industry 4.0 technologies [7] for further improvement and/or innovation of manufacturing operations. [8–13] present limited insight into the co-existence of both approaches, focusing on smart products, smart machines and augmented operators and cyber-physical JIT delivery respectively. This paper aims to offer a more holistic account of lean production and Industry 4.0 integration, presenting actual industrial Proofs-of-Concept (PoCs) from an explorative case study.

Table 1. Recent literature addressing Industry 4.0 and lean production integration

Paper	Main contribution
[8]	This research work explores the co-existence of lean production and Industry 4.0 in a smart network of machines, products, components, properties, individuals and ICT systems of a smart factory value chain
[9]	This research work explores the Industry 4.0 offers as an estimated benefit for stabilizing lean processes with Industry 4.0 applications, and presents an Industry 4.0 impact matrix on lean production systems as a useable evaluation framework. The matrix considers elements of lean production systems with Industry 4.0 technologies and gives a first estimation of impact
[10]	This research work conducts an analysis of interdependencies between the principles of lean production systems and Industry 4.0 based on the structuring of Industry 4.0 elements into technologies, systems and process-related characteristics of 260 use cases of applied Industry 4.0 technologies in the German industry
[11]	This research work describes the co-existence of lean production and the implementation of Industry 4.0 technologies in a plot that it is drawn between drawbacks of lean and advantages of Industry 4.0
[12]	This research work examines the relationship between lean production practices and the implementation of Industry 4.0 in Brazilian manufacturing companies based on a survey to 110 companies of different sizes and sectors, at different stages of lean production implementation. Findings indicate that lean production practices are positively associated with Industry 4.0 technologies and their concurrent implementation leads to larger performance improvements. Furthermore, the contextual variables investigated do matter to this association, although not all aspects matter to the same extent and effect
[13]	This research work emphasizes the interaction between lean production and Industry 4.0 and proposes a methodology, which provides guidance for Industry 4.0 under lean production environment. Moreover, Industry 4.0 technologies and automation oriented lean production applications are also included
[14]	This research work describes a practical approach to interlink the lean method world with the cyber-physical world. It combines the lean methodological approach with the Industry 4.0 technology-driven vision

Table 2. Industry 4.0 technologies: commonly accepted definitions [7, 15]

Autonomous robots	The evolution of traditional robots opened the way to new collaborative solutions of robots (i.e. CoBots) that are able to work together with humans in a safe and efficient way. Human-Robot Interaction (HRI) can enable high productivity [16]. Moreover, embedded intelligence in robots can allow them to learn from human activities, improving their autonomy and flexibility
Simulation	Simulation tools can be widely used along all the value chain, starting from product design to operations management. Modelling and simulation tools are crucial for the development of digital engineering and virtual representation of products and processes, in order to identify in advance potential issues, avoiding cost and resource wastes in production [7]
Horizontal- and vertical integration	As defined in [17], horizontal integration refers to the creation of a global value network through the integration and the optimization of the flow of information and goods between company, suppliers and customers. The vertical integration, instead, is the integration of functions and departments of different hierarchical levels of the single company creating consistent flow of information and data
Industrial Internet of Things	Industrial Internet of Things (IIoT) enables the communication among every device inside and outside the factory. [18] defines IIoT as a "non-deterministic and open-network in which auto organized intelligent entities and virtual objects will be interoperable and able to act independently pursuing their own objectives (or shared ones) dependently on the context, circumstances or environments"
Cybersecurity	In order to guarantee the security of the large amount of data collected, stored and communicated via IIoT, cybersecurity strategies are one of the major challenges for the future [19]
Cloud computing	Cloud computing is related to the ICT-infrastructure that allows the ubiquitous access to data from different devices. Cloud can be treated as a service and support collaborative design, distributed manufacturing, collecting innovation, data mining, semantic web-technology and virtualization [20]
Additive manufacturing	Additive Manufacturing (AM) consists in a cluster of technologies that enable to produce small batches of products with a high degree of customization by adding rather than removing material from a solid block. The reduction of scrap material, a quicker market launch due to the rapid prototyping, a higher production flexibility and a lower number of required tools are the major advantages of this technology [21]
Augmented reality	Augmented reality (AR) allows the creation of a virtual environment in which humans can interact with machines using devices able to recreate the workspace. Interesting applications of AR are related to the training of workers and the support in manual production activities [22]
Big data analytics	Big data is characterized by volume, variety and velocity (the 3Vs), and it requires new techniques of data processing and analysis [23]. Visualization, analysis and sharing of data are at the basis of analytics that support decision-making and improve self-awareness and self-maintenance of the machines

2   Literature Review

This paper addresses the co-existence and potential integration mechanisms of *Industry 4.0 technologies* [7] with existing industrial lean production programmes. This section provides an overview of relevant literature combining the fields of lean production and Industry 4.0 (see Table 1).

From literature, it is clear that *Lean Production* and *Industry 4.0* can be successfully integrated. In fact, it appears that the realization of lean principles can be further enhanced from the support offered by innovative digital technologies and cyber-physical systems, which are the major contributions introduced by Industry 4.0. Moreover, it is possible to consider the two approaches as complementary, because the strength of *lean manufacturing* that is based on participation and standardized practices can take advantage of the collaborative environment and structured data collection and analysis offered by Industrial Internet of Things (IIoT) and Cyber-Physical System (CPS) technologies. In order to better clarify the opportunities of combining lean production and Industry 4.0, we first provide a brief description of the technologies that are considered as the pillars of Industry 4.0 (see Table 2) [7, 15].

3   Research Methodology

A single, exploratory case study approach is adopted, taking insight into the current *Industry 4.0 programme (i.e. Digital Transformation)* of an Italian producer of automotive parts and brake systems: Brembo S.p.A. – http://www.brembo.com/en.

A selection of ongoing Industry 4.0 initiatives and *Proof-of-Concept (PoC) pilots* were discussed with representatives of the company, including: Operations Director, Industry 4.0 Programme Manager, Continuous Improvement Manager, Shift Supervisors and Lean-Lab Coordinator.

By providing valuable insights from this explorative use case, this paper is able to highlight several ways in which Industry 4.0 technologies can be used to support and further develop a company's existing lean production programme.

4   Exploratory Case Description

With approximately 9,000 employees distributed across 15 countries and 19 industrial production sites, the company achieved a turnover of €2.2 billion in 2016, following successive growth year-on-year in the previous ten years. Delivering OEM and after-sales parts and systems to the major automotive companies, and with an existing *lean production programme* (since 2008) and lean production *"office"* with eight *lean-labs* worldwide, the company demonstrates a clear understanding of its value propositions and major value streams.

The company established an Industry 4.0 committee and programme management team in 2015, and currently has more than 50 on-going Industry 4.0 initiatives, managed by "Digital Factory Project Managers" and executed by "Digital Factory Engineers". The "Digital Personnel" works closely with personnel from the lean programme office to ensure the alignment of both initiatives. An example of this collaboration is the company's lean-lab, which has recently been redesigned to cater for two core types of *lean-training,* the first for the more traditional human-intensive areas such as manual production and assembly operations, and the second for more Industry 4.0 relevant, capital-intensive areas like robotics and automation.

This investigation focuses on the company's activities in the machining and assembly operations in the Italian factory, which has approximate 1,000 employees and produces in excess of 2,600,000 units per year. The factory has approximate 50 CNC machines and 50 assembly lines. We examine the company's Industry 4.0 proofs-of-concept in machining, powder coating, and quality control operations, in addition to the company's proof-of-concept for data management and e-learning. All four proofs-of-concept have been envisioned as strategic applications of Industry 4.0 technologies (see Table 3), and have been constructed as experiments implemented in the Brembo Factory located at Curno in Bergamo, Italy, in order to promote organizational learning. It is anticipated that the outcome and results of each PoC will be evaluated based on its contribution towards the company's Profit and Loss (P&L) statement and strictly measured in terms of Return on Investment (ROI) before successful implementations are eventually rolled-out worldwide.

Table 3. Strategic applications of Industry 4.0 technologies at Brembo S.p.A.

Proof-of concept	Autonomous robots	Simulation	Horizontal- and vertical integration	Industrial internet of things	Cybersecurity	Cloud computing	Additive manufacturing	Augmented reality	Big data analytics
PoC A	●		●	●					●
PoC B	●		●	●					
PoC C			●	●					●
PoC D		●	●	●				●	●

4.1 PoC A: Machine Cell Automation and Smart Tool Management

Adoption of Industry 4.0 technologies [7] for automating machining and assembly operations shows extensive signs of promise for supporting both JIT and RFH systems. Applying a modular concept for machine cell automation based on standardisation and further machine improvement has resulted in improved performance in Quality, Cost, Delivery and Safety (QCDS) metrics. Robots are used for picking and visual inspection of raw metal-castings, as well as deburring. In-line quality inspection is also automated with use of integrated Coordinate Measuring Machines (CMMs), which has allowed 1/11 parts to be inspected instead of 1/100 without increasing the cycle time.

In the future, the company will realise autonomous set-ups – but today continue to work with the lean practice of Single Minute Exchange of Dies (SMED) for continuous reduction of set-up time. All machine cells are also AGV-ready (Automated Guided Vehicle), suggesting a move towards unmanned logistics in the near future.

In addition to the efforts in machine cell automation, the company has also marked every tool with a unique identification, allowing for "Smart Tool Management".

A database tracks the location and remaining lifecycle of each tool in real-time and generates a tool-wear forecast, allowing for more effective and efficient planning for tool replenishment in the tool preparation area. A production supervisor suggested, *"Operators in the tool preparation area are now able to prepare replenishment before the machine operator realizes the need"*.

The movement toward "Smart Tool Management" has resulted in at least 30% reduction in tool-inventory – and has an even greater effect with regard to tooling cost because of moving from fixed lifetime tool changes to condition-based tool-life.

4.2   PoC B: Powder Coating Automation

Following an analysis of the causes for poor quality in the powder coating department, the company realised that the masking and unmasking operations were responsible for generating a significant amount of defects. For this reason, the masking and unmasking operations have been fully automated using a high degree of innovation and robotics – resulting in significant cost savings and a swift return on investment. The process must manage 600,000 pieces per year, with a range of 15 colours and 30 different geometries, requiring 12 set-ups per day.

4.3   PoC C: Quality Control Digitization

The company has developed a "Smart Quality" concept, which involves the digitization of all dimensional quality control checks. This system also involves a 300-parameter in-line paperless CMM check. Before, there was a significant paper trail with regard to recording results of quality control, and the quality engineers/supervisors would have to physically search for documents from machine-to-machine. Now, the shift supervisor has a single access point (his/her PC) and receives a push warning via an on-line app on his smartphone should the pre-determined workflow render this necessary. This resulted in a paperless Quality Management System – with real-time Statistical Process Control (SPC), real-time process capability analysis, and real-time alerts in case of defect-detection.

4.4   PoC D: Data Management and e-Learning

The final proof-of-concept is the "Analytics Platform", which connects all production lines on a common database and web-platform. A set of touch-screen dashboards situated directly in the shopfloor provides an instantaneous overview of the state of operations throughout the factory, in real-time. This allows for full real-time traceability per unit (including individual parameter information and test results), as well as web-analytics for shopfloor monitoring of both product and process. Because the information is collected and stored on a web-platform, workflows can be defined for various events, such as the detection of defects. For example, when a defective part is detected, automation in the production cell will remove the part from the line, and the system can deploy a push-message to the shift supervisor's smartphone. This system secures a fast flow of information to key stakeholders, offers broad visibility and provides a hierarchical escalation mechanism in the event of unplanned event detection. Most importantly in terms of the "Respect-for-Human" principle, the web-platform guides the production operator to act in the correct way.

The system also supports an *e-learning mechanism* for operator training. Digital instructions are provided across several levels – including safety, machine installation/ set-up procedures, machine maintenance procedures, and assembly procedures/work instructions. Each instruction is based on a 3D digital model of the machine, – and provides an animation that allows the operator to repeat the instruction in real life, acting as a self-assessment and test of understanding. This system was used to accelerate the opening and ramp-up of production in the company's new factory in Mexico.

5 Findings and Discussion

Findings were organized according to the seminal work of Sugimori et al. [4], that describes TPS as the aggregation of two sub-systems: Just-in-Time (and Jidoka[1]) system and Respect-for Human System. These sub-systems are subsequently broken down into a sub-set of actions, as shown in Table 4. It is also suggested the enabling functionality of Industry 4.0 technologies for the various "lean production constructs" – on which the lean production programmes of many companies are based.

Table 4. Enabling functionality of Industry 4.0 technologies

Lean production constructs	Enabling functionality of Industry 4.0 technologies
Just-in-Time (and Jidoka*) System	
Reduction of cost through elimination of waste	Data analytics provides new and novel ways in which to plan and execute production and coordinate the upstream supply chain to support the Just-in-Time principle
Withdrawal by subsequent processes	Enterprise-wide connectivity via a data analytics platform provides instantaneous real-time signalling for production and replenishment
One piece production and conveyance	Shopfloor web-analytics tools provide suitable infrastructure for "track-and-trace" of one-piece-flow, providing real-time information and visibility of production operations AGVs provide functionality for automatic conveyance of single units of work without the need for building physical conveyor lines
Levelling of production	Through the adoption of smart automation technologies and big data analytics, *Heijunka* becomes much more realizable, allowing for greater optimization capabilities of planning and scheduling tasks, which are now supported by real-time monitoring of tasks execution. This enables minor adjustments to the schedule given unexpected or unforeseen events in production as well as turbulence in actual demand versus forecast

(continued)

---

[1] The term 'Jidoka' as used at Toyota means, "To make the equipment or operation stop whenever an abnormal or defective condition arises".

Table 4. (*continued*)

Lean production constructs	Enabling functionality of Industry 4.0 technologies
Elimination of waste from overproducing	Data analytics platform provides real-time remote visibility of the status of operations, preventing and highlighting potential causes of waste such as overproduction
Control of abnormality	In-line testing of products using automated coordinate measuring machines (CMMs) and subsequent digitalization of quality control documentation eliminates the burden of the previous, heavily manual quality assurance tasks The intelligent automation of manual tasks that produce high-level of scrap and rework leads to significant cost savings
Respect-for-Human System	
Full utilization of workers capabilities	The e-learning platform offers a digital environment (i.e. a virtual lab) for the operators training, which is combined with a physical laboratory for accelerating the upskilling and reskilling of operators
Elimination of waste movement by workers	AGVs are supporting operators in reducing their unnecessary (non-added value) movements within the shopfloor
Considerations to workers safety	The e-learning platform primary goal is to ensure that all operators and associates are well trained in safety procedures in their respective operations areas, not just on physical production and assembly procedures
Self-display of workers' ability	The combination of the e-learning platform and the physical laboratory supports a competency-based training programme that allows assessing the operators and associates in his/her knowledge and skills, on applying such knowledge, for conducting different work instructions

6 Conclusions and Further Research

This paper provides a review of lean production in light of emerging Industry 4.0 technologies. Specific reflections have been made regarding the potential of these technologies to build on existing lean production programmes and serve as enablers for leaner production. In particular, an exploratory case study of an Italian company operating in the automotive sector has been discussed in order to present some evidence from an actual implementation of Industry 4.0 proofs of concept. From the case study, the potential of digital technologies to support key lean manufacturing constructs emerged. This paper aimed at providing the foundations for further research, which can be towards a more detailed framework for "Digital Lean" or "Lean 4.0".

In terms of limitations of the work, we recognize that from a single case study, it is difficult to make accurate theoretical generalisations of the topic(s) under exploration. Therefore, further case studies are required to verify the significance of the propositions presented in this paper. In addition, as the results presented in this paper cannot be considered exhaustive and fully extendible to all possible industrial realities, further development will include the enlargement of the sample considering different sectors in the B2B and B2C contexts, as well as extending the analysis to different tiers of the supply chain.

Acknowledgements. The authors would like to acknowledge the support of Brembo S.p.A. Industry 4.0 Programme Management Team for sharing their vision on *"lean production, digital lean manufacturing* and *Industry 4.0"*, as well as the Research Council of Norway for financial support in the project "Lean Management". Thanks also to the University of Bergamo, Italy – CELS Research Group – for the invitation as visiting research professors (non-Italian co-authors).

References

1. Netland, T.H.: Exploring the phenomenon of company-specific production systems: one-best-way or own-best-way? Int. J. Prod. Res. **51**, 1084–1097 (2013)
2. Womack, J.P., Jones, D.T.: Lean Thinking: Banish Waste and Create Wealth in Your Corporation. Free Press, New York (1996)
3. Netland, T.H., Powell, D.J.: A lean world. In: Netland, T.H., Powell, D.J. (eds.) The Routledge Companion to Lean Management. Routledge, New York (2017)
4. Thoben, K.-D., Wiesner, S., Wuest, T.: "Industrie 4.0" and smart manufacturing – a review of research issues and application examples. Int. J. Autom. Technol. **11**(1), 4–16 (2017)
5. Sugimori, Y., Kusunoki, K., Cho, F., Uchikawa, S.: Toyota production system and kanban system – materialization of just-in-time and respect-for-Human system. Int. J. Prod. Res. **15** (6), 553–564 (1997)
6. Liker, J.K.: The Toyota Way: 14 Management Principles from the World's Greatest Manufacturer. McGraw-Hill, New York (2004)
7. Mittal, S., Khan, M.A., Romero, D., Wuest, T.: Smart manufacturing: characteristics, technologies and enabling factors. J. Eng. Manufact. (2017)
8. Mrugalska, B., Wyrwicka, M.K.: Towards lean production in Industry 4.0. Procedia Eng. **182**, 466–473 (2017)
9. Wagner, T., Herrmann, C., Thiede, S.: Industry 4.0 impacts on lean production systems. Procedia CIRP **63**, 125–131 (2017)
10. Dombrowski, U., Richter, T., Krenkel, P.: Interdependencies of Industrie 4.0 & lean production systems: a use cases analysis. Procedia Manufact. **11**, 1061–1068 (2017)
11. Karamveer, S.: Lean production in the era of Industry 4.0. In: Logistics Engineering and Technologies Group - Working Paper Series 2017-005 (2017). SSRN: https://ssrn.com/abstract=3068847 or http://dx.doi.org/10.2139/ssrn.3068847
12. Tortorella, G.L., Fettermann, D.: Implementation of Industry 4.0 and lean production in Brazilian manufacturing companies. Int. J. Prod. Res. (2017). http://doi.org/10.1080/00207543.2017.1391420
13. Satoglu, S., Ustundag, A., Cevikcan, E., Durmusoglu, M.B.: Lean production systems for Industry 4.0. Industry 4.0: Managing The Digital Transformation. SSAM, pp. 43–59. Springer, Cham (2018). https://doi.org/10.1007/978-3-319-57870-5_3
14. Prinz, C., Kreggenfeld, N., Kuhlenkötter, B.: Lean meets Industrie 4.0 – a practical approach to interlink the method world and cyber-physical world. Procedia Manufact. **23**, 21–26 (2018)
15. Rüßmann, M., et al.: Industry 4.0: the future of productivity and growth in manufacturing industries. http://www.inovasyon.org/pdf/bcg.perspectives_Industry.4.0_2015.pdf

16. Thoben, K.D., Wiesner, S., Wuest, T.: "Industrie 4.0" and smart manufacturing: a review of research issues and application examples. Int. J. Autom. Technol. **11**(1), 4–19, https://doi.org/10.20965/ijat.2017.p0004
17. Kagermann, H., Wahlster, W., Helbig, J.: Recommendations for implementing the strategic initiative Industrie 4.0 - securing the future of german manufacturing industry. Acatech, National Academy of Science and Engineering (2013)
18. Zuehlke, D.: Smart factory: towards a factory-of-things. Annu. Rev. Control **34**, 129–138 (2010)
19. Khan, A., Turowski, K.: A survey of current challenges in manufacturing industry and preparation for Industry 4.0. In: Abraham, A., Kovalev, S., Tarassov, V., Snášel, V. (eds.) Proceedings of the First International Scientific Conference "Intelligent Information Technologies for Industry" (IITI'16). AISC, vol. 450, pp. 15–26. Springer, Cham (2016). https://doi.org/10.1007/978-3-319-33609-1_2
20. Park, H.S.: From automation to autonomy - a new trend for smart manufacturing. In: Katalinic, B., Tekic, Z. (eds.), DAAAM International Scientific Book (2013)
21. Bhatia, U.: 3D printing technology. Int. J. Eng. Scie. **3**, 327–330 (2015)
22. Syberfeldt, A., Holm, M., Danielsson, O., Wang, L., Brewster, R.L.: Support systems on the industrial shop-floors of the future operators' perspective on augmented reality. Procedia CIRP **44**, 108–113 (2016)
23. Kang, H.S., et al.: Smart manufacturing: past research, present findings, and future directions. Int. J. Precis. Eng. Manufact.-GrePoen Technol. **3**(1), 111–128 (2016)

Big Data Analytics for Logistics and Distributions Using Blockchain

Benedito Cristiano A. Petroni[1]($\boxtimes$) (iD),
Elisângela Mônaco de Moraes[2] (iD), and Rodrigo Franco Gonçalves[2] (iD)

[1] Universidade Paulista, Jundiaí, Brazil
benedito.petroni@docente.unip.br
[2] Universidade Paulista, São Paulo, Brazil
elisangela.moraes@docente.unip.br,
rofranco212@gmail.com

Abstract. The volume of data generated is increasing. Companies capture large amounts of bytes of information about customers, vendors, products, sensory components, and especially their manufacturing operations. However, important problems, such as the Supply Chain Management processes, present difficulties regarding the security, integrity and validity of information generated in different databases. Blockchain technology presents itself as a disruptive process control technology where, through Smart Contracts, it provides transaction reliability and assures the parties involved that its purpose is strictly adhered to. Meanwhile, Big Data is offered as a solution to analyze all the information originated from the operations generated. In this article, as a contribution, possibilities of information generation will be presented, with the interaction of Blockchain, Cyber Physical Systems, Internet of Things technologies in function of the Supply Chain Management processes, so that they can later be analyzed through Big Data, giving users better controls and decision management in favor of improving their business.

Keywords: Blockchain · Big data analytics · Cyber Physical Systems

1 Introduction

Industry 4.0 has led to several discussions concerning industrial processes, services and controls, and is considered a new potential to affect industries in their business, projects, manufacturing and deliveries [2]. Logistic management, a major part of an SCM system, has over the years ceased to be a simple activity of conferring and transporting products between companies, becoming a complex structure of collaborative analysis among all departments involved in its process. Despite logistical management, numerous devices and sources generate every second a large amount of unstructured data in the most diverse databases for its operations, and in addition, the amount of data created each year is much larger than the one created previously [1], thus requiring an attention to an effective analysis of its contents, mainly regarding security, integrity and reliability of the information. New technologies have promoted research that seeks to transform SCM processes and bring about changes in the way we produce, market,

I. Moon et al. (Eds.): APMS 2018, IFIP AICT 536, pp. 363–369, 2018.
https://doi.org/10.1007/978-3-319-99707-0_45

buy, consume and mainly how we control our goods and products, [4], allowing analyzes of the necessary information that can corroborate in future decisions. There is currently a growing interest in companies to gain insight into the origins of consumer products and the demand for sustainable transportation, where products are imported and sold with the limited information of a label addressing the origins of manufacturing or production [5]. It was traumatic for many managers not to have real-time information on product supply in the gondola or delivered to an end consumer through channels specifically set up for such purpose as e-commerce [19]. The SCM processes represent all the links involved in the creation and distribution of goods, from raw materials to the finished product that will be in the consumer's possession. Supply chains can presently span hundreds of stages and dozens of geographic locations, making it very difficult to trace events or investigate incidents [6], thereby ensuring the safety and integrity of the entire process. Modern vehicles in intelligent transport systems can communicate with each other, as well as roadside infrastructure units, in order to increase transport efficiency and road safety. For example, there are techniques to alert drivers in advance about traffic incidents and to help them avoid congestion, [7]. On the other hand, threats to such systems may limit the benefits of such technologies, as they rely on technological environment boundaries, poorly connected and mainly centralized information. In this article, issues such as the decentralization of information regarding SCM, security and integrity will be provoked by the proposal of integration of technologies such as blockchain, Internet of Things- IoT, Cyber Physical Systems- CPS and Big Data in its favor.

2   The Literature

2.1   Industry 4.0

The evolutionary process of the German initiative, the Industry 4.0 is bringing to organizations new perspectives and improvements in services and production methods.

After two or three years of discussions on Industry 4.0, many companies currently have smart factory active designs projects [10]. The Industry 4.0 focused on the establishment of manufacturing components and intelligent objects as well as new production processes [11]. Technologies that capture the exclusive needs of factory floor users will decide the future of this new world, and yet with the possibility of deeply analyzing all user information.

Internet of Things – IoT
In organizations, the Internet is allowing a huge leap in productivity because the emerging IoT is the first intelligent infrastructure revolution in history, wich will connect every device, company, residence, vehicle in an intelligent network in an Internet as a network communications, energy, transport, and all of them are embedded in a single operating system [12].

Although recent developments have made IoT a reality, there are a number of challenges to be addressed in order to realize its full potential and to bring tangible benefits to society, the environment, the economy and individual citizens. [13] Divices will be able to make intelligent decisions, so that many workflows will be automated in new ways, resulting in significant time and cost savings [19]. However, true revolution can happen if all devices are controlled for example by a platform, in the blockchain case, where instead of direct user control it can be using Smart Contracts, with the conditions and rules of the business that must be dealt with before a transaction is included in the blockchain [19]. Therefore, IoT and Industry 4.0 are being increasingly interlinked in order to create more opportunities by providing new types of services and business models of value chain interaction [16].

Cyber Physical Systems
The multiple and distinct behavioral modalities with the interaction of one with the other object in a multitude of ways that change according to the application context [18], are part of the context of the CPS. Its operation involves different fields, such as network of distributed sensors, intelligent network [15], medical monitoring, process control system among others, being the communication capacity between virtual objects and processes with real object and production processes one of the most important of this technology [14]. In CPS all computing and communication layers are incorporated in all types of objects and structures in the physical environment [13]. According to [17], the CPS consider in their implementation a combination of embedded hardware and software technologies, and in its interaction with the physical world it is considered the use of large monitoring structures composed of networks of sensors and actuators for the execution of the tasks.

2.2 Blockchain

Blockchain technology fits into a relatively new research area in different forms and possibilities for applications in a new generation of transactional applications. Its popularization is directly linked as being the basis of the model of the Bitcoin crip-tosmoeda created by Satoshi Nakamoto, where in a file somewhere represents the transactions carried out and registered.

Each blockchain, such as that used by the Bitcoin cryptomoeda is distributed, running on volunteer computers around the world, so there is no central database, [3]. In essence, the blockchain is a public book that contains information about each transaction made within a system known as peer to peer, or point to point [5].

Blockchain is an incorruptible ledger that stores all data exchanges that occur on the network, built over time and maintained by the collaboration of all of us in a particular network - the user can be sure that the data is accurate [3].

This technology is being viewed as a revolutionary solution, addressing modern technology concerns such as decentralization, trust, identity, data ownership, and datadriven decisions. While actively looking for the best way to store, organize and process Big Data, block-chain technology provides a significant contribution, [20]. A certain process, being manufacturing or logistic, will have its registration in a block of records and from this, all its contents will become immutable, that is, no more changes are allowed, thus guaranteeing security and integrity in the process.

In this process, all network members can check all their transactions in the block chain, if no consensus on the validity of the new block is reached, the block will be rejected [6]. Similarly, if there is a consensus that the transactions in the block are valid, the block is added to the chain, thereby forming a specific blockchain that can be applied to SCM and logistics processes.

The guarantee of this process is in the generation of a cryptographic file -hash (file that ensures the integrity of the information) that is generated for each block, which contains not only transaction logs, but also the hash of the previous block, creating a block interdependence linking to a chain thus forming the blockchain.

2.3   Big Data Analytics

Big Data is the term that describes a huge, structured, and generally unstructured set of data that requires real-time analysis, independent of the storage medium. An important aspect in this respect is the efficient management of business processes and risks [8].

Some concepts are common in terms of definitions found as: Reference to large volumes of data (>1 bytes Peta), different types of structured and unstructured data, faster generation of data through different sources and new ways of storing, process, analyze, visualize and integrate the data. There are a variety of definitions found on Big Data and similarly it repeats with respect to Big Data techniques and technologies.

There are some Big Data aspects [15]: Big Data Analysis techniques, Big Data techniques and visualization. Organizations in many industrial sectors can take advantage of these important data to facilitate the discovery of new ideas, with the effective use of large data, has the potential to transform economies, providing a new wave of productivity growth involving SCM, as well as the controls of distribution and delivery to the end user.

3   Blockchain Applied in SCM and Logistics Processes

As a critical issue, one of the elements of the SCM, logistics is treated taking into account some security risks and with a direct tendency to centralize its operations, because even with supporting technologies - IoT, CPS and cloud computing, these can temporarily be unavailable due to attacks, performance limitations and even improper operations, [9].

With this, blockchain technology presents itself as a great potential to improve processes and security models in the SCM area, especially in logistics. However, according to some recent studies on trends in SCM and logistics, the blockchain is known only by some experts and still in a small number by those who search for implementation plans [14]. This technology enables intelligent devices with relevant information from manufacturing processes to be programmed for actions in defined circumstances without risk of error and tampering, by implementing Smart Contracts. With this, it is possible to record all transactions that occurred with Smart Contracts in its ledger of all SCM processes. Still, according to the inherent characteristics of blockchain technology, such as the execution of Smart Contracts, it is not only possible to apply it to productive processes, but also to consider how these technologies are applied in practically the entire production chain, as can be observed in Fig. 1 below:

As explained in Fig. 1, all SCM processes such as manufacturing, storage and distribution are executed according to certain rules derived from the Smart Contracts

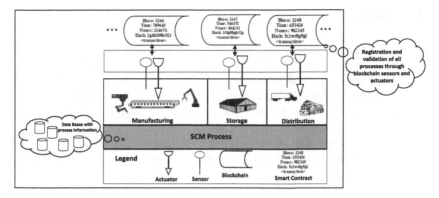

Fig. 1. Blockchain applied to SCM processes

executed on the blockchain platform, on all the validation processes by the network members and the interaction with IoT and CPS components.

Thus, blockchain aggregates all computing resources in the resolution of previously intractable problems, for example, more refined real-time transport management and control [9], with the integrity and security of the information until the final consumer with its records. In this way, it is possible to efficiently guarantee the security, integrity and authenticity of the entire block chain.

Once all the information has been stored, they can be analyzed in detail through Big Data. In Fig. 2 below, all the information from the validated and secure SCM processes by the blockchain platform as well as all the processes that have been stored in several databases, using Big Data technology, analysis of information can be carried out in order to obtain knowledge stored in the aid in the decision-making process.

Fig. 2. Analysis of information by big data.

Thus, through Big Data, all the information contained in the databases can be processed and analyzed, but remains private or semi-private [15], and through mass collaboration and cryptographic mechanisms all information has become secure, in this way, all the records of the blocks contained in the blockchain platform will be analyzed.

4   Conclusion

With the article information, it has been shown that, with the advent experienced by IoT and elements of the CPS everything can be registered, informed and stored. Blockchain technology through Smart Contracts and encrypted storage can authenticate all stages of the production and logistics chain, that is, from the manufacturing process, from the modes of transport to the final consumer, registering in the books with security, transparency and integrity.

Big Data technology will be able through its analytical techniques provide valueadded to companies with knowledge for improvements in manufacturing processes and future decision making. As blockchain technology is still considered embryonic, new studies are sure to emerge to further explore possibilities and needs with further detailed investigations of the applications.

References

1. Ayed, A.B., Halima, M.B., Alimi, A.M.: Big data analytics for logistics and transportation. In: 2015 4th International Conference on Advanced Logistics and Transport (ICALT), Valenciennes, pp. 311–316 (2015)
2. Hofmann, E., Rüsch, M.: Industry 4.0 and the current status as well as future prospects on logistics. Comput. Ind. **89**, 23–34 (2017)
3. Tapscott, D., Tapscott, A.: Blockchain: como a tecnologia por trás do Bitcoin está mudando o dinheiro, os negócios e o mundo. SENAI-SP Editora, São Paulo (2016)
4. Dickson, B.: Blockchain has the potential to revolutionize the supply chain. Techcrunch (2016). https://techcrunch.com/2016/11/24/. Accessed 12 Nov 2017
5. Sadouskaya, K.: Adoption of blockchain technology in supply chain and logistics. Unpublished Bachelor's thesis, Kymenlaakso University of Applied Sciences, Kotka, Finland (2017)
6. Petersen, M., Hackius, N.: Mapping the sea of opportunities: blockchain in supply chain and logistics (2017)
7. Ming, L., Zhao, G., Huang, M., Kuang, X., Li, H., Zhang, M.: Security analysis of intelligent transportation systems based on simulation data. In: 2018 1st International Conference on Data Intelligence and Security (ICDIS), South Padre Island, TX, USA, pp. 184–187 (2018)
8. Niesen, T., et al.: towards an integrative big data analysis framework for data-driven risk management in industry 4.0. In: 49th Hawaii International Conference System Sciences (HICSS) (2016)
9. Yuan, Y., Wang, F.Y.: Towards blockchain-based intelligent transportation systems. In: IEEE 19th International Conference on 2016 Intelligent Transportation Systems (ITSC), Rio de Janeiro, pp. 2663–2668 (2016)
10. Zezulka, F., Marcon, P., Vesely, I., Sajdl, O.: Industry 4.0 - an introduction in then phenomenon. IFAC-Papers OnLine **49**(25), 8–12 (2016)
11. Rajkumar, R., Lee, I., Sha, L. Stankovic, J.: Cyber-physical systems: the next computing revolution. In: Design Automation Conference, Anaheim, CA, vol. 7, pp. 731–736 (2010)
12. Yang, L.: Industry 4.0: a survey on technologies, applications and open research issues. J. Ind. Inf. Integr. **6**, 1–10 (2017)

13. Scheuermann, C., Verclas, S., Bruegge, B.: Agile factory - an example of an industry 4.0 manufacturing process. In: IEEE 3rd International Conference on Cyber-Physical Systems, Networks, and Applications, Hong Kong, pp. 43–47 (2015)
14. Kersten, W., Seiter, M., von See, B., Hackius, N., Maurer, T.: Trends and strategies in logistics and supply chain management – digital transformation opportunities. DVV Media Group, Hamburg (2017)
15. Manyika, J., et al.: Big Data: the Next Frontier for Innovation, Competition, and Productivity. McKinsey Global Institute, New York City (2011)
16. Bertaglia, P.: Desmistificando a manufatura 4.0, disponível em. https://www.linkedin.com/pulse/desmistificando-manufatura-40-paulo-roberto-bertaglia/. Accessed 02 Apr 2018
17. Garay, J.R.B.: CyberSens: uma plataforma para redes de sensores em sistemas ciber-físicos. 2012. Tese (Doutorado em Sistemas Eletrônicos) - Escola Politécnica, Universidade de São Paulo, São Paulo (2012)
18. Khaitan, S.K., et al.: Design techniques and applications of cyber physical systems: a survey. IEEE Syst. J. 9(2), 350–365 (2014)
19. Herrera-Joancomartí, J., Pérez-Solà, C.: Privacy in bitcoin transactions: new challenges from blockchain scalability solutions. In: Torra, V., Narukawa, Y., Navarro-Arribas, G., Yañez, C. (eds.) MDAI 2016. LNCS (LNAI), vol. 9880, pp. 26–44. Springer, Cham (2016). https://doi.org/10.1007/978-3-319-45656-0_3
20. Karafiloski, E., Mishev, A.: Blockchain solutions for big data challenges: a literature review. In: IEEE EUROCON 17th International Conference on 2017 Smart Technologies, Ohrid, pp. 763–768 (2017)

A Study on the Integrations of Products and Manufacturing Engineering Using Sensors and IoT

Dahye Hwang⬡ and Sang Do Noh(✉)

Sungkyunkwan University, Suwon, South Korea
sdnoh@skku.edu

Abstract. In recent years, studies on smart manufacturing using ICT have increased significantly, and much attention has been paid to CPSs, IoT, sensors, industrial data analytics and artificial intelligence as core technologies. In particular, CPSs are one of the core technical elements in smart manufacturing, and a variety of studies on CPSs are underway. Accordingly, a large number of technical developments and applications related to intelligent and autonomous facilities, the prediction of factory operation, machinery factories and quality issues and proactive responses have been made. The new paradigm in smart manufacturing can be defined as customisation, connectivity and collaboration. The goal of smart manufacturing is to perform right decision making autonomously by connecting intelligent design, the efficient manufacture of customized products in accordance with the analysis of market and customer demand, sales, the user's use and the service sector. The paper presents the concept, framework, configuration and implementation method of a CPS that is performed intelligently based on the IoT, smart sensors and industrial data analytics from manufacturing preparation and execution.

Keywords: Cyber-physical system (CPS) · Internet of Things (IoT)
Data analytics · Smart manufacturing · Smart product

1 Introduction

Much attention has been paid to information and communication technology (ICT), which has been consistently advanced through the Fourth Industrial Revolution. Accordingly, cyber–physical systems (CPSs), big data, artificial intelligence and the Internet of Things (IoT) have arisen as the main technical innovations, which have changed existing industrial structures significantly [1].

Industrie 4.0 is a strategy to respond to changes in society, technology, the economy, the ecosystem and politics faced by manufacturing in Germany with all efforts by combining ICT capabilities. In South Korea, the Manufacturing Innovation 3.0 program has been underway nationally to build and promote smart factories where all business processes of planning, design, production, distribution and sales are integrated through ICT and custom-tailored products are manufactured with minimum cost and time [2]. A CPS is a core technology that configures and operates smart manufacturing. It is a system that monitors, controls and regulates changes in physical environments

© IFIP International Federation for Information Processing 2018
Published by Springer Nature Switzerland AG 2018. All Rights Reserved
I. Moon et al. (Eds.): APMS 2018, IFIP AICT 536, pp. 370–377, 2018.
https://doi.org/10.1007/978-3-319-99707-0_46

autonomously by combining network technology with physical elements, such as machinery and workers as well as the surrounding environments [3]. Accordingly, a variety of studies have been conducted on CPSs. In particular, a large number of technical developments and applications related to intelligent and autonomous facilities, the prediction of factory operation, machinery factory and quality issues and proactive responses have been made [4].

The study presents a framework that connects and integrates product and manufacturing through the CPS and introduces an application of the framework to a cosmetic company.

2 Research Background

Smart manufacturing refers to a strategy that combines technologies complexly to connect and operate facilities and factories and operation systems with the CPS concept for personalized manufacturing and operation excellence. Personalized manufacturing aims to provide customized products and services for operation and individual consumers collaboratively by combining facilities, factories and manufacturing information with services. Operation excellence aims to improve productivity, quality and cost via optimal responses to various changes rapidly and intelligently by sharing and utilizing production information and knowledge in real time.

Smart manufacturing can be defined as customization, connectivity and collaboration [5]. Customization represents an attribute of the market or demand side, while connectivity and collaboration represent attributes of the supply side as all components and participants in the value chain are connected in real time.

2.1 Product Design in Smart Manufacturing

Research on Smart Product Design. Urtnasan et al. proposed a parameter derivation methodology to derive the design parameters of a universal ear shell for a hearing aid [6]. To reduce its time and cost, their study derived design parameters, and customer usage and product information are inputted, and machine learning algorithm is applied to train the data.

Harvard business review defined three elements that compose smart products [7]. A smart connected product consists of physical components, smart components, such as sensors and a data repository, and connectivity components. The capabilities of a smart connected product can be defined by four improvements: monitoring, the autonomous function control, optimization and diagnosing.

A study called 'Designing for Manufacturing's Internet of Things' introduces a case study on a smart connected product with the example of Dell [8]. Dell attached radio frequency identification (RFID) tags to each of 4,000 trays in the manufacturing process to deliver assembly information on the products. Through this process, Dell was able to collect various pieces of information more accurately than before. However, limitations such as lack of standardization of networks and interfaces, the security of information leakage, the deficient infrastructure of IoT equipment exist.

A study entitled 'Enabling process mining on sensor data from smart products' applied a process-mining methodology to Philips smart feeding bottles to discover patterns of customer behavior and propose a utilization measure [9]. In the above study, the log data of users were analyzed via the process-mining methodology using temperature and gyro sensors in the smart feeding bottle, thereby dividing the process into preparation, feeding and aftercare and deriving detailed sub-processes. This process is expected to help product designers as well as provide services to customers.

Three Main Elements of Smart Products. In smart manufacturing, as the advancement of ICT has influenced products, control software has been embedded in products, which have become more intelligent and serviceable through connection to the Internet [10].

Smart products can record information, such as the movement paths of products, using embedded RFID and classify product information through unique product ID. Furthermore, smart products influence the surrounding environment and monitor the surrounding environment and their own status to exchange information. Smart connected products can be divided into three components: physical components, such as product design; smart components, such as sensors and embedded software; and connectivity components for external services for products and data exchange.

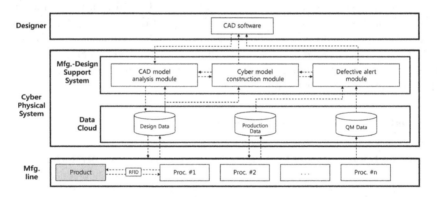

Fig. 1. Framework for product–manufacturing integration

3   Integration Framework for Product and Manufacturing

The paper aims to design a CPS where the product and manufacturing are integrated. The basic framework including the product and manufacturing phase in the product life cycle is shown in Fig. 1, which shows activities and data flows. Collected information is stored on a cloud in an integrated manner, and feedback is given to product designers utilizing the collected information.

In the paper, it is assumed that facilities with IoT sensors and database storing product process information are supporting data delivery among products, production facilities and processes through product IDs. In the production phase of the framework, a module that utilizes data obtained during manufacturing is designed, which plays a role as middleware that connects designers and production data.

In the production phase, design information and production information on the product is shared and utilized through communications between the product and facility using RFID [11]. To achieve this, an RFID tag is attached to every product while an RFID reader is attached to every facility. The production information on the product is fetched from the cloud by tagging the RFID of the product via the facility reader before the process starts. After a process is performed according to the production information, actual processing information and quality information on the product are collected and transferred to the cloud again.

If a defect occurs during the process, the ID of the defect is tagged, and up-to-date cumulative actual processing information is delivered to the data analysis module. In the data analysis module, the defect process and causes of the defect are analyzed and the analysis results are stored in the cloud. The cumulative past production data are utilized in a new product design of a similar product line to give feedback to designers about the defect rate, defect causes and ratio of past products for each process.

Flexible manufacturing can be achieved as the production schedule is changed according to production information on the product whenever the processes are performed in contrast to the traditional manufacturing, where processes are performed according to the pre-determined production schedule.

3.1   Data Model Structure and Database

Figure 2 shows data schema of product-manufacturing integrations. It contains basic information on the product, such as the product no. (product ID), location of the CAD file, drawing information and product classification, and the parameter information contains design parameters and parameter values used in CAD modelling. In addition, data on defects, such as the presence of defects, defect causes and defect processes that occurred during the production phase, are added with regard to products in past production. The product data stored in the cloud (or database) are collected constantly in the design and production phases and transferred to the cyber model construction module whenever design verification is requested.

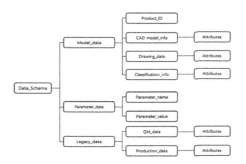

Fig. 2. Data schema of product–manufacturing integrations

3.2   Cyber Model Construction Module

The cyber model construction module plays a role in extracting design data, such as parameters from the CAD model of a new product and creating and transferring integrated data. Product ID, product classification information and parameter information, which are set in the CAD model, are verified in the cyber model construction module. The module also includes an extraction process of matching values in the CAD model. The integrated model data, including a matched value with each of the information names, are automatically created, and the created integrated model data are transferred to the database.

3.3   CAD Model Analysis Module

The CAD model analysis module receives design data for past and new products from the cloud and predicts a design. The past and new product design data are compared based on the production data and quality management data of past manufactured products, thereby predicting expected problems or the defect rate during production.

3.4   Defect Alert Module

The defect alert module displays the design variables, and defects are predicted in the CAD model analysis module in the CAD model run by the CAD program. Furthermore, defect rates, parameters and its values with which defects are predicted are displayed on the dashboard in real time so that designers can easily utilize the product design feedback from manufacturing phase.

4   Implementation

Bottles of cosmetics from a Korean company were employed as a verification target of the study. A product is designed by utilizing the designer dashboard based on the past production data in a similar product line followed by the manufacturing phase in the factory. An RFID is attached to each of the products and facilities. The facility tags the ID of the RFID card attached to the product for communication between the facility and product. Once the facility reads the product ID, manufacturing information on the product (input solution, input amount, and processing temperature etc.) is read from the cloud, and a process is performed according to the manufacturing information. Once the process is complete, the facility collects data (actual input solution, actual input amount, and actual processing temperature) performed in the actual process and transfers the information to the cloud. If a defect occurs during the process, the defect information is delivered to the data analysis module, in which defect occurrence processes and causes are analyzed. The analyzed data are delivered to the cloud, and the data are utilized to provide feedback on the expected defective part in the design screen using a dashboard form when similar products are manufactured next. The design dashboard displays a defect rate per process, defect causes and ratio and analyses 3D

CAD files of the newly designed product, thereby displaying the part where the defect is expected by highlighting it (Fig. 3).

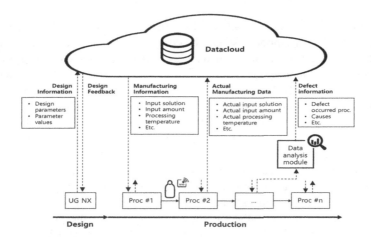

Fig. 3. Virtual smart factory based on real cosmetic factory

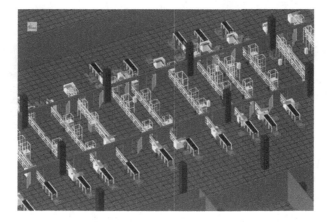

Fig. 4. Scenario of implementation

Assuming that the environment was a smart factory where a real-time data collection system was applied, the testbed was constructed to verify the concept based on scenarios. To prove the concept and need for the product CPS proposed in the present study, the proof of concept (POC) was conducted with cosmetics products (lotion, balancer and cream) and filling and assembly processes in a Korean company.

Since the POC could not be performed at a factory where CPS was implemented perfectly, the testbed was constructed by linking a physical testbed that replaces the actual processes with a virtual factory implemented by QUEST simulation. In the physical testbed, the RFID attached to the product is tagged to the RFID reader of the process facilities and the information of the product is read. Virtual testbed was implemented through the QUEST, which simulated a real factory as shown in Fig. 4. The study employed an RFID reader and Mifare1K Card from Advanced Card Systems.

For CAD software, NX 7.5 was used. First, a CAD file of the target product is fetched from the design support system. The design parameters and values in the model inputted through the CAD analysis module are extracted. Once the data extraction of the CAD model is complete, the past design data collected previously are fetched, and then the data of the newly designed CAD model and old data are compared. After each piece of design information is inputted into the cyber model construction module, the extracted data and related data of the past product data are matched, and the defect rate is predicted through the matched information. If the analysis prediction result is available, the defect rate is displayed on the dashboard through the defect alert module, and the predicted defect location is visualized by highlighting in NX. The manufacturing starts after re-designing to complete a design without the predicted defect.

Facilities in the filling process and lid assembly process which are the target processes, are displayed in the testbed as shown in Fig. 5, and the products are moved along the conveyor at a lot-level. Here, when the RFID reader attached to the facility tags the RFID card in the product, QUEST responds by running the production simulation.

Fig. 5. Physical testbed with cosmetic products, RFID tags and readers and virtual testbed implemented by QUEST

Data collected during production simulation is stored in the database for use in the next product design. When a designer inputs a newly designed CAD model file, the CAD model analysis module is executed to extract the data in the corresponding model. Cyber model construction is the key activity that the overall Virtual testbed implemented by QUEST defect rate is generated through product data analysis in the same product line based on the new product data, and parameters where the defect is predicted are provided. Defect prediction results, in which the parameter variables where an abnormality occurs, predicted defect code and cause of the defect are displayed on the dashboard once the part that corresponds to the parameter where the defect is predicted is selected on NX screen. Using the displayed information, the designer can understand and improve the design more intuitively by comparing the current design parameters and defect rates and ones changed.

5 Conclusion

The present study proposed a framework by which smart manufacturing can be implemented utilizing big data collected via the IoT during manufacturing and verified the study content through a case study on a cosmetics company in Korea. However, it has a limitation regarding data items since it employs the manufacturing information of the virtual smart factory.

In future research, user's use history which is gathered by smart product itself, may be employed to product design phase to reflect user needs. So far, it has been hard to gather accurate use history from user since qualitative or indirect methods were used for investigation of user experiences. Big data analytics based on real use history is quantitative and direct method, so it may offer a new point of view in product development.

On the other hand, extended data will be employed to increase the accuracy of the analysis results and a study on new product development other than similar product lines will be conducted through trend prediction using social network and factor analysis.

References

1. Lee, K., Lee, G., Song, B.: KEIT PD issue report. Trend of Smart Factory Technology, Korea Evaluation Institute of Industrial Technology, Cheonan (2015)
2. Hyundai Research Institute: Upgrading Manufacturing Industry U.S. Japan Germany Manufacturing Industry R&D policy trend and Implication. Hyundai Research Institute, Seoul (2014)
3. Sha, L., Gopalakrishnan, S., Liu, X., Wang, Q.: Cyber-physical systems: a new frontier. In: Machine Learning in Cyber Trust, pp. 3–13. Springer, Boston (2009). https://doi.org/10.1007/978-0-387-88735-7_1
4. Anderl, R., Picard, A., Albrecht, K.: Smart engineering for smart products. In: Abramovici, M., Stark, R. (eds.) Smart Product Engineering, pp. 1–10. LNPE. Springer, Heidelberg (2013). https://doi.org/10.1007/978-3-642-30817-8_1
5. Shin, D., Jeong, B., Bo, J.: Smart Manufacturing, 1st edn. Epress, Seoul (2017)
6. Urtnasan, E., Jeon, Y.-Y., Park, G.-S., Song, Y.-R., Lee, S.-M.: A study on design parameters for ready-made ear shell of hearing aids. Korean Inst. Electr. Eng. 60(5), 1055–1061 (2011)
7. Harvard Business Review. https://hbr.org/2014/11/how-smart-connected-products-are-transforming-competition. Accessed 06 Apr 2018
8. Cognizant: Designing for Manufacturing's 'Internet of Things'. Cognizant, US (2014)
9. Van Eck, M.L., Sidorova, N., Van der Aalst, W.M.P.: Enabling process mining on sensor data from smart products. In: 2016 IEEE Tenth International Conference on Research Challenges in Information Science, RCIS, pp. 1–12 (2016)
10. Kang, S., Jun, J., Kim, H., Jun, I.: A research on design-manufacturing-service interoperation architecture for managing lifecycle of smart-connected products. In: Korean Institute of Information Scientists and Engineers, pp. 638–641 (2015)
11. Han, C.: Constitution and Principle of RFID System, 1st edn. Microsoftware, Seoul (2006)

Towards a Platform for Smart Manufacturing Improvement Planning

SangSu Choi[1(✉)], Thorsten Wuest[2],
and Boonserm (Serm) Kulvatunyou[3]

[1] IGI, LLC, Clarksburg, MD 20871, USA
Sangsu.choi@igiamerica.com
[2] Industrial and Management Systems Engineering, West Virginia University,
Morgantown, WV 26506-6070, USA
thwuest@mail.wvu.edu
[3] Systems Integration Division, National Institute of Standards and Technology,
Gaithersburg, MD 20899-1070, USA
boonserm.kulvatunyou@nist.gov

Abstract. The manufacturing industry is transitioning towards smart manufacturing systems (SMS). Small and medium size manufacturers (SMMs) are particularly behind in this transition, plagued by lack of knowledge and resources. Several smart manufacturing capability assessment and maturity models exist to guide the transition. However, support for choosing the right assessment is lacking. This paper proposes a web-based, open source platform for smart manufacturing assessment to support SMMs in this transition. The platform allows for free self-assessments of the current maturity levels and developments of continuous improvement plans that are customized to the manufacturers' unique characteristics. The platform also allows for sourcing of third-party technologies and services relevant to the improvements. More importantly, it will learn, rate, and recommend improvements and services based on past data. The platform is designed to be extensible and scalable to ultimately serve manufacturing enterprises of all industries.

Keywords: Smart manufacturing · Smart factory · Industrie 4.0
Cyber-physical production system · Smart manufacturing assessment
Smart manufacturing readiness

1 Introduction

The world is moving towards the next industrial revolution where manufacturing enterprises are seeking for performance improvements through a new level of interconnectivity within their own production environments and value chains. The core of the current industrial revolution is the development of smart manufacturing systems (SMS). SMS are built on the intersection of cutting-edge Information Technology (IT) and Operation Technology (OT) such as Internet of Things (IoT), big data, cloud computing, machine learning, additive manufacturing, CNC machine tools, and collaborative robots [1, 2].

I. Moon et al. (Eds.): APMS 2018, IFIP AICT 536, pp. 378–385, 2018.
https://doi.org/10.1007/978-3-319-99707-0_47

A smart manufacturing system is ultimately realized by integrating several of these core technologies in a customized and value-adding way. SMS must be developed harmoniously based on a combination of IT/OT technologies that fit each individual company's unique manufacturing environment. A recent study by West Virginia University (WVU) [3] on Small and Medium-Size Manufacturers' (SMMs) smart manufacturing adoptions found that the vast majority of SMMs do not possess the required resources and are struggling in taking the critical first step of their own smart manufacturing journey. They need systematic assessment methodologies to better understand their needs and build a solid foundation for their own, value-adding SMS.

Several smart manufacturing and Industrie 4.0 manufacturing system assessment methods and capability maturity models are available. These methods and models evaluate a manufacturing enterprise from various perspectives with differing applicability to various sizes and maturity of the enterprise. There are also still limited wealth of information supporting the usages and derived values of these methods and models. Sorting through them will require expertise and resources SMMs typically lack. Using outside consultants can also be cost prohibitive and too risky for many SMMs.

This paper introduces a smart manufacturing improvement planning system that aims to systemize smart manufacturing consulting services, to be easily utilized by manufacturing companies. In the next section, related works are provided. Then, an overview of the platform is given, followed with discussion of the future work and finally conclusion.

2   Related Works

Over the past decade, frameworks or models for business and process maturity assessment have been developed within the manufacturing sector. Technology readiness level (TRL) [5] represents the maturity of a technology for commercial adoption. Similarly, manufacturing readiness level (MRL) [6] reflects the characteristics of manufacturing process technology. Supply chain readiness level (SCRL) [7] provides a way to assess the ability of the supply chain to operate and to achieve specific operational performance goals. It is associated with characteristics within fifteen categories that discretely provide an improvement roadmap for design and operation of a supply chain.

More recently as the new industrialization paradigms such as smart manufacturing and Industrie 4.0 have been developed, models for respective readiness and maturity assessments have also been proposed. Weber et al. [8] presented a model for data driven manufacturing in the context of Industrie 4.0 that consists of six maturity levels (0-Nonexistent IT Integration, 1-Data and System Integration, 2-Integration of Cross-Life-Cycle 3-Data and Service-Orientation, 4-Digital Twin, 5-Self-Optimizing Factory). Lee et al. [9] developed an assessment framework in the context of smart factory that consists of Leadership, Process, System and Automation, and Performance Criteria. In addition, they introduced the effects based on 20 case studies of South Korean SMEs.

Carolis et al. [10] introduced the Digital REadiness Assessment MaturitY (DREAMY) model that focuses more on the digitalization of an enterprise. It aims to assess a manufacturing enterprise readiness level for the digital transformation and to develop a roadmap for prioritizing investments. Smart manufacturing system readiness level (SMSRL) [4] was developed at the National Institute of Standards and Technology (NIST) as an index that measures a manufacturing company's readiness for improving manufacturing system performance using data intensive smart manufacturing technologies. It measures the readiness in four aspects including ICT, performance management, organization, and information connectivity. Li et al. [11] introduced an assessment model using MESA MOM Capability Maturity Model (CMM) [12] and suggested a way to reduce the time and resources consumption for applying the CMM to manufacturing enterprises by replacing the lengthy yes/no questionnaires with multiple-choice and providing various kinds of improvement strategies.

Although various smart manufacturing assessment models are being developed, their applicability issues remain, particularly regarding SMMs special requirements. SMMs typically need trainings to conduct assessments internally. Alternatively, consulting services may be used. Both options add more loads to the SMMs scarce resources. For these reasons, SMEs need a clear value proposition and a mechanism to evaluate the trustworthiness of consulting services.

To solve these problems, it is necessary to develop an assessment platform that enables manufacturers to either conduct a self-assessment with a very intuitive, step-by-step user interface, or provide access to assessment models and community-evaluated consulting services. The platform should allow users to develop subsequent improvement plans and share success values.

3 Smart Manufacturing Assessment System

3.1 SMAS Architecture

This assessment system is being developed based on the MEAN stack (MongoDB, Express.js, Angular 4, and Node.js). It will be an open source, web-based, free

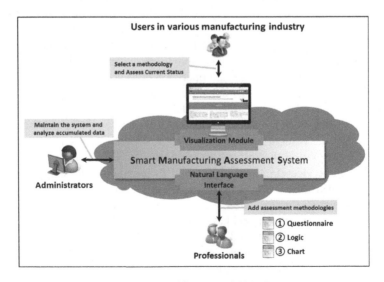

Fig. 1. Architecture of SMAS

self-assessment system for manufacturing companies. It will provide a platform to host various SMS assessment methodologies [e.g., 4, 8, 9], reflecting the diversity of manufacturing companies and their individual, often domain specific requirements.

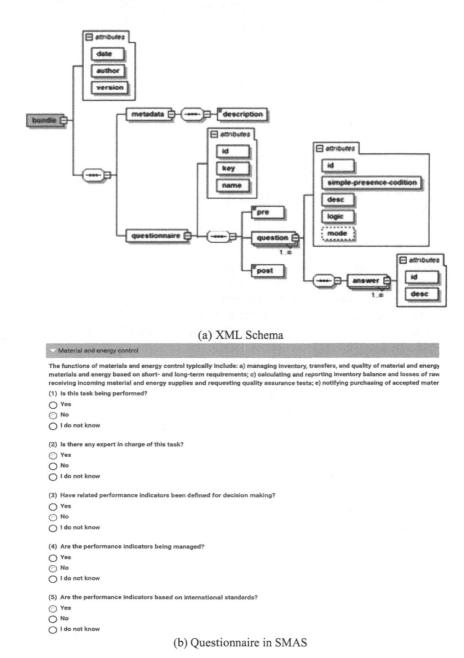

(a) XML Schema

Material and energy control

The functions of materials and energy control typically include: a) managing inventory, transfers, and quality of material and energy materials and energy based on short- and long-term requirements; c) calculating and reporting inventory balance and losses of raw receiving incoming material and energy supplies and requesting quality assurance tests; e) notifying purchasing of accepted mater

(1) Is this task being performed?
- Yes
- No
- I do not know

(2) Is there any expert in charge of this task?
- Yes
- No
- I do not know

(3) Have related performance indicators been defined for decision making?
- Yes
- No
- I do not know

(4) Are the performance indicators being managed?
- Yes
- No
- I do not know

(5) Are the performance indicators based on international standards?
- Yes
- No
- I do not know

(b) Questionnaire in SMAS

Fig. 2. XML schema for assessment models and SMAS user interfaces

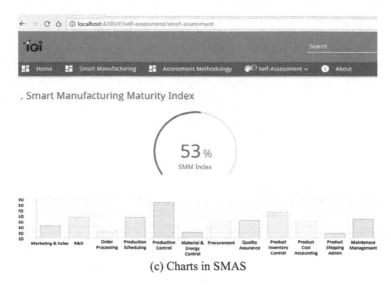

(c) Charts in SMAS

Fig. 2. (*continued*)

Manufacturing enterprises can intuitively compare their current smart manufacturing readiness to reference models and peers, adopt improvement strategies, get technologies and services recommendations that have been community-vetted, and generate improvement roadmap systemically on the platform.

Figure 1 shows the system architecture. Professionals can add assessment methods into SMAS by a convenient procedure. A bundle that consists of a detailed description, questionnaires, computation logics, and charts are defined using a standard XML schema shown in Fig. 2(a). The mounting of an assessment model is completed uploading XML files using the neutral language interface of SMAS. Manufacturing users select one of the assessment models to conduct their assessment as shown in Fig. 2(b). Intuitive charts indicating the current status are provided as shown in Fig. 2 (c). Improvement plans are automatically presented based on the assessment results. Administrators can analyze accumulated data and generate industry, regional, or national level benchmarking reports without revealing individual manufacturer's identity.

3.2   Assessment Methodologies

Two assessment methods are currently equipped in SMAS prototype. The first model is SMSRL [4] that seeks to provide an evaluation of how manufacturers manage/improve their performances and the available infrastructure to support related activities. SMSRL method is based on a formal reference model for factory improvement activities called FDI [13] and evaluates manufacturers in four aspects including organizational maturity, performance management maturity, IT maturity, and information connectivity maturity as shown in Fig. 3. Consolidating these four categories into a single measure creates a maturity index reflecting a manufacturer's readiness to deploy smart manufacturing solutions or to participate in a network of smart manufacturers.

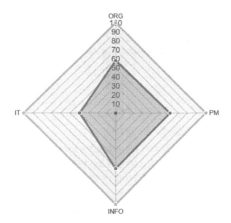

Fig. 3. Four aspects of SMSRL

The second unique methodology is developed by WVU's Smart Manufacturing Lab and focuses specifically on the needs of manufacturing SMEs. The WVU assessment and maturity model is unique in several aspects: (i) it reflects the lower baseline several manufacturing SMEs have when it comes to Smart Manufacturing (adding a 'level 0'), (ii) it merges a readiness index with a maturity model, and (iii) integrate building blocks and toolkits that can be combined in a modular fashion based on the individual maturity and assessment outcome. The model will be set around five organizational dimensions and five maturity levels. The model is informed by a recently conducted in-depth study of the current state of the art of Industrie 4.0/Smart Manufacturing maturity/assessment/readiness models and the learning from WVU's recent SME study [3].

3.3   Discussion

The choices of assessment methods included in SMAS prototype validated its scalability to address different needs varied by sizes and maturities of manufacturers. The SMSRL method is applicable to a more mature typically of medium to large sizes manufacturer, while the WVU method is applicable to a less mature typically of a small size manufacturer. Going forward, SMAS will provide user-friendly interfaces (UI) for professional or admin users to conveniently add various assessment methods. SMAS will be developed as a scalable open source platform with a high degree of openness and collaboration as shown in Fig. 4 [14]. Manufacturing users will intuitively compare different SMS technologies and services on the platform. Suitable solutions are matched with individual manufacturers requirements by a machine learning algorithm. The machine learning will use data from a peer review system and success stories associated with the past technologies and services adoptions. Thereby the effectiveness of suggestions will improve with scale and over time. SMAS will allow manufacturers to assess their smart manufacturing level for free by themselves. Guidelines including tools, advice and counsel on how to invest wisely will be provided separately by industry.

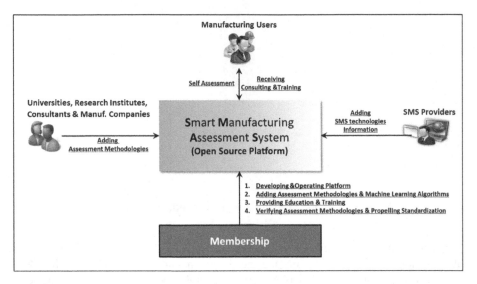

Fig. 4. Concept of platform

SMAS services will sustain by charging advertising and/or transaction fees from trainings, consulting services, technologies offered on the platform. They will be propelled by developments and standardizations of assessment methodologies and increasing utilizations.

4   Conclusions

A smart manufacturing assessment system called SMAS for manufacturing enterprises, especially SMMs, is being developed. SMAS will be released in the near future as an open source platform. Through this platform, technologies, knowledge and information related to SMS will be widely shared. It will also provide appropriate assessment methodologies and best practices for various industries and national users. Accumulated big data from manufacturing users will be analyzed, and it can be used for developing appropriate government support policy and SMS technology roadmap. This platform will help manufacturing companies improve SMS understanding and build their own smart factories. Creating a coherent suite of assessment methods or showing their differences and relationships remain a challenge. In our future work, we plan to investigate the possibility of using the three smart manufacturing dimensions, namely smart factory, value chain, and digital thread proposed by [15] as a guidance.

Disclaimer. Any mention of commercial products is for information only; it does not imply recommendation or endorsement by NIST.

References

1. Thoben, K.D., Wiesner, S., Wuest, T.: Industrie 4.0 and smart manufacturing–a review of research issues and application examples. Int. J. Autom. Technol. **11**(1), 4–16 (2017)
2. Kang, H.S., et al.: Smart manufacturing: past research, present findings, and future directions. Int. J. Precis. Eng. Manuf.-Green Technol. **3**(1), 111–128 (2016)
3. Wuest, T., Schmid, P., Lego, B., Bowen, E.: Overview of smart manufacturing in West Virginia. Bureau of Business & Economic Research, West Virginia University (2018)
4. Jung, K., Kulvatunyou, B., Choi, S., Brundage, M.P.: An overview of a smart manufacturing system readiness assessment. In: Nääs, I., et al. (eds.) APMS 2016. IAICT, vol. 488, pp. 705–712. Springer, Cham (2016). https://doi.org/10.1007/978-3-319-51133-7_83
5. Dubos, G.F., Saleh, J.H., Braun, R.: Technology readiness level, schedule risk, and slippage in spacecraft design. J. Spacecr. Rockets **45**(4), 836–842 (2008)
6. Ward, M.J., Halliday, S.T., Foden, J.: A readiness level approach to manufacturing technology development in the aerospace sector: an industrial approach. Proc. Inst. Mech. Eng. Part B: J. Eng. Manuf. **226**(3), 547–552 (2012)
7. Tucker, B., Paxton, J.: SCRL-model for human space flight operations enterprise supply chain. In: Aerospace Conference 2010, pp. 1–9. IEEE (2010)
8. Weber, C., Königsberger, J., Kassner, L., Mitschang, B.: M2DDM–a maturity model for data-driven manufacturing. Proc. CIRP **63**, 173–178 (2017)
9. Lee, J., Jun, S., Chang, T.W., Park, J.: A smartness assessment framework for smart factories using analytic network process. Sustainability **9**(5), 794 (2017)
10. De Carolis, A., Macchi, M., Negri, E., Terzi, S.: A maturity model for assessing the digital readiness of manufacturing companies. In: Lödding, H., Riedel, R., Thoben, K.-D., von Cieminski, G., Kiritsis, D. (eds.) APMS 2017. IAICT, vol. 513, pp. 13–20. Springer, Cham (2017). https://doi.org/10.1007/978-3-319-66923-6_2
11. Li, Q., Brundage, M., (Serm) Kulvatunyou, B., Brandl, D., Do Noh, S.: Improvement strategies for manufacturers using the MESA MOM capability maturity model. In: Lödding, H., Riedel, R., Thoben, K.-D., von Cieminski, G., Kiritsis, D. (eds.) APMS 2017. IAICT, vol. 513, pp. 21–29. Springer, Cham (2017). https://doi.org/10.1007/978-3-319-66923-6_3
12. Brandl, D.: MESA MOM Capability Maturity Model Version 1.0. White Paper #53, MESA International White Paper (2016)
13. Jung, K., Choi, S., Kulvatunyou, B., Cho, H., Morris, K.C.: A reference activity model for smart factory design and improvement. Prod. Plan. Control **28**(2), 108–122 (2017)
14. Menon, K., Kärkkäinen, H., Wuest, T.: Role of openness in industrial internet platform providers' strategy. In: Ríos, J., Bernard, A., Bouras, A., Foufou, S. (eds.) PLM 2017. IAICT, vol. 517, pp. 92–105. Springer, Cham (2017). https://doi.org/10.1007/978-3-319-72905-3_9
15. Leiva, C.: Three perspectives converge on smart manufacturing. Internet article, February 2018. http://advancedmanufacturing.org/17797-2/

Manufacturing Execution Systems: The Next Level of Automated Control or of Shop-Floor Support?

S. Waschull$^{(\boxtimes)}$, J. C. Wortmann, and J. A. C. Bokhorst

University of Groningen, PO Box 800, 9700 AV Groningen, The Netherlands
s.waschull@rug.nl

Abstract. Manufacturing Execution Systems (MES) are at the heart of industrial organizations' endeavors. While MES were traditionally positioned as an integration technology to bridge the shop-floor with higher level business systems, their current focus seems to be on the digitization of shop-floor activities for the collection, analysis and exchange of real-time information. Still, there remains dispute on the role of MES, specifically with respect to the functions they support in relation to other information systems in the automation pyramid, and their resulting interactions with humans. While MES are often positioned as the top layer of automated control of manufacturing processes, it is perceived by others as an integrated decision support system for the shop-floor. This study aims to shed light on the role of MES to either automate or to augment human tasks. Based on insights of a case study, we found that MES are neither automatic control nor solely decision support. MES' main role is the creation and maintenance of digital twins of products. This involves human interaction, which closely resembles work related to computer-aided engineering (CAE) systems. We expect that work in the sphere of MES will therefore increasingly resemble engineering work.

Keywords: Manufacturing execution systems · Automation pyramid
Digital twin · Shop-floor support

1 Introduction

The collection and analysis of large volumes of data generated throughout the product lifecycle is of growing importance for organizations. In line with that, more and more different forms of manufacturing execution systems (MES) have been implemented during the last decades [1] to deal with data in order to decrease cost, increase quality and meet efficiency requirements [2]. MES are also facilitators for implementing recent developments resulting from Industry 4.0 [3] and hence play a key role as an enabler of further innovation in manufacturing. Broadly speaking, MES focus on the digitization of shop-floor activities to monitor, document and report information on the transformation of raw materials into finished goods in an integrated manner, enabling the control and optimization of production processes in near real time [4–6] Whereas enterprise resource planning (ERP) systems focus on the horizontal integration across business functions, MES focus on the vertical integration of manufacturing processes

I. Moon et al. (Eds.): APMS 2018, IFIP AICT 536, pp. 386–393, 2018.
https://doi.org/10.1007/978-3-319-99707-0_48

with business processes by bridging enterprise information systems and the actual shop-floor [5]. This architectural view is commonly summarized in an automation pyramid that classifies and separates industrial systems [4]. MES then represent the middle layer in between ERP as a system of decision support, and the shop-floor mostly concerned with automated control [1]. However, this positioning leads to ambiguity on the role of MES and its interactions with other systems and with humans: *Is MES a new layer of automated process control, or a system for business support?*

The literature provides two perspectives. MES are sometimes positioned as systems to enable the vision of the automated lightless factory as promoted during the era of Computer Integrated Manufacturing (CIM). This perspective emphasizes the automation of all activities in the sphere of MES and shifts the focus for human tasks towards higher level business support [7]. Alternatively, MES are referred to as systems of decision support, similar to ERP, enabling empowered humans to take decentralized and well informed decisions on aspects of shop-floor control [8]. Several researchers already claimed that the automation pyramid will be transformed over the next years into a more decentralized and less rigid structure [9], but no further details were provided. Furthermore, it seems that MES functions are also supported by other information systems, leading to redundancy between these systems [10]. Despite a wide usage of MES, there are still unanswered questions such as: What is the exact role of MES? How do MES relate to (or how can they be differentiated from) other industrial systems in the automation pyramid? Are MES the next level of automated process control or of decision-support? What are implications for human tasks? These questions will be addressed in this research.

The next section provides an overview of the literature on MES and the role of MES as an integration layer. To further explore this empirically, Sect. 3 presents a case study at an aerospace company currently involved in the development of a MES. Based on the findings in Sect. 4, a discussion is provided in Sect. 5. Finally, Sect. 6 concludes.

2   What Is the Role of MES?

The automation pyramid classifies industrial systems into distinct layers as can be seen in Fig. 1 [4, 11]. On the uppermost level, ERP takes on the role of the transactional backbone of all business processes and databases of a company [12].

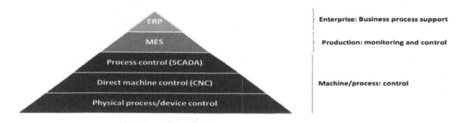

Fig. 1. Automation pyramid

ERP supports the execution of business processes, such as order fulfillment or inventory control [13]. The bottom levels of the pyramid relate to automated control and are specifically hardware oriented, e.g. sensors, programmable logic controllers (PLC), and supervisory control and data acquisition (SCADA) systems. Control here concerns direct autonomous control actions with real-time sensors and actuators [14]. The middle level, i.e. where MES are positioned, is said to be bridging the gap between these upper and lower levels in the pyramid. The MESA standard defines several functions for MES, e.g. operations scheduling, dispatching, data collection, labour or quality management [1, 6, 16]. Despite standards, organizations are still struggling to define and demarcate the MES functionalities from other information systems available within the same layer (MES) and also across layers. This is because these information systems partly provide similar functions, e.g. document management (in PDM), inventory management (in ERP) or product tracking/dispatching (with control automation) [10]. In addition, even though there is a need to exchange data between manufacturing engineering and the shop-floor itself (e.g. the bill of material list, manufacturing instructions, control programs or possible non-conformances) [15], it is surprising to observe that industrial information systems supporting production innovation and their interactions with MES have been largely ignored in the automation pyramid. Computer-aided engineering (CAE) or product life cycle management (PLM) are such systems. Even though production definition management has been defined as a major aspect of MES in the ISA95 standard, it remains vague how and to what extent product innovation plays a role in aspects of MES, or how the design of product innovation systems is influenced by their usage in MES. To mention just one example, Engineering Change Management cannot be ignored in MES, but ISA95 does not seem to acknowledge this fact.

Finally, the interactions of MES with humans and their involvement in the control loop has not received much attention in the literature [16]. This is surprising considering that as Industry 4.0 takes shape, humans are required to be highly flexible and skilled to be able to work in a more complex and dynamic environment [17]. Hereof, two diverging perspectives on the role of MES and its interactions with humans can be described depending on how MES are approached in the pyramid. From the perspective of automated control, MES are described as a tool to achieve a fully automated and integrated manufacturing environment [7], as has been envisioned by the CIM movement [18]. This perspective views MES as the top layer of automated process control, extending control of the shop-floor components to control of all shop-floor control activities. In this view, MES and not humans eventually control the execution of manufacturing. From a different perspective, namely top-down, MES are presented as shop-floor decision support systems similar to ERP [8]. In this light, MES' main role is to collect, process and report information on various shop-floor activities in an integrated manner, to aid production monitoring and control shop-floor operations [6]. Workers can optimize their control decisions by providing accurate and timely information, and can react quickly [8]. Opposed to the light-free factory promoted in CIM, humans then remain essential in the activities located in the sphere of MES.

In order to increase our understanding of the role of MES in the automation pyramid, we conducted an in-depth case study. The case study presented next focuses on a factory on its way to digitization while maintaining an important role for humans.

3   Case Study

This study is part of a larger in-depth longitudinal case study focusing on the impact of digitization on work. The case company is an aerospace company, which designs and manufactures discrete lightweight structures for the aerospace defense industry. The case provides the unique opportunity to study both the design and the implementation process of a MES. The first author of this paper has been involved as project team member for three years now and collected data through interviews, observations and archival documents.

3.1   Rationale for MES Implementation

The company operates under high variety, and is characterized by high quality and compliance requirements. In absence of a MES, the company currently works with different often isolated information systems on the shop-floor. The manufacturing planning and execution management is still highly manual and paper based. ERP and product lifecycle management (PLM) systems form the backbone of all manufacturing activities. Translating business and engineering requirements to the shop-floor and exchanging information between these two systems is, for a large part, accomplished by humans through an array of different paper based documents, databases and applications, e.g. weekly schedules and manufacturing instructions. Based on the current shop-floor control system, the following rationales for a MES were identified.

Shop-Floor Control. Manufacturing planning, scheduling and dispatching requires human expertise and human decision-making to synchronize high-level planning to existing capacity on the shop-floor (e.g. man-hours, machine capacity). Moreover, the case company has much difficulty to obtain accurate and real-time information on the position and status of production orders and production resources (e.g. machines, tooling) to facilitate optimal shop-floor control and to quickly react to changes.

Quality Improvements and Information Sharing. Currently, it is difficult to carry out many types of analysis for quality improvement activities and to learn from past decisions. First, registrations of as-built information (on the specific production process and product) are to a great degree still done on paper. It is hence difficult to conduct root-cause analyses and to connect quality issues in the line to the actual problems. Second, the company is working with islands of automation and disparate information systems (e.g. excel databases, functional information systems). Various functions (i.e. planning, engineering, dispatching) work independently and do not share information. Information is hence not transparent and shared to a limited extent.

Engineering Data Structure and Manufacturing Instructions. Engineering data (technical product specifications) are input for detailed manufacturing instructions created by the engineering department for each individual product. Currently, these instructions consist of multiple long PDF documents. They are non-standardized and instructions differ in syntax and structure. This results in a lot of manual labor when engineering changes need to be implemented and released. In addition, the use of multiple long instructions makes that operators either do not properly read the instructions, or spend a high share of their time looking for the right information. The following section describes the MES system architecture developed by the case company to overcome the stated problems, commencing with the digitization of manufacturing processes.

3.2 MES Architecture at the Case Company

The MES developed by the case company comprises the following computer applications: (1) a manufacturing process designer (MPD) to create and maintain manufacturing instructions based on engineering data, (2) a shop-floor manager (SFM) to control manufacturing activities, (3) a shop-floor viewer (SFV) to present manufacturing instructions to the operator and for digital registrations and (4) a registration manager (RM) to create a digital product dossier of as-built information.

Manufacturing Process Designer (MPD). The MPD is a system used by manufacturing engineering for production definition management, i.e. creating and managing manufacturing capabilities of processes and equipment. The MPD provides a digital library to create and maintain manufacturing instructions. Its data structure distinguishes manufacturing processes into standardized operations and processes (i.e. activities and tasks), equipment data (machines, materials) and customer specifications (authorizations required, quality items). The standardization of instructions and the resulting data model enables a more efficient implementation of engineering changes. These changes now only need to be made once and are valid for all related products and near real-time on the shop-floor. The system also keeps track of releases, resulting in different versions of instructions. Design engineering data (e.g. drawings) are maintained in the existing PLM system. Ultimately, the aim of the MPD is to move production engineers from thinking in preparation of long, heterogeneous verbose design documents to thinking in reusable, visual and modular process activities that are essential input for the detailed control and execution of processes.

Shop-Floor Manager (SFM). The SFM takes on a central function in the MES architecture. The SFM takes on functions of dispatching (e.g. resource allocation, clustering) and control by tracking and monitoring the status and progress of production orders. It is closely integrated with the MPD, which provides the "as planned" product data.

Shop-Floor Viewer (SFV). The SFV supports the workers on the shop-floor by providing manufacturing instructions developed in the MPD, i.e. the process flow, bill of material items and technical specifications. The operators are guided through the manufacturing process in a sequential manner, by following instructions and providing registrations when required (e.g. lot-numbers, product measurements, quality controls). The system automatically checks if these registrations are according to specifications; if workers are authorized and if a non-conformance is detected, the process stops and appropriate actions are taken.

Registration Manager (RM). During the creation of the product, an RM captures all "as-built" data per production order in a digital file, resulting in the creation of a product digital twin. This digital twin includes three data categories, namely (1) general production order information (e.g. customer, quantity, production order) and release notes on instructions used, (2) planned production execution data (routings, processes, resources) and (3) as-built data of the manufacturing execution (actual activity and task flow with task times), BOM items and other customer specifications (quality items, certificates to perform and to release). To some extent, as-built data is dependent on various manual registrations provided through the SFV (e.g. approved control checks, reports, product measurements, environmental conditions).

4 Findings

MES are supporting humans in their job. MES are neither a top layer of automated control nor a purely decision support system. Through collecting and synthesizing data on the status of production orders, we find that MES' main function is the creation of digital twins of products that contain all relevant product related information on a low level of aggregation, i.e. operating parameters, environmental data. The product digital twin ensures that the product in use is monitored in real-time, relevant data is transparent, a historical record is built up, and data sources are integrated into one file. Other functions as outlined in the MESA standard are either executed manually or taken over by other information systems, and more or less integrated in the new MES architecture.

To build the product digital twin, input is required from several sources. One is input from sensor data and automatic controllers, others are detailed manufacturing instructions or other design documents. This shows that MES should be closely integrated with systems of product innovation. The execution of manufacturing is defined by engineers with the help of CAE to develop manufacturing instructions to support shop-floor workers in the production. Input for the CAE is delivered by the PLM, which means that PLM should be naturally linked with CAE in MES. In addition, insights from the MES must be reported back to CAE to enable the creation of improved instructions and process/product designs.

At the case company, humans receive an important role in the activities evolving around the creation and analysis of the product digital twin data. The digital product twin serves humans to make well-informed decisions regarding quality, shop-floor control and resource management. Humans even seem to take on a stronger role regarding the optimization of their processes due to the availability of digital product twin data and its data analysis possibilities. Data can be analyzed or potentially simulated to adjust and optimize scheduling and dispatching decisions, to connect quality issues to their root-cause, or to perform continuous improvement activities. Hence, human interaction with MES is abundant and humans are found to still play an essential role in all stages of the control loop at the case company, i.e. data collection, analysis and decision making.

5 Discussion

In this paper, we aimed to clarify the role of MES in the automation pyramid. MES' main function is the collection and reporting of data and it centers on the creation of digital twins of products. Hence, we propose that MES should therefore not be positioned as a layer in between ERP and control systems in the automation pyramid, and that the hierarchical nature of industrial systems should be reconsidered, which is in line with general statements seen in earlier literature [9]. Systems of product innovation (CAE, PLM), execution management (MES) and business support (ERP) augment workers in industrial production and are clearly disparate from control systems that focus on automation aspects. We therefore adapt the top layer of the automation pyramid in Fig. 2 to a comprehensive top layer. Here, the digital twin is central in the sphere of MES. It receives and reports information from and to other integrated industrial systems. Moreover, this study showed that MES are currently designed to support humans in their work. In the sphere of MES, humans will increasingly focus on activities evolving around the digital twin. Depending on the industry and the level of automation of companies, this level of involvement will vary. To some degree, the type of work in the sphere of the digital twin (e.g. registering, checking) will increasingly resemble engineering work. This means that remaining work in the sphere of MES could become more complex and might lead to higher skill requirements.

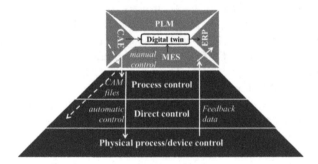

Fig. 2. Adjusted top layer of the automation pyramid

6 Conclusion

MES play a crucial role in the creation and maintenance of the digital twin of a product. MES should also be closely integrated with systems of product innovation to create the digital twin. MES is neither business support nor automatic control. Human interaction with MES is found to be essential in all stages of the control loop. Work in the sphere of MES will increasingly resemble work traditionally referred to as engineering work. In that sense, operators will then not only be involved in the production of the physical product, but also in the creation and maintenance of the digital twin. Future research should further elaborate and validate with more cases to obtain a more holistic picture. It would also be interesting to further elaborate which functions in the MESA standard are central to MES, and which are redundant.

References

1. Harjunkoski, I., Nyström, R., Horch, A.: Integration of scheduling and control-theory or practice? Comput. Chem. Eng. **33**, 1909–1918 (2009)
2. Rondeau, P., Litteral, L.A.: The evolution of manufacturing planning and control systems: from reorder point to enterprise resource planning. Prod. Inventory Manag. J. **42**, 1–7 (2001)
3. Arica, E., Powell, D.J.: Status and future of manufacturing execution systems. In: Proceedings of the 2017 IEEE IEEM, pp. 2000–2004 (2017)
4. ISA: ANSI/ISA 95: Enterprise-Control System Integration Part 3: Activity Models of Manufacturing Operations Management (2005)
5. Romero, D., Vernadat, F.: Enterprise information systems state of the art: past, present and future trends. Comput. Ind. **79**, 3–13 (2016)
6. de Ugarte, B.S., Artiba, A., Pellerin, R.: Manufacturing execution system – a literature review. Prod. Plan. Control **20**, 525–539 (2009)
7. Huang, C.: Distributed manufacturing execution systems: a workflow perspective. J. Intell. Manuf. **13**, 485–497 (2002)
8. Naedele, M., Chen, H., Kazman, R., Cai, Y., Xiao, L., Silva, C.V.A.: Manufacturing execution systems: a vision for managing software development. J. Syst. Softw. **101**, 59–68 (2015)
9. Monostori, L.: Cyber-physical production systems: roots, expectations and R&D challenges. Proc. CIRP **17**, 9–13 (2014)
10. Schmidt, A., Otto, B., Österle, H.: A functional reference model for manufacturing execution systems in the automotive industry. In: Wirtschaftsinformatik Proceedings, p. 89 (2011)
11. Williams, T.J.: The Purdue enterprise reference architecture. Comput. Ind. **24**, 141–158 (1994)
12. Shehab, E.M., Sharp, M.W., Supramaniam, L., Spedding, T.A.: Enterprise resource planning: an integrative review. Bus. Process Manag. J. **10**, 359–386 (2004)
13. Wortmann, J.C.: Evolution of ERP systems. In: Bititci, U.S., Carrie, A.S. (eds.) Strategic Management of the Manufacturing Value Chain. ITIFIP, vol. 2, pp. 11–23. Springer, Boston, MA (1998). https://doi.org/10.1007/978-0-387-35321-0_2
14. Shobrys, D.E., White, D.C.: Planning, scheduling and control systems: why cannot they work together. Comput. Chem. Eng. **26**, 149–160 (2002)
15. Ben Khedher, A., Henry, S., Bouras, A.: Industrialization and manufacturing steps within the global product lifecycle context. In: Vallespir, B., Alix, T. (eds.) APMS 2009. IAICT, vol. 338, pp. 400–408. Springer, Heidelberg (2010). https://doi.org/10.1007/978-3-642-16358-6_50
16. Pacaux-Lemoine, M.-P., Trentesaux, D., Rey, G.Z., Millot, P.: Designing intelligent manufacturing systems through Human-Machine Cooperation principles: a human-centered approach. Comput. Ind. Eng. **111**, 581–595 (2017)
17. Gorecky, D., Schmitt, M., Loskyll, M., Zühlke, D.: Human-machine-interaction in the industry 4.0 era. In: Proceedings of the 2014 12th IEEE International Conference on Industrial Informatics, INDIN 2014, pp. 289–294 (2014)
18. Cagliano, R., Spina, G.: Advanced manufacturing technologies and strategically flexible production. J. Oper. Manag. **18**, 169–190 (2000)

Construct an Intelligent Yield Alert and Diagnostic Analysis System via Data Analysis: Empirical Study of a Semiconductor Foundry

Yi-Jyun Chen, Yen-Han Lee, and Ming-Chuan Chiu[(✉)]

National Tsing Hua University, No. 101, Section 2,
Kuang-Fu Road, Hsinchu 30013, Taiwan
mcchiu@ie.nthu.edu.tw

Abstract. As semiconductor manufacturing technology advances, the process becomes longer and more complex. A critical issue is to determine how to avoid yield loss at an early stage or to diagnose the cause of yield loss soon, in order to save more money. Traditional statistical regression analysis and correlation analysis are unable to quickly and easily figure out the causes of process anomalies and potential problems. This study aims to construct an intelligent yield alert and diagnostic analysis framework combined within a big data analysis architecture. Through an intelligent detection and early warning mechanism, instant detection of yield anomalies and automatic diagnostic analysis based on good/bad wafer classification, we can effectively and rapidly find out the factors that may cause process variation to help quickly clarify the causes of abnormal product yield. The case study in this paper uses real-world data from a foundry in Taiwan. We hope to provide engineers and domain experts with a reference framework for building a yield analysis system to help improve the yield of semiconductor manufacturing and enhance the competitiveness of high-tech industries.

Keywords: Big data analysis · Yield analysis · Regression analysis
Correlation analysis

1   Introduction

The concepts of Smart Factory and Industry 4.0 have recently drawn increasing attention in Taiwan's semiconductor industry. The semiconductor industry in Taiwan plays an important role in the global market and has a leading position especially in the fields of wafer foundry, packaging, and testing. Due to strong global competition, implementation of smart manufacturing to increase the efficiency of production processes, increase the automation of equipment, and enhance data analysis capabilities is not just an option but is a necessary action.

The advances in semiconductor process technology required to reach the Nano-node have made the process more complex and lengthier. In the wafer manufacturing process, huge amounts of production records and process parameters data have

© IFIP International Federation for Information Processing 2018
Published by Springer Nature Switzerland AG 2018. All Rights Reserved
I. Moon et al. (Eds.): APMS 2018, IFIP AICT 536, pp. 394–401, 2018.
https://doi.org/10.1007/978-3-319-99707-0_49

accumulated and must be analyzed. A semiconductor fab must use various types of dynamic data analysis collected from the automated production machines to early predict the equipment status of possible production problems and abnormal state by referring to the history data. If it is possible to adjust the equipment immediately to correct the wrong status, the fab can reduce huge losses caused by interruption of production due to errors in the production flow.

It is critically important to understand how to utilize the huge production records and process parameters data. This research aims to propose an intelligent yield alert and diagnostic analysis framework that can intelligently detect and alert the abnormal situations at an early stage for the semiconductor industry. The framework is based on and validated with the data collected from shop floor of a semiconductor foundry company in Taiwan.

The second section of this study is a review of the literature concerning big data, and the applications of big data in the industry. The third section proposes to construct an intelligent yield warning and diagnosis analysis model using a big data analysis architecture and apply this model to the semiconductor wafer manufacturing industry. The Sect. 4 verifies the validity and feasibility of the research model with a semiconductor foundry's products, which come from two stages of trial production and mass production. Section 5 concludes the contribution of this research and suggests future research directions.

2 Literature Review

Big Data is a concept that has been used extensively over the past decade in the enterprise for data analytics, business intelligence and statistical applications. The field has matured due to the rapid growth in the quantity of data, the decline in data storage costs, the advancement of software technology and maturity of cloud environment Data analysis from previous insights of historical data can predict future outcomes, or even innovate, creating business models never seen before.

The characteristics of big data are known as 3Vs: Volume, Velocity and Variety (Eaton *et al.* 2012). These are similar to the data types in semiconductor industry. The first "V" represents that the massive amount of data. The second one is about how fast the data is generated. The last one means there are various types of data. Due to the lengthy and complicated wafer process, a lot of data is generated during manufacturing. Each machine at each station in each step of process could generate data, so there is a high velocity of generating data. Data generated from different machine could be in different forms, such as images or numerical.

As a result, some papers utilize big data to solve semiconductor factory problems. The applications of big data can be roughly divided into three types: realizing existing data, enhancing the competitiveness of enterprises through data and using data as the foundation and core services to subvert traditional industries (Li 2016). Learning how to extract useful knowledge from the data is very important. The authors designed experimental data mining to extract helpful information from data automatically collected in the process (Chien *et al.* 2014a). The next challenge is to use the data generated in semiconductor manufacturing. The authors recommend utilizing FDC and

MES data to enhance the overall usage effectiveness, and have developed a framework for that data (Chien *et al.* 2014b). Other tools for data mining in semiconductor industry have been developed for decades (Kusiak 2001). Or combine two data mining approaches to extract pattern of data in semiconductor industrial to improve yield (Hsu and Chien 2007). Further propose a framework to solve the problems such as root cause detection in semiconductor industrial (Chien and Chuang 2014). Gradually develop a systematic approach to solve problems.

3   Intelligent Yield Alert and Diagnostic Analysis Framework in Semiconductor Industry

This research proposed an intelligent yield alert and diagnostic analysis system (see Fig. 1). The first stage of this model is the abnormality detection and early warning mechanism. The detection is based on each piece of wafer yield test data returned daily from the production line. The second stage of the model is to diagnose the cause and alert the operator to any suspicious factors.

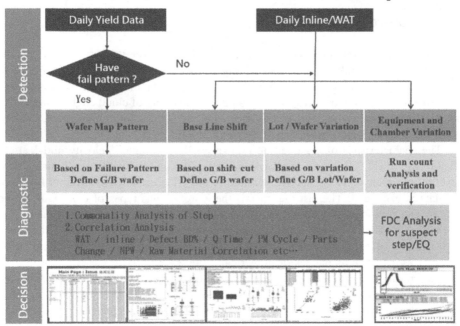

Fig. 1. Intelligent yield alert and diagnostic analysis model

3.1 Abnormality Detection and Early Warning Mechanism

The yield of semiconductor wafers is calculated based on the ratio of defective and functioning wafers. A probe is used to test the electrical characteristics of each of the crystal grains in the wafer and their connections in the circuit. There is a special pattern in the Wafer Bin Map (WBM) to determine whether there is an abnormality in the process of wafer manufacturing. The yield data includes different fault codes (Bin #/Bin Group), which respectively represent the meanings of different electrical characteristics of the grain. Therefore, it is possible to classify the yield abnormalities according to different fault codes. The WBM is not the only data source we can use to find different abnormal phenomena in the yields. Other methods we investigated include: base Line Shift, lot to lot variation, wafer to wafer variation, and equipment and chamber variation.

Wafer Bin Map. First, we used Novelty Detection (Pimental et al. 2014) to see if there are unknown patterns in the new wafer bin map to determine whether the classification model needs to be retrained. If there is no need to retrain the model, wafer yield data will undergo Radon Transform to do data transformation and feature extraction. We can get important features from this graph. Then we use an SVM as a classification model. We separate the two groups of wafers into Random Pattern (G0) and Non-Random Pattern (G'). Finally, we divide the Non-pattern (G') group into clusters of G1, G2,... Gk according to their wafer pattern characteristics. We use Calinski-Harabasz Criterion (Calinski and Harabasz 1974) to determine the number of clusters.

Baseline Shift. In practice, the yield test data returned by the production line every day are sorted according to the test time, and the product yield rate will vary over time. If the exact position of the yield change can be accurately identified, it can quickly clarify the time when the abnormalities occur. This study detected baseline deviations through Change Point Analysis (Killick and Eckley 2014) as shown in Fig. 2.

Lot-to-Lot and Wafer-to-Wafer. In practice, we will find that products often have variations between lots to lots, or variations within batches, from wafer to wafer. Therefore, this study uses quadrant analysis as shown in Fig. 3 to classify and select the variations between lots or wafers. The plot shows the Lot Mean (Fail Bin Loss Lot Mean) along the X axis and Lot Stdev (Fail Bin Loss Lot Stdev) as the Y axis. Two-dimensional quadrants are the median of Lot Mean and median of Lot Stdev as shown in Fig. 3.

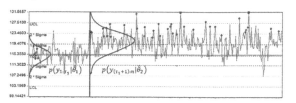

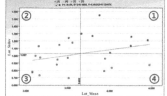

Fig. 2. Baseline shift detection

Fig. 3. Quadrant analysis of lot mean and lot Stdev.

Equipment and Chamber Variation. On the actual production line, there are many differences between the individual machines in the same class of machine group, and these differences may alter the yield of products. Therefore, this study uses Statistic Matching Methodology and Mean Matching to check if there are differences between the machines. The concept of this method is as shown in Fig. 4, there are significant variations of machine Tool4 so the yield loss of products produced by Tool4 may come from those variations. In the second stage of the model we will do further analysis to confirm this hypothesis.

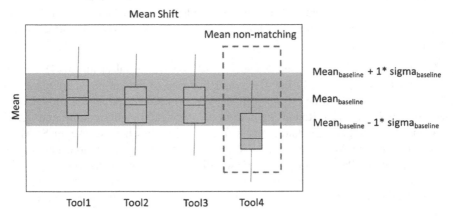

Fig. 4. Equipment and chamber variation

3.2   Suspicious Factor Decision Model

Due to the complexity of the process, our first step was to identify doubtful sites that may cause abnormality in yields through commonality analysis and correlation analysis. Then, our second step as to go through the intelligent yield alert and diagnostic analysis model-suspicious factor decision model to further confirm and filter out the real cause of the abnormality. There are three steps to the suspicious factor decision model:

Long Trend Performance Analysis. Since each step of the diagnostic analysis can only explain part of the abnormal phenomenon, all wafers within the same time period must be sorted by production time to show the trends of yield changes.

Run Count Analysis. This step of the suspicious factor decision model is to find equipment and chamber variation. After listing the possible variability of the machines, we will analyze the run count of the wafers passing through the machine to further verify that the wafer yield will significantly drop when the number of wafers passing the same machine increases.

Fault Detection and Classification (FDC). The basic FDC is to inspect the specifications of equipment and to use statistical process control (SPC) to control machine parameters. The advanced FDC is to use a time-series model according to univariate analysis or multivariate statistical analysis to view the feature information for a particular time segment in the process. Based on the data from process equipment, measurement equipment, wafer acceptance test (WAT), and yield, data mining and analysis are used to find diagnostic rules, modeling, and perform immediate diagnosis and control.

4 Case Study

This study validates the framework with an empirical study conducted in a fab in Taiwan. The model is designed to quickly clarify issues in the pilot production yield, speed up the rate of increasing yield, and quickly diagnose the problem of mass production anomalies and avoid their abnormal expansion.

The empirical data covers historical production records of plot production products (product A) and mass production products (products B and C). We prepared the data by arranging it, establishing whether it is relevant and integrating it in advance, then storing it in the big data analysis platform.

We used the intelligent yield alert and diagnostic analysis framework in semi-conductor industry mentioned in Sect. 3. In the first stage, we use the Wafer Bin Map Pattern for identification and classification, the Base Line Shift testing, variation test between batches and wafers, Equipment and Chamber Variation test and other methods to construct the yield abnormality detection and early warning system. In the second stage, each abnormal type of Good and Bad Lot/Wafer are selected to carry out a diagnostic analysis of the yield abnormal factors' commonality and correlation. For the factors found by the diagnosis, we used a cross-validation of the machines run count and FDC analysis of long-term trends to determine the final suspicious factors to help engineers narrow the scope of exploration yield anomalies.

The experimental results show that Equipment and Chamber Variation can be effectively aberration and other anomalies. The problems discovered are shown in Table 1, which were found by the yield abnormalities detection and early warning system, Wafer Bin Map Pattern, baseline shift, lot to lot variation, and wafer to wafer variation.

These anomalies cover nearly 80% of the daily abnormalities generated in the plant, so the system can effectively help engineers to quickly sort out the abnormalities of daily products. At the same time, through the diagnostic analysis system, the scope of suspicion of anomalies can effectively be reduced to help engineers to quickly identify and confirm the causes of daily product anomalies.

Table 1. Description of empirical case

Case	Product	Product type	Problem type	Yield (↑)
A1	A	Pilot	Baseline shift	0.7%
B1	C	Mass	Baseline shift	0.19%
B3	A	Pilot	Baseline shift	0.09%
B2	A	Pilot	Map pattern	0.05%
A3	B	Mass	Baseline shift	0.03%
A3	B	Mass	Baseline shift	0.03%

This model was applied to 78 actual cases a year which are from important customers. The performance is as shown in Table 2. The average analysis time of a case was reduced from 13 days to 3.5 days, which greatly improved the efficiency of the analysis of the abnormality. At the same time, product A improved the yield rate by 7.08%, and the improvement of yield of product B was 3.94%. Every die in average improved the yield rate by 3%, bringing a potential profit of 10 million to the company.

Table 2. Improvement of the cases

#	Improvement	Before	After
1	Average analysis time/per case	13 days	3.5 days
2	Product A yield	d1	d1 + 7.08%
3	Product B yield	d2	d2 + 3.94%

5   Conclusion

This study builds on the manufacturing and process data collected during the wafer fabrication process to provide an early warning of abnormal production, and helps diagnose anomalies and thus increase yield. According to the semiconductor wafer manufacturing yield testing data, this paper proposes a model construction of yield anomaly warning and analysis of abnormal factors diagnosis. Through the two stages of the model, we can find out the types of abnormal phenomena and yield variation at an early stage, and then conduct a diagnostic analysis upon the abnormal yield factor and cross-validate the hypothesis to find out the final suspicious factors causing issues.

The contribution of this study is to develop an effective yield anomaly detection and diagnosis model. It can shorten the analysis time to find out cause of defect, and help engineers to narrow down scope of suspicious factors and to improve the quality of decision making.

Due to the lengthy and complicated characteristics of semiconductor manufacturing process, many variables influence the model, which also may affect each other. In future research, we can focus on the process of interaction between the front-end and back-end to study the diagnosis of cross-site interaction impact factor. At the same time, we advise keeping a record of correct analyses found in previous each anomaly case. This helps to build an abnormal case database and establish an index that can be used to improve the accuracy of detection and diagnosis through machine learning and search techniques. In addition to finding anomaly factors, the wafer fab's most frequently asked question is whether or not to look for ways to study the golden path for best-in-class wafers, and we can do more to study the most effective process flow to find that path.

References

Chien, C.-F., Chang, K.-H., Wang, W.-C.: An empirical study of design-of-experiment data mining for yield-loss diagnosis for semiconductor manufacturing. J. Intell. Manuf. **25**(5), 961–972 (2014a)

Chien, C.-F., Chuang, S.-C.: A framework for root cause detection of sub-batch processing system for semiconductor manufacturing big data analytics. IEEE Trans. Semicond. Manuf. **27**(4), 485–488 (2014)

Chien, C.-F., Diaz, A.C., Lan, Y.-B.: A data mining approach for analyzing semiconductor MES and FDC data to enhance overall usage effectiveness (OUE). Int. J. Comput. Intell. Syst. **7**(2), 52–65 (2014b)

Calinski, R. B., Harabasz, J.: A dendrite method for cluster analysis. Commun. Stat. **3**, 1–27 (1974)

Eaton, C., Deroos, D., Deutsch, T., Lapis, G., Zikopoulos, P.: Understanding Big Data: Analytics for Enterprise Class Hadoop and Streaming Data. McGraw-Hill Companies, New York (2012)

Hsu, S.-C., Chien, C.-F.: Hybrid data mining approach for pattern extraction from wafer bin map to improve yield in semiconductor manufacturing. Int. J. Prod. Econ. **107**(1), 88–103 (2007)

Kusiak, A.: Rough set theory: a data mining tool for semiconductor manufacturing. IEEE Trans. Electron. Packag. Manuf. **24**(1), 44–50 (2001)

Killick, R., Eckley, I.: Changepoint : an R package for changepoint analysis. J. Stat. Softw. **58**(3), 1–19 (2014)

Li, J.: Industrial Big Data the Revolutionary Transformation and Value Creation in Industry 4.0 Era. CommonWealth, Taipei (2016)

Pimentel M.A.F., Clifton D.A, Clifton L., Tarassenko L.: A Review of Novelty Detection. Sign. Process. **99**, 215–249 (2014)

The Industrial Ontologies Foundry Proof-of-Concept Project

Boonserm (Serm) Kulvatunyou[1]([⊠]), Evan Wallace[1],
Dimitris Kiritsis[2], Barry Smith[3], and Chris Will[4]

[1] Systems Integration Division, National Institute of Standards and
Technologies, Gaithersburg, USA
{serm,evan.wallace}@nist.gov
[2] EPFL, Lausanne, Switzerland
dimitris.kiritsis@epfl.ch
[3] State University of New York, Buffalo, USA
phismith@buffalo.edu
[4] Dassault Systemes, Vélizy-Villacoublay, France
chris.will@3ds.com

Abstract. The current industrial revolution is said to be driven by the digitization that exploits connected information across all aspects of manufacturing. Standards have been recognized as an important enabler. Ontology-based information standard may provide benefits not offered by current information standards. Although there have been ontologies developed in the industrial manufacturing domain, they have been fragmented and inconsistent, and little has received a standard status. With successes in developing coherent ontologies in the biological, biomedical, and financial domains, an effort called Industrial Ontologies Foundry (IOF) has been formed to pursue the same goal for the industrial manufacturing domain. However, developing a coherent ontology covering the entire industrial manufacturing domain has been known to be a mountainous challenge because of the multidisciplinary nature of manufacturing. To manage the scope and expectations, the IOF community kicked-off its effort with a proof-of-concept (POC) project. This paper describes the developments within the project. It also provides a brief update on the IOF organizational set up.

Keywords: Smart manufacturing · Industrie 4.0 · Ontology · IOF
Industrial Ontologies Foundry

1 Introduction

The current industrial revolution is said to be driven by the digitization that exploits connected information across all aspects of manufacturing [1]. Standards have been recognized as an important enabler; meanwhile, ontology is considered as the next generation standard for connected information. Although there have been ontologies developed in the industrial manufacturing domain, they have been disparately developed with inconsistent principles and viewpoints. Hence, existing industrial ontologies are incoherent and not suitable for the connected information goal.

I. Moon et al. (Eds.): APMS 2018, IFIP AICT 536, pp. 402–409, 2018.
https://doi.org/10.1007/978-3-319-99707-0_50

With successes in developing coherent ontologies in the biological, biomedical, and financial domains [2–4], an effort called Industrial Ontologies Foundry (IOF) has been formed to pursue the same goal for the industrial manufacturing domain [5]. Modern manufacturing, particularly with today's complex cyber-physical products and materials, however, requires diverse disciplines of engineering, information technology, and management. This nature makes the scoping and development of coherent ontology for the industrial manufacturing domain a mountainous challenge. To manage scope and expectations, the IOF community has devised a proof-of-concept (POC) project with the aim to prove the viability and values of the endeavor. This paper describes the developments within the POC project.

The paper first describes the IOF formation, organizational structure, and aims of its subgroups. It then describes the POC process, discusses current results, and finally concludes with future plans.

2 IOF Formation and Organization

The first IOF workshop was organized in December 2016 at the National Institute of Standards and Technology (NIST), Gaithersburg, USA [6]. Thereafter, the community has had weekly conference calls and yearly workshops [7, 8].

Following the workshop in 2017, the IOF charter has been drafted and became available on its web site as a community draft [9]. One of the most important messages from the charter that makes IOF unique from other standard organizations that have published engineering ontologies is the intention of the IOF for its ontologies to be freely open. Although the current charter stops short at indicating a particular intellectual property licensing agreement, the community recognizes the need for such an encompassing ontology to be freely reusable, so that the corresponding information can be truly connected. The intention of the community has always been gravitating toward one of the royalty free licenses (e.g., variations of the creative commons licenses [10], which only require some recognitions).

The charter also outlines goals that include not only publishing the freely available ontologies, but also providing principles, guidelines, and governance processes such that a suite of ontology modules can grow in an interoperable fashion. One of the components to enable this is the organizational structure of the IOF community.

The community has devised three kinds of committees: a governance board (GB), a technical oversight board (TOB), and working groups (WGs). There is one GB, one TOB, and as many WGs as deemed necessary by the community. To ensure interoperability, these boards have overlapping personals as shown in Fig. 1, where each circle represents the membership of each board.

The primary role of the GB is to maintain the health and effective operation of the IOF organization. It sets the overall policy and manages legal aspects of the business. The other important role for the GB is to resolve conflicts unresolvable by the TOB.

TOB members are responsible for setting ontology principles and design guidelines used across the WGs. They have an important role to ensure that modules of the IOF ontologies developed by each WG are interoperable and consistent.

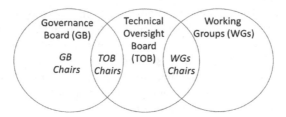

Fig. 1. IOF organizational structure

Each WG develops an ontology or a suite of ontologies of the IOF ontologies vetted by the TOB. Some WGs may be responsible for developing or adapting cross-cutting, domain independent ontologies such as for time or units of measurement. Figure 2 shows types of ontologies anticipated within the IOF ontologies. A WGs may exist for the foundation ontology, each of bubbles, or a group of bubbles in the figure. The top two layers reflect specializations of the IOF ontologies for a particular use that may be private or licensed (developing such specializations is considered out of scope for the IOF).

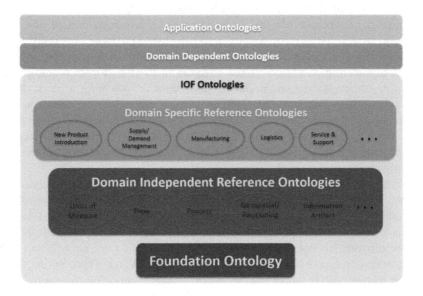

Fig. 2. Architecture of the IOF ontologies [9]

We can observe from Fig. 2 that it is a challenge to establish the scope of each WG, particularly at the Domain Specific Reference Ontologies level as information about a manufactured product overlaps across its life cycle phases and operational areas involved in development and manufacturing of the product. On the other hand, starting from bottom up looking at the choices of foundation ontology (e.g., BFO [11], DOLCE [12]) and Domain Independent Reference Ontologies carry a risk of developing something don't meet the requirements of the domain. To manage such risk and challenge, the IOF community has agreed to start with a proof-of-concept (POC) project, which set the scope based on a consensus rather than the life cycle or operation areas of manufacturing and devised both bottom-up and top-down groups to test the feasibility and values of IOF ontologies. The next section describes this ongoing activity.

3   IOF POC

The IOF proof-of-concept (POC) project was intended to test the feasibility of IOF goals. Therefore, the objectives of the POC included not only producing a small, initial ontology, but also testing the organizational structure (described above) and producing and testing drafts principles and guidelines.

To set the scope, the POC started by asking for most interested manufacturing-related terms from the community. To set a very low bar, textual definitions were optional. Terms submitted should have a use case behind them so that a proof-of-value (POV) can be performed once the ontology is available. Each submission could include up to 50 terms in virtually any form of structured or unstructured file format. After collecting all the submissions, 20 terms were to be identified based on the frequencies of matches across the submissions. Each term has a (synonym) set of closely-matched terms; therefore, we call the output of this step the top-20 sets.

Getting the Top-20 Sets

At the time of this writing, 23 submissions were received, some of which went over the 50-term limit. Submission topic areas included product life cycle management, general manufacturing, manufacturing process, material (in the sense of material science), supply chain management, logistics, shop floor automation, manufacturing resources, production system engineering and analysis, and additive manufacturing.

To identify the top-20 sets, first submissions were transcribed into a web-based collaborative ontology editing tool [13] using a Simple Knowledge Organization System (SKOS) representation [14]. In a few cases, submissions were provided in an Web Ontology Language (OWL) [15] format. The tool was able to import these, then SKOS concept assertions were manually added to their class URIs. In this way, all terms could be mapped using the SKOS *closeMatch* relationship.

This led to the second step, creating a rough mapping. The objective of this mapping was not to do semantic alignment, but rather to set a scope for the POC. Hence, mappers were instructed to be quite liberal with their mapping and to not be concerned with the concept hierarchy. One relative rich submission was copied as a starting point for a canonical terminology (i.e. the IOFPOC skos:ConceptScheme) for mapping. The mapping task was divided among four individuals who performed the mapping consecutively, and the target for completion was a few weeks.

Even with the rough mapping in mind, it was not a trivial work for the last individual because the canonical grew as unmapped terms were added to it. The last individual reported that the search functionality in the tool became very handy. At the finish, the canonical had over 600 terms. Table 1 below shows the resulting top-20 sets.

Due to space limitation, only the terms and counts are shown. Table 2 shows definitions provided for the term set with the most matches. Complete result will be available on the IOF web site [5].

Table 1. The top-20 sets of closely matched terms

	Term set	Count
1	Product, Physical product, Product material, Manufactured product	13
2	Material, Material object, Engineered material	12
3	Manufacturing machine, Processor, Machinery, Machine tool, Machine, Mechanism, Machine, Workstation	10
4	Tool, Tools, Tooling, Manufacturing tool	9
5	Assembly, Part, Composition	8
6	Part, Physical part, Sub assembly, Product component, Component	8
7	Process, Transformation	8
8	Supplier, Supplier provider or vendor, Material supplier	8
9	Transportation process, Move, Movement, Transfer, Transport, Act of transportation, Transport	8
10	Quality, Indicator, General KPI, Quality, Engineering quality, Physical quality	7
11	Requirement, Requirement specification, Control	7
12	Assembly process, Assembly operation, Technological pair positioning, Joining, Act of assembly	6
13	Customer, Business customer	6
14	Feature, Materials property, CAD model feature	6
15	Process plan, Work instructions, Manufacturing method, Operation, Process plan, Manufacturing process plan	6
16	Resource	6
17	Task, Activity, Operation	6
18	Design, Design process	5
19	Equipment, Machinery	5
20	Fixture, Work holder	5

Discussion

It can be seen from Table 1 that judging only by the label, the terms in each set are quite semantically close to each other. However, Table 2 demonstrates that each submission in the set gave a variety of definitions; and a few distinct notions (or concepts) may be refactored from the set. All but three of the submissions provided textual definitions; though two of those three provided subsumption hierarchies. Due to the richness of the semantics provided in the submission, the mapping result frequently yielded closely related notions within each set. That is, we observed that notions in the same set were often either close to each other in a subsumption hierarchy, an action or process of another notion in the set, or a mereologically related notion to another notion in the set. There are however other complex cases where similar terms are used for

Table 2. Textual descriptions for the most frequent set

Term	Textual description
Physical product	Subclass of spatial region (derived from the class axiom)
Product	Product (for manufacturing industry) is a Material Object, manufactured to satisfy a need of the market (e.g. to be sold in order to provide profit and support customers by covering their needs)
Product	The output of a manufacturing process
Product	A material entity or service that is developed to be sold
Product	This is a tangible object manufactured to satisfy a need of the market. For the specific mould maker, common products are: moulds, dies, and high precision parts
Product	Material and/or service sold to others. Note that in manufacturing enterprises 'product' often refers to a product type or class, which in supply chains may be differentiated by packaging, but 'product' may also refer to a product instance
Product	A goods, idea, method, information, object or service created as a result of a process and serves a need or satisfies a want. It has a combination of tangible and intangible attributes (benefits, features, functions, uses) that a seller offers a buyer for purchase
Product material	A material entity produced by man or machine, including raw material, parts, semi-finished product, and finished product
Manufactured product	A product that is created via a manufacturing process
Product	A product is the subject of the activity
Product	Desired output or by-product of the processes of an enterprise. Note 1 to entry: A product can be an intermediate product, end product, or finished goods from a business perspective. [SOURCE: IEC 62264-1:2013-01, 3.1.27]
Product	No definition provided

overlapping notions and similar terms are used for subtly distinct notions. An example of the former case can be observed in Table 2 where 'product' was used exclusively for physical object, both physical object and service, only desired (or designed) output, and both desired and undesired (by-product) output. An example of the latter case is 'material'. In one notion, it is a chemical composition, while in the other, it is a part, assembled component, or raw substance (e.g., metal powder) supplied to the manufacturing activity.

Next Step

In the next step, the IOF community is creating a WG to formalize these top-20 sets. Two kinds of WGs are in the plan, top-down and bottom-up. At the time of this writing, a top-down WG has been formed. Its approach is to classify the notions in the top-20 set using the Basic Formal Ontology (BFO) [11] and conversely to see if BFO needs changes.

The formations of the bottom-up WGs are driven by use cases. At this time, the TOB is soliciting use cases from the community. With use case information, the TOB will cluster use cases together to form bottom-up WGs.

Both types of WGs will allow the submitters an opportunity to complete their submissions with detail textual definitions before the WGs proceed. It is expected that each bottom-up WGs would consider notions beyond the top-20 set. They will take the focal point at ensuring that the harmonized definitions or ontology in each bottom-up domain board satisfy their functional requirements and viewpoints. It is unclear at this point whether each bottom-up WG will produce a more formal definition (or model) such as class diagram or even an ontology. They will however perform gap analysis between their notions and the output from the top-down group by classifying their notions with respect to the top-down view. It is yet to be determined whether the gap analysis will be performed concurrently across all the bottom-up groups or sequentially. The community seems excited about what is coming before them.

4   Conclusion and Future Plans

The IOF is a growing community. After a round of inactivity elimination, over 60 participants have registered and are actively involved with representative across all populous continents except Africa. Both the contingent governance (5 seats) and technical oversight (12 seats) boards consist of diverse representatives from private companies, research institutes, academia, and standard development organizations. Both boards have a lot of deliverables lying ahead. The governance board should set up membership policies, development infrastructure, and intellectual property policy. The technical oversight board should draft ontology design rules (e.g., naming convention, minimal ontological commitment, URIs, versioning) and design principles (e.g., modularity, interaction with existing standards). It is anticipated that the proof-of-concept (POC) project, which is still ongoing, will be the platform for developing these documents. At the present time there is no fee to participate in the IOF; however, the governance board is tasked with developing a business model to sustain the community given a successful POC. Interested individual are invited to submit a request for participation on the IOF web site.

Acknowledgement and a Disclaimer. The authors wish to thank all the Industrial Ontologies Foundry (IOF) members who have contributed their expertise and content to the founding of IOF and the POC project. Any mention of commercial products is for information only; it does not imply recommendation or endorsement by NIST.

References

1. The Economist: April 21 issue on the Third Industrial Revolution (2012)
2. Open Biological and Biomedical Ontology Foundry Web Site. http://obofoundry.org. Accessed 11 July 2018

3. Financial Industry Business Ontology press release. http://www.edmcouncil.org/downloads/20171026_FIBO_Release.pdf. Accessed 11 July 2018
4. FIBO spec page. https://www.edmcouncil.org/financialbusiness. Accessed 11 July 2018
5. Industrial Ontologies Foundry (IOF) Website. https://sites.google.com/view/industrialontologies/home. Accessed 11 July 2018
6. Kulvatunyou, B., Morris, K.: Working Towards an Industrial Ontology Foundry to Facilitate Interoperability. http://blog.mesa.org/2017/03/working-towards-industrial-ontology.html. Accessed 11 July 2018
7. Ivezic, N., et al.: 2017 NIST/OAGi Workshop: Enabling Composable Service-Oriented Manufacturing Systems. NIST Advanced Manufacturing Series 100-15 (2018)
8. NIST/OAGi Workshop Enabling Composable Service-Oriented Manufacturing Systems. https://www.nist.gov/news-events/events/2018/04/2018-nistoagi-workshop-enabling-composable-service-oriented-manufacturing. Accessed 11 July 2018
9. IOF Charter. https://sites.google.com/view/industrialontologies/about/charter. Accessed 11 July 2018
10. Creative Common Licenses. https://creativecommons.org/licenses/. Accessed 11 July 2018
11. Smith, B., et al.: Basic Formal Ontology Home Page. http://ontology.buffalo.edu/bfo/. Accessed 11 July 2018
12. Gangemi, A., Guarino, N., Masolo, C., Oltramari, A., Schneider, L.: Sweetening ontologies with DOLCE. In: Gómez-Pérez, A., Benjamins, V.R. (eds.) EKAW 2002. LNCS, vol. 2473, pp. 166–181. Springer, Heidelberg (2002). https://doi.org/10.1007/3-540-45810-7_18
13. Mobi - a decentralized, federated and distributed graph data platform for teams and communities. https://github.com/matonto/matonto. https://creativecommons.org/licenses/. Accessed 11 July 2018
14. W3C: Simple Knowledge Organization System Reference (2009)
15. OWL Document Overview. https://www.w3.org/TR/owl2-overview/. Accessed 11 July 2018

The Lean Production System 4.0 Framework – Enhancing Lean Methods by Industrie 4.0

Uwe Dombrowski and Thomas Richter[⊠]

Institute for Advanced Industrial Management, Technische Universität
Braunschweig, 38106 Braunschweig, Germany
th.richter@tu-bs.de

Abstract. Industrie 4.0 is one of the major approach towards an increased production effectiveness. For the evaluation of Industrie 4.0 impact on production systems and the followed implementation, a common understanding of all participants and interdisciplinary stakeholders of Industrie 4.0 projects is required. A common and application-orientated framework might support the common understanding. However, a general, common and application-orientated has not been invented and described so far. Furthermore, it has been analyzed, that Lean builds the basis for the implementation of Industrie 4.0. Thus, this paper presents an application-orientated Industrie 4.0 framework and the interdependencies of Industrie 4.0 and Lean Production Systems (LPS), resulting in the Lean Production framework 4.0 (LPS 4.0). Based on this LPS 4.0, a toolbox respectively a catalogue of LPS methods, enhanced by using the Industrie 4.0 framework, has been developed - the LPS 4.0 method catalogue. This supports companies to identify Industrie 4.0 potentials and evaluate the individual benefits of Industrie 4.0.

Keywords: Lean Production Systems · Industrie 4.0 · Industry 4.0
Framework industrie 4.0

1 Introduction

Due to the volatile and globalizing market as well as the accompanying intensified competition, manufacturing companies face new challenges in terms of cost, quality and time. The increasing number of competitors and the change from the seller's to the buyer's market, enable customers to choose from a variety of different products with a high degree of freedom. This increases the need for individual products, whereby a constant cost and quality level is demanded. Thus, the importance of an economic production in lot size 1 will increase for manufacturing companies in the future. This trend can be summarized under the term 'mass customization'. In order to remain competitive as a manufacturing company in high-wage countries like Germany, processes along the entire value chain have to be designed in a productive, efficient and flexible way. To cope the above mentioned continuous increasing challenges, the approach of Industrie 4.0 has been presented at the Hanover Fair in 2011. Industrie 4.0 can be defined as "real time, intelligent and digital networking of people, equipment and objects for the management of business processes and value-creating networks" [1].

I. Moon et al. (Eds.): APMS 2018, IFIP AICT 536, pp. 410–416, 2018.
https://doi.org/10.1007/978-3-319-99707-0_51

A detailed literature analysis from 2017 shows the need, that LPS are building the basis for Industrie 4.0 and the successful implementation of modern information and communication technologies [2]. However, according to a study from 2017, Industrie 4.0 has not been successfully established within the production and companies struggle with the operational implementation of Industrie 4.0 elements [3]. The most important aspects, which hinder especially small- and medium sized companies implementing Industrie 4.0 elements, are the missing understanding of Industrie 4.0 and the absent idea of using Industrie 4.0 elements within the own company and enhancing the individual Lean Production Systems (LPS) and processes. Thus, a practical Industrie 4.0 framework is needed to get a common understanding of Industrie 4.0.

2 Industrie 4.0 Framework

Since the publication of the Industrie 4.0 in 2011, the approach has been under strong discussion and research in science, economics and politics. Many articles regarding Industrie 4.0 have been published, trying to interpret the term Industrie 4.0, including several terms, definitions and description [4]. However, an explicit and consistent understanding and common view is a necessary prerequisite for the Industrie 4.0 implementation. Linguistic and conceptual inaccuracy and misunderstandings are obstacles and hindrances regarding the implementation of Industrie 4.0. [5].

According to a study, 50% of the analyzed companies stated, that the complexity of Industrie 4.0 is a major obstruction implementing Industrie 4.0. [6, 7] To address the mentioned hinders and challenges, a simple and application-orientated framework of Industrie 4.0 needs to be developed. As a consequence, the framework needs to be reduced in complexity and more application-orientated in comparison to the already existing models, which have an IT background and are focusing on the technical aspects of Industrie 4.0 (for example RAMI [8], SIMMI 4.0. [9]).

The IPO-model (Input-Process-Output) is a widely used and common approach for describing the structure of IT processes. Even in the Industrie 4.0, the IPO-model will still be valid and be kept in principle. However, the data acquisition (Input) on the shopfloor (I), the transformation and distribution, the processing & analysis (Process) (II), as well as the output and utilization of these data (Output) (III) will change in the Industrie 4.0. Data will be collected on the shop floor (through sensors or human machine interfaces (HMI)). These data are processed via the Internet of Things (IoT) to be stored, saved and analyzed in cloud servers. That basically means that the collected data are directly and in real time transferred to cloud computers via the internet of things, without using the currently existing automation pyramid and its interfaces and layers (field, control, supervision, management and ERP). Within these cloud computers, data will be analyzed by smart algorithms, pre-defined rules and artificial intelligence. Afterwards, these data will be transferred by the Internet of Things directly to actuators or HMI on the shopfloor level. Thus, the process on the shopfloor level is either controlled by these data automatically or these data are provided by HMI to enable workers on the shopfloor to adjust and adopt process [10] – supported by assistant systems and tools like for example smart glasses (Fig. 1).

Another crucial aspect while implementing Industrie 4.0 is the IT-Security and the Management of the IT-Interfaces. Thus, an Industrie 4.0 framework needs to consider the IT security and the management of IT Interfaces as well. Due to the real-time, intelligent and digital networking of people, equipment and objects, some specific process "features" or "attributes" (IV) will be available, which generate the actual value for the management of business processes [11]. Typical "features" or "attributes", for example, are "traceability/real-time", "data consistency", "smart data", "vertical integration", and "horizontal integration". However, these "features" or "attributes" are a result of the company's individual production system, processes and Industrie 4.0 application.

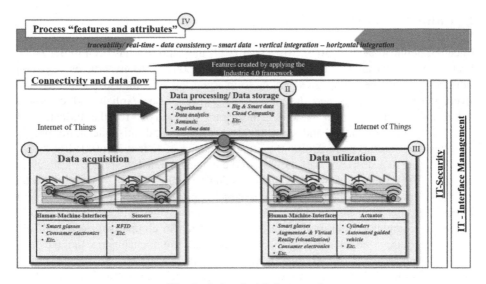

Fig. 1. Industrie 4.0 framework

3   Lean Production System 4.0

Lean Production System 4.0 Framework
In the past, companies have introduced Lean Production Systems (LPS) to create efficient and target-orientated processes. Thus, processes and procedures of manufacturing companies are currently designed according to Lean principles and methods. LPS can be described as "an enterprise-specific methodical system of rules for the continues orientation of all enterprise processes to the customer in order to achieve the largest by the enterprise management" [12] and pursues the goal of a systematic and continuous reduction of non-value-adding activities and the alignment of all processes to the customer's perspective. [13] LPS are targeting to achieve a continuous improvement process (CIP) within the entire enterprise. [12] In the meantime, LPS have been established in almost all industries and has become an industry standard with the publication of the VDI 2870. Nowadays, 90% of manufacturing companies have

already implemented the principles and methods of a LPS in the production environment [14, 15]. The processes and procedures of these companies are often structured and organized according to the LPS principles, using different company-specific individual configured methods of the LPS.

A detailed literature analysis by [2] shows, that the application of modern information and communication technologies (ICT) into LPS can improve the performance of Lean Productions Systems by gaining more efficient production and logistics processes. 2/3 of the analyzed articles have stated explicitly, that Lean builds the basis for Industrie 4.0 [2]. Therefore, Industrie 4.0 needs to be integrated into the existing LPS framework and a catalogue of the enhanced LPS methods is required.

The LPS framework (Fig. 2 – left side) with its structure of goals, processes, principles, methods and tools will still applicable for future production systems [1]. Nevertheless, the data management and the provision of the required data is a prerequisite to generate the actual Industrie 4.0 potential and benefit within the management of processes. People, equipment and objects do have a certain need for specific information to take decisions and adjust processes. Therefore, data will be collected, processed and provided to all related and relevant stakeholders of the processes. Thus, the "data management - provision of information /data" has been integrated in the process layer of the LPS 4.0 framework (see Fig. 2 – right side). This data management and the application of the IPO-model will lead to specific "features" and "attributes". These "features" and "attributes" will have a direct benefit while managing the business processes and the existing methods and tools of current LPS will be enhanced and sophisticated by Industrie 4.0 [1, 2] and will lead to a new maturity of these methods and tools and the entire LPS.

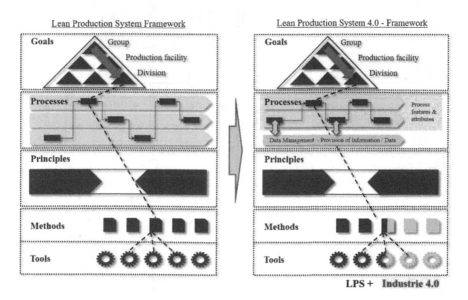

Fig. 2. Lean production system 4.0 framework

Lean Production System 4.0 Methods

As stated above, a common catalogue of sophisticated and enhanced LPS methods supports companies to identify Industrie 4.0 potentials and to configure the individual LPS 4.0. Based on the integration of Industrie 4.0 elements into LPS, some of the existing and known LPS methods of the VDI-Guideline 2870 [12] will be enhanced and sophisticated. However, Industrie 4.0 has a different impact on specific methods, some are influenced more than others and some might have higher potential by

Table 1. Lean production system 4.0 method catalogue

Method catalogue LPS 4.0	Quality	Cost	Time	Risk	Potential	Effort
Digital 5S	●●●	●●	●●	●	●●	●
Dynamic/flexible standards	●	●●	●●	●●	●●	●●
Data & digital supported shop floor Management	●●●	●●●	●●●	●	●●●	●●
Data & digital supported 5 W-Analysis	●●●	●	●●	●	●●●	●●
Data & digital supported 8D-Report	●●	●●	●●	●	●●●	●●
Data & digital supported A3 Sheet	●●	●●	●●	●	●●●	●●
Data & digital supported Ishikawa	●●	●●	●●	●	●●●	●●
Digital Poka Yoke	●●●	●●	●●	●	●●●	●●●
Short term feedback loops	●●	●	●●	●	●●	●●
Data driven process control	●●●	●	●	●●	●●	●●
Simultaneous engineering	●●●	●●	●●●	●●	●●	●●
Data & digital supported Continuous Improvement Process (CIP)	●●●	●●●	●●●	●●	●●●	●●●
Dynamic milk-run	●	●●	●●	●●	●●	●●●
Dynamic KANBAN	●	●●	●●●	●●	●●	●●
Digital twin	●●●	●●●	●●●	●●●	●●●	●●●
Digital factory and process planning	●●	●●	●●	●	●●	●
Real-time value stream analysis:	●	●●	●●●	●	●●●	●●●
Live Sankey Diagram	●	●●	●●●	●	●●●	●●●
Short term layout adaption	●	●●	●●●	●	●●●	●●●
Data & digital supported Total Productive Maintenance	●●●	●●●	●●●	●●	●●●	●●●
Worker assistant systems	●●●	●	●●	●●	●●●	●●
Smart autonomous assistant systems // Algorithms	●●●	●●●	●●●	●	●●●	●●●
One piece flow // realtime production planning	●●●	●●●	●●●	●●	●●	●●●
JIS/JIT	●	●●	●●	●	●●●	●●●
Real-time leveling	●	●	●●	●●	●●	●●
Data driven waste analysis	●	●●●	●●●	●●●	●●●	●●●
Autonomation / online analysis	●●●	●●	●●	●	●●●	●●
SMED	●	●●	●●●	●	●●	●
Target management	●●	●●	●●	●	●●	●●
IT Security	●●	●●	●●	●●	●●	●●
Interface Management	●●	●●	●●	●●	●●	●

●●● high

●● medium

● low

applying Industrie 4.0 than others. The impact analysis has been done quantity wise by analyzing 260 existing German Industrie 4.0 use cases from a data base of the "Plattform Industrie 4.0"[1] in the first step. [2, 16] In the second step, the results have been analyzed quality wise with an interview of five production engineers and eight Industrie 4.0 scientist, who evaluated the impact from Industrie 4.0 on the specific Lean Production System Methods with the impact factor from 0 (now impact) to 5 (high impact). Based on the evaluation, LPS methods with an impact factor higher than 2 have been further developed and described to LPS 4.0 methods.[2] Furthermore, some additional methods, supplementing the described LPS methods in the VDI 2870, needs to be taken into consideration and have to be part of the LPS 4.0 method catalogue as well. The LPS 4.0 methods have been evaluated regarding the goal-contribution (quality, cost, time) and the risks, the potential and the effort while implementing and performing the method by the above mentioned participant group of production engineers and Industrie 4.0 scientists. The derived LPS methods and the evaluation is shown in Table 1. The catalogue serves production engineers and production planners to get a brief overview of the methods and supports the identification of potentials for the individual processes according to the distinct production system. Nevertheless, the configuration of the individual company's LPS 4.0 requires a specific implementation procedure to ensure an efficient and systematical implementation of the LPS 4.0 methods.

4 Review and Outlook

Within this paper, a general and application-orientated Industrie 4.0 framework has been presented. The Industrie 4.0 framework supports a common understanding of all (interdisciplinary) stakeholders of Industrie 4.0 and LPS projects, independent of the specific background of the project members. As a LPS is a prerequisite for Industrie 4.0, a LPS 4.0 framework has been developed. It is shown, that the "features" and "attributes" of Industrie 4.0, which will be generated by connecting people, equipment and objectives in real-time, have a direct impact on managing the business processes within LPS. Furthermore, LPS 4.0 methods have been developed and evaluated. This evaluation serves as a basis for generating and evaluating ideas of Industrie 4.0 applications in individual processes and LPS. Nevertheless, the individual configuration and implementation of Industrie 4.0 respectively the LPS 4.0 requires a systematical implementation procedure. The evaluated LPS 4.0 method catalogue could be integrated into this systematical implementation procedure. The development of that systematical

---

[1] Plattform Industrie 4.0 is a joint project founded in 2013 by the associations BITKOM, VDMA and ZVEI with the aim of developing and implementing the high-tech strategy of Germany. In 2015, the project has been taken over by the BMBF and BMWi to take additional social and political aspects into account. Within the organization of the Plattform Industrie 4.0, there are various working groups investigating the future project Industry 4.0. https://www.plattform-i40.de/.

[2] The evaluation has been done by 13 Industrie 4.0 experts. To secure the evaluation and the results, the amount of participants could be enlarged regarding the quantity and the background.

implementation procedure is part of current research activities at the Institute for Advanced Industrial Management - Technische Universität Braunschweig - Germany.

References

1. Dombrowski, U., Richter, T.: Supplementing lean production systems with information and communication technologies. In: Proceedings of the Flexible Automation and Intelligent Manufacturing Conference, FAIM 2016, pp. 654–661 (2016)
2. Dombrowski, U., Richter, T., Krenkel, P.: Interdependencies of Industrie 4.0 & lean production systems. In: A Use Cases Analysis. proceedings of the Flexible Automation and Intelligent Manufacturing Conference, FAIM 2017, pp. 1061–1068 (2017)
3. Staufen, A.G.: Industrie 4.0-Index (2017). https://www.staufen.ag/fileadmin/HQ/02-Company/05-Media/2-Studies/STAUFEN.-studie. Accessed 15 June 2018
4. Tschöpe, S., Aronska, K., Nyhuis, P.: Was ist eigentlich Industrie 4.0? Zeitschrift für wirtschaftlichen Fabrikbetrieb 110(3), 145–149 (2015)
5. Pfrommer, J., et al.: Begrifflichkeiten um Industrie 4.0 – Ordnung im Sprachwirrwarr. Fraunhofer IOSB, RWTH Aachen, Siemens AG, TU Dresden, Karlsruhe (2014). http://publica.fraunhofer.de/eprints/urn_nbn_de_0011-n-2905334.pdf. Accessed 1 June 2018
6. Beck, A.: Industrie 4.0 - Wo steht Deutschland?, Bitkom (2018). https://www.bitkom.org/Presse/Anhaenge-an-PIs/2018/Bitkom-Pressekonferenz-Industrie-40-23-04-2018-Praesentation-2.pdf. Accessed 15 June 2018
7. Statista GmbH: Industrie 4.0 in Deutschland (2017). https://de.statista.com/statistik/studie/id/21467/dokument/industrie-40-in-deutschland-statista-dossier/. Accessed 15 June 2018
8. Sendler, U., et al.: Industrie 4.0. Beherrschung der industriellen Komplexität mit SysLM. In: Sendler, U. (ed.) Industrie 4.0. Xpert.press, pp. 1–19. Springer, Heidelberg (2016). https://doi.org/10.1007/978-3-642-36917-9_1
9. Leyh, C., Schäffer, T., Forstenhäusler, S.: SIMMI 4.0 – Vorschlag eines Reifegradmodells zur Klassifikation der unternehmensweiten Anwendungssystemlandschaft mit Fokus Industrie 4.0. Multikonferenz Wirtschaftsinformatik (MKWI), pp. 981–992 (2016)
10. Siepmann, D.: Industrie 4.0 – Fünf zentrale paradigmen. In: Roth, A. (ed.) Einführung und Umsetzung von Industrie 4.0, pp. 35–46. Springer, Heidelberg (2016)
11. Dombrowski, U., Richter, T.: Ganzheitliche Produktionssysteme und Industrie 4.0. Zeitschrift für wirtschaftlichen Fabrikbetrieb 111(12), 771–774 (2016)
12. VDI 2870: Ganzheitliche Produktionssysteme - Grundlagen, Einführung und Bewertung. Beuth-Verlag (2870) (2012)
13. Dombrowski, U., Mielke, T. (eds.): Ganzheitliche Produktionssysteme. Aktueller Stand und zukünftige Entwicklungen. VDI-Buch. Springer, Berlin (2015). https://doi.org/10.1007/978-3-662-46164-8
14. Glass, R., Seifermann, S., Metternich, J.: The spread of lean production in the assembly, process and machining industry. In: Proceedings of the CIRP Conference, vol. 55, pp. 278–283 (2016)
15. Staufen, A.G.: 25 Jahre Lean Management. Lean Gestern, Heute und Morgen (2015)
16. Dombrowski, U., Richter, T., Krenkel, P.: Wechselwirkungen von Ganzheitlichen Produktionssystemen und Industrie 4.0. Eine use-case-analyse. Zeitschrift für wirtschaftlichen Fabrikbetrieb 112(6), 430–433 (2017)

AR/VR-Based Live Manual for User-Centric Smart Factory Services

Minseok Kim[1], Kyeong-Beom Park[1], Sung Ho Choi[1],
Jae Yeol Lee[1(✉)], and Duck Young Kim[2]

[1] Chonnam National University, Gwangju 61186, South Korea
jaeyeol@jnu.ac.kr
[2] UNIST, Ulsan 44919, South Korea

Abstract. Although several physical implementations of the smart factory have been introduced, a viable implementation or platform has not been proposed to make human workers perceive smart factory services more effectively and naturally with respect to task assistance. In this paper, we propose an AR/VR-based Live Manual, a new approach to provide workers with user-centric smart manufacturing services in IoT-enabled smart factory testbeds. The proposed live manual can make both on-site and remote workers do their tasks more effectively by utilizing and synchronizing AR with VR, which can help them to make better decisions. The synchronized dual view between AR and VR can help workers to understand the situation more easily and clearly depending on the worker's contexts and manufacturing situations.

Keywords: AR/VR-based live manual · Smart manufacturing services
Augmented reality · Virtual reality · Smart factory

1 Introduction

One of the key themes in Industry 4.0 is to build a new manufacturing ecosystem (e.g., smart factory) through the fusion of smart manufacturing systems and information communication technology (ICT). The new manufacturing ecosystem refers to a customer-oriented production system that can incorporate ICT technology into the existing manufacturing services to effectively and actively reflect the user's demands and requirements [1, 2].

To manufacture products, various production processes such as machining, assembly and inspection should be performed [3, 4]. In order to be more productive and safe while performing tasks, the worker must be able to accurately and effectively recognize the manufacturing situation and the operation status of related facilities. The operating conditions of the facilities change in real time due to internal factors such as facility failure and external factors such as production status or customer requirement change. For this reason, it is very difficult for the worker to recognize all working situations and to acquire all related knowledge. Therefore, it is essential to provide relevant and user-centric visual information to workers in a form appropriate to their working situations [5, 6].

© IFIP International Federation for Information Processing 2018
Published by Springer Nature Switzerland AG 2018. All Rights Reserved
I. Moon et al. (Eds.): APMS 2018, IFIP AICT 536, pp. 417–421, 2018.
https://doi.org/10.1007/978-3-319-99707-0_52

With the advent of smart augmented reality (AR) and virtual reality (VR) devices, AR and VR have been widely applied to a variety of fields such as entertainment, game and education. In particular, in manufacturing industries, AR and VR are considered to play an important role in providing more user friendly visual information to the worker for task assistance and monitoring [7–9]. However, it is almost impossible to provide user-oriented manufacturing services without considering the worker's location, the status of manufacturing facilities, and worker's role and situation [5, 6, 9].

In this paper, we propose an AR/VR-based Live Manual, a new approach to provide workers with user-centric manufacturing services regarding worker's contexts and situations by combining AR, VR, and deep learning in IoT-enabled smart factory testbeds. The proposed live manual can be executable in various mobile and wearable devices, and has been successfully applied to two smart factory testbeds. Section 2 overviews the proposed approach. Section 3 presents the proposed AR/VR-based Live Manual with some implementation results. Section 4 concludes the paper with some remarks.

2 Proposed AR/VR-Based Live Manual

This paper proposes an AR/VR-based Live Manual to more effectively provide user-centric manufacturing services such as information visualization, monitoring, and sharing for task assistance and maintenance in the IoT-enabled smart factory environment. Figure 1 presents the research goal and framework of the proposed live manual. We aim to provide an AR/VR-enabled mediator to workers in smart factory testbeds built in two cities such as Ulsan and Gumi, South Korea as shown in Fig. 1.

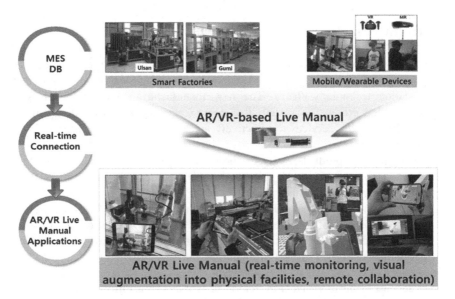

Fig. 1. Proposed AR/VR live manual for supporting various kinds of user-centric task assistance.

The AR/VR-based Live Manual supports the visual augmentation of manufacturing information acquired from the related manufacturing execution system (MES) in real time into physical artifacts through AR/VR technology depending on the user context or situation. The deep learning technology has also been utilized to find the worker's location and to detect physical facilities in the factory to overcome the limitation of the conventional marker-based AR. The AV/VR Live Manual consists of five main modules: *Human-Machine Interface, AR/VR Visualization, Detection and Recommendation, Information View Management,* and *Interaction with Information* modules. Based on the five modules, the AV/VR Live Manual enables to track and recognize physical facilities and products using a deep learning-based object detection, to analyze the detected results and relevant manufacturing information retrieved from MES and working environment, and to embed the analyzed information into the worker's display of smart devices, rendered in AR and VR.

3 AR/VR-Based Live Manual with Deep Learning-Based Object Detection

One of the key features of the AR/VR Live Manual is to make workers do their tasks more effectively by combining and synchronizing AR and VR. Furthermore, the deep learning method is applied to support physical object detection and to suggest recommendation for task assistance by analyzing manufacturing information, user contexts and result of the object detection.

For the traditional marker-based AR, it is essential that the facility or its surrounding environment must have a planar surface to attach AR markers. To make worse, to support different perspective-based recognition, multiple markers must be attached, which is almost impossible in the real environment. For this reason, the object detection without markers is also supported by applying a deep learning method such as YOLO [10] as shown in Fig. 2. This method can overcome the inherent problem of the marker-based AR.

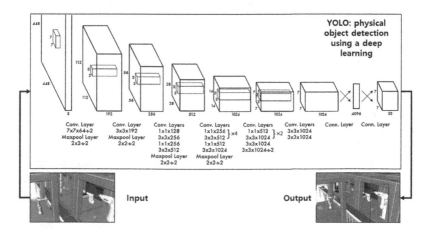

Fig. 2. Applying the deep learning-based object detection to AR [10].

Based on the detected facilities and the worker's context, the live manual can retrieve related manufacturing information, filters the relevant information required for the worker, and augments it into corresponding physical facilities or products through smart and wearable devices. For this purpose, another machining learning method with an auto encoder (AE) is used, which can recommend a necessary task or suggest an appropriate information depending on the worker's role [11].

Another key feature of the AR/VR Live Manual is to provide a synchronized dual view in addition to the main AR view. In particular, the dual view can be switched, and the VR can be the main view if the worker needs alternative information than augmented information, which can complement the AR view. Therefore, the worker can more effectively monitor and analyze the manufacturing information depending on the situation of the working environment. Figure 3 presents the implementation of the AR/VR-based Live Manual in two different modules of the smart factory testbeds.

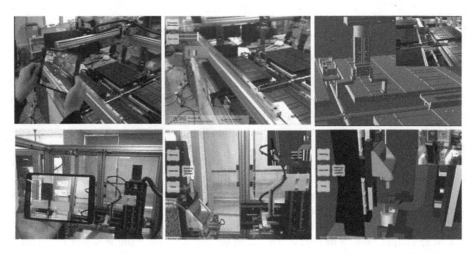

Fig. 3. Implementation of AR/VR-based live manual using handheld devices that has been applied to two different smart factory modules; the live manual supports dual views that can complement AR and AR as they are visually synchronized each other.

We have developed the AR/VR-based Live Manual for providing user-centric manufacturing services, which has been applied to the two real smart factory testbeds built in two cities. The two testbeds can produce different types of BLDC motors and handpieces, respectively. In addition to the AR-based task assistance with the dual view and the deep machine learning, the proposed approach can also support different functionalities such as VR-based smart factory simulation with a high immersion using VR HMDs such as HTC Vive™, world-in-miniature (WIM)-based visualization, mixed reality (MR)-based visualization and monitoring of physical artifacts using wearable glasses such as MS HoloLens™. In particular, when a remote collaboration is performed, it is possible to interoperate with the on-site worker with the AR module. Using different level of functionalities, on-site workers and remote workers can monitor real-time manufacturing information more easily and perform required tasks more effectively.

4 Conclusion

In this paper, we proposed the AR/VR-based Live Manual, a unified approach to provide human workers with smart factory services in IoT-enabled testbeds. The proposed live manual system can be executable in various smart and wearable devices by taking advantage of combining and synchronizing AR and VR. In addition, it can make workers do their tasks more effectively as the proposed approach can provide situation-adaptive visualization with respect to the worker's surrounding contexts and manufacturing situations. The dual view conversion between AR and VR helps on-site workers to switch the live manual to either VR- or AR-focused mode using smart and wearable devices. We have also developed several AR/VR-based live manual modules using smart glasses. We are currently designing a more concrete platform for supporting various AR/VR-based task assistance. We are also evaluating the usability and usefulness of the proposed approach.

Acknowledgements. This work was supported by the Basic Science Research Program through the National Research Foundation of Korea (NRF) funded by the Ministry of Education (NRF-2016R1D1A1B03934697) and the Development of IIoT-based manufacturing testbeds for the Korean manufacturing equipment industry funded by the Ministry of Science and ICT (2015-0-00374).

References

1. Lee, J., Bagheri, B., Kao, H.-A.: A cyber-physical systems architecture for Industry 4.0-based manufacturing systems. Manufact. Lett. **3**, 18–23 (2015)
2. Wang, S., Wan, J., Li, D., Liu, C.: Knowledge reasoning with semantic data for real-time data processing in smart factory. Sensors **18**(2), 471 (2018)
3. Peniche, A., Diaz, C., Trefftz, H., Paramo, G.: Combining virtual and augmented reality to improve the mechanical assembly training process in manufacturing. In: Proceedings of the 6th WSEAS International Conference on Computer Engineering and Applications, pp. 292–297 (2012)
4. Wang, X., Ong, S.K., Nee, A.Y.C.: Multi-modal augmented-reality assembly guidance based on bare-hand interface. Adv. Eng. Inf. **30**(3), 406–421 (2016)
5. Henderson, S., Feiner, S.: Exploring the benefits of augmented reality document for maintenance and repair. IEEE Trans. Vis. Comput. Graph. **17**(10), 1355–1368 (2011)
6. Webel, S., et al.: An augmented reality training platform for assembly and maintenance skills. Robot. Auton. Syst. **61**, 398–403 (2013)
7. Zhu, Z., Branzoi, V., Wolverton, M., Murray, G., Vitovitch, N., Yarnall, L.: AR-mentor: augmented reality based mentoring system. In: Proceedings ISMAR, pp. 17–22 (2014)
8. Liu, C., Cao, S., Tse, W., Xu, X.: Augmented reality-assisted intelligent window for cyber-physical machine tools. J. Manufact. Syst. **44**, 280–286 (2017)
9. Kim, M., Choi, S.H., Park, K.-B., Lee, J.Y., Cho, Y.-J.: Conceptual framework for providing manufacturing UX using context awareness and dual reality. ICIC-ELB **9**(1), 53–59 (2018)
10. Redmon, J., Divvala, S., Girshick, R., Farhadi, A.: You only look once: unified, real-time object detection. In: Proceedings CVPR 2016, pp. 779–788 (2016)
11. Zhang, S., Yao, L., Xu, X., Wang, S., Zhu, L.: Hybrid collaborative recommendation via semi-autoencoder. arXiv preprint arXiv:1706.04453 (2017)

Active Role-Based Database System for Factory Planning

Uwe Dombrowski, Christoph Imdahl$^{(\boxtimes)}$, and Alexander Karl

Institute for Advanced Industrial Management (IFU), Technische Universität
Braunschweig, Langer Kamp 19, 38106 Brunswick, Germany
c.imdahl@tu-bs.de

Abstract. The globalization of markets and the paradigm shift to mass customization lead to a turbulent planning environment. For companies, this results
in an increased planning frequency and an increased volume of planning data in
the factory planning process. Solutions are the concepts of the Digital Factory
and the Digital Shadow. In the context of these two concepts, database systems
must be integrated into systematic planning tools in order to make continuous
and active use of factory planning knowledge and to reduce the amount of data
to the required. Against this background, the paper proposes a concept for the
development of an active role-based database system that converts information
from various sources into manageable restrictions and filters them by assigning
them to the relevant planning phase and to the responsible employee in the
company. To validate the concept, the database system is integrated in a factory
planning table. A use case shows, that in combination with the planning table,
the database system reduces the planning time of factories and at the same time
improves planning quality by integrating stored planning knowledge.

Keywords: Digital Factory · Database system · Factory planning

1 Global Factors Influencing Factory Planning Processes in Companies

Due to the globalization of markets and the paradigm shift in production from mass
production to customized mass production, product cycles and the degree of individualization as well as the complexity of products have been decreasing for years [1, 2].
As a result, companies' planning processes have to meet customer demands for more
variants, in the shortest possible delivery times and maximum transparency across the
entire business processes [3, 4]. Under these circumstances, there is an increase in
planning frequency, the volume of planning data raises and requires its exchange
through further interfaces along the value chain. Therefore, new methods and instruments have become necessary in order to master the increasingly complex product and
production development processes economically [1]. One solution is the systematic use
of planning methods and virtual planning and validation in order to implement the
modifications in the existing or new factory after successful evaluation [3–5].

I. Moon et al. (Eds.): APMS 2018, IFIP AICT 536, pp. 422–430, 2018.
https://doi.org/10.1007/978-3-319-99707-0_53

2 Digital Factory and Digital Shadow

The mentioned solution approach is summarized under the concept of the Digital Factory. According to the widely accepted VDI 4499 definition, the Digital Factory is an approach that includes digital models, methods and tools that support early parallelization and digital processing from product development and production planning to virtual start-up and operation [1]. Therefore, the Digital Factory is a digital model of the physical structure of a factory but does consider non-physical aspects such as existing knowledge as well [4, 6]. The goal is an integrated planning, evaluation and continuous improvement of the essential structures and processes of the real factory in relation to the product [1]. Accordingly, data integration and digital plausibility checks, can increase the planning speed by approx. 20% and the planning quality by 10 to 15% [7, 8]. Due to further developments in data processing in the digital age, the concept of Digital Shadows has gained in importance beside the Digital Factory [9]. The Digital Shadow is a digital image of the real-time data in production, development and other areas with sufficiently detailed accuracy [10]. Therefore, the Digital Factory is the static digital image of the factory and is created from historical data of the real factory, while the Digital Shadow is a real-time model of the factory. The simulations of both approaches help to achieve improvements in the current factory, so both concepts are closely linked [9]. In the future, factory planning with the Digital Factory and the Digital Shadow will require the intelligent use of existing digital data to extract planning knowledge and integrate it into the planning process [11]. For this purpose, database tools must be created to systematically convert planning data into stored planning knowledge and to use it actively across all planning phases of the factory planning process [3, 5, 12]. In addition, the tools must have a human-oriented visualization in order to include all persons who must be jointly involved in solving specific tasks [5, 13].

3 Meaning of Database Systems for Factory Planning

A database system consists of a database and a data management system. These two components enable the structuring, storage and provision of data and thus the automation of planning steps [14]. The planning of a factory is divided into creative processes and routine tasks. For the creative processes, the participative factory planning approach is mostly used, in which all planners work together on the same planning status to create many creative variants with high planning quality [4]. Therefore, the objective of database systems is to automate routine tasks such as calculations or the consideration of requirements in order to create more freedom for creative tasks [15].

Database systems support the factory planning process with the following functions:

- Collection of planning know-how from experienced employees and continuous improvement of the database through further project experience
- Knowledge accumulation is supported by structured and retrievable data
- Offering predefined modules, such as social rooms or standard workstations in libraries.

With these functions, database systems enable even inexperienced planners to quickly plan different variants of production layouts with high quality and compare these planning alternatives [15].

However, the use cases show that current database systems only provide planning knowledge passively, which means that the planner must actively extract the information from the database himself. The database system described below differentiates itself at this point by making the planning knowledge actively available, since it continuously checks the planning status according to validity in real time. The appropriate planning knowledge is then assigned and provided to the responsible employee. In participative, creative planning processes, planners therefore know immediately whether the planning status is valid and which changes must be made.

4 Design of an Active Role-Based Database System for Factory Planning

In accordance with the requirements elaborated in the previous section, this paper proposes a design for a database system for factory planning. In summary, the aim of the database system is to intuitively support the planner in the respective factory planning phase by actively providing planning knowledge to the relevant employee during the planning process. To achieve this goal, the functional principle of the database system shown in Fig. 1 consists of four modules. These pursue four subgoals in order to enable active provision of planning knowledge.

1. Building a Database by capturing data and knowledge for factory planning from different sources in different fields for the factory planning procedure.
2. Validating the planning status by structuring the data into requirements, transferring it into logical arguments and linking it to planning objects.
3. Actively providing and filtering unfulfilled requirements by factory planning and role in the company.
4. Enable the traceability of requirements to their original document in order to prove that special requirements have been planned.

The four modules are explained in detail in the following subsections.

4.1 Module 1: Capturing Data

In Module 1 information relevant to the factory planning process must be collected from different sources in different fields. This step generates the factory planning-specific database, which is structured and filtered in the following modules. The database requires the following data:

Type of Information: The type assigns they can be assigned to the subject areas. Examples in the factory planning process are e.g. environmental, work safety, etc.

Source: Indicates the document in which the original claim was formulated and is readable.

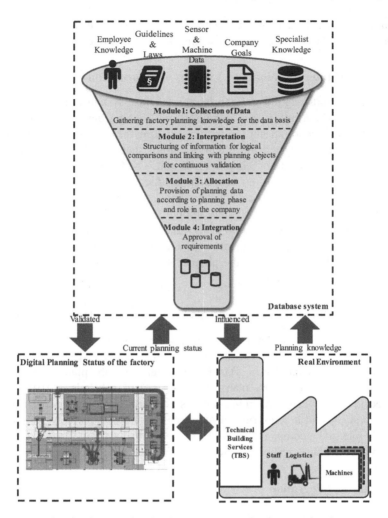

Fig. 1. Concept for the database system for factory planning

Specific Page: Specifies the exact location of the information in the original document in order to avoid longer search effort for sources with several pages.

Publisher: Can be persons, organizations or entities who have written the information.

Revision Level: Displays the current status of the information and allows the system to add and update information.

Serial Number: Enables the unique determination of the information if several requirements can be recorded from one source. The unique identification of data is an important premise for the database.

Original Text of the Requirement: Literally describes the content of the information and is therefore unaltered, since the information is available without interpretation.

With the specified data, requirements can be recorded, clearly determined and traced back to the exact place of origin within the original document.

4.2   Module 2: Interpretation and Linking of Information

In module 2, the most significant step of the database system is performed by converting the information into if-then conditions and linking them to specific planning objects, such as production machines. In this structure, the database system can use the data from the real factory and the digital planning status to check whether the production requirements have been taken into account. The following steps are performed for this structuring process. In the first step, production requirements are determined from the information stored in the database. These requirements are formulated with as few words as possible in order to avoid ambiguities. Once the requirement has been formulated, it must be converted into a logical if-then comparison. Finally, this condition is linked to an object or element in the factory so that the system can check the requirement. The link also shows the planner what needs to be changed so that the planning status becomes valid.

4.3   Module 3: Allocating Requirements in the Factory Planning Process

In order to process the large number of restrictions formed in the factory planning process, it is necessary that the requirements for the factory and production planning are filtered and made available in a targeted manner. First, the planning knowledge is filtered according to the factory planning phase so that only relevant information is considered in the respective planning process. To ensure that the unfulfilled requirements are processed in a goal-oriented manner, they are then actively assigned to the responsible role in the company. The roles in the company are in turn linked to one or more employees, who is responsible for the unfulfilled requirement.

4.4   Module 4: Integration of Requirements

The last module is a release process that checks new factory or production requirements and changes before they are taken into account in the planning process. The purpose of the approval process is to prevent incorrect or obstructive requirements from slowing down the planning process or reducing the quality of planning. The release is carried out by the factory planner as he has the know-how to check the relevance of the data, tasks and restrictions and to decide whether the classification in the planning phase is correct.

5   Use Case: Participative Factory Planning with the IFU Factory Planning Table 4.0 and the Database System

As already explained in Sect. 3, the concepts of the Digital Factory and the Digital Shadow require new forms for planning workplaces. One widely used approach is participative factory planning [4]. Planning tables have established themselves as

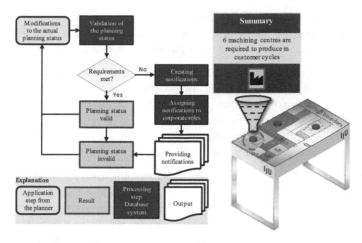

Fig. 2. Application cycle of the database system on the IFU factory planning table 4.0

helpful assistance systems for this creative form of factory planning, because they allow a group of planners to plan simultaneously at the same planning stage.

The IFU factory planning table 4.0 was developed at the Institute for Advanced Industrial Management (IFU) of the Technische Universität Braunschweig. Figure 2 shows the functional principle of the planning table with the application cycle of the database system. The aim of the IFU factory planning table 4.0, in the context of participatory factory planning, is to include all knowledge carriers in the planning process in order to implement a valid layout within the shortest planning time with the best planning quality. For this purpose, the table has a 65-in. touch display on which parallel cooperation is possible. On this multi-touch interface, users can insert objects using Marker with 3D representations and design the layout by moving the markers and using gestures on the touch surface. The application cycle shows that every time the planners modify the planning status, by adding new objects or changing the layout, the database system checks whether all requirements for the factory that are linked to objects have been met. If all requirements have been met, the planning status is evaluated as valid. For all unfulfilled requirements, a message is generated from the short description and shown to the responsible employee in the summary on the display. With cameras under the planning table, employees can be identified by their badges, so that the logged in employee only receives notifications concerning his role in the company. If the planner needs more detailed information in addition to the general description, the planning table provides the linked source for the requirement. This application cycle enables planners to work through the planning processes for a new factory step-by-step on one planning status and generate a valid, evaluated layout within less time.

In a factory planning project with a medium-sized company, the combination of IFU factory planning table 4.0 and database system was used. The aim of the project was to check the initial layout derived from an existing production plant for optimality and validity so that the construction project could begin. With the initial layout, new variants were created in a workshop with the planning group consisting of eight people at the planning table. In addition to several smaller requirements, the developed database system was able to avoid serious planning errors and adding value by:

- Consideration of an additional machining center, due to the reduction of the customer cycle through the new production program
- Correct dimensioning of the driveways for loading and unloading of goods from the newly planned continuous flow rack
- Shift participants' focus to finding creative solutions to requirements rather than thinking about unnoticed problems.

To illustrate how it works, Table 1 shows an excerpt from the database system for the listed requirements.

The generated variants from the workshop were then summarized into a valid planning status that combines most of the benefits. In this way, a very good and valid planning status for the start of the construction project could be planned in a two-week project. The use case shows the relevance of the active provision of information by the developed database system in the participative factory planning process in order to create space for the creative planning processes and to achieve a high planning quality.

Table 1. Extract of the database system with described requirements

Collection of data				Interpretation and linking				Allocating		Integration
Type of information	Source	Serial number	Original text	Short description	Logical equation	Linked object	Value	Factory planning step	Role	Approved
Material flow	Production program	1_1	The analysis indicates that 6 machining centres and 4 assembly stations are required for production in customer cycles	6 machining centres are required for production	If number of linked objects <6, then False	Machining center	FALSE	Layout planning	Production planner, CEO	Yes
Logistics	Technical document	2_1	The track for loading and unloading must be 2.5 m wide	The track for loading and unloading must be 2.5 m wide	If distance of an object to the linked object <2.5 m, then False	Flow rack	FALSE	Layout planning	Production planner, CEO	Yes
Work safety	Directive	3_1	The escape route must be free	The escape route must be free	If the distance of an object to the linked object = 0, then False	Escape route	FALSE	Layout planning	Safety officer, logistics specialist	Yes

6 Summary and Outlook

With the concepts of the Digital Factory and the Digital Shadow, the use of digital planning tools has become an essential success factor in the factory and production planning of manufacturing companies. Especially the reduction of the provided data to the most essential data for the specific process will gain more and more importance. The presented database system enables the storing of planning knowledge and continuous monitoring of the planning status. It differs from existing database systems primarily in the active provision of planning knowledge which is filtered according to factory planning phase and role, so that an active and sustainable use of stored knowledge is possible. The use case shows that implementing the database system in a factory planning tool, such as the planning table, leads to a faster and more creative planning process with higher planning quality. This allows the planning process to focus on the disclosure of implicit expert knowledge of the employees. The disadvantage of such a system is the increased initialization effort, therefore future research is mainly needed to automate the initialization and updating of the database with the requirements through the direct coupling of the database with the real production via digital shadow.

References

1. VDI 4499: VDI 4499 Part1: Digital Factory – Fundamentals (2008)
2. Hu, S.J., et al.: Assembly system design and operations for product variety. CIRP Ann. – Manuf. Technol. **60**(2), 715–733 (2011)
3. Bley, H., Fritz, J., Zenner, C.: Die zwei Seiten der Digitalen Fabrik. ZWF **101**(1–2), 19–23 (2006)
4. Dombrowski, U., Bothe, T., Tiedemann, H.: Visionen für die Digitale Fabrik. ZWF **96**(3), 96–100 (2001)
5. Westkämper, E., Bischoff, J., Briel, R., von Dürr, M.: Factory digitalizing: an adapted approach to a digital factory planning in existing factories and buildings. Werkstattechnik Online **91**, 304–307 (2001)
6. Gregor, M., Medvecky, S.: Digital Factory – Theory and Practice. Engineering the Future: Sciyo (2010)
7. Kühn, W.: Digital Factory - Integration of Simulation Enhancing the Product and Production Process towards Operative Control and Optimisation. Electrical, Information and Media Engineering, University of Wuppertal, Wuppertal (2006)
8. Haller, E., Schiller, E.F., Hartel, I.: Impact of the digital factory on the production planning process. In: Zülch, G., Jagdev, H.S., Stock, P. (eds.) Integrating Human Aspects in Production Management. IICIP, vol. 160, pp. 73–84. Springer, Boston, MA (2005). https://doi.org/10.1007/0-387-23078-5_6
9. Wohlfeld, D., Weiss, V., Becker, B.: Digital shadow – from production to product. In: Bargende, M., Reuss, H.-C., Wiedemann, J. (eds.) 17. Internationales Stuttgarter Symposium. Proceedings, pp. 783–794. Springer, Wiesbaden (2017). https://doi.org/10.1007/978-3-658-16988-6_61
10. Bauernhansl, T., Krüger, J., Reinhart, G., Schuh, G.: WGP-Standpunkt Industrie 4.0. WGP, Darmstadt (2016)

11. Deuse, J., Eigner, M., Erohin, O., Krebs, M., Schallow, J., Schäfer, P.: Intelligente Nutzung von implizitem Planungswissen der Digitalen Fabrik. ZWF **106**(6), 433–437 (2011)
12. Zäh, M.F., Patron, C., Fusch, T.: Die Digitale Fabrik. ZWF **98**(3), 75–77 (2003)
13. Eigner, M., von Hauff, M., Schäfer, P.D.: Sustainable product lifecycle management: a lifecycle based conception of monitoring a sustainable product development. In: Hesselbach, J., Herrmann, C. (eds.) Glocalized Solutions for Sustainability in Manufacturing, pp. 501–506. Springer, Heidelberg (2011). https://doi.org/10.1007/978-3-642-19692-8_87
14. Kemper, A., Eickler, A.: Datenbanksysteme: Eine Einführung. De Gruyter, 10th edn. München (2015)
15. Bracht, U., Geckler, D., Wenzel, S.: Digitale Fabrik, 2nd edn. Springer, Heidelberg (2018). https://doi.org/10.1007/978-3-662-55783-9

Industry 4.0 – Collaborative Cyber-physical Production and Human Systems

A Method to Assess Social and Human Factors of Production Innovations

Stanisław Strzelczak$^{(\boxtimes)}$ ⓘ and Stanisław Marciniak

Faculty of Production Engineering,
Warsaw University of Technology, Warsaw, Poland
{s.strzelczak,iosp}@wip.pw.edu.pl

Abstract. This paper examines human and social factors of production innovations. An assessment method is proposed to be used for various purposes at the enterprise level. The method is built upon a theoretically justified model that relates human and social endowments to the production innovations as well as the outcomes. The approach derives from the resource based viewing of a strategy process. The holism of assessment is assured by the consideration of crucial interdependencies, the consistency of assessment and the integrity of assessment.

Keywords: Holistic assessment · Innovations · Human factor
Social factor

1 Introduction

Contemporary business environments require dynamic, innovative and evolutionary capabilities. In such circumstances the effective utilization and the development of human and social capital become key success factor for the sustained competitive performance of industrial firms [1]. Technological change and diffusion (especially in reference to the exponential technologies), rapid innovations and deregulation have eroded the recognized entry barriers, like: technological supremacy, economy of scale, patent protections and government regulations.

Traditionally the economic capital, which comprises financial and material assets, such as equipment and plants, has received all the attention of theory, research, and business practice. In a new economy that recognizes the value from intangible sources, both scholars and managers appreciate equally the importance of human and social capital for economic returns [2].

This paper explores the impact of human and social factors to the innovativeness of industrial firms. We propose a theoretically grounded model that relates human and social endowments to the production innovations as well as the ultimate outcomes. The model is used as the basis for a method for assessing impacts of the both intangible factors. By following the septuple pattern 'objectives-context–perspectives–modules–subjects–metrics-methods', a reference procedure for a structured assessment was developed. The holism of evaluation is assured by taking into account the viewpoints of all

I. Moon et al. (Eds.): APMS 2018, IFIP AICT 536, pp. 433–441, 2018.
https://doi.org/10.1007/978-3-319-99707-0_54

stakeholders as well as all crucial interdependencies between the factors and the primary and secondary effects, and also by securing the consistency and integrity of assessment.

2 Background

The notion of human capital pertains to knowledge, skills and other abilities of individuals that allow for changes in action and economic growth [3]. Basically human capital is developed through education and training. The literature provides evidence of a positive correlation between the human capital, measured by education level and work experience, and the economic performance [4]. Human capital is an important source of competitive advantage to the individuals, organizations and societies [5].

Existing research distinguishes different types of human capital [2]. *Firm-specific human capital* is expertise, skills and abilities valuable within a specific firm. They may give an advantage over competitors if they are not transferable to other firms [6]. *Industry-specific human capital* pertains to know-how gathered by learning and experience specific to an industry. It may stimulate innovativeness through social networking and exchanges of tacit know-how among the main players in that industry [7]. Especially the proximity, both in a 'cultural' and geographical sense, within a region or industry, matters in terms of innovation as the exchange of tacit knowledge requires a high degree of mutual understanding [7, 8]. *Individual-specific human capital* comprises education, vocational training, experience and psychological capital (self-efficacy, creativity, attitudes, resilience, etc.) [1]. The psychological component can be developed following the UX theory, e.g. using mastery experiences, performance attainments, arousal, social persuasion or vicarious experiences [2].

The importance of aligning human capital and corporate strategy with the performance has been supported by an extensive research evidence [9, 10]. Literature recognizes country level contributions to the human capital, including educational, social, cultural, and welfare factors [1, 11].

Social capital refers to the networking, relationships and trust, industrial relations[1], associational activities[2] and collective behavior[3]. Unlike the economic view that perceives humans as a resource, social capital applies a sociological view of human actions occurring in groups and teams [2]. The central proposition in the literature on social capital is that networking and relationships provide valuable resources and endowments that can be utilized for the good of an individual or a collectivity [10]. Social capital, like the human one, is being referred to different levels, including the individual, organizational, and societal. At the organizational level, social capital can be defined as the value to an organization from networking and relationships possessed by its members and engaged in collective activities [12]. Prior research emphasizes the

---

[1] Industrial relations are relationships and interactions between employees and employers.

[2] Associational activity pertains to the attitudes common in a society to associate or socialize.

[3] Collective behavior refers to the attitudes to cooperate and subordinate self-interest for that of the collectivity. Norms of civic and social behavior delimit selfish behavior and encourage individuals to exhibit higher care and concern for the good of public or organizations.

role of social capital for innovation and business performance [10, 12], as well as the development of human capital [5].

Literature provides an extensive evidence of positive associations of innovations with the human and social capital, including the following correlating factors:

- level of human capital [2, 10];
- external networking, especially for the collaborative innovations [7, 8];
- level of proximity, especially for the collaborative innovations [7, 8];
- level of interpersonal and interorganizational trust [2, 7];
- industrial relations [13];
- level of associational activities, both in a company and among organizations [2];
- norms (or level) of collective behavior [2].

The above dependencies apply to radical innovations and continuous improvements.

The assessment and relating of human and social capital with innovations requires quantitative measurement of the factors considered, taking into account the benefits and risks. Measurement of the value derived from intangible sources is a challenge, since it is usually difficult to separate the specific contributions of human and social capital. Literature suggests using direct measures of particular items (natural metrics or Likert-type scales), both leading and lagging, to evaluate specific impacts of human and social factors on innovation and business performance [2]. Adaptation of asset valuation measures (market-to-book ratio, Tobin's Q, etc.) and the method of calculated intangible value (CIV) is also recommended by some authors [14].

Some suggested ways to measure and evaluate social capital involve the size, structure and composition of networks [1]. Another approach derives from the Social Network Analysis (SNA) and suggests such measures as: reciprocity, propinquity, multiplexity, homophily and completeness [15]. Also the theories of social and economic networks offer a range of dynamic models to relate social capital and innovations (e.g. the Axelrod model can be used to analyze the spread of knowledge [16]).

Several innovation indicators are suggested in the literature, like: amount of patents innovations and improvements (both filed and implemented), expenditures and resources dedicated to innovations, level of using innovations, industry-specific yardsticks, outputs and outcomes generated through innovations [2].

3 Human and Social Factors vs. Innovations and Performance

According to the literature review in Sect. 2, existing theories perceive human and social factors as essential resources to sustain a competitive advantage. According to the relational view [17] and the theory of factor endowments [18], human and social capital is supplemented by the networking and environmental endowments. This setup is compatible with the resource-oriented structure of the strategy base, which entangles ends (outcomes – competitive performance) and means: resources and strategic capabilities, including innovativeness [19]. Thus, a holistic framework can be derived to relate the human and social factors, the innovativeness and the performance.

Holistic assessment respects all stakeholders by the multi-perspective viewing of a domain [19]. In reference to the paradigm of new economy, we can identify the following perspectives for assessment of the ultimate effects: (i) economic (financial performance and capital turnover); (ii) social (welfare, safety, law observance and civic norms), (iii) ecological; (iv) customer and market; (v) operational; (vi) development (learning, innovation, growth); (vii) sustainability (resilience, vulnerability).

By adapting the reference framework of operations strategy presented in [19] and integrating the aforementioned items of human and social capital, a contextual model was developed that combines: (i) leading factors: internal resources and external endowments; (ii) lagging factors: human and social capital; (iii) outputs - strategic capability of interest: innovativeness; (iv) outcomes: internal and external performance (Fig. 1). The latter item represents the ultimate effects, as perceived by stakeholders.

Own resources embrace all tangible and intangible assets that contribute to the human and social capital [19]. Organization refers to configuration, allocation, location, layout and links of own resources or sites. It determines the internal exchanges that enhance human and social capital. External endowments are contributions from the networking of a firm and from environment. The base of strategy is complemented with particular strategic abilities, including the dynamic and evolutionary capabilities and the innovativeness [19]. The latter item is included in the proposed model.

The model was populated with all items of human and social capital and other items suggested in literature. This way a comprehensive contextual setup of factors and effects was obtained, which enables to develop dedicated models for assessments of interdependencies of factors and effects. These can be formulated as influence maps, then possibly as functional models. Apart of the strategy process, other contexts of

Leading factors			
INTERNAL RESOURCES		EXTERNAL ENDOWMENTS	
OWN RESOURCES	ORGANIZATION	NETWORKING	ENVIRONMENTAL
Work conditions Remuneration Work safety Organizational culture	Roles of sites Linking of sites Mutual learning	Relationships Trust Interorganizational behavior Connectivity Learning exchanges Cultural exchanges Agglomeration Similarities/Proximity	Learning/Competence Educational Cultural Legal Supports/subsidies Associational activities Collective behavior Welfare and social safety Similarities/Proximity

Lagging factors	
HUMAN CAPITAL	SOCIAL CAPITAL
Knowledge Skills Experience Psychological capital	Industrial relations Organizational / Associational behavior Trust Collective behavior

Outputs – strategic capability
INNOVATIONS
Radical innovations Continuous improvement

Outcomes						
INTERNAL AND EXTERNAL PERFORMANCE						
Economical	Sociological	Ecological	Customers and markets	Operational	Development	Resilience & vulnerability

Fig. 1. Reference map of human and social conditioning of innovations - strategy view

using the model can be suggested, like: manage and control processes, performance management, planning and controlling the development of human and social capital, innovations management, assessment of locations (along the operations strategy process), benchmarking and inter-firm comparisons (IFC), other analytics and research.

4 Holistic Approach to Assessment

Holistic approach claims that parts of a whole are in idiosyncratic interdependencies that cannot exist independently of the whole or cannot be understood without any reference to the whole, i.e. by inferring from knowledge about the regularities governing the parts [19, 20]. Holistic assessment has to take into account: perspectives of all stakeholders, all important factors and effects, all crucial dependencies (trade-offs, offsets, discrepancies etc.) [19]. It is comprehensive but also pragmatically selective - not unjustifiably reductionist and consistent.

Consistency of assessment, depending to a context, pertains to three aspects [19]. Time-consistency determines phasing of assessment, e.g. according to a strategy life-cycle (ex ante, reviewing, ex post) or innovation life-cycle (ideation, research, development, implementation, exploitation and improvement, abatement, disposal). Spatial consistency determines objects of assessment, considering the vertical (hierarchical) and horizontal extent (punctual vs. 'cradle-to-cradle'). Scope-consistency determines subjects of assessment, considering the functional (economic, social, ecological customer and market, operational, development, resilience and vulnerability) and causal extent (leading factors, lagging factors, final effects). By considering a given context the above items can be chosen accordingly. Apart of consistency, specific fits are crucial to avoid dysfunctional assessments [21]: (i) complexity fit: reflects whether the setting of assessment adequately considers the trade-offs and other critical interdependencies of factors and effects; (ii) measurement fit: consistency of applied metrics with the measured characteristics; (iii) aggregation-granularity dilemma: too detailed assessments and too aggregated measures increase the assessment effort and the difficulty to address complexities, while using too focused measures reduces diagnostic power and directing function of the assessment; (iv) informational fit: conformance with the support from legacy ICT systems; (v) methodical fit: conformance of assessment with the legacy systems and processes of manage and control.

The adequacy and correctness of assessment depend to a large extent on the competences involved. In this regard the quality of assessment relies on the dynamics and balance between technical and social controls. It is more likely that humanistic organizations that leverage reciprocity and participative approach will exhibit more competent assessments than the Weberian, leadership-based or neo-liberal organizations.

5 Measurement of Factors and Effects

This section outlines a framework to evaluate social and human factors of production innovations, which was derived from the model presented in Sect. 3. The measures were derived from literature, They are ordered according to scope, module (sub-range) and subject of assessment (Table 1). Non-specific measures are not considered.

Table 1. Measures to assess social and human factors of production innovations

Scope	Module	Subject	Measure
External endowments	Environmental	Learning and cultural exchanges	Checklist/Levels or ratios
		Accessible competence	Checklist/Levels or ratios
		Education	Checklist/Levels or ratios
		Legal	Checklist
		Supports/subsidies	Checklist/Level
		Associational activities/Collective	Benchmark/Level
		behavior	Salaries<Average salary>
		Welfare	Unemployment<Ratio>
		Social safety	Benchmark
		Similarities/Proximity	
	Networking	Relationships/Trust	Checklist/Level
		Interorganizational behavior	Benchmark/Reciprocity index
		Connectivity	Multiplexity/Completeness
		Learning and cultural exchanges	Checklist/Level
		Agglomeration	Checklist/Level/Propinquity
		Similarities	Checklist/Level/Homophily
		Proximity	Checklist/Level/Propinquity
Internal endowments	Own resources	Work conditions	Checklist/Level
		Remuneration	Benchmark/Reciprocity index
		Work safety	Checklist/Level
		Organizational culture	Checklist/Level
	Organization	Roles of sites	Exchanges<Checklist/Level>
		Linking of sites	Links<Checklist/Level>
		Mutual learning	Exchanges<Checklist/Level>
Human capital	Competence	Knowledge/Skills/Experience	Items<Checklist>/Level
	Psychological capital	Self-efficacy/Creativity/Attitudes/Resilience	Checklist/Level
Social capital	Social behavior	Industrial relations	Actions<Checklist/Level>
		Organizational behavior	Items<Checklist/Level>
		Trust	Level
		Collective and associational behavior	Items<Checklist/Level>
	Collective behavior	Norms of civic behavior	Benchmark
Innovations	Radical innovations	Actions	Expenditures; Number of projects
		Outputs	Patents filed/implemented Benefits<Checklist/Level>
	Continuous improvement	Actions	No. of Kaizen events/Quality circles
		Outputs	Number or effects of improvements
Outcomes	Economic	Efficiency, Growth/Welfare	Percentages indicate ratios
	Social	Work continuity/safety	Percentages indicate ratios
	Ecological	Consumption/depletion of natural resources	Eco-efficiency/Intensity ratios/Percentages indicate ratios
		Waste/Pollution	
	Customer & market	Competitiveness	Percentages indicate ratios
	Operational	Efficiency/Costs/Quality	Level/Ratios
	Development	Intellectual capital/Exports	Percentages indicate ratios
	Resilience and vulnerability	Risks	Risk metrics
		Contingencies	Checklist/Level

The framework provides a reference to be tailored, detailed or extended along different assessments, including: performance management, planning and controlling the development of human and social capital, management of innovations, assessment of locations, benchmarking and IFC, business and economic analytics and also research.

6 A Method of Assessment

This section outlines a method to assess social and human factors of production innovations. The phasing of the method was adapted from the pattern 'objectives-context–perspectives–modules–subjects–metrics-methods'. The method itself is derived from the model presented in Sect. 3 and assumes using the measurement framework presented in Sect. 5. The holism of assessment is secured through including indispensable steps to identify all factors and effects as well as by considering important dependencies between them. In regard to the consistency of assessment, the method relies on involvement of the relevant competencies, which depends on the dynamics and balance between technical and social controls in the focal organization.

The method assumes seven phases (Fig. 2). Firstly objectives and context are contextualized. Normally objectives are derived from the strategy. Then perspectives of assessment are defined in regard to the setup of stakeholders and the constraints identified, accordingly. Altogether the first two phases enable to obtain in a holistic way the base for further assessment. The third phase consists in identification, then causal modelling of all factors and effects. Next, a structure of measures is developed, then functional models of the domain. Fifth phase provides input information to the assessment through data collection analytics. The evidence for assessment is then verified, possibly modified, and approved. The last phase consists in implementation of results through deployment, then monitoring and reactive (corrective) activities.

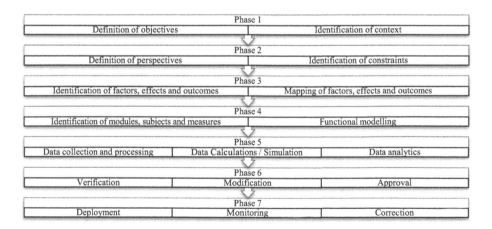

Fig. 2. Phased procedure of assessing human and social factors of production innovations

The above reference framework can be customized and detailed to a specific procedure in accordance with the current perspective and context (as indicated in Sect. 3), the required aspects of consistency (Sect. 4) and measurement (Sect. 5), and the purpose of using the method determined by the context of its use (Sect. 3). The method exemplifies a full-blown holistic approach to assessment.

7   Summary and Further Work

This paper proposes a method to assess human and social factors of production innovations. It is based on a model derived from a strategy framework, which is based on the resource-based view. The key constructs in the model are human and social capital. The model is equipped with a measurement framework. The solution is derived from the existing research evidence. The design of method assures holistic assessment through comprehensive and multi-perspective viewing of the domain, consideration of all important factors, effects and complexities, as well as integrity of assessment.

The contribution of this paper lies in an original holistic approach to assessment of human and social factors of innovations. The proposal is sound, as it synthesizes the existing research evidence. It is also viable and universal in the sense that it matches to various contexts of its use. As yet the approach relies on theoretical justification and requires further validation. Another need for further examine the factors and effects and their interdependencies using the phenomenological research. The empirical validation of the method provides another challenge.

References

1. Luthans, F., Luthans, K.W., Luthans, B.C.: Positive psychological capital: beyond human and social capital. Bus. Horiz. **47**(1), 45–50 (2004)
2. Dakhli, M., De Clercq, D.: Human capital, social capital and innovation: a multi-country study. Universiteit Ghent Working Paper, No. 2003/211 (2003)
3. Becker, G.: Human capital. National Bureau of Economic Research, New York (1964)
4. Gimeno, J., Folta, T., Cooper, A., Woo, C.: Survival of the fittest? Entrepreneurial human capital and the persistence of underperforming firms. Adm. Sci. Q. **42**, 750–784 (1997)
5. Coleman, J.S.: Social capital in the creation of human capital. Am. J. Sociol. **94**, S95–S120 (1988)
6. Barney, J.B.: Firm resources and sustained competitive advantage. J. Manage. **17**(1), 99–120 (1991)
7. Strzelczak, S.: Modularized innovations in cluster-based innovation networks in China. In: Brzóska, J., Pyka, T. (eds.), Modernity of Industry and Services Under Crisis and New Challenges, pp. 229–242, TNOiK Katowice, Katowice (2013)
8. Taylor, R., Morone, P.: Innovation, networks and proximity: an applied evolutionary model. In: Proceedings of the 4th European Meeting on Applied Evolutionary Economics (EMAEE), 19–21 May 2005, The Netherlands (2005)
9. Harter, J.K., Schmidt, F.L., Hayes, T.L.: Business-unit level relationship between employee satisfaction, employee engagement, and business outcomes: a meta-analysis. J. Appl. Psychol. **87**(2), 268–279 (2002)

10. Nahapiet, J., Ghoshal, S.: Social capital, intellectual capital and the organizational advantage. Acad. Manage. Rev. **23**, 242–266 (1998)
11. Prais, S.J.: Productivity, Education and Training: an International Perspective. Cambridge University Press, Cambridge (1995)
12. Adler, P.S., Kwon, S.-W.: Social capital: prospects for a new concept. Acad. Manage. Rev. **27**(1), 17–40 (2002)
13. Hashimoto, M.: The industrial relations system in Japan: an interpretation and policy implications. Manage. Decis. Econ. **12**, 147–157 (1991)
14. Dzinkowski, R.: The value of intellectual capital. J. Bus. Strat. **21**(4), 3–4 (2000)
15. Lai, G., Lin, N., Leung, S.: Network resources, contact resources, status attainment. Soc. Netw. **20**, 159–178 (1998)
16. Barrat, A., Berthélemy, M., Vespignani, A.: Dynamical Processes on Complex Networks. Cambridge University Press, Cambridge (2010)
17. Dyer, J.H., Singh, H.: The relational view: cooperative strategy and sources of interorganizational competitive advantage. Acad. Manage. Rev. **23**(4), 660–679 (1998)
18. Porter, M.E.: Competitive advantage, agglomeration economies, and regional policy. Int. Reg. Sci. Rev. **19**(1-2), 85–94 (1989)
19. Strzelczak S.: Integrated assessment of operations strategy. Scientific Papers of Silesian University Technology, Series: Organization & Management, no. 116, pp. 95–108 (2018)
20. Marciniak, S.: Evaluation of functioning of an innovating enterprise considering the social dimension. In: Lödding, H., Riedel, R., Thoben, K.-D., von Cieminski, G., Kiritsis, D. (eds.) APMS 2017. IAICT, vol. 513, pp. 372–379. Springer, Cham (2017). https://doi.org/10.1007/978-3-319-66923-6_44
21. Strzelczak, S.: Integrated assessment of 'Green–Lean' production. Int. J. Autom. Technol. **11**(3), 815–828 (2017). https://doi.org/10.20965/ijat.2017.p0815

A Literature Review on Human Changeover Ability in High-Variety Production

Christopher Ketelsen(✉) , Rasmus Andersen , Kjeld Nielsen ,
Ann-Louise Andersen , Thomas D. Brunoe , and Sofie Bech

Department of Materials and Production, Aalborg University, Aalborg, Denmark
christopherketelsen@gmail.com

Abstract. The business strategy of Mass Customization, enabled by e.g. Reconfigurable Manufacturing and Changeable Manufacturing is based on the fundamental premise; to achieve high operational efficiency, while producing high-variety products in small batches and with short product-life cycle of the unique products. To efficiently achieve this premise in manufacturing systems, all levels of changeability must be addressed. This paper investigates a fundamental sub-set of this changeability, which has not been addressed comprehensively by academia; the human changeover ability on workstation level. Based on a literature review, this paper identifies seven human related challenges which must be addressed to be able to manage high-variety and low-volume efficiently on a changeover ability level. This leads to a subsequent literature review that aims at investigating possible approaches and solutions for the identified challenges. Overall seven approaches and solutions have been identified which address five of the seven identified challenges. This leaves two challenges open; the forgetting and learning curve. These two challenges are therefore proposed for further research to be at the cutting edge of an emerging challenge organizations striving for high-variety production will meet.

Keywords: Changeover ability · Human changeover ability · Changeability
Changeable manufacturing · Mass customization

1 Introduction

High-variety production, often related to the business strategy of Mass Customization has experienced increased attention throughout the last decade both in academia [1], as well as in the industry [2]. The requirement to produce a higher variety of products, accompanied by decreasing production volume relative to both the batch-sizes in production as well the overall product-life-cycle (PLC) of products, causes challenges for traditional dedicated manufacturing systems [3]. To cope with these conditions, changeability has to be developed on all structural levels spanning from the supply-chains agility to the workstations changeover ability [4]. Arguably, changeability has to be developed bottom-up, with the changeover ability being the fundament for all other changeability-levels [5]. Changeover ability is hereby defined as *"[…] the operative ability of a single machine or work-station to perform particular operations on a known work piece or subassembly at any desired moment with minimal effort and*

© IFIP International Federation for Information Processing 2018
Published by Springer Nature Switzerland AG 2018. All Rights Reserved
I. Moon et al. (Eds.): APMS 2018, IFIP AICT 536, pp. 442–448, 2018.
https://doi.org/10.1007/978-3-319-99707-0_55

delay" [4]. Addressing changeover ability on the workstation level therefore becomes crucial in order to strengthen a factory's changeability [6]. Achieving changeover ability requires both physical, logical and human enablers [7]. Physical changeover ability relates to the machines and equipment, whereas the logical changeover ability relates to the planning and scheduling of the system components. Human changeover ability relates to the human, and more specifically the operator on the workstation level. Focus for the human changeover ability is the operators' ability to cope with a large variety of tasks both cognitively as well as skill wise. All of the three enablers have to be addressed in order to achieve comprehensive changeability [8]. While physical changeability enablers have been widely addressed in research on lower structuring levels of the factory including the workstation [9], focus on addressing the human enabler remains limited. To investigate this gap in literature, this review has the purpose to address the requirements that must be fulfilled to achieve human changeover ability. Subsequently, existing literature addressing these requirements will be reviewed to investigate the current state-of-art. This will lead to an assessment and documentation of gaps between the investigated requirements and the methods presented in existing literature, which will suggest viable new research directions. The research questions for this paper are:

RQ1: Which requirements does high variety production impede for the human changeover ability?
RQ2: Which solutions exist to address challenges on human changeover ability?
RQ3: Which gaps between literature and requirements are required to be closed?

2 Requirements for Human Changeover Ability in High-Variety Production

This section presents challenges that must be addressed to achieve human changeover ability in high-variety production environments. Focus in this article will be on the human changeover ability in traditional factories, which still constitute the majority of industry [10]. The following section will be built around the challenges caused by the increased variety and the accompanied reduced volume respectively. The challenges within each field have been identified by reviewing literature, which often indirectly address the implied challenges caused by them.

2.1 Requirements Caused by Increased Product Variety

Increasing the variety of products offered by a company affects the manufacturing systems significantly, as variety proliferates on all levels and creates new requirements for processes and the workstations that perform these processes [11]. Intuitively, the increased amount of product varieties increases the amount of unique production configurations in the manufacturing systems. For operators, this increases the number of different configurations that must be operated [12]. It therefore requires broader skillsets of the operators to operate the manufacturing system. As a further consequence of the increased variety, time between operating the same configuration increase, which challenges the operator in recalling the specifics of each configuration. This phenomenon is referred to as the forgetting curve and is related to increased re-work and decreased efficiency as a function of increased time and other tasks in between performing the same configuration [13]. Another challenge for the human changeover ability, is the increased automation as an enabler for the production systems change-ability [4]. Automation thereby in general has the purpose to automate simple and routine operations currently performed by operators. This increases the density of the complex and undefinable operations left for the operators, resulting in overall more complex work tasks for the operator [13]. Finally, with the increased automation, the interaction between operator and machines will become of increased importance. This requires the operators acquire skills to interact with the interface of the machines and furthermore be adaptable and flexible to resolve problems with the machines [6].

2.2   Requirements Caused by Decreased Volume

Apart from the requirements related to the increased variety, the reduced production volumes also affect the operators' changeover ability. This holds true for both day-to-day operations, as well as for the whole PLC. By reducing the production batch volumes in day-to-day operations, the number of changeovers performed relative to the overall production quantities are increased. Apart from reducing the overall efficiency of the manufacturing system, this also increases the workload of the operators, if performed manually. It is therefore required to find an efficient solution to decrease the changeover times to achieve the desired number of changeovers with the available resources. Relative to the reduced volume and implicitly length of the PLC connected to the mass customization paradigm, the learning curve of operators relative to new production configurations gets challenged [16]. To operate and changeover to a new production configuration efficiently, several repetitions and sufficient operation time are required [17]. By reducing the PLC of the unique production configurations, the amount of repetitions and operation time get decreased corresponding. This thereby increases the amount of comparably inefficient production time of a product on the learning curve relative to the fully efficient production time [18]. This emphasizes the requirement for faster learning of new production configurations to achieve satisfactory production efficiency for the overall PLC. The decreased PLC further challenges the current approach to continuous improvement (CI) initiatives. In a simplified version, CI initiatives are based on historical learnings, which are converted into new procedures to improve processes and increase efficiency. Reducing the PLC, will correspondingly reduce the time where learnings can be converted into improvements, within the lifetime of a production configuration.

3   Solutions for Human Changeover Ability in High-Variety Production

Based on the challenges identified in the previous section, this section introduces how these are addressed by research with the purpose to identify shortcomings and gaps in relation to achieving changeover ability in the context of high-variety production. The findings are summarized in Table 1.

3.1 Solutions for Variety Related Challenges

Four different approaches have been identified in literature to address three out of the four variety related challenges. The first presented approach is competence training, focusing on increasing the competencies of the operators [19–21]. By training, a deeper understanding of the required competence is gained, instead of memorizing the skill in focus. Even though not reducing the workload, this approach thereby increases the holistic insight and interpretation of various tasks thereby enabling intuitive operation of a larger variety of tasks. This approach can be applied to three different challenges, respectively to broaden the operators' skillset, optimize the execution of complex tasks or to equip the operator with competencies for the interaction with the machines of the manufacturing system. By upskilling operators, their work motivation and morale gets increased, while simultaneously dependency of the specific human likewise is increased for the organizations point of view [15]. Another approach to address the mentioned challenges is by introducing information systems based on augmented technology to assist the operator [12, 19]. Instead of storing the complexity and required knowledge at the operator, it can be stored and communicated by the information system. This decreases the dependency of the specific operator, but likewise also the motivation and knowledge. Apart from the knowledge-based approaches, two organizational approaches must be foretaken to address the density of complex tasks. To handle the increased complexity, the operators are required to have corresponding autonomy and empowerment [4, 12, 22]. This requires the operators both to take responsibility for demanding decisions and furthermore get allocated the corresponding authority to do so. To support the described autonomy, a flat organization is required to enable the operators to rapidly take complex decisions [4, 12].

3.2 Solutions for Volume Related Challenges

There have been identified three approaches to address two out of the three presented volume related challenges. First, the Single minute of exchange (SMED) methodology can be applied to optimize changeover procedures and processes and reduce the duration of the single changeovers to free capacity for the increased amount [16]. Yet, this approach concerns retrospective improvement. To achieve proactive improvements of the changeovers, the design-for-changeover approach can be applied in design of products or processes [16]. In order to address the decreased CI effect relative to the PLC, compressed kaizen events in the early phases of the PLC can be suggested [23]. This initiative enables to rapidly improve the new production configurations and correspondingly reap the benefits in the subsequent PLC. Yet, this approach requires high amount of commitment and resources of the organization for each production configuration, which may, when considering reduced PLC's, result in negative economic impact.

3.3 Research Gap

Based on the literature review summarized in Table 1, two of the seven challenges are not addressed sufficiently in literature, respectively the learning and forgetting curve.

Even though both concepts are addressed in their respective subject area, and furthermore on a general operations management level, their impact on increasing product variety and decreased production volume are not addressed and solutions are not found. It is therefore required to investigate the effect of both the learning and forgetting curve on the changeover ability of the human operators in high-variety production environments. Without further research on the presented challenges, companies striving for increased product variety and decreased production volume will be able to achieve changeover ability on both the physical and logical yet lack the human aspect. With one enabler lacking, this will hinder the company's changeability and result in inefficient business processes, undermining the overall objective.

Table 1. List of approaches addressing the presented challenges

Challenge / Approach	Variety related challenges				Volume related challenges		
	Broader skillset	Forgetting curve	Density of complex tasks	Human/ machine	Increased changeovers	Decreased learning curve	Decreased CI effect
Competence Training	X		X	X			
Augmented technology	X		X	X			
Autonomy			X				
Flat organization			X				
SMED					X		
Design for change-over					X		
Kaizen events							X

To address the presented challenges, research directed towards digital assistance systems can be suggested. These systems must be designed to deliver the required information necessary for the operators for either faster learning or avoidance of forgetting in an easy understandable way. This requires joint effort in research between operations management, cognitive psychology and software-development. Inspiration can be drawn from research within the field of conducting assembly instructions, where major overlaps relative to investigated challenges and solutions are present [24].

4 Conclusion

Human enablers of changeability have been neglected by academia in the rise of production philosophies striving for higher production variance and lower production volumes. This paper has shed light on seven challenges related to human changeability and more specifically human changeover ability on workstation level. A literature review on the seven discovered challenges within several academic areas revealed approaches and solutions for five of the seven challenges, leaving two challenges unresolved; the forgetting curve and the learning curve. It can therefore be concluded that further research must be conducted which addresses these specific challenges in the light of human changeover ability in a production environment. Corresponding approaches and solutions must be devised to be at the cutting edge of an emerging challenge organizations striving for mass customization will meet.

References

1. Fogliatto, F.S., Da Silveira, G.J.C., Borenstein, D.: The mass customization decade: an updated review of the literature. Int. J. Prod. Econ. **138**, 14–25 (2012)
2. Slamanig, M.: Einleitung. In: Produktwechsel als Problem im Konzept der Mass Customization, pp. 1–16, Gabler, Wiesbaden (2011)
3. Koren, Y., Shpitalni, M.: Design of reconfigurable manufacturing systems. J. Manufact. Syst. **29**, 130–141 (2011)
4. ElMaraghy, H.A., Wiendahl, H.-P.: Changeability - an introduction. In: ElMaraghy, H.A. (ed.) Changeable and Reconfigurable Manufacturing Systems, pp. 3–24. Springer, London (2009). https://doi.org/10.1007/978-1-84882-067-8_1
5. Owen, G.W., Matthews, J., McIntosh, R.I., Culley, S.J.: Design for changeover (DFC): enabling flexible and highly responsive manufacturing. In: Fogliatto, F.S., da Silveira, G.J.C. (eds.) Mass Customization: Engineering and Managing Global Operations, pp. 247–273. Springer, London (2011). https://doi.org/10.1007/978-1-84996-489-0_12
6. Wiendahl, H.-P., ElMaraghy, H.A., Nyhuis, P., et al.: Changeable manufacturing - classification, design and operation. CIRP Ann. Manufact. Technol. **56**, 783–809 (2007)
7. Deif, A.M., ElMaraghy, W.H.: A systematic design approach for reconfigurable manufacturing systems. In: ElMaraghy, H.A., ElMaraghy, W.H. (eds.) Advances in Design, pp. 219–228. Springer, London (2006). https://doi.org/10.1007/1-84628-210-1_18
8. Rösiö, C.: Supporting the Design of Reconfigurable Production Systems. Mälardalen University (2012)
9. Andersen, A.-L., Brunoe, T.D., Nielsen, K.: Reconfigurable manufacturing on multiple levels: literature review and research directions. In: Umeda, S., Nakano, M., Mizuyama, H., Hibino, H., Kiritsis, D., von Cieminski, G. (eds.) APMS 2015. IAICT, vol. 459, pp. 266–273. Springer, Cham (2015). https://doi.org/10.1007/978-3-319-22756-6_33
10. Verzijl, D., Dervojeda, K., Jorn, S.-K.-F., et al.: Smart factories capacity optimisation, p. 17 (2014)
11. Elmaraghy, H., Schuh, G., Elmaraghy, W., et al.: Product variety management. CIRP Ann. Manufact. Technol. **62**, 629–652 (2013)
12. Gehrke, L., Kühn, A.T., Rule, D., et al.: A discussion of qualifications and skills in the factory of the future. In: Hann Messe 2015, p. 28 (2015)
13. Jaber, M.Y., Bonney, M.: Lot sizing with learning and forgetting in set-ups and in product quality. Int. J. Prod. Econ. **83**, 95–111 (2003)
14. Wiendahl, H.-P., Reichardt, J., Nyhuis, P.: Production requirements. Handbook Factory Planning and Design, pp. 29–62. Springer, Heidelberg (2015). https://doi.org/10.1007/978-3-662-46391-8_3
15. Waschull, S., Bokhorst, J.A.C., Wortmann, J.C.: Impact of technology on work: technical functionalities that give rise to new job designs in Industry 4.0. In: Lödding, H., Riedel, R., Thoben, K.-D., von Cieminski, G., Kiritis, D. (eds.) APMS 2017. IAICT, vol. 513, pp. 274–281. Springer, Cham (2017). https://doi.org/10.1007/978-3-319-66923-6_32
16. McIntosh, R., Owen, G., Culley, S., Mileham, T.: Changeover improvement: reinterpreting Shingo's "SMED" methodology. IEEE Trans. Eng. Manage. **54**, 98–111 (2007)
17. Anzanello, M.J.: Selecting relevant clustering variables in mass customization scenarios characterized by workers' learning. In: Fogliatto, F.S., da Silveira, G.J.C. (eds.) Mass Customization: Engineering and Managing Global Operations, pp. 291–304. Springer, London (2011). https://doi.org/10.1007/978-1-84996-489-0_14

18. Elmaraghy, W.H., Nada, O.A., Elmaraghy, H.A.: Quality prediction for reconfigurable manufacturing systems via human error modelling. Int. J. Comput. Integr. Manufact. **21**, 584–598 (2008)
19. Wiendahl, H.-P.: Systematics of changeability. In: Wiendahl, H.-P., Reichardt, J., Nyhuis, P. (eds.) Handbook Factory Planning and Design, pp. 91–118. Springer, Heidelberg (2015). https://doi.org/10.1007/978-3-662-46391-8_5
20. Gerst, D.: Designing workplaces from a work organizational perspective by detlef gerst. In: Wiendahl, H.-P., Reichardt, J., Nyhuis, P. (eds.) Handbook Factory Planning and Design, pp. 169–195. Springer, Heidelberg (2015). https://doi.org/10.1007/978-3-662-46391-8_7
21. Acatech Kompetenzentwicklungsstudie Industrie 4.0 (2016)
22. Lall, M., Torvatn, H., Seim, E.A.: Towards Industry 4.0: increased need for situational awareness on the shop floor. In: Lödding, H., Riedel, R., Thoben, K.-D., von Cieminski, G., Kiritsis, D. (eds.) APMS 2017. IAICT, vol. 513, pp. 322–329. Springer, Cham (2017). https://doi.org/10.1007/978-3-319-66923-6_38
23. Farris, J.A., Van Aken, E.M., Doolen, T.L., Worley, J.: Critical success factors for human resource outcomes in Kaizen events: an empirical study. Int. J. Prod. Econ. **117**, 42–65 (2009)
24. Claeys, A., Hoedt, S., Van Landeghem, H., Cottyn, J.: Generic model for managing context-aware assembly instructions. IFAC-PapersOnLine **49**, 1181–1186 (2016)

A Conceptual Digital Assistance System Supporting Manual Changeovers in High-Variety Production

Rasmus Andersen[(✉)] [ID], Christopher Ketelsen [ID], Kjeld Nielsen [ID],
Ann-Louise Andersen [ID], Thomas D. Brunoe [ID], and Sofie Bech

Department of Materials and Production, Aalborg University, Aalborg, Denmark
therasmusandersen@gmail.com

Abstract. The advent of production strategies such as Mass Customization and Changeable Manufacturing requires that production systems be increasingly flexible towards diverse customer needs. Although humans remain the most flexible entity in modern production systems, the increasing complexity of these systems presents a challenge for the operators with regards to remaining efficient. Research related to Industry 4.0 has promoted the application of digital assistance systems, as a method of augmenting human operators to handle the complexity of these production systems better. However, no digital assistance system that supports human operators in performing manual changeover operations in complex production systems has been identified. This paper, therefore, presents a conceptual digital assistance system, which utilizes information about two consecutive production configurations, and processes this data through an algorithm, to determine which specific changeover operations are required to perform a changeover most efficiently. Potentials of implementing the proposed digital assistance system are briefly introduced, and topics for further research are outlined.

Keywords: Digital assistance system · Changeover ability · Changeability
Changeable manufacturing · Mass customization

1 Introduction

The production strategy of Mass Customization, which focuses on offering customers individualized products at near mass production costs, has become increasingly relevant since the 1980's, where a shift in market circumstances has challenged the practice of traditional mass producers in many industries [1]. To cope with these changed circumstances, many companies see the ability to adapt to changes in production mix and volume as providing superior competitive advantages [2]. From a production perspective, one of the enablers of mass customization concerns robust processes, which can be achieved through changeability. In seminal works on the subject, changeability is defined as "[…] the characteristics to accomplish early and foresighted adjustments of the factory's structures and processes on all levels, due to change impulses, economically" [3]. Although changeability must permeate all levels of the

I. Moon et al. (Eds.): APMS 2018, IFIP AICT 536, pp. 449–455, 2018.
https://doi.org/10.1007/978-3-319-99707-0_56

factory, its foundation constitutes the workstation level performing the actual operations [4], meaning that to obtain changeable production systems, the individual stations comprising the system must themselves be changeable. Enablers of changeability on the station level are changeover ability, which relates to the individual work station's ability to process a given part or component as efficiently as possible in terms of both time and resources [3]. Although changeover ability can be facilitated using automation [3] most changeovers are still performed by human operators [5]. The increase in product variety and simultaneous decrease in production batch sizes, resulting from introducing Mass Customization to a production system, has a negative effect on the learning and memory performance of the human operators [6, 7]. Besides these impacts, six additional challenges for human operators in relation to changeover ability have been identified [8]. Based on a review of existing literature Ketelsen et al. [8] concluded that there are two overall gaps concerning solutions to support human operators. These are related to overcoming the negative effects of increased task variety and decreased task repetition. Research related to human operators in Industry 4.0 points towards utilization of digital information [9] or assistance systems [10–12] as solutions for augmenting human operators to better manage the increasing complexity of modern production systems. Assistance systems have been classified as one of five major research branches within Industry 4.0 [13]. However, despite this recognition, no solutions have been identified, which directly address the issue of assisting human operators in efficiently handling manual changeover tasks in high-variety settings. Failing to support operators cognitively results in a hampered ability to deliver a high variety of products cost effectively [8], which in turn decreases the competitiveness of a company. Recognizing this gap, this paper presents a concept for a digital assistance system designed to support human operators in efficiently carrying out highly varying manual changeover tasks. The remainder of the article is structured as follows; Sect. 2 introduces digital assistance systems in the context of high-variety manufacturing. Then, Sect. 3 presents the conceptual design and functioning of the proposed digital assistance system. Section 4 discusses potential improvements to be gained from implementing the proposed assistance system. Finally, Sect. 5 points out directions for further research related to the development of the digital assistance system.

2   Digital Assistance Systems

Although fully automated and autonomous production systems are gaining increasing interest, this does not translate to the complete exclusion of humans from the production system [14]. Despite advances in manufacturing technology, the human is still recognized as the most flexible entity in a production system [11]. However, as outlined above, human operators are still subject to certain limitations mainly related to their cognitive abilities. Together with the increased complexity of modern production systems, the need to support human operators in their work tasks is, therefore, essential [10, 12, 13, 15]. In the Operator 4.0 typology proposed by Romero et al. [15] one of the eight archetypes of the typology is the "Augmented Operator". This archetype encompasses the use of digital assistance systems as a means of offloading cognitive work for human operators. Specifically, this is realized through digital assistance systems utilizing augmented reality as a facilitator for integrating humans and computer systems on the factory floor [15]. Augmenting operators can be accomplished using mobile smart devices [11] that are connected to different data sources within the factory [13], and can thus be considered as a type of cyber-physical system [7]. A digital assistance system relies on the ability to collect and display data from multiple data sources within the company [13] in order to present these to the operators in an efficient and easily understandable way [11]. This involves catering to the individual preferences of human operators [10, 11] by designing the digital assistance system to support multi-modal information presentation [12]. Furthermore, to increase the usability of the digital assistance system, it is suggested that design of the user interface is inspired by apps for smartphones and tablets since most operators will be familiar with these interfaces [11]. Reviewing literature on digital assistance systems have produced several solutions related to augmenting human operators in a product assembly scenario (e.g. [7, 12]). However, no literature was identified, which addresses this issue in a manual production changeover scenario.

3 Conceptual Assistance System in Support of Manual Changeover Operations

The purpose of the proposed digital assistance system is to support human operators in performing complex changeovers, whether it is on individual workstations or entire production lines, in order to achieve changeability. Figure 1, left side, presents a flowchart illustrating the functioning of the digital assistance system in transforming individual production configurations into actionable changeover tasks. First, information about the next product changeover is obtained. Then, based on this information, the corresponding production configuration for each of the products is extracted from a database. Hereafter, an algorithm analyzes the two production configurations and filters out any identical rows, representing specific configurations of settings, across them. This produces a new table containing only the actual changes that must be made to the current production configuration to change over to the next, as per the production plan. The changeover operations are then analyzed by a second algorithm, which matches sets of individual changeover operations with continuous improvement initiatives logged in another database. These initiatives are then appended to the relevant changeover operation. The result is then visualized for the human operators performing the changeover. Following this brief introduction to the functioning of the digital assistance system, the aspects of collecting, processing, and presenting the data for the digital assistance system is explained in more detail.

3.1 Information Gathering

The digital assistance system relies on data from three different sources, which are the production planning module in the enterprise resource planning (ERP) system, the production configuration database, and the changeover instruction database. The production planning module in the ERP system provides the digital assistance system with the current production plan, from which the unique product IDs for the product being

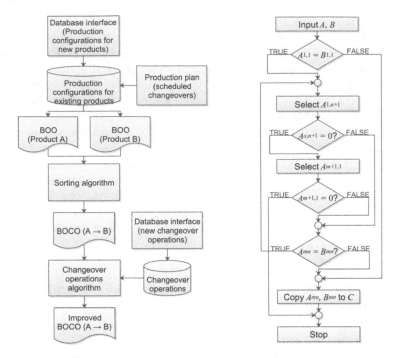

Fig. 1. (Left side) flowchart of the digital assistance system. (Right side) sorting and filtering algorithm illustrated following drawing style of Tausworthe [16].

changed from as well as the product being changed to can be obtained. The instruction database contains structured data about all changeover instructions for existing product variations. This database is updated through a database interface where changes to existing instructions are applied centrally and then automatically propagate to the changeover instructions for all related product variants. The database interface also allows the creation of changeover instructions for new product variants.

3.2   Information Processing

Part of augmenting human operators through the digital assistance system is done by processing data to deliver context-specific and timely data. The data processing is performed by algorithms, which provide a means of computing a solution to a problem, based on an explicitly defined computational process [17]. The first algorithm that is applied to the data is concerned with sorting and filtering the production configuration settings based on both the product that is changed from, as well as the product that is changed to. The purpose of the algorithm is to filter out any setup constants across the two setup configurations. This leaves only the relevant changeover tasks to be performed for that specific changeover. Figure 1, right side, presents a flowchart detailing the functioning of the algorithm, using symbols and drawing styles following Tausworthe [16]. First, the algorithm loads the two matrices A and B, containing the production configurations or bill-of-operations (BOO) for the product being changed from and the product being changed to, respectively. Then, the algorithm successively evaluates each row, m, and all variables, n, in A against its corresponding counterpart B. Thus, for every row the algorithm evaluates the value of A_{nm} against the value of B_{mn}. If the evaluation returns TRUE, the algorithm registered a constant prompting it to proceed to the next variable. The algorithm proceeds by evaluating every remaining variable in the current row, and if no FALSE conditions are returned, the row is marked as a constant across the two production configurations, thereby prompting the algorithm to ignore it and proceed to the next row. However, if any of the variable evaluations returns a FALSE, the algorithm copies the two configurations to a new matrix C. This behavior is performed successively until all rows have been processed, after which the algorithm stops. Hereafter, the individual changeover operations are applied to the sets of production configurations, forming a document containing all the operations necessary to perform a changeover between two given production setup configurations, as illustrated in Fig. 1, left side. It is proposed that the resulting document is referred to as the bill-of-changeover-operations (BOCO).

Extending the processing power of the digital assistance system further, machine learning could be utilized by the system to acquire knowledge of how to best present information to the users based on their previous interaction with the system. This would provide the assistance system with the ability to present varying detail levels of changeover instructions to the operators based on their experience or based on data analyses of, e.g., error prone changeover operations [18].

3.3   Information Presentation

The final aspect of the digital assistance system is the user interface, which is the part of the system that the human operator will interact with. It is, therefore, an essential aspect of a digital assistance system, as even an assistance system with a powerful data processing ability will be of little use if this data cannot be communicated efficiently to the operator. It is proposed that the digital assistance system interacts with users through a touchscreen interface on a tablet, as it is expected that smaller smart devices will have insufficient display size to communicate the processed changeover instructions efficiently. Alternatively, with the prevalence of augmented reality technology it has been proposed that an even higher level of digital assistance would be provided by progressing from tablet-based instructions to augmented reality glasses [19]. However, regardless of the choice of smart devices to visualize changeover instructions, Mattsson et al. [20] found that humans prefer graphical rather than text-based instructions for assembly work. The changeover instructions are, therefore, to be presented primarily as graphical entities, with the option of switching between multiple modes of graphics, such as animations or figures.

4   Conclusion

In this paper, a conceptual digital assistance system supporting manual changeovers in high-variety production was proposed to increase changeability in production. Since the digital assistance system is still in a conceptual stage, there are not yet actual results from implementation to report. However, literature presents several aspects related to production performance, where a digital assistance system is expected to deliver improved results. Hold et al. [7] state that the primary purpose of a digital assistance system is to improve productivity, which in turn results in a positive influence on key performance indicators like the overall equipment effectiveness [13]. More specifically, for the described conceptual digital assistance system, the general benefits mentioned by Romero et al. [15] may translate into faster and more consistent changeover times. This may be attributed to the reduced cognitive load on the operators caused by the focused changeover instructions. Furthermore, a digital assistance system may reduce errors made by operators [15] by assisting them with choosing the correct setups and tools [7]. The authors expect that improvements of the same parameters are possible through the implementation of the proposed digital assistance system as well. Besides the potential benefits, implementing the conceptual digital assistance system in a high-variety production setting may incur extensive costs related to the production of the required changeover instructions. However, research suggests the possibility of using reconfigurable instruction sequences to facilitate cost-effective, high-variety instructions [21].

5 Further Research

For the conceptual digital assistance system introduced in this paper to fulfill the above-described potentials, additional work is needed. First, further research into how the briefly described continuous improvement element of the system should be designed is required. This is particularly important as the ability of the operators to share experiences and best-practices with their colleagues is essential for the performance of the production system [11]. Once a prototype of the digital assistance system has been finished, real-life experiments in a production company are required to validate the potentials of the digital assistance system regarding increasing production performance. Looking even further into the future, the potential of utilizing changeover data from the digital assistance system to optimize production planning is seen as a relevant research topic.

References

1. Koren, Y.: Reconfigurable manufacturing systems. In: The Global Manufacturing Revolution, 1st ed., pp. 227–252. Wiley, Hoboken (2010)
2. Andersen, A., Larsen, J.K., Brunoe, T.D., et al.: Exploring requirements and implementation of changeability and reconfigurability in danish manufacturing. In: 51st CIRP Conference on Manufacturing Systems Exploring, pp. 665–670. Elsevier B.V. (2018)
3. ElMaraghy, H.A., Wiendahl, H.-P.: Changeability - an introduction. In: ElMaraghy, H.A. (ed.) Changeable and Reconfigurable Manufacturing Systems, pp. 3–24. Springer, London (2009). https://doi.org/10.1007/978-1-84882-067-8_2
4. Owen, G.W., Matthews, J., McIntosh, R.I., Culley, S.J.: Design for changeover (DFC): enabling flexible and highly responsive manufacturing. In: Fogliatto, F.S., da Silveira, G.J.C. (eds.) Mass Customization: Engineering and Managing Global Operations. Springer Series in Advanced Manufacturing, pp. 247–273. Springer, London, London (2011). https://doi.org/10.1007/978-1-84996-489-0_12

5. Brunoe, T.D., Andersen, A.-L., Nielsen, K.: Reconfigurable manufacturing systems in small and medium enterprises. In: Bellemare, J., Carrier, S., Nielsen, K., Piller, F.T. (eds.) Managing Complexity. Springer Proceedings in Business and Economics, pp. 205–213. Springer, Cham (2017). https://doi.org/10.1007/978-3-319-29058-4_16
6. Jaber, M.Y., Bonney, M.: Lot sizing with learning and forgetting in set-ups and in product quality. Int. J. Prod. Econ. **83**, 95–111 (2003)
7. Hold, P., Erol, S., Reisinger, G., Sihn, W.: Planning and evaluation of digital assistance systems. Proc. Manuf. **9**, 143–150 (2017)
8. Ketelsen, C., Andersen, R., Nielsen, K., et al.: A literature review on human changeover ability in high-variety production. In: Advances in Production Management System (2018, submitted)
9. Dean, P.R., Tu, Y.L., Xue, D.: An information system for one-of-a-kind production. Int. J. Prod. Res. **47**, 1071–1087 (2009)
10. Lall, M., Torvatn, H., Seim, E.A.: Towards industry 4.0: increased need for situational awareness on the shop floor. In: Lödding, H., Riedel, R., Thoben, K.-D., von Cieminski, G., Kiritsis, D. (eds.) APMS 2017. IAICT, vol. 513, pp. 322–329. Springer, Cham (2017). https://doi.org/10.1007/978-3-319-66923-6_38
11. Gorecky, D., Schmitt, M., Loskyll, M., Zühlke, D.: Human-machine-interaction in the industry 4.0 era. In: Proceedings - 2014 12th IEEE International Conference on Industrial Informatics, INDIN 2014, pp. 289–294 (2014)
12. Claeys, A., Hoedt, S., Van Landeghem, H., Cottyn, J.: Generic model for managing context-aware assembly instructions. IFAC-PapersOnLine **49**, 1181–1186 (2016)
13. Prinz, C., Kreimeier, D., Kuhlenkötter, B.: Implementation of a learning environment for an industrie 4.0 assistance system to improve the overall equipment effectiveness. Proc. Manuf. **9**, 159–166 (2017)
14. Al-Ani, A.: CPS and the worker: reorientation and requalification? In: Jeschke, S., Brecher, C., Song, H., Rawat, Danda B. (eds.) Industrial Internet of Things. SSWT, pp. 563–574. Springer, Cham (2017). https://doi.org/10.1007/978-3-319-42559-7_23
15. Romero, D., Stahre, J., Wuest, T., et al.: Towards an operator 4.0 typology: a human-centric perspective on the fourth industrial revolution technologies. In: CIE 2016 46th International Conference on Computers and Industrial Engineering, pp. 1–11 (2017)
16. Tausworthe, R.C.: Standardized development of computer software (1977)
17. Cormen, T.H., Leiserson, C.E., Rivest, R.L., Stein, C.: Introduction to Algorithms. MIT Press, Cambridge (2001)
18. Schuhmacher, J.: Machine learning for user learning. In: Mensch und Computer, 1013 (2017)
19. Fischer, H., Engler, M., Sauer, S.: A human-centered perspective on software quality: acceptance criteria for work 4.0. In: Marcus, A., Wang, W. (eds.) DUXU 2017. LNCS, vol. 10288, pp. 570–583. Springer, Cham (2017). https://doi.org/10.1007/978-3-319-58634-2_42
20. Mattsson, S., Fast-Berglund, A., Li, D.: Evaluation of guidelines for assembly instructions. IFAC-PapersOnLine **49**, 209–214 (2016)
21. Reisinger, G., Komenda, T., Hold, P., Sihn, W.: A concept towards automated data-driven reconfiguration of digital assistance systems. Proc. Manuf. **23**, 99–104 (2018)

Softbots Supporting the Operator 4.0 at Smart Factory Environments

Ricardo J. Rabelo[1], David Romero[2(✉)], and Saulo Popov Zambiasi[3]

[1] UFSC - Federal University of Santa Catarina, Florianopolis, Brazil
ricardo.rabelo@ufsc.br
[2] Tecnológico de Monterrey, Monterrey, Mexico
david.romero.diaz@gmail.com
[3] UNISUL - University of Southern Santa Catarina, Florianopolis, Brazil
saulopz@gmail.com

Abstract. This paper investigates how software robots, also known as softbots, can support the Operator 4.0 in smart factory environments, helping in the interfacing between smart machines and computer information systems with the aims of supporting the Operator 4.0 in different tasks at the shop floor. The work uses a reference framework called ARISA, which allows the derivation of softbots for given domains. An experimental setup and its results are presented in a testing scenario of a softbot to support the Operator 4.0 concept.

Keywords: Industry 4.0 · Operator 4.0 · Human cyber-physical systems
Human-machine interfaces · Smart factories · Social internet of things
Services and people · Software robots · Softbots
Socially sustainable manufacturing

1 Introduction

Industry 4.0, or *cyber-physical production systems,* is a new concept being gradually adopted by manufacturing enterprises in order to increase their general efficiency and sustainability while coping with the need of highly customized and shorter lifecycles products and emerging product-service systems [1]. Benefiting from the advances on industrial automation, information and communication technologies (ICTs) and control and management models – shopfloor systems and equipment have turned into much more active entities within the wider, intensively collaborative and smarter production environment that characterizes the Industry 4.0 scenario [2].

A number of core-systems' design principles have been considered as a must to be supported by manufacturing enterprises when adopting Industry 4.0 architectures, platforms and technologies [1–3]: interoperability, modularity, virtualization, real-time information, service-orientation, and decentralization/autonomy.

Although much emphasis has been put on the "automation and control" part of the digitalization process of production systems, including on the so-called *cyber-physical systems,* many research works in literature have underestimate the impact of the Industry 4.0 on the workers and, at the same, on the new systems' requirements needed

I. Moon et al. (Eds.): APMS 2018, IFIP AICT 536, pp. 456–464, 2018.
https://doi.org/10.1007/978-3-319-99707-0_57

to support the new types of human-machine interactions arisen with such new systems generation (i.e. human cyber-physical systems) [4–6].

The concept of *Operator 4.0* [4, 5] has emerged to embrace this issue, promoting a balanced and/or symbiotic interaction between humans and machines. It aims to support a socially sustainable manufacturing workforce environment in the factories of the future, where "smart and skilled operators should perform not only 'cooperative work' with robots, but also 'work aided' by machines as and if needed, by means of human cyber-physical systems, advanced human-machine interaction technologies and adaptive automation towards 'human-automation symbiosis work systems'" [4].

In spite of the conceptual advances on the *Operator 4.0* area (e.g. [4–6]) and based on a literature review about it, it has been realized that larger efforts are necessary *to implement* the *Operator 4.0 vision.* This is the underlying motivation of this paper: How to 'translate' this concept into practice?

A number of approaches can be used for that. One of them is via *software robots.* A software robot, also known as *softbot,* can be generally defined as a virtual system deployed in a given computing environment that automates and helps humans in the execution of some tasks with variable levels of intelligence and autonomy [7].

In this direction, this paper presents a proof-of-concept and qualitative work that aims at investigating at which extent 'softbots' can support the implementation of the *Operator 4.0 concept,* particularly the *Smarter Operator 4.0 type* [5]. This is a type which is helped by softbots as *Intelligent Personal Assistants (IPAs)* to interface with smart machines and robots, computers, databases and other information systems so as to aid the operator in the execution of different tasks in a human-like interaction. This type of Operator 4.0 is grounded on the essentials of Industry 4.0 reference architectures design principles (viz. *Reference Architecture Model for Industrie 4.0 - RAMI 4.0* (Germany) and *Industrial Internet Reference Architecture - IIRA* (USA)).

A *reference framework* for deriving instances of 'softbots' was conceived in a previous work [8] and it was used to create a prototype of a "Smarter Operator 4.0".

This paper is organized as follows. Section 1 has presented the problem and the paper's goal. Section 2 gives a brief review about softbots and related works. Section 3 describes a reference framework and the model used to derive softbots. Section 4 presents the developed prototype and some current results. Section 5 summarizes the conclusions so far got as well as the main next steps of this research.

2 Softbots and Related Works

The research on *softbots* is not really new[1], but their "popular usage" in industry is. Literature [9–14] shows their increasing use by large software-houses (e.g. Microsoft, Apple and Google) mainly from the last decade on. *Softbots* are becoming more and more used by general companies, for example in the traveling, health, banking and government sectors, where *softbots* interacts with users to solve problems, to clarify issues, etc. – typically using 'chatbots' or 'intelligent personal assistants' (IPAs).

---

[1] First chatbot, named: Eliza (1996) – by Massachusetts Institute of Technology (MIT).

A number of relevant *softbot implementations* (AI-based chatbots or IPAs) have been developed since then, such as 'Cortana' [9], 'Sandy' [10], 'Siri' [11], 'PAL' [12], 'Narval' [13], and 'Alexa' [14]. Their applications cover several different specific goals, like recalling users about different daily appointments and tasks; performing repetitive business activities autonomously on behalf of the user; searching for solutions of problems through the Internet considering users' profile, problem's context and historical data; proposing solutions for unexpected situations via machine learning techniques; among others.

Actually, two basic types of *chatbots* can be found in literature [15]: *(a) Rule-based chatbots,* programmed to recognize certain terms and patterns from which they can respond with pre-set answers (e.g. MS-Office Assistant *Clippy*); and *(b) Artificial Intelligence (AI)-based chatbots,* which are considered as 'artificial brains' using sophisticated cognitive and natural language processing capabilities for understanding the context, intent and emotion(s) of users' requests, and that evolves as they interact and learn from conversations with users (e.g. Microsoft AI *Cortana*).

A *softbot* can implement many different things within several domains. Romero et al. [5] have identified eight categories of possible applications where human operators might be aided by *intelligent software* in Industry 4.0 [4, 6]. Its interaction with humans can be provided by different means, like web-browsers and desktop computers, mobile devices, holography, augmented reality, natural language, haptics, etc.

BCG [16] has recognized the importance of *software assistance* in the Industry 4.0 and outlined ten so-called 'use cases' scenarios to be supported: *(a) Big-data-driven quality control,* where 'softbots' can make use of data analytic techniques to support quality engineers in analysing real-time and historical quality-control data, identifying quality issues and their causes and pinpointing ways to minimize product failures and waste; *(b) Robot-assisted production* and *(c) Self-driving logistics vehicles,* where 'softbots' can oversee all the industrial entities operations (viz. smart machine tools, robots, co-bots, belt-conveyors, AGVs (i.e. automated guided vehicles) and human operations) on the shopfloor in order to guarantee humans and machines safety in advanced human-machine interactions (HMIs) and the overall manufacturing system's productivity; *(d) Production line simulation,* where 'softbots' can provide proactively production planners with insights on how to optimize and support all operational demands; *(e) Smart supply network,* where 'softbots' can provide supply network managers with real-time monitoring (e.g. track & trace) and simulation (e.g. what-if scenarios) capabilities to enable companies to react or even anticipate disruptions in the supply network, and therefore, adjust the network in advance or in real-time as conditions change; *(f) Predictive maintenance,* where 'softbots' can support service technicians with automated remote alerts, delivered in their mobile devices, based on real-time monitoring of smart equipment and with intelligent embedded prognostics algorithms as troubleshooting assisting means; *(g) Machine-as-a-service* and *(h) Self-organizing production,* where 'softbots' can support production managers with information about the location, condition, availability, etc. of smart equipment for assisted production management (i.e. coordination and optimization of the utilization of each production asset), *(i) Additive manufacturing of complex parts,* where 'softbots' can help industrial designers to determine the "printability" of given 3D-objects acting as "printability checkers" using machine learning techniques, and *(j) Augmented work, maintenance, and service,* where 'softbots' can help to dispatch (i.e. find, sort, filter and deliver) the right information to the operator in abundant information environments (the smart factory) as part of digital assistance systems.

Schwartz et al. [17] proposed a concept of "hybrid teams" to face the increasing need for higher-level collaboration between humans, smart industrial equipment and software so as to better underpinning Industry 4.0 requirements (see also [6]).

Older but very powerful approaches, as *multi-agent systems* and *holonic systems,* seem to be 'rediscovered' after their boom in the end of 90 s in a time where Internet-based ITs were just flourishing [18]. Their intrinsic properties are pretty much in line with the Industry 4.0 architecture design principles, especially in what the decisions' decentralization and the autonomy of equipment and industrial entities is concerned. Several works [e.g. 18–20] were developed based on those approaches, where agents could virtualize and represent industrial entities from any type in such way they could be able to reason about the current shopfloor status, to autonomously provide real-time information to other systems, to dynamically establish opportunistic consortia to collaborate, and to solve problems via e.g. negotiation strategies.

Despite the relevance of all those mentioned works, the ones presenting real implementation of *softbots (or equivalent)* were not properly devised to cope with *Industry 4.0* and *Operator 4.0 scenarios.* On the other hand, the works presenting implementations related to Industry 4.0 were neither devised to cope with *Operator 4.0 scenarios* nor to support *softbots* to help humans in their activities.

3   Softbots Reference Framework – Supporting the Operator 4.0

A *reference framework* called 'ARISA', presented in [8], has been used to develop the intended proof-of-concept *Smarter Operator 4.0 type* as a *softbot implementation.* This framework was chosen due to its main intrinsic properties, which offers some support to implement (at different levels of depth) the core design principles of Industry 4.0 architectures (Table 1).

The *ARISA Reference Framework* is actually the implementation of the *ARISA Reference Model* in concrete software artefacts so as to support particular derivations, as the envisaged IPA (see Fig. 1).

In very general terms and in a high-level view, the model has as elements: the *User* interacts with his/her IPA using proper interfaces – *User Applications* (e.g. Gmail, Twitter, text-consoles, etc.); a *Toolbox* (general programming & configuration tools to derive particular IPAs); and *Legacy Applications* (enterprise's applications that can be involved in the business processes the derived IPA should interact with). The *Personal Assistant Manager* represents the IPA's core, being responsible to define, configure and manage the right access and execution of all internal IPA's entities. The *Services Federation* involves all registered software services that can be involved in the IPA execution regarding its goals and related business processes. The *Interoperability Services* refer to all software required to support the interoperability between the systems and general computing artefacts used once an IPA is derived. The *Toolbox*

Table 1. ARISA: supporting core-design principles of industry 4.0 architectures

Interoperability	• It is strongly based on open-IT standards and integration patterns, facilitating interoperability with human end-users, other softbots, with other shopfloor entities and systems (including legacy systems), and with other enterprise systems (e.g. ERPs, Amazon Cloud and Facebook 's APIs)
Modularity	• The used services can be implemented from scratch, but can also use services provided by open digital software services ecosystems or IT business partners, by means of static or dynamic services compositions • New services can be added and other ones can be deleted from the softbot without damaging its internal architecture • The softbot's internal architecture can be designed following the 3-Tiers or MVC models, and its user interface can be showed through different devices (e.g. mobile devices). Yet, the different model's layers can be deployed at different servers
Virtualization	• It allows the derivation of instances-of 'softbots' for different domain applications
Real-time Information	• A softbot can perform several actions simultaneously and asynchronously
Service- orientation	• Its instances are natively designed under the Service-Oriented Architecture (SOA) model, meaning that a given softbot is internally composed of a set of built-in (distributed) software services, such as communication ways (as Twitter, webmail, text entry and voice); and standards reports, for e.g. communication auditing. It is also open to implement as many services as needed for particular applications
Decentralization/autonomy	• The softbot's behaviour (including the autonomy and intelligence levels) can be variable and implemented for different scenarios

comprises all the supporting tools, execution engines and computing environments involved in the integration and deployment of the IPA's elements.

ARISA is organized in the *SOA (Service Oriented Architecture)* style, meaning that all the IPA's elements are modelled and implemented as software services. By default, the IPA is designed to work under the 3-Tiers model, being the many of the involved services physically separated into presentation, process and data layers.

A number of activities have to be carried out in order to derive an IPA. To be emphasized the activities related to define the IPA's business processes and activities to be executed (i.e. *what*) of a given problem area; the IPA's behaviour (i.e. *how* and *when* to do the *what*); the IPA's resources (i.e. *which* internal or external software services will execute the *what*, where services can be coded in different languages, like in *PHP*); and the IPA's execution places (i.e. *where*), when it is necessary to endow it with the ability to 'travel' through the network to execute some of their tasks in another server or equipment, as a mobile agent [21]).

ARISA has a specific programming shell to do that (one of the Toolbox's tools). It can be seen as a lower-level *BPM (Business Process Management)* modelling in the form of *if-then-else-end* statements to express the business process' logic as well as the respective internal and external services to be invoked (see Fig. 2). A *BPEL (Business Process Execution Language)* file is then generated, which runs quite well regarding that only *web-services* and *SOAP* protocol are supported in this current implementation version.

4 Experimental Setup and Results

Considering that this is a proof-of-concept work and regarding the *Operator 4.0 typology,* a small scenario to support the *Smarter Operator 4.0 type* was built up.

ARISA is actually an academic prototype and it is not very easy to derive instances of softbots and to configure it, which requires an expert on IT.

The devised testing scenario comprises a lathe machine and its CNC controller, its respective *Operator 4.0,* and a buffer that feeds the smart machine considering a given batch-size of raw parts to be machined.

The business process (BP) was designed to monitor the number of parts in such way the machining can keep operating only if there is a minimum number of parts (10) of type *'101'* in the buffer. There is a sensor in the buffer which counts this number. This information is sent out (via a emulated *Profinet* Industrial Network) to the CNC controller's wrapper (compliant to the ISO 9506 MMS/VMD) when the buffer reaches the minimum level so that a *'purchasing order'* (business process of id *'80'*) can be triggered and performed by the IPA close to the part's supplier (called hypothetically as *'John Doe Ltda'*). This transaction will cost $25.00.

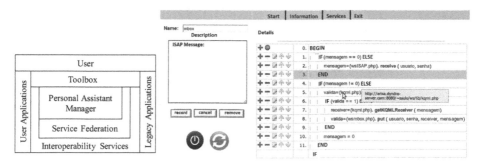

Fig. 1. ARISA reference model

Fig. 2. Interface for the IPA management

However, this supplier does not have the required total amount of parts and the IPA autonomously decide to look for another supplier. It finds the supplier *'Sora konpyuuta'* company in the enterprise's supplier catalogue, but the cost of this transaction (for the 17 required additional parts) is $28.00. The *Operator 4.0 – 'Mr. Saulo'* is notified that there are 17 parts needed to be purchased, via an order '81', to complete the BP production.

Three basic use cases were supported: (i) The IPA manages the whole mentioned process scenario and keep the *Operator 4.0* informed about the purchasing success via the IPA's graphical interface, using the *Gtalk* tool (Fig. 3); (ii) the *Operator 4.0* interacts with the IPA via text or voice in his/her mobile phone asking about how many orders are still pending in that machine, using the *Twitter* tool. In this case, the IPA answers that the order '84' is still opened, and it is related to '14' units of product '101' with a cost of $28.00 (Fig. 4); and (iii) the IPA (the ARISA Personal Assistant) publishes as a report a summary of its daily activities, using a *blog* tool (see Fig. 5).

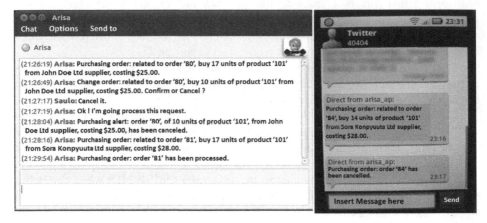

Fig. 3. IPA's graphical interface   **Fig. 4.** Operator 4.0 mobile phone

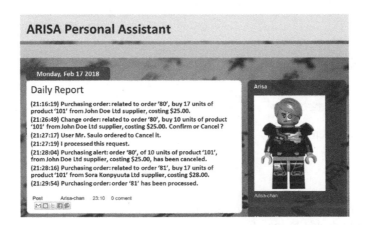

Fig. 5. IPA's daily report

5 Conclusions and Further Research

This paper has presented a proof-of-concept on how *softbots* could be used as a feasible approach to implement the *Smarter Operator 4.0 type* [6]. The implemented *softbot* was derived from a reference framework called 'ARISA', which natively supports the Industry 4.0 architectures design principles.

The development of 'human-automation symbiosis' offers advantages for the sustainability of the manufacturing workforce in Industry 4.0, improving operational excellence, inclusiveness, satisfaction and motivation, safety and continuous learning.

A use case scenario was implemented in a controlled and emulated shopfloor environment. Based on this, it can be said that *softbots* can fulfil several of the "Smarter Operator 4.0 type" interfacing requirements with other industrial entities.

The *softbot prototype* could perform the actions as planned and hence could assist the human operator in some tasks, both in terms of interacting with him/her when needed and by automating tasks execution on behalf of him/her. These were the general performance indicators used to evaluate this current version of the prototype.

Important to mention that part of this successful results was due to the ARISA framework, which uses many integration patterns as well as supports a high-level of flexibility and configurability when deriving instances-of IPAs.

There are some technological limitations in the developed prototype. For example, there is no support for security, semantic interoperability, advanced voice processing, robust natural language recognition, advanced usability techniques, and adaptive softbot's behaviour. On the other hand, thanks to the intrinsic SOA-based architecture of derived softbots, and to the fact that the internal architecture is open, standard-based and scalable, those limitations can be mitigated using specific services for that, which in turn can be invoked from external/proper services providers.

The implemented scenario was relatively simple, covering a business process related to the general management of an equipment, including both human interactions and automatic actions by the IPA. In a real-case scenario the modelling of all the necessary business processes and interaction with human can be very hard to conceive, model, implement and maintain. Besides that, business processes are very different to each other, meaning that critical actions may have to be supervised or authorized by humans before being taking. All this requires deep training of workers.

This is an ongoing work. Next main steps comprise improvements on the voice and natural language recognitions, evaluation of softbots in other types of the *Operator 4.0 typology,* and deeper analysis of integration approaches between the softbot and real smart industrial equipment's wrappers and controllers.

References

1. Hermann, M., Pentek, T., Otto, B.: Design principles for industry 4.0 scenarios. In: Proceedings of the 49th IEEE Hawaii International Conference on System Sciences, pp. 3928–3937 (2016)
2. Lee, J., Bagheri, B., Kao, H.A.: Recent advances and trends of cyber-physical systems and big data analytics in industrial informatics. In: Industrial Informatics. IEEE (2014)

3. Mittal, S., Khan, M.A, Romero, D., Wuest, T.: Smart manufacturing: characteristics, technologies and enabling factors. J. Eng. Manuf. (2017). https://doi.org/10.1177/09544054 17736547

4. Romero, D., Bernus, P., Noran, O., Stahre, J., Fast-Berglund, Å.: The operator 4.0: human cyber-physical systems and adaptive automation towards human-automation symbiosis work systems. In: Nääs, I., et al. (eds.) APMS, vol. 488, pp. 677–686. Springer, Cham (2016). https://doi.org/10.1007/978-3-319-51133-7_80

5. Romero, D., Stahre, J., Wuest, T., Noran, O., Bernus, P., Fast-Berglund, Å., Gorecky, D.: Towards an operator 4.0 typology: a human-centric perspective on the fourth industrial revolution technologies. In: Proceedings of the International Conference on Computers and Industrial Engineering, pp. 1–11 (2016)

6. Romero, D., Wuest, T., Stahre, J., Gorecky, D.: Social factory architecture: social networking services and production scenarios through the social internet of things, services and people for the social operator 4.0. In: Lödding, H., Riedel, R., Thoben, K.-D., von Cieminski, G., Kiritsis, D. (eds.) APMS 2017. IAICT, vol. 513, pp. 265–273. Springer, Cham (2017). https://doi.org/10.1007/978-3-319-66923-6_31

7. Kim, J.H.: Ubiquitous robot. In: Reusch, B. (ed.) Computational Intelligence, Theory and Applications. Advances in Soft Computing, vol. 33, pp. 451–459. Springer, Heidelberg (2005)

8. Zambiasi, S.P., Rabelo, R.J.: A proposal for reference architecture for personal assistant software based on SOA. IEEE Latin Am. Trans. 10(1), 1227–1234 (2012)

9. Cortana. https://developer.microsoft.com/en-us/cortana

10. Sandy. https://boingboing.net/2007/11/14/i-want-sandy-perfect.html

11. Siri. https://www.apple.com/ios/siri/?cid=oas-us-domains-siri.com

12. PAL, DARPA PAL Project. http://pal.sri.com/

13. Narval, C.N.: The Intelligent Personal Assistant or How the French Linux Gazette is Built. https://linuxgazette.net/issue59/chauvat.html

14. Alexa. https://developer.amazon.com/alexa

15. Monchalin, E.: (2017). https://atos.net/en/blog/an-introduction-to-chatbots

16. BCG Boston Consulting Group. https://www.bcg.com/pt-br/publications/2015/technology-business-transformation-engineered-products-infrastructure-man-machine-industry-4.aspx

17. Schwartz, T., Zinnikus, I., Krieger, H.U., Bürckert, C.: Hybrid teams: flexible collaboration between humans, robots and virtual agents. In: Klusch, M., Unland, R., Shehory, O., Pokahr, A., Ahrndt, S. (eds.) Multiagent System Technologies. LNCS, vol. 9872, pp. 131–146. Springer, Cham (2016)

18. Rabelo, R.J., Camarinha-Matos, L.M.: Negotiation in multiagent dynamic scheduling. Robot. Comput.-Integr. Manuf. J. 11(4), 303–310 (1994)

19. Barata, J., Camarinha-Matos, L.M.: Coalitions of manufacturing components for shop floor agility. Int. J. Netw. Virtual Organ. 2(1), 50–77 (2003)

20. Van Brussel, H., Wyns, J., Valckenaers, P., Bongaerts, L.: Reference architecture for holonic manufacturing systems. Comput. Ind. 37(3), 255–274 (1998)

21. Wangham, M.S., Fraga, J.S., Rabelo, R.J., Lung, L.C.: Secure mobile agent system and its application in the trust building process of virtual enterprises. Multiagent Grid Syst. J. 1(1), 147–168 (2005)

A Fundamental Study on the Effect of Visual Guidance to Inspectors Using Visual Indicator on Defect Detection in Visual Inspection Utilizing Peripheral Vision

Ryosuke Nakajima[1(✉)], Kosuke Fujie[2], Takuya Hida[2], and Toshiyuki Matsumoto[2]

[1] Seikei University, Tokyo, Japan
nakajima@st.seikei.ac.jp
[2] Aoyama Gakuin University, Kanagawa, Japan
a5711069@aoyama.jp, {hida,matsumoto}@ise.aoyama.ac.jp

Abstract. In recent years, it is reported that a number of inspectors in the visual inspection process of industrial products utilized not only the central vision but also the peripheral vision. The visual inspection has been realized with both efficiency and accuracy. However, for the inspectors of many manufacturing industries to adopt this method, visual guidance is necessary for visual attention. Therefore, to obtain the fundamental knowledge for training of the visual inspection method, this study considers the effect of visual guidance on the defect detection performed by inspectors using visual indicators. Specifically, the presence or absence of visual guidance, defect location, and defect characteristics (luminance contrast between defect and inspection model and size) are designed as experimental factors. Further, the effect on inspection accuracy is evaluated with six subjects. As a result, it is clarified that the presence or absence of visual guidance does not affect the defect detection regardless of the defect location and defect characteristics. That is, the visual guidance is not an impediment to inspection accuracy; it is suggested that the visual guidance is an effective tool for the education and training of the visual inspection method utilizing peripheral vision.

Keywords: Visual inspection · Peripheral vision · Visual guidance

1 Introduction

To supply high-quality products to the market, manufacturing industries provide as much attention to product inspection as to processing and assembly. Two types of inspections exist: functional inspection and appearance inspection. In functional inspection, the effectiveness of a product is inspected. In appearance inspection, small visual defects such as scratches, surface dents, and unevenness of the coating color are inspected. The automation of functional inspection has advanced because it is easy to determine whether a product works [1, 2]. However, it is not as simple to establish

© IFIP International Federation for Information Processing 2018
Published by Springer Nature Switzerland AG 2018. All Rights Reserved
I. Moon et al. (Eds.): APMS 2018, IFIP AICT 536, pp. 465–472, 2018.
https://doi.org/10.1007/978-3-319-99707-0_58

standards to determine whether the appearance of a product is defective. First, many different types of defects exist. Second, the categorization of a product as non-defective or defective is affected by the size and depth of the defect. Third, some products have recently become smaller and more complex. Finally, the production has shifted to high-mix, low-volume production. It is thus difficult to develop technologies that can capture small defects and create algorithms that can identify multiple types of defects with high precision. Therefore, appearance inspection still strongly depends on human visual inspection [3–6].

As visual inspection is performed by humans, inspection efficiency and inspection accuracy differ among different inspectors. This is a common problem in many manufacturing industries. Recently, a visual inspection method utilizing peripheral vision was proposed [7–11], and the effectiveness of the method has been reported by manufacturing factories [12]. Human vision can be divided into two ranges. Central vision is the $1°$–$2°$ range of vision on either side of the center of the retina. The remaining range is known as peripheral vision. The spatial resolution of human vision decreases significantly with the increase in this angle from the center of the retina [13]. The visual inspection method utilizing peripheral vision involves two steps: First, a wide spatial range is searched by peripheral vision; subsequently, the type of defect is decided using the high-spatial resolution of the central vision. Thus, low-level processes such as sampling and clustering are processed using peripheral vision, whereas high-level processes such as discrimination are processed using central vision, such that the amount of information to be processed is reduced. This allows for efficient visual information processing to be realized [14]. The visual inspection method utilizing peripheral vision which can be realized high inspection efficiency and accuracy has been expected.

Based on the background above, in order to widely adopt the inspection method to the inspectors of many manufacturing industries, the authors considered the effect of inspection area, inspection time, eye movement, viewing distance, and other factors on defect detection [15–17]. The authors have also developed a training system to educate and to train inspectors using computers [18]. Through these studies, to educate and train the visual inspection method utilizing the peripheral vision, it is necessary to appropriately determine the points to be fixed, attention/consciousness range, and visual timing. It is found that to visual guidance for visual attention is necessary. However, it is possible that the visual guidance using a visual indicator affect an impediment to inspection efficiency and inspection accuracy, and their relationship has not been clarified.

Therefore, to obtain fundamental knowledge for the training of the visual inspection method, this study considers the effect of visual guidance on inspectors using visual indicators for defect detection. Specifically, an experiment is implemented using the presence or absence of visual guidance, defect location, and defect characteristics (luminance contrast between defect and inspection model and size) as experimental factors. The effect of these factors on the inspection accuracy is examined.

2 Experimental Design

2.1 Experimental Tasks

The experimental subjects are tasked with visually inspecting a model that is displayed on a monitor (MF403KIT42inch, METASIGN Inc.). A model with height and width both equal to 300 mm is used. The background color of the inspection model is set to an achromatic color (RGB values: (50, 50, 50)).

If no defect is detected, the subject presses the SPACE KEY on the keyboard, and the next inspection model is displayed. If a defect is detected, the subject presses the ENTER KEY. The experimental layout is shown in Fig. 1. To ensure a uniform visual distance between each subject and the inspection model, the chin holder is placed at a distance of 400 mm from the inspection model to fix the head position of a subject.

2.2 Experimental Factors

Presence or Absence of Visual Guidance
The presence or absence of the visual guidance is set to two different patterns. The inspection model with a black 10 mm diameter circle (as a fixation point) is set as the presence of visual guidance (Fig. 2-a). On the other hand, the inspection model without a black circle is set as the absence of visual guidance (Fig. 2-b). To lead the inspection utilizing peripheral vision, the subjects are requested to focus only on the center of the inspection model during the experiment.

Defect Locations
The inspection model is divided into sixteen parts (4 × 4 horizontally and vertically), and the defect is located at the center of either one of those parts. As shown in Fig. 2-c, the parts are divided into four areas, from area ① to area ④, according to the distance from the fixation point.

Defect Characteristics
The defect characteristics are defined by the luminance contrast between the inspection model and the defect, and by the size. The shape of all defects is circular. The luminance contrast of each defect is one of the three following levels: 0.10, 0.15, and 0.20. The defect size is specified by a diameter of 0.50 mm, 0.75 mm, and 1.00 mm. These defects are determined by assuming the standard of the appearance inspection. The list of defects using this experiment is shown in Fig. 3.

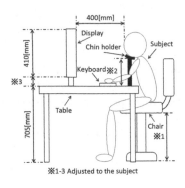

Fig. 1. Experimental layout

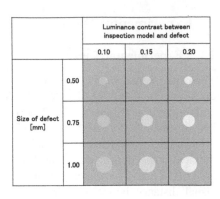

Fig. 3. Defects using the experiment

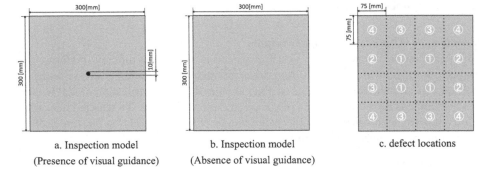

a. Inspection model
(Presence of visual guidance)

b. Inspection model
(Absence of visual guidance)

c. defect locations

Fig. 2. Inspection model and defect locations

2.3 Experimental Procedure

Six subjects, aged between 21 and 24 years, are employed in this experiment. Only subjects with a corrected eyesight score (decimal visual acuity) higher than 1.0 were employed. To familiarize the subjects with the experiment, an overview was provided and the experiment procedure was explained. In addition, the subjects were requested to perform some preliminary experiments. In the experiment, the task was to inspect 288 inspection models (144 non defective, 144 defective) for each case with the presence or absence of visual guidance.

The experimental room temperature was set between 18 °C and 24 °C, and the humidity was set between 40% and 60%. Since the luminance of the inspection model and the defect were affected by the external and internal light (such as fluorescent lighting), the experiment was implemented in a dark room. A written statement of the purpose and contents of the experiment was provided to the subjects, and informed consent was obtained from all subjects.

Using the results of the experiment, obtained using the aforementioned procedures, the defect detection rate was calculated, which is the number of detected defects divided by the number of total defects. It is expressed by Eq. (1) and is used as the evaluation index of the inspection accuracy.

$$Defect\,detection\,rate\,[\%] = \frac{Numuber\,of\,detected\,defects}{Number\,of\,total\,defects} \qquad (1)$$

3 Experimental Results

3.1 Individual Characteristics of Subjects

Using the defect detection rate, the effect of the presence or absence of visual guidance is examined. Owing to the possibility that the individuality of the subject might influence the results, the uniformity of the results for all subjects is verified.

The defect detection rate of each subject is shown in Fig. 4. As a result of the Smirnov–Grubbs test shows no outlier values in the defect detection rates of any of the subjects. Therefore, the data from six subjects are used.

3.2 Effect of Visual Guidance on Inspection Accuracy

To analyze the effect of the presence or absence of visual guidance on the inspection accuracy, three-way ANOVA (analysis of variance) is executed with the presence or absence of visual guidance (2), defect location (4), and defect characteristics (9) as the factors. The ANOVA table is shown in Table 1. As a result, a significant difference is not observed for the main effect of the presence or absence of visual guidance, and their mutual interactions. On the other hands, a significant difference of 1% is observed for the main effect of the defect locations, defect characteristics, and their mutual interactions. The relationship between each experimental factor is shown in Fig. 5.

From the above, it is clarified that presence or absence of visual guidance does not affect the defect detection, regardless of the defect locations and the defect characteristics. That is, it is found that the visual guidance is not an impediment to inspection accuracy.

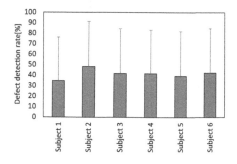

Fig. 4. Defect detection rate for each subject

Table 1. ANOVA for defect detection rate

Factor	Sum of squares	Degrees of freedom	Mean square	F-value	Significant difference
Subject(S)	0.70	5	0.14		
Presence or absence of visual guidance(A)	0.01	1	0.01	0.27	
S × A	0.17	5	0.03		
Defect location(B)	12.90	3	4.30	65.43	**
S × B	0.99	15	0.07		
Defect characteristics (C)	47.02	8	5.88	146.88	**
S × C	1.60	40	0.04		
A × B	0.03	3	0.01	0.45	
S × A × B	0.36	15	0.02		
A × C	0.17	8	0.02	0.95	
S × A × C	0.89	40	0.02		
B × C	6.69	24	0.28	10.84	**
S × B × C	3.09	120	0.03		
A × B × C	0.44	24	0.02	1.13	
S × A × B × C	1.94	120	0.02		
Total	76.99	431			

$p < 0.05$: *, $P < 0.01$: **

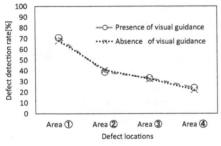

a. Relationship between presence or absence of visual guidance and defect locations

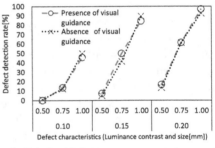

b. Relationship between presence or absence of visual guidance and defect characteristics

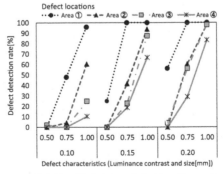

c. Relationship between defect locations and defect characteristics

Fig. 5. Interaction between experimental factors

4   Conclusion

To obtain fundamental knowledge for the training of the visual inspection method, this study considered the effect of visual guidance on the inspectors using a visual indicator on the defect detection, experimentally. As a result, it is clarified that the presence or absence of the visual guidance does not affect the inspection accuracy (the defect detection), regardless of the defect location and the defect characteristics. That is, the visual guidance is not an impediment to inspection accuracy. It is suggested that the visual guidance is an effective tool for the education and training of the visual inspection method utilizing peripheral vision.

As future tasks, we will consider in more detail the method of efficient education and training of the visual inspection method utilizing peripheral vision, including the knowledge garnered from this study. Further, we will also consider the work design and the standardization of the visual inspection method utilizing peripheral vision.

Acknowledgement. This study was supported by Grant-in-Aid for JSPS Fellows (14J09642), JSPS Grant-in-Aid for Research Activity Start-up (16H07202), Special Research of Faculty of Science and Technology in Seikei University.

References

1. Aoki, K.: Review on in-process inspection. J. Jpn. Soc. Non-Destr. Insp. **63**(8), 433–435 (2014)
2. Aiyama, H.: Review on magnetic particle, penetrant and visual testing. J. Jpn. Soc. Non-Destr. Insp. **63**(8), 384–390 (2014)
3. Nickles, G.M., Melloy, B.J., Gramopadhye, A.K.: A comparison of three levels of training designed to promote systematic search behavior in visual inspection. Int. J. Ind. Ergon. **32**, 331–339 (2003)
4. Yeow, P.H., Sen, R.N.: Ergonomics improvements of the visual inspection process in a printed circuit assembly factory. Int. J. Occup. Saf. Ergon. **10**(4), 369–385 (2004)
5. Lee, F.C., Chan, A.H.: Effects of magnification methods and magnifier shapes on visual inspection. Appl. Ergon. **40**(3), 410–418 (2009)
6. Chang, J.J., Hwang, S.L., Wen, C.H.: The development of a training expert system for TFT-LCD defects inspection. Int. J. Ind. Eng. Theory Appl. Pract. **16**(1), 41–50 (2009)
7. Sasaki, A.: Syuhenshi Mokushikensahou [1]. Japan Inst. Ind. Eng. Rev. **46**(4), 65–75 (2005)
8. Sasaki, A.: Syuhenshi Mokushikensahou [2]. Japan Inst. Ind. Eng. Rev. **46**(5), 61–68 (2005)
9. Sasaki, A.: Syuhenshi Mokushikensahou [3]. Japan Inst. Ind. Eng. Rev. **47**(1), 55–60 (2006)
10. Sasaki, A.: Syuhenshi Mokushikensahou [4]. Japan Inst. Ind. Eng. Rev. **47**(2), 53–58 (2006)
11. Sasaki, A.: Syuhenshi Mokushikensahou [5]. Japan Inst. Ind. Eng. Rev. **47**(3), 67–72 (2006)
12. Sugawara, T., Shinoda, S., Uchida, M., Sasaki, A., Matsumoto, T., Niwa, A., Kawase, T.: Proposal of a new inspection method using peripheral visual acuity focusing on visibility and inspection angle of defective items during product inspection. J. Japan Ind. Manage. Assoc. **62**(4), 153–163 (2011)
13. Ikeda, M.: Meha Naniwo Miteiruka. Heibonsya, Tokyo (1999)
14. Yoshida, C., Toyoda, M., Sato, Y.: Vision system model with differentiated visual fields. Inf. Process. Soc. Japan **33**(8), 1032–1040 (1992)

15. Nakajima, R., Tanida, K., Hida, T., Matsumoto, T.: A study on the relationship between defect characteristics and conspicuity field in visual inspection. Jpn. J. Ergon. **51**(5), 333–342 (2015)
16. Nakajima, R., Shida, K., Matsumoto, T.: A study on the effect of inspection time on defect detection in visual inspection. In: Prabhu, V., Taisch, M., Kiritsis, D. (eds.) APMS 2013. IAICT, vol. 414, pp. 29–39. Springer, Heidelberg (2013). https://doi.org/10.1007/978-3-642-41266-0_4
17. Nakajima, R., Shida, K.: A study on the effect of different presentation method on defect detection rate in visual inspection. J. Soc. Bio Mech. Japan **36**(4), 234–240 (2012)
18. Nakajima, R., Inagaki, I., Matsumoto, T.: Development of a training system for visual inspection method utilizing peripheral vision. J. Japan Ind. Manage. Assoc. **66**(3), 267–276 (2015)

Digitalizing Occupational Health, Safety and Productivity for the Operator 4.0

David Romero[1(✉)], Sandra Mattsson[2], Åsa Fast-Berglund[2],
Thorsten Wuest[3], Dominic Gorecky[4], and Johan Stahre[2]

[1] Tecnológico de Monterrey, Monterrey, Mexico
david.romero.diaz@gmail.com
[2] Chalmers University of Technology, Gothenburg, Sweden
{sandra.mattsson,asa.fasth,johan.stahre}@chalmers.se
[3] West Virginia University, Morgantown, USA
thwuest@mail.wvu.edu
[4] Switzerland Innovation, Biel, Switzerland
dominic.gorecky@switzerland-innovation.com

Abstract. Industry 4.0 technologies, such as enterprise wearables, can foster better industrial hygiene to keep operators healthy, safe, and motivated within emerging cyber-physical production systems. This paper provides an optimistic perspective on opportunities evolving from wearable devices in an Industry 4.0 workplace environment to support occupational health, safety and productivity for the Operator 4.0. Examples of technical solutions, and their associated application scenarios, are presented showcasing how enterprise wearables may foster detection of situations that involve potential occupational risks before they actually occur at smart shopfloors.

Keywords: Industry 4.0 · Operator 4.0 · Occupational health & safety
Human cyber-physical systems
Human-automation and human-machine interfaces · Smart wearables
Socially sustainable manufacturing · Industrial hygiene

1 Introduction

Digitalization, and the paradigm shift associated with it, is shaping the future of work. This specifically includes new challenges and opportunities for occupational health, safety, and productivity for the well-being of the Operator 4.0 [1]. In this context, Industry 4.0 technologies such as *enterprise wearables*[1] [2] can foster better *industrial hygiene* to keep operators healthy, safe, and motivated within emerging smart and social shopfloors [3, 4]. Real-time monitoring of a range of Operator 4.0 vital signs and her/his surrounding workplace environment is currently being facilitated by wearable sensors [5] as well as a sensing and social shopfloor (i.e. ambient intelligence) [3, 4]. This is the basis for the development of *Occupational Health and Safety (OHS)* applications for [6]: (i) *alerting* workers of possible exposure to risks factors like

---

[1] e.g. exoskeletons; body-sensors; mixed reality glasses; smart- watches, helmets, handsets; location trackers.

© IFIP International Federation for Information Processing 2018
Published by Springer Nature Switzerland AG 2018. All Rights Reserved
I. Moon et al. (Eds.): APMS 2018, IFIP AICT 536, pp. 473–481, 2018.
https://doi.org/10.1007/978-3-319-99707-0_59

toxins, high temperatures, or noise levels; (ii) *emergency stops* of heavy machinery; (iii) *anti-ergonomic body movements and postures* – in order to avoid strain or injury; and/or (iv) *monitoring* of cognitive and physical workloads to avoid *Muri*^{2} (overburden).

Discussing real-time monitoring (tracking) of operators generally implies visiting topics such as data related privacy and labour regulations [7]. However, taking an optimistic perspective, and delimiting legal and regulatory matters, wearable trackers (and associated data) have the potential to drive positive changes in smart workplaces.

This paper explores examples of technical solutions, and their associated application scenarios, which could be used as preventive and proactive approaches to enable detection of situations of potential occupational risks before they actually occur at smart shopfloors. This exploration is seen in the context of supporting the Operator 4.0 in her/his daily routines and jobs (i.e. labour polyvalence), considering the operators' cognitive and physical well-being together with the achievement of production objectives, as work complexity may increase within smart shopfloors of the new Industry 4.0 workplace environment.

2   The Healthy Operator 4.0 and Her/His Smart Workplace

The *Operator 4.0* is defined as "a smart and skilled operator who performs not only 'cooperative work' with robots, but also 'work aided' by machines as and if needed. This may be achieved by means of human cyber-physical systems, advanced human-machine interaction technologies and adaptive automation towards 'human-automation symbiosis work systems' " [1]. The sub-type *Healthy Operator 4.0* uses smart wearable solutions (i.e. wearable trackers for health-related metrics) including data analytics capabilities together with advanced Human-Machine (HMI) and Human-Automation Interfacing/Interaction (HAI) technologies, to utilize her/his bio-data (i.e. physiological data). Thus, driving positive change in terms of improved productivity, well-being, and proactive safety measures at smart workplaces [1].

The *Healthy Operator 4.0 type* emerged within the *Operator 4.0 typology* [1], in response to rising concerns about increasing workforce stress levels and state of psycho-social health [8, 9]. Further, the *Healthy Operator 4.0* concept addresses new potential physical risks [10, 11] in emerging, cyber-physical production environments being 'disrupted' by the introduction of new Industry 4.0 technologies (e.g. autonomous and collaborative robots, augmented reality and virtual reality, artificial intelligence, big data analytics, internet of things, etc.) and new work-methods [12].

In this context, the *operators' well-being,* incl. OHS, job satisfaction, work-related affect, and workforce productivity [13] has rarely been *operationalized* in the past due to limitations in measurability of the phenomenon directly and in real-time. This has changed with new smart wearable technologies [14, 15] (with processing, data storage and communication capabilities) and ambient intelligence [15] at the smart shopfloors.

---

^{2} *Muri* occurs when operators are utilized (overworked) for more than 100% to finish their tasks.

The next sub-sections discuss how the *cognitive and physical workload* of a *Healthy Operator 4.0* can be measured using wearable devices and how the operator can be 'strategically' managed using *Artificial Intelligence (AI)* to predict and enhance the operator's health. The AI can be included in a *Cyber-Physical Production System (CPPS)* [16], which comprises both Internet of Things (IoT) and smart applications.

2.1 Reducing the Operator's Cognitive Workload

Cognitive load can be defined as a multidimensional construct representing the mental efforts involved in performing a particular task and their effects on the operator's cognitive system. Two such constructs are: (i) the *causal dimension* – reflecting the interaction between task and operator characteristics, and (ii) the *assessment dimension* – reflecting measurable concepts of mental load, mental effort, and performance [17].

In order to assess (or measure) *cognitive workload,* this paper adopts the operator's perceived view of her/his workstation considering mental load and performance [18]. The operators perceived view is assessed through *perceived production complexity,* which is defined as "the interrelations between product variants, work content, layout, tools and support tools and work instructions, as perceived by the operators" [18]. Moreover, Industry 4.0 production lines are characterized by highly- flexible and adaptable manufacturing systems that support mass-customization and personalization strategies. As a result, Industry 4.0 production lines create an increasingly complex production and high-variance working environment for the operator, thus increasing the mental effort required from her/him to perform the tasks [19]. An increase in perceived production complexity is not negative for the operators' health per definition, nevertheless, it is important to study what variable relations affect the increase [18].

One way to cope with *production complexity,* and therefore support the operator's cognitive workload in her/his daily job, is by means of *Smart Cognitive Support Tools (SCST)*[3] (e.g. augmented reality-based tools and other intelligent HMIs). *SCSTs* can present information in a more intuitive way to the *Operator 4.0* as and if needed. This is enabled by 'AI capabilities' for aided decision-making and understanding of the cognitive task at hand [19, 21, 22]. The *SCSTs* can also present information in real-time to the operator that is adapted to her/his cognitive load level (e.g. if a disturbance occurs information regarding that is presented to the operator in terms decision support). For example, *cognitive workload* can be relieved by assessing the operator's well-being at work using smart wearables (i.e. body-sensors for assessing changes in the operator's cognitive states based on skin conductance, blood-pressure, heart-rate, breathing and/or temperature measurements or by assessing eye-movement) [23]. In parallel her/his cognitive-load can be managed by addressing the cognitive tasks allocated to her/his job to keep the operator at an ideal 'stress level', without under- or over-whelming her/him. This could be achieved by associating new variations to an Operator 4.0's routine whose vital data suggest she/he is bored with her/his current

---

[3] *SCSTs* are assisting tools that use AI capabilities to leverage innate human abilities, e.g. visual information processing, to improve human understanding and cognition of challenging problems [adapted from 20].

routines, or on the other extreme, provide less variety to the Operator 4.0 who is overwhelmed by new tasks, indicated by e.g. perspiration and high-pulse rate.

2.2   Reducing Operators' Physical Workload

Physical load – can be defined as the physical effects of mechanical forces on the human body [23]. Furthermore, *physical workload* can be assessed (or measured) in terms of "biomechanical events occurring in the human body" [23]. Hence, today, *wearables* can provide a wide range of sensors that measure acceleration, motion and stress (e.g. number of steps, time during day when the operator is standing/sitting, and work-pace), which can be associated with the operators' physical workload. This opens up new opportunities to measure the *Operators 4.0* exposure to various mechanical forces in real-time, to always support the practice of proper ergonomics during daily working routine(s). Moreover, *smart sensors* can be used to increase adaptability between humans and robots in order to create truly collaborative environments.

The *Healthy Operator 4.0* aims to provide sustainable solutions for workers through both a personalized design process and customized recommendations of ergonomic work-routines. That way, the operators' health and productivity can be increased in a sustainable fashion. Several theoretical benefits emerge from this development, besides the overall goal of healthier employees: (i) less sick-days, (ii) lower risks of work- accident/injury related law-suites, (iii) better planning of staff availability when operator health can be predicted based on sensory input, and (iv) lower personnel turnovers.

2.3   HCA, HAI, and HMI as Means to Support Smart Workload Management

This sub-section introduces relevant enabling means for supporting smart workload management in the factories of the future, taking advantage of new human-centred automation design approaches [24] and human-machine interfaces [25, 26].

Human-Centred Automation (HCA) [24] is defined as "automation designed to work cooperatively with human operators in pursuit of stated objectives". HCA emphasizes that automation functionality should be designed to support human performance and human understanding of the automation system. This means that automation systems must support both cognitive and physical workload of the operator [24]. In order to do this, *Human-Automation Interaction (HAI)* is needed and is defined as "the way a human controls and receives information from automation" [25]. *Automation* is then defined as "the execution by a machine agent of a function previously carried out by a human" [26]. Moreover, *Human-Machine Interfaces/Interactions (HMI)* are defined as interfaces/endeavours that allow user inputs to be translated into signals for machines. They, in turn, provide required results to the user, ranging from knowledge discovery to information visualizations in recent cyber-physical world(s) at 'smart shopfloors'.

In [3, 21], Romero et al. explore how 'intelligent' HMIs, as well as adaptive and human-in-the-loop control systems (i.e. HAIs) can support the development of *Human-Automation Symbiosis (HAS) work systems* for the Operator 4.0. *HAS work systems* aim to offer the *Healthy Operator 4.0* the inherent advantages of smart cognitive, physical, and hybrid, automation-aided systems. Such systems can provide sustainable relief of physical and mental stress for the operator, as and if needed. That way, production objectives and productivity goals do not get compromised. Neither does the health and safety of the Operator 4.0 [21].

3   Digitally-Enabled OHS and Enhanced-Productivity Scenarios

This section explores three examples of scenarios where digitally-enabled OHS and enhanced-productivity solutions support the *Healthy Operator 4.0* to stay healthy, safe, and highly-productive in emerging Industry 4.0 manufacturing systems.

3.1   Smart Exoskeletons in Industry 4.0 Assembly Lines

Exoskeletons are wearable assistance devices powered by a system of electric motors, pneumatics, levers, hydraulics, or a combination of technologies that allow for limb movement with increased strength and endurance (i.e. physical load) [27]. *Smart exoskeletons* are a type of exoskeletons that have been instrumented with 'smart on-body-sensors' for behavioural and biomechanical modelling with the intention of real-time monitoring and recognition of anti-ergonomic body movements and postures in order to avoid strains or injuries in operators.

From the perspective of a digitally-enabled OHS scenario, *smart exoskeletons* can help operators to improve their postures and to reduce work-related injuries while performing manual tasks, e.g. when an operator has to lift heavy parts and restrain them into the assembly position. Complementary, from the perspective of an enhanced-productivity scenario, *smart exoskeletons* can reduce currently required human physical efforts during many manual tasks. Resulting reductions in strenuous and tiring work have the potential to reduce work fatigue and increase operators' productivity.

More generally, any kind of physical activity, such as lifting, pushing, pulling, carrying, moving, manipulating, holding or restraining objects, is considered to be a manual task [28]. Any kind of similar physical activity may cause musculoskeletal disorders (MSDs). MSDs represent a central issue for operators and public health [29]. Hence, *smart exoskeletons* can identify conditions under which the risk of work-related MSDs is high(er), so that the operator can then either be provided with multimodal (e.g. visual, auditory and tactile) feedback and recommendations in order to change risky or critical postures. Another option is that the exoskeleton intervenes actively and supports the limb movement with supplementary strength and endurance.

The continuous collection of (personal) ergonomic assessment data over time and scale will also help to build-up a comprehensive database of occurring manual tasks and postures. This database enables the system to learn about risky and critical work conditions that can be generalized as new ergonomic guidelines at the same time that will allow the development of adequate interventions for each operator.

3.2   Adaptive Collaborative Robots (Co-bots) in Industry 4.0 Assembly Lines

Adaptive co-bots are collaborative robots that dynamically adapt to the human's pace, stress-level, and experience [30]. *Adaptive co-bots* can result in co-bots working more efficiently and seamlessly with their human partners, consequently, increasing their overall productivity [30]. From both perspectives, a digitally-enabled OHS and an enhanced-productive scenario, *adaptive co-bot systems* will monitor the operators' cognitive and physical workloads and work proactively [31] to avoid *Muri*. This is made possible through available *smart wearable body-sensors* at the *Operator 4.0* measuring skin conductance – using an electro-dermal activity sensor, body-motion – using accelerometers and gyroscopes, and/or heart-rate – using a pulse sensor, which will send data to an AI-system that optimises the cognitive and physical help depending on the status of the operator, e.g. pace, stress-level and experience. Hence, an *adaptive co-bot* will change its speed and number of tasks performed, depending of the operator's health status. More generally, if an operator indicates signs of fatigue (e.g. longer cycle-times or bad quality), an AI-system can take over the tasks while the operator can decrease her/his cognitive and physical workload. When the *adaptive co-bot* receives indication that the operator has recovered, it can start providing the operator with more tasks again. This can even out cycle-time and quality of products, but also decrease sick-leaves related to stress and over-load (e.g. burn-out) of the operators. In addition, the *adaptive co-bot* will support the operator when she/he needs to do another task (e.g. solving a disruption in the production line).

Using *adaptive co-bots* as a supporting element in work-systems, provides the opportunity to adjust the degree of assistance based on a variable automation level [32] and respond to human restrictions individually [33]. Hence, there is little consideration of the operator's individual performance parameters to design her/his workstation-orientated to personal capabilities and ergonomics [33] today. More research is needed to fully create collaborative and adaptable workstations for the *Healthy Operator 4.0*.

3.3   Smart Personal Protective Equipment in Logistics 4.0 Environments

The purpose of *Personal Protective Equipment (PPE)* is to reduce worker exposure to hazards, when engineering and administrative controls are not feasible or effective to reduce such risks to acceptable levels. Present PPEs can be considered as 'passive' protective equipment that aims to reduce the severity of an injury in case of an accident. Nevertheless, and from a perspective of a digitally-enabled OHS scenario, a new generation of *Smart PPEs* is emerging. These are mainly driven by the development of *smart wearables* and the arrival of *work environmental sensors* to the industrial workplaces towards *ambient intelligence* [15], manifested as *smart workplaces,* thanks to the measurement of environmental parameters – using temperature, humidity, noise, workplace light, air-quality and/or motion sensors, and of workers' location and vital body functions – using smart wearable body-sensors and location trackers. Such is the case of *intelligent container ports* where *Smart PPEs* interact with in motion *smart containers* and *smart cranes* to 'actively safeguard' the harbour staff also in motion at the terminal by alerting them of dangerous situations (e.g. walking by accident under a container being lift/transported by a crane).

Overall, *Smart PPEs* aim to 'actively' prevent and ensure workers health and safety by alerting workers of possible exposure to risks factors like toxins, high temperatures, or noise levels as well as dangerous (smart) objects moving nearby [34]. From the perspective of an enhanced-productivity scenario, *Smart PPEs* can improve operators' productivity by making it easier for the *Operators 4.0* to get alerts and communicate with each other thanks to wearable computing (i.e. the *Social Operator 4.0* [1]).

4   Conclusions

The vision of the *Operator 4.0* [1], i.e. the *Healthy Operator 4.0,* may seem futuristic. Nevertheless, many workers constantly wear personal and private activity trackers, smart watches and other wearables containing micro-gyroscope technology, heart-rate monitoring capability and GPS-positioning functionality. Yet, in today's production environments, productive use of this new abundance of data has not been exploited, neither for the benefit of the workers, nor for corporate reasons. This paper provides an optimistic perspective on future opportunities emerging from 'enterprise wearables' in an Industry 4.0 workplace environment that may soon be realised. Through typical case descriptions, the authors aim to attract the attention of industry management involved in analysing how available resources and technologies can be used to address everyday concerns for worker well-being. In addition, by raising the awareness of such cases some of them might become reality.

While this is intended as a visionary paper, the authors are aware that some of the core limitations are not necessarily technical in nature. Having access to personal data and information includes a significant potential for misuse of data – e.g. predicting a worker's health to base a promotion or contract-termination decision on the acquired data. Such legal and ethical topics need urgent public discussion among inter-disciplinary groups of experts. Problems should be addressed by experts on philosophy and legal issues as well as on social and humanities matters, in addition to the 'usual line of suspects' from business, computer science, and engineering. In addition, the acceptability of the operators need to be studied. New technologies should always be introduced to the operator in a cooperative manner and the effects of the application of the *Healthy Operator 4.0* should be clearly presented.

Forthcoming work involves bringing the illustrated example scenarios to 'life' and carefully evaluating their technological feasibility. First evaluations can be done in a lab setting, for proof-of- concept investigations. Later, assessments should be made with industrial partners in real-world smart shopfloors, to analyse return on investment and potential non-technical issues e.g. employee acceptance.

References

1. Romero, D., et al.: Towards an operator 4.0 typology: a human-centric perspective on the fourth industrial revolution technologies. In: Proceedings of the International Conference on Computers & Industrial Engineering (CIE46), Tianjin/China, pp. 1–11 (2016)
2. Pavón, I., Sigcha, L.F., Arezes, P.M., Costa, N., de Arcas, G, Lopez-Navarro, J.M.: Wearable technology for occupational risk assessment: potential avenues for applications. In: Occupational Safety and Hygiene VI, pp. 447–452, CRC Press (2018)
3. Romero, D., Wuest, T., Stahre, J., Gorecky, D.: Social factory architecture: social networking services and production scenarios through the social internet of things, services and people for the social operator 4.0. In: Lödding, H., Riedel, R., Thoben, K.-D., von Cieminski, G., Kiritsis, D. (eds.) APMS 2017. IAICT, vol. 513, pp. 265–273. Springer, Cham (2017). https://doi.org/10.1007/978-3-319-66923-6_31
4. Kassner, L., Hirmer, P., Wieland, M., Steimle, F., Königsberger, J., Mitschang, B.: The social factory: connecting people, machines and data in manufacturing for context aware exception escalation. In: 50th Hawaii International Conference on System Sciences (2017)
5. Perera, C., Liu, C.H., Jayawardena, S.: The emerging internet of things marketplace from an industrial perspective: a survey. IEEE TETEC 3(4), 585–598 (2015)
6. Liberty Mutual Insurance by Quartz Creative: Tailor Made to Reduce Risk: Wearables Technology in the Workplace. https://qz.com/1087388
7. Schall Jr., M.C., Sesek, R.F., Cavuoto, L.A.: Barriers to the adoption of wearable sensors in the workplace: a survey of occupational safety and health professionals. Hum. Factors 60, 351–362 (2018). https://doi.org/10.1177/0018720817753907
8. Buffet, M.A., Gervais, R.L., Liddle, M., Eeckelaert, L.: Well-being at work: creating a positive work environment. J. Personal. Soc. Psychol. 84(4), 822–848 (2013)
9. Salanova, M., Libano, M., Llorens, S., Schaufeli, W.: Engaged, workaholic, burned-out or just 9-to-5? towards a typology of employee well-being. Stress Health 30, 71–81 (2014)
10. Matthias, B., Oberer-Treitz, S., Staab, H., Schuller, E., Peldschus, S.: Injury risk quantification for industrial robots in collaborative operation with humans. In: 41st International. Symposium on and 6th German Conference on Robotics (ROBOTIK), pp. 1–6 (2010)
11. Vasic, M., Billard, A.: Safety issues in human-robot interactions. In: IEEE International Conference on Robotics and Automation (ICRA), pp. 197–204 (2013)
12. BCG Boston Consulting Group. https://www.bcg.com/pt-br/publications/2015/technology-business-transformation-engineered-products-infrastructure-man-machine-industry-4.aspx
13. Page, K.M., Vella-Brodrick, D.A.: The 'what', 'why' and 'how' of employee well-being: a new model. Soc. Indic. Res. 90(3), 441–458 (2009)
14. Bernal, G., Colombo, S., Al Ai Baky, M., Casalegno, F.: Safety: designing IoT and wearable systems for industrial safety through user centered design approach. In: 10th International Conference on Pervasive Technologies Related to Assistive Environment, p. 163. ACM (2017)
15. Podgorski, D., Majchrzycka, K., Dabrowska, A., Gralewicz, G., Okrasa, M.: Towards a conceptual framework of OSH risk management in smart working environments based on smart PPE, ambient intelligence and the internet of things technologies. Int. J. Occup. Saf. Ergon. 23(1), 1–20 (2017)
16. Sameer, M., Muztoba, K., Romero, D., Wuest, T.: Smart manufacturing: characteristics, technologies and enabling factors. J. Eng. Manuf. (2017). https://doi.org/10.1177/09544 05417736547
17. Löscher, I., Axelsson, A., Vännström, J., Jansson, A.: Eliciting strategies in revolutionary design: exploring the hypothesis of predefined strategy categories. Theor. Issues Ergon. Sci. 19(1), 101–117 (2018)

18. Mattsson, S., Tarrar, M., Fast-Berglund, Å.: Perceived production complexity: understanding more than parts of a system. Int. J. Prod. Res. **54**(20), 6008–6016 (2016)
19. Fast-Berglund, Å., Stahre, J.: Cognitive automation strategy for reconfigurable and sustainable assembly systems. Assem. Autom. **33**(3), 294–303 (2013)
20. Walenstein, A.: Foundations of cognitive support: toward abstract patterns of usefulness. In: Forbrig, P., Limbourg, Q., Vanderdonckt, J., Urban, B. (eds.) DSV-IS 2002. LNCS, vol. 2545, pp. 133–147. Springer, Heidelberg (2002). https://doi.org/10.1007/3-540-36235-5_10
21. Romero, D., Bernus, P., Noran, O., Stahre, J., Fast-Berglund, Å.: The Operator 4.0: human cyber-physical systems & adaptive automation towards human-automation symbiosis work systems. In: Nääs, I., et al. (eds.) IFIP Advances in Information and Communication Technology. IFIPAICT, vol. 488, pp. 677–686. Springer, Cham (2016). https://doi.org/10.1007/978-3-319-51133-7_80
22. Mattsson, S., Fast-Berglund, Å., Åkerman, M.: Assessing operator wellbeing through physiological measurements in real-time – towards industrial application. Technologies **5**(4), 223–232 (2017)
23. Winkel, J., Mathiassen, S.E.: Assessment of physical work load in epidemiologic studies: concepts. Issues Oper. Consid. Ergon. **37**(6), 979–988 (1994)
24. Billings, C.E.: Aviation Automation: The Search for a Human-Centered Approach. CRC Press, Boca Raton (1996)
25. Sheridan, T.B., Parasuraman, R.: Human-automation interaction. Rev. Hum. Factors Ergon. **1**(89), 89–129 (2015)
26. Parasuraman, R., Riley, V.: Humans and automation: use, misuse, disuse, abuse. Hum. Factors: J. Hum. Factors Ergon. Soc. **39**(2), 230–253 (1997)
27. Sylla, N., Bonnet, V., Colledani, F., Fraisse, P.: Ergonomic contribution of ABLE exoskeleton in automotive industry. Int. J. of Ind. Ergon. **44**(4), 475–481 (2014)
28. Council for Occupational Safety and Health (COSH): Code of Practice: Manual Tasks. Government of Western Australia, Department of Commerce, Perth (2010)
29. Burgess-Limerick, R.J.: Ergonomics for manual tasks. Australian Master of OHS and Environment Guide, CCH Australia, North Ryde, pp. 261–278 (2007)
30. Görür, O., Rosman, B., Sivrikaya, F., Albayrak, S.: Social cobots: anticipatory decision-making for collaborative robots incorporating unexpected human behaviors. In: ACM/IEEE International Conference on Human-Robot Interaction (2018)
31. Görür, O., Rosman, B., Hoffman, G., Albayrak, S.: Toward integrating theory of mind into adaptive decision-making of social robots to understand human intention. In: Workshop on the Role of Intentions in Human-Robot Interaction (2017)
32. Fasth, Å., Lundholm, T., Mårtensson, L., Dencker, K., Stahre, J.: Designing proactive assembly systems – criteria and interaction between automation, information, and competence. In: CIRP Conference on Manufacturing Systems (2009)
33. Thomas, C., Stankiewicz, L., Grötsch, A., Wischniewski, S., Deuse, J., Kuhlenkötter, B.: Intuitive work assistance by reciprocal human-robot interaction in the subject area of direct human-robot collaboration. Procedia CIRP **44**, 275–280 (2016)
34. Frost & Sullivan: Wearables and Smart Personal Protection Equipment (PPE) Technologies for the Industrial Market (2016)

A Framework for Process Model Based Human-Robot Collaboration System Using Augmented Reality

Hwaseop Lee, Yeeyeng Liau, Siku Kim, and Kwangyeol Ryu$^{(\boxtimes)}$

Pusan National University, Busan 46241, South Korea
{hslee,yeeyeng85,siku.kim,kyryu}@pusan.ac.kr

Abstract. The concept of smart factory is being applied into traditional manufacturing system. Since factory automation is applied gradationally, Human-robot collaboration (HRC) system is becoming an important issue. In order to construct an effective HRC system, clear communication with the human workers and the robots has to be considered. This research proposed a conceptual framework of process model based HRC system for efficient human-robot collaboration in a semi automation process to produce electric motors. We applied a process modeling methodology for capturing collaborative features, activity and resource flow in the manufacturing process. The model defined by the proposed methodology is the data storage to contain process information and interface between the human workers and robots to provide accurate information in the appropriate context. Furthermore, machine vision technology is implemented to recognize specifications of work in process (WIP) parts. The recognized parts are mapped with the correct work order and work instruction manual defined by the proposed model. In order to reduce human worker's errors, the extracted work information is transmitted to the worker through the augmented reality device. The proposed HRC system is expected to be able to support the construction of a semi automation system that can reduce errors of human workers and ensure production flexibility.

Keywords: Augmented reality · Human-robot collaboration · Machine vision
Process modeling

1 Introduction

This research proposed a conceptual framework of human-robot collaboration (HRC) system for semi-automated process to produce electric motors. This process consists of automated machines, a handling robot, and a human worker. The automated machines conduct processing operations such as cut off, drilling, facing and etc. The robot assists the human worker in the material handling operation. The robot picks up the parts from each automated machine and locates on the pallets, then transfers the partial processed parts to the assembly section which performed by a human worker. In the current practice, there are no interaction between the robot and human worker on the part information. Human worker does not receive information of the type of parts that are picked up by the robot in advanced, i.e. before the part arrives at assembly

© IFIP International Federation for Information Processing 2018
Published by Springer Nature Switzerland AG 2018. All Rights Reserved
I. Moon et al. (Eds.): APMS 2018, IFIP AICT 536, pp. 482–489, 2018.
https://doi.org/10.1007/978-3-319-99707-0_60

section, especially when changeover of part model. Hence, delay occurred when the human worker needs to measure and identify the part.

In this paper, machine vision technology is applied to identify the part in collaboration process. When image processing through machine vision is completed, accurate work order and part information corresponding to the extracted image should be defined. We defined the work order and part information using Part-flow based Manufacturing Process Modeling (PMPM) which can express process flow and part flow at the same time [1]. In order to transmit the tracked data to the worker immediately, we used the augmented reality (AR) device to transmit work order information and product specification information. This study proposes a conceptual framework of HCR system using a process model and AR interface.

2 Literature Reviews

2.1 Human-Robot Collaboration in Assembly Operation

Human-robot collaboration is one of new trends in the field of industrial robots as a part of strategy Industry 4.0. Full automation has limitation in achieving the required production demand due to the high complexity in process and flexibility of equipment to cope with the rapid response. Hence, HRC which has advantage to maximize the flexibility in production became one of the important trends in current industrial application. Human-robot collaboration is a system in which a robot and a human are collaborating on a same task which combines benefits from both human and robot in a joint task [2]. HRC system plays an important role to increase flexibility to cope with wide variety of products and the frequent changeover in equipment to cope with the fluctuating demand [3]. In HRC workstation, the collaborative robot must have the capability to sense the existence of human, i.e. with appropriate safety mechanism that defines the ability to collaborate with human without safety cage.

Machine Vision for Assembly. Machine vision system consists of image capture device, lighting and computer with image processing software [4]. Machine vision systems enable flexibility in automation by providing the machine capability of "see" and think. From the existing researches, the main application of machine vision system is quality monitoring for wide range of industries such as electromechanical parts [5], textile manufacturing [6], pharmaceutical [7], food packaging [8], steel making industry [9] and etc. Teck et al. [10] integrated machine vision system into automation systems to provide product data which assists the decision making of the production system. Gao et al. [11] developed machine vision to track and calibrate the coordinates of fast moving battery lid in automated sealing rings assembly system. The application of machine vision with the robot in the assembly system increased the efficiency and robot adaptability to the environmental changes and enable real-time adjustment of robot motion.

AR for Assembly. AR is a technology derived from a field of VR, which refers to a computer graphics technique that superimposes virtual contents created in 3D in the real world of the user [12]. Since the augmented reality technology models and matches only the required virtual objects based on the real-time image of the actual manufacturing environment, the construction cost and time for 3D models necessary for implementing a new manufacturing system can be drastically reduced.

Kollatsch et al. [13] discussed about an AR based application for mobile devices realizing a user-friendly and problem-oriented visualization of information. However, this research has limitations in simply suggesting the AR-based concept introduced for visualizing the process value of mobile devices. Further, Wang et al. [14] presented about a novel human Cognition-based interactive Augmented Reality Assembly Guidance System is proposed to investigate how AR can provide various modalities of guidance to assembly operators for different phases of user cognition process during assembly tasks. In addition, Danielsson et al. [15] implemented an environment in which an untrained worker using AR in a human-robot collaboration environment. This research, however, has a problem that various errors occur during assembly due to misunderstandings of the instructions of the test person.

Although many studies have been conducted to utilize the strength of the AR technology in the manufacturing system implementation, there is a lack of an AR system which can be properly utilized in the manufacturing system.

2.2   Part-Flow Based Manufacturing Process Modeling: PMPM

PMPM is a modeling tool for visualizing and visualizing man (worker), machine, material (parts), and method (activity) of collaborative manufacturing process. It can clearly define the order of the manufacturing operations that make up the process and its execution objects. This method consists of 6 notations for activity expression and 10 notations for part expression. It can provide functions to record parts' history and to manage parts status by using part notations. and this method can define collaborative activities in each process. The flow of parts and the flow of work can be determined identically or independently. It is possible to define changes in characteristics such as changes in the number of management units of parts and merging of parts. It also allows a clear definition of objects using manufacturing facilities. It is manufacturing process-oriented modeling methodology. In this paper, we used PMPM to store process information and track part information.

3   Process Model Based HRC System

3.1   System Framework

Figure 1 shows data flow diagram of the proposed process model based HRC system. Electronic motor manufacturing process consists of four automated workstations which perform coil forming and cap machining and assembly of electric motor by human worker. Two types of material handling methods are used in the process: (1) using conveyor to transfer parts between automated workstations; (2) a robot collects the partial complete components from these workstations on a pallet and transfers to assembly workstation. PMPM modeling methodology is used in this study to build the digital model for this process. The PMPM model stores information about work order, parts flow, and task performing objects. When the part arrives at the assembly process, the operator recognizes the part through the AR device. In this paper, the machine vision is integrated in AR interface to identify the parts in the assembly model. After the parts are identified, the work order such as assembly sequence, parts required and production quantity corresponds to the identified part is extracted from the PMPM model and transmitted to the AR interface. The PMPM modeling simulates the start time of each workstation in the order of minimizing the production cycle time. The coordination of processing time among the workstations and the material handling time by robot i.e. part pick-up time at each automated workstation and delivery time to human assembly workstation by robot is important to ensure the smooth flow and avoid stacking of part and idle time at each station especially the human assembly work-station. Hence, the real-time production status at the human assembly workstation has to be sent to the robot via AR interface to "call" for parts and "stop" input of parts. Besides, this method also can reduce overproduction at each automated workstation and part shortage with the updated finished parts quantity.

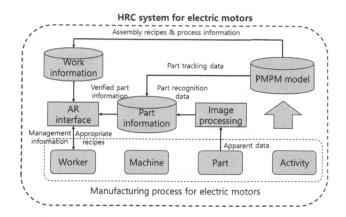

Fig. 1. Data flow of system framework.

3.2 Implementation

PMPM Modeling. The first step is to model the electronic motor assembly process using PMPM. Figure 2 shows the result for modeling the target process. Rectangles are the tasks performed by automated machines. Rounded rectangles and octagons are the collaborative works of the robot and the worker. As shown in Fig. 2, the type and number information of the input and output parts are defined in the model. Therefore, this model plays a role as an important data engine that has main information of HRC system and is used to track part information and verify image processing results. From PMPM modeling, the human worker who performs the assembly is updated with the real-time type of model and quantity during the production in each automated workstation via the AR device. Hence, PMPM modeling acts as communication interface between the automated workstation and human worker who performs the assembly.

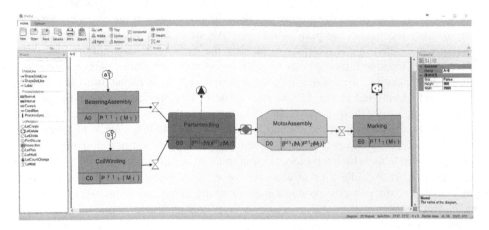

Fig. 2. PMPM model for electric motors.

Image Processing. The electric motor models are differentiated according the size of case and the size of cap. The dimension of cap and case are shown in Table 1. Since the outer shapes of the parts are similar, there are possibility for human worker assemble the wrong combination. The measurement using Vernier caliper every time before the assembly process reduce the productivity of the operation. Hence, part measuring using machine vision system is proposed to increase the accuracy of part identification and increase the productivity of the assembly process. In order to achieve these, the vision system must be capable to acquire the image for part detection as close as human vision [16]. The steps in image processing involved to identify cap and measure the dimension of the cap arrived at the assembly section are shown in Fig. 3. First, the image is captured by the Augmented Reality interface and send to MATLAB image processing software. Image processing is performed using image processing toolbox in MATLAB. The image processing starts with converting the image acquired to gray scale image. Then, the image is converted to binary image for edge detection using Canny method. Since the cap is in round shape, the 'imfindcircles' function is used to identify the shape with defined radius range. Finally, the identified cap is marked and the radius is measured in pixels (see Fig. 4). The algorithm needs further improvement to remove the shadow of the image captured and to provide measurement in centimeters.

Table 1. Types of raw material and measurement for processing.

Magnet	Coil	Inner diameter of bearing	Outer diameter of case	Length of case
6ø	6.5ø	1.5 mm	14ø	35 mm
8ø	8.5ø	2 mm	16ø	37 mm
-	-	-	-	39 mm

AR Interface Development. In this study, app development environment is built. Based on Android, an app is developed that uses an image target and a virtual button

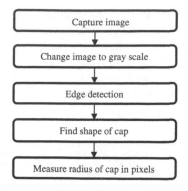

Fig. 3. Image processing for identify and measure cap.

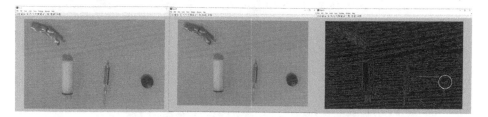

Fig. 4. Visualization of image processing steps.

which are linked to a tracker by camera rendering by using Vuforia and Unity. The developed application visualizes actual factory data and pre-analyzed simulation data to the manager and visualizes them to the human worker in real time through the AR device. Managers can make manufacturability decisions and verify production plans through pre-simulation. In addition, real-time log data preprocessing and data exchange environment can be constructed by data linkage between log data from manufacturing facilities and MES.

To build an AR interface, we used the Vuforia module by using the Unity engine. Unity is a virtual/augmented reality production tool which has the advantage of creating mobile AR programs regardless of iOS or Android. This is expected to be effective in the manufacturing field where various AR equipment are combined. The user can monitor real-time information of the identified part. The information is predefined and can be freely set according to the characteristics of the operator and each part.

Figure 5 shows the pilot program screen of the AR interface. It provides the assembly recipes and process information stored in the database to the operator using the AR through the part information verified by image processing. The developed AR application allows process values to be stored and analyzed to show process-related information to the operator or administrator. Thus, the user does not need extensive knowledge of the machine and the control device, and the production process is not disturbed. The collected data can be displayed to the user in real time or can be evaluated later. Process data is stored in the database and can be retrieved from other applications. The traditional monitoring system provides operators with a simple signal on the designated board, but the AR based interface provides the operator with real-time status of the plant and makes the work more efficient. The operator can virtually overlap the plant parameters and process state at the actual location of the sensor/equipment/actuator. It can also visualize information about areas that are generally inaccessible or dangerous.

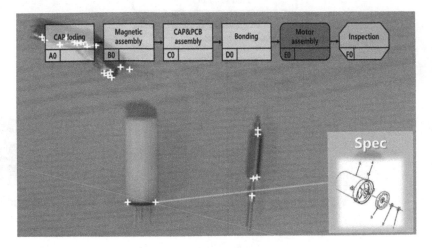

Fig. 5. AR interface pilot program.

4 Conclusion

In this paper, we proposed process model based HRC system using AR interface. We defined the work order, parts flow, and collaboration information of the electronic motor assembly process using the part-flow based manufacturing process modeling (PMPM). The PMPM model is used to act as an interface between human worker, automated processing machines and material handling robot through the identification of parts and corresponding work sequences. Hence, integration of AR devices and image processing is needed to capture parts information efficiently. Image processing technique used to extract features of component from the image captured using AR device and feedback the result of part identification to human workers via AR device. The proposed system is expected to reduce human error in part model identification and work sequence. Furthermore, production flexibility that able to cope with frequent model changeover can be achieved. The main contributions of this framework are the data management using process model and the use of image processing to increase the part recognition of AR. However, since this study is an early stage, it is necessary to verify the proposed framework and define practical problems through application.

References

1. Lee, H., Ryu, K., Son, Y.J., Cho, Y.: Capturing green information and mapping with mes functions for increasing manufacturing sustainability. Int. J. Precis. Eng. Manufact. **15**(8), 1709–1716 (2014)
2. Faber, M., Bützler, J., Schlick, C.M.: Human-robot cooperation in future production systems: Analysis of requirements for designing an ergonomic work system. Procedia Manufact. **3**, 510–517 (2015)
3. Thomas, C., Matthias, B., Kuhlenkötter, B.: Human-robot collaboration-new applications in industrial robotics. In: International Conference on Competitive Manufacturing (COMA), pp. 293–299, Stellenbosch (2016)
4. Malamas, E.N., Petrakis, E.G., Zervakis, M., Petit, L., Legat, J.D.: A survey on industrial vision systems, applications and tools. Image Vis. Comput. **21**(2), 171–188 (2003)
5. Di Leo, G., Liguori, C., Pietrosanto, A., Sommella, P.: A vision system for the online quality monitoring of industrial manufacturing. Opt. Lasers Eng. **89**, 162–168 (2017)
6. Cho, C.S., Chung, B.M., Park, M.J.: Development of real-time vision-based fabric inspection system. IEEE Trans. Industr. Electron. **52**(4), 1073–1079 (2005)
7. Možina, M., Tomaževič, D., Pernuš, F., Likar, B.: Automated visual inspection of imprint quality of pharmaceutical tablets. Mach. Vis. Appl. **24**(1), 63–73 (2013)
8. Duan, F., Wang, Y., Liu, H.: A real-time machine vision system for bottle finish inspection. In: ICARCV 2004 8th Control, Automation, Robotics and Vision Conference, vol. 2, pp. 842–846. IEEE, Kunming, China (2004)
9. Yun, J.P., Choi, D.C., Jeon, Y.J., Park, C., Kim, S.W.: Defect inspection system for steel wire rods produced by hot rolling process. Int. J. Adv. Manuf. Technol. **70**(9–12), 1625–1634 (2014)
10. Teck, L.W., Sulaiman, M., Shah, H.N.M., Omar, R.: Implementation of shape-based matching vision system in flexible manufacturing system. J. Eng. Sci. Technol. Rev. **3**(1), 128–135 (2010)
11. Gao, M., Li, X., He, Z., Yang, Y.: An automatic assembling system for sealing rings based on machine vision. J. Sens. **2017**, 12 p. (2017). Article ID 4207432. https://doi.org/10.1155/2017/4207432
12. Azuma, R., Baillot, Y., Behringer, R., Feiner, S., Julier, S., MacIntyre, B.: Recent advances in augmented reality. IEEE Comput. Graphics Appl. **21**(6), 34–47 (2001)
13. Kollatsch, C., Schumann, M., Klimant, P., Wittstock, V., Putz, M.: Mobile augmented reality based monitoring of assembly lines. Procedia CIRP **23**, 246–251 (2014)
14. Wang, X., Ong, S.K., Nee, A.Y.C.: Multi-modal augmented-reality assembly guidance based on bare-hand interface. Adv. Eng. Inform. **30**(3), 406–421 (2016)
15. Danielsson, O., Syberfeldt, A., Brewster, R., Wang, L.: Assessing instructions in augmented reality for human-robot collaborative assembly by using demonstrators. Procedia CIRP **63**, 89–94 (2017)
16. Peña-Cabrera, M., Lopez-Juarez, I., Rios-Cabrera, R., Corona-Castuera, J.: Machine vision approach for robotic assembly. Assem. Autom. **25**(3), 204–216 (2005)

Management of Reconfigurable Production Networks in Order-Based Production

Johannes be Isa[1]($\boxtimes$), Helge Epha[2], Stefan Braunreuther[3],
and Gunther Reinhart[4]

[1] Fraunhofer IGCV, Provinostr. 52, 86153 Augsburg, Germany
johannes.be.isa@igcv.fraunhofer.de
[2] Technical University of Berlin, Straße des 17. Juni 135. 17,
10623 Berlin, Germany
[3] University of Applied Sciences Augsburg,
An der Hochschule 1, 86161 Augsburg, Germany
[4] Technical University of Munich,
Bolzmannstraße 15, 58748 Garching, Germany

Abstract. High market volatility as well as increasing global competition in manufacturing lead to a growing demand for flexible and agile production networks. Advanced production systems in turn conduct high capital expenditure along with high investment risks. However, the latest developments of information and communication technology in production environments carry promising optimization opportunities.

The approach of this paper is to apply reconfigurable production networks for scalable capacity and low capital expenditure by adapting "Production planning as a service". Therefore, a genetic algorithm was applied to solve a complex optimization problem. At the end of this work, a prototypical application of the discussed subject is shown on a world-leading household appliance manufacturer.

Keywords: Production planning · Reconfigurable production networks
Mass-customization

1 Introduction and Motivation

The current global market situation is characterized by shorter delivery times, higher timeliness as well as high demand volatility [1]. Further saturated markets lead to a trend of customer individualized products in the consumer business sector [2]. In addition, the industry business sector shows a significant trend to higher individualization based on various technical requirements. These trends lead to an increasing number of product variants [2]. High number of variants in turn lead to large inventories in the make-to-stock (MTS) production approach. The MTS approach is very promising and ensures very fast delivery times for the mass production of standardized products. However, this mode of operation bears the risk of overproduction and unsold products in the stock [3].

To tackle this major challenge, manufacturing companies combine the MTS with the make-to-order (MTO) production approach. The combination of the MTS and

I. Moon et al. (Eds.): APMS 2018, IFIP AICT 536, pp. 490–497, 2018.
https://doi.org/10.1007/978-3-319-99707-0_61

MTO approaches have been discussed since the mid-1990s [3, 4]. The fact that production forecasts are still very poor is traced back to unforeseeable market shifts and shorter product lifecycles. This expresses the need for fast adaptable production networks to ramp up production capacity in very short timeframes [5].

The latest innovations in information technology can be seen as enablers of fast and reliable communication between production sites [2]. This paper discusses an approach to order optimization based on the idea of a Production-as-a-Service concept.

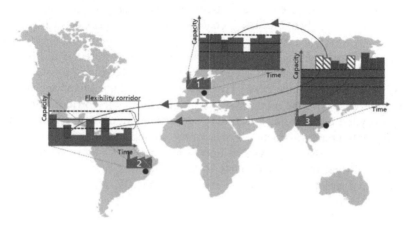

Fig. 1. Model of a simple global production network, characterized by various supply and demand of capacities [6].

Figure 1 shows a model of a simple global production network. Very typical utilization rates are given; some manufacturing sites have too many free capacities, e.g., factory 2 in the figure, others run an excessive workload, e.g., factory 3. Both of these scenarios are far from an optimal operating strategy [6]. To reach a better solution, a short and mid-term exchange of production orders should be considered. Therefore, reconfigurable production systems are promising. The evaluation of the optimal network reconfiguration will be automatically fulfilled by an applied genetic algorithm.

2   State of the Art

The fundamentals of reconfigurable production systems and production networks in a scalable context are further discussed for a greater understanding of the following reconfiguration aspects in the next chapters.

2.1   Reconfigurable Production Systems

The idea of *reconfigurable manufacturing systems* (RMS) for quick reactions to market changes started with Koren et al. in the late 1990s [7]. At that time, the majority of applied operation concepts were based on product-specific machining plants and dedicated manufacturing lines (DML). Today, many manufacturing companies still use these concepts; however, some enterprises have decided to install and run flexible manufacturing systems (FMS) [3].

Initially, *dedicated manufacturing lines* are developed for specific products on a mass production scale [5]. The general system as well as the machine structure of the DML concepts are planned and fixed before the start of production. Consequently, DMLs are characterized by fixed capacity limits and lacking responsiveness due to changing conditions [7]. In very stable markets with high batch sizes, it is possible to run such a production system in a cost-efficient way. Fast-changing market circumstances cannot be handled with DML concepts as briefly suggested in Fig. 1.

The *flexible manufacturing systems* were developed to remedy the disadvantages of the lacking ability to change the machine structure and the missing flexibility of the DML concept. The FMS allows adjustments within a predefined flexibility corridor (see Fig. 1). In contrast to the DML, a corridor is given and not a fixed specific number. This allows you to run the production system in a profitable corridor. Modifications, which go beyond the predefined flexibility corridor, go along with high time and cost efforts. Reconfigurable production systems may comprise several systems, e.g., processing machines, assembly systems and transportation systems. That implies the advantages of dynamic and adjustable systems in terms of capacity, functionality, technology and structure within a cost-effective manner [7–10].

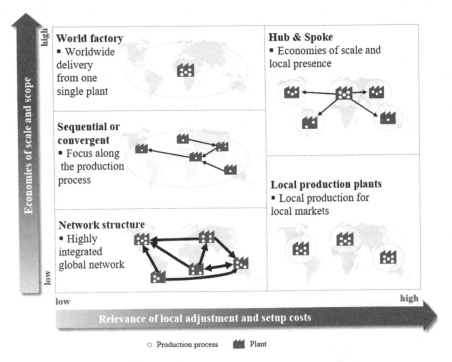

Fig. 2. Different phenotypes of production networks [8].

2.2   Production Networks

The research field of production networks is quite broad and covers various subject areas, e.g., social, economic, environmental and technical aspects. Many questions concerning the strategic set up of those production networks have been discussed in research [3]. The operation and adaptability of those complex production networks are seldom discussed [6]. Hence, there are various descriptions of the term production network. The following definition of Röhrs is technical but generally valid:

A production network can be seen as a network where nodes adopt subtasks of a production process and maintain service exchange relations based on material and information flow [11].

In Fig. 2, a very common distinction between production networks in phenotypes can be found. These phenotypes were described by Abele [8]. Further, the figure shows, on the one hand, the importance of the *economies of scale and scope* and, on the other hand, the importance of *local features and transactional costs*.

So far, the short and mid-term move from one phenotype to another has not been investigated in-depth [10]. In the following, this idea will be briefly disscused.

3   Reconfigurable Production Networks

Reconfigurable production networks are a promising concept to solve the current and future challenges in production. They consist of highly flexible factories with reconfigurable manufacturing and assembly systems, and they offer the ability of network reconfiguration. The modularity of RMS allows a reconfiguration of capacity, functionality and technology within minutes or hours according to market demands and required products [10]. Due to the increased usability and mobility of the individual elements, reconfigurable production networks enable an agile production in a volatile and competitive environment. Moreover, they increase the possibility of distributing the product portfolio across locations.

The increased technical capabilities of reconfigurable production networks prescribe new requirements for production planning. Westkämper & Zahn recommended a fundamental change from resource-based to capability-based production planning [12]. Thereby, the degrees of freedom in detailed planning can be increased while the planning accuracy is constant. Automated production planning is feasible based on processing, resource, order and activity models. A core element is a comparison of the processing steps to be manufactured and the available capabilities in the production network. The following concepts applied different algorithms – mainly linear programming, genetic algorithms and game theories – to solve the optimization problem of production planning:

Hees developed a method for the mid-term production planning of RMS based on mixed-integer linear programming (MILP) [10]. The concept aims to align capacity supply and demand. The order allocation within a RMS defines a combinatorial auction designed by Suginouchi [13]. Bensmaine et al. configured a non-dominated sorting genetic algorithm II (NGSA-II) to identify a suitable machine configuration for a defined set of orders [14]. The majority of the described concepts focus on the selection of the optimal configuration of the network, RMS and order allocation.

Supply and demand for each period are known and form the basis for the opti-mization process, which mainly targets minimal production costs.

However, all concepts are limited by the subtasks of production planning and exhibit the following essential weak points: Execution of resource-based instead of capability-based production planning; consideration of limited hierarchy levels of a production network and limited dimensions of changeability (product, operation, capacity). What is not taking into account were factory-specific resource differences and logistic expenditures.

A new holistic approach is required to fulfill the requirements of production planning in reconfigurable production systems.

4   Approach of Production Planning to Reconfigurable Production Systems

A concept for capability-based production planning in reconfigurable production sys-tems will be developed. The core element is a genetic algorithm (GA) to solve the problem of optimal order allocation [15].

The requirements of the developed concept are as follows: Orders with a high variety of products and demand have to be allocated to the resources of an established reconfigurable production network. Thereby, on the one hand, production costs have to be minimized and delivery dates fulfilled, and, on the other hand, the three dimensions of changeability for all hierarchy levels of the production network have to be considered [16].

The selected approach combines the expedient elements of the concepts described in chapter 3 with new elements to fulfill the requirements. It follows the overall approach of capability-based production planning. The basic design comprises the three function modules: order consolidation, capability availableness and order allocation.

The resource model represents the capabilities and characteristics of all resources in the production network (see Fig. 3). Various modules Mm are combined into resource configurations RCr and provide the specific capabilities for each work station. The supply of capacity for each RCr is derived from the capacity profiles of the required modules. Consequently, each RCr owns various technology vectors $TVRr,j$. A con-figuration matrix stores technical and planning configurations for all RCr in the pro-duction network. The order model represents the entire manufacturing process and the capability demand for each processing step. Analogous to the resource model, tech-nology vectors $TVDd,i$ represent the capability demand. Moreover, quantity, delivery date and location are stored information in the order model. The system model defines production network, factory, RMS and module as the five hierarchy levels of a reconfigurable production network. The numerous variations of the manufacturing process for a product are compiled in a process variations graph. The first function module, order consolidation, initiates the planning process by merging all orders with the same product, delivery date and location to a production order, except orders with a starting time within the frozen zone or high urgency.

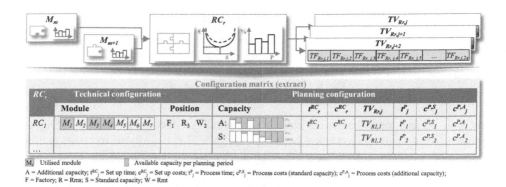

Fig. 3. Configuration matrix representing supply of capabilities and capacity.

The concept of demand-capability comparison based on technology vectors is the core element of the module capability availableness. If all corresponding technology factors of $TVD_{d,i}$ and $TVR_{r,j}$ comply with the comparative operators, an RC_r is capable of fulfilling the demand of a production order (see Fig. 4.). Subsequently, the supply of capacity for all capable RC_r is determined to update the configuration matrix. As a result, only capable and available RC_r are included in the following scheduling process.

comparative operators		
$TF_{Dd,i,k}$	Op.	$TF_{Rr,j,k}$
Process	⊆	Process
Material	⊆	Material
Geometry	⊆	Geometry
Dimension	<	Workspace
Dimension	>	Min. Dimension
Surface structure	<	Surface structure
Weight	<	Weight

$TV_{Dd,i}$ = Technology vector i of processing step d; $TV_{Rr,j}$ = Technology vector j of resource configuration r; $TF_{Dd,i,k}$ = Technology factor k of $TV_{Dd,i}$; $TF_{Rr,j,k}$ = Technology factor k of $TV_{Rr,j}$

Fig. 4. Demand-capability comparison.

Order allocation is executed by a modified NSGA-II. Following the evolutionary principle "survival of the fittest", the algorithm identifies near-optimal solutions for an optimization problem using the operator's selection, termination, recombination, mutation and substitution. The starting point is a randomly generated initial population of individuals, each representing a valid solution. A fitness function controls the optimization process. In the following, the developed approach is described in detail:

Each individual is a combination of a variable number of genes consisting of alleles representing the order allocation ($TVD_{d,i}$ and $TVR_{r,j}$), category of capacity ($x_{i,t}$), job-split factor (JS_{dijl}), branching points in the manufacturing process ($and_{d,i}$) as well as scheduling priority (rank) (see Fig. 5).

Fig. 5. Generic model of individuals.

The present optimization objective is minimal production costs, consisting of process, set up and transportation costs (see Fig. 6.). The majority of the costs can be integrated into the GA-operators through individual constraints requiring a repair function and a modified fitness function. The repair function ensures the complete representation of all production orders within an individual regarding the lot size of the processing steps and the manufacturing process. A decoding heuristic generates a valid order allocation, which dispatches every production order lot of an individual into a machine schedule according to the information given in each related gene, starting with the gene of highest scheduling priority. The fitness function subsequently evaluates the quality of the solution by calculating the sum of the objective and penalty functions. Adherence to delivery dates increases the calculated fitness value.

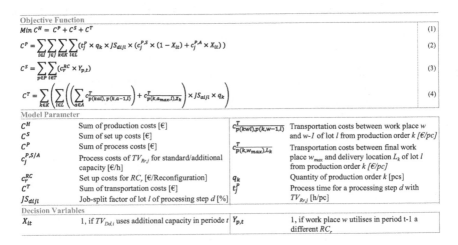

Fig. 6. Objective function of the optimization problem.

Initial population, substitution, termination and selection are implemented in line with the general principles of an NSGA-II. Two different mutation operators were selected: In mutation 1, some genes were randomly selected and mutated in $TVRr,j$, xi,t or $JSdijl$ to increase the diversity of individuals. In mutation 2, a pair of genes was randomly selected and swapped to modify the scheduling priority.

A Prototypical Application in the Production of Household Appliances

The developed approach was successfully applied in the replicated reconfigurable production network of a household appliance manufacturer, consisting of four factories and three target markets. The system for production planning was able to reduce the overall production costs, although improvements in runtime and detail level of costs are required.

5 Conclusion

The presented approach of reconfigurable production networks holds significant potential in order-based production. Especially issues concerning the utilization rate of various production sites by short and mid-term production planning show benefits. The genetic algorithm based on a configuration matrix and a demand-capacity comparison solves the problem of optimal order allocation.

To sum up, this paper showed a good opportunity to react fast to high market volatility in the order-based production by intelligent reconfiguration of an existing production network.

References

1. Abele, E., Reinhart, G.: Zukunft der Produktion. Herausforderungen, Forschungsfelder, Chancen. Hanser, München (2011)
2. Reinhart, G.: Industrie 4.0. Geschäftsmodelle, Prozesse, Technik. Hanser, München (2017)
3. Wiendahl, H.-P.: Betriebsorganisation für Ingenieure. Hanser, München (2010)
4. Piller, F., Tseng, M.M.: The Customer Centric Enterprise. Advances in Mass Customization and Personalization. Springer, Heidelberg (2003). https://doi.org/10.1007/978-3-642-55460-5
5. Atug, J., Hees, A., Wagner, M., Braunreuther, S., Reinhart, G.: Production planning for customer innovated products. In: International Conference on IEEM. IEEE, New Jersey (2016)
6. Atug, J., Braunreuther, S., Reinhart, G.: Rekonfiguration von Produktionsnetzwerken. wt Werkstatttechnik online, vol. 108. Springer, Düsseldorf (2018)
7. Koren, Y., et al.: Reconfigurable manufacturing systems. CIRP Ann. **48**, 527–540 (1999)
8. Abele, E., Meyer, T., Näher, U., Strube, G., Sykes, R.: Global Production: A Handbook for Strategy and Implementation. Springer, Heidelberg (2008). https://doi.org/10.1007/978-3-540-71653-2
9. Wiendahl, H.-P.: Wandlungsfähigkeit: Schlüsselbegriff der zukunftsfähigen Fabrik. In: wt-online, vol. 92, no.4, pp. 122–127 (2002)
10. Hees, A.: System zur Produktionsplanung von rekonfugrierbaren Produktionssystemen. Utz Verlag, Munich (2017)
11. Röhrs, A.: Produktionsmanagement in Produktionsnetzwerken. Lang, Frankfurt (2003)
12. Westkämper, E., Zahn, E.: Wandlungsfähige Produktionsunternehmen. Das Stuttgarter Unternehmensmodell. Springer, Berlin (2009). https://doi.org/10.1007/978-3-540-68890-7
13. Suginouchi, S., Kokuryo, D., Kaihara, T.: Value co-creative manufacturing system for mass customization. Proc. CIRP **63**, 727–732 (2017)
14. Bensmaine, A., Dahane, M., Benyoucef, L.: A non-dominated sorting genetic algorithm based approach for optimal machines selection in reconfigurable manufacturing environment. Comput. Ind. Eng. **66**, 519–524 (2013)
15. Deb, K., Pratap, A., Agarwal, S., Meyarivan, T.: A fast and elitist multiobjective genetic algorithm: NSGA-II. IEEE Trans. Evol. Comput. **6**, 182–197 (2002)
16. Hochdörffer, J., Berendt, C.V., Lanza, G.: Resource-based reconfiguration of manufacturing networks using a product-to-plant allocation methodology. In: Proceedings of the International Conference on Competitive Manufacturing CIRP COMA, vol. 6, pp. 511–516 (2016)

Author Index

Printed in the United States
By Bookmasters